EXPLORING THE WORLD

2nd Edition

Nona Starr, CTC

TheTravelinstitute

Brief Contents

Table of Contents

Dear Future Travel Professional:

Congratulations on your decision to enter the travel and tourism industry. We, at The Travel Institute, applaud your decision and wish you a fulfilling and prosperous career.

As you can imagine, travel and tourism evolves as quickly as the world changes. Politics, economics, geography, weather, cultural events, and a host of other factors continually affect travel and tourism businesses. Accordingly, the paramount role of The Travel Institute is to encourage and facilitate professional development and continuous learning for individuals at all career stages.

The Travel Institute's professional designation and certification programs address core and advanced knowledge requirements needed by all travel professionals.

The Travel Institute maintains a unique position in the world of travel and tourism. We are the only professional, not-for-profit industry organization that is politically neutral and open to all. We strive to provide a forum for healthy debate of industry issues.

Visit www.thetravelinstitute.com to learn about membership, especially student membership, and all of the benefits available to each and every member of our Institute family.

Sincerely,

Scott Ahlsmith, CTC
Chairman of the Board of Trustees
The Travel Institute

148 Linden Street, Suite 305, Wellesley, MA 02482 • tel: 781.237.0280 • 800.542.4282 • fax: 781.237.3860 • www.thetravelinstitute.com

Preface

The second edition of *Exploring the World* is a practical, comprehensive, and up-to-date text designed to serve the needs of students planning careers in the travel, tourism, and hospitality industry. In writing the new edition we have aimed

- To stimulate students' imagination and build on their spirit of adventure and love of travel while developing geographic literacy.
- To give readers information about the world's most visited destinations plus an overview of less popular locations.
- To help students match travelers and destinations and develop selling skills that they can apply on the job.
- To give students hands-on practice in using traditional print and contemporary electronic resources.

What's New in the Second Edition

This new edition of *Exploring the World* is not only thoroughly updated but also shortened and polished to help students learn about destinations more easily. Students can now find basic facts about a state or country—from its capital and currency to airport codes—in the Fact File, which begins on page 417. Worksheets have been expanded to include exercises that help students develop their ability to match travelers and destinations, counter objections, and respond to common requests. These worksheets have been moved to a new *Student Workbook*, which also includes lists of Web sites and other resources to help students develop their research skills.

Coverage and Organization

Exploring the World emphasizes those destinations that are most important to travelers while introducing students to the world of travel, tourism, and hospitality. The book is divided into fifteen chapters. Chapter 1 reviews the fundamentals of geography, both physical and cultural. Chapters 2–4 are devoted to the United States. Chapters 5–8 examine Canada, Bermuda, the Bahamas, the Caribbean islands, Mexico, Central America, and South America. Chapters 9–12 explore Europe. Chapters 13–15 look at destinations in Africa, the Middle East, Asia, and the Pacific.

To facilitate learning, each of Chapters 2–15 follows a similar path:

- Each chapter begins with an overview ("The Environment and Its People") of the region's physical environment and historical background.
- This introduction is followed by sections that describe specific destinations and their attractions, emphasizing what travelers are likely to want to see and do.
- The next section ("Planning the Trip") examines issues that arise when arranging trips. It explores the role of the tour operator, the best time to travel, what clients need to know to prepare for a trip, and choices for transportation and accommodations.
- Finally, selected chapters conclude with a supplementary section that briefly discusses countries that are less popular destinations.

Appendices provide additional information. Appendix A is the Fact File. It gives a country's area, capital, airport code, population and density, language, currency, time zone, and affiliations such as membership in the European Union. Appendix B gives codes for major airports. Appendix C lists films that feature the destinations.

Learning Aids and Special Features

To help students develop an effective learning strategy, each chapter includes

- **Learning Objectives,** which identify goals for the chapter.
- A **Check-Up** at the end of each major section to encourage students to check that they have grasped the section's major points. For sections on destinations, the Check-Ups outline a region's key attractions for travelers.
- A **Chapter Wrap-Up** at the end of each chapter to encourage students to review what they have learned. Each Chapter Wrap-Up includes (1) a **Summary,** which reviews the Objectives that opened the chapter, and (2) **Questions for Discussion and Review.**

Within the text, other features ease the task of mastering information. Key places and terms are emphasized in **boldface type** when they are introduced. Destinations that are in bold in the text are featured on the maps, and the definitions of key terms are reviewed in the **Glossary of Geographical Terms** at the end of the book.

In addition, pronunciation guides are given when commonly used place-names and terms are introduced. These phonetic spellings use Americanized, not native-language, pronunciations. They appear in italic type in parentheses; for example, Jamaica (*juh MAY kuh*). The syllable or syllables with the most stress are printed in capital letters.

Other special features of *Exploring the World* include the following:

- Visual aids. *Exploring the World* offers a multitude of photographs, figures, and tables. The photographs emphasize landmarks. Maps provide visual summaries of the cities, attractions, and physical features discussed in the text. Each of Chapters 2–15 includes a Milestones chart, which outlines major events in the region's history, emphasizing those that affected the travel industry.
- **Close-Ups.** These boxes take a closer look at the most popular destinations. Each box addresses these questions: Who is a good prospect for a trip to the destination? Why would they visit this destination? Where specifically would they go? When is the best time to go? Most boxes offer a sample itinerary. Finally, each box includes one objection or question often raised by travelers and a sample response.
- **Profiles.** These highlight an area's cuisine, shopping lures, sports attractions, or activities of special interest.

- Margin notes. Trivia facts and anecdotes are noted in the margin to add to the student's enjoyment.
- **On-the-Spot** role-plays. These true-to-life scenarios present challenging face-to-face situations and provide hints on how to deal with travelers' concerns.

The Student Workbook

The Workbook, new with the second edition, has content and worksheets that reinforce students' learning. Each chapter has

- A **Resources** section that provides an extensive list of Web sites.
- A section listing an area's sites of geographic and cultural importance.
- Suggestions for classic and contemporary background reading.
- **Review quizzes** concentrating on the geography and attractions of each chapter's destination.
- A worksheet dealing with traveler's **questions** to help students develop their ability to match travelers and destinations, counter objections, and respond to common requests.
- A **map exercise**.
- A **research exercise** that calls on students to find information either from classroom resources or on the Internet. The exercises help students identify documentation requirements and health concerns and plan travel logistics.
- **Looking Back**—a review of the chapter.

The Instructor's Resource Manual

Instructors can use *Exploring the World*'s Instructor's Resource Manual to help them plan lectures and to reinforce their teaching strategies. Among the tools included are

- Chapter outlines.
- Suggestions for end-of-chapter discussion questions.
- Answers to Workbook exercises.
- Suggestions for classroom activities.
- Chapter-by-chapter test banks and answer sheets.

The Travel Institute's Geography for Travel Professionals Test

The Travel Institute offers an optional, but recommended, testing service exclusively to students who complete a course of study using *Exploring the World*. Students who pass the test, a 100-question, multiple-choice examination that is administered by instructors and scored by the Institute, receive The Travel Institute's Exploring the World Test Certificate, a travel industry credential that can be useful in the job search process. For more information about The Travel Institute's Exploring the World testing program or any of the Institute's other programs, please contact

The Travel Institute
148 Linden Street
Wellesley, MA 02482
Phone: 781-237-0280
www.thetravelinstitute.com

Acknowledgments

Special thanks to the following educators who provided evaluations of *Exploring the World.* Their assistance was invaluable.

- Marty Sarbey de Souto, CTC, Vista Community College
- Jean Marshall, CTC, New Hampshire Technical Institute
- Pat Schultz, CTC, Northwestern Business College

CHAPTER 1

Destination Geography

- Location: Finding a Destination
- Place: Describing the Environment
- Interaction: Exploring Cultures
- Movement: Understanding Tourism
- Learning about the Destination

OBJECTIVES

When you have completed Chapter 1, you should be able to

1. Describe the key features of maps and the system of time zones.
2. Locate the land and water masses of the earth, and describe the major landforms.
3. Explain the factors that influence the climate of a destination.
4. Describe how cultural geography influences tourism.
5. Identify key sources of information used in planning trips.

Travel professionals have many skills. They question effectively, listen actively, and communicate clearly. But communication skill is not enough. People working in the industry must know what to communicate. Success requires factual knowledge of places where people want to go. Other chapters in this book describe the destinations; this chapter reviews the terms used in the descriptions. The terms come from the science of **geography**, which is the study of the relationships between people and their environments.

Geography has two main divisions: physical geography and human geography. **Physical geography** is the study of the earth's natural features and the processes that shape it. **Human geography** focuses on people and their patterns of settlement and activity. **Destination geography** is the application of geographic knowledge to the travel, tourism, and hospitality industry.

The earliest geographers collected information by exploring the world. Today, geographers use data transmitted from satellites and analyzed by computers. But like their predecessors, modern geographers address four basic questions about places on the earth:

- Where is it? What is its *location*, its position on the surface of the earth?
- What are the characteristics of the *place*? What are its landforms—features of the earth's surface such as plains and mountains? What is its environment? What are the water, climate, and vegetation like, and how do they interact?
- How do the people *interact* with their environment? What are the people like, and how do they live?
- How do things on earth *move* from one place to another? In particular, how do people travel to and from a destination?

These questions point to the enduring themes of geography: location, place, interaction, and movement. This chapter examines each of these four themes.

Location: Finding a Destination

Where is it? How far is it? How long will it take to get there? Almost anyone who is thinking about taking a trip will want answers to these questions. For the answers, people rely on tools created by geographers.

Mapping the World

The basic tool that allows people to locate destinations is the frame of reference created by geographers to plot the position of places on the earth. They constructed an imaginary grid of horizontal and vertical lines around the planet.

The term *geography* comes from a Greek word that means "writing about or describing the earth." The discipline probably began with the observation that places and people on earth differ from one another.

Latitude and Longitude The starting points of this grid are (1) the North and South Poles, which mark the two ends of the earth's axis, and (2) the equator, the imaginary horizontal line that circles the earth midway between the poles, as you can see in Figure 1.1. The equator separates the world into the Northern and Southern Hemispheres. To these starting points mapmakers add horizontal lines called parallels and vertical lines called meridians.

Parallels are the horizontal lines that measure **latitude**, the distance

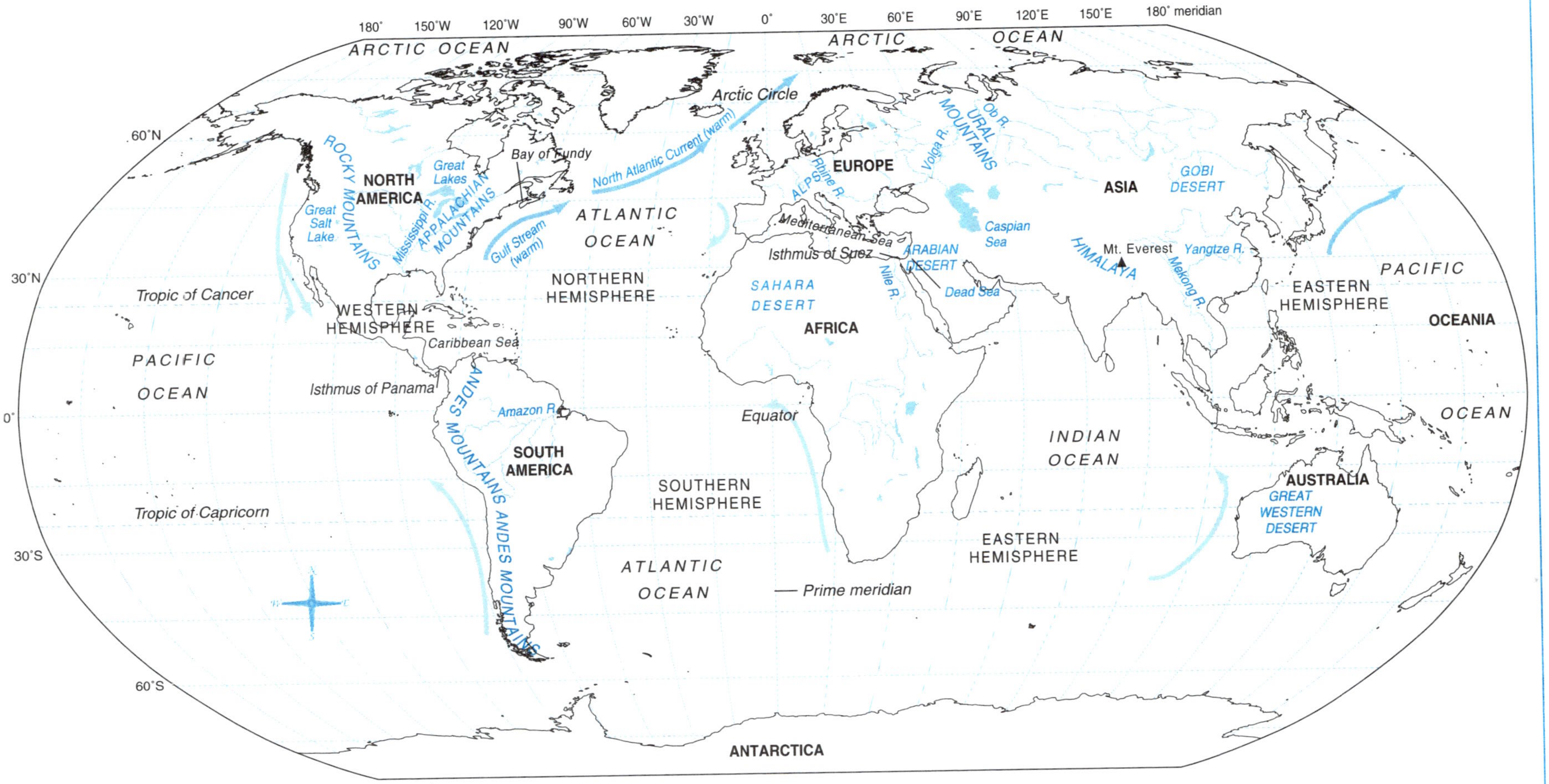

FIGURE 1.1 Earth

▲ National park or other site
1 inch = 2,316 miles (3,726 km)

north or south of the equator. The equator is the 0° line of latitude. Each line of latitude is an equal distance from the equator at all points.

Meridians are the vertical lines that measure **longitude**, the distance east or west from the first or **prime meridian**, which is defined as the 0° line of longitude. In 1884, by international agreement, geographers decided that the meridian passing through Greenwich, England, would be the prime meridian. The **180° meridian** is in the middle of the Pacific Ocean on the opposite side of the world from Greenwich. The half of the earth east of the prime meridian to 180° longitude is the **Eastern Hemisphere**. The half of the earth west of the prime meridian to 180° longitude is the **Western Hemisphere**.

Globes, Maps, and Projections With the frame of reference provided by latitudes and longitudes, geographers create globes and maps. A globe is a scale model of the earth on which shapes, areas, distances, and directions are represented. But globes are too bulky to be carried around. Maps are more practical because they are easy to carry, to store, and to reproduce. Maps are representations on a flat surface of a whole or part of an area.

Today, **cartography**, or mapmaking, has been revolutionized by aerial photography, satellites, and computers. A collection of computers and software known as a **geographic information system (GIS)** can record, retrieve, analyze, and manipulate information gathered by satellites. The GIS user asks for information; the computer guides the user toward answers. The process is called **interactive mapping**.

The *Global Positioning System* (*GPS*) is a worldwide navigation system that uses radio signals broadcast by satellites. Developed for military use in the 1970s, the GPS is now widely available to the public. A computerized radio receiver in an airplane, ship, car, or other vehicle uses satellite signals to calculate its own position. This should make people who are reluctant to ask for directions very, very happy.

Despite technology, no map is perfect. An average map produced by the U.S. Geological Survey contains a million items of data, but it still leaves something out. All maps simplify reality. Mapmaking requires the transfer of information about the round earth onto flat paper, a process called **projection**. A map might show area, shape, scale, or direction accurately—but it cannot show all of these characteristics at the same time without distortion.

Suppose you want to find the shortest route between New York and Paris. If you look at a map, you might think that the shortest way is straight across the Atlantic. In fact, the shortest route is to fly north, as you can see in Figure 1.2, on a curved path. This route is a **great circle route**, which is a phrase used by airline navigators to refer to the shortest distance between two points. When a string is stretched between any two points on a globe, it marks the great circle route. If you use a ruler to connect the same two places on a flat map, the route is different and looks shorter because of the distortion caused by projecting a round object onto a flat surface.

Using Maps

To get the most out of a map, you must know how to interpret it. Maps usually include the following aids:

- The **compass rose**, a symbol in the corner of a map indicating the map's orientation. Usually, maps put north at the top, but this is just a convention.
- A **key**, or **legend**, explaining the symbols used on the map. In this book a star is used to indicate a country's capital, circles are used to show other cities, and different types of lines are used to indicate rivers and political boundaries.
- A **scale** indicating the relationship between the distances on the map and the actual distances on the earth. For example, 1 inch on the map might represent 100 miles (161 km).

FIGURE 1.2

The Globe from a Different Perspective

To see the effect of different projections, contrast the size and shape of North and South America in this map and in Figure 1.1. Also notice the example of a circle route that is plotted here.

- Varying colors to differentiate features such as elevation, water, or vegetation.

Calculating Time

Suppose you board a plane and fly eastward from Atlanta, Georgia, leaving at 9:00 PM EST. Seven hours later you land in Frankfurt, Germany, in midmorning sunshine with bustling traffic, although your watch says it is only 4:00 AM. What happened? Why isn't it still dark? The answer involves the rotation of the earth. Time changes with distance.

Once people began traveling great distances, they had to grapple with the fact that distance and time are related. People divided the day into twenty-four hours as long ago as the 14th century. But even in the late 19th century, people still operated according to local sun time. As trains began to crisscross the continent, a system for coordinating time became essential.

An international conference in 1884 in Washington, D.C., solved the problem. Time around the globe was standardized against the time at the prime meridian at Britain's Royal Observatory at Greenwich, England. The world was divided into twenty-four time zones, each approximately 15° of longitude in width and each differing by one hour from the next. In 1918 the U.S. Congress applied this system to the United States, establishing official time zones.

To understand the time system, you need two tools: a 24-hour clock and a map of the world's time zones. The **24-hour clock** eliminates the AM/PM distinction and provides a different numeral for each hour of the day, as Figure 1.3 shows. Figure 1.4 shows the world's time zones. The time at Greenwich is

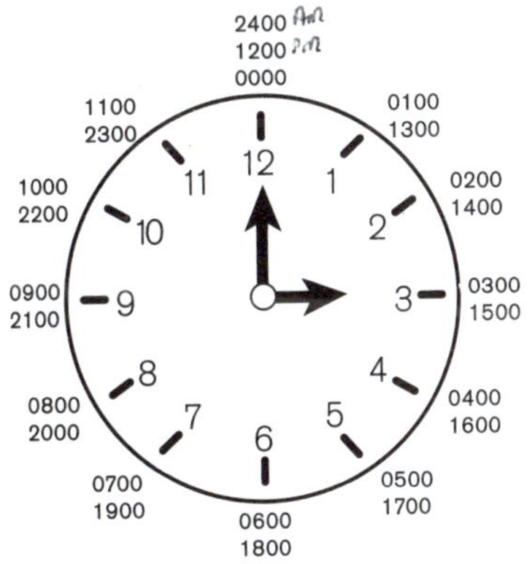

FIGURE 1.3 24-Hour Clock

On the 24-hour clock each day begins at 0000 (midnight) and progresses through each hour of the day from 0100 (1:00 AM) to 2300 (11:00 PM). The last two digits give the minutes. To convert 24-hour time to AM/PM time, subtract 1200 from hours later than noon. To convert AM/PM time to the 24-hour clock, add 1200 to hours after noon.

called **Greenwich Mean Time** (**GMT**, also called *Universal Time*). The time elsewhere in the world is expressed as "plus or minus GMT." Zones east of Greenwich are plus GMT; zones west of Greenwich are minus GMT.

Where do the pluses begin and the minuses stop? The location 180° east of Greenwich, which is twelve time zones ahead of GMT, is also the location 180° west of Greenwich, twelve time zones behind GMT. So when it is noon at Greenwich on October 14, at this location it would be midnight on both October 14 and October 13! To fix the problem, the point 180° from Greenwich was named the **international date line**, and the time zone there was divided in half. Thus the world is actually divided into twenty-three full zones and two half zones; the twelfth zone west and the twelfth zone east are each half a zone wide. At any time, two calendar days are in effect in the world. Travelers crossing the international date line in a westward direction, toward Japan, add a day (Sunday becomes Monday). When they return, they subtract a day (Sunday becomes Saturday).

FIGURE 1.4 World Time Zones

On the 24-hour clock each day begins at 0000 (midnight) and progresses through each hour of the day from 0100 (1:00 AM) to 2300 (11:00 PM). The last two digits give the minutes. To convert 24-hour time to AM/PM time, subtract 1200 from hours later than noon. To convert AM/PM time to the 24-hour clock, add 1200 to hours after noon.

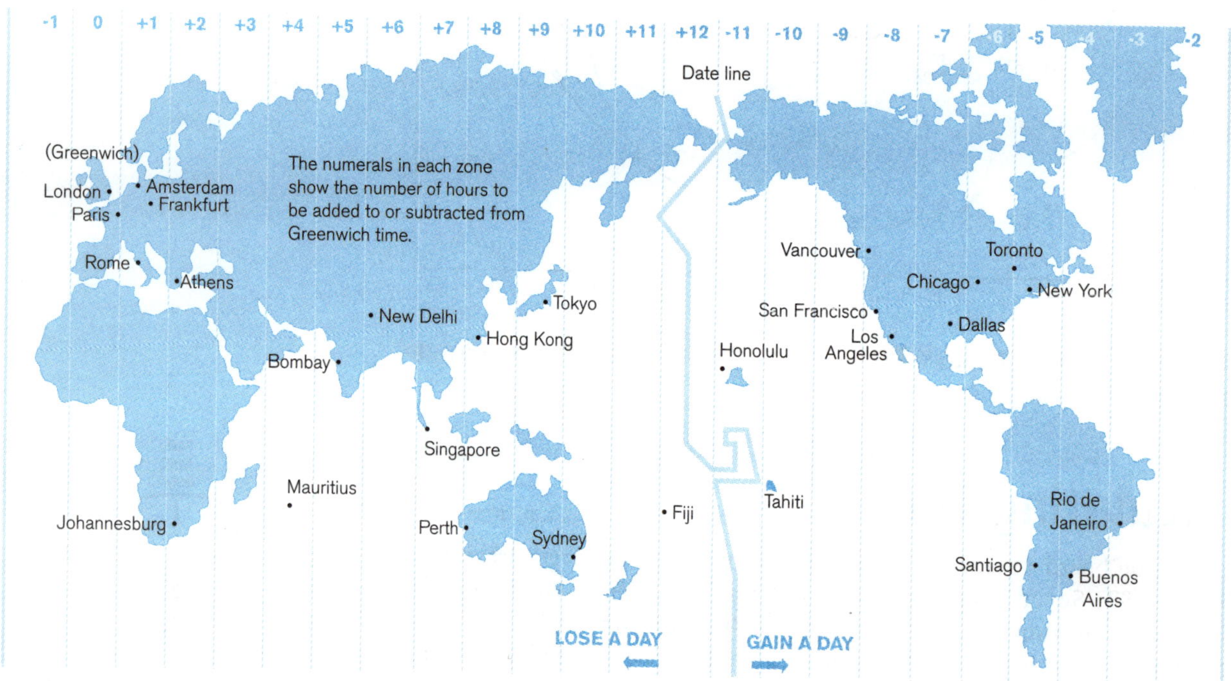

To Calculate the Time Difference

1. For each location, find the local time and its relationship to GMT on an international time chart.
2. If both locations are either ahead of GMT (GMT+) or behind GMT (GMT–), subtract the smaller from the larger figure.

   For example, Toronto is GMT –5 and San Francisco is GMT –8. Subtracting 5 from 8 gives 3, so there is a 3-hour time difference between the two locations.
3. If the local time is ahead of GMT (GMT+) at one location and behind GMT (GMT–) at the other location, add the figures.

For example, New York is GMT –5 and Rome is GMT +1. Adding 5 plus 1 gives 6, so there is a 6-hour time difference between the two locations.

To Calculate the Elapsed Travel Time

1. Convert departure and arrival times to 24-hour clock time.
2. Subtract the departure time from the arrival time.
3. When traveling east, subtract one hour for every time zone crossed. When traveling west, add one hour for every time zone crossed. The result is the actual travel time.

For example, suppose the departure time from Paris is 12:15 PM and the arrival time in New York is 1:25 PM. Converted to 24-hour clock time, the departure time is 1215 and the arrival time is 1325. The difference is 1 hour and 10 minutes. Because 6 time zones are crossed going west from Paris to New York, add 6 hours to the result. Thus the elapsed travel time in this case is 7 hours and 10 minutes.

The time at any particular place is called its **local time**. Using the system of time zones, you can determine the local time for any place in the world. You can also determine how long it will take to get to a destination, or the **elapsed travel time**. Figure 1.4 describes how to make these calculations.

The calculations can get complicated for some destinations and at certain times of the year. Some countries, such as India, set their standard times fifteen or thirty minutes from the time designated by the international system. Other countries, such as China, put the entire country in a single time zone. Furthermore, many places—but not all—move their clocks during part of the year to create what is called **daylight saving time** or **summer time**. Not all areas, even within the United States, adopt the time change. Of those that do, different countries may make the change on different dates.

In 1935 Pan American World Airways' seaplane the *China Clipper* left San Francisco for the first flight across the vast Pacific, destination Manila. The plane needed to refuel along the way. On one island, the airport was closed when the plane arrived. Someone had been confused by the date line, and the plane was not expected until the next day!

✔ CHECK-UP

The imaginary grid used for locating places on earth includes

- ✔ The North and South Poles.
- ✔ The equator, which separates the globe into Northern and Southern Hemispheres.
- ✔ Parallels, which measure latitude, the distance north or south of the equator.
- ✔ Meridians, which measure longitude, the distance east or west of the prime meridian.

The earth's time zones

- ✔ Are measured from the prime meridian in Greenwich, England.
- ✔ Are one hour apart.
- ✔ Meet in the Pacific at the international date line.

Place: Describing the Environment

Over time, great forces formed the features of the earth. Even today, the earth moves at **faults**, which are breaks in the earth's crust, its outermost layer. Earthquakes, volcanoes, weathering, erosion, and the buildup of sediment continue to reshape the earth's surface. As a result, the earth offers a rich variety of types of land, water, and climates. For many people, these environmental variations offer the key reason for travel.

The Land

Thirty percent of the earth is land. Traditionally, the earth's great land areas have been divided into seven **continents**. From largest to smallest, they are **Asia**, **Africa**, **North America**, **South America**, **Antarctica**, **Europe**, and **Australia**. The **Ural Mountains** divide Europe and Asia along a line running south and then west from northern Russia (look again at Figure 1.1). The term *continent* is imprecise, however. Some geographers put Europe and Asia together as one continent, **Eurasia**. Also, geographers use the term **Oceania** to refer not only to the thousands of scattered islands in the Pacific but also to Australia and New Zealand.

The edge of land that borders the ocean along a continent or an island is called the **coast**, **seacoast**, or **shore**. Land actually extends outward beyond the

According to a 1988 proclamation by U.S. President Ronald Reagan, "The territorial sea of the United States henceforth extends to 12 nautical miles (22 km) from the baselines of the United States determined in accordance with international law."

TABLE 1.1 Kinds of Islands

Type	Description
Continental	Land broken away from a continent.
Barrier island	Built from sediment along a continent's coastline.
Coral island	Low, flat island formed by living coral polyps.
Atoll	Circular ring of coral in the open sea found chiefly in the Pacific.
Volcanic island	Formed by eruptions of volcanoes on the ocean floor.

White Range, Ancash, Peru

coast, gently sloping underwater. The area where the sea meets the land is the **continental shelf**. Because a country's legal jurisdiction is limited to its territory, countries claim as much of their continental shelves as they can. How much of the shelf falls under a country's legal jurisdiction influences activities from fishing and oil drilling to when a cruise ship can open its casinos and shops.

Geographers treat islands near a continent as part of the mainland; for example, Great Britain and Ireland are considered part of Europe. An **island** is a body of land completely surrounded by water and above water at high tide. Table 1.1 describes the various types of islands. A group of islands clustered together is an **archipelago** (*arc kuh PEL uh goh*).

Here are other terms that describe the land:

- An **isthmus** is a narrow bridge of land that connects two large landmasses. The Isthmus of Suez joins Africa to Asia. The Isthmus of Panama joins North and South America.
- A **peninsula** is land that extends from a continent and is almost surrounded by water. Florida is a prime example.
- A **reef** is a ridge of rocks or sand at or near the surface of the water along the coast. **Coral reefs** are ridges built by tiny sea animals called corals.
- A **panhandle** is a narrow projection of a larger territory into another's land surface. In the United States, Florida, Texas, Oklahoma, and Idaho have panhandle territories.

Features of the Land

Although each continent is unique, all share two basic features. First, each has old, geologically stable regions called shields. A **shield** is an area of the earth's crust that formed during its early history. Shields are relatively flat regions and are usually found in the interiors of continents.

Second, each continent also has younger, more active regions marked by mountains. A **mountain** is a landform higher than its surroundings with some kind of peak or summit. North and South America have young, high mountain ranges (the **Rockies** and the **Andes**, respectively) rising near their west coasts. The steep, young **Alps** and the **Himalaya** extend eastward across Eurasia. The earth's highest mountain is **Mount Everest** in the Himalaya; it soars 29,035 feet (8,850 m) above sea level. Older mountain systems, such as the **Appalachians** in eastern North America and the **Urals** of Eurasia, tend to be worn down and hence less steep.

Other landforms include **hills**, which are generally more rounded and not as high as mountains, and **valleys**, which are depressions between hills or mountains. Movements of the earth's crust produce **rift valleys**, valleys that formed when the land sank between two parallel faults. A **canyon** is a deep, narrow valley with steep sides. Canyons are generally cut by water.

The **fall line** is the place near a continent's edge where the land drops from a higher elevation to the coastal plain. **Plains** are flat or gently rolling lands. At the fall line, rivers generally have waterfalls or rapids. As a result, ships cannot navigate upstream unless a canal and locks are built.

Plateaus are another type of flatland. A **plateau**, also called a **tableland**, is higher than the surrounding land and has at least one steep side, called a **cliff**.

Water

About 70 percent of the earth's surface is water. Water is essential to life, and the distribution of water has far-reaching effects. Throughout history, the location of navigable rivers and good coastal harbors has shaped the flow of people, goods, and ideas from place to place. When leisure time is available, people seek out water for play or relaxation.

Ninety-seven percent of the earth's water is found in the **ocean**, an interconnected body of salt water. The world ocean has four subdivisions: in order of size, the **Pacific**, **Atlantic**, **Indian**, and **Arctic**. Each ocean includes smaller bodies of water called **seas**, **gulfs**, and **bays**. A **strait** is a narrow passage of water that connects two larger bodies of water. For example, the Strait of Gibraltar connects the Atlantic Ocean and the Mediterranean Sea. **Lagoons** are narrow water bodies that form between the mainland and barrier islands or reefs; most are connected to the ocean by tidal inlets.

The ocean is a dynamic place, moved by tides, waves, and currents. **Tides** are the rhythmic rise and fall of the ocean waters that occur twice each day as a result of the gravitational pull of the moon and sun. **Waves**—movement on the ocean's surface—are created by wind, not by tides. **Currents** are cold or warm rivers of water that flow within the ocean.

Currents are caused by the rotation of the earth, moving air, and differences in water temperature within the ocean. The currents are of two kinds: some (*thermohaline currents*) flow from the ocean's surface to the bottom and back; others (*wind-driven currents*) flow horizontally. The earth's spin causes currents to curve to the right north of the equator and to the left south of the equator, a tendency known as the **Coriolis effect**.

Only about 3 percent of the earth's water is fresh, not salty. Of fresh water, more than two-thirds is frozen in **glaciers**, huge masses of ice that move slowly over land. This movement accounts for the formation of the greatest number of the world's **lakes**, which are bodies of water surrounded by land. Glaciers form lakes by cutting valleys and leaving deposits that dam the water formed by the glacier's melting ice.

Other lakes form on **karst**, an area of land underlain by limestone that is honeycombed with sinkholes, underground streams, and caves. Karst is found throughout the world, but it is best developed in humid climates. In the United States, karst occurs in Missouri, Kentucky, Indiana, and Florida.

Lakes are either of salt or fresh water. Freshwater lakes that have both incoming and outgoing streams do not become salty; the **Great Lakes** between Canada and the United States are examples. At inland seas that have no outlets, water is lost by evaporation, and salt gradually builds up. Thus the Middle East's **Dead Sea**, the **Caspian Sea**, and Utah's **Great Salt Lake** are very salty.

A **river** is a ribbon of water flowing over the land. Some rivers flow continuously; others flow intermittently. The beginning of a river is called its **source** or **headwater**. The source may be ice melting in a glacier, snow melting on a mountain, an overflowing lake, or a spring bubbling from the ground.

From its source, a river flows downhill. Smaller streams, called **tributaries**, flow into the river. Where the river and its tributaries tumble over rocks and down steep bluffs, **rapids** and **waterfalls** occur. Farther downstream, as its slope levels out, the river begins to flow more slowly. It gradually widens and builds a broad **floodplain**. As it nears the ocean, the river may form a marsh. As a river flows along, it picks up **sediment**, which is the solid matter that water, ice, and wind transport and deposit. The end of a river is its **mouth**. Where a river empties into a larger body of water, it slows down, often dropping its sediment to form a fertile **delta**, which is a flat, low-lying plain, at the river's mouth. Prime examples are the deltas of the **Mississippi, Nile, Volga**, Ganges, **Yangtze**, and **Mekong**. Not all rivers have deltas. In some areas, powerful ocean waves and currents sweep the material away as soon as it is deposited. Other rivers do not carry enough sediment to form deltas.

Earthquakes and volcanoes under the ocean can cause a **tsunami** (*sue NAHM ee*), a wave that can move through the water at 400 miles (644 km) an hour and reach a height of more than 100 feet (30 m) near the shore. Tsunamis are sometimes mistakenly called "tidal waves," but they have no connection with tides and are usually caused by earthquakes or volcanoes.

One of the most devastating tsunamis in recent history occurred December 26, 2004. At least 162,000 people were killed and more than 1.5 million people were displaced when their homes were destroyed by the tsunami, which affected 15 countries. Damage was concentrated in the Indian Ocean, with its effects felt in Thailand, Indonesia, Malaysia, Sri Lanka, India, and as far away as the east coast of Africa.

It is uncertain how long it will take for rebuilding to occur and for tourists to return to the popular beach resorts in southeast Asia.

The tsunami was triggered by a magnitude 9.0 earthquake in the Indian Ocean off the western coast of northern Sumatra, Indonesia.

In a few rivers, high tide sometimes begins with a **tidal bore**—an abrupt front of high water from the sea rushing up the mouth of a river. The **Amazon** has a tidal bore, although the bore of the **Bay of Fundy** in Canada is the most famous.

Weather and Climate

One of the first questions a traveler is likely to ask is "What will the weather be like there?" Strictly speaking, the question is unanswerable because weather is what's happening now. It can be described by six features: (1) temperature, (2) atmospheric pressure, (3) wind, (4) humidity, (5) precipitation, and (6) clouds.

- **Temperature** is the degree of hotness or coldness as measured by a thermometer. The **Fahrenheit scale** is used in the United States, but almost all other countries use the **Celsius**, or **centigrade**, scale. For most vacationers, a temperature below 64° F (18° C) is too cool for sitting around doing nothing; a temperature above 86° F (30° C) is too hot for active sport.
- **Atmospheric pressure** is the weight of the atmosphere as measured by a barometer. Changes in pressure signal shifts in weather.
- **Wind** is the movement of air caused by the uneven heating of the earth by the sun.
- **Humidity** refers to how much water vapor the air contains. Most people find high humidity very uncomfortable.
- **Precipitation** is rain, sleet, hail, or snow formed when water and winds interact with temperature.
- **Clouds** consist of tiny water droplets or ice crystals. Cloudy days as a rule are cooler than clear ones. The opposite is true at night because clouds act as a blanket keeping the earth warm.

As the earth rotates around the sun, its tilt causes the seasons—spring, summer, autumn, and winter—each with special light, temperature, and weather patterns that repeat themselves yearly. The seasons in the Northern Hemisphere are the opposite of those in the Southern Hemisphere, and not all parts of the earth have four distinct seasons.

Climate is the average of weather conditions in an area over a long period of time. Climates are the product of (1) latitude, (2) elevation, (3) topography, and (4) distance from water. Each set of conditions forms a climate type (see Table 1.2).

Latitude To understand how latitude affects climate, note that the sun's rays reach the earth most directly at the equator. The farther you go from the equator, the cooler it gets. The farthest points from the equator where the sun appears directly overhead are 23.5 degrees in either direction. These points are the Tropic of Cancer, the line of latitude about 23.5 degrees north of the equator, and the Tropic of Capricorn, the line of latitude about 23.5 degrees south of the equator. The lands between the Tropic of Cancer and Tropic of Capricorn are known as the tropics.

In addition, latitude influences climate because winds vary with latitude. **Trade winds** are the constant winds that blow from the northeast toward the equator in the Northern Hemisphere and from the southeast toward the equator in the Southern Hemisphere. The **westerlies** are currents of air high above the earth that blow from the southwest in the Northern Hemisphere and from the northwest in the Southern Hemisphere. Westerlies steer storms from west to east across middle latitudes.

The heat index is the combination of temperature and relative humidity that the National Weather Service puts together to warn individuals of possible health threats.

By international agreement, hurricanes are called **typhoons** west of 180° in the Pacific Ocean and **cyclones** in the Indian Ocean.

ON THE SPOT

The Outerbridge family (two adults and two children, ages three and five) is looking for a winter vacation destination. They would like to go to Bermuda for a January beach vacation. They had had a wonderful time there eight years ago on their June honeymoon. They are looking for a family resort on the beach so that their children can swim. What do you know about Bermuda in January that you should tell the couple?

Bermuda is in the Atlantic Ocean off the coast of North Carolina. Although the island is caressed by the Gulf Stream and enjoys a mild climate, in January Bermuda is in the midst of its winter. Many of the beachfront resorts are closed for renovations. Using a map as a sales tool, you might point out Bermuda's geographic location and suggest an island closer to the equator.

TABLE 1.2 Types of Climate

Climate	Characterization
Tropical wet	Always hot and humid. Heavy precipitation.
Tropical wet and dry	Always hot with alternate wet and dry seasons.
Semiarid	Hot to cold. Light precipitation.
Desert	Hot to cool. Very little precipitation.
Subtropical dry summer	Hot, dry summers and mild, rainy winters.
Humid subtropical	Warm to hot summers and cool winters.
Humid oceanic	Warm summers and cool winters. Moderate precipitation.
Humid continental	Mild summers and cold winters. Moderate precipitation.
Subarctic	Short, cool summers and long, cold winters.
Tundra	Always cold with brief chilly summers. Little precipitation.
Icecap	Always cold. Precipitation almost always snow.

Jet streams are part of the westerlies. A cooperating jet stream can shorten the time it takes an airplane to fly east from California. Flying against a jet stream usually makes a flight heading west take longer.

Elevation If latitude were the only variable that affected climate, generalizing would be easy. But other factors also shape climate. The higher a place is, the colder it is. For every 1,000 feet (304.8 m) in elevation, the temperature drops about 3.5° F (1.9° C). For example, Mount Kenya in Kenya—Africa's second-highest mountain—is on the equator. It soars 17,058 feet (5,199 m). The climate is tropical at the base and polar on its twin peaks, where snow falls throughout the year. Global warming is melting the mountain's glaciers and affecting the snow melt.

Note that elevation and altitude are both measures of distance above sea level, but **altitude** refers to height in the atmosphere, and **elevation** refers to height on the surface of the earth.

Topography The earth's surface features also influence climate, particularly the development of clouds and precipitation. Mountains block or funnel the winds that bring clouds and rain. Lands on the **leeward** side of mountains—the protected side away from the wind—tend to be dry; they are said to be in a *rain shadow*. For example, the eastern part of the state of Washington is in the rain shadow of the Cascade Range and is a semiarid region. On the western side of the mountains, Pacific winds bring ample rainfall, and the area is lushly forested. Some of the rainiest places on earth are on windward slopes, those facing the wind. The **windward** side of anything is the direction from which a wind is blowing.

Distance from Water Water regulates climate because it is slow to change temperature. Thus oceans and large lakes have a steadying influence on climate. Winds blowing from the water bring cooler air in summer and warmer air in winter. Because an ocean's water is warmest near the equator, currents that begin there and flow north carry warm water. The Coriolis effect causes the water on the east coast of a continent to be warmer than the water on the west.

The **Gulf Stream** (shown in Figure 1.1) illustrates how a current influences climate. Its warm water originates in the western Caribbean and flows along the U.S. East Coast. It turns northeast after it reaches Cape Hatteras in North Carolina. There its path becomes twisted as it meets cold water from the north. Some parts drift toward Europe and form the **North**

Atlantic Current. Thanks to the current's lingering warmth, the British Isles and western Europe have a milder climate than has Canada's province of Labrador on the same latitude.

Vegetation

Climate and vegetation have a close relationship. The world's vegetation can be divided into four broad categories: forest, grassland, desert, and tundra.

Forests of both evergreen and deciduous trees grow on every continent except Antarctica. About 5 percent of the earth is covered by **rain forests**. These are moist, densely wooded areas. Annual rainfall is about 80 inches (200 cm) and sometimes as high as 400 inches (1,000 cm). Vegetation in a rain forest consists of broadleaf evergreen trees, vines, and sparse undergrowth. The soil is typically shallow and nutrient poor. Once denuded, it does not renew itself easily. There are temperate as well as tropical rain forests. In the temperate rain forest, trees are lower and less dense than in the tropical rain forest, and there is more change with the seasons.

Tropical rain forests are found primarily in parts of South and Central America, central Africa, and southeast Asia. The largest rain forest is in the Amazon basin of South America.

Grasslands are flat or rolling open areas where grasses are the natural vegetation. Examples are the prairies of North America, the savannas of Africa, and the vast steppe that stretches in a wide band across much of eastern Europe and western and central Asia.

A **desert** is any region that supports little plant life because of insufficient moisture. The earth has cold deserts, such as the Arctic and the Antarctic, as well as hot ones. It is believed that no rain has fallen in Antarctica for 2 million years. In warm desert areas, underground water may provide an **oasis**, a small area of vegetation. About one-third of the world's land surface is desert.

Tundra is a cold region characterized by low vegetation. There are two kinds: *alpine tundra*, which is associated with high elevation, and *Arctic tundra*, which exists primarily in extreme northern latitudes. **Permafrost**, a layer of permanently frozen ground beneath the earth's surface, is a characteristic of Arctic tundra. Forests that begin south of the Arctic tundra are called **taiga**. Vast evergreen forests like those in Russia and Canada grow in the taiga area.

✔ CHECK-UP

Major features of the earth include

- ✔ The continents, in order of size: Asia, Africa, North America, South America, Antarctica, Europe, and Australia.
- ✔ The world ocean, divided into the Pacific, Atlantic, Indian, and Arctic.

Climate reflects the interaction of

- ✔ Latitude.
- ✔ Elevation.
- ✔ Topography.
- ✔ Distance from water.

Interaction: Exploring Cultures

From the beginning of time, people have interacted with the geography of their land to create ways of living called **cultures**. Every feature of an area's way of life—including language, religion, dress, diet, arts, manners, recreation, and government—is part of its culture. Culture includes all learned behavior. The study of how people and the environment interact and the cultures that result is called *cultural geography.*

Throughout the world the way people live is always a response to their physical and cultural environment. Cultural change is usually the result of contact and the sharing of ideas, practices, and artifacts. Barriers to contact between people have helped cultural differences survive. Natural barriers such as deserts, mountains, forests, and oceans often restricted the movement of people and ideas. People also have created artificial barriers, such as the Great Wall of China, to keep "foreigners" from entering their territory. Passports, visas, and security procedures are examples of modern artificial barriers.

Travel and tourism have played a part in producing cultural change. The ease of transportation and communication today has reduced cultural isolation, but cultures still differ in fascinating ways. The diversity of cultures offers both attractions and obstacles to tourism.

Great Wall of China

Cultural Attractions

What aspects of a culture are most likely to attract travelers? Religion, food and beverage, arts, and recreation motivate many people to visit particular destinations.

Perhaps no aspect of culture does more to both divide and unite people than religion. Places of worship often tell the story of a people. Travelers interested in the history of a religion and the architecture it has inspired are drawn to religious sites throughout the world.

Almost any visitor is likely to savor at least one aspect of a culture: its food. What people originally ate in an area depended on what was grown there. Although most foods are now widely available, people tend to cling to their habits regarding both what they eat and how they prepare it. Besides the food itself, meal hours, service expectations, and tipping customs also vary from culture to culture.

The arts are usually considered to be the highest expression of a country's culture. These include not only the fine arts—such as literature, music, painting, sculpture, drama, and dance—but also motion pictures, photographs, pottery, weaving, and architecture. The structures in which we live not only tell of the great people and powerful kingdoms of history but also open a window into the everyday life of humankind. Much about a culture can be read from the famous buildings and layout of its cities.

Sports also reflect an area's culture. Examples include soccer in Europe and South America; horse racing in the Middle East; bull fighting in countries with a Spanish background; and, oh yes, football in the United States. Future chapters will describe forms of recreation that have special attractions for tourists.

"In traveling, a man must carry some knowledge with him if he would bring any home."

—Samuel Johnson

Many North and South American cities follow a grid pattern that is rarely seen in older European and Asian cities. Why? The reason dates back to when the continents were being colonized. In 1573 Philip II of Spain decreed the *Laws of the Indies*, which set out procedures for planning towns and their surroundings. The laws stated that cities should be laid out in a grid fashion.

Cultural Complications

Government and language are two additional aspects of an area's culture that may attract the visitor, but these can also discourage and complicate travel. Governments discourage travel when they fail to keep the peace, enact unjust policies, or enforce regulations that make traveling across their borders difficult. Language differences can be just as troublesome. About 3,000

Chinese is the language spoken by the largest number of people. English is spoken over the greatest area.

languages are spoken around the world today. Travelers are best advised to pack a sense of humor along with their foreign dictionaries and just enjoy their linguistic mistakes.

In many lands, travelers should also be prepared to encounter numerous small differences in daily life—such as money, electrical voltage, mealtimes, and the side of the road used for driving. One of the differences most frequently encountered is the system used for weights and measures; Table 1.3 offers some hints on how to deal with it.

✔ CHECK-UP

Aspects of a country's culture that attract tourists include

- ✔ Religion.
- ✔ Food and beverage.
- ✔ The arts.
- ✔ Recreation.

Aspects of culture that complicate travel include

- ✔ Government policies and regulations.
- ✔ Language differences.
- ✔ Everyday customs, such as systems of weights and measures.

Movement: Understanding Tourism

Geographers are interested in how things move across the earth—whether those things are water, birds, plants, or people. Our interest is the movement of travelers. A staggering number of people are traveling today, and the travel, tourism, and hospitality industry is constantly changing to meet their needs and attract yet more travelers.

An outrigger in Indonesia

The Growth of Tourism

After World War II, economic prosperity, paid vacations, transportation advances, and a hotel/motel building boom gave people spare money, time to spend it, better ways to travel, and more satisfactory places to stay. Domestic travel increased as new model cars and the interstate highway system enticed people from their homes. International travel expanded as people wanted to

TABLE 1.3 Conversion Factors for Weights and Measures

When You Know	Multiply By	To Find
miles	1.609	kilometers
kilometers	0.621	miles
square miles	2.590	square kilometers
square kilometers	0.386	square miles
feet	30,480	centimeters
centimeters	0.394	feet
degrees Fahrenheit	5/9 after subtracting 32	degrees Celsius
degrees Celsius	9/5 and then add 32	degrees Fahrenheit

see places they had heard about or been to during the war. The media directed this time, money, and desire toward travel. The first films made on location appeared in the 1950s. About the same time, television brought tantalizing pictures of interesting destinations into the living room.

In the 1990s, global spending on travel and tourism more than doubled. More countries became accessible to tourists. Corporate travel soared, while rising incomes gave people the opportunity for leisure travel. Travel, tourism, and hospitality remain the only "products" that customers are happy to buy without seeing or touching them.

The number of jobs directly or indirectly supported by the business is incalculable. But despite their importance, travel, tourism, and hospitality are fragile industries, depending on economic prosperity and political stability. They have the advantages of being global products, but all the disadvantages of being both nonessential and expensive. Yet they have weathered every storm to date.

Planning a Trip

Why do travelers choose one destination for a trip rather than another? Table 1.4 lists some of the most frequent reasons travelers cited for their choices. The Close-Up discusses factors to keep in mind when you are promoting international travel.

If travelers go abroad, they must meet the regulations of foreign governments regarding border crossings. Often they must consider political conditions and health concerns. These regulations and concerns vary over time, and we do not attempt to describe them for each country. Instead, in the Workbook we offer suggestions about where to find up-to-date information and exercises to give you practice using the sources.

Three key elements in planning a trip are discussed in each chapter: what a traveler might see and do at the destination, options for transportation, and choices for accommodations. The more you know about each of these elements, the better you can meet the needs of travelers.

What to See and What to Do For some people, travel itself is recreational. For others, what they do during the trip provides the recreation. Shopping ranks high among the things travelers like to do. Look for the Profiles in each chapter that discuss attractions such as the shopping opportunities and the cuisine of a destination. There has been a huge increase recently in *special interest travel,* which consists of trips focused on a particular activity or subject. Interests range from physical adventures such as hiking or water sports to gambling, wine tasting, cooking, and theater.

Transportation Leisure travelers have many transportation options. They can choose to go by plane, ship, train, automobile, or motorcoach. Long-distance sea travel today is rarely an option, although ferries continue to provide plenty of water transportation. When people travel by ship, they usually do so for the sake of the cruise itself. The ship, in a sense, has become the destination. Cruise lines have introduced itineraries and ship features that appeal to all tastes and pocketbooks.

Train travel is an option even in North America, where services have lagged behind those of Europe and Japan. Specialty trains that use trains for transportation and accommodations but stop for sightseeing have grown in popularity.

ON THE SPOT

Senior citizens Mr. and Mrs. Fairbairn are concerned about health issues while traveling. Although both are in good health, they have heard too many horror stories from friends about problems encountered in foreign countries, and they want to be prepared. Their question to you is "How do we get medical help abroad?"

Advise them to ask their own doctor and dentist for a list of reliable practitioners at the destination. If neither can provide names, they should find the nearest university teaching hospital or call the U.S. embassy or consulate for a recommendation. The nonprofit International Association of Medical Assistance to Travelers (IAMAT) can provide valuable services in the event of illness. Membership is free, but the group relies on donations.

TABLE 1.4

Factors Cited Most Often for Choice of Vacation Destination

Reason	Percentage Who Cited
Beautiful scenic place	50%
Good weather and climate	43%
Been there before	41%
Lots of things to do	39%
Very relaxing place	39%
Reasonable cost of hotels/meals	38%
Good place for family	32%
Safe and secure place	30%
People speak English	25%*
Great place to shop	24%*

*Other factors not listed here were cited more frequently.
Source: NFO Plog/*Travel Weekly*, November 2003

Many destinations offer unusual forms of transportation: monorails at theme parks; hovercrafts across channels, harbors, and bays; helicopter rides over scenic regions; cog rails (gears that connect small trains to the rail bed, allowing the trains to climb a hill); funiculars (counterbalanced cable rail cars used on steep inclines; one car ascends as the other descends); and ski lifts in mountain territory. There are also camel rides in the desert, elephant rides in the jungle, horseback rides at guest ranches, raft rides through white water, river and sea kayaking, and bicycle treks. The book highlights special forms of transportation in each chapter.

Accommodations Around the world people can find hotels that are just like those in North America, but they can also find accommodations that reflect the area's culture and provide special travel experiences. This book will mention some famous hotels and discuss the unique accommodations found in each destination.

Tours Transportation, accommodations, and activities are put together and priced by tour operators in a process called *packaging*. Packaged tours can be divided into three categories: independent, hosted, and escorted.

- An **independent tour** is a prepaid package of three travel elements. The elements are usually air, ground transportation at the destination, and lodging. Travelers on an independent tour never see anyone from the tour company; they present vouchers provided by the tour operator or travel

CLOSE-UP: PROMOTING INTERNATIONAL TRAVEL

Who is a good prospect for international travel? International travel requires time, money, and desire. If time and money are available, why do some people travel and some people stay at home? Why don't both types of people have desire? To find the answers, *qualifying* the traveler becomes the most important part of the travel sale. You must question the prospective travelers before suggesting destinations. You can pick up clues by asking such questions as "Where have you been before that you enjoyed?" or "If you could go anywhere in the world, where would you like to go?"

Where would they go? It is possible to define the character of destinations in terms of the types of people they appeal to. The timid traveler is generally happiest nearest home, visiting a beach, theme park, or gambling resort for a bit of fun. The adventurous traveler seeks the new, the exciting, or the destination with a lot of personal challenges, such as travel in a developing country or some sort of physically demanding adventure.

When is the best time to go? A destination's seasons obey no hard-and-fast rules, but they are generally set on the basis of demand as high, low, or shoulder. Each season has its attractions and drawbacks.

- **High season** is the time when a destination is in most demand. Prices are at their highest, and crowds are at their worst. The climate of the traveler's home influences the traveler's choice. For example, it is the temperature back home that makes winter the high season for the Caribbean, not the temperature of the Caribbean, an area where temperatures fluctuate little.
- **Low season** is an area's time of least demand. Prices are lower, and there is less crowding. Between the Thanksgiving and Christmas holidays is usually a low season for travel.
- **Shoulder season** is a time when demand is neither high nor low. Shoulder seasons occur in spring and fall. They are times of good value, chancy weather, and middling crowds and are growing more and more popular with travelers who have no time constraints and can go when they wish.

Your clients make the following objection: "You are suggesting a trip to France for our vacation. Although we love the country, we have been there several times. Isn't there someplace new we can visit?" How would you respond? To renew an experienced traveler's interest, you do not always have to suggest a new destination. You might repackage the tried and true. Suggest taking a new mode of transportation, such as a barge tour, or concentrating on a special interest such as a wine, cooking, or bicycle tour.

FIGURE 1.5 Evaluating Tour Packages

Here are some guidelines for evaluating tour packages.

Itineraries

How many times will the traveler have to pack and unpack?

How many days will be spent in each destination?

Will the travelers be able to see the destination in depth, or will they have time for only a quick overview?

Hotels and Location

Most tour companies categorize their hotels as tourist, first class, or deluxe. Does the tour company's category mesh with industry ratings?

Where is the hotel in relation to the city center?

What amenities are offered?

Meals

Are they included? If so, how many?

Are menus set, or can travelers order à la carte?

Sightseeing

Is sightseeing included or "optional" (at extra cost)?

Do excursions "view" (just drive by) or "visit" (stop and enter) an advertised attraction?

Transportation

Are the motorcoaches small vans or large coaches?

Do they have bathrooms? Will the guide rotate seats?

Travel Time per Day

Is the traveler OK with the amount of movement? Few people enjoy traveling more than eight hours a day.

Terms and Conditions

What does the brochure say about cancellation penalties, final payment requirements, and tour inclusions and exclusions?

---

counselor to the supplier of the transportation or lodging facility. At the destination they are free to do as they wish.

- **Hosted tours** include the same prepaid elements as independent tours. The difference is that a host is available at the destination to assist the travelers. Hosted tours primarily go to one destination such as to a resort or to London.
- The **escorted tour** is a structured program of prepaid transportation, lodging, sightseeing, and certain meals accompanied by a person who meets the travelers at the destination and stays with them for the duration of the trip. Usually, participants on an escorted tour are part of a group, although it is possible to have a private escorted tour. Group size varies. Movement characterizes an escorted tour, and a key benefit is having the escort to help with logistics. Tour escorts know the territory and how to smooth over difficulties.

At first glance many tour packages may look alike, but in fact, there are usually subtle variations that can spell the difference between a satisfied traveler and a potential lawsuit. See Figure 1.5 for help in evaluating tours.

✔ CHECK-UP

Key divisions of the travel industry are
- ✔ Business travel.
- ✔ Leisure travel.

Elements of a trip include
- ✔ What to see or do.
- ✔ Transportation.
- ✔ Accommodation.

Learning about the Destination

Destination geography is a complex subject, immense and ever changing. You cannot depend on personal experience. One expert suggests that if you have not been someplace in two years, you have not been there.

Only through continuous education can we keep up with change. Personal travel, training programs, Global Distribution Systems (GDSs), the Web, books, magazines, TV, films, videos, and networking with peers are ways to learn about destinations. You should become familiar with the following key types of sources:

- *Atlases and dictionaries.* For spelling and pronunciation of place-names, see a specialized dictionary such as *Merriam Webster's Geographical Dictionary.*
- *Government resources.* When questions involve safety, health, or customs and documentation regulations, it is best to turn to authoritative sources such as U.S. government agencies and publications—for example, the State Department and Centers for Disease Control.
- *Guidebooks.* Time-specific information is more easily updated on Web sites than in books, but printed guidebooks are best at portraying a country's history and culture.
- *Travel suppliers and trade associations.* Brochures and seminars created by travel suppliers offer a wealth of information. Trade associations that are especially useful sources include the *Cruise Line International Association (CLIA),* which is the trade organization of the cruise industry, as well as the *United States Tour Operators Association (USTOA)* and the *National Tour Association (NTA),* both prestigious associations of international and domestic tour operators.
- *Trade and consumer magazines.* Trade papers such as *Travel Weekly, Travel Agent, Travel Trade, Tour and Travel News,* and the trade association magazines are directed to those who work within the industry. Publications for the general public that offer good travel information include the travel columns of the *New York Times,* other major newspapers, and *Condé Nast Traveler.*

Chapter 1 of the Workbook that supplements this textbook provides a fuller outline of the basic sources of information about destinations. For capsule information about each country discussed in this book, see Fast Facts (Appendix A) on page 417.

As you begin to know where to go or the person to ask to get answers to your questions, you are developing vital research skills. Each chapter of the Workbook includes a Resources box with a list of Web sites and worksheets designed to give you practice. The old saying "Practice makes perfect" still holds. Technology may shorten distances, but the person who wants to see what's over the next hill will always be around, needing information and seeking the travel professional who can provide the answers.

CHAPTER WRAP-UP

SUMMARY

Here is a review of the objectives with which we began the chapter.

1. **Describe the key features of maps and the system of time zones.** All maps must simplify and distort reality to represent three-dimensional space in two dimensions. Key features of any map include its scale and projection. Mapmakers must choose a geographic grid as the frame of reference for plotting the position of places on earth. Lines of longitude and latitude mark the grid. One line of longitude—the prime meridian at Greenwich, England—is the reference point for the system of time zones. At each time zone, the time differs by one hour, expressed as plus or minus GMT (Greenwich Mean Time). The international date line where the zones meet is 180° from Greenwich in the Pacific.

2. **Locate the land and water masses of the earth, and describe the major landforms.** The major landmasses are the seven continents: Asia, Africa, North America, South America, Antarctica, Europe, and Australia. The world ocean has four subdivisions: the Pacific, Atlantic, Indian, and Arctic. Features of the land include geologically stable regions called shields and younger, more active regions marked by mountains. Other key landforms include hills, valleys, canyons, plains, and plateaus.

3. **Explain the factors that influence the climate of a destination.** The farther away a destination is from the equator, the less sunlight the region receives. Thus latitude is a dominant influence on climate. The higher the elevation, however, the lower the temperature is. Large bodies of water moderate a nearby climate. Within the ocean, currents carry warm and cold water to various destinations. Vegetation and climate interact. The principal kinds of vegetation are forest, grassland, desert, and tundra.

4. **Describe how cultural geography influences tourism.** To many people, the diversity of cultures is an incentive to travel. Religion, food, the arts, and recreation are aspects of cultures that are particularly likely to attract tourists. Differences in language, in government regulations, and in ways of handling daily tasks such as driving are among the aspects of cultures that can complicate travel.

5. **Identify key sources of information used in planning trips.** Information is available electronically or in print. The U.S. government provides information related to health and safety abroad. Atlases, dictionaries, guidebooks, travel suppliers, trade associations, and trade and consumer magazines are also important sources.

QUESTIONS FOR DISCUSSION AND REVIEW

1. Why are location and place important geographic themes?
2. Why does the temperature of a place or region depend on its elevation?
3. If people living in regions with a lot of snow build homes with pointed roofs, in what region might they build homes with flat roofs? Why?
4. Why do people create cultural barriers?
5. Can you think of anything in your food preferences that you would relate to your cultural background?

1) use of maps + knowing the 24 hr clock + the international date line help to pinpoint a location; help the traveler determine how long the trip will take. Place describes environmental features, (topography), which can affect the types of activities + the climate.

2) The higher the elevation, the lower the temp.

3) Places w/ little precip

4)

5)

CHAPTER 2

The Eastern United States

- New England
- New York
- Mid-Atlantic States
- The South
- Florida
- The Gulf States

OBJECTIVES

When you have completed Chapter 2, you should be able to

1. Describe the environment and people of the eastern United States.
2. Identify the main attractions of the region, matching travelers and destinations best suited for each other.
3. Provide or find the information needed to plan a trip to the eastern United States.

The United States is the world's fourth-largest country, outstripped by Canada and Russia in physical size, by India in population, and by China in both respects. Still, within its shores are most types of natural environments, people from every corner of the globe, and countless travel attractions.

Bordered by Canada and Mexico, the United States spans the North American continent from east to west. Its states can be classified in many ways. This book presents them in three chapters, moving from east to west. The eastern United States is the topic of Chapter 2. Chapter 3 examines the states of the Great Lakes, Great Plains, and Texas. Chapter 4 looks at the Mountain and Pacific states as well as Alaska and Hawaii. Areas that are governed by the United States but are not states—Puerto Rico, the U.S. Virgin Islands, Guam, and American Samoa—are discussed in Chapters 6 and 15.

The eastern United States includes twenty-two states and the District of Columbia, and it stretches from the Canadian border south to the Gulf of Mexico and from the Atlantic Ocean west to the Mississippi and Ohio Rivers. Figure 2.1 is a map of the region. This chapter first takes a broad look at the region's environment and culture; then it describes places to see and things to do. The chapter ends with a review of elements to consider in planning a trip to these destinations. See the Fact File in Appendix A for a list of the states in alphabetical order.

The Environment and Its People

Geographically and culturally, the eastern states vary significantly. From north to south, the region includes the New England states of **Maine**, **New Hampshire**, **Vermont**, **Massachusetts**, **Rhode Island**, and **Connecticut**; **New York**; the Mid-Atlantic states of **New Jersey**, **Pennsylvania**, **Delaware**, and **Maryland**; the southern states of **Virginia**, **West Virginia**, **North Carolina**, **South Carolina**, **Georgia**, **Tennessee**, and **Kentucky**; **Florida**; and to the west, the Gulf states of **Alabama**, **Mississippi**, and **Louisiana**.

It was in the east that the United States began, so the area is rich in historic attractions. The region owes much of its success to its plentiful natural resources, the hard work of its pioneers, and a rich cultural mix.

PROFILE

East Coast National Millennium Trails

The U.S. Department of Transportation selects these driving and hiking trails because they reflect their region's history, culture, and character.

- *American Discovery Trail*. This route from Cape Henlopen State Park in Delaware to Point Reyes National Seashore in California has more than 10,000 historic sites.
- *Appalachian National Scenic Trail*. This continuous footpath stretches through fourteen states from Maine to Georgia.
- *Civil War Discovery Trail*. Through twenty-seven states and the District of Columbia, this trail traces the political, social, and military aspects of the Civil War.
- *Underground Railroad*. This is the route traveled by escaping slaves seeking freedom.
- *Unicoi Turnpike Trail*. This path over the southern Appalachians played a significant role in the fur and hide trade between the Cherokee and European traders.

The Land

Most of the eastern states border the Atlantic Ocean or the Gulf of Mexico, with coastal plains extending inland from the shore. Much of the coastal plain of New England and New York lies beneath the sea; almost all that remains is a series of peninsulas and islands, most notably **Cape Cod** in Massachusetts and **Long Island** in New York State.

South of New York the coastal area is different. From Long Island to Florida, gently sloping beaches are protected in their battle with the ocean by a line of barrier islands and sandbars that runs parallel to the shore. In the southern states the coastal plain is called the **tidewater**, and it is broad and low-lying, with many swampy areas. Inshore, river valleys flooded by the sea created estuaries (an **estuary** is an arm of the sea at the mouth of a river), such as Chesapeake Bay on the coast of Maryland and Virginia. Farther south, Florida, a long, flat, swampy peninsula, juts from the mainland. A narrow ribbon of sandbars, coral reefs, and barrier islands protects its shore.

FIGURE 2.1

Eastern United States

FIGURE 2.2

Milestones of the History of the Eastern United States

1513 Ponce de León lands on the Florida coast and claims the region for Spain.

1607 The first permanent English settlement is established in Jamestown, Virginia.

1620 The Pilgrims settle on Cape Cod.

1664 Dutch New Amsterdam becomes the English colony of New York.

1776 The Continental Congress adopts the Declaration of Independence.

1791 President Washington selects a site for the Federal District.

1803 Thomas Jefferson makes the Louisiana Purchase.

1825 The Erie Canal links New York City and the Midwest.

1861–1865 The Civil War takes place.

1896 Henry Flagler's East Coast Railway reaches Miami.

1903 The Wright brothers make the first successful powered airplane flight near Kitty Hawk, North Carolina.

1931 The Empire State Building opens in New York City.

1934 John D. Rockefeller Jr. funds the restoration of Williamsburg, Virginia.

1940 The Pennsylvania Turnpike, the nation's first multilane, limited-access highway, opens.

1978 Atlantic City, New Jersey, opens casinos.

2001 Terrorists destroy New York City's World Trade Center and damage the Pentagon in Washington, D.C.

2004 World War II Memorial opens on the Mall in Washington, D.C.

West of the coastal plain, the area south of Maryland to Georgia has a region of rolling, hilly land known as the **Piedmont** (*PEED mahnt*)—French for "foot of the mountain." It is separated from the coastal plain by a distinct *fall line*, the place where rivers plunge into waterfalls and rapids, marking the limit of inland travel for ships. The Piedmont ends when it meets the **Appalachian** (*ap uh LAY chuhn*) **Mountains**.

The Appalachians stretch from southeast Canada to Alabama and include many mountain ranges. In the northeast, the ranges are the **White Mountains** in New Hampshire, the **Green Mountains** in Vermont, and the **Adirondack** (*ad uh RAHN dak*) and **Catskill Mountains** in New York. The **Alleghenies** extend from central Pennsylvania through western Maryland, eastern West Virginia, and western Virginia. The **Blue Ridge Mountains** stretch from southeastern Pennsylvania across western Maryland, Virginia, North and South Carolina, and northwest Georgia. Other ranges include the **Great Smoky Mountains**, which got their name from the smoky haze that usually covers them.

West of the mountains, the fertile Great Valley extends from the Hudson River Valley to Alabama. The Great Valley includes the Cumberland, Lebanon, and Lehigh Valleys in Pennsylvania, the Shenandoah (*shehn uhn DOH uh*) Valley in Virginia, the Valley of East Tennessee, and the Coosa River Valley in Alabama.

Farther west is the vast basin of the **Mississippi-Missouri** and **Ohio Rivers**. The Mississippi flows 2,340 miles (3,766 km) from its source in northwest Minnesota to its mouth in the Gulf of Mexico in Louisiana. Through the centuries the river has brought huge amounts of sediment, building a delta where the river meets the gulf.

The Climate

The climate of the eastern United States ranges from subtropical in Florida to humid continental in the northern states. New England and New York are noted for their cold winters, warm summers, and a broad daily range of temperatures. Cold, snowy winters linger from November to May. Springs, summers, and falls are short. Each state has regional variations.

The Mid-Atlantic states have a four-season climate. In low elevations near the coast, the region has hot, muggy summers from June to September, pleasant falls from October to November, cold winters from December through early March, and springs with beautiful floral displays. The climate in higher elevations is cooler in summers and colder in winters.

The South and the Gulf states have a subtropical climate with hot, humid summers, mild winters, and precipitation in all seasons.

Hurricanes cause havoc in an extensive area along the Atlantic Coast and the Gulf of Mexico. The official hurricane season is from June to November.

The People and Their History

The people now known as Native Americans had been living in North America for thousands of years before foreign explorers arrived in the 1500s. The New World offered opportunities for wealth, power, and adventure, and before long the newcomers were outnumbering the Native Americans and overwhelming their culture (see Figure 2.2).

At first, settlers came from northwestern Europe, especially Spain, Great Britain, Ireland, the Netherlands, Germany, and France. To farm the fertile land, slaves were brought from Africa to the southern plantations. Wherever they settled, the immigrants brought the place-names, architectural styles, food preferences, and speech patterns of their ancestral homes to the new land. In some areas, such as mountainous regions or islands, geographic barriers allowed unique cultures to develop.

By the 17th and 18th centuries, the British governed the lands along the Atlantic, except for Florida. In 1776 thirteen colonies challenged the world's most powerful empire. They defeated Great Britain and created the United States. Most of the eastern states were part of this birth of the nation; however, Tennessee, Kentucky, Florida, Alabama, Mississippi, and Louisiana did not become states until later.

Disputes between the North and the South ended in the Civil War (1861–1865). Rebuilding was painfully slow in the South; meanwhile the North entered a time of great industrial expansion. The need for labor encouraged immigration from Italy, Scandinavia, and Eastern Europe.

The southern states remained poor well into the 20th century. In the period after World War II, federal programs such as the interstate highway system, the movement of corporations south in search of less expensive labor and land for factories, and the civil rights movement brought immense change to the region. The southern states became not only prosperous but also leaders in the country's growth.

✔ CHECK-UP

Major features of the eastern United States include

- ✔ Flat coastal plains.
- ✔ Barrier islands off the coast.
- ✔ Piedmont, particularly noticeable from Maryland south to Georgia.
- ✔ Appalachian Mountain System with its many ranges.
- ✔ Continental basin of the Mississippi-Missouri and Ohio River systems.
- ✔ Mississippi delta.
- ✔ Climate ranging from subtropical to humid continental, with many variations.

The culture of the eastern United States is notable for

- ✔ Submergence of Native American culture by European cultures.
- ✔ Influence of settlers' ancestral cultures on development.
- ✔ Diverse architectural styles, culture preferences, and speech patterns.

New England

Six states—Maine, New Hampshire, Vermont, Massachusetts, Rhode Island, and Connecticut—make up New England. Figure 2.3 shows a map of the region. In the 17th century English colonists brought democratic values and an emphasis on education that remain strong traditions.

Maine, New Hampshire, and Vermont are mountainous and rural, especially toward the Canadian border, where evergreen forests dominate the landscape. Their village greens, white churches with tall steeples, covered bridges, and small inns are the essence of New England. In fall, the colors of the woods are justly famous. In winter, the mountains are magnets for winter sports. Spring, locally called "mud season," is short. In summer, skis and skates are exchanged for hiking boots, mountain bikes, fishing rods, and canoe paddles. Craft fairs, antique shows, and theater and music programs flourish in July and August.

FIGURE 2.3 New England

Massachusetts, Rhode Island, and Connecticut are more urban. Their terrain is rolling, with the sea in the east and hills in the west. Their historical sites are attractive destinations for individuals and families exploring America's colonial past.

Maine

Maine's relatively unspoiled natural beauty is a key attraction. Forests cover nearly 90 percent of the interior. In the east, long fingers of the mainland extend miles into the sea. The jagged coastline is home to thousands of small islands. **Augusta** is the state's capital.

In western Maine's rugged north woods, the **Allagash Wilderness**

Waterway is a white-water canoe paddler's dream. It stretches south from the Canadian border 92 miles (148 km) through dense forests, where primitive campsites line the banks. Slightly to the east of the Allagash in Baxter State Park, **Mount Katahdin** is the northern end of the Appalachian Trail.

Most of Maine's tourist attractions are on the coast. Mount Desert Island (from the French word meaning "bare" and pronounced like the English word *dessert*) is a national treasure. Sixty percent of the island is **Acadia National Park**, which is a small park compared to western ones, but one of the most visited. Attractions include Cadillac Mountain—the highest point on the Atlantic Coast between Labrador, Canada, and Rio de Janeiro, Brazil—and miles of hiking trails. The town of **Bar Harbor** near the park's entrance provides shops, restaurants, and accommodations.

Down the coast, **Camden** and **Rockland** are embarkation ports for the windjammers (sailing ships) that cruise off the coast from mid-May to mid-October. Seven of the windjammers represented by the Maine Windjammer Association are designated National Historic Landmarks. Farther south, near the New Hampshire border, the resort of **Ogunquit** (*oh GUNG quit*) has a wide expanse of beach—but don't expect warm water! From **Portland**, Maine's largest city, ferries run to the nearby Casco Bay Islands.

What makes the tourist shiver seems to make one Maine native—the lobster—very happy. The cold-water lobster grows claws, something warm-water lobsters do not. For centuries the lobster was considered food for the poor only.

New Hampshire

cap-Concord - Rural - White mts, winter skiing, fall-foliage, summer-lakes, hiking

Unlike Maine, New Hampshire has little coastline. Its southeast corner meets the Atlantic for only 18 miles (29 km). The state's natural harbor, **Portsmouth**, became a thriving community during the 17th and 18th centuries and then fell into neglect. Rescued, the area is now a restoration of an early waterfront community called Strawbery Banke.

West of Portsmouth are **Manchester**, the state's largest city, and the capital, **Concord**. Concord's domed State House is the country's oldest in continuous use.

From Concord, roads lead north to the state's travel attractions. In the middle of the state, spreading west from the Maine border, is the Lake Region; it is home to 237 lakes and ponds as well as ski resorts (see the Profile on ski resorts). **Laconia** on **Lake Winnipesaukee** (Native American for "Smiling Waters") is a summer destination. North of the lakes, travel on the Kancamagus Highway from North Conway in the east to Lincoln in the west is a popular way to view the fall foliage.

Mount Washington, the highest peak in the Northeast, rises in the Presidential Range of the White Mountains. P. T. Barnum once described its view as "the second-greatest show on earth." On a nice day in summer, its summit can be reached by foot, automobile (toll road), or the 1869 cog railway. The mountain's weather is treacherous, with record-breaking winds. Many have died on its slopes.

Vermont

Rural, Green Mts, cap. Montpelier, winter-skiing, fall-foliage, summer-lakes, hiking, maple syrup

West of New Hampshire is Vermont, one of the most historic and beautiful states. It has no ocean seashore, but its northwestern edge borders **Lake Champlain**, which it shares with New York State and Canada. Thick evergreen forests cover the slopes of the Green Mountains. The state's stony soil makes farming difficult but yields useful minerals. The Vermont Marble Exhibit in Proctor displays locally quarried marble and shows how the raw material is turned into a carved and polished product.

➤ PROFILE

New England Ski Resorts

The year 2003 saw 57.6 million visitor days at U.S. ski resorts. Here's a sampling of New England's resorts. For more information, visit www.skiresorts.com.

Maine

- ➤ Sugarloaf, a "turbo tubing" park, with tunnels in the snow for fast sledding.
- ➤ Sunday River, conveniently near Portland.

New Hampshire

- ➤ Attitash, where snowboarding is almost as popular as downhill skiing.
- ➤ Bretton Woods, the White Mountains' largest resort.
- ➤ Jackson, center of cross-country skiing.
- ➤ Waterville Valley, with condos on the slopes.
- ➤ Wildcat, New Hampshire's highest lift-served summit.

Vermont

- ➤ Killington, the largest ski complex east of the Mississippi.
- ➤ Mount Snow, with trails for novices and a tubing park.
- ➤ Smugglers' Notch, with facilities for those seeking terrain for practice.
- ➤ Stowe, suitable for both beginners and experts.
- ➤ Stratton Mountain, which claims to make more snow than any other eastern resort.
- ➤ Sugarbush, with ample accommodations nearby.

Vermont remains mostly rural. Its cities have stayed small; the capital, **Montpelier** (*mahnt PEEL yuhr*), has fewer than 10,000 residents. **Burlington**, on the shores of Lake Champlain, is the largest city.

The state's year-round resort industry has thrived since the 19th century. City folks come for the cool lakes and mountain air, fall foliage, and snowy slopes. Some of the East's largest winter resorts are in Vermont (see the Profile on page 27). The state is also known for its covered bridges, called "wishing" or "kissing" bridges. The bridges had to be "high enough and wide enough to take a load of hay."

To discover Vermont, travelers should leave the interstates and drive on the back roads. In the middle of the state, Route 100 passes through the **Mad River Valley**, a beautiful four-season area famed for its resorts. The road from Warren to Waitsfield is especially scenic.

Vermont is the largest U.S. producer of maple sugar. "Sugaring off" begins when the snow starts melting in March. People gather at sugarhouses to watch syrup being made from maple sap.

Massachusetts

Massachusetts is the hub of New England tourism. Many tours begin and end in the capital, **Boston**, which is also the region's largest city.

Boston

Rich in culture and history, Boston is a patchwork of distinctive neighborhoods, such as the North End, an Italian enclave; Beacon Hill, original home of the "Proper Bostonians"; the sophisticated Back Bay; the multicultural South End; colorful Chinatown; the Theater District; and Kenmore Square, center of student life.

Things to see and do in Boston include

- Riding the swan-shapted, pedal-powered boats (in season) on a lagoon in the Public Garden.
- Walking the Freedom Trail, a self-guided tour that winds through the city, passing sixteen landmarks in the founding of the nation.
- Visiting the waterfront. Its attractions include Faneuil (various pronunciations include *FAN nel*, *FAN you ill*, and *fan YUL*) Hall and Quincy Market, which offers food stalls, restaurants, boutiques, bars, pushcarts, and street entertainment. Nearby are hotels, the New England Aquarium, and ferries to Boston Harbor Islands National Recreation Area and State Park. The completion of the city's "Big Dig," a massive construction project, has opened the waterfront to the development of new parks and other attractions.
- Viewing a museum. Choices include the Museum of Fine Arts, the Isabella Stewart Gardner Museum, the Museum of Science, and the John F. Kennedy Library.
- Attending the Boston Symphony or a Boston Pops concert.
- Cheering a team. Fenway Park is home to baseball's Red Sox; the Fleet Center hosts professional and college sports.

In 1929 Arthur Fiedler (1894–1974) instituted free concerts by professional musicians at the Hatch Shell on the banks of the Charles River. The Boston Pops' season highlight is the Fourth of July concert, which ends with Tchaikovsky's *1812 Overture*, complete with church bells, cannons, and elaborate fireworks.

Cambridge

The Charles River separates Boston from the city of **Cambridge**. Cambridge is a college town. Harvard (1636), the first college in the colonies, and MIT make the city a center of technology research. Harvard has one of the country's finest university art collections in its museums: the Fogg Art Museum, the Arthur M. Sackler Museum, and the Busch-Reisinger Museum. Another Cambridge sight is the Henry Wadsworth Longfellow House. In good weather, street life in Harvard Square provides entertainment into the wee hours.

Lexington and Concord

On April 19, 1775, about 70 Minutemen waited for more than 700 British soldiers as they heeded Paul Revere's warning, "The

British are coming." Today, visitors to Lexington and Concord can stop by Buckman Tavern, where the Minutemen met; see the Lexington Battle Green, where the "shot heard round the world" started the American Revolution; and travel the Battle Road through Minuteman National Historical Park to Concord's Old North Bridge.

In the 1800s, Concord was home to influential American authors. Ralph Waldo Emerson, Louisa May Alcott, Nathaniel Hawthorne, and Henry David Thoreau lived there. Nearby is Walden Pond, the inspiration for Thoreau's book *Walden*.

The North Shore In **Salem**, north of Boston, the Salem Witch Museum traces the witchcraft hysteria that gripped the town in the 1690s. Salem also has a glorious seafaring history preserved at the Salem Maritime National Historical Site. Tourists can also visit the House of Seven Gables, the setting for Nathaniel Hawthorne's novel of that name.

Gloucester, on the coast of Cape Ann, 27 miles (43 km) northeast of Boston, is home to several museums and whale-watching excursions. It is the home port featured in the thrilling film *The Perfect Storm*.

Plymouth South of Boston, sites near the town of Plymouth commemorate the Pilgrims' settlement of New England in 1620. Their supposed landing site, Plymouth Rock, has been moved several times but now rests here. Plimouth Plantation re-creates the settlement with costumed interpreters who speak in 17th-century dialect, with settings and food demonstrations that are about as authentic as possible.

Cape Cod The Cape is the large bent arm of land that extends from the Massachusetts mainland. Its small shingled "Cape Cod" houses, salt marshes, lakes, cranberry bogs, sandy beaches, and cooling breezes make it a favorite vacation area. Some of its treasured beaches have been declared a National Seashore. **Provincetown**, at the tip of the Cape, is known as an artists' and writers' colony. Ferries to the islands of **Martha's Vineyard** and **Nantucket** leave from **Wood's Hole** and **Hyannis.** The islands are low-key, upscale resorts with homes of the rich and famous, as well as small hotels and B&Bs to delight today's vacationers.

The Berkshires Two to three hours by car to the west of Boston, the **Berkshire Hills** are home to the sounds of music and also art, theater, and dance. The Boston Symphony Orchestra at **Tanglewood**, the Berkshire Choral Festival at Sheffield, the Norman Rockwell Museum at **Stockbridge**, and the Jacob's Pillow Dance Festival at Becket are joined by a number of smaller yet vital companies and performance centers.

Rhode Island

Summer beaches parks mansions Cap Providence

Although it takes just forty-five minutes to drive from one end of Rhode Island to the other, the smallest state in the nation has miles of beaches, parks, historic attractions, and some of the world's most magnificent mansions.

Providence The capital of Rhode Island enjoyed a major facelift in the 1990s. Providence's revitalization included the rerouting of two rivers and the building of pedestrian walkways and Venetian-style footbridges around Waterplace Park.

ON THE SPOT

The Folsoms live in Alabama and would like to take a driving trip to New England during the first week of October. But they are having trouble making hotel reservations and have heard that the roads are very congested and that all the leaves will have fallen by October 1. They ask you if they should reconsider their plans. How would you respond?

You might suggest that the Folsoms consider flying to Boston and then taking a motorcoach tour for relaxation, assured reservations, and price control. The motorcoach driver will know the best routes for seeing scenery and for avoiding traffic. The tour operator has blocked hotel space. The Folsoms also will benefit by knowing how much the trip will cost. When will the leaves fall? Well, no one can say for sure, but early October is usually a time of peak color.

Architect Richard Morris Hunt was asked to build a summer "cottage" for the Vanderbilt family in Newport, Rhode Island. The cottage wound up with seventy rooms—thirty-three of which were set aside for household staff and the maids and valets of guests.

Newport Located south of Providence, Newport is called the *Queen of American Resorts.* In its mansions, the Gilded Age of 19th-century millionaires reached its peak. The Breakers is Newport's most frequently visited home. Other houses open to visitors are Marble House, Chateau-sur-Mer, the Elms, Kingscote, and Rosecliff. At Christmas the houses are beautifully decorated. The Cliff Walk, a national historic trail, passes in back of the mansions along the bluffs overlooking the sea and allows the walker glimpses of a different world.

Other Newport sights include the International Tennis Hall of Fame, the Museum of Yachting, and the Touro Synagogue National Historic Site, which is the oldest Jewish house of worship in the United States. Music festivals draw large crowds: in July, the Newport Music Festival of classical music; in August, the Newport Jazz Festival; and in late August, the Newport Folk Festival. A popular excursion from Newport is the one-hour ferry trip to **Block Island** to see the National Wildlife Refuge and Mohegan Bluffs.

Connecticut

casinos

Proximity to New York City has made Connecticut home to some of America's wealthiest people, but the state is more than the city's bedroom. Much of Connecticut is open land, with rolling hills in the northwest. The Connecticut River flows south through the state's center into Long Island Sound, where sailboats from the marinas along the shore test the wind.

Hartford is Connecticut's capital and hometown to several insurance companies. Here, tourists can visit the Victorian mansion where Samuel Clemens (1835–1910) wrote *The Adventures of Tom Sawyer* (1876) using his pseudonym Mark Twain. Nearby is the farm where the author of *Uncle Tom's Cabin*, Harriet Beecher Stowe (1811–1896), lived until her death.

Tourism is most evident along the coast. **New Haven** is the home of Yale University and the Peabody Museum of Natural History. New London hosts the U.S. Coast Guard Academy. **Mystic** recalls Connecticut's seafaring tradition; the seaport has been rebuilt to look like a whaling village of the 1800s.

Inland near Ledyard, the Mashantucket Pequot Tribal Nation's **Foxwoods**—the world's largest casino complex—and nearby Mohegan Pequot Tribe's Mohegan Sun casino compete for the traveler's dollar. A part of the Foxwoods complex, the Mashantucket Pequot Museum is an enormous interactive facility that tells a very different story of the settling of America.

✔ CHECK-UP

New England includes

- ✔ Maine; its capital is Augusta.
- ✔ New Hampshire; its capital is Concord.
- ✔ Vermont; its capital is Montpelier.
- ✔ Massachusetts; its capital and New England's largest city is Boston.
- ✔ Rhode Island; its capital is Providence.
- ✔ Connecticut; its capital is Hartford.

For travelers, highlights of New England include

- ✔ Colorful fall foliage.
- ✔ Skiing in Maine, New Hampshire, and Vermont.
- ✔ Freedom Trail in Boston.
- ✔ Scene of the American Revolution's "shot heard round the world" in Lexington.
- ✔ Music in the Berkshires.
- ✔ Mansions of the Gilded Age in Rhode Island.
- ✔ Seafaring traditions of Mystic, Connecticut.

New York

New York is bounded by Vermont, Massachusetts, and Connecticut on its east; New Jersey and Pennsylvania on its south; and **Lakes Erie** and **Ontario** on its west and northwest. (See Figure 2.4 for a map.) A popular vacationland, the state has a coastline along the Atlantic plus the Hudson River, forested mountains, shining lakes, historic attractions, and extensive sports facilities.

The Cities

New York has six cities with populations over 100,000: **Albany** (the state's capital), Buffalo, Rochester, Syracuse, Yonkers, and, of course, **New York City**.

Statue of Liberty, New York City

New York City The country's largest city—known affectionately as the *Big Apple*—New York City attracts millions of business and leisure visitors a year. When people talk about New York, they are usually referring to Manhattan, the oldest of the city's five boroughs. The other boroughs are the Bronx, Brooklyn, Queens, and Staten Island.

Manhattan is a rocky island surrounded by the East River, New York Harbor, the Hudson, and the narrow Harlem River. It has one of the world's great natural harbors. The city is built on a simple grid pattern. Except in Lower Manhattan, streets intersect at right angles and those going east-west are numbered. North-south avenues have names and numbers. Fifth Avenue is the city's spine. Streets to its west are known as the West Side; streets to the east are on the East Side. Uptown is the area north of 59th Street. A hotel in Midtown is convenient for tourists. Lower Manhattan means south of 34th Street. In parts of Lower Manhattan, streets have names and follow the original colonial

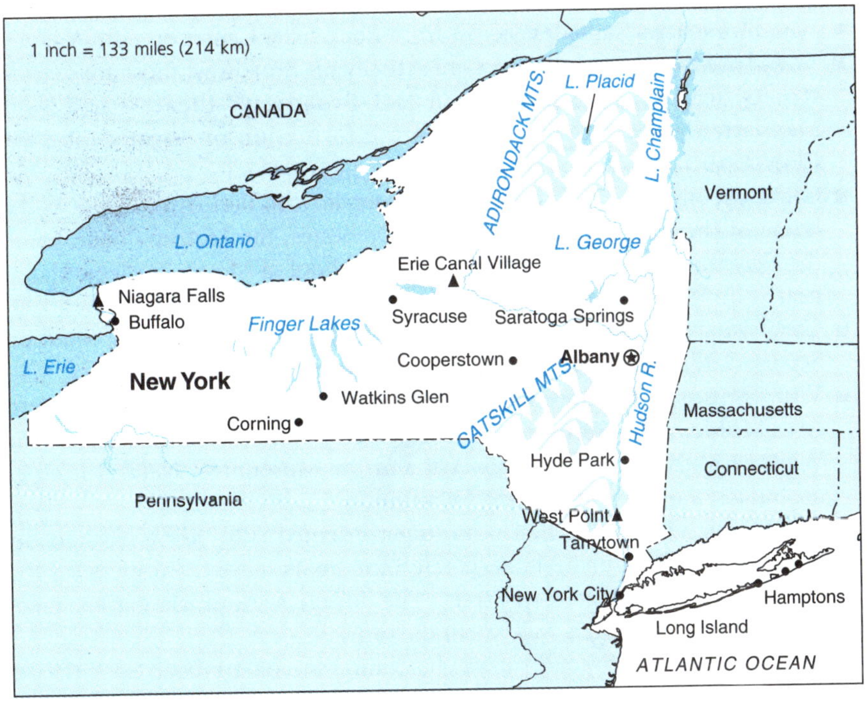

FIGURE 2.4 New York State

paths. Wall Street, the city's financial center, follows the line of fortifications erected by the Dutch, who built the colony.

Broadway slants across Manhattan. Wherever it crossed a major street going north, a square was laid out—Union, Madison, Herald, and Times.

Things to see and do in New York City include the following:

- Go to the foot of the island. There, Battery Park is the site of Castle Clinton, the departure point for the ferries to Liberty and Ellis Islands. The Statue of Liberty on Liberty Island has been partially off-limits to visitors for both security concerns and structural needs. Tourists can ride a ferry to the island and explore the statue's base.
- Take a boat ride to Ellis Island, the gateway to America between 1892 and 1924. The island's museum tells the immigrants' stories through films, photos, artifacts, and a children's learning center.
- See the Brooklyn Bridge. The completion of the bridge in 1883 opened access to Brooklyn on Long Island. No bridge of its size had ever been built.
- Visit the site of the twin towers of the World Trade Center, destroyed by terrorists in 2001. Plans for the buildings' replacement, the Freedom Tower, call for a structure with a spire that will pierce the sky and provide office space up to the 60th floor.
- While in Lower Manhattan, visit the South Street Seaport (an area of shops and markets along the East River), Little Italy, Chinatown, SoHo (*so*uth of *Ho*uston Street—a trendy area of galleries and boutiques), and Greenwich Village, the former bohemian area gone upscale.
- Tour United Nations Headquarters, on the East River between 42nd and 48th Streets.
- Ride to the top of Midtown's 102-story Empire State Building for a spectacular view.
- Visit the city's backyard. In 1853 the city acquired wasteland north of 57th Street; it became Central Park. The park, which runs from 59th to 110th Streets, includes a zoo and restaurants, as well as concert and sports areas.
- See Rockefeller Center, on Fifth Avenue between 48th and 51st Streets. It is the world's largest privately owned business and entertainment facility, the home of NBC and Radio City Music Hall. Tours are available.
- View St. Patrick's Cathedral, across from Rockefeller Center on Fifth Avenue.
- Attend the theater. Few theaters are actually on Broadway; most are on side streets near Times Square or in "off-Broadway" theaters in Lower Manhattan and Brooklyn. (For more information on theaters, see the Close-Up).
- Catch up on culture. The Lincoln Center for the Performing Arts is the home of the New York Philharmonic Orchestra, the Metropolitan Opera, the New York City Ballet, and the Juilliard School of Music. Carnegie Hall is nearby on West 57th Street.
- Cheer your favorite. The city has all the major sports franchises. Madison Square Garden hosts everything from dog shows to wrestling matches.
- Visit a museum. The Metropolitan Museum of Art, the Museum of Modern Art (MoMA), the Solomon R. Guggenheim, the Frick Collection, the Whitney Museum of American Art, and the Museum of Natural History are but a few of the outstanding museums.
- Take a tour. One of the best ways to get oriented is to take a city tour by motorcoach. Or tour by boat. Circle Line boats leave from piers on the Hudson River at West 43rd Street. The voyage around Manhattan takes about three hours and is well worth the time.
- Visit other boroughs by taxi, subway, bus, limousine, or ferryboat. Coney Island lies at the southern tip of Brooklyn, the Bronx has the Zoo, Queens is home to

New York City's tallest buildings are built on the island's rock core. The skyline of Manhattan dips markedly between Lower and Midtown Manhattan, reflecting the once-marshy area between.

Radio City Music Hall is the world's largest indoor theater. The home of the dancing Rockettes has a seating capacity of 5,900.

CLOSE-UP: NEW YORK CITY

Who is a good prospect for a trip to New York City? A city visit would appeal to couples on a honeymoon or those celebrating an anniversary or other special occasion. Especially good prospects are groups. The group setting provides security for those for whom the big city might be overwhelming if taken as an individual. Museum goers, theater devotees, shoppers, gourmets, and similar special interest groups are excellent prospects.

Why would they visit New York City? It offers something for every taste, for the sophisticated as well as for those visiting a big city for the first time. New York's glamour and excitement provide a real getaway from normal life for most people. Business travelers are drawn to the many corporate headquarters.

Where would they go? New York City can be superficially experienced in two to three days, but there is plenty to do to occupy a longer trip or a repeat visit. Suggest that travelers take a city sightseeing tour to get oriented. You might recommend one of the city's famous musical theater productions. Several Web sites provide theater information. If tickets have not been ordered in advance (it is wise to do so for hit shows), suggest that travelers try for last-minute tickets from the booth in Times Square, from the theater's own box office, or through broker services (for an extra charge). Plans for the second day might include a museum trip, a ride to the top of the Empire State Building, shopping, or a visit to United Nations Headquarters or the Stock Exchange.

For convenience visitors should stay in a Midtown hotel. The ability to walk to shops and theaters saves time and money.

When is the best time to visit? Because seeing New York City usually involves much walking, spring and fall are the optimum seasons to visit. Each season has its attractions, however. December is the time to see the beautiful holiday decorations and perhaps take in the Christmas show at Radio City Music Hall. Many people visit for a special event—Macy's Thanksgiving Parade, for example, or a sports event, or the dog or cat shows. On weekends the streets are less crowded. Hotels sometimes offer lower rates on weekends or other times when they are not filled with business travelers.

A timid traveler to the big city asks, "Is there any truth to the rumor that chocolate in our checked baggage will set off an alarm at airport security devices?" How would you respond? New York City's airports have some of the country's strictest security procedures. Travelers will benefit from any advice that helps to smooth their trip. A regular-size chocolate bar isn't likely to set off any alarms, but blocks of chocolate, cheese, jars of peanut butter or jelly, stacks of books, or thick leather shoe soles may set off the screening devices because they can mimic the density of plastic explosives. The Transportation Security Administration recommends that you "avoid packing food and drink items in checked luggage." Also, pack books horizontally and place shoes single-file atop your clothes. For more rules and regulations, go to www.tsa.gov.

La Guardia and John F. Kennedy International Airports, and the ferry ride to Staten Island has one of the city's finest views. Of the city's two train stations, Penn Station is the home of Amtrak and commuter trains to Long Island. Grand Central Station handles commuter trains to the northern suburbs.

- Watch a cruise ship sail down the Hudson. Ships dock at West Side piers and at ports in Bayonne (New Jersey) and Brooklyn. During the summer and fall, ships depart to Bermuda and Canada, and the *Queen Mary 2* sails to Europe.

Buffalo New York's second-largest city is **Buffalo**, a port on Lake Erie and the Niagara River. It is the gateway to the honeymoon capital of an earlier era, Niagara Falls. The falls are accessible from both the U.S. and Canadian sides and are described in more detail in Chapter 5.

Other Places to Visit

Exploration of upstate New York can be interesting, relaxing, and fun. The large state has much to see.

Syracuse grew famous in 1825 as the hub of the Erie Canal, which linked the Hudson River and the Great Lakes. Cruises on the canal operate from spring to fall.

The Hudson River Valley From New York City north beyond Albany, the Hudson River flows through a beautiful valley. The river is flanked by terraces backed by mountains. The valley was the setting for Rip Van Winkle's long sleep in the story by Washington Irving (1783–1859). Both Irving's home in **Tarrytown** and the Rockefeller estate, Kykuit, are open to the public. Boats cruise up the Hudson from Manhattan to **West Point**, the home of the U.S. Military Academy. Farther north near Poughkeepsie is **Hyde Park**, home of Franklin D. Roosevelt (1882–1945). The river shaped the nation's history, and its beauty produced the Hudson River School (1825–1875), a group of landscape painters who helped shape the country's image. The art of this era is displayed in museums throughout the state. While in the area, visitors should consider taking a meal at one of the restaurants operated by the Culinary Institute of America, considered to be the country's most prestigious culinary school.

Saratoga Springs North of Albany, **Saratoga Springs** is noted for its mineral springs, racetracks, and cultural activity. The *Queen of Spas* has harness racing from April to January and thoroughbred racing in August. The Saratoga Performing Arts Center is the summer home of the New York City Ballet and Opera and the Philadelphia Orchestra.

Erie Canal In the town of Rome, 30 miles from Lake Ontario, **Erie Canal Village** is a reconstructed village of the early 1800s where tourists can take a mule-drawn boat ride on the canal. Part of the 524-mile Erie Canalway National Heritage Corridor, the waterway played a key role in turning New York City into a center for commerce, industry, and finance. A catalyst for growth in the Mohawk and Hudson Valleys, the canal also helped open up western America for settlement.

The Shore, Mountains, and Lakes On weekends and during summer months, the seaside towns of eastern Long Island are filled with people looking to escape the big city. On the south shore of the island, the summer resorts of the **Hamptons** (Southampton, Bridgehampton, and East Hampton) attract the seriously rich with beautiful homes, fine restaurants, polo fields, and a busy social life.

The Adirondack Mountains of northern New York have hundreds of lakes, waterfalls, and fishing streams. Nineteenth-century millionaires chose this wilderness to build "camps," complete with rustic charm and armies of servants. A few of the lavish vacation homes survived, some still owned by the families that built them, others operating as summer camps or conference centers. The village of **Lake Placid**, site of the 1932 and 1980 Winter Olympics, has excellent facilities for every type of winter sport.

To the south, about a two-hour drive from Manhattan, the Catskill Mountains form a semicircular chain west of the Hudson River. The Catskills are known for their resorts, where many entertainers got their start. The past lives on at Mohonk Mountain House, a rambling hotel built by two Quaker brothers in 1869. The resort specializes in themed weekends such as mystery whodunits.

West-central New York features the **Finger Lakes**—eleven long, narrow lakes. Wineries and summer auto racing at **Watkins Glen** are among the area's attractions. Two small museums of special interest near the Finger Lakes are the National Baseball Hall of Fame and Museum in **Cooperstown** and the Corning Glass Center in **Corning**, home of Steuben glass, America's premier art glass.

✔ CHECK-UP

New York City's attractions include

- ✔ Broadway and off-Broadway theater.
- ✔ Statue of Liberty and Ellis Island.
- ✔ Finest stores and restaurants.
- ✔ Outstanding museums such as the Metropolitan Museum of Art, MoMA, the Guggenheim, and the Museum of Natural History.
- ✔ View from the Empire State Building and other skyscrapers.
- ✔ Walks around Central Park, Times Square, Greenwich Village, and Wall Street.

Fun things to do in upstate New York:

- ✔ Bet on a winner at Saratoga.
- ✔ Taste wine near the Finger Lakes.
- ✔ Take a ride on the Erie Canal.
- ✔ Visit historic homes in the Hudson River Valley.

Mid-Atlantic States

New Jersey, Pennsylvania, Delaware, and Maryland are part of the Atlantic *megalopolis*—the urban corridor that runs from Washington, D.C., to Boston. By size and landscape, each state is geographically different (see Figure 2.5). **Washington, D.C.**, is the federal district carved out of Maryland and Virginia.

New Jersey

The small state of New Jersey, sandwiched between New York and Pennsylvania, has always been a transportation hub. **Newark** is the largest city, and Newark Airport is one of New York City's major gateways. Travelers can

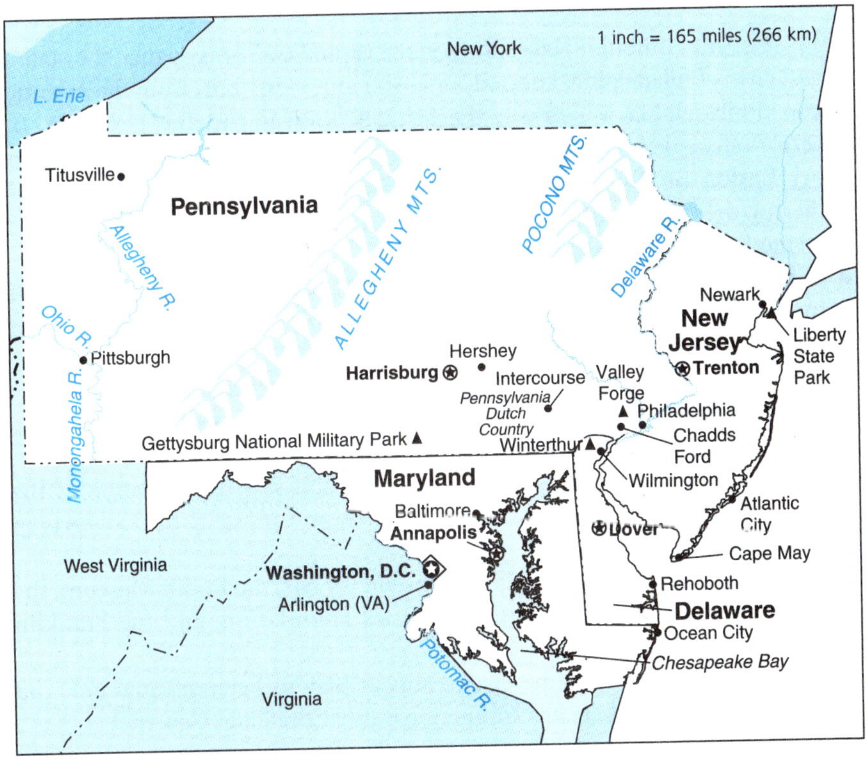

FIGURE 2.3

Mid-Atlantic States

access the Statue of Liberty and Ellis Island from New Jersey's **Liberty State Park** without the hassle of going into Manhattan.

Northeast of the capital, **Trenton**, the state is densely populated and highly industrialized. In contrast, the state's southern region is a truck-farming area, growing food for the cities—hence the nickname, the *Garden State*. Part of southern New Jersey is an area of rivers, swamps, and stunted pines called the *Pine Barrens;* it is one of the largest wilderness areas east of the Mississippi.

Most of the coastline is a long, narrow sandbar with white sandy beaches. **Atlantic City** is by far the best-known shore resort. Its location near New York and Philadelphia has made it *America's Favorite Playground* for more than a century. Day-trip tourists drive in or arrive on motorcoach tours for casino action twenty-four hours a day. The town hosts the Miss America Pageant each September.

Atlantic City's Boardwalk and Steel Pier link the city with its past. The Boardwalk of the Monopoly game still has rolling-chair rides and saltwater taffy shops as well as glitzy casinos.

Other beach resorts include Ocean City, Seaside Heights, Wildwood, and **Cape May**, which claims to be the country's oldest seaside resort. Located on a peninsula at the southernmost tip of the state, the town has more than 600 Victorian homes and is a National Historic Landmark. Many of the houses are charming small hotels.

Pennsylvania

Across the Delaware River from New Jersey, Pennsylvania extends westward to the shores of Lake Erie. William Penn was granted control of the region in 1681 and founded a colony based on Quaker principles of tolerance and democracy.

Pennsylvania's fortunes came from its rich soil and its access to water. In the east there are beautiful stretches of farmland and woodland. In the west deposits of coal and minerals helped to make the state a great industrial and manufacturing center. And for access to water, Pennsylvania has three of the country's busiest ports: Philadelphia is one of the world's largest freshwater ports; Erie is a major Great Lakes port; and Pittsburgh provides access to the extensive inland waterway system.

The U.S. oil industry got its start in 1859 in northwest Pennsylvania near Titusville, when Edwin L. Drake built the first commercial oil well.

Philadelphia Although **Harrisburg** is the capital of Pennsylvania, the state's largest city is Philadelphia. Located some 100 miles (161 km) from the Atlantic Ocean, Philadelphia is between the Schuylkill River and the Delaware. In America's struggle for independence, it seems all the great events happened in either Boston or Philadelphia. With its historic attractions, museums, and orchestra, the city is a cultural center.

Highlights of Philadelphia include:

- Independence National Historic Park, with copies of the Declaration of Independence and the Constitution on display. Nearby is the famous cracked Liberty Bell.
- Society Hill, a historic district with hundreds of restored homes.
- Penn's Landing, a gathering place for evening entertainment.
- South Street, a center of restaurants, clubs, and galleries.
- Academy of Music, the oldest U.S. opera house still in use, home of the Philadelphia Orchestra. In summer, the orchestra presents free concerts in Fairmont Park.
- Museums such as the Philadelphia Museum of Art, the Rodin Museum, the Academy of Natural Sciences, the Barnes Foundation, and the Franklin Institute.
- Professional football and baseball teams at play in Veterans Stadium, and hockey and basketball teams competing in the CoreStates Center.

The Poconos The Poconos are a low range of hills in the state's northeast. They are known for resorts with heart-shaped beds, bubble-filled champagne-glass-shaped whirlpools built for two, and winter and summer sports facilities. About 15,000 puckered honeymooners pass through its fabled tubs each year. The upper Delaware River on the border between New York and Pennsylvania is a National Scenic and Recreational River.

Brandywine Valley Southeastern Pennsylvania meets northern Delaware in the Brandywine Valley, about 45 minutes from Philadelphia. It is an area of natural beauty, small museums, antique shops, and charming B&Bs. Longwood, one of the world's great gardens, was part of Pierre du Pont's estate, and he bequeathed it to the public. **Chadds Ford**, the scene of the Revolutionary War's Battle of Brandywine Creek, is home to the Brandywine River Museum. It displays the works of the Wyeth family as well as other valley artists.

Valley Forge National Historic Park About 25 miles (40 km) northwest of Philadelphia, Valley Forge is a shrine of the American Revolution. No battles were fought here, but some 2,500 soldiers died of disease and cold during the winter of 1777–1778, when George Washington brought his men here to rest and be trained after defeats at Brandywine and Germantown.

Pennsylvania Dutch Country To the west of Valley Forge is Lancaster County, center of the farms of the Amish, Mennonites, and Dunkers. These are the "plain people" (usually called the *Pennsylvania Dutch*) who fled religious persecution in Germany and established flourishing farms while forgoing modern conveniences. A patchwork of fields with quaint barns—often decorated with hex signs—sits against a backdrop of wooded hills. The center of tourism is the town of **Intercourse.**

Two area attractions are **Hershey** and **Gettysburg.** In 1903 Milton S. Hershey purchased a cornfield in Hershey and started to make candy. He was a pioneer in the mass production of milk chocolate, turning it from an expensive luxury into an affordable, everyday treat. *Chocolatetown, USA*, has a visitors' center and amusement park. Near Pennsylvania's southern border is Gettysburg National Military Park, the site of the Civil War's bloodiest battle and Abraham Lincoln's moving address.

Pittsburgh In western Pennsylvania, near the Ohio border, Pennsylvania's second-largest city, Pittsburgh, began as a frontier outpost. It became the world's major producer of steel; generated wealth for Andrew Mellon, Andrew Carnegie, and Henry Frick; played a part in the labor movement; battled pollution; and is a model for urban renewal.

Much of downtown Pittsburgh lies in a wedge-shaped area called the *Golden Triangle*, a point of land where the Allegheny and Monongahela Rivers meet to form the Ohio. At the western tip of the Triangle—the Point—old buildings were torn down to develop scenic Point State Park and an office complex called Gateway Center.

A hill called Mount Washington overlooks downtown. It features observation decks and restaurants with spectacular views of the city and its rivers. Small cable cars, called "inclines" by Pittsburghers, carry visitors up and down the mountain.

The city's museums include one for native son Andy Warhol as well as the Frick Museum and the Museum of Natural History at the Carnegie Institute. Heinz Field is home to the Pittsburgh Pirates; PNC Park is home to the Steelers.

The Pennsylvania Dutch were called "Dutch" because the word *Deutsch*, which means "German," was misinterpreted.

Streetlights in Hershey, Pennsylvania, are shaped like Hershey kisses.

The Johnstown Flood National Memorial in Pennsylvania is on the location of the South Fork Dam. When the dam broke in 1889, it caused one of the worst natural disasters in American history, killing 2,200.

Delaware

The *First State* to sign the Constitution, Delaware is the second-smallest state. Its Atlantic beach resorts attract city dwellers from Baltimore and Washington, D.C. Its capital is **Dover**, but **Wilmington**, which is almost on the Pennsylvania border, is the largest city. **Rehoboth** on the Atlantic is a popular beach resort.

Delaware's history is closely connected to the E. I. du Pont Company, the manufacturer of chemicals and chemical products. Tourists can visit sites connected to the du Pont family, including **Winterthur**, Henry du Pont's mansion. Its exhibits feature American antiques and decorative arts.

Maryland

Maryland has a most unusual shape. Its Eastern Shore is low and flat, separated from the mainland by the Chesapeake Bay, which cuts deep into the state. Maryland's mountainous west forms a straight-line border with Pennsylvania to the north and a jagged border with Virginia and West Virginia in the south and west.

Captain John Smith said of Maryland, "Heaven and earth never agreed better to form a place more perfect for man's habitation." In Maryland, tourists will find 17th-century churches that reflect the colonists' search for religious freedom and guides in colonial attire eager to talk about the accomplishments of the settlers.

Annapolis, the capital, has an attractive harbor and hosts the impressive U.S. Naval Academy. The Academy—a National Historic Landmark—has been a part of the town's life since 1845. The city is a good starting point for a tour of the laid-back Eastern Shore. The Chesapeake Bay's ragged eastern shoreline lures sailors of all abilities. The skipjack sloops that used to bring home the oyster catch now offer cruises lasting anywhere from a few hours to a few days. Passengers might be treated to a stop at an informal crab shack for dinner. **Ocean City** is the state's busy beach resort.

Maryland's largest city, **Baltimore**, lies on the Patapsco River, about two-thirds of the way up Chesapeake Bay. Cruise ships sail from its busy port in spring, summer, and fall on their way to Bermuda and other destinations. For tourists, Baltimore's attractions include the following:

- Harborplace, a complex of shops and restaurants.
- Maryland Science Center.
- Port Discovery, a children's museum.
- National Aquarium, with thousands of fish, reptiles, and birds.
- Fort McHenry National Monument, the star-shaped fort where Francis Scott Key (1779–1843) wrote "The Star-Spangled Banner" while watching the British bombard the fort during the War of 1812.
- Preakness Stakes, a horse race run each May at the Pimlico racetrack.
- Camden Yards, home of the Baltimore Orioles baseball team.

The District of Columbia

Southwest of Baltimore, near the meeting of the Potomac and Anacostia Rivers, Washington, D.C., rises from bottomland along the rivers to a series of low hills in the north. Much of the original swampy land had to be filled in. President George Washington chose the site for the nation's capital—the first planned city—and appointed commissioners and surveyors to design the city.

One was Major Pierre Charles L'Enfant (1754–1825), the son of a court painter from Louis XVI's court at Versailles. L'Enfant placed the principal buildings and squares, which he connected by grand avenues named after the states, within a grid of streets.

L'Enfant's high-handed ways caused much conflict, and he was fired. However, his plans were on their way. In 1909 L'Enfant was reburied with honors in Arlington National Cemetery.

Washington, D.C., is one of the country's most popular tourist destinations. Its attractions are many. Top sites include

- The National Mall, the central feature of L'Enfant's plan. The Mall's lawn leads from the U.S. Capitol to the Washington Monument to the banks of the Potomac. The National Park Service continually sponsors festivals and concerts on the grass.
- The White House, home to the president. Depending on security needs, citizens and school groups can arrange for tours through their senators and representatives.
- The Lincoln, Jefferson, Vietnam, and World War II Memorials at the foot of the Mall.
- The Smithsonian Institution, sometimes called "our nation's attic" for its range of collections. The Smithsonian administers museums and galleries in Washington (nine on the Mall), the National Zoo, and the Cooper-Hewitt Museum in New York City. For years the Smithsonian's Air and Space Museum was its most popular attraction, but only about 10 percent of its collection could be exhibited. In 2003 the Steven F. Udvar-Hazy (*OOD var HAH zee*) Center opened next to Dulles Airport in Virginia. Hundreds of aircraft and space artifacts, including the Space Shuttle *Enterprise*, are on display.

Jefferson Memorial, Washington, D.C.

- The Holocaust Museum, devoted to remembering the murder of Jews and other minorities by the Nazis from 1933 to 1945.
- Ford's Theatre, where Lincoln was shot.
- The John F. Kennedy Center for the Performing Arts, designated by Congress as the National Cultural Center and official memorial to President Kennedy. The center includes an opera house, a concert hall, theaters, two restaurants, and conference facilities.

The *capital* is a city and the *capitol* is a building. The capitol is located in the capital. To remember the difference, think about the *o* in *capitol* as being the dome of a capitol building.

Springtime is tourist season, as school groups by the thousands descend on the city. The big question is always: When will the Japanese cherry trees bloom? They are planted around the Tidal Basin. Depending on whether winter was mild or harsh, the buds open sometime in late March or early April.

Many of Washington's sights are across the river in Virginia. Out toward Dulles International Airport is Wolf Trap Farm Park for the Performing Arts, the only national park devoted to the performing arts. Arlington National Cemetery is the burial ground for the nation's military and includes the Tomb of the Unknowns and the grave of President Kennedy. The Changing of the Guard ceremony is conducted twenty-four hours a day. To the southeast of the cemetery is the Pentagon—the world's largest single building—which was built during World War II as the headquarters of the U.S. armed forces. Damage done by the terrorist attack in 2001 has been repaired and is undetectable.

Martha Washington's grandson built a mansion in Arlington, Virginia. His daughter married Robert E. Lee. When Lee refused the offer to command the Union forces in the Civil War and rode south to Richmond, the estate was confiscated and the grounds used for the burial of war dead, becoming Arlington National Cemetery.

Mount Vernon, George Washington's beautifully preserved home, is south of the District along the Potomac in Virginia. After the White House, it is America's most visited historic home. There, Washington enjoyed the life of a successful planter, and there he died. George and Martha are buried on the grounds.

✔ CHECK-UP

The Mid-Atlantic region includes

- ✔ New Jersey; its capital is Trenton, but its largest city is Newark.
- ✔ Pennsylvania; its capital is Harrisburg, but its largest city is Philadelphia.
- ✔ Delaware; its capital is Dover, but its largest city is Wilmington.
- ✔ Maryland; its capital is Annapolis, but its largest city is Baltimore.
- ✔ District of Columbia, the capital of the United States.

For travelers, highlights of the Mid-Atlantic region include

- ✔ Atlantic City and its casinos.
- ✔ Cape May resorts.
- ✔ Independence National Historical Park in Philadelphia.
- ✔ Pennsylvania Dutch Country.
- ✔ Brandywine Valley.
- ✔ Baltimore's Harborplace.
- ✔ Smithsonian Museums in Washington, D.C.
- ✔ George Washington's Mount Vernon.

The South

The South includes Virginia, West Virginia, North Carolina, South Carolina, Georgia, Tennessee, and Kentucky (see Figure 2.6). The "Old South" has become a popular and valuable tourist commodity. Throughout the region historic homes and gardens are open to the public, and beach and mountain resorts cater to just about every vacation need.

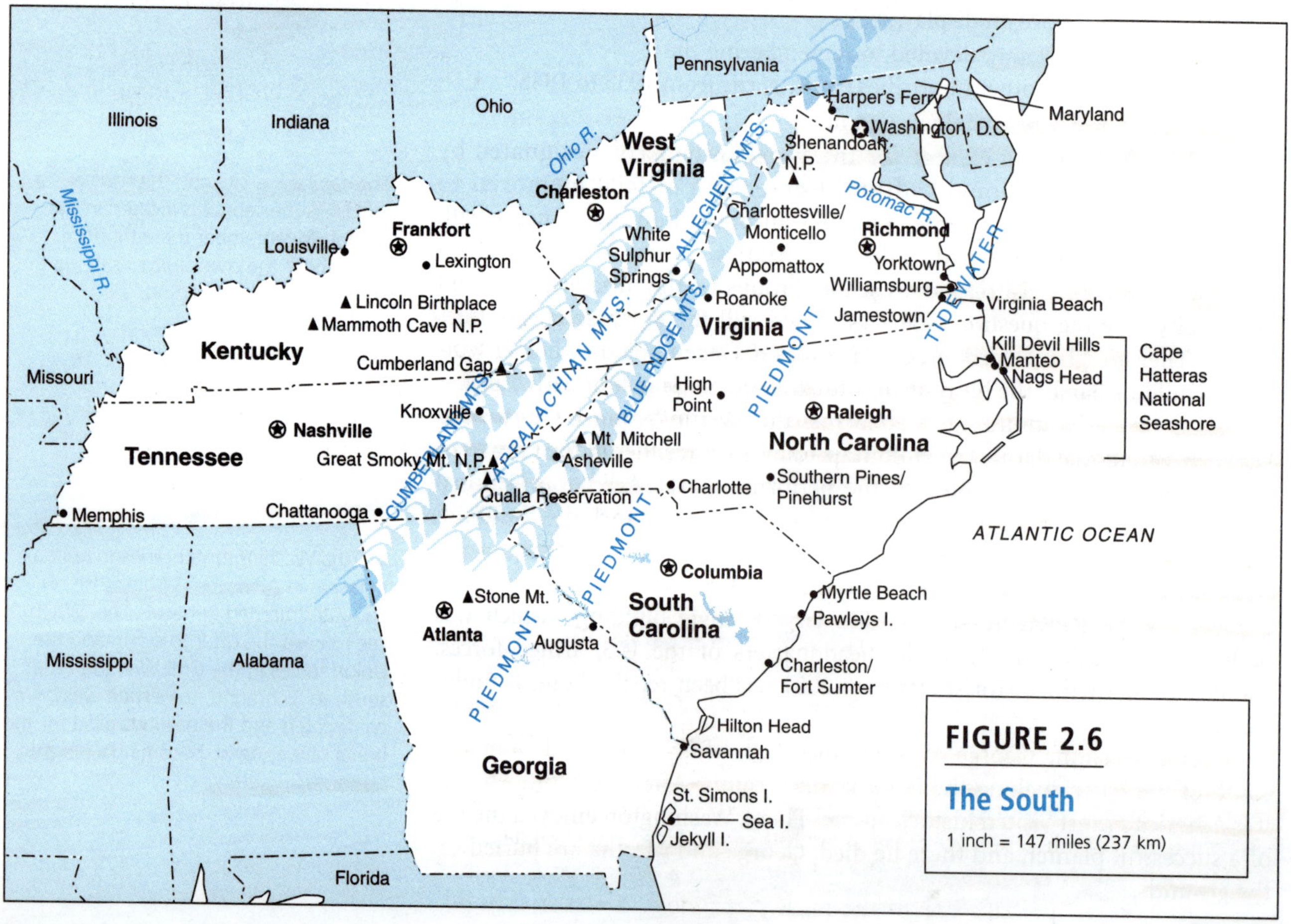

FIGURE 2.6

The South

1 inch = 147 miles (237 km)

Virginia

The plantation society of Tidewater Virginia produced some beautiful homes and small cities. A tour of historic sites is easy to combine with relaxation at one of the resorts.

Reenactments of battles, as well as monuments, memorials, and preservation efforts, have kept the memory of the Civil War South alive throughout the region. Thousands of reenactors don costumes, camp out, get dirty, eat food of the period, and fight mock battles.

The Tidewater In Virginia's Tidewater, **Yorktown, Jamestown,** and **Williamsburg** form the *Historic Triangle* between the York and James Rivers. In 1607, 104 Englishmen created Jamestown, the first permanent English colony in America. Visitors can board one of the full-scale replicas of the three tiny ships that brought the colonists to the new land. At Yorktown in 1781, Lord Cornwallis surrendered in the last major battle of the Revolutionary War. Yorktown today is a small village with colonial-era architecture, but it is in Williamsburg that the colonial period comes to life. Because Williamsburg was Virginia's capital from 1699 to 1780, its taverns were forums for such leaders as Thomas Jefferson, Patrick Henry, George Mason, George Washington, and Richard Henry Lee.

When **Richmond** was named the capital during the Revolution, Williamsburg began a long decline. By the early 20th century, the town was in sad shape. The rector of a local church persuaded John D. Rockefeller Jr. (1874–1960) to purchase the town and rebuild it in its colonial form. In 1934, partially restored but mostly rebuilt, Colonial Williamsburg opened to the public. It was the first restoration to use costumed guides to interpret colonial life.

Colonial Williamsburg, Virginia

From Williamsburg the road east leads to the ocean. Boasting miles of beachfront, **Virginia Beach** is Virginia's largest city. Flanking the concrete Boardwalk, hotels face the ocean as far as the eye can see.

Shenandoah Valley Flanked by the Blue Ridge and Allegheny Mountains, the Shenandoah Valley is part of the Great Valley. Crowning the Blue Ridge between Front Royal and Waynesboro, **Shenandoah National Park** is the closest national park to the population centers of the East.

For a continuous scenic drive, the traveler can take Skyline Drive along the crest of the Blue Ridge Mountains and connect with the Blue Ridge Parkway to the south. Stopovers off the parkway might include visits to **Monticello** ("little mountain"), the Palladian-style home Thomas Jefferson designed and built for himself outside Charlottesville, or a tour of a Civil War battlefield. The National Park Service administers such historic sites as the Booker T. Washington National Monument in **Roanoke** and **Appomattox Court House**, where the agreement on the terms of surrender in the Civil War took place.

Many Civil War battles have two names because the Confederates named them after the nearest settlement and the Union forces named them after the nearest body of water.

West Virginia

West Virginia nestles deep into the Appalachians. It separated from Virginia and became a state in 1861 when its small farmers, who had no interest in keeping slaves, voted against secession. It has a history of poverty and isolation, but it offers beautiful scenery and an abundance of outdoor sports. **Charleston** is the capital and largest city.

Several places are worth a visit. At **Harper's Ferry**, geography and history have influenced each other for more than 250 years. Here the Potomac and Shenandoah Rivers crash through the mountains in a drama that Thomas Jefferson declared "perhaps one of the most stupendous scenes in nature."

Here George Washington established an armory to help safeguard the new republic. But what most folks remember about the town took place in 1859. Fiery abolitionist John Brown attempted to seize the armory as a first step in his revolutionary scheme to rid the nation of slavery. His plan failed, Brown was hanged, and his actions further divided the nation over the issue of slavery. During the Civil War, the town changed hands eight times, eventually becoming the base of Union operations for invasions into the Shenandoah Valley.

For those who like their confrontations with nature tied up with a bow, the National Historic Landmark Greenbrier Resort in **White Sulphur Springs** offers superior deluxe accommodations, a spa, golf, tennis, and much more in a beautiful mountain setting. The original hotel opened in 1858 but had to be razed and rebuilt in 1913. During World War II, the resort was an internment facility for German and Japanese diplomats awaiting exchange and then a hospital for war-wounded. In April 1948 it reopened as a hotel with guests including the Duke and Duchess of Windsor, Mr. and Mrs. John Jacob Astor, Bing Crosby, and young Congressman John F. Kennedy.

North Carolina

Raleigh Blue Ridge Golf, beaches

North Carolina is a region of rural delights and modern urban centers. **Raleigh** is the capital, but **Charlotte** is the largest city. The main tourist attractions, however, are outside the cities. Golf and shopping at factory outlet stores are among the diversions for visitors (see the Profiles on pages 43 and 53), but the beaches along the state's coast and the mountains along its western border are the major tourist destinations.

According to legend, Nags Head got its name from the islanders' practice of tying lanterns to the necks of ponies and marching them along the dunes at night. The swinging lights deceived ship captains into running aground, where their cargo was seized.

The Outer Banks A string of narrow islands and peninsulas called the Outer Banks lies along the coast. This is the site of the **Cape Hatteras National Seashore**, the Atlantic's most extensive stretch of undeveloped seashore. It boasts the largest sand dunes in the East and the tallest of America's lighthouses. Tricky winds and dangerous tides helped give the cape at the southern end of the Banks its nickname as the *Graveyard of the Atlantic*. In 1903, in **Kill Devil Hills**, the wind helped the Wright brothers make the first powered airplane flight. Accommodations are in **Nags Head**.

Nearby on **Roanoke Island**, an English colony was established in 1585 and then disappeared without a trace. Its story is told from June through August in the outdoor play *The Lost Colony*, near the town of **Manteo**.

Thomas Wolfe (1900–1938) grew up in Asheville, North Carolina. Much of Wolfe's novel *Look Homeward, Angel* was set in the town and his home—a boarding house operated by his mother.

The Mountains Once a hunting ground for the Cherokee, the western mountains enticed people from the lowlands to come to escape the summer heat before air-conditioning was invented. Today, the region is a booming retirement and resort region. From Virginia, the Blue Ridge Parkway leads south to **Asheville**, where George W. Vanderbilt built his 250-room French château, Biltmore House, representing American domestic architecture at its most grandiose. The Biltmore Estate provides a magical setting for the mansion and acres of gardens masterfully landscaped in 1888 by Frederick Law Olmsted. The historic Grove Park Inn in Asheville is but one place for visitors to stay while seeing Biltmore. Near Asheville is **Mount Mitchell** (6,684 feet/2,037 m), the highest summit of the Appalachians.

At the Blue Ridge Parkway's end lie the Smoky Mountains. The **Great Smoky Mountain National Park** is one of the most heavily visited of the country's national parks. Visitors can travel to the **Qualla Reservation**, the home of the Eastern Cherokee.

South Carolina

South Carolina has many features of the South of pre–Civil War days. From the Up Country of the western hills to the Low Country along the coast, the state boasts beautiful scenery and many historic sites. The coastal plain includes many areas of swamp. Barrier islands are resort and retirement areas despite being exposed to occasional hurricanes. **Columbia** is the capital and largest city.

Charleston Charleston is on a peninsula between the Ashley and Cooper Rivers on the coast. Despite fires, hurricanes, tornadoes, earthquakes, bombardment by guns from land and sea in several wars, and two military occupations, Charleston has retained its beauty. In one historic moment in 1861, Confederate troops attacked **Fort Sumter** in the city's harbor, triggering the Civil War.

The city is renowned for its architecture, especially the elegant homes lining the Battery along the harbor. Many people visit the city's Old and Historic District during the Festival of Houses and Gardens in March and April. The *Spoleto Festival of the Arts* in May or June each year uses the historic sites as performance venues.

Golf has been a local preoccupation since 1786, when residents established the South Carolina Country Club, the first golf course and golf club in America. The nearby resorts of Edisto Island, Seabrook Island, Wild Dunes on the Isle of Palms, and Kiawah (*KEY ah wah*) Island have more than twenty courses.

Beach Resorts The northern part of South Carolina's coastline, from the North Carolina border to Pawleys Island, is called the *Grand Strand*. Here, **Myrtle Beach** has developed into a golf and tennis center. More than ninety courses have been carved from the wooded sand hills. Country/western music lovers enjoy the area's clubs. Peak months for visitors are July and August, but the beach beckons from late spring through October.

South of the Strand, saltwater marshes adjoin the coast, and tidal rivers cut far inland. Among the many coastal islands is **Hilton Head**, a master-planned community with upscale resorts.

Charleston's homes were ingeniously adapted to its hot and humid climate. The "single house" is one room wide, with two rooms on each floor, placed so that its gabled end, rather than its front, faces the street to catch the prevailing breeze.

➤ PROFILE

Southern Golf Resorts

A golf package usually includes tee times, accommodations, carts, and a rental car. Some well-known courses include

- In North Carolina, Pinehurst/Southern Pines, with more than thirty courses and the PGA World Golf Hall of Fame.
- In South Carolina, courses along the Grand Strand and at Hilton Head, as well as around Charleston and Edisto Island, Seabrook Island, Isle of Palms, and Kiawah.
- In Georgia, Saint Simons Island and the Augusta National Golf Course, home of the Masters tournament.
- In Florida, courses on both coasts from north to south.
- In Alabama, the Robert Trent Jones Golf Trail, a series of courses that stretches the length of the state.

Georgia

Georgia was the last of the original thirteen colonies to be founded. It has the largest land area of any state east of the Mississippi. Mountains and ridges along the northern border slope southward to red clay hills, then to flat coastal plains. Much of Georgia is a mild, sunny land of pines, magnolias, and moss-draped trees.

Atlanta The commercial and transportation center of the Southeast, Georgia's capital is in the foothills of the Blue Ridge Mountains in northern Georgia. Atlanta's airport is one of the world's busiest. Things to see include

- CNN Center, with broadcast studios as well as the Omni sports coliseum.
- National headquarters for the Centers for Disease Control.
- Coca-Cola Company's headquarters and visitors' center.
- Five Points, the traditional heart of the city.
- Underground Atlanta, a shopping and entertainment complex below street level just south of Five Points.
- Martin Luther King Jr. National Historic Site, which includes King's

birthplace, the Ebenezer Baptist Church where he preached, and the King Center, with his tomb.

- Peachtree Street, Atlanta's most famous street, running from downtown northward.
- Robert W. Woodruff Arts Center, housing the Atlanta Symphony, the Alliance Theater Company, and the High Museum.
- Carter Presidential Center, on a hill overlooking the city.
- Facilities for football's Atlanta Falcons and baseball's Atlanta Braves.
- **Stone Mountain**, outside Atlanta, the largest stone mountain in the United States. Sculptures on the mountain depict Civil War figures Jefferson Davis, Robert E. Lee, and Stonewall Jackson.

Coca-Cola was invented in Atlanta in 1886.

Savannah Thanks to its founder, James Oglethorpe, Savannah has unusual charm. He designed the city as a series of wards in which commercial and residential buildings centered on a public square. Twenty-two of Oglethorpe's original squares survive, bordered by handsome town houses and landscaped with live oaks, azaleas, fountains, and statues. The Historic Society had to fight hard to preserve the city's heritage, but they won. Savannah now has the nation's largest national landmark district.

The Golden Isles Once winter resorts for America's rich, Georgia's barrier islands attract attention only once in a blue moon. The only islands accessible by car are the three known as the Golden Isles—**Saint Simons Island**, **Jekyll Island**, and **Sea Island**—connected by a causeway to the mainland at Brunswick. Saint Simons is the largest and most populated of the three. Sea Island is connected to Saint Simons by a short causeway. On Sea Island, the Cloister Resort and Spa is where presidents and executives have vacationed for decades. From 1886 until 1942, Jekyll Island was the exclusive preserve of millionaires, but their descendants lost interest, sold out, and let the common folk in.

Some of the Golden Isles are home to the descendants of slaves who escaped mainland plantations and preserved an independent black culture on the islands. Residents use the local patois, a version of English called *Gullah*, and places have names that derive from West Africa.

The southeastern corner of Georgia is occupied by the Okefenokee (*OH kuh fuh NOH kee*) Swamp, one of the last natural swamps in the United States. Its water trails can be explored on flat-bottomed boats that slip quietly through the mysterious jungle-like terrain.

Tennessee

Tennessee borders eight states. (Look again at Figure 2.6.) The **Cumberland Gap** in northeast Tennessee forms a major break in the Appalachian Mountain chain. First used by animals in their migrations and then followed by Native Americans, the Gap was the first and best road west for the settlement of the country's interior. Daniel Boone used it as he blazed the Wilderness Road into Kentucky.

In the eastern third of the state, **Knoxville** and **Chattanooga** are western gateways to the Great Smoky Mountains National Park.

Central Tennessee includes the capital, **Nashville**, a crossroads both geographically and culturally. President Andrew Jackson's home, The Hermitage, is nearby. Western Tennessee slopes down to the Mississippi. **Memphis**, the state's largest city, is in the southwest corner, on the Mississippi River.

Music is the theme behind many of Tennessee's attractions. Folk songs and bluegrass came from the mountains. The "blues" developed in the Mississippi delta region and became known in the early 1900s after W. C. Handy began to publish songs. Gospel and rock also came from the river region. Country took over Nashville. This musical heritage draws tourists to several sites:

- Nashville, the performance and recording center that has been known as *Music City U.S.A.* since the Grand Ole Opry started its weekend radio broadcasts in 1925. The Country Music Hall of Fame displays everything from Elvis's 1960s gold Cadillac to Minnie Pearl's straw hat with dangling price tag.
- Memphis, the site of Graceland, Elvis Presley's home. The estate resembles a small theme park, complete with his mansion, his automobiles, shops, and his grave.
- Memphis's Beale Street, where Handy performed, a National Historic District and a lively entertainment area.
- Mud Island, also in Memphis. A pedestrian bridge and a monorail lead from downtown to this island park with its Mississippi River Museum.

Kentucky

Kentucky is known for horses, bourbon, fried chicken, and bluegrass music. Its capital is **Frankfort**. The Ohio River forms the state's long northern border. Its eastern border touches the Appalachian Mountains. To the west the state borders the Mississippi River. Coal is mined in eastern and western counties.

The center of the state is *Bluegrass Country*. The nickname comes from the variety of grass that produces a small blue flower in early spring. Thoroughbred horses graze on the lush grass around **Lexington**. There, the Kentucky Horse Park includes a daily parade of more than forty breeds of horses and opportunities to watch training.

On the first Saturday in May, the Kentucky Derby is held at Churchill Downs in **Louisville**, the state's largest city. The Derby is the country's oldest continuously run horse race. Thousands of trackside spectators and millions of television viewers watch the "run for the roses," which refers to the blanket of roses presented to the winning horse and jockey.

The Kentucky Derby in Kentucky, the Preakness in Maryland, and the Belmont Stakes in New York make up the famous Triple Crown of horse racing.

The **Abraham Lincoln Birthplace National Historic Site** is south of Louisville near Hodgenville. Continuing south, travelers will find **Mammoth Cave National Park**, the world's longest known cave system. Park rangers guide visitors on varying tours through miles of corridors on five levels. Easy tours to the best dripstone formations as well as challenging Wild Cave tours are available.

✔ CHECK-UP

The southern states include

- ✔ Virginia; its capital is Richmond, but its largest city is Virginia Beach.
- ✔ West Virginia; its capital and largest city is Charleston.
- ✔ North Carolina; its capital is Raleigh, but its largest city is Charlotte.
- ✔ South Carolina; its capital and largest city is Columbia.
- ✔ Georgia; its capital and the South's transportation hub is Atlanta.
- ✔ Tennessee; its capital is Nashville, but its largest city is Memphis.
- ✔ Kentucky; its capital is Frankfort, but its largest city is Louisville.

For travelers, highlights of the South include

- ✔ Restoration of Colonial Williamsburg.
- ✔ Civil War history.
- ✔ Skyline Drive and the Blue Ridge Parkway.
- ✔ Place of first flight in Kill Devil Hills, North Carolina.
- ✔ America's largest private home, Biltmore House in Asheville, North Carolina.
- ✔ Architecture of Charleston, South Carolina, and Savannah, Georgia.
- ✔ Beaches and coastal islands of North and South Carolina and Georgia.
- ✔ Grand Ole Opry and Graceland in Tennessee.
- ✔ Mammoth Cave and Bluegrass Country in Kentucky.

Florida

Both the Atlantic Ocean and the Gulf of Mexico border Florida (see Figure. 2.7), a peninsula with more coastline than any other state except Alaska. The northwest part of the state, called the *Panhandle*, extends along the shore of the Gulf of Mexico. Rivers and creeks cut through the state, and it is dotted with springs, lakes, and swamps. **Lake Okeechobee** (*oh kee CHOH bee*), the largest lake in the southern United States, feeds the **Everglades**, the great swamp that covers much of south Florida. The **Keys** make up the state's southernmost part. These small coral islands curve southwestward for about 150 miles (241 km) off the mainland from Miami.

Visitors have been seeking Florida and its Fountain of Youth for centuries. The Spanish were the first. In 1821 the United States gained Florida from Spain, and pioneers moved in. The Seminole Indians fiercely resisted and were forcefully displaced to reservations in the West. Not all the Seminoles left; some retreated deep into the Everglades.

The Native American tribes driven into the Everglades opened the Miccosukee Resort—south Florida's first legal gambling casino—on reservation ground.

In the 1880s, two railroad tycoons, Henry B. Plant and Henry M. Flagler, visited Florida as tourists and ended up building luxurious resort hotels and transportation empires. Plant built a railroad that connected **Tampa** with the north and established the West Coast's tourist industry. Flagler's Florida East Coast Railroad expanded to the upscale resort of **Palm Beach**, then to **Miami**, and finally—on a string of bridges over the keys—to **Key West**. At each stop, Flagler created resort hotels that served as the foundations for communities and, in the case of Miami, a city.

Throughout the state, sports opportunities are endless. Greyhound and horse racing, jai alai, and polo all have their fans. Several major league baseball

FIGURE 2.7 Florida

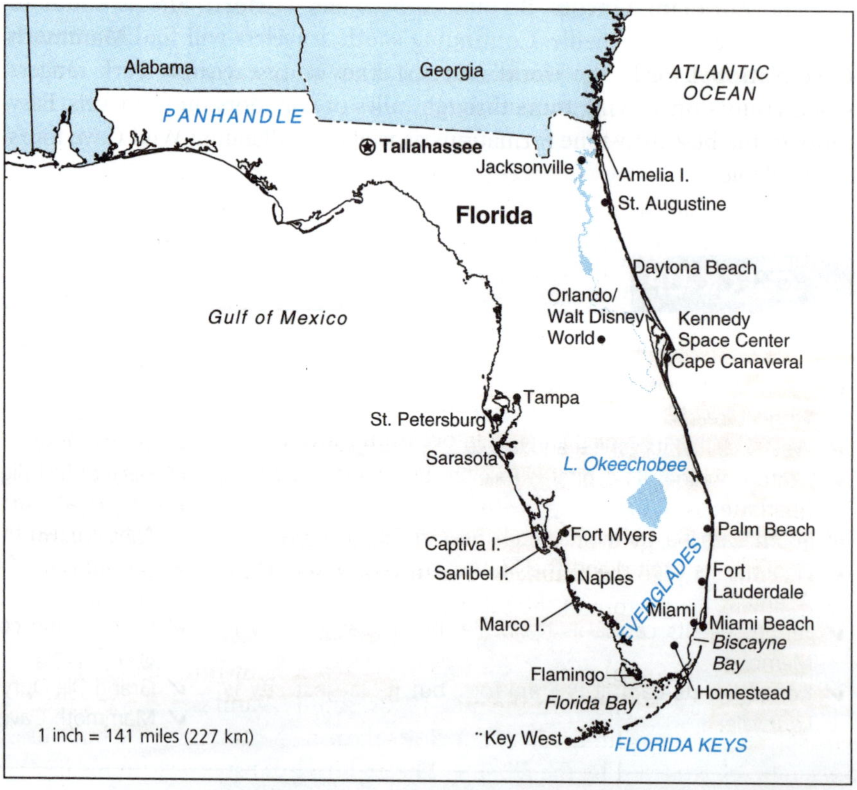

teams have held spring training near St. Petersburg since 1914. The state has more than 1,000 golf courses. And of course, every possible thing to do on or in the water is available.

Northern Florida

Florida's capital, **Tallahassee**, is in the Panhandle. The largest city is **Jacksonville**, in the northeast corner of the state. **Amelia Island**, near Jacksonville, is a resort known for its tennis facilities. Nearby **St. Augustine** is called *America's Oldest City.* The Spanish explorer Ponce de León is believed to have landed there in 1513. The excavated grounds of the original colony contain remnants of the settlement as well as an Indian burial ground.

A theme park is an amusement park where architecture, decoration, costumes, entertainment, music, food, shops, and other elements suggest an identity for the entire attraction.

Central Florida

Before 1971, tourists would drive rapidly through the orange groves around **Orlando** on their way south to the beaches. Then, in 1971, **Walt Disney World** opened in Lake Buena Vista, and nothing has been the same since. Walt Disney World attracts millions of visitors. Its theme regions are the Magic Kingdom, EPCOT Center, MGM Studios, and the Animal Kingdom, an adventure and safari park.

A week barely gives enough time for all that there is to see and do in central Florida (see the Close-Up). Other attractions include Universal Studios, working studios with a theme park; Sea World, a marine park; Pleasure Island, an adult entertainment complex with nightclubs, stage shows, and live concerts; and, at a bit of a distance to the east on the Atlantic Coast, the **Kennedy Space Center**.

Cinderella's Castle, Walt Disney World, Florida

South Florida

Florida's second-largest city, **Miami** (*my AM ee*), is on Biscayne Bay, west of the ocean. Miami is a busy commercial city, not a resort. Miami International Airport serves as a gateway between the United States and Latin America. Today, the city is a mosaic of ethnic backgrounds. More than 55 percent of the population is foreign born, and Spanish is the most commonly spoken language.

The city's attractions include Little Havana at *Calle Ocho* (Eighth Street) and Vizcaya Museum, the Mediterranean mansion on Biscayne Bay built as a winter home in 1916 for James Deering, a Chicago industrialist. At that time Miami's population was less than 10,000. The annual Orange Bowl football game on or near New Year's Day is a major draw. The city hosts the Miami Dolphins (football) and the Florida Marlins (baseball). Miami is one of the most important cruise ship ports. On occasion more than ten huge ships may be docked at its piers.

Miami Beach

Located on a thin barrier island across Biscayne Bay, Miami Beach is connected to the mainland by causeways. In 1912 rock and sand were pumped from the bottom of the bay and spread over mangrove roots and soft sand to create the city.

South Beach (SoBe) is the area of Miami Beach known for its Art Deco hotels and vibrant nightlife. In the mid-1930s, south Miami Beach was called *God's Waiting Room.* Hundreds of small hotels and apartments were built to house retirees attracted by the climate. The architectural style was influenced by the Paris *Exposition des Arts Décoratifs*. More than 800 of these hotels, now refurbished and rebuilt, remain in the Art Deco Historic District between 6th and 23rd Streets from Ocean Drive to Lennox Avenue. North of SoBe, Miami Beach turns into a long stretch of hotels and luxury high-rise condominiums.

Fort Lauderdale North of Miami Beach, Fort Lauderdale is also attracting attention. The Seminole tribe, in partnership with a hotel chain, has built a hotel and casino on its reservation just fifteen minutes from downtown. The city's cruise ship port, Port Everglades, can handle the largest ships. It was the destination for the *Queen Mary 2*'s first transatlantic voyage. All this plus an artificial reef, a long stretch of walkable beach, busy nightlife, and trendy shopping on Las Olas Boulevard have made Fort Lauderdale an attractive destination.

Visitors can see the Everglades on airboat rides operated by descendants of the Miccosukee tribe or from nature trails built on boardwalks that lift travelers safely above the swamp and its crocodiles.

The Everglades A popular day trip from Miami is to **Everglades National Park**, one of the country's few subtropical regions. The Everglades extend from Lake Okeechobee to Florida Bay and the Gulf of Mexico. From the highway, they appear as an endless prairie. The main visitors' center and park headquarters is southwest of **Homestead**. It marks the beginning of a road that meanders through sawgrass prairie, hardwood hammock, cypress swamp, and lakes and ends at **Flamingo** on the edge of Florida Bay.

Key West Key West is the last key on the string of coral islands to the south of Miami, the southernmost city in the continental United States. Once home to

CLOSE-UP: CENTRAL FLORIDA

Who is a good prospect for a trip to central Florida? Families and the young at heart are good prospects. The theme parks have rides and attractions to suit old and young. It really is a treat to see a child get a hug from Mickey Mouse. The area has special appeal to school groups.

Why would they visit central Florida? The area has some of the world's most extensive theme parks and a range of hotels, shopping, and food facilities for all tastes. For those from northern climes, it offers an opportunity to see different vegetation. (The coconut palm does not grow this far north, but orange trees do.) Golf and tennis are available, as well as most water sports.

Where would they go? Orlando is the area's gateway airport. Walt Disney World in Lake Buena Vista dominates the area, although attractions such as Sea World and Universal Studios do excellent business as well.

A week is not too long to spend in the area. A typical itinerary includes three or four days in Walt Disney World and the rest spent visiting nearby attractions or pursuing special interests such as golf or shopping. (There are many outlet malls in the area.)

On a ten-day visit, tourists can spend a day at the Kennedy Space Center on the Atlantic Coast. They might add a cruise on one of the Disney ships. Participants are transferred to the port at Cape Canaveral. If they were staying at a Disney resort, there is no second check-in; baggage is sent ahead to their cabin. Resort room keys even open shipboard staterooms.

Orlando package tours generally include air, transfers or a rental car, accommodations, and admission tickets to various attractions.

When is the best time to go? Winters can be cool, with rain; summers are hot and humid. Early spring offers the best weather in central Florida. But to have the best chance of avoiding crowds, visitors might come instead between Labor Day and mid-December or in May before Memorial Day, avoiding any holidays. The parks are crowded during school and summer vacations.

How would you respond if the travelers said: "Our children are too young to spend all day walking around the park. Isn't the admission ticket awfully expensive if we can stay only a few hours?" The admission tickets allow people to leave the park and reenter later that day. Many people with young children come during the early morning, leave before or after lunch, return to their hotels for nap time or a swim, and then return in the evening with their strength restored.

pirates and freebooters, it is 100 miles (161 km) southwest of where the Keys join the mainland north of Key Largo and about 90 miles (145 km) from Cuba. The Overseas Highway to Key West is built on the footings of Flagler's railroad, which was destroyed in 1935 by one of the severest hurricanes on record.

Key West is also the name of the most distant island's town. In the 1820s, its citizens earned a good living salvaging the vessels that ran aground on the Florida Reef. Wood, fixtures, and portholes from stranded ships were used in local homes. Today, Key West is a resort, a cruise ship port, and the land of Hemingway, sunset celebrations on Mallory Pier, and Jimmy Buffett's "Margaritaville." Duval Street is the main thoroughfare, going from the Atlantic Ocean to the Gulf of Mexico.

Brilliantly colored marine and plant life inhabit the John Pennekamp Coral Reef State Park just south of Key Largo. Visitors can swim, snorkel, fish, take scuba diving lessons, and ride in glass-bottom boats.

Florida's West Coast

Tampa and **St. Petersburg** are cities of Florida's central West Coast. Tampa is a cruise port. **Sarasota** is the region's cultural capital, thanks to the generosity of the Ringling family of circus fame, who left their art collection to be displayed at the Ringling Museum of Art.

South from Sarasota, **Sanibel** and **Captiva** are low-lying islands in the Gulf of Mexico well known to seashell collectors. They are connected to the mainland by a causeway at **Fort Myers**. Sanibel's J. N. "Ding" Darling National Wildlife Refuge has foot and bicycle trails and kayak and canoe routes. More to the south, **Naples** has golfing, shopping, and fishing opportunities. Its dependency, **Marco Island**, is a model of ecological preservation.

A conch (*konk*) is a large mollusk with a spiral shell. People who were born and raised in Key West like to call themselves Conchs. The Conch Train is the little open-air tram that tours the town's points of interest.

✔ CHECK-UP

Florida's natural attractions include

- ✔ Beautiful sandy beaches lining miles of coastline.
- ✔ Mild winter climate.
- ✔ One of the most interesting and unusual swamps, the Everglades.
- ✔ Florida Keys.

Florida's draws include

- ✔ Extensive sports facilities.
- ✔ Luxurious hotels and resorts.
- ✔ South Beach on Miami Beach.
- ✔ Central Florida theme parks, especially Walt Disney World.

The Gulf States

The Gulf of Mexico is the great curved arm of the Atlantic Ocean bordered by five states (see Figure 2.8). Of these, Alabama, Mississippi, and Louisiana share a culture that sets them apart, a culture that includes Spanish, French, and Old South influences.

Alabama

For many years King Cotton ruled Alabama, but in the 1900s industry pushed in, and **Birmingham**, the state's biggest city, became a center of the iron and steel industry. Paying homage to Vulcan (the Roman god of fire and metalworking), the world's largest cast-iron statue overlooks the city.

Alabama's attractions include

- The **U.S. Space and Rocket Center** at Tranquility Base in Huntsville.
- **Montgomery**, the capital and the first capital of the Confederacy.
- Monuments of the civil rights movement: the Dexter Avenue King Memorial Baptist Church in Montgomery; the route of a march from **Selma** to Montgomery taken by King and about 30,000 others in 1965 to demand equal voting rights for African Americans.
- **Mobile**, on the Gulf of Mexico. During late March and early April, the city's Azalea Trail winds past blooming bushes. The city is a cruise ship port.
- The Golf Trail, a series of golf courses spaced a few hours from one another.

After the boll weevil destroyed cotton crops in the South at the beginning of the 20th century, farmers were forced to diversify. They switched from cotton to peanuts. As a result, they grew more prosperous and erected a monument in Enterprise, Alabama, to the beetle. Its inscription says, "In profound appreciation of the boll weevil and what it has done as the herald of prosperity."

Mississippi

Jackson

History

Casinos

From the Alabama border, Mississippi stretches west to the Mississippi River. In the north, visitors can see **Oxford**, the town captured fictionally in the writings of William Faulkner (1897–1962). His Greek Revival home is open to the public.

The **Natchez Trace Parkway**, administered by the National Park Service, starts at the state's northeast corner and winds its way diagonally across the state. This ancient pathway, originally an Indian trail, was used by flatboat men who sailed downriver to Natchez, sold everything—including their boats—and walked home on the trace.

Jackson, in central Mississippi, is the capital and the state's cultural heart. West of Jackson, on the river, lies the **Vicksburg National Military Park**, where a Union victory was a major turning point in the Civil War. Farther south, also on the river, is **Natchez**. In spring and fall, tours of houses that existed before the Civil War attract visitors. Natchez-under-the-Hill is a colorful area of pubs, gift shops, restaurants, and dockside casinos.

FIGURE 2.8

The Gulf States

The Mississippi Gulf Coast is a popular vacationland. White-sand beaches lined with hotels and casinos attract vacationers from spring to late fall. **Gulfport** and **Biloxi** began permitting "offshore" gambling in the late 1980s. To fulfill the letter of the law, hotels are constructed on land, with casinos built on piers extending into the sea.

Louisiana

The name *Louisiana*—after the French king Louis XIV—originally applied to the whole Mississippi River basin, which was settled by French colonists in 1699. After losing the territory to England and Spain, then regaining the region, the French sold the territory to the United States in a transaction known as the Louisiana Purchase. In 1812 the southern part of the territory became the state of Louisiana. To this day, French and Spanish influences can be seen throughout the state.

New Orleans Louisiana's largest city is bordered on the north by Lake Pontchartrain (*PAHN chuhr trayn*) and on the south by the Mississippi River, about 75 miles (121 km) upriver from the Gulf of Mexico. Its location on an enormous crescent of the river created its nickname, the *Crescent City*. Another city nickname is the *Big Easy*, which describes perfectly the city's relaxed pace and flair for having a good time.

A strong embankment, a *levee*, protects New Orleans from the river. Because of the high water table, cemetery tombs were built above ground so coffins would not float to the surface after a hard rain. Modern burial practices have conquered the problem, but ornate family tombs continue to be popular. New Orleans's newest streetcar line, the Canal line, takes travelers from the French Market to the most famous cemeteries.

New Orleans's districts have unique characteristics and attractions. The easiest way to picture the city is to divide it into two main sections: uptown and downtown. The dividing line is Lee Circle. Below Lee Circle are the French Quarter, Warehouse Arts District (a formerly rundown section that is now a trendy area of restaurants, shops, museums, hotels, and businesses), and the Central Business District. Above Lee Circle are Uptown and the Garden District. Casinos are located along the river.

The **French Quarter**, the *Vieux Carré* (*view kah RAY*), is the heart of the tourist's New Orleans. The old quarter is laid out along the river. Here the *Creoles* (which can mean people with any blend of French, Spanish, West Indian, and African ancestry) built their town houses, cathedral, marketplace, and theaters. And here, served by slaves, they developed one of North America's most sophisticated cities.

Exploration of the French Quarter begins in Jackson Square, dominated by the St. Louis Cathedral. Bawdy Bourbon Street, stretching from Canal Street to Esplanade Avenue, is famous for its bars, jazz clubs, strip joints, and tacky novelty shops. On most nights it is a pedestrian mall packed with revelers.

Many visitors come to New Orleans to hear music. Preservation Hall in the Quarter is renowned for traditional jazz, but all styles are performed. Even funerals call for music, with a jazz band playing dirges on the way to the cemetery and swinging on the way back. Each year the town has music festivals. The New Orleans Jazz and Heritage Festival is held in April or May.

The Garden District is an area of beautiful homes. A fun way to see the area is by streetcar. Tennessee Williams immortalized the streetcars in his play *A Streetcar Named Desire*. No line named *Desire* runs today, but visitors enjoy rides on the St. Charles Avenue line. Its cars have been included in the National

➤ PROFILE

Cuisine of the Eastern United States

Each region of the country has special dishes and its own style of cooking. Visitors might like to sample

- Real maple syrup on their pancakes in New England.
- Seafood fresh from the ocean: lobsters, clams, and scallops in New England; crab from the Chesapeake; and shrimp and oysters from the Gulf.
- Bagels and falafel sandwiches from the street stalls of New York City.
- Pretzels, shoofly pie, and scrapple in Amish country.
- Cheese steak sandwiches in Philadelphia.
- Peanuts fixed every which way in Virginia and Georgia.
- Colonial dishes in Williamsburg.
- Charleston's she-crab soup made from crab and roe.
- Cuban cuisine in Miami and stone crabs at Joe's on Miami Beach.
- Key lime pie in Florida.
- Pecan pie from its home in Mississippi.
- Beignets (deep-fried donuts covered in powdered sugar) with dark-roasted coffee, laced with chicory, at Café du Monde in New Orleans.
- Cajun cooking, particularly gumbo and jambalaya, in Louisiana.

New Orleans is famed for its restaurants. One—Antoine's—has maintained its reputation under the watchful eye of a single family through the Civil War, Prohibition, World War II, and the cyberage. Its chefs created the classic Oysters Rockefeller (oysters on the half-shell topped with spinach and seasonings).

New Orleans bars have twenty-four-hour liquor licenses; closing time is strictly random. Visitors can take their drinks from club to club as long as the drink is in a plastic "go cup" rather than a glass or metal container.

Register of Historic Places. On the route you can visit the Superdome, one of the world's largest indoor sports arenas, and the Audubon Zoo.

Probably New Orleans's best-known event, **Carnival** lasts for one to two months, exploding in its final days in a wild party to end all parties. There are private balls and public parades held in the French Quarter and other parts of the city day and night. Mardi Gras ("Fat Tuesday") is the final day, the last party before Ash Wednesday, the beginning of Lent. A word of warning: the party can get rowdy.

The *Delta Queen* on the Mississippi

River Road The River Road follows the Mississippi between New Orleans and **Baton Rouge,** the state's capital. Plantations are sited on both sides of the river. Several antebellum homes built in "Steamboat Gothic" style are open to the public. **Nottoway** was the South's largest plantation home; now it is a restaurant and inn. It is also possible to see the plantations on a steamboat tour up the river from the city.

Cajun Country West of the city is the romantic landscape of the Teche, Atchafalaya, and Vermilion **bayous,** which are swampy backwaters of a river or a lake. The bayous are the home of the Cajuns, descendants of the French settlers called Acadians who were driven out of Canada by the British during the 1750s. Many settled in southern Louisiana near **Lafayette,** a town west of New Orleans. Visitors can tour bayou settlements, sample the spicy cuisine, and hear some foot-stomping music.

✔ CHECK-UP

The Gulf states include
- ✔ Alabama; its capital is Montgomery, but its largest city is Birmingham.
- ✔ Mississippi; its capital and largest city is Jackson.
- ✔ Louisiana; its capital is Baton Rouge, but its largest city is New Orleans.

Highlights of the Gulf states include
- ✔ Cajun culture of the Louisiana bayous.
- ✔ Carnival in New Orleans, Louisiana.
- ✔ Gambling in Mississippi.
- ✔ Mississippi River and the River Road.
- ✔ Monuments of the civil rights movement in Alabama.

Planning the Trip

Observing the traveler's needs and interests are the keys to planning a trip. Whatever the activity and whatever the destination in the eastern states, information is readily available. It can be obtained from industry sources or state tourist offices. (Web sites are listed in the Resources boxes in the Workbook.) The United States has no government-supported tourism office; almost all U.S. travel and tourism promotion is conducted at state and local levels.

When to Go

Cities operate no matter what the weather, and in winter their shops, museums, theaters, and clubs are places of retreat when the outdoors is less than welcoming. Upstate New York is known for low winter temperatures and deep snow, and the mountains of western Pennsylvania can also have heavy snow. In general, spring and fall are the most desirable seasons for sightseeing in the cities of the north. Christmas decorations have a special appeal almost everywhere. Fall is certainly the peak time to visit New England, and spring is the time to view the Mid-Atlantic's gardens.

A satisfying resort vacation depends on the weather. Ski resorts list snow depths on the Web for those who are especially choosy. Some resorts even have cameras on their slopes that allow a preview of conditions. Predicting sunshine for a beach vacation is always difficult. In south Florida, ideal vacation conditions exist between December and May, when temperatures average between 60° and 85° F (16° and 30°C) and rainfall is scant; in summer, torrential rainstorms often occur in late afternoon. In winter, even south Florida has days too chilly for the surf. North of Florida, high season for most beach resorts is from late May to September.

Sometimes a special event or the avoidance of crowds is more important than weather for timing a trip. For the least crowds, the time to travel to central Florida is between Labor Day and the start of Christmas vacation, except on any holiday; for Williamsburg, January through March. To avoid mosquitoes and high humidity, winter is the best time to visit Florida's Everglades.

Preparing the Traveler

Travelers who "know before they go" seem to have the most satisfying vacations and become the industry's desired commodity—repeat visitors. Even a few safety reminders, clothing hints, or a friendly tip about food or what to see or do or buy can benefit a traveler. See the Profiles on the cuisine (page 51) and shopping opportunities (page 53) in the eastern United States.

Transportation

The eastern United States has every mode of transportation: plane, train, motorcoach, and private car. Time and money usually determine what is best.

By Air Despite security concerns, air travel is usually the quickest way to get to most destinations. Airports are connected to their city centers by taxis, limousines, vans, buses, and sometimes even water shuttles. A smooth transfer from an airport to a city center starts a trip on a pleasing note. Transfer information is available on the Web.

By Water Taking a cruise has become one of the most popular ways to vacation in the United States. Destinations include cities up and down the East Coast as well as offshore islands and international ports. New York City, Philadelphia, Baltimore, Norfolk, Charleston, and Mobile host ships in season, but Florida is the cruise center. Its major ports are Miami, Port Everglades (Fort Lauderdale), Port Canaveral (Disney Cruises), Tampa, and Jacksonville, with ships departing almost daily for the Bahamas, the Caribbean, and Mexico, as well as on more extensive itineraries. (These destinations will be covered in Chapters 6 and 7.)

New Orleans is another attractive port for travelers. The voyage on the Mississippi to the Gulf passes old Cajun cottages and flaming oil rigs. Voyages upstream on old-fashioned paddleboats appeal to history fans.

By Rail Amtrak is the independent semipublic corporation that operates U.S. passenger trains. It provides rail service along the East Coast from Boston to

➤ **PROFILE**

Shopping in the Eastern United States

Some well-known destinations in the East include

- Freeport, Maine, home of mail-order giant L. L. Bean, "open 24 hours a day, 365 days a year," the centerpiece of more than 100 outlet stores.
- New York City, which features the boutiques of Madison Avenue for upscale shopping and stores in Lower Manhattan for bargains. Do *not* buy a Rolex watch from a street vendor!
- Northeast Philadelphia, where Franklin Mills Mall is the number one tourist destination in Pennsylvania.
- Shops of the Smithsonian Museums in Washington, D.C., for posters, books, and unique treasures.
- High Point, North Carolina, the hub of America's furniture-manufacturing industry, where more than a hundred factories have retail outlets.
- Nashville, Tennessee, home of the Opry Mills megamall.

Amtrak's official name is the National Railroad Passenger Corporation; its popular name comes from the words *America*, *travel*, and *track*.

ON THE SPOT

It is only natural that when discussing a destination, potential travelers will ask, "Have you been there?"

The answer should always be the truth. But even if you have been to the destination many times, there could be recent changes. Respond, "What do you need to know? The resources of the industry enable me to find out just about anything you might like to know." The travelers may in fact simply be looking for such information as which days an attraction is open or when a ferry leaves—facts you might know or can easily find out.

Visitors to Williamsburg can stay in one of the small colonial houses. It is a popular, though not inexpensive, choice for many.

Miami. High-speed trains such as the Acela (*ah CELL a*) Express operate on the busy Northeast Corridor between Boston, New York City, and Washington, D.C. Outside the corridor, rail travel is not usually convenient and certainly not time efficient. On a long-distance route, the price is rarely competitive with flying.

Amtrak's Auto Train operates nonstop overnight service from Lorton, Virginia (just south of Washington, D.C.) to Sanford, Florida (near Orlando). The train leaves daily at 1640 and arrives the next morning at 0900. Typical passengers include travelers who cannot fly or drive owing to disabilities and snowbirds who want their cars but also want to avoid the 900-mile (1,521 km) drive.

By Road Personal car travel continues to be the preferred mode of transportation within the United States. Most people vacation within 150 miles (241 km) of home and use the family car as transportation. Automobile organizations such as AAA provide maps and itineraries, and local tourism offices are invaluable sources of destination information.

For longer trips rental cars fill the gap. Travelers fly to their destinations and rent a car on arrival. Visitors to New York City do not need a car, but visitors to most other cities do. Public transportation is sometimes excellent, sometimes nonexistent. In Washington, D.C., open-air blue-and-white shuttle buses called Tourmobiles circulate around the sites. Tickets are valid all day and entitle the visitor to unlimited on and off boarding. Other cities are copying the shuttle bus concept.

In central Florida a rental car is useful unless travelers are staying at a resort within Walt Disney World, where buses, monorail trains, and boats circulate. Hotels outside the park have shuttles, but a car is useful for visits to restaurants and other attractions.

Accommodations

North America is the home of the modern hotel, and choices can range from basic budget motels along the highway to some of the world's finest resorts. It is easy to choose a deluxe property. The difficult hotel choice is the request for a "charming, centrally located property at low cost."

Hotels that cater to corporate travelers during the week often offer attractive packages for leisure travelers on weekends. During peak seasons or when cities host special events, reservations are imperative and room rates are at their highest.

Travelers to big cities—especially New York—may be surprised to see how small the rooms are, even at deluxe hotels. Of course, guests can upgrade to a suite. Lower-priced accommodations may be available at less convenient locations outside a city's center, but staying there means incurring additional time and transportation costs.

Upscale B&Bs have sprouted up throughout the country. Although they are usually located in the countryside or in small cities, some B&Bs are even found in the big cities.

CHAPTER WRAP-UP

SUMMARY

Here is a review of the objectives with which we began the chapter.

1. **Describe the environment and people of the eastern United States.** The coastline of the eastern United States varies from Maine's rugged and irregular

shore to the gently sloping beaches found from Long Island to Florida and the Gulf of Mexico. From New Jersey to Florida, a line of barrier islands and sandbars protects the coast in its endless battle with the ocean. Florida is part of the coastal plain.

The Piedmont, evident from Maryland to Georgia, stretches from the coastal plain to the base of the Appalachian Mountain System, which extends from Canada to Alabama. The system includes separate ranges: the White, Green, Adirondack, Catskill, Allegheny, Blue Ridge, and Great Smoky. West of the mountains is the great continental basin formed by the Mississippi-Missouri and Ohio River systems.

The climate of the eastern United States ranges from subtropical in Florida to cold continental in the states bordering Canada. Within each region there is great variation. Hurricane season is from June to November.

Five hundred years of immigration have produced a country with a combination of shared and separate cultures. Immigrants brought the place-names, architectural styles, food preferences, and speech patterns of their ancestral homes to the new land, where they were adapted and changed to suit local needs.

2. **Identify the main attractions of the region, matching travelers and destinations best suited for each other.** For family fun, the theme parks of central Florida are a favorite choice. For those looking for outdoor activities, the mountains of New England and the coastal beaches are appealing. Good beaches are almost everywhere along the coast from Long Island to Mississippi. Florida's coastline is one big sand pile. For those who want activity after the sun goes down, Rehoboth, Ocean City, Virginia Beach, Myrtle Beach, and certainly Miami Beach provide a great deal. For something quieter, the island resorts of South Carolina, Georgia, and the west coast of Florida fit the request.

   Casinos are found at Foxwoods in Connecticut, at Atlantic City in New Jersey, at Native American resorts in Florida, and in Gulfport or Biloxi, Mississippi, and New Orleans, Louisiana.

   For history buffs, Boston, New York's Hudson River Valley, Philadelphia, Virginia's Historic Triangle, Charleston, Savannah, and Natchez have special appeal.

   Nightlife is ample in New York City, Atlantic City, Miami, New Orleans, Memphis, Nashville, and New Orleans.

3. **Provide or find the information needed to plan a trip to the eastern United States.** For most destinations, flying to the region and then renting a car for local touring makes the best use of valuable time. For each season, there is someplace in the eastern United States appropriate for a vacation. Logistical information is available through industry sources or on the Internet.

QUESTIONS FOR DISCUSSION AND REVIEW

1. New Orleans is a destination magnet for those who enjoy author Anne Rice's *Vampire Chronicles*. What books have you read that influenced your interest in a city or area?
2. Bring in a consumer travel publication, and choose an article about a destination. What in particular caught your eye? How does the writer encourage you to travel to the destination? What logistical facts are missing from the article? What would you do if a traveler referred to an article and wanted to go to a destination or event that you knew nothing about?

CHAPTER 3

The Midwest

- The Great Lakes States
- The Great Plains States
- Texas

OBJECTIVES

When you have completed Chapter 3, you should be able to

1. Describe the environment and people of the Midwest.
2. Describe the main attractions of the region, matching travelers and destinations best suited for each other.
3. Provide or find the information needed to plan a trip to the area.

Throughout the 18th and 19th centuries, the United States expanded westward. The region stretching west from the Ohio and the Mississippi Rivers to the Rocky Mountains became the states of the Midwest. Although not a tourist draw like Florida or Las Vegas, the region has vibrant cities, scenic wilderness, Native American landmarks, and pioneer history.

The Environment and Its People

This chapter considers fifteen states as part of the Midwest. As Figure 3.1 shows, six of the states have borders on the Great Lakes: **Ohio, Indiana, Michigan, Illinois, Wisconsin**, and **Minnesota**. Eight states are part of the region known as the Great Plains: **Iowa, Missouri, Arkansas, Oklahoma, Kansas, Nebraska, South Dakota**, and **North Dakota**. Although the plains extend into **Texas**, its border on the Gulf of Mexico, immense size, and southwestern culture give it stand-alone status.

The Land

Great waterways border the Midwest on the east, south, and north. On the east, the **Mississippi River** is the country's principal inland waterway. "Old Man River" empties into the Gulf of Mexico. In the north are the **Great Lakes**, North America's largest lakes. They were created by the action of glaciers many centuries ago. Of the five lakes—**Superior, Michigan, Huron, Erie,** and **Ontario**—only Lake Michigan is entirely in the United States. The other lakes are shared by the United States and Canada.

In February 1987, Chicago's Lake Shore Drive was closed by floods for the first time. Storm winds had driven the water from Lake Michigan. A warm winter had melted ice barriers that usually protect the city.

Plains stretch from the Appalachian Highlands in the east to the Rocky Mountains in the west. Glaciers covered the region during the Ice Age. They stripped the topsoil from parts of Michigan, Minnesota, and Wisconsin and carved out thousands of lakes. Today, much of this area is heavily forested. Farther south—in parts of Illinois, Indiana, Iowa, and Ohio—the glaciers flattened the land and deposited rich soil ideal for farming.

The plains slope upward in the west and get progressively drier. The region's west, called the **Great Plains**, has vast grasslands. Few trees grow in the area. Some rugged hills, including the **Black Hills** of South Dakota, rise out of the plains.

In the southeast, the **Ozark-Ouachita** (*WAHSH ih taw*) **Highlands** rise from the plains and form a scenic landscape in southern Missouri, northwest Arkansas, and eastern Oklahoma. The highlands include forested hills, artificial lakes, and many underground caves and gushing springs.

Texas begins with coastal plains along the Gulf of Mexico on the east and rises gradually to meet the Great Plains in the northwest. A large part of the Great Plains is within the **Texas Panhandle**, the part of the state that juts northward alongside New Mexico and Oklahoma. The western part of the Panhandle is a high plateau called the *Llano Estacado* ("Staked Plains"), an area that extends into New Mexico and the Panhandle of Oklahoma.

The Climate

Weather reports of the Great Lakes region always seem to forecast either

FIGURE 3.1
The Midwest
National capital
State capital
City
National park or other site
1 inch = 236 miles (380 km)
CANADA
Montana
Missouri R.
North Dakota
GREAT PLAINS
Bismarck
Minnesota
L. Itasca
L. Superior
Michigan
L. Huron
St. Paul
Wisconsin
L. Michigan
Michigan
Wyoming
BLACK HILLS
Pierre
South Dakota
Mississippi R.
Madison
Lansing
GREAT PLAINS
Iowa
L. Erie
Nebraska
Missouri R.
Des Moines
Illinois
Indiana
Ohio
Columbus
Colorado
Lincoln
Indianapolis
Missouri
Springfield
Kansas
Topeka
Ohio R.
West Virginia
Jefferson City
Cahokia Mound
GREAT PLAINS
Missouri R.
Ohio R.
Kentucky
Virginia
LLANO ESTACADO
OZARK-OUACHITA HIGHLANDS
PANHANDLE
Oklahoma City
North Carolina
GREAT PLAINS
Tennessee
Mississippi R.
New Mexico
Little Rock
Oklahoma
South Carolina
LLANO ESTACADO
Arkansas
Mississippi
Alabama
Georgia
Texas
Rio Grande
Louisiana
Austin
Florida
Rio Grande
MEXICO
Gulf of Mexico
CUBA

FIGURE 3.2

Milestones in Midwestern History

700 BC The Adena culture builds large mounds in what is now southern Ohio.

1682 Spanish missionaries build churches in Texas.

1803 The Louisiana Purchase almost doubles the size of the country.

1804 Lewis and Clark pass through South Dakota on their expedition to the Pacific Ocean.

1811 Work begins on the National Road, which will link the East and the Midwest.

1800s St. Louis, Missouri, becomes the gateway to the West.

1866 Oil is discovered in Texas near Nacogdoches.

1871 The Chicago fire destroys much of the city.

1885 The world's first metal-frame skyscraper, the ten-story Home Insurance Building, is constructed in Chicago, Illinois.

1927 Gutzon Borglum begins work on Mount Rushmore National Monument.

1963 President Kennedy is assassinated as he rides through Dallas.

1964 The Lyndon B. Johnson Space Center in Houston makes southeastern Texas a center for space research.

1990s Branson, Missouri, emerges as one of the most popular motorcoach destinations.

1995 Rock 'n' Roll Hall of Fame opens in Cleveland.

1999 Chicago fills its streets with cow statues.

severe cold in winter or extreme heat in summer. Keep in mind the local variations. Ideas that latitude determines climate are shaken when you are chilled to the bone in Milwaukee one day in late fall while a coat may not be needed directly across Lake Michigan in the Michigan fruit belt. The prevailing winds from the west pass across the lake and absorb the heat stored in the water during the summer.

The Great Plains are wide open to cold polar air from the Arctic and warm, humid air from the Gulf of Mexico. Winters are cold, with blizzards; summers are warm, with frequent heat waves.

Texas draws warm air from the Gulf. In most of the state, winter comes and leaves before wearing out its welcome. Only January and February can be called winter. During March and April wildflowers splash the plains and deserts with carpets of color. The eastern part of Texas is wetter than the west. Hurricanes come in from the Gulf of Mexico, and tornadoes occur along *Tornado Alley*, the belt of land that stretches across Texas, Oklahoma, Kansas, Nebraska, and Iowa. This region has the world's highest incidence of tornadoes.

The People and Their History

Mystery surrounds the earliest inhabitants of the Midwest (see Figure 3.2). Ohio, Wisconsin, and Illinois have more than 30,000 sites with prehistoric ruins. The people of the region—called "mound builders"—formed large piles of earth as burial places and as platforms for important buildings. Most mounds are found in the valleys of the Mississippi and Ohio Rivers and near the Great Lakes. The mound at **Cahokia** in southern Illinois is the largest remaining. Its base is larger than that of Egypt's Great Pyramid.

The Native American tribes who came after the mound builders were displaced by the westward expansion of the young United States. Treaties with the Indians forbade settlement, but after the Louisiana Purchase, nothing could stop the pioneers. They settled on Indian lands, and bitter fighting occurred. In the 1850s, the government tried buying land from the Indians and settling the tribes on reservations. When the Homestead Act of 1862 provided cheap land for new settlers and land grants for the railroads, more settlers moved in, pushing the tribes out yet again.

After the Civil War came the glory years for the cowboy. The great south Texas cattle drives began in the late 1860s when ranchers rounded up the longhorn cattle that had been left to roam during the war.

The final period of settlement lasted until 1910. Meanwhile, the industrial cities on the Great Lakes were growing rapidly and attracting immigrants from throughout the world. Life on the frontier seems colorful when we look back on it today, but the people who settled there found it difficult and dangerous—and even dull at times.

✔ CHECK-UP

Major features of the environment of the Midwest include

- ✔ The Great Lakes, the world's largest group of freshwater lakes.
- ✔ The plains extending from the Mississippi to the Rockies.
- ✔ The Ozark-Ouachita Highlands between the interior plains and the coastal lowlands.
- ✔ "Tornado Alley" across Texas, Oklahoma, Kansas, Nebraska, and Iowa.

The history of the Midwest includes

- ✔ Extensive prehistoric settlements.
- ✔ Gradual expansion of U.S. borders during the 18th and 19th centuries.

The Great Lakes States

Ohio, Indiana, Michigan, Illinois, Wisconsin, and Minnesota occupy the northern part of the country's heartland (see Figure 3.3). They are called the Great Lakes states because their northern borders touch four of the Great Lakes—Lakes Erie, Huron, Michigan, and Superior. These states have some of the nation's great industrial cities, as well as extensive wilderness areas.

Ohio

Lake Erie in the north and the winding **Ohio River** on the east and south are Ohio's borders. The state is a highly urbanized industrial giant. Its three major cities are **Columbus**, the capital and largest city, which is in the heartland; **Cincinnati**, in the south on the Ohio River; and **Cleveland**, in the north on Lake Erie.

Fountain Square is the heart of downtown Cincinnati. Its riverfront area includes Public Landing (with showboats and cruises) and Riverfront Coliseum and Riverfront Stadium, homes of professional baseball and football teams.

Cleveland has a fine Museum of Art, one of the country's best symphony orchestras, and the Rock 'n' Roll Hall of Fame. The latter celebrates American rock music by honoring its popular performers, producers, songwriters, and disc jockeys. The phrase "rock and roll" was coined by the Cleveland disc jockey Alan Freed in 1951, so it is fitting that Cleveland is home to this attraction.

FIGURE 3.3

The Great Lakes States

1 inch = 241 miles (388 km)

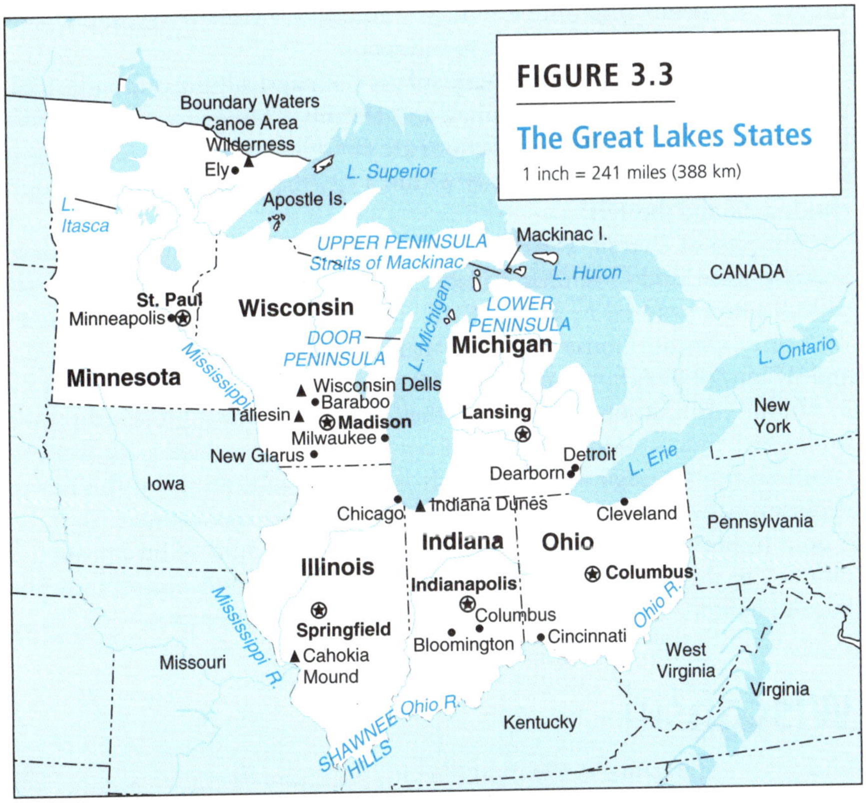

ON THE SPOT

Kelly MacCluer is a successful businesswoman in her middle thirties who is leading a busy life in Omaha. She is going to a business meeting in Cleveland that requires her to stay over the weekend. She is wondering what to do in her free time.

Cleveland offers early-20th-century architecture, museums, performing arts institutions, and a multitude of diverse neighborhoods. For some fun Kelly might try a Saturday morning visit to the Rock 'n' Roll Hall of Fame on the shores of Lake Erie in the North Coast District. If she wants to shop, she might head to the city center, an area called the Tower City District. Its focal point is Tower City Center, a renovated train terminal that is now an upscale shopping mall. Energy permitting, she might continue to the Warehouse District, a popular entertainment destination and Cleveland's premier downtown neighborhood, where warehouses have been converted into loft apartments and condominiums. Along both banks of the Cuyahoga River, the area known as the Flats is home to restaurants, nightclubs, and riverboats.

In the evening Kelly might go to Playhouse Square Center, the country's second-largest performing arts center, which offers the Cleveland Opera, Ohio Ballet, The Second City, Broadway productions, the Great Lakes Theatre Festival, and hundreds of concerts throughout the year. Suggest that she use the Web to see what attractions strike her fancy.

Indiana

Intense settlement occurred along the Ohio River, Indiana's southern boundary, during the first half of the 19th century. The people were mainly farmers. Southern Indiana is a region of forest, limestone outcrops, and attractive valleys. Artists were attracted to its scenic beauty, especially to the picturesque wilds of Brown County between **Bloomington** and **Columbus.**

Indiana's northwest corner, which includes the curve of Lake Michigan, was an expanse of huge sand dunes and wild rice swamps before the area was industrialized during the late 19th century. Remnants of the dunes were saved by formation of the **Indiana Dunes National Lakeshore**, making the area a popular summer beach destination.

Auto racing fans head to the center of the state to **Indianapolis**, the capital and largest city, home of the Indianapolis 500. The auto race is held each year on Memorial Day weekend. Tours are available when the Speedway is not in use. Indianapolis is a sports-minded town with excellent facilities for professional football, basketball, and hockey.

About 50 miles (80 km) south of Indianapolis is Columbus, one of the country's most interesting planned cities. Many of the world's best architects designed its buildings (beginning in 1942 with Eliel Saarinen), making the city a textbook example of modern architecture. Walking and bus tours are available.

The National Road, which extended from Cumberland, Maryland, to Vandalia, Illinois, was the 19th century's main road. It was replaced by Interstate 70. Cities east of Indianapolis retain numerous structures from the National Road era.

Good prospects for trips to the Indy 500 include attendees at local Nascar races and customers of sporting goods or automobile stores. To learn about auto racing or any other special interests, you might start by buying magazines devoted to the subject.

Michigan

North of Indiana and Ohio, Lake Michigan divides the two peninsulas that make up the state of Michigan. The peninsulas are linked by one of the world's longest suspension bridges across the **Straits of Mackinac** (*MACK i naw*).

The rugged **Upper Peninsula** was a hub of the French fur trading empire in the 18th century. In the 19th and 20th centuries, deposits of iron and copper fueled the automotive industry around Detroit. Today, the Upper Peninsula is a haven for backpackers and moose.

The mitten-shaped **Lower Peninsula** is both agricultural and industrial, the site of both **Lansing**, the capital, and **Detroit** ("Motor City"), the state's largest city. Among Detroit's attractions are Hitsville USA, a draw for Motown fans, and Renaissance Center, a city within a city that includes a hotel, shops, restaurants, and theaters.

Just west of Detroit, **Dearborn** has the Automotive Hall of Fame, Henry Ford Museum, and Greenfield Village. The latter includes historic buildings collected and restored by Henry Ford. Structures include Thomas Edison's laboratory, the courthouse where Abraham Lincoln practiced law, and Orville and Wilbur Wright's home and bicycle shop.

In the 1800s, steamship travel on the Great Lakes brought tourists to Lake Michigan's dunes. **Mackinac Island** became a summer haven for wealthy families from Chicago and Detroit. It is at the northern tip of the Lower Peninsula between Lakes Huron and Michigan. No cars are allowed. All travel is done by horse-drawn carriage, by bicycle, or on foot. Perched on a high bluff overlooking the straits, the Grand Hotel is the island's dominant structure. The huge white wood building opened in 1887 and is still going strong.

Working in a sanitarium in Battle Creek, Michigan, in 1906, W. K. Kellogg developed a flaking process for grain called "corn flakes." A patient, C. W. Post, developed his own line of cereals based on foods he was served there. Thus began the breakfast cereal business centered in Battle Creek.

Wisconsin

Wisconsin was the final destination of many European immigrants, and it has the country's strongest German heritage. It is a beautiful region, with dairy farms producing a variety of products. Wisconsin practically overflows with curds and hops. Milk and beer may not be a good tasting mix, but they have been good for the economy.

Milwaukee, on Lake Michigan, is the state's largest city. The Germans who settled the city in the 1840s developed the mammoth breweries that made Milwaukee famous. Most of the breweries have moved on. Tours of the Pabst Mansion give visitors a taste of how the beer barons lived at the end of the 19th century.

Wisconsin's capital, **Madison**, is beautifully sited on five lakes about 75 miles (121 km) west of Milwaukee. Within an hour or so from Madison, visitors can reach **Wisconsin Dells**, a resort area; **Baraboo**, home to Circus World Museum; **Taliesin**, Frank Lloyd Wright's (1867–1959) home and studio; and **New Glarus**, also known as *Little Switzerland*.

Due north of Milwaukee, jutting into Lake Michigan, is the **Door Peninsula**. Here Wisconsin becomes a wilderness with few towns. The Door Peninsula got its name from the dangerous channel at its tip, which the French called *Death's Door*.

In Wisconsin's far northwest are the **Apostle Islands**. They are one of only four sites that have been designated by Congress as national lakeshores. Misnamed by French missionaries who thought the islands numbered twelve instead of twenty-two, the heavily forested Apostles are in Lake Superior. Visitors can thread their way through sea caves; hike among ancient hemlocks and pines; camp on islands populated with deer, bear, and great blue herons; visit century-old lighthouses; and see the wrecks of sunken ships. The islands are reached by boat through the village of Bayfield.

National lakeshores are the Indiana Dunes, Indiana; Pictured Rocks, Michigan; and Sleeping Bear Dunes, Michigan; as well as the Apostle Islands, Wisconsin.

Illinois

Since the 19th century, Illinois has been the center of trade, transportation, and communications for the middle of the continent. The *Land of Lincoln* is also part of the great Midwestern Corn Belt. Vast prairie covers most of the state. In the capital, **Springfield**, Abraham Lincoln married and began his legal career. **Chicago**, the state's largest city and the nation's third largest, is in the northeast corner.

Chicago, Illinois

Chicago

Chicago is the hub of the Midwest. Poet Carl Sandberg (1878–1967) called Chicago the *City of Big Shoulders*, and the city does do things in a big way. It has the world's largest grain market and some of its tallest buildings; its O'Hare Airport is one of the world's busiest.

The city is at the mouth of the Chicago River at the southern end of Lake Michigan. The wind can blow fiercely off the lake, giving Chicago its nickname of the *Windy City*. (Others credit the nickname to the "windy" speeches of the city's politicians.) The land is flat, and streets are built on the grid model. State Street divides east from west; Madison Street divides north from south. The two streets form the base lines of Chicago's street-numbering system.

The area south of the Chicago River is called *The Loop*, a name derived from the elevated railroad built in the 1890s to encircle the business district. The Loop contains the financial district and many of the architectural masterpieces that mark the evolution of the skyscraper.

When Chicago filled its streets with life-sized cows painted by local artists, the Visitors' Bureau estimated that businesses benefited by more than $200 million because people came to town to see the cows, demonstrating the power of a well-advertised attraction.

In 1871 Chicago suffered perhaps its most historic event: Mrs. O'Leary's cow kicked over a lantern and set a fire. The fire's origin may be a legend, but

William Le Baron Jenney designed the ten-story Home Insurance Building (1885) in downtown Chicago, considered the first metal-framed skyscraper. Instead of thick walls, a steel frame supported the building. The steel frame is basic to modern design.

in fact, the fire devastated the city. It also created space. While rebuilding, architects solved engineering problems that made the skyscrapers of New York City possible.

The city attracts millions of tourists each year. Here are some of the places they come to see:

- North America's tallest building, the 110-story Sears Tower.
- Street sculpture by such masters as Calder, Miró, Chagall, Oldenburg, and Picasso.
- Sandy beaches within walking distance of downtown.
- Grant Park along the lake, with the Field Museum of Natural History, the John G. Shedd Aquarium, the Adler Planetarium, and the Art Institute of Chicago.
- Lincoln Park and its zoo.
- Water Tower and Pumping Station, landmarks that survived the Great Fire.
- Michigan Avenue with its Magnificent Mile of shops, hotels, and restaurants.
- The Gold Coast, a residential area on the Near North Side.
- Jackson Park, with the Museum of Science and Industry, the city's most popular attraction since the building was erected for the World Expo of 1893.
- Robie House, an example of Frank Lloyd Wright's prairie houses, built in 1909.
- After-dark activities including football, baseball, hockey, and basketball in their seasons; the Chicago Symphony and Chicago Opera; improvisational theater; and summer entertainment in the parks.

➤ PROFILE

Cuisine of the Midwest

Regional specialties of the area include

- ➤ Deep-pan pizza in Chicago.
- ➤ Cheese and dairy products made in Wisconsin.
- ➤ German cuisine in Milwaukee.
- ➤ Wild rice from Minnesota, Michigan, and Wisconsin—not a true rice, but a wild aquatic grass with brown-black seeds that requires long cooking.
- ➤ Prime beef from Omaha.
- ➤ Mexican food in Texas.

Other Attractions Illinois also has historic and scenic attractions outside the Windy City. Visitors can see John Deere's original blacksmith shop at Grand Detour, west of Chicago. Here, in 1837, Deere successfully forged the self-scouring steel plow, an invention that opened the prairie to farming. It replaced the pioneers' cast-iron plows, which were sluggish in turning the gummy soil. The Shawnee Hills of southern Illinois and the rolling hills of Jo Daviess County in northwestern Illinois have beautiful scenery. Near the state's southwest border is Cahokia Mound, the largest prehistoric ruin north of Mexico.

Minnesota

The *Land of 10,000 Lakes* is a destination for those who enjoy the outdoors. Minnesota's north is a vast wilderness. **Lake Itasca**, in north-central Minnesota, is the source of the mighty Mississippi.

The metropolitan area known as the *Twin Cities* is one of the cleanest and most livable in the nation, although it is one of the coldest as well. The Twin Cities are **St. Paul**, Minnesota's capital, and **Minneapolis**.

Farnsworth House in Plano, Illinois, outside Chicago, was designed by architect Ludwig Mies Van Der Rohe. The home is considered one of the world's five greatest pieces of modern architecture. Unfortunately for occupants, the glass house leaves them and their everyday doings open to view. One owner woke up to find tourists peering into his bedroom.

The cities began as frontier towns with German, Irish, and Scandinavian immigrants. St. Paul is the smaller of the two cities but very attractive. Minneapolis, the state's largest city, has theaters, nightclubs, a year-round sports program, and the Nicollet Mall, a pedestrian mall lined with shops, restaurants, and entertainment. An elaborate system of indoor skywalks connects the downtown buildings. Minneapolis also has a distinguished symphony and the Guthrie Theater, which offers premiers by American playwrights.

The largest shopping mall in the country, the Mall of America, is a hop, skip, and a jump from the Minneapolis Airport. It is home to more than 520 stores, dozens of restaurants, nightclubs, an indoor roller coaster, a mini-golf course, and Underwater World (a walk-through aquarium). The mall, which opened its doors in August 1992, attracts visitors from as far away as Asia who come to shop, shop, shop.

Outdoorsmen are drawn to the **Boundary Waters Canoe Area Wilderness** in the north, bordering Canada. It has 1,500 miles (2,414 km) of mapped canoe routes but not a single road. Entrance is usually from **Ely**, north of Duluth.

✔ CHECK-UP

The Great Lakes states include

- ✔ Ohio; its capital and largest city is Columbus.
- ✔ Indiana; its capital and largest city is Indianapolis.
- ✔ Michigan; its capital is Lansing, but its largest city is Detroit.
- ✔ Wisconsin; its capital is Madison, but the largest city is Milwaukee.
- ✔ Illinois; its capital is Springfield, but its largest city is Chicago.
- ✔ Minnesota; its capital is St. Paul, but the largest city is Minneapolis.

For travelers, highlights of the Great Lakes include

- ✔ Mysterious mounds.
- ✔ Rock 'n' roll in Cleveland.
- ✔ Auto racing in Indianapolis.
- ✔ Motown and Mackinac in Michigan.
- ✔ Chicago, the city of Big Shoulders and home of the skyscraper.
- ✔ Frank Lloyd Wright's prairie houses.
- ✔ Guthrie Theater and the Mall of America in Minneapolis.

The Great Plains States

By the 20th century, the Great Plains states—Iowa, Missouri, Arkansas, Oklahoma, Kansas, Nebraska, South Dakota, and North Dakota—were the country's agricultural heartland (see Figure 3.4). Many sites of historic interest have been carefully preserved and attract local tourists as well as travelers on cross-country pilgrimages.

Iowa

Iowa is bordered by the Mississippi River on the east and the Missouri River on the west. It is a showcase of America's fertile plains and small towns. **Des Moines**, the capital and largest city, is in the center of the state. The city's state fair has attracted millions of visitors each August since 1886 to view livestock exhibitions and food contests.

Other places to visit include the **Amana Colonies**, seven villages with small museums and popular restaurants located southwest of **Cedar Rapids**, and **Effigy** (*EHF uh jee*) **Mounds National Monument**. Its rounded mounds are shaped in the image of animals. Riverboats on the Mississippi and Missouri offer sightseeing, dining, family entertainment, and gambling.

Missouri

South of Iowa is Missouri. Like Iowa, it is bordered by the Mississippi and Missouri Rivers. The beautiful Ozarks straddle Missouri's southern border with Arkansas. **Jefferson City** is the capital, but **St. Louis** and **Kansas City** are better known.

Gateway Arch, St. Louis, Missouri

St. Louis In the early 1800s, St. Louis was the gateway to the West for pioneers assembled at outfitting towns before they began their trek. The city is on the western bank of the Mississippi River. It is the country's largest inland port.

St. Louis's outstanding monument is **Gateway Arch**, one of the nation's tallest memorials. Elevators carry visitors to the top. Underground, beneath the Arch, the Museum of Westward Expansion explains America's westward movement. Riverboat cruises on the Mississippi leave from near the arch.

Other attractions include Laclede's Landing, a shopping and entertainment area by the river, and Union Station, an architectural masterpiece. A few miles west of downtown, Forest Park was the site of the Louisiana Purchase Exposition in 1904 and is now the location of the city's Art Museum, Science Center, and Zoological Park.

The Busch family has given St. Louis its stadium, its Cardinals, Grant's Farm (an animal park on the Busch estate), and its favorite brew. A tour of the

FIGURE 3.4

The Great Plains States

Anheuser-Busch brewery's facilities shows state-of-the-art equipment housed in a National Historic Landmark building dating from 1891. Visitors can see the Clydesdale horses, watch the brewing process, and sample the beer.

St. Louis was home to W. C. Handy, Josephine Baker, Chuck Berry, Tina Turner, Miles Davis, and the ragtime composer Scott Joplin. Clubs continue the music tradition. For classics lovers, the St. Louis Symphony, the second-oldest orchestra in the country, maintains its musical reputation.

In 1904 the Louisiana Purchase Exposition in St. Louis, Missouri, introduced hot dogs, iced tea, and ice cream cones to the United States. Electricity was also new, and the fair's grand buildings blazed with light.

Kansas City Located on Missouri's western border, Kansas City is the state's largest city. It was a pioneer gateway that became a reception center for cattle and produce. The Hallmark Crown Center is the heart of downtown. To the east is **Independence**, the hometown of President Harry S. Truman, the site of the Truman Library, and the beginning of the Santa Fe Trail, which was one of the longest commercial routes of the frontier era. From there the wagon trail headed west to Santa Fe, New Mexico.

Hannibal A two hours' drive northeast from St. Louis along the river brings the traveler to Hannibal, the childhood home of Mark Twain/Samuel Clemens. Clemens's white clapboard boyhood home is restored and serves as the centerpiece of a complex dedicated to the author.

The greatest earthquake to strike the continental United States occurred on December 16, 1811, in New Madrid, Missouri.

Branson In the 1960s, Hugo and Mary Hershend opened a small old-time Arkansas village attraction. Today, Branson has more than 20,000 hotel rooms and music and entertainment venues lining a 4-mile (6 km) strip. It is the country's leading destination for motorcoach tours.

CLOSE-UP: A PADDLE-WHEEL VOYAGE

Who is a good prospect for a steamboat cruise? Those who would like a slow-paced journey into America's heartland in luxurious comfort are good prospects. The longer cruises attract the mature market.

Why would they take a river cruise? A steamboat adventure is a destination for those who just want to have some fun, watch the scenery float by, learn some history, relax, listen to onboard music, and enjoy the company of others with similar tastes.

Where would they go? Travelers have a choice of cruises on the Mississippi, Cumberland, and Ohio River systems. One departing from St. Louis, Missouri, headed north on the Mississippi might follow this itinerary.

Day 1 Fly to St. Louis from home. Embark and set sail in the late afternoon.

Day 2 Floating on the river.

Day 3 Port call to Hannibal, Missouri, Mark Twain country.

Day 4 On the river.

Day 5 Port call to Dubuque, one of Iowa's oldest cities.

Day 6 Port call to LaCrosse, Wisconsin, at the junction of the Black and Mississippi Rivers.

Day 7 Port call to Red Wing, Minnesota, 40 miles (64 km) south of St. Paul.

Day 8 St. Paul, Minnesota. Disembark for the return trip home.

When is the best time to visit? Spring and fall are the best times to cruise up or down the river.

How would you respond if the travelers say the following: "We don't know much about the cities on the itinerary. How can we find out what to do?" Like any cruise line, steamboat companies offer optional excursions in each port. You can help the travelers find the information they need about each port. They can then use the cruise line's Web site to see if the ship offers what they want. If there is a fit, travelers can book online (within thirty days of departure) and be assured of having a place on the tour of their choice. Or if they prefer to wait until they are onboard, they can sign up after listening to the ship's cruise director give a talk about each destination.

Arkansas

Arkansas is a state of mountains, thick forests, and fertile farmland. In many ways, the state resembles West Virginia. Both have great natural beauty and a mountain culture, each is the most mountainous state in its region, and both are often neglected by travelers heading for other locations.

The Mississippi River forms Arkansas' eastern border. The **Ozark Plateau** and **Ouachita Mountains** in northern and western Arkansas are known as the *Highlands*. **Little Rock**, the capital and largest city, is near the state's center.

The town of **Hot Springs** is southwest of Little Rock. It has been one of the country's best-known natural spas for more than a century. Grand old hotels feature baths in spring waters, which many people believe help cure certain ailments. When visitors are not soaking in one of the town's thermal springs, they can visit a racetrack, browse through shops and galleries, or hike through the Ouachita National Forest.

A diamond mine open to the public is near Murfreesboro, Arkansas. Tourists sometimes find diamonds, which they are permitted to keep.

Oklahoma

Oklahoma is on the classic cross-country route to California or Arizona. The interstates take visitors through the cities of Tulsa and Oklahoma City, the state's capital. Oklahoma City's National Cowboy and Western Heritage Museum showcases western art, with works by Charles Russell and Frederic Remington. The site of the tragic terrorist bombing in 1995 is now a memorial in the heart of downtown.

Oklahoma is the home of more Native American tribes than any other state. The *Trail of Tears* marks the route taken by Native Americans in the 1830s when President Andrew Johnson forced the Cherokees to march from North Carolina, Tennessee, Georgia, and Alabama to reservations in the West. Displays in the Cherokee Heritage Center in **Tahlequah** detail the hardships of the trip.

Tornado-chasing tours are possible in Oklahoma.

Kansas

Rural agricultural Kansas is located at the geographic center of the country. The state appeals to those wanting to see the heartland, prairie flora and fauna, and reminders of frontier days. **Topeka**, the capital, is in the eastern part of the state near the Missouri border. **Wichita**, the largest city, is in south central Kansas.

Visitors can see ruts made by wagons on the Sante Fe and Chisholm Trails and visit former cavalry bases such as Forts Riley and Scott. In **Dodge City** they can view Front Street and Boot Hill Cemetery as they were in the 1870s. The Eisenhower Library and Museum is open to visitors in **Abilene**.

An estimated 20 million buffalo roamed the Great Plains in the 1860s. Some twenty-five years later, hunters in pursuit of hides had reduced the population to fewer than 100,000.

Nebraska

Nebraska is part of the agricultural heartland of the Great Plains. **Lincoln**, the state capital, and **Omaha**, the largest city, are both in the eastern part of the state. Nebraska's west has huge sand hills dotted with cliffs, bluffs, and valleys, an area where the farmlands stop.

Nebraska's history provides several sites of interest. Highways follow the historic Oregon and Mormon Trails, roads carved by pioneers on the way west. Nebraska's history includes the story of the tough farmers whose homes were built of sod because the grassy land had few trees. The state is home to **Scotts Bluff** and **Chimney Rock** (near Baynard), both natural landmarks that marked the trails for the pioneers, and the **Homestead National Monument** (near Beatrice), the site of one of the first pieces of land claimed under the Homestead Act. Scout's Rest Ranch, near North Platte, was the home of Buffalo Bill, the famous scout and showman. His popular Wild West Shows rehearsed there.

Omaha has been revitalized. Along with shiny high-rises and waterfront development, the city has a new performing arts center, an ever-expanding bohemian district known as Old Market, and a huge convention center and arena. Omaha is no longer the cow town of yore, but steak still rules. The famous local product is proudly advertised on every meat-bearing menu in town.

In Omaha, the Henry Doorly Zoo is Nebraska's number one tourist attraction. The site includes the Lied Jungle, claimed to be the world's largest indoor rain forest, and the Desert Dome, the world's largest indoor desert.

South Dakota

North of Nebraska is South Dakota. **Pierre** (*peer*) is the capital, and **Sioux Falls** is the largest city. Farms and ranches cover about nine-tenths of the state. The eastern part has prime farmland, with corn so high the town of **Mitchell** has a Corn Palace to honor it. Each year the building's exterior is totally decorated with corn, grasses, and grain.

The Missouri River flows southward through the middle of the state. West of the river are the state's attractions for tourists, including the weirdly beautiful **Badlands**—small, steep hills and deep gullies formed by water erosion—and the **Black Hills.**

Rapid City is the gateway to the Black Hills. When gold was discovered in the Black Hills in 1876, prospectors rushed to the area, and the little town of **Deadwood** grew. Deadwood gained a reputation as the most brawling, lawless settlement on the frontier. Reminders of the early days include legalized gambling and the Mount Moriah Cemetery, where Calamity Jane and Wild Bill Hickok are buried.

Caves are also part of the Black Hills experience. **Jewel Cave National Monument** and **Wind Cave National Park** are worth exploring.

The Black Hills' biggest tourist attraction by far, however, is the **Mount Rushmore National Monument**. Sixty-feet-high heads of four presidents (George Washington, Thomas Jefferson, Theodore Roosevelt, and Abraham Lincoln) have been blasted out of the mountain.

Mt. Rushmore, South Dakota

North Dakota

North Dakota is the country's least-visited state. Unprotected by western mountains, it has the coldest average temperature in the country. It has no cross-country highways and no large cities. **Bismarck** is the capital, but **Fargo** is the largest city.

In the fall, hunters are attracted to streams and lakes where migrating waterfowl stop on their way south. **Theodore Roosevelt National Park** is a favorite summer resort area in the state's west. Lewis and Clark passed through. Travelers can visit interpretive centers and sites commemorating the famous journey that opened up the West.

From 1804 to 1806, U.S. Army officers Meriwether Lewis and William Clark explored the wilderness of what is now the northwest United States. Lewis and Clark's journals describe the natural resources and native peoples of the West.

✔ CHECK-UP

The Great Plains states include

- ✔ Iowa; its capital and largest city is Des Moines.
- ✔ Missouri; its capital is Jefferson City, but its largest city is Kansas City.
- ✔ Arkansas; its capital and largest city is Little Rock.
- ✔ Oklahoma; its capital and largest city is Oklahoma City.
- ✔ Kansas; its capital is Topeka, but Wichita is the largest city.
- ✔ Nebraska; its capital is Lincoln, but its largest city is Omaha.
- ✔ South Dakota; its capital is Pierre, but its largest city is Sioux Falls.
- ✔ North Dakota; its capital is Bismarck, but Fargo is the largest city.

For travelers, highlights of the Great Plains include

- ✔ View of the Mississippi from the top of the Gateway Arch in St. Louis, Missouri.
- ✔ Entertainment in Branson, Missouri.
- ✔ Faces on Mount Rushmore in the Black Hills of South Dakota.
- ✔ Wilderness exploration in North Dakota.

Texas

Six flags have flown over Texas: those of Spain, France, Mexico, Texas Republic, the Confederacy, and the United States. Sandy beaches in the southeast stretch along the Gulf of Mexico, and coastal plains extend inland to meet the Great Plains to the north in the Texas Panhandle. The waters of the Rio Grande form the border with Mexico (see Figure 3.5).

The Cities

Several Texas cities are tourist attractions. This overview takes them alphabetically.

Austin Austin is the state's capital, its educational center, and a gateway to Texas Hill Country. Its capitol building is taller than the U.S. Capitol and is considered by many to be quite as grand. The Lyndon Baines Johnson Library, which houses documents and souvenirs of the president, is on the campus of the University of Texas in Austin. This and other colleges give the city a young attitude. Perhaps that is why Austin bills itself as the *Live Music Capital of the World.* Evening entertainment includes music performed in clubs along Sixth Street, the restored historic district.

The city is on the Colorado River. Seven dams north of Austin contain the Colorado, thus creating seven artificial lakes, which provide fine recreational facilities.

Austin is also home to the Wildflower Research Center, founded by Lady Bird Johnson—an appropriate site because Texas is the state with the most wildflowers.

Corpus Christi On Texas's Gulf Coast, Corpus Christi is a popular playground for golf and tennis players. It's also known for fishing and windsurfing competitions.

Dallas/Fort Worth One of the country's largest cities, Dallas sprawls in all directions. Most visitors go to the John F. Kennedy Memorial Plaza and Dealey Plaza, site of the assassination. Downtown also houses the Dallas Museum of Art and Deep Ellum, a restored warehouse district of blues and

FIGURE 3.5 Texas

jazz clubs, galleries, restaurants, and stores. The fifty-story Reunion Tower has an observation terrace and a revolving restaurant. Other attractions are the DeGolyer Estate (built by an oil baron) and the West End Historic District's shops, restaurants, and museums. Southfork Ranch, site of the long-gone TV series *Dallas,* continues to be a popular tourist attraction.

An impressive collection of Art Deco buildings constructed for the 1936 Texas Centennial graces Fair Park—home to the Cotton Bowl stadium, the state fair, and museums. The fair takes place each September/October and offers exhibits, Broadway musicals, livestock shows, and a huge midway.

Dallas meets Fort Worth 30 miles (48 km) to the west. The Dallas/Fort Worth Airport is between the two cities. Much more western in spirit than sophisticated Dallas, Fort Worth started as a military outpost and then became a cow town where cattlemen brought their herds to be shipped. Though still active in cattle sales, Fort Worth's stockyards are today better known as a tourist attraction, part of the Stockyards National Historic District.

For some Texas-style fun, an excursion to Billy Bob's in Fort Worth is in order. Billed as the world's largest honky-tonk, with a 6,000-person capacity, it has an indoor rodeo rink, bull riding, miles of bar rails, really tacky gift shops, dance floors, and country/western entertainment.

El Paso The state's westernmost city is beside the Rio Grande in a desert pass between the mountains. The largest U.S. city on the Mexican border, El Paso is actually closer to cities in New Mexico, Arizona, and southern California than it is to other Texan cities. San Jacinto Plaza, a bustling symbol of the city's Spanish and Mexican heritage, is in the heart of downtown. About 70 percent of El Pasoans have Hispanic ancestry, and both English and Spanish are spoken in much of the city.

Houston The country's fourth-largest city and the state's largest, Houston has been an oil city since "black gold" was discovered in nearby Beaumont in

In the late 1860s, San Antonio was the starting point of the Chisholm (*CHIHZ uhm*) Trail north to the Kansas stockyards.

The Alamo, San Antonio, Texas

ON THE SPOT

Mr. and Mrs. Daley from Chicago are planning a one-week family vacation during the school spring vacation period. Their sports-loving children are a girl, age 13, and a boy, age 11. During past vacations they have gone to the beach, taken a cruise, and visited Disney World; now they are looking for something different. Do you have any suggestions?

Perhaps the Daleys would enjoy a one-week ranch stay in the Hill Country of Texas. They could fly from Chicago to either Austin or San Antonio, see the local sights, and then rent a car to drive to one of the many ranches in the Hill Country. Most ranches offer daytime activities that the active family would enjoy: horseback riding, hiking, swimming, and tennis. Dining is usually family style, which lets guests get to know each other. Nighttime entertainment might be square dancing or a visit to a local festival.

1901. Today, it is a center of oil and natural gas technology and the home of NASA's Lyndon B. Johnson Space Center.

The 50-mile-long (80 km) Houston Ship Canal links the city with the Gulf of Mexico, making Houston a busy commercial port. **Galveston Island**, southeast of Houston on the Gulf of Mexico, was known as the "Wall Street of the Southwest" in the second half of the 19th century. More than fifty historic buildings in Galveston's former commercial district have been restored and interspersed with restaurants, shops, and galleries. Galveston is a popular cruise ship port.

San Antonio The top vacation attraction in Texas is San Antonio, the country's ninth-largest city. The city proudly proclaims its Spanish as well as its cow-town origins. In 1718 Spanish missionaries established the mission of San Antonio de Valero, later renamed the Alamo. Here, in 1836, a band of Texas volunteers defied a Mexican army led by General Santa Anna for thirteen days of siege. One month after the Alamo's defeat, Texans, led by Sam Houston, won the Battle of San Jacinto using the battle cry "Remember the Alamo."

The narrow San Antonio River winds through the heart of the city. The banks of the river have been developed into the *Paseo del Rio* ("River Walk"), an area of hotels, restaurants, bars, and shops. Small boats take tourists along the river.

La Villita ("Little Town") is a 250-year-old Spanish settlement in the center of downtown. It was here that Mexican General Cos was said to have surrendered San Antonio to Texas revolutionaries. Other attractions include displays at the Institute of Texan Cultures and four beautiful old missions in San Antonio Missions National Historical Park.

Other Places to Visit

Hill Country Ranch vacations are widely available in the Hill Country between San Antonio and Austin. The town of **Bandera** bills itself as the *Cowboy Capital of the World,* as much for the number of its dude ranches as for the cowboys who call the town home. The beauty of this part of the state comes as a surprise. It is an area of low hills, pastures, and oak-studded landscape rich in rivers and lakes. It is especially beautiful in spring when the land is a sea of purplish bluebonnets (the state flower). Year-round fishing, rodeos, and square dances fill relaxed days and nights.

German immigrants settled the Hill Country in the mid-1800s. The old country heritage is visible in its wursthouses, festivals, and architecture.

Padre Island South of Corpus Christi, Padre Island National Seashore is a barrier island off the mainland, one of the nation's last natural seashores. Each end of the narrow sand pile has parks and resorts. In between, the National Seashore preserves an unblemished stretch of sand that draws shell collectors, snorkelers, and divers.

Big Bend National Park At a bend in the Rio Grande to the west, Big Bend National Park is the state's last great wilderness area. Route 385 leads from Persimmon Gap, the north entrance to the park, down to the Panther Junction Visitor Center. The road follows a trail once used by Comanche Indians, army expeditions, settlers, and miners. Bird-watchers delight in the park's many species. El Paso is the gateway to Big Bend.

✔ CHECK-UP

Texas's principal cities include
- ✔ Austin, its capital.
- ✔ Dallas, site of the state fair.
- ✔ El Paso, the largest U.S. city on the Mexican border.
- ✔ Houston, the state's largest city and home to space technology.
- ✔ San Antonio, the state's number one visitor attraction.

For travelers, highlights of Texas include
- ✔ River Walk in San Antonio, Texas.
- ✔ A ranch stay in the Hill Country.
- ✔ Big Bend National Park.
- ✔ Beautiful beaches of Padre Island.

Planning the Trip

The Midwest has good transportation, modern accommodations, familiar culture, and a variety of attractions. The region has great appeal for those interested in exploring America's heartland.

When to Go

A driving trip is best timed for spring or fall. Spring is a good time to visit Texas to see the desert bloom in the Hill Country.

Preparing the Traveler

You might recommend that travelers borrow a video from the library or view a destination's Web site to get a feel for a destination.

Transportation

The region is well served by air carriers, car rental firms, and local destination management companies offering tours and transportation.

By Air The airlines provide good service to the region's largest cities. Chicago (United), Minneapolis (Northwest), Houston (Continental), and Dallas (American) are airline hubs. Travelers from smaller cities usually have to change planes in an intermediate city. Regional carriers serve the small towns.

By Water Although most people do not think of the Midwest as a cruise destination, day and longer cruises ply the Great Lakes, and old-fashioned steamboats operate on the Mississippi and its tributaries. Leaving from ports such as New Orleans and St. Louis, the Delta Queen Steamboat Company re-creates the life of Mark Twain on the *Delta Queen* (a National Historic Landmark) and the more modern *Mississippi* and *American Queens*. Voyages from three to fourteen nights travel the Mississippi, Ohio, Tennessee, and Cumberland Rivers. Galveston, Texas, is a port for Caribbean cruises.

By Road Private or rental cars are useful for destinations outside a city, and fly-drive trips that include air transportation, rental car, and hotel

➤ PROFILE

Shopping Opportunities in the Midwest

Shopping possibilities in the Midwest include
- ➤ In Chicago, State Street, North Michigan Avenue's *Magnificent Mile*, and the specialty stores in Old Town, Lincoln Avenue, and New Town.
- ➤ In St. Louis, elegant regional shopping malls, including Plaza Frontenac and the St. Louis Galleria.
- ➤ In Ohio, the towns of Lebanon and Waynesville, known as the *Antiques Capital of the Midwest*. For Amish specialties, the best area is around Fredericksburg in Wayne County.
- ➤ In Minnesota, the Mall of America.
- ➤ In Dallas, all the shopping centers (more per capita than any other U.S. city) and the original Neiman Marcus.
- ➤ In San Antonio, stores with Mexican folk art.

accommodations are appropriate for most travelers. Motorcoach tours operate throughout the region.

By Rail Chicago is a major U.S. rail hub, for both freight lines and Amtrak. Few trains cross the country directly, however; most passengers must change trains in Chicago. Allow plenty of time between connections. If passengers miss a connection, the next train probably will not go until the next day.

Accommodations

The Midwest offers the full range of accommodations. The majority of hotels are modern and part of national and international chains. During special events such as the Indy 500, hotels often require a minimum stay. Most hotel rates are quoted European Plan (EP), that is, no meals are included. Accommodations such as ranches and resorts offer American Plan (AP), including all meals, or Modified American Plan (MAP), including some meals, usually breakfast and dinner.

CHAPTER WRAP-UP

SUMMARY

Here is a review of the objectives with which we began the chapter.

1. **Describe the environment and people of the Midwest.** Glaciers created the Great Lakes, carving the thousands of lakes of northern Michigan, Minnesota, and Wisconsin. West of the Mississippi the land rises slowly through the plains, with fertile farmland becoming drier grassland to the west. The Ozark-Ouachita Highlands separate the plains and the southeast coastal lands. Texas rises slowly from the Gulf of Mexico as part of the Great Plains in the area called the Texas Panhandle.

   Near the Great Lakes the region's original inhabitants left great earthen mounds in the river valleys. The Native American tribes who lived there after them were mostly forced onto reservations by the late 1800s as pioneers arrived.

2. **Describe the main attractions of the region, matching travelers and destinations best suited for each other.** Travelers tend to see the Midwest on cross-country driving trips or business trips. Chicago, of course, is a major draw, with museums, shops, restaurants, and nightlife. Throughout the region, displays of Native American and pioneer heritage and culture are big attractions. The motorcoach tour is popular with groups visiting such attractions as Branson. South Dakota's Black Hills and Badlands attract many to their unusual scenery, Mount Rushmore, caves, and Old West mining towns. Texas's attractions range from the white-sand beaches of Padre Island to ranches in the Hill Country to vibrant cities, some with old-fashioned cowboy nostalgia.

3. **Provide or find the information needed to plan a trip to the area.** State tourist boards are helpful sources for festival dates and special activities.

QUESTIONS FOR DISCUSSION AND REVIEW

1. Which of these states have you visited? What attracted you to the destination?

2. How would you promote Indiana if you were working for its tourist board?

3. Why do you think more than 6 million people visit Branson each year? How did the region become such a major attraction? What would you do to make Branson attractive to younger visitors?

CHAPTER 4

The Western States, Alaska, and Hawaii

- The Mountain States
- The Pacific States
- Alaska
- Hawaii

OBJECTIVES

When you have completed Chapter 4, you should be able to

1. Describe the environment of the western states.
2. Summarize the special physical attractions of Alaska and Hawaii.
3. Describe the region's attractions, matching travelers and destinations best suited for each other.
4. Provide or find the information needed to plan a trip to the western states, Alaska, or Hawaii.

"Go West, young man," said New York newspaper publisher Horace Greeley in 1851. The country took his advice, developing the land from the Rockies to the Pacific and on to Alaska and Hawaii.

Today, these regions are some of the country's most popular destinations. The magnificent national parks, towering mountains, fascinating deserts, Native American cultures, Pacific Coast beauty, and sophisticated cities lure both domestic and international travelers. Alaska and Hawaii are destinations of contrast. Alaska is spirit, space, and wilderness. Hawaii is fire, cultural diversity, and sea. This chapter explores the special qualities of these newest parts of the United States.

The Environment and Its People

The western states can be broadly divided into Mountain states and Pacific states. The Mountain states are **Montana, Idaho, Wyoming, Colorado, New Mexico, Arizona, Utah,** and **Nevada.** They fill the continent from the Canadian to the Mexican border west of the Great Plains. The Pacific states—**California, Oregon,** and **Washington**—border the world's largest ocean (see Figure 4.1).

Alaska is in the far northwest corner of North America. A map of the state superimposed on one of the continental United States would reach from the Atlantic to the Pacific and from Canada to Mexico. Despite its great size, Alaska has a relatively small population; only Wyoming has fewer people.

Hawaii is an archipelago near the middle of the North Pacific. In terms of landmass, the islands are smaller in total area than Massachusetts.

The Land

The **Rocky Mountains** are North America's largest mountain system. They extend from northern Alaska to northern Mexico, with peaks more than 14,000 feet (4,267 m) high.

West of the Rockies—from Washington south to the Mexican border—is the driest part of the country. It is an area of plateaus, basins, and ranges—specifically, the **Columbia Plateau,** the **Colorado Plateau,** and the **Great Basin.** The region's unusual landforms include natural bridges, arches of solid rock, and the great river gorge called the **Grand Canyon,** formed by the **Colorado River.** To the south are the **Sonora** and **Mojave** (*mo HAH vee*) **Deserts.** To the north of the Grand Canyon is the **Great Salt Lake,** a salty shallow lake.

To the west are more mountains. The **Cascade Mountains** in the north and the **Sierra Nevada** in the south run north-south through western Washington and Oregon and most of California. West of the Cascades and Sierras are broad fertile valleys including Washington's **Puget Sound Lowlands,** Oregon's **Willamette Valley,** and California's **Central Valley.** The **Columbia River** forms part of the boundary between the states of Oregon and Washington.

West of the valleys, mountains called the **Coast Ranges** line the Pacific from the southern part of California through Oregon and Washington into Canada and Alaska. In many places, they rise abruptly from the sea. In other areas, particularly in southern California, they back off behind coastal plains. Deep bays along the coast include **Puget Sound, Columbia River Bay, San Francisco Bay,** and **San Diego Bay.** The West Coast has few barrier islands.

The Continental Divide passes through the Rocky Mountains. It is an imaginary line that separates streams that flow into the Pacific from those that flow into the Atlantic.

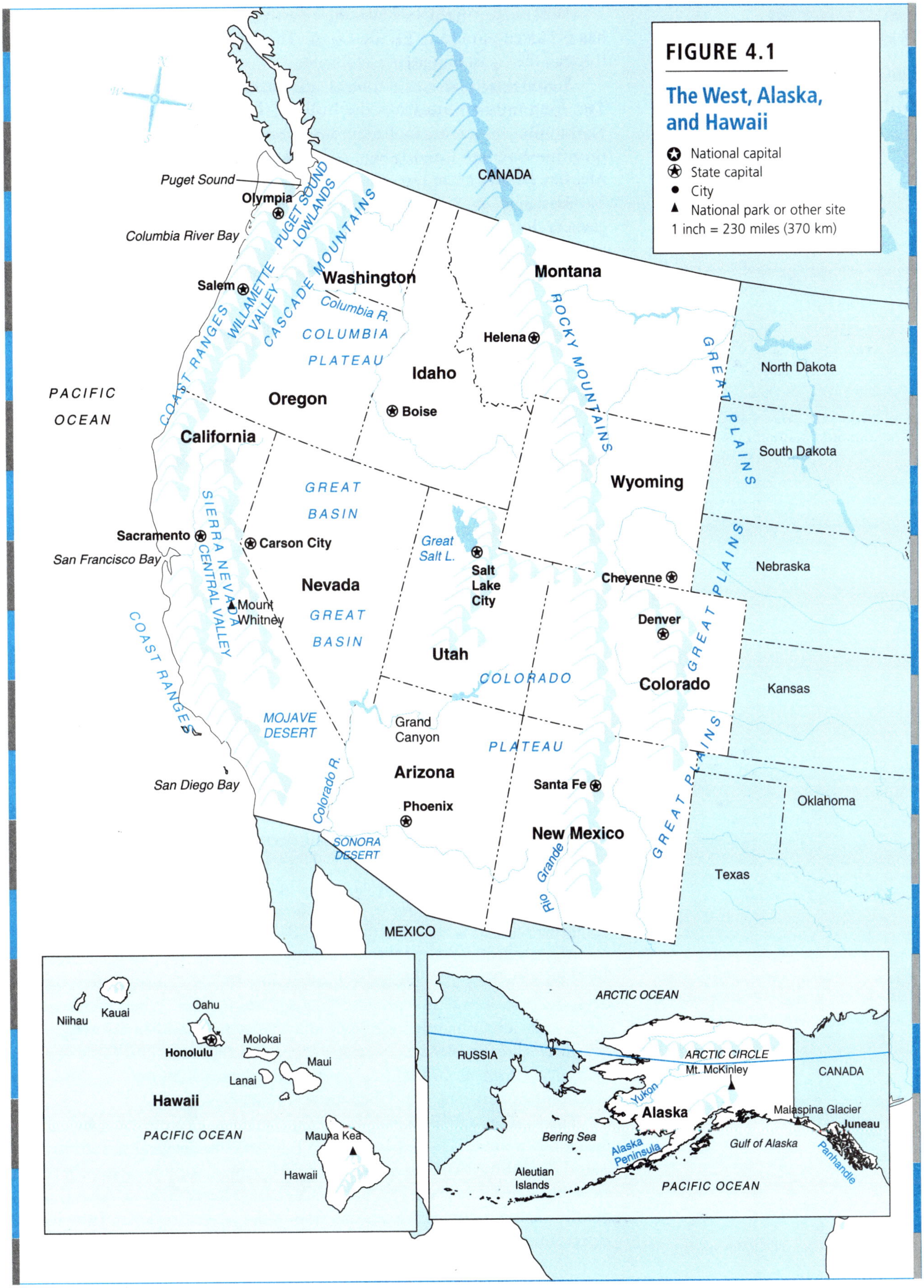

FIGURE 4.1

The West, Alaska, and Hawaii

> **➤ PROFILE**
>
> **Western National Millennium Trails**
>
> These hiking trails were selected by the U.S. Department of Transportation to reflect the history, culture, and character of the West:
>
> - *The Great Western Trail*, from the Canadian to the Mexican border.
> - *The Iditarod National Historic Trail*, the longest and oldest commerce trail in the United States. It travels the state of Alaska for 938 miles (1,509 km).
> - *Juan Bautista de Anza National Historic Trail*, the route followed by the Spanish explorer in 1775–1776.
> - *Lewis and Clark National Historic Trail*, the explorers' path from St. Louis to the mouth of Oregon's Columbia River.
> - *North Country Trail*, defining the northern rim of the continental United States, from New York to North Dakota.

Most of the continent's earthquake activity during the past hundred years has occurred along the Pacific Coast. The famous San Andreas Fault runs through the Coast Ranges of California.

Mountains, tundra, rain forests, and glaciers dominate Alaska's landscape. Two long tails extend from the bulk of the state. On the southeast, the **Panhandle**—a narrow mountainous coastal strip with numerous offshore islands—borders Canada. On the west, the **Alaska Peninsula** and the **Aleutian Islands** extend into the North Pacific toward the coast of Siberia.

Alaska has some of North America's highest mountains. From them large glaciers descend to the sea. Most of the glaciers are along the coast in the south and southeast. **Malaspina** is North America's largest glacier.

The Hawaiian Islands are the peaks of an underwater mountain chain; some are still active volcanoes. Lush forests cover the slopes. Hawaii has industries, but its greatest asset is its natural beauty.

The Climate

On the continent the amount of precipitation decreases as you go west. The Rocky Mountains receive heavy snow, but western snow is dry. Much of the moisture is drawn out as storms travel east over the Sierras and across deserts before hitting the Rockies. The resulting snow creates the famed powder conditions that resort promoters love to talk about. Occasionally, the Rockies have a warm dry wind—the **Chinook**—which raises temperatures and quickly melts snow.

Much of the Mountain states have low precipitation, particularly in the Southwest, where large areas of Arizona, Nevada, New Mexico, Utah, and Colorado are desert or semi-desert. High summer temperatures are made more bearable by low humidity.

The Pacific Northwest coast is the least sunny part of the country. (A local saying is "The rain in Spain stays mainly in Seattle.") Rainy season is between September and April. During the summer the traveler can expect cool nights and pleasantly warm days. Winters are not as cold as other places on the same latitude, but snow does fall.

California's north coast has a climate similar to that of the Pacific Northwest, but temperatures increase and rainfall decreases as you go south. The cold California Current flows south along the coast, cooling the region and causing frequent fogs. Southern California enjoys mild and moderately wet winters and warm to hot and dry summers. Mountain areas have heavy snow. Southeastern California's climate is similar to that of the desert regions of Arizona.

> Alaskan hotels and cruise ships provide thick curtains to create dark for sleeping during the long days of spring and early summer.

Alaska's extremes occur in its interior and north. South coastal areas are less cold in winter but subject to heavy rain and snow. In summer, Alaska's days are long, warm, and punctuated regularly by rain. When it shines, the sun does its job brilliantly for twenty hours a day from mid-May through July. Fall is the shortest of Alaskan seasons; in but a few days, howling winds rip every leaf from its branch. In winter, the days are short—in the north practically nonexistent—and the long nights are cold.

The weather in the Hawaiian Islands is warm and comfortable from April through November. December through February are the coolest months. The islands' southwest coasts are relatively dry; their rainy season is between November and February. The northeast coasts receive heavier rainfall in all months. Some mountain slopes are among the wettest regions of the world. Hurricanes come between May and November, but severe storms are less frequent than in the Caribbean or the western Pacific.

The People and Their History

Spain colonized the Southwest in the 1500s, and the area reflects its Spanish heritage (see Figure 4.2). In 1848 the United States gained the Southwest by winning the Mexican-American war. The country had now acquired all the land of the contiguous forty-eight states. Eventually, the Native Americans of the region would be sent to reservations, mostly in semiarid or mountainous regions.

Settlement of the West was speeded by reports of gold and silver. The prospectors needed supplies. To fill the need, the Union Pacific Railroad started from the east and the Central Pacific from the west to build a transcontinental system. The tracks met at Promontory, near Ogden, Utah, in 1869. With the railroads came the period of the cattle kings, but by 1885, the cattle boom was over. By 1912, the last of the western territories gained statehood.

The Alaska natives fared somewhat better than the natives in the "lower forty-eight." The United States bought Alaska from Russia in 1867 for $7.2 million. When Alaska became a state in 1959, the tribes secured economic and political power through their settlement of land claims. In Alaska today, there is a resurgence of native pride and culture.

Alaska's pioneers built ports, towns, and even railroads. But what they did not build—and have not built to this day—is roads. Transportation was by dogsled in the winter and water routes in the summer. The distances were simply too great and the population too small for highways. World War II helped make parts of the state more accessible. Fearful that the Japanese would invade via the Aleutians, the U.S. government built the Alaska Highway in 1942 as a military supply route. It also built gravel landing strips in tiny hamlets. Pilots flying small planes equipped to land on both water and primitive runways linked town and country and changed everything. People could get in—and out.

Isolation from the outside world ended for Hawaii in 1778 when British ships, commanded by Captain James Cook, discovered the islands. After Cook, waves of European traders and missionaries brought disease, firearms, and different beliefs.

The islands kept their political independence for a century. A monarchy was established in 1795 by King Kamehameha I (1758–1819) and lasted until 1893, when Queen Lili'uokalani (1838–1917) was overthrown by a force led by Americans who wanted a government more sympathetic to their commercial goals. Hawaii became a republic headed by Sanford B. Dole. In 1959 Hawaii became the fiftieth state.

Today, the state is a community of people with many backgrounds. The native Hawaiian culture, however, remains one of the islands' many attractions.

FIGURE 4.2

Milestones of Western, Alaskan and Hawaiian History

1540 Father Junípero Serra establishes the first California mission.

1725 Tsar Peter the Great commissions Vitus Bering, a Danish navigator, to explore the North Pacific. Bering reaches Alaska.

1778 Captain James Cook of the British navy visits the Sandwich Islands (Hawaii).

1784 Russians establish settlement in Alaska on Kodiak Island.

1849 The California Gold Rush begins.

1867 United States buys Alaska from Russia.

1869 Transcontinental railroad is completed.

1872 Yellowstone preserved as the world's first national park.

1896 Gold discovered in Alaska.

1906 San Francisco's earthquake and fire.

1910 D. W. Griffith makes Hollywood's first film: *In Old California*.

1916 National Park Service authorized by Congress.

1931 Nevada legalizes gambling.

1941 Japanese attack Pearl Harbor, plunging United States into World War II.

1959 Alaska and Hawaii become states.

1981 Introduction of personal computers greatly affects the travel and tourism industry.

1989 *Exxon Valdez* oil spill in Alaska.

2003 Iditarod Sled Dog Race rerouted due to lack of snow.

2004 A federal regulation allows Norwegian Cruise Lines to sail within the Hawaiian Islands without making a detour to a foreign port.

✔ CHECK-UP

Features of the West include

- ✔ Rocky Mountains, North America's highest mountain system.
- ✔ Desert regions in the Southwest.
- ✔ Mountains lining the Pacific Coast.
- ✔ Fertile valleys between the coastal ranges and the inland mountains.
- ✔ Area of earthquake and volcanic activity.
- ✔ Native American and Spanish background.

Features of Alaska and Hawaii include

- ✔ Alaska's vastness and harsh winter climate.
- ✔ Hawaii's compactness and ideal vacation climate.
- ✔ Diversity of ethnic backgrounds.

The Mountain States

A land of scenic splendor with ghost towns and cow towns, ski resorts and guest ranches, modern cities and small villages, salt lakes and rivers that cut canyons, the Mountain states offer a panorama of America. Figure 4.3 shows the region's eight states.

Montana

Although most of Montana belongs to the Great Plains, it is the mountains that give *Big Sky Country* its extraordinary beauty. This was the territory of prospectors and copper barons. The miners founded **Butte** (*byoot*) on one of the world's largest copper deposits, "the richest hill on earth." The capital, **Helena** (*HEHL uh nuh*), is north of Butte.

FIGURE 4.3

The Mountain States

At Montana's northern border is **Glacier National Park**. The park has two areas: Waterton Lakes National Park in Canada and the larger Glacier National Park in Montana. The *Going-to-the-Sun Highway* crosses the park's spectacular alpine landscape and is one of America's most scenic drives.

Billings, Montana's largest city, is a regional gateway and accommodations center. **Little Bighorn National Monument** is an hour southeast of Billings. There, on a scorching June afternoon in 1876, Lt. Col. George Armstrong Custer pitted his troops against 2,000 Sioux and Cheyenne warriors led by Crazy Horse, Gall, and Sitting Bull. Custer's soldiers died to the last man.

Frequently called *Little Switzerland* or the *American Alps*, Glacier National Park is prime hiking territory.

Idaho

Idaho's capital and largest city, **Boise** (*BOY zee*), is in the state's south. The central part of the state is almost exclusively national forest and wilderness. Two of the largest regions are the **Selway-Bitterroot Wilderness Area** and the **Frank Church River of No Return Wilderness Area. Hells Canyon**, America's deepest gorge, is on the Snake River about 100 miles (161 km) south of Lewiston.

Idaho is a particularly good match for those who want real adventure on white water, pack trips on horseback, fishing, and wilderness hikes. A raft trip on the Selway is one of the country's most coveted white-water experiences. The U.S. Forest Service allows only one party a day to launch its rafts. Rafting season is May 15 through July 31.

Ketchum and **Sun Valley**, in south central Idaho, are developed resorts. Before there was Vail or Aspen, there was Sun Valley, one of the West's first ski resorts. Ketchum is an old mining town beloved by Ernest Hemingway, who is buried there.

Built in 1936 by Averell Harriman, then chairman of the board of Union Pacific Railroad, Sun Valley was created as a way to fill trains during off-season winter months.

Wyoming

The Great Plains meet the Rocky Mountains in Wyoming. The Rockies sweep across the state in several ranges and include the Bighorn and Laramie Mountains. Between the mountains are treeless basins dotted with lonely towers of rock called *buttes.* Parts of three great river systems—the Missouri, the Colorado, and the Columbia—start in Wyoming.

Cheyenne Wyoming's capital and largest city, Cheyenne (*shy AN*) is in the southeast corner near the Colorado border. The city relives its Wild West past during *Frontier Days,* a ten-day festival held each July since 1897. Parades, square dancing, and country/western entertainment highlight the country's largest rodeo. Those passing through at other times can visit the Cheyenne Frontier Days Old West Museum.

Rodeo is North America's own sport, and there is a rodeo nearly every day and night somewhere in Wyoming from June to Labor Day.

Yellowstone Yellowstone National Park takes up Wyoming's northwest corner. In 1872 the area was preserved for posterity as the world's first national park.

One of the park's most famous attractions is Old Faithful, a **geyser** (a spring that throws up hot water). The intervals between eruptions vary from about 30 to 120 minutes; a sign in the visitors' center gives the next likely time. Some 200 other geysers erupt occasionally, blowing fountains of hot water and steam with a distinctive rotten egg smell.

Most of Yellowstone's landscape was created by volcanic eruptions more than 60,000 years ago. A large mass of molten rock, called **magma**, lies beneath the surface of the park, furnishing the heat for the park's geysers and hot springs. The park also has a magnificent canyon and dramatic waterfalls. The Grand Canyon of the Yellowstone River provides some of the park's best views.

Five entrances lead to the park. Spur roads connect the entrances to the Grand Loop Road through the heart of the park. It criss-crosses the Continental Divide. Unfortunately, summer traffic can turn park roads into wilderness gridlock. Less crowded winter adventures are becoming increasingly popular.

Accommodations within the park are booked solid during the peak summer months. The Old Faithful Inn, considered the largest log building in existence, overlooks Old Faithful.

Devil's Tower in Wyoming's northeast was designated the country's first national monument in 1906. The rock monolith rises from the prairie like a huge tree stump. It was used as the alien landing site in the film *Close Encounters of the Third Kind*.

Grand Teton The John D. Rockefeller Jr. Memorial Parkway links Yellowstone with Grand Teton National Park to the south. Many consider the Tetons to be North America's most majestic mountains. The Teton Range rises abruptly from a green valley named **Jackson Hole**. Attractions include horseback riding and hiking; in addition, the Snake River is well known to anglers and rafters. In winter, Jackson Hole is a popular ski resort. Accommodations are available at guest ranches and at the town of **Jackson**.

Colorado

The Great Plains cover the eastern half of Colorado. The Rocky Mountains begin west of **Denver**, the capital and largest city. Colorado is a year-round destination. A day or two in Denver, winter sports, a stay on a guest ranch, hikes in the national parks, a river-rafting trip, a drive to Pikes Peak, and exploration of a cliff dwelling are just some of the activities that could be packed into a satisfying vacation.

Denver Denver has been the center of one mineral boom after another; the most recent involved oil and gas. Most of the downtown high-rise buildings did not exist before 1978. The city was part of the Old West, filled with wagon trains, cowboys, gamblers, and gunfighters. As the town settled down, the elegant Brown Palace Hotel (1892) was built, one of the first hotels with an atrium. Larimer Square, a Victorian block of shops and cafés, is the gateway to the Lower Downtown District, also known as LoDo. Denver has the western branch of the U.S. Mint and the Molly Brown House Museum. Brown became a heroine in 1912 when she survived the sinking of the *Titanic*.

In 1995 Denver opened the country's first major new airport in twenty-five years. The airport is the gateway to the mountain resorts and is equipped to handle special needs—a baggage carousel for skis, for example.

Many people like to stay in Denver a day or two so they can adjust to the altitude before traveling on to the mountains. Although Denver is a mile high, it is still far lower than the mountain resorts. Travelers with respiratory problems should be cautioned.

If people are going to spend the night in Denver before going on to a ski resort, they might need to return to the airport because the resort shuttles depart from the airport.

Boulder Northwest of Denver, Boulder is at the foothills of the Rockies, home to the University of Colorado. Northwest of Boulder is **Rocky Mountain National Park**, Colorado's most popular attraction. Reaching heights of 12,183 feet (3,713 m), Trail Ridge Road crosses the park and forms one of the highest continuous highways in North America. The village of Estes Park is on the edge of the park.

Colorado Springs South of Denver, Colorado Springs is home to the U.S. Air Force Academy and the lavish Broadmoor Hotel. West of the town, **Pikes Peak** at 14,110 feet (4,301 m) is probably the most famous mountain in the Rockies, even though thirty Colorado peaks are higher. Visitors can get to the top by toll road, by cog railway, on horseback, or on foot.

In 1893 a Wellesley College professor, Katherine Lee Bates, rode by wagon to the top of Pikes Peak and was inspired to write the words to "America the Beautiful."

Ski Resorts Colorado is a premier ski destination. **Aspen** and **Vail** are just the best known of many resorts (see Table 4.1). Excellent natural conditions plus snowmaking capabilities allow the ski season to last from November through April.

Mesa Verde National Park Southwestern Colorado is *Four Corners* country, where Utah, Colorado, New Mexico, and Arizona come together.

TABLE 4.1 Ski Resorts

State	Resort	Characterization
California	Heavenly Valley	10,000 rooms; access via Reno, Nevada
	Mammoth	30,000 beds; California's most popular resort
	Squaw Valley	Near Lake Tahoe; access via Reno
Colorado	Aspen	World-famous resort
	Beaver Creek	Suitable for families; 10 miles (16 km) west of Vail
	Breckenridge	For skiers of all abilities; year-round resort
	Buttermilk	Popular with beginners
	Club Med	Two resorts: Copper Mountain and Crested Butte
	Copper Mountain	Award-winning trails for all abilities
	Crested Butte	Excellent facilities; north of Gunnison Airport
	Howelsen	Facilities for ski jumping
	Keystone	Claims the longest ski season; west of Denver
	Steamboat Springs	Distinctly western heritage
	Telluride	Snowboarding
	Vail	Famous resort 100 miles (161 km) west of Denver
Idaho	Sun Valley	Upscale resort 150 miles (241 km) from Boise
Montana	Big Sky	South of Bozeman
New Mexico	Taos	Native American culture
Utah	Alta	26 miles (42 km) south of Salt Lake City
	Deer Valley	In Park City
	Park City	27 miles (43 km) east of Salt Lake City
	Snowbird	45 minutes from the SLC airport
Wyoming	Jackson Hole	Small resort with a magnificent setting

Mesa Verde National Park is the only park devoted exclusively to archaeology.

Here, Mesa Verde ("Green Table") National Park features the impressive dwellings of a people called the *Anasazi*—"the ancient ones." Centuries ago the Anasazi built houses along the walls of a huge mesa under an overhanging cliff. The canyon homes, which resemble modern apartment blocks, were built between A.D. 900 and 1200. Cliff Palace, the largest house, has more than 200 rooms. Until 1884, when the dwellings were discovered, no one had heard of the Anasazi. The mystery of this ancient people and why they vanished has yet to be explained.

New Mexico

Plains cover the eastern third of New Mexico. The Rockies bisect the state, extending from Colorado south to the Mexican border. The Rio Grande runs down the state's center. In some places in summer, the river is no more than a trickle. In the south the river turns east and forms the border between Texas and Mexico.

New Mexico's colorful past is the foundation for many of its attractions. Spanish settlers contributed place-names, church architecture, food, customs, and holidays. Native Americans have established a research center to study their lore and artifacts. Near their *pueblos*—villages built of stone or adobe with flat roofs—the tribes operate casinos.

Hatch, New Mexico, is the chili capital of the world, producing 8,000 acres of the hot fruit. Red or green chilies are added to many dishes in New Mexico. Watch out!

Albuquerque Albuquerque (*AL buh kur kee*) is New Mexico's largest city. Although the city has skyscrapers, many low, flat-roofed adobe houses help the city keep its western character.

For nine days in October, Albuquerque's skies blossom. The Balloon Fiesta attracts thousands of colorful hot-air balloons and a huge crowd. After the fiesta, near Albuquerque, travelers can still "get their kicks on Route 66," as Nat King Cole told us. Or travelers can take the Sandia Crest National Scenic Byway (also known as the *Turquoise Trail*) east of the city and head north through old mining towns such as **Cerrillos**, a center of turquoise mining, to **Santa Fe**, the state's capital.

Commissioned in 1926 and paved in 1937, Route 66 once ran for 2,448 miles (3,939 km) through eight states from Chicago to Santa Monica, California. It provided an east-west road for travelers before the interstates were built.

Santa Fe The continent's oldest capital (1610), Santa Fe served as the seat of government for Spain, Mexico, the Confederacy, and the United States. The Plaza is the heart of the small city below the Sangre de Cristo Mountains. After New York and Los Angeles, Santa Fe ranks as the third-largest art market. A promenade along Canyon Road—a narrow street of galleries, shops, and outdoor cafés—is a must. The Santa Fe Opera performs each summer at an open-air theater set in a natural bowl in the hills.

Taos Taos has been an artists' mecca since 1898 when two painters stopped to fix a broken wagon wheel and stayed to create the Taos Society of Artists. In later decades D. H. Lawrence, Ansel Adams, and Georgia O'Keeffe settled there. In winter, Taos is the center of New Mexico's ski industry. Northeast of the town in the foothills, the Taos pueblo provides a cultural diversion from skiing and shopping. The pueblo's multistoried adobe buildings have been continuously inhabited for more than a thousand years. They are open daily to visitors except during tribal rituals.

Carlsbad Caverns These huge caves are in the southeast of the state near the Texas border. Lighted trails offer visitors an opportunity to see fantastic rock formations. Hundreds of thousands of bats fly out of the caverns at dusk and return at dawn.

North of Carlsbad is **Roswell**. In 1947 an unidentified flying object crashed north of this desert town. The first press release reported that it was a spaceship; later stories called it a weather balloon. Who knows? To commemorate the event just in case, Roswell hosts a UFO Festival each July.

Arizona

Arizona was the last of the mainland forty-eight states to join the Union, but people lived in the arid area for at least 25,000 years. Today, more than one-fourth of the state is Navajo, Hopi, and Apache land. The tribes operate the state's casinos. The state also features some of the world's most luxurious resorts and spas as well as golf courses that draw fans from around the world. City slickers might prefer to go west to one of the many dude ranches, which range from rustic to positively plush.

Phoenix Arizona's capital, Phoenix, is a mix of Spanish, Native American, and western cultures. The city grew around Camelback Mountain. Greater Phoenix is divided into three sections: Phoenix and the West Valley; **Scottsdale** and the Northeast Valley; and Mesa, Tempe, and the East Valley.

Phoenix is a popular retirement and resort center. In winter, golf and tennis are lures, and the weather is delightful. When guest ranches up north close because of cold weather, local ranches are enjoying high season. Summers are extremely hot and dry.

Clustered in Scottsdale's Downtown Arts District are hundreds of galleries, studios, and small museums. The town is also a shrine to modern architecture, the site of Frank Lloyd Wright's Taliesin West. Begun in 1937, it served as Wright's winter home and studio. Visitors can walk the grounds and choose from a variety of tours. Reservations are needed.

Phoenix boasts the greatest number of five-star luxury hotels in the country. Wright even designed one, the Arizona Biltmore, described as the *Jewel of the Desert.*

Tucson Tucson (*TOO sahn*)—south of Phoenix and just 60 miles (97 km) north of the Mexican border—has winter sunshine, mountains, and desert vegetation. The El Presidio District and the Tucson Museum of Art are highlights of downtown.

West of the city, the Arizona-Sonora Desert Museum is a must-see for anyone who wants to understand the desert. National parks surround the city. One, the **Saguaro National Park**, is dedicated to the preservation of the stately saguaro cactus. About 100 miles (161 km) southeast of Tucson is **Tombstone**, the site of the notorious gunfight between the Earp brothers and rustlers at the OK Corral.

Grand Canyon The Colorado River enters Arizona from Lake Powell on the Utah border and forms Arizona's border with California. The river has been busy for millions of years cutting one of the seven wonders of the natural world, the Grand Canyon.

The canyon can be approached from either the North Rim or the South Rim. The less crowded North Rim is open only from mid-May through October. The south entrance, coming from **Flagstaff**, is the more popular. On the route to the canyon, the road climbs steadily across flat scrubland. Suddenly, there is a vast open space—the canyon—more than a mile (1.6 km) deep in places, 277 miles (446 km) long, and as much as 18 miles (29 km) wide.

➤ PROFILE

National Parks of the Western United States

The following are the most visited national parks in the western United States, in the order of the number of visitors, beginning with the most popular:

- *Golden Gate National Recreation Area*, California.
- *Lake Mead National Recreation Area*, Arizona and Nevada.
- *Grand Canyon National Park*, Arizona.
- *Olympic National Park*, Washington.
- *Yosemite National Park*, California.
- *San Francisco Maritime Historical Park*, California.

Source: National Park Service, Department of the Interior.

Arizona is in the Mountain Standard Time Zone (GMT – 7). Most of the state does not participate in daylight saving time. The only exception is the Navajo Nation in the northeast corner of the state.

Grand Canyon, Arizona

Curiously, the average stay at the Grand Canyon is less than four hours.

Reservations for rooms at Phantom Ranch—accessible only by foot, mule, or Colorado River raft—are taken up to twenty-three months in advance; the lodging is often fully booked a year in advance. Same-day requests are by wait-list, in case there is a cancellation.

Many of today's residents of Canyon de Chelly live in *hogans* (one-room Navajo structures) and raise crops on the canyon's floor.

Bathers find it hard to sink in the Great Salt Lake because the high salt content keeps them floating.

White-water river rafting trips take adventurers through the canyon. Trails for hiking and mule-back treks run down the canyon's side. Trails from north and south connect a vertical mile below the rim at Phantom Ranch, where weary travelers find cabins, a dining hall, and a campground. The Havasupai Indians have been residents for 700 years and are now keepers of the official tourist flame.

Spring and fall are the best times to visit. In summer, the deeper one goes into the canyon, the hotter it gets. Winter brings snow.

Outside the park the closest airport and accommodations are in Flagstaff. Just south of Flagstaff, the tourist and artist mecca of **Sedona** is nestled in spectacular red rock formations.

Navajo Nation East of Flagstaff is Navajo Nation, covering more than 25,000 miles of Arizona, New Mexico, and Utah. It is considered a sovereign nation, where Navajo is still the native tongue.

Canyon de Chelly (*de SHAY*) is the one of the tribe's holiest places, a landscape of sheer sandstone cliffs containing hundreds of prehistoric sites. The canyon is best known for its multistoried cliff dwelling made of sun-dried clay and stone by the Anasazi people between A.D. 700 and 1300. In the 13th century, the inhabitants mysteriously deserted the canyon. No one lived there until about 1750, when the Navajo moved in. The canyon is open year-round, although tourist season peaks in the summer. The canyon floor is accessible only to hikers, horseback riders, and people in four-wheel-drive vehicles on tours led by a park ranger or an authorized Navajo guide.

West of Canyon de Chelly, the **Painted Desert** extends along the Little Colorado River. The Painted Desert includes the **Petrified Forest National Park** on the border of Navajo Nation near the town of Holbrook.

Straddling the Arizona-Utah border, the rock formations of **Monument Valley** rise from the floor of a broad valley. The ancient wonder has been the backdrop for dozens of classic western films, starting with John Ford's 1939 masterpiece, *Stagecoach*.

Utah

Utah is north of Arizona. Its eastern part is mountainous. The region west of the mountains is one of the country's driest. Between these regions, in a valley rimmed by mountains, is the capital and largest city, **Salt Lake City**.

Salt Lake City The proud Mormon heritage of Salt Lake City, founded by Brigham Young (1801–1877), is everywhere in sight. At the heart of the city, Temple Square is dominated by the monumental Temple. The Temple is open only to church members, but on Sunday mornings and Thursday nights, the Tabernacle is open to all and rings with the voices of the renowned choir. Nearby, lavish Beehive House was the official residence of Young and one of his twenty-seven wives.

The Great Salt Lake The briny shallows of an immense lake form the northwestern boundary of Salt Lake City. After the Dead Sea, the Great Salt Lake has the world's saltiest water. It stretches 92 miles (148 km) to the north and is about 48 miles (77 km) wide.

The Great Salt Lake Desert extends west from the lake to Nevada. Near the Nevada border are the **Bonneville Salt Flats**, where land speed records are frequently set.

Resorts Utah's ski areas are in the mountains a short distance east of Salt Lake City: Alta, Deer Valley, Park City, and Snowbird. South of the city, the winding Alpine Scenic Loop road leads to **Provo** and **Sundance**, a community associated with the actor Robert Redford. Each January the prestigious Sundance Film Festival premieres films made by independent filmmakers.

National Parks East of Salt Lake City, near the Colorado border, is **Dinosaur National Monument.** In the southeast of the state, **Canyonlands**, Utah's largest national park, has miles of dirt prospectors' roads. It has entrances near **Moab**, which has become a popular destination for mountain bikers. **Arches National Park**, 5 miles (8 km) northeast of Moab, is a photographer's paradise. Local outfitters arrange for off-road vehicles to follow biking parties with food, water, and portable showers.

Zion and **Bryce Canyon** are in the state's southwest. Zion's outstanding scenery includes petrified sand dunes and rock faces in brilliant colors. Bryce Canyon is a series of natural amphitheaters eroded into the edge of a plateau. Bristle-cone pines atop the plateau have lived for thousands of years.

Nevada

The Nevada tourist board divides the state into *Reno-Tahoe Territory* in the northwest, *Cowboy Country* in the north, *Pony Express Territory* across the state's center, *Pioneer Territory* in the south, and *Las Vegas Territory* in the southeast corner. In a nutshell, these divisions describe Nevada.

Reno-Tahoe Territory From magnificent **Lake Tahoe** to historic **Virginia City**, the Reno-Tahoe Territory contains many of Nevada's most scenic and historic areas as well as **Carson City**, the capital. Lake Tahoe (*TAH hoh*) is a beautiful oval-shaped glacial lake that lies in a valley of the Sierra Nevada on the California-Nevada border. **Reno** was Nevada's original gambling and divorce capital. Virginia City is 25 miles (40 km) southeast of Reno. In the 1860s, the city's Comstock Lode produced one of the West's great gold and silver mining booms. The town maintains the character of that time.

Las Vegas Gambling is legal in many other states, but Las Vegas remains the world's gambling capital. It is also the state's largest city, the country's fastest-growing city, and America's most popular adult playground. It started out as a Mormon mission. The railroad came through in 1905, and the town thrived as a center for mining operations. In the 1930s, the federal government began construction of **Hoover Dam**, and small casinos opened to help the workers wile away their time. In 1931 Nevada's state government legalized gambling and prostitution and minimized the requirements for marriage and divorce. This brought real prosperity.

Gangster "Bugsy" Siegel might be called the founding father of modern Las Vegas. In 1946 he built the Flamingo Hotel on the newly named Strip, and the new city was born. Las Vegas Boulevard, the hub of the Strip, is lined with glittering casinos, show palaces, and extravagantly luxurious hotels. In the 1990s, old hotels were torn down to make way for huge theme hotels with 3,000 to 5,000 rooms. Bugsy wouldn't recognize his city anymore, but the millions who visit each year know and love it.

Things to see and do in Las Vegas include

- Gambling (everywhere).
- Attending a lavish stage show with superstars.

ON THE SPOT

"I know I'm calling at the last minute. I have only a few days' vacation this year, and I've been watching the ski conditions in the mountains, and they look great! Can you suggest a resort where I don't have to stay a whole week to qualify for a discount plan? I'd like to go on a weekend, but I'm somewhat flexible if it helps keep the price down."

Like other travelers, skiers are taking shorter but more frequent vacations, and resort packages are changing accordingly. The average stay for a ski vacation is 4.7 nights. Increasingly common are last-minute bookings since travelers find current weather forecasts and snow conditions on the Internet. Ski travel is highly seasonal—busiest during the Christmas–New Year's period, quieter in early January and again after mid-March. Rates for lodging and lift tickets are lower Monday through Thursday. Even the most exclusive resorts offer discounts on everything from ski lifts to complete packages.

"If you aim to leave Las Vegas with a small fortune, go there with a large one."

—Anonymous American saying

Las Vegas has a monorail that travels from the MGM Grand at the south end of the Strip to the convention center. Plans are to extend the train routes to downtown as well as out to McCarran Airport.

- Fulfilling your fantasy. Dance with fountains choreographed to show tunes (at the Bellagio). Ride in a gondola (at the Venetian). Observe Las Vegas from on high (at the Stratosphere). View a city skyline (New York, New York). Watch pirates battle showgirls (Treasure Island). See a volcano explode (Mirage). Get married at 2:00 AM (many wedding chapels).
- Visiting Hoover Dam on the Colorado River on a day trip.

✔ CHECK-UP

The Mountain states include
- ✔ Montana; its capital is Helena, but its largest city is Billings.
- ✔ Idaho; its capital and largest city is Boise.
- ✔ Wyoming; its capital and largest city is Cheyenne.
- ✔ Colorado; its capital and largest city is Denver.
- ✔ New Mexico; its capital is Santa Fe, but its largest city is Albuquerque.
- ✔ Arizona; its capital and largest city is Phoenix.
- ✔ Utah; its capital and largest city is Salt Lake City.
- ✔ Nevada; its capital is Carson City, but its largest city is Las Vegas.

For travelers, highlights of the Mountain states include
- ✔ Gambling in Las Vegas, Reno, or Tahoe.
- ✔ Hearing the Mormon Tabernacle Choir in Salt Lake City.
- ✔ Relaxing at a winter resort in Phoenix or Tucson.
- ✔ Seeing the Grand Canyon.
- ✔ Skiing in Idaho, Wyoming, Colorado, or Utah.
- ✔ Viewing the unspoiled wilderness of Idaho and Montana.
- ✔ Touring a Native American adobe pueblo in New Mexico.
- ✔ Visiting Yellowstone and the Grand Tetons in Wyoming.

The Pacific States

The states that border the Pacific—California, Oregon, and Washington—share one of the country's most scenic regions. They feature spectacular cities and a lifestyle envied throughout the world, and they are among America's leading tourist destinations. See Figure 4.4 for a map of the region.

California

Death Valley has long been prized for its unique wildlife and desert beauty. Its summers are notorious for temperatures in excess of 120° F (48° C).

California's geography includes just about every type of landscape except Arctic tundra. It contains the highest point on the forty-eight contiguous states, Mount Whitney, and the lowest point on the continent, Death Valley. The state is shaped like a long trough. In the middle is the Central Valley, with the Sierra Nevada to the east and the Coast Ranges along the Pacific. The capital is Sacramento.

The Hotel del Coronado, with its ornate gingerbread trim and numerous domes, has housed royalty and celebrities since 1888. It is now a National Historic Landmark.

San Diego San Diego is Los Angeles without the smog and San Francisco without the fog. Its bay is one of the West's great natural harbors, home to the U.S. Navy and cruise ships. Fingers of land jut into the bay to guard fine beaches. The city is on flat land near the sea, but hills and mountains appear to the east. The luxurious Hotel del Coronado sits on a narrow peninsula that extends into the harbor.

Things to see and do in San Diego include
- A view of the city from Cabrillo National Monument, commemorating Juan Cabrillo, a Portuguese explorer who led the first European expedition to explore the coast of what is now California. Whale watchers come to the

FIGURE 4.4

The Pacific States

headland in late December to see the annual migration from Arctic waters to southern climes.

- A stop at Balboa Park. These 1,200 acres in the heart of town offer fifteen museums, botanical gardens, and the famous San Diego Zoo.
- The beach, deep-sea fishing, or whale watching.
- The Gaslamp Quarter, an area of restored Victorian buildings, for dining, shopping, and entertainment.
- Shelter Island, a man-made strip of land in the harbor known for its marinas, resorts, restaurants, and shops.
- Sea World at Mission Bay, an aquatic theme park.
- A trip south to **Tijuana** (*tee WHAN uh*), Mexico.

- A journey on a camino real ("royal road"; a road built by the Spanish explorers to connect capital cities). Father Junípero Serra (1713–1784) blazed California's *Camino Real*, now Route 101, and established a chain of missions along the road. Its signs have a mission symbol.

Los Angeles The *Entertainment Capital of the World* was founded in 1781 on a flat plain with the ocean to the west and mountains to the east. Its streets were laid out on a grid, centered on a plaza. The first settlers were cattle ranchers.

Today, the country's second-largest city uses the entire coastal plain and even jumps mountain ranges to find land for its ever-growing suburbs. The city stretches for more than 60 miles (96 km) from south to north.

Downtown L.A. has been likened to an empty doughnut hole. Most of what people associate with the city takes place outside the city center—the movielands of Burbank and Hollywood to the north, the theme parks of Anaheim to the southeast, the beach communities of Santa Monica and Malibu to the west. With the 2003 opening of the Walt Disney Concert Hall (designed by Frank Gehry), hopes for a vital center were finally realized. Nearby is the Los Angeles Music Center with its Dorothy Chandler Pavilion and the Museum of Contemporary Art.

Distances between L.A.'s attractions can be intimidating. At rush hour, even getting on the freeway means waiting your turn for stoplight-controlled access. Although the city has a subway and other public transportation, a car is a necessity.

Other things to see in Los Angeles include

- **El Pueblo de Los Angeles**, the center of the old Spanish settlement, with Olvera Street, a colorful Mexican marketplace.
- **Hollywood** and the hillside Hollywood sign, originally a real estate advertisement; La Brea Tar Pits, rich fossil deposits; Mann's Chinese Theater, with footprints of the stars; the Boulevard Walk of Fame; NBC Studios, with tours and tickets; and the Hollywood Bowl, with outdoor concerts.
- **Universal Studios Hollywood**, a theme park and reputedly the world's largest film studio. A tram tour of film sets includes a simulated earthquake, a collapsing bridge, and a surprise attack from King Kong.
- **Beverly Hills**, an enclave of palatial homes with Rodeo (*roh DAY oh*) Drive, whose exclusive shops are for those with big paychecks. City tours take tourists past "Homes of the Stars."
- The original **Disneyland** and **Knott's Berry Farm** in Anaheim, 28 miles (45 km) south of Los Angeles.
- **The Getty Center**, perched atop a ridge and looking out over Los Angeles to the Pacific. This art museum is a work of art itself.
- **The beach communities of Malibu, Santa Monica, and Venice**, as well as **Long Beach**, the permanent dock of the first *Queen Mary*, which is now a hotel. Cruise ships leave from the Long Beach piers for sailings to Hawaii, down the coast to Mexico, and to other destinations.

A 1910 Los Angeles Chamber of Commerce advertisement aimed at luring the film industry noted, "Cold rain and slushy snow do not tend to the proper mental condition for the best creative work."

On a clear day in winter, Los Angeles County is one of the few places in the world where you can ski in the morning and bask on the beach in the afternoon. **Big Bear** and **Lake Arrowhead** in the San Bernardino Mountains are nearby ski resorts.

Up the Coast You can fly or drive eight hours on the interstate from Los Angeles to San Francisco, but you would be missing one of life's great scenic experiences by not driving the Pacific Coast Highway, California State Highway 1. It snakes along the coast through a region often called *America's Riviera*. Travelers should plan a trip of at least two or three days.

The road runs north from Los Angeles through Malibu and Ventura. Ventura harbor is home to the **Channel Islands National Park**, five islands along the coast accessible only by boat.

Highway 1 passes **Santa Barbara**, a city with a beautiful mission, following the Santa Ynez (*ee NEZ*) Mountains to Lompoc. At Morro Bay the highway turns toward the sea to reach San Simeon and **Hearst's Castle**, the mansion built by the newspaper magnate William Randolph Hearst (1863–1951). He employed buyers to travel the world to stuff his home with priceless works of art. Tours (with reservations recommended) explore different parts of the house and estate. Buses collect visitors from the huge car parks and take them up to the castle.

The personality and career of William Randolph Hearst are believed to have inspired Orson Welles's 1941 film, *Citizen Kane*.

The road goes north until it reaches breathtaking **Pfeiffer Big Sur State Park**. The village of **Carmel-by-the-Sea** has a classic mission and dates back to the 1770s. Carmel is the start of the 17-mile (27 km) drive (toll) along the Monterey Peninsula. On the drive, golfers might want to stop to see the Pebble Beach course. At the end of the drive, the coastal resort of **Monterey** has Fisherman's Wharf, the Steinbeck Museum, an annual jazz festival, and the Monterey Bay Aquarium located on Cannery Row.

From Monterey, Highway 1 continues north to San Francisco, but people in a hurry veer inland to Route 101. At the base of San Francisco Bay, the city of **San Jose** is the center of the aerospace industry and the high-tech complexes of **Silicon Valley**.

Golden Gate Bridge, San Francisco

San Francisco The most beautiful of American cities seems designed for the traveler. It has everything: scenery, history, climate, shopping, culture, fine dining, and nightlife. Sometimes, without warning, the earth even moves.

Sprawled over steep hills, the city fills a narrow peninsula, with the Pacific Ocean backed by the coastal mountains to the west and San Francisco Bay to the east. The only gap in the mountains is the Golden Gate Strait, the entrance to the spectacular harbor. In 1937 the Golden Gate Bridge opened and linked the headlands.

Mexican soldiers and settlers sailed into San Francisco Bay in 1775 and established the Presidio (military fort). Streets were laid out in grid fashion. When the Gold Rush started in 1849, the city's population was about 850. By the end of 1850, it had reached 12,000. Another grid pattern was started at a 45-degree angle from the original line along Market Street, which forms the meeting point between the city's two grids.

When the transcontinental railway reached the city in the 1880s, San Francisco had a second boom. The metropolitan district expanded across the Bay Bridge east to **Oakland** and **Berkeley** (home of the University of California at Berkeley) and north across the Golden Gate to Sausalito in Marin County.

Viewers are surprised that San Francisco's Golden Gate Bridge—one of the city's most famous sights—is not golden but reddish orange.

On April 18, 1906, perhaps one of the best-known earthquakes in recorded history—but by no means the most severe—destroyed the area from the waterfront to Market Street. Broken gas pipes caused fires that raged uncontrolled for three days. But within ten years the city had rebuilt.

Things to see in San Francisco include

- Chinatown, 25 square blocks of colorful shopping and restaurants.
- Fisherman's Wharf, with restaurants, shops, hotels, and lots of tourists.
- Ghirardelli Square, an old chocolate factory transformed into restaurants and shops.
- Golden Gate Park, with the Japanese Tea Garden and the M. H. de Young Museum.
- Lombard Street, the *Crookedest Street in the World*.
- North Beach and SoMa (south of Market), for lively nighttime entertainment.
- Palace of the Legion of Honor, an art museum.

When parking facing downhill in San Francisco, the car's wheels must be turned toward the curb to keep the auto from rolling. When parking facing uphill, the wheels must be turned away from the curb.

- Telegraph Hill, with Coit Tower and a view of the city.
- The top of the Mark Hopkins Hotel.
- Union Square, center for hotels and shops.
- Alcatraz, the famous prison. Boats leave from a pier near Fisherman's Wharf.

San Francisco is a walker's city, but distances are considerable and visitors require occasional lifts by bus, taxi, or the famous cable cars, which debuted in 1873. The cars are the only National Historic Landmarks that move. The Powell-Hyde Line offers some of the best views and most thrilling curves; it takes riders to Fisherman's Wharf.

Marin County Going north across the Golden Gate Bridge, a trip to Marin County should include stops at **Point Reyes National Seashore** and **Muir Woods National Monument**. At Point Reyes, the *Earthquake Trail* follows the San Andreas Fault.

Muir Woods is the best place near the city to see the redwood trees, *Sequoia sempervirens*. The redwoods and the giant sequoia are the only remaining types of sequoia (*sih KWOY uh*), a tree that ranks among the earth's largest and oldest living things. The redwoods grow near the Pacific from central California north of San Francisco into the southern part of Oregon; the giant sequoia grows only on the western slopes of the Sierra Nevada at elevations from 5,000 to 7,800 feet (1,500 to 2,380 m). Giant sequoias do not grow as tall as redwoods, but their trunks are larger.

The North Coast The *Redwood Highway* (US 101) stretches from San Francisco to the Oregon border. The area includes the grape-growing counties of Mendocino, Lake, Sonoma, and Napa. The town of **Napa**, with its lovely Victorian homes, is the gateway to the famous wine-producing valley. Roads are lined with the neat rows of vineyards that belong to the region's wineries;

CLOSE-UP: CALIFORNIA

Who is a good prospect for a trip to California? Almost any domestic or international traveler is a good prospect for a trip to California. It suits young and old, families and individuals, and it offers attractions and accommodations to fit every taste and budget.

Why would they visit California? The state has climate, scenery, history, museums, theme parks, shops, fine dining, theater, sports, and nightlife.

Where would they go? You might plan a fly-drive trip, beginning in either San Francisco or San Diego. If the travelers decide to start in San Francisco, hold off on the car rental pickup while they are in the city. If they begin the trip in San Diego, you can arrange car pickup at the airport. Several days in either city would make a good beginning. From San Francisco, the travelers could take day tours to see Muir Woods or the wine country. When city time is over, they could pick up a rental car and drive down the coast to Los Angeles, taking three or four days, stopping at small hotels or B&Bs along the way.

When is the best time to visit? California has a very agreeable climate: sunny and dry with only short periods of relatively cold weather in the mountains in winter. The coast can have fog anytime throughout the year. Rain occurs between November and March. San Diego and Palm Springs are particularly attractive in winter to those who live in northern states. San Francisco and the wine country are always in season. Northern California and the mountains are the most affected by seasonal change.

The travelers say, "I've heard that Yosemite is crowded and you can't use your car. How do we get around?" How would you respond? The National Park Service has taken steps to prevent overcrowding in the parks. In Yosemite, the NPS has cut the number of campers permitted in Yosemite Valley and is providing public transportation around the most popular sites.

most offer tours and tastings (for a fee). The wine country has small hotels and B&Bs, mineral springs and spas, fine restaurants, and beautiful scenery. The state has other grape-growing areas, many in the San Joaquin Valley.

The Parks **Yosemite** (*yoh SEHM ih tee*) **National Park** is southeast of San Francisco on the western slope of the Sierra Nevada. It is one of the country's most beautiful and most visited parks, but crowds can dull the pleasure. Although the park has miles of trails, most tourists crowd into Yosemite Valley to see the famous sights: the Big Trees; waterfalls such as Ribbon (the country's highest), Bridal Veil, Vernal, and Upper and Lower Yosemite; and rock masses such as Half Dome and El Capitan. High-water season in spring is the best time to see the waterfalls.

Four hours south of Yosemite by car are **Kings Canyon National Park** and **Sequoia National Park**. They have many of the same wonders as Yosemite. The region includes Mount Whitney and groves of giant sequoias. Open year-round, the parks are at their peak in spring and fall. Access is from Fresno; there is no access from the east.

Joshua Tree National Park is in the Mojave Desert east of Los Angeles. The Joshua tree is a tall cactus with outstretched arms. Near Joshua Tree is **Palm Springs**, 115 miles (185 km) southeast of Los Angeles. It is a fashionable desert resort with homes of the rich and famous. Summer is low season in Palm Springs due to high temperatures.

ON THE SPOT

Mr. and Mrs. Stanford are planning a vacation to the San Francisco area and are interested in seeing the redwood trees. Where would they go, and what suggestions do you have for their trip?

Since the Stanfords will be in San Francisco, you might suggest they rent a car and drive up the coast to see the redwoods, the seascapes, and the charming towns between San Francisco and the Oregon border. Cross the Golden Gate Bridge to see the redwoods at Muir Woods National Monument. Then switch to the coastal road, California Route 1, for the drive to Oregon. The redwoods get bigger and the seascapes more dramatic as you go. A good overnight stopover is around Mendocino and Fort Bragg. California Route 1 reconnects with 101. On their return they can travel through the wine valleys.

Oregon

The Cascade Mountains divide Oregon (the *Beaver State*) into eastern and western sections. Eastern Oregon resembles the plateaus and plains of Wyoming and Nevada. Western Oregon has lush green forests, snowcapped mountains, and rugged rivers.

In the north the Columbia River and its tributary the Snake flow west across the state until they join the **Willamette** at Portland and empty into the Pacific. At **Astoria** the Columbia's mouth forms the West Coast's only deepwater harbor between San Francisco and the entrance to Puget Sound. Nearby is Fort Clatsop, where Lewis and Clark ended their expedition across the continent. Modern-day explorers can trace their route from the confluence of the Snake and Columbia on stern-wheelers.

Highway US 101 hugs the Pacific shore. Small fishing and lumbering towns have become artist colonies filled with B&Bs and small inns. Steep cliffs rise along much of the wave-swept coast. Parts have sandy beaches, but the water is cold. Inland, 15 miles (24 km) north of the California border, **Ashland** is home to the Oregon Shakespeare Festival. America's largest celebration of the Bard, it runs eight months of the year.

Most of Oregon's cities, including **Salem**, the capital, and **Portland**, the largest city in the northwest of the state, are in the Willamette (*will AM ette*) Valley. The Willamette River divides Portland, the *City of Roses*. Pioneer Square is the heart of the city. Portland's annual *Rose Festival* takes place in early June.

Less than an hour's drive south of Portland, more than a hundred wineries are open to the public. An hour east of Portland by road is the stunning **Columbia River Gorge**. The river's waterfalls include mighty **Multnomah Falls**. A circle trip from Portland could visit the gorge, the falls, and **Mount Hood**. The snow-covered mountain towers above the Cascade Range. Lunch at Timberline Lodge on Mount Hood is a pleasant break. Timberline offers year-round skiing.

Yosemite's luxury hotel, the Ahwahnee, is a tribute to Native American art. Built in 1927, the Ahwahnee blends right into the landscape and is one of the most prestigious hotels in the national parks.

Astoria is the Northwest's oldest settlement. It was established in 1811 by John Jacob Astor's Pacific Fur Company.

Space Needle, Seattle, Washington

On May, 18, 1980, Mount St. Helens in the Cascade Mountains south of Seattle became the first volcano to erupt in the continental United States in more than sixty years.

Washington

Like Oregon to its south, Washington is divided by the Cascades. The Puget Sound lowlands lie between the Cascades and the Coast Range. The snowcapped Olympic Mountains are in the state's northwest corner.

With innumerable waterways on its coast and mountain wilderness down its spine, Washington is a center for adventure travel. It is known for both environmental awareness and high-tech industry. Microsoft, the computer giant, and Boeing, the aircraft manufacturer, are the area's largest employers.

Olympia is the capital of Washington, but **Seattle** is the largest city. It is located on Puget Sound, about 100 miles (161 km) south of the Canadian border.

Proximity to the Pacific makes Seattle a premier port for Asian trade; Seattle's mountains and lakes make it a premier city for its residents. **Mount Rainier** is the volcano that looms over Seattle on clear days. Seattle's cultural center, Benaroya Hall, hosts the Seattle Symphony, opera, and the Seattle Repertory Theater.

Downtown Seattle has four distinct sections: the retail shopping area; Belltown, the area north of the retail section; "The Market," as Pike Place Farmer's Market is called by locals; and Pioneer Square, the birthplace of the city. The original Starbucks opened in The Market in 1971.

Boats leave from the piers below The Market for harbor cruises. From The Market, one can also walk to the monorail station in Westlake Center and travel to Seattle Center and the Space Needle. The spire was built in 1962 for the Seattle World's Fair. It provides views of the city and its surrounding natural beauty.

✔ CHECK-UP

The Pacific states include

- ✔ California; its capital is Sacramento, but its largest city is Los Angeles.
- ✔ Oregon; its capital is Salem, but Portland is the largest city.
- ✔ Washington; its capital is Olympia, but its largest city is Seattle.

For travelers, highlights of the Pacific states are

- ✔ Visiting the San Diego Zoo.
- ✔ Experiencing the beauty of the California coast on State Highway 1.
- ✔ Seeing the Golden Gate Bridge and temporarily visiting Alcatraz in San Francisco.
- ✔ Sipping wine in Napa or Sonoma County.
- ✔ Viewing a giant tree in Yosemite, Kings Canyon, or Sequoia National Park.
- ✔ Cruising on the Columbia River from Portland.
- ✔ Viewing Seattle from the Space Needle.
- ✔ Seeing the rugged coast of the Pacific Northwest.

Alaska

Physically separated from the "lower forty-eight," Alaska is called the *Last Frontier* for good reason. A very special part of the United States, Alaska, with its northern latitudes, pastel light, Native Americans, lack of roads, and miles of wilderness, has a magical quality. Moose, caribou, bears, whales, seals, eagles, and snowy owls bring tourists face to face with nature. Figure 4.5 shows a map of the state.

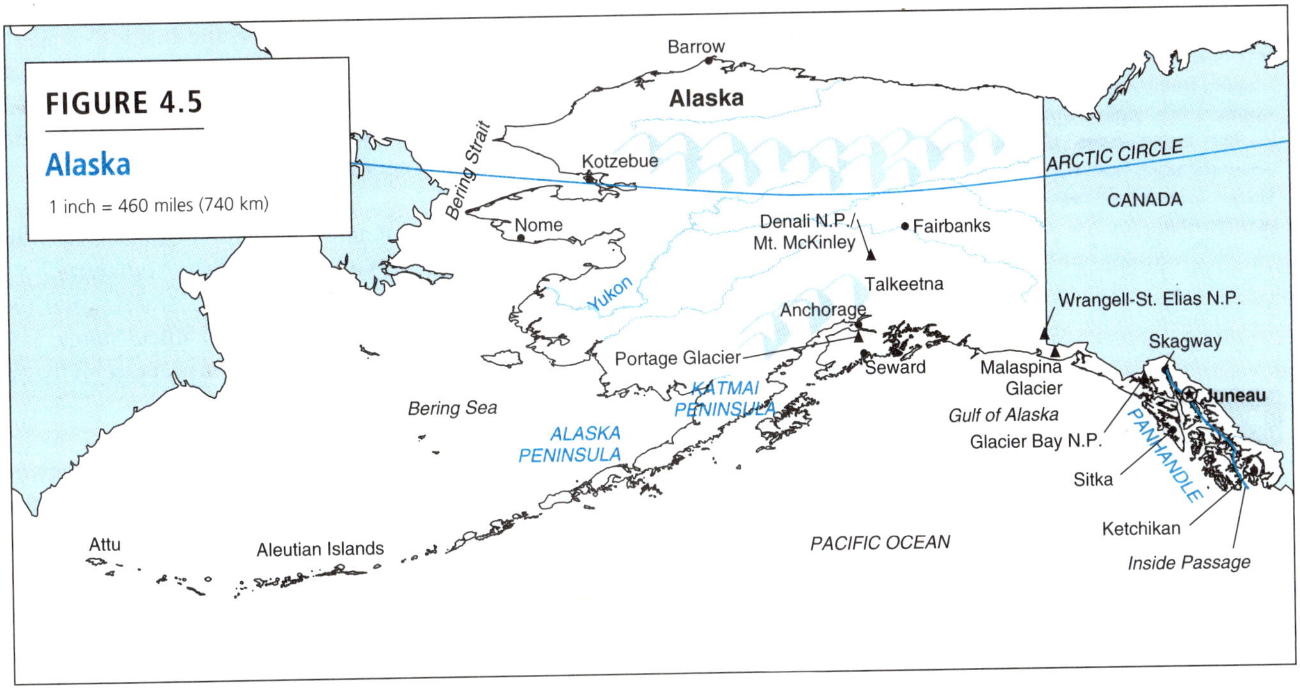

FIGURE 4.5

Alaska

1 inch = 460 miles (740 km)

Alaska's nearest neighbors are Canada and Russia. Some of its citizens live closer to Japan than to their own state capital, **Juneau** (*JOO noh*). Alaska is 80 percent owned by the federal government, and less than 1 percent of the state has been developed.

Once, Alaska was called "Seward's Folly," named for the secretary of state who purchased it from the Russians for $7.2 million in 1867. Alaska's image changed dramatically when gold and oil were discovered. Long after North Slope oil runs out, the glaciers and forests and caribou will be there, more sought after than ever in a world where true wilderness is fast disappearing.

Any area so vast with so many attractions must be divided into regions. Alaska's regions are the southwest, the Panhandle, south central Alaska, the interior, and the far north.

Tourism is Alaska's second-largest employer, after the oil industry. Fishing ranks third.

The Southwest

The **Aleutian Islands** stretch farther west than Hawaii. **Attu** is just 53 miles (85 km) across the **Bering Strait** from Russia. Everything from king crab to salmon to most of the fast-food fish America eats comes from the turbulent seas of southwest Alaska.

The Panhandle

The strip of coastal land in the southeast called the Alaska Panhandle includes tall mountains and ice fields. The coast is cut by hundreds of small bays and narrow, steep-sided inlets called **fjords**. One-third of visitors to Alaska come for a cruise on the **Inside Passage**, a water route through the islands and strip of mainland that make up the Panhandle. Passenger ships ply the waters from late May to early September. The passage runs from Seattle, Washington, to the Alaskan towns of Haines and Skagway, although at present most cruise ships leave from Vancouver, Canada. Because there are no roads along the coast, the waterway is also called the **Alaska Marine Highway**, and ferries sail it year-round.

Cruising on the Inside Passage, Alaska

Totem poles are among southeast Alaska's treasures. They are sorted into various kinds: legend poles represent folklore; history poles tell about a clan; memorial poles honor a person; and shame poles ridicule someone for acts of wrongdoing.

➤ PROFILE

Alaska's National Parks

Alaska has seven national parks and two national forests:

- Chucgach National Forest along the south central coast.
- Denali National Park encircling Mount McKinley.
- Gates of the Arctic National Park, about as far north as you can go.
- Glacier Bay National Park on the Inside Passage.
- Katmai National Park on the peninsula southwest of Anchorage.
- Klondike Gold Rush National Historical Park near Skagway.
- Sitka National Historical Park on the outside of the Inside Passage.
- Tongass National Forest in the Panhandle.
- Wrangell-St. Elias National Park in the southeast sector of the mainland.

Ketchikan From Vancouver, Canada, the first port on the Inside Passage is Ketchikan, an old fishing camp for the Tlingit Indians. Creek Street, once known to loggers and fishermen as the place for whiskey and women of the night, now houses gift shops and galleries. Excursions from town go to Saxman, where residents practice totem carving.

Sitka Northwest of Ketchikan, Sitka is not actually on the Inside Passage but on the western coast of Baranof Island. Founded as New Archangel by a Russian fur trader in 1804, it was the chief town of Russian America and the site of the formal transfer of Alaska from Russia to the United States. The onion-bulb spire of reconstructed Saint Michael's cathedral is about all that is left of the occupation.

Juneau There are no roads to Juneau; everyone has to get there by plane or ship. From January through April, the legislature convenes. In summer, cruise ship passengers descend. Sometimes as many as seven ships a day are in the harbor. Shore excursions visit the **Mendenhall Glacier** northwest of town. Helicopter or floatplanes provide spectacular ways to see the glaciers. Other activities include rafting, salmon fishing, trail biking, kayaking, and hiking.

Glacier Bay National Park and Preserve West of Juneau, near the northern end of the Panhandle, is Glacier Bay. Here, glaciers drop icebergs into the water with a sound described as "white thunder." The process is known as **calving**. In the sun, ice crystals absorb all colors but blue, which they reflect, creating the glacier's shades of color. Seals recline on icebergs. Humpback whales flock there in the summer. Access to the bay is by cruise ship or charter boat. The cruise lines eagerly seek permits to enter the bay.

Skagway As part of the Klondike Gold Rush National Historical Park, Skagway has been restored to what it was during the Yukon gold rush. When gold was discovered in Canada's Yukon Territory in 1896, prospectors came by sea to Skagway and then hiked 40 miles (64 km) over the White Pass to Lake Bennett, where they built boats for the 500-mile (805 km) trip to the gold fields. The White Pass & Yukon Railroad was built in 1898 to help shorten the journey. Today's tourists ride the vintage trains on sightseeing trips.

South Central Alaska

South central Alaska includes **Seward**, the debarkation and embarkation point for many Alaskan cruises, and the **Katmai Peninsula**, leading to the Alaska Peninsula. This region is also the location of the country's largest national park, **Wrangell-St. Elias National Park**, and of Alaska's largest city, **Anchorage**.

Wrangell-St. Elias National Park Edging the Gulf of Alaska, Wrangell-St. Elias is more than six times the area of Yellowstone. Four mountain chains meet here, and the park has nine of the country's sixteen tallest peaks. The park is open year-round, but most people visit between mid-May and mid-September, when lodges and guide services are operating. Many visitors fly in with bush pilots.

Anchorage Sited on an arm of the sea, Anchorage is a modern city, home to

269,000 people and about 2,000 moose. It is the base for the companies working in the oil fields of the North Slope and a busy modern city with an international airport.

Anchorage is also the starting point for "The Last Great Race on Earth," the *Iditarod Trail Sled Dog Race.* Held each March, the 1,047-mile (1,685 km) race restarts up the trail in Wasilla and ends in **Nome.** Around 75 mushers and 1,500 dogs enter the Iditarod each year. If trail conditions are favorable, the winning team gets to Nome in ten to twelve days.

Portage Glacier is an hour's drive south from Anchorage. Icebergs visible from the parking lot float in a lake formed from the glacial runoff. The highway to Portage follows the Turnagain Arm. It got its name when Captain Cook, looking for the Northwest Passage, learned that he had come to a dead end and had to "turn again."

In 1964 one of the most powerful earthquakes ever recorded in North America (8.4 on the Richter scale) hit the Anchorage area. Buildings crumbled and pavement fell 30 feet (9 m) in a few seconds. A tsunami (*soo NAH mee*) shattered the ports of Anchorage, Seward, and Valdez.

Although Alaska has plenty of snow, the short hours of winter daylight and unreliable weather make most skiers choose other destinations. Aleyeska ski resort is close to Anchorage and popular with locals.

The Interior

The interior of Alaska goes on and on. **Talkeetna** is the jumping-off point for **Denali National Park and Preserve.**

CLOSE-UP: ALASKA

Who is a good prospect for a trip to Alaska? Soft- and hard-adventure lovers would be delighted with the destination. Good prospects include those who have cruised before, those who have taken trips through the national parks of the West, and those who display an interest in spectacular scenery and nature at its best. Alaska is often the trip of a lifetime. It appeals to families and travelers celebrating an anniversary or special occasion.

Why would they visit Alaska? The pioneer spirit that propelled people across the prairies continues to push the adventurous traveler. Most city dwellers will never come face to face with a moose; in Alaska, chances are good that they will.

Where would they go? You might recommend a cruise up the Inside Passage and a land extension to see Denali. The trip begins in Vancouver, Canada, where travelers board their cruise ship for the voyage north.

Day 1 Travel to Vancouver, Canada; board the ship for an afternoon departure.

Day 2 Sail the Inside Passage; watch for whales and wildlife.

Day 3 Ketchikan, famous for salmon and totem poles.

Day 4 Juneau, the state capital.

Day 5 Glacier Bay, an up-close encounter with an iceberg.

Day 6 Skagway, entrance to the gold fields.

Day 7 Cruise the Gulf of Alaska.

Day 8 Disembark in Seward; transfer by motorcoach to Anchorage.

Day 9 Anchorage–Denali. Journey to Denali via Matanuska Valley. Stop in Wasilli, where you visit the Iditarod Race Museum and see a few of the racing dogs.

Day 10 Denali. Spend the day in the park. Experienced guides drive you through the park in search of moose, bear, and wolves while detailing the area's history.

Day 11 Denali. Day at leisure in the park.

Day 12 Denali–Fairbanks. Spend the morning in the park; then board the Alaska Railroad for your journey to Fairbanks.

Day 13 Fairbanks. A riverboat tour on the Chena and Tanana Rivers. The stern-wheeler stops to visit an early Athabascan settlement.

Day 14 Fly back to Anchorage for connections home.

When is the best time to visit? Winter is long, dark, and harsh. Unless travelers have some specific interest such as the Iditarod Trail Sled Dog Race (March) in mind, the tourist season is from June to early September.

The travelers make the following objection: "Won't Alaska be cold?" How would you respond? It normally isn't cold during tourist season (June through September), although evenings can get cool. With daylight twenty hours a day, June and July get quite warm, especially inland. Travel into some of the glaciers can be chilling.

The south summit of Denali, the highest point in North America, was first reached by climbers in 1913.

Denali The official name of the North America's highest mountain is **Mount McKinley**, although many prefer its Athabascan name, *Denali*. Alaska's premier symbol of wilderness is its most popular tourist attraction.

The mountain is notorious for playing hide-and-seek. Only 25 percent of visitors actually see it. More than half the mountain is permanently covered in snow. August mornings offer the best chance for a view. It is a rare afternoon that the mountain does not cloud up. Other attractions are caribou, sheep, moose, wolves, and grizzly bears. The local joke is that the three most common animals are the moose, the bear, and the mosquito. Bug spray is a traveler's necessity.

Fairbanks Fairbanks is Alaska's second-largest city, the interior's service and supply center. It is located near the geographic center of Alaska. The city has a small-town atmosphere and remains close to its gold rush roots.

The Far North

Most of northern Alaska is undisturbed; approximately two-thirds of it lies above the Arctic Circle. The northernmost point, **Barrow**, is almost 1,300 miles (2,090 km) south of the North Pole. Tours sometimes visit (by air) the village of **Kotzebue** above the Arctic Circle on their way to **Nome**, which is on the Seward Peninsula below the circle.

✔ CHECK-UP

Alaska's regions include

- ✔ The southwest, the Aleutian Islands.
- ✔ The Panhandle, with the capital, Juneau.
- ✔ South central Alaska, with Anchorage, the largest city.
- ✔ The interior, with Denali and Fairbanks.
- ✔ The far north, mostly undisturbed land.

For travelers, highlights of Alaska include

- ✔ Face-to-face encounter with nature.
- ✔ Mount Denali.
- ✔ White thunder of glaciers as they calve into the sea.
- ✔ Whales, seals, bears, and unspoiled nature along the Inside Passage.

Hawaii

The Hawaiian Islands are about 2,400 miles (3,862 km) southwest of the U.S. mainland, making them the country's most southern state. On the same latitude as central Mexico, Hawaii is a tropical paradise.

The ancestors of the Hawaiians sailed to the state from other Pacific islands more than 2,000 years ago. Their culture was built on respect and reverence for the land. When New England missionaries arrived in 1820, they were scandalized by the islanders' culture, especially the *hula* ("dance" in Hawaiian). The missionaries focused on the dance, but it is the chant—the words—that are important. The Hawaiians had no written language and relied on the hula to preserve their history and mythology. For years the hula was performed only in secret. Today, hula and chant festivals draw fans to events with tickets sold a year in advance. It is but one example of the appeal that the native Hawaiian culture holds for both islanders and visitors.

The Hawaiian alphabet has only twelve letters. Every word ends in a vowel. Pronounce every syllable. The accent of most words falls on the next-to-last syllable.

Most of Hawaii's islands are too small to support development. Figure 4.6 shows its six main islands. From east to west they are **Hawaii** (*huh WAH ee*), **Maui** (*MOW ee*), **Molokai** (*moh loh KAH ee*), **Lanai** (*lah NAH ee*), **Oahu** (*oh AH hoo*), and **Kauai** (*kah oo AH ee*).

Hawaii

The Big Island lends its name to the entire state. It is the largest of the islands—in area three times larger than Rhode Island—and its volcanoes keep making new land. Hawaii is also the most diverse island. It affords visitors the rare opportunity to experience bone-dry desert conditions, tropical rain forests, and snowcapped mountains, all in one day.

Hilo (*HEE low*), the island's port, is on the northeast side of the island, the wetter side. Its gritty black-sand beaches are a direct result of volcanic action.

The Resorts

The Hilo area of Hawaii has small hotels, but no major resorts. Hawaii's resorts are on the island's west coast, where the Kona-Kohala Coast offers beautiful beaches, luxury hotels, big-game fishing, and world-class golf courses. The black-lava beaches of the **Kohala Coast** host Mauna Kea, the hotel built in 1965 that set the standard for Hawaii's many super-resorts. The Kohala Coast ends where the serrated **Kona Coast** begins.

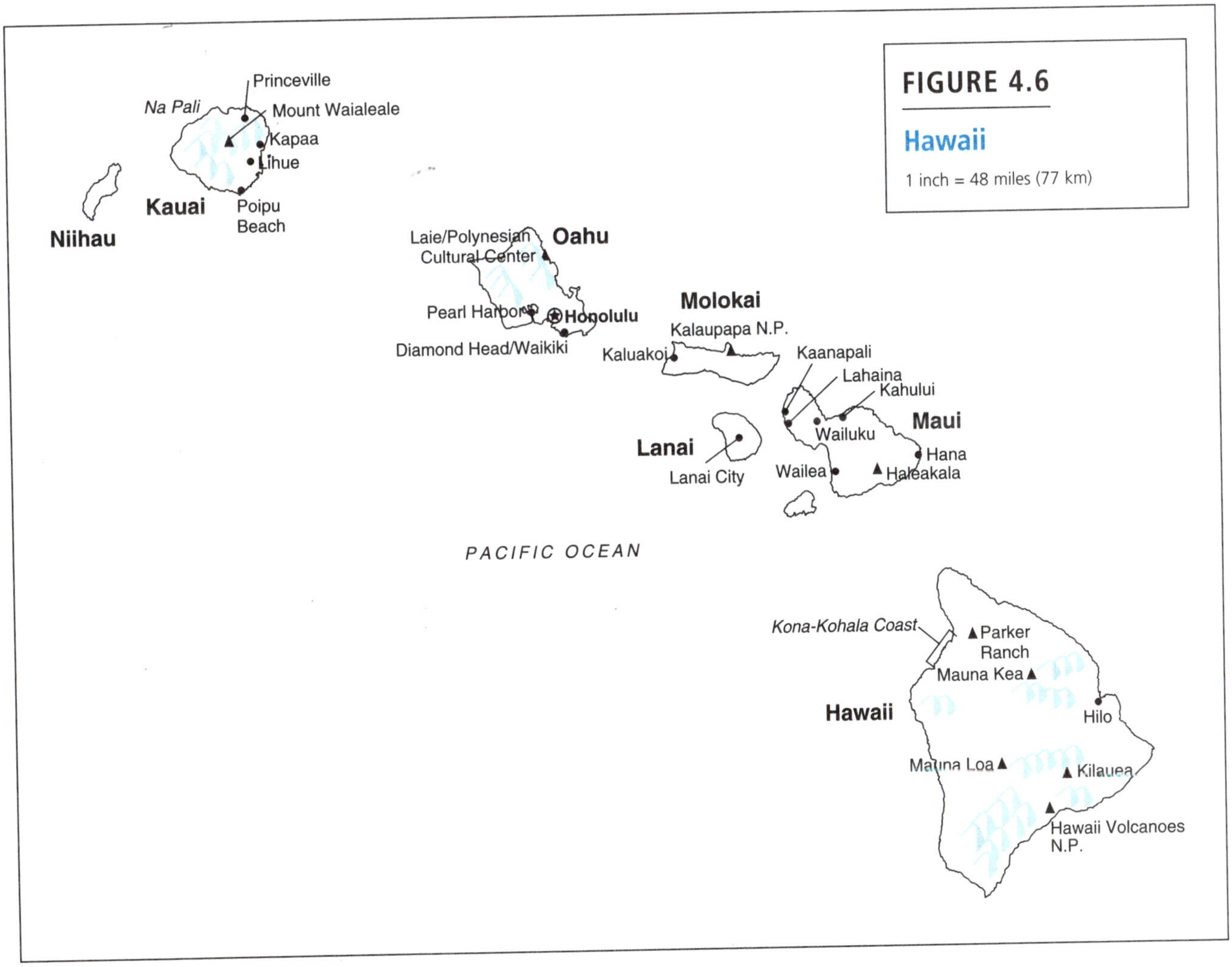

FIGURE 4.6

Hawaii

1 inch = 48 miles (77 km)

When visitors arrive in Hawaii, they traditionally receive *leis* (necklaces of flowers strung together) as a sign of welcome.

Activities Hawaii might also be called the *Volcano Island*. Five volcanoes, two of which—**Mauna Loa** and **Kilauea**—remain active, contributed to its formation. **Hawaii Volcanoes National Park** is on the southeast side of the island. The park has an amazing variety of ecosystems and climatic conditions and offers hiking and driving tours.

A third volcano, **Mauna Kea**, now dormant, is the world's tallest mountain when measured from the ocean floor. Native Hawaiians view the mountain as sacred, the home of the god Pele. In winter, the higher reaches of the mountain are snowcapped. Visitors come to Mauna Kea at night to see the sky. The air is extraordinarily thin, dry, and clear, with no light pollution to obscure the heavens. Telescopes on the summit include the world's largest optical and infrared scope.

The island's western side has coffee farms and cattle ranches. Travelers can visit the Coffee Living History Museum. The visitor center at **Parker Ranch** offers a look at Hawaii's *paniolo* (cowboy) history. John Parker established the ranch in 1847, and it is now one of the largest privately owned spreads in the United States.

Maui

Maui was formed from two volcanoes connected by an isthmus, which is the "valley" of its nickname, the *Valley Isle*. **Kahului** *(kah ha LEW ee)*, the site of the airport and the island's largest town, is on the north coast of the isthmus. Direct flights from the mainland changed Maui from a quiet to a bustling island. The Kahului area has moderately priced hotels, but most vacationers head for the beach resorts.

When vacationing in Hawaii, men often buy brightly colored aloha shirts, and women look for muumuus. A *muumuu* is the loose floor-length dress that was introduced by the missionaries. The *holomuu* is a fitted version. When all dressed up, tourists attend a *luau* with Hawaiian food, music, and the hula.

The Resorts West Maui is the more developed part of the island. **Kaanapali** was Maui's first planned resort, and the area has a range of hotels and family-style condominiums. To the south is the town of **Lahaina** (*la HINE uh*), a National Historic Landmark. Lahaina is a little bit of New England, complete with clapboard houses. In the 19th century, Lahaina welcomed not only Yankee whalers but also New England missionaries. Sugar production revived Lahaina's economy after electricity replaced the need for whale oil in lamps. However, sugar production is now unprofitable, and Maui's last crop was harvested in 1999.

On the southwest coast, **Wailea** (*why LAY uh*) has luxurious resorts and condos, championship golf courses, and crescent beaches. Its tennis stadium hosts major tournaments. In addition, there is horseback riding, sailing, snorkeling, windsurfing, diving, and kayaking.

Activities **Haleakala** (*hal ee AH kuh lah*) is an extinct volcano on the southeastern end of the island. A paved road goes to the top. After watching the sunrise, visitors can begin the popular 38-mile (61 km) bicycle ride back to sea level. Riders coast all the way, controlling their descent with oversized brakes.

The *Hana Highway* is a narrow twisting road along Maui's rugged windward coast. **Hana** is as distant from south and west Maui's beach resorts in style as it is geographically. Situated at the eastern end of the island, Hana has changed little in the past decades, providing a touch of Old Hawaii for residents and visitors.

Late January is the peak of Hawaii's annual whale season, when thousands of humpbacks return to the warm waters off Maui. The giant whales make the long trip from their summer home in Alaska to ensure that their calves are born in Maui. Whale-watching boats offer excursions under the watchful eyes of the Hawaiian Center for Whale Research.

Country roads travel through green forests to cattle ranches and farms where the famous Maui onion grows. **Wailuku** is the gateway to beautiful Iao (*yow*) Valley. The valley is the home of the stone column nicknamed *Iao Needle*, set amid wild orchids and giant ferns.

ON THE SPOT

Your clients are asking for a new place to vacation. They have been to Europe and are not ready to go back right now. They want a place that is steeped in history and jam-packed with cultural experiences. But they also want it to be safe, familiar, and warm.

Suggest they think about Hawaii. The same islands that offer perfect beaches, fine climate, limitless sporting choices in and out of the water, and nonstop golf also abound with history that predates the discovery of the Americas.

Molokai

Historically, the *Friendly Island* has been a place of refuge. In the 19th century, lepers were exiled to Molokai. On the northern coast, at the base of a sea cliff on an isolated peninsula, is **Kalaupapa National Park**. This is the place where, in the 1870s, Belgian priest Father Damien founded a settlement dedicated to treating those suffering from Hansen's disease—leprosy. The ride to the colony is a dramatic journey via mule down a 26-mile (42 km) switchback trail cut into the cliffs. Travelers must make advance arrangements for the trip through the Molokai Mule Ride.

On Molokai's southern coast, visitors can see the remains of the summer house of King Kamehameha V. **Kaluakoi** on the island's western shore is the area of resorts.

Lanai

Once a private island owned by the Dole Hawaiian Pineapple Company, Lanai—the *Secluded Island*—today is a secluded luxury resort. The isle is a place for sport fishing, ocean kayaking, and outstanding tennis and golf. Bicycling, horseback riding, and hiking are also major activities. **Lanai City**, the town and site of the airport, is in the island's center.

Oahu

Oahu means *Gathering Place*, and the phrase certainly describes the island. **Honolulu**, the capital, is the only real city in the archipelago. Oahu is the island for those who want nightlife and activity along with their beautiful beaches. It is a popular honeymoon and vacation destination for Asian visitors. Outside Honolulu, Oahu becomes rural.

Aloha means love in the Hawaiian language. The word is used for many things, including hello and good-bye.

Honolulu In Honolulu's bustling downtown, Iolani Palace is the only royal palace on U.S. soil. The Victorian structure, with its thrones and crowns, is open to the public. Exhibits in the Bishop Museum detail the island's history.

Other attractions in and around Honolulu include

- **Pearl Harbor**, a U.S. Navy base. The U.S.S. Arizona Memorial stands over the place where the battleship *Arizona* was sunk on that sad Sunday morning, December 7, 1941, when Japanese planes attacked Pearl Harbor and plunged the United States into World War II.
- The Aloha Tower, a waterfront landmark. It was the arrival port when sea travel was the only way to get to the islands. Now it is a port for cruises around the islands.
- The shopping areas of Kalakaua Avenue, Kilohana Square, the Ala Moana Center, and the Kahala Mall.
- The Kahala residential district, with mansions owned by the rich and famous.

■ Shangri La, the home built by tobacco heiress Doris Duke in 1938. It is now a museum showcasing her collection of Islamic art.

Waikiki Beach, Oahu

The Resorts **Diamond Head**, the extinct volcano that is Oahu's familiar landmark, overlooks famous **Waikiki Beach**, with its stretch of high-rise hotels. The hotels range from elegant to touristy. Some built in the early 20th century—the Moana and the Royal Hawaiian—still stand. The "Pink Palace," as the Royal Hawaiian is known, was built in 1927 by Matson Navigation to house its passengers.

Other Attractions Oahu's north shore is the gateway to the island's renowned surfing beaches, including the treacherous *Banzai Pipeline.* Winter brings huge waves that challenge the world's best surfers. In summer, the water is safe for snorkelers and swimmers.

Access to the north shore is along Route 83, the *Kamehameha Highway* to **Laie**. Laie is home to the Mormon Temple, Brigham Young University, and the **Polynesian Cultural Center**, Hawaii's most visited attraction. The center is a complex of re-created Polynesian villages where students from the university perform native songs and dances, demonstrate arts and crafts, prepare traditional foods, and explain the customs, rituals, and ceremonies of their islands: Fiji, Tonga, Samoa, Tahiti, Marquesas, New Zealand, and Hawaii.

Tourists on the north shore can also visit the Dole Plantation, take its Pineapple Express train ride, and view the plantation's garden.

The wettest place on earth is Mount Waialeale on the island of Kauai. The average annual rainfall there is 460 inches (1,168 cm).

Kauai

The greenest and oldest island in the Hawaiian archipelago, Kauai is essentially a single volcano that rises from the ocean floor. It is called the *Garden Island* because of its lush vegetation, the result of a potent mixture of sunshine and rainfall. Two-thirds of Kauai is impenetrable. Dozens of streams flow from rainy **Mount Waialeale** (*why AHL ee AHL ee*) through deep canyons to the sea. The rugged **Na Pali** (*pali* means "cliffs") on the northwest coast make it impossible to build a road entirely around the island.

Kapaa is the largest town; **Lihue** (*lih HOO ee*) is the airport site. Hotels are concentrated on **Poipu Beach**, in **Princeville** on the north shore, and around Lihue.

Visitors to Kauai enjoy dazzling beaches and challenging golf courses. The Wailua River boat trip brings them to Fern Grotto, where weddings are performed and a group sings the Hawaiian wedding song. An island oddity is the beach called Barking Sands; walking on it when it is dry sometimes produces a sound like a barking dog. Kauai was the setting for the old film *South Pacific* and for a newer one, *Jurassic Park*.

Passengers on ships leaving Hawaii toss their leis into the water. Tradition says that if your lei drifts away from land, you have seen the last of the islands. If your lei floats ashore, you will return.

✔ CHECK-UP

The Hawaiian Islands include
- ✔ Hawaii, the Big Island, with several active volcanoes.
- ✔ Maui, the Valley Isle, with Lahaina, the old whalers' village.
- ✔ Molokai, the Friendly Island.
- ✔ Lanai, the Secluded Island.
- ✔ Oahu, the Gathering Place, with Honolulu, the major city.
- ✔ Kauai, the Garden Island, known for its lush vegetation.

For travelers, highlights of Hawaii include
- ✔ Attending a luau on Waikiki Beach.
- ✔ Golfing at a top resort.
- ✔ Learning to do the hula.
- ✔ Remembering Pearl Harbor.
- ✔ Riding a bicycle down the slopes of Haleakala.
- ✔ Watching lava flow from an active volcano.

Planning the Trip

A trip to the Mountain states, the Pacific Coast, Alaska, or Hawaii is a special vacation. The destinations are popular with independent travelers, although every kind of tour is also available. For travelers to Alaska, a tour that combines a cruise with an extension to Denali brings many benefits.

When to Go

Winter is an ideal time to visit Phoenix, Tucson, San Diego, Los Angeles, Palm Springs, and the mountain ski resorts. San Francisco and the wine country are good in almost any season. Summer is best for a trip to the Southwest, the Northwest, or one of the northern national parks, although crowds are at their peak then. Trips are often planned to coincide with events such as the Rose Bowl in Los Angeles, the Rose Festival in Portland, the Balloon Fiesta in Albuquerque, or the opera season in Santa Fe.

The months of June to early September are Alaska's season, but an off-season visit, if the weather cooperates, can be something special. Hawaii, in contrast, is a suitable destination at any time.

Preparing the Traveler

Travelers often have questions about what to wear. It depends on the traveler's lifestyle. For the areas discussed in this chapter, casual clothes and comfortable shoes are usually in order. City visits may require more formality, however, and fine restaurants often require men to wear a jacket and tie.

For Alaska during summer, casual layered clothing is in order for daytime wear. It can get both hot and cold. Cruise passengers need to bring along dress-up clothes for evening celebrations. Hawaiian vacations call for colorful resort clothing. Bug spray and binoculars are handy for Alaska, and sunscreen is a must for Hawaii.

Transportation

The airlines provide ample east-west travel. Although one tourist board fielded an inquiry about driving conditions from California to Hawaii, the islands and Alaska are destinations served best by plane or ship.

By Air In general, the state's capital will have the region's largest airport. See the Fact File in Appendix A for an alphabetical list of the states, their capitals, and airport codes.

Anchorage is Alaska's principal international airport, but small planes and charter air reach almost every town throughout the state.

Honolulu is Hawaii's largest international airport. From there interisland flights provide connections. Kahului on Maui has traffic to and from the United States, Canada, and other destinations. West Maui has a small airport, and there is an airport in Hana. On the Big Island, Kona has flights from North America and Japan.

➤ PROFILE

Shopping in the West, Alaska, and Hawaii

Shopping opportunities range from upscale shopping in the cities to souvenir finds along the way:

- Western clothing and art in the Mountain states.
- Fashion's latest designs in California's cities.
- Native American pottery, rugs, kachina dolls, and jewelry in the Southwest.
- Art and handcrafted jewelry in Santa Fe.
- Colorful resort clothing, macadamia nuts, Kona coffee, and wood products in Hawaii.
- Native American handicrafts made from ivory, jade, fur, or bone (identified by a silver hand logo); woven baskets; and miniature hand-carved totem poles.

By Water Inland water adventures include white-water rafting through the Grand Canyon, on the Snake, and on the wilderness rivers of Idaho. Informal cruises on Oregon's Columbia River are also popular, especially in fall.

Cruise lovers might leave from ports in Long Beach (Los Angeles) or San Diego. For anyone who is concerned about seasickness, Alaska's Inside Passage is a good choice. The protected route produces little motion. The cruise season is from May to mid-September. At present most cruises originate in Vancouver, British Columbia, because of the U.S. Passenger Services Act (PSA) of 1886. Ships carrying a foreign flag—such as most cruise lines—have been prohibited from sailing from one U.S. port to another unless the itinerary includes a specified number of foreign ports in between. Cruise lines are testing the rules and lobbying Congress for change.

A chain of ferries, known as the Alaska Marine Highway, connects coastal communities in that state. The service is an official highway system. The state's "blue canoes," as they are called, are a budget-priced alternative to cruise ships. The ferries, which take cars, have cabins for about half the passengers. Those without cabins sleep in chairs or in sleeping bags on the decks. The southern terminus is in Bellingham, Washington, an hour north of Seattle. The complete trip lasts from a Friday night to a Monday morning. A ticket allows its holder to stop off at any port along the way. The end of the line is Skagway or Haines.

For cruises to and within the Aloha State, travelers can leave from the Pacific Coast or fly to Honolulu and take a leisurely voyage around the islands. Norwegian Cruise Lines (NCL)—at present the only U.S.-flagged ship in Hawaii—sails within the islands. A special rule allows NCL to cruise within the islands without having to visit foreign ports in between.

"Cruise everywhere else in the world before visiting Alaska," experienced passengers often advise, "because once you've seen Alaska, everything else pales by comparison."

By Rail Although U.S. trains are not up to European standards of luxury and convenience, rail tours in western America offer reasonable comfort and some spectacular scenery. The coastal route between Los Angeles and San Francisco is especially scenic. Independent companies offer short rides on vintage trains in many other scenic locations.

The Alaska Railroad operates daily between Anchorage, Fairbanks, and Denali Park, taking about eight hours from Anchorage and four hours from Fairbanks to the park. Connections to the state ferry system can be made at Seward and Whittier.

By Road Fly-drive vacations are popular ways to see the Mountain and Pacific states, but the automobile earns only a supporting role in Alaska. Travelers who want a rental car in Alaska must always ask about the drop-off fee if they want to rent a car in one city and leave it in another. One traveler wanted to rent in Anchorage and drive the Alaska Highway to Seattle, where the car would be dropped off. The drop-off fee would have been in the range of the price of the car.

The Alaska Highway travels through some of the most pristine countryside in the Americas. Without hurrying, travelers can drive from Fairbanks to Seattle in six to ten days.

Car rental is popular in Hawaii, but the islands are crowded and traffic jams are common. Some resorts offer complimentary shuttle services.

➤ PROFILE

Cuisine of the West, Alaska, and Hawaii

Specialties of the western United States and Alaska include

- Chilies with, on, and hidden in everything in New Mexico.
- Rainbow trout and buffalo and elk steaks in Colorado.
- Salmon in Washington, Oregon, and Alaska.
- Sourdough bread and seafood on the wharf in San Francisco.
- California wines from the Napa and Sonoma Valleys.

In Hawaii, try

- *Laulau*, spinach-like chopped taro leaf, fish, and pork or chicken, wrapped in ti leaves and steamed.
- Macadamia nuts, Kona coffee, and sweet Maui onions.
- *Poi*, a starchy food made by pounding the cooked underground stem of the taro plant until it becomes a paste. Tourists get a taste at a luau.

Accommodations

Arizona and California have some of the world's most tempting luxury properties. Unique hotels include the properties in the national parks. The stately hotels were carefully preserved for decades, but time has taken a heavy toll.

The old dude ranch ain't what it used to be. True, guests can ride a horse into meadows spangled with wildflowers, chow down at a chuck wagon barbecue, sit by a campfire beneath the stars, and bunk in a log cabin. But in parts of the West, ranches are turning into deluxe resorts with such amenities as golf, tennis, and spas. Most require a one-week minimum stay.

Alaska's hotels range from modern chains to rustic lodges. Informality is the rule in most places.

Hawaii's properties range from budget condominiums to super-deluxe resorts. Spa vacations are a large segment of Hawaii's market. A spa experience is a natural choice for upscale travelers looking for relaxation.

CHAPTER WRAP-UP

SUMMARY

Here is a review of the objectives with which we began the chapter.

1. **Describe the environment of the western states.** The Rockies, North America's largest mountain system, rise in the Mountain states to the west of the Great Plains. Immediately west of the Rockies, the land is a mix of basins, plateaus, and mountains. The Colorado River created the Grand Canyon in Arizona on its way from the mountains to the sea.

   Two major mountain ranges run north to south through the Pacific states. The Coast Ranges line the Pacific. To their east are broad fertile valleys. Farther east are the Cascade Range in the north and the Sierras in California.

2. **Summarize the special physical attractions of Alaska and Hawaii.** Alaska is a land of mountains; glaciers; cold, rushing rivers; tundra; vast space; and extremes of winter temperatures. Alaska's physical attractions lure the adventurous traveler. Hawaii is also a mountainous land, but one with tropical vegetation and space limited by water. Its natural events include erupting volcanoes. The islands have little temperature variation. Hawaii's physical attractions lure both the person wishing total relaxation on a beach and the one wanting soft adventure.

3. **Describe the region's attractions, matching travelers and destinations best suited for each other.** The western states offer outstanding outdoor adventure opportunities such as white-water rafting, winter sports, hiking, and city adventures to such places as Phoenix, Denver, San Diego, Los Angeles, San Francisco, Portland, and Seattle. For those who want gambling, there are Las Vegas and Reno; for nightlife, Las Vegas, Los Angeles, and San Francisco; for museums, Los Angeles and San Francisco; and for scenery, the Grand Canyon, the national parks, and the entire Pacific coast.

   Alaska's attractions are for travelers who want to see the best that nature provides. Cruises on the Inside Passage appeal to those who want their experience cushioned by the comforts of a deluxe resort. Hawaii appeals to travelers looking for a relaxing vacation in beautiful surroundings with shops, restaurants, deluxe hotels, golf, and water sports of every variety.

4. **Provide or find the information needed to plan a trip to the western states, Alaska, or Hawaii.** Logistical information is available through industry computers and tourist board Web sites. Tour operators and cruise lines play an important part in providing information and planning itineraries to Alaska and Hawaii.

QUESTIONS FOR DISCUSSION AND REVIEW

1. People talk about the West Coast lifestyle. How would you explain it to a traveler from a different region?

2. Alaska and Hawaii offer contrasting vacation experiences. What qualifying questions would you ask to fit the destination to the traveler?

3. As far back as the Civil War, North American newspapers used maps so that the public would know where places were. How could you use maps as sales tools for this region? Some things to consider: time zones, latitude, population density, and resort location.

CHAPTER 5

Canada

- The Atlantic Provinces
- Québec
- Ontario
- The Prairie Provinces
- British Columbia
- The North

OBJECTIVES

When you have completed Chapter 5, you should be able to

1. Describe the environment and people of Canada.
2. Identify Canada's provinces, territories, and most-visited sites.
3. Describe Canada's attractions, matching travelers and destinations best suited for each other.
4. Provide or find the information needed to plan a trip to Canada.

Canada crowns the North American continent. It extends from the Atlantic Ocean in the east to the Pacific Ocean in the west. The Arctic Ocean borders its north. A journey from east to west crosses six time zones. It is the second-largest country in the world (after Russia), but Canada has only about one-tenth as many people as its southern neighbor, the United States. Nearly four-fifths of the land is uninhabited. Most Canadians live within a few hundred miles of the U.S. border.

For travelers, Canada offers something for almost any taste. Some will be attracted by the diverse culture of its vibrant cities; others will welcome the peace of its vast countryside. The country is separated into ten provinces (political divisions similar to the states of the United States) and three territories (see Fact File in Appendix A).

The Environment and Its People

"My country isn't a country, it's the winter," wrote Canadian folk poet Gillet Vigneault. In fact, Canadian winters are long, and the far north of Canada is an icebox. But Canada is as varied as it is vast.

The Land

Canada's most northerly point lies just 500 miles (805 km) from the North Pole, while its most southerly point (on Lake Erie) is on the same latitude as Rome and northern California. In the north, icecaps and **permafrost** (a permanently frozen layer of ground) lie beneath the surface, and much is **tundra**, where no trees grow. South of the tundra are the evergreen forests of spruce and fir known as **taiga**. The **Yukon**, **Northwest Territories**, and **Nunavut** are Canada's northern territories.

To the south the landscape varies from west to east. On the Pacific Coast in **British Columbia**, mountains, coastal islands, lakes, fjords, and lush green forests lure the nature lover. A series of mountain ranges runs parallel to the western coast. At the eastern edge of these ranges, the **Canadian Rockies** offer some of North America's most spectacular scenery. East of the Rockies are the prairies of **Alberta**, **Saskatchewan**, and **Manitoba**. These rippling lands produce colossal amounts of wheat, not to mention significant quantities of oil and natural gas.

At the heart of Canada is a huge inland sea, **Hudson Bay** (see Figure 5.1). The provinces of **Ontario** and **Québec** surround the bay and extend southward to border the United States. The dominant geographic feature is the **Canadian Shield**. This mass of ancient rock sweeps in an arc around Hudson Bay from far northwest to far northeast. During the Ice Age, glaciers advanced and retreated over the area, scraping the surface down to its present level, hollowing out lakes and removing most of the existing soil. Along its southern rim, the shield forms the **Laurentian Mountains**.

At the eastern edge of Canada, along the Atlantic, are **Newfoundland and Labrador**, **Nova Scotia**, and **New Brunswick**. An extension of the Appalachians gives these provinces rugged hills and plateaus as well as a rocky coastline broken by fjords, coves, and bays. In contrast, the province of **Prince Edward Island** in the Gulf of St. Lawrence has gently rolling terrain.

➤ PROFILE

Adventure in Canada

Spectacular opportunities for outdoor activities are available throughout Canada's provinces and territories. Here are some popular things to do:

- ➤ Watch the whales in New Brunswick or Newfoundland.
- ➤ Hike in rugged Cape Breton Highlands National Park, Nova Scotia.
- ➤ Golf on Prince Edward Island.
- ➤ Ski in the Laurentian Mountains of Québec.
- ➤ Canoe in Ontario (which claims to have more canoe routes than any other region).
- ➤ Watch polar bears in Churchill, Manitoba.
- ➤ Ride a sno-coach on the Athabasca Glacier, Alberta.
- ➤ Pan for gold or watch grizzlies in the Yukon.

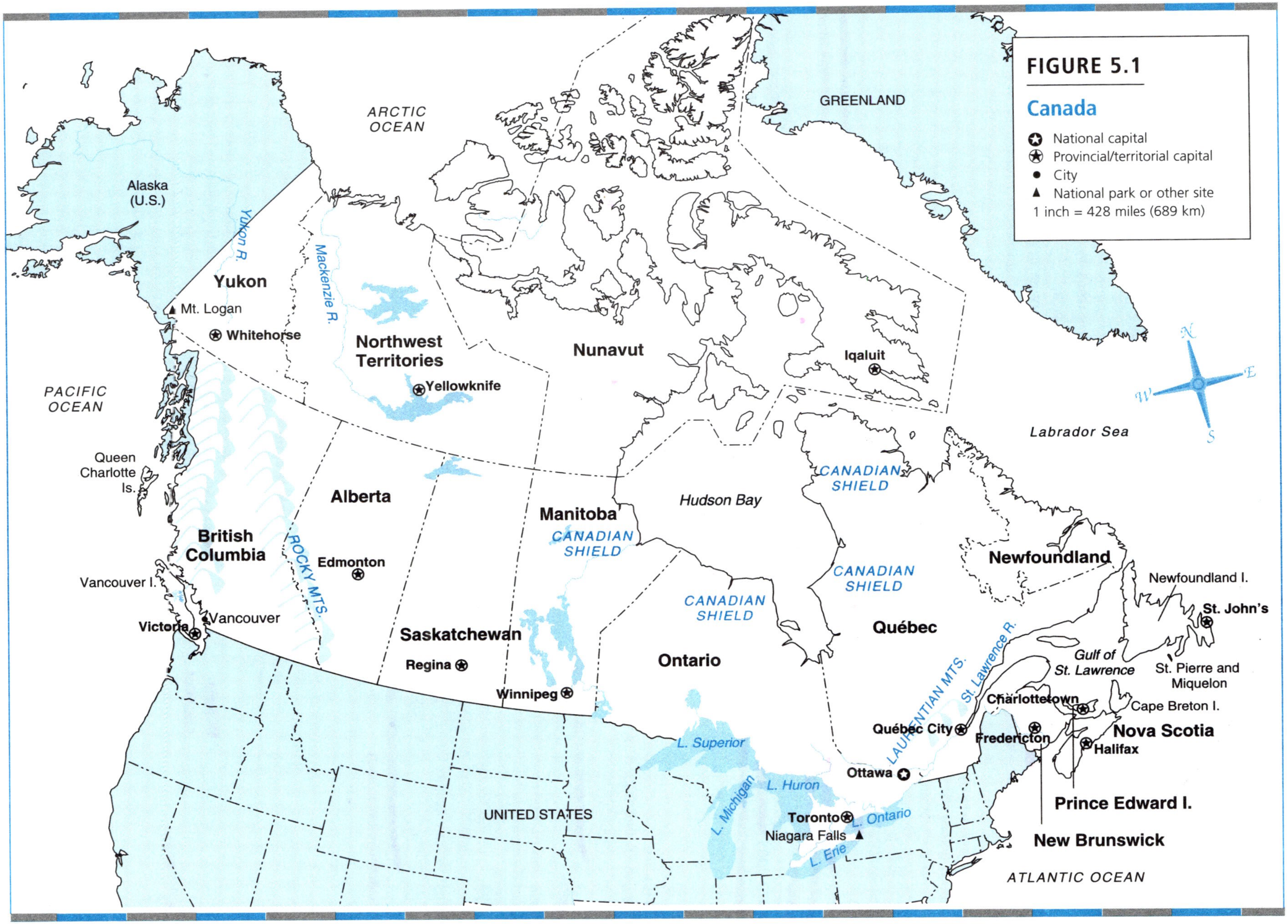
FIGURE 5.1
Canada
National capital
Provincial/territorial capital
City
National park or other site
1 inch = 428 miles (689 km)
ARCTIC OCEAN
PACIFIC OCEAN
ATLANTIC OCEAN
Labrador Sea
Hudson Bay
GREENLAND
Alaska (U.S.)
UNITED STATES
Yukon
Northwest Territories
Nunavut
British Columbia
Alberta
Saskatchewan
Manitoba
Ontario
Québec
Newfoundland
Nova Scotia
Prince Edward I.
New Brunswick
Yukon R.
Mackenzie R.
Mt. Logan
Whitehorse
Yellowknife
Iqaluit
Queen Charlotte Is.
Vancouver I.
Vancouver
Victoria
ROCKY MTS.
Edmonton
Regina
Winnipeg
CANADIAN SHIELD
CANADIAN SHIELD
CANADIAN SHIELD
CANADIAN SHIELD
L. Superior
L. Michigan
L. Huron
L. Ontario
L. Erie
Toronto
Niagara Falls
Ottawa
Québec City
LAURENTIAN MTS.
St. Lawrence R.
Gulf of St. Lawrence
Charlottetown
Fredericton
Halifax
Cape Breton I.
St. Pierre and Miquelon
Newfoundland I.
St. John's
N
E
S
W

FIGURE 5.2

Milestones in the Making of Canada

c. AD 1000 Vikings explore the Atlantic coastline.

1497 Sponsored by the English king, Italian navigator John Cabot/Giovanni Caboto (1450–1499) sights Cape Breton Island.

1534 French explorer Jacques Cartier (1491–1557) discovers the St. Lawrence River and claims Canada for France.

1700s Frenchmen known as *coureurs de bois* ("wood-runners") become the backbone of the fur-trading system.

1759 British forces capture Québec and take control of Canada in the decisive battle of the French and Indian War.

1776 English Loyalists who do not support the American Revolution move to Canada.

1870–1905 Manitoba, British Columbia, and Saskatchewan become provinces.

1901 World's first transatlantic radio signals are sent from Newfoundland to England.

1910s Ukrainians, Czechs, Slovaks, Poles, Hungarians, and Serbs migrate to Alberta and Saskatchewan.

1931 Canada becomes an independent nation.

1954 Construction begins on the St. Lawrence Seaway.

1968 Parti Québécois is founded. The French separatist movement begins.

1995 The Canadian Parliament recognizes Québec as a distinct society.

1999 Canada creates the self-governing Inuit territory of Nunavut.

Canada's name comes from *kanata*, an Iroquois word that means "village" or "community."

Within this vast land some important waterways are

- **Lakes Ontario, Erie, Huron,** and **Superior**, which are shared with the United States.
- The **St. Lawrence River**, which carries the waters of the Great Lakes to the Atlantic Ocean. The river is called the *Mother of Canada* because it was the route of explorers, fur traders, and colonists. The **St. Lawrence Seaway**—a system of canals, locks, and dams—allows ships to sail from the Atlantic to the Great Lakes.
- The **Yukon River**, North America's third-longest river, which flows across the Yukon and Alaska to the Bering Sea.

Canada has the world's longest navigable coastline, about one-tenth of the world's forest, and about one-fifth of the world's remaining wilderness outside of Antarctica. With this landscape Canada offers one of the best places in the world for outdoor adventures (see the Profile).

The Climate

Weather across Canada varies immensely from east to west. Parts of eastern Canada have short snowy winters, mild springs, warm summers, and long autumns. The cold Labrador Current flowing south along the Atlantic Coast keeps the coastal region relatively cool during the summer. When the cold current meets the warm water of the Gulf Stream, fogs form along the coast. In southern Ontario, the Great Lakes temper both winter cold and summer heat. The landlocked prairies have bitterly cold and long winters but warm to hot summers. The Rockies have short summers and long, severe winters. The Pacific Coast around Vancouver has mild winters and often heavy rainfall.

Only the most adventurous go to Canada's far north, where winters are long, dark, and bitterly cold, and snow flurries are not unknown even in August. Summers have twenty-four hours of daylight.

The People and Their History

The people of the Arctic are perhaps the most distinctive of Canada's native people. Until recently they were called *Eskimos*. The term used today is Inuit (*IHN yoo iht*), which means "the people."

Canada's other original inhabitants, the *First Nations*, are the people who used to be called *Indians*. Although they belong to many nations, each with its own language and culture, members have joined together to assert their identity. From the totem poles and wood carvings of the west coast to the basketwork of the east coast, First Nation communities use art not only for expression of their cultures but also for commercial development.

The French and British established Canadian settlements in the early 1600s (see Figure 5.2). Their competition for dominance ended in the late 18th century when the British won control. In the 19th century, Britain's Canadian colonies formed the Dominion of Canada. Settlers pushed west, and new provinces were formed. In 1931 Canada became an independent nation.

Many Canadians trace their heritage to the First Nations, to British or French settlers, or to English Loyalists from the United States who came north because they did not support the American Revolution. Others are descendants of eastern European immigrants who helped propel Canada's westward expansion in the late 19th and early 20th centuries. Recently, people from southern Europe, Asia, South America, and the Caribbean have made Canada their home.

Canada's cultural diversity provides attractions for visitors, but it has also brought tensions within the country. Best known is the Anglo-French divide. In 1774 Britain recognized the right of French Canadians to retain aspects of their culture, including their language. Québec has kept its distinctiveness ever since, and some people have sought independence from Canada. The country's diversity should be clear in the following sections, as the attractions of each of the provinces and territories are outlined.

✔ CHECK-UP

Features of Canada's environment include

- ✔ Canadian Shield, a rocky region that covers about half of eastern Canada.
- ✔ Mountains in western Canada.
- ✔ Icecaps and tundra in the far north.
- ✔ Rocky coastline with fjords along both the Pacific and the Atlantic.
- ✔ Prairies east of the Rockies.
- ✔ Vast forests and wilderness areas.
- ✔ Subarctic climate in more than half the country.

Canada's culture is notable for

- ✔ Its democratic government.
- ✔ Its multiculturalism.

The Atlantic Provinces

Four provinces—Newfoundland, Nova Scotia, Prince Edward Island, and New Brunswick—border the Atlantic and are known as the Atlantic or Maritime provinces (see Figure 5.3). Most of the people live in coastal settlements. The fishing villages attract visitors with their bays, coves, inlets, cliffs, and peaceful way of life.

Newfoundland and Labrador

Canada's easternmost province, Newfoundland (*NOO fund land*) includes both the island of Newfoundland and **Labrador** on the mainland. Labrador is largely undisturbed wilderness, remote even by Canadian standards.

Newfoundland is three times the size of New Brunswick, Nova Scotia, and Prince Edward Island combined, but it receives only about as many visitors in a year as Toronto does in a weekend. It attracts the vacationer who is seeking the rugged outdoors. Hunting and fishing camps are accessible by small plane.

St. John's Newfoundland's largest city is St. John's. Located on the east side of Newfoundland Island, it is the easternmost city in North America. In fact, St. John's is closer to Ireland than it is to Toronto. In 1901 St. John's Signal Hill was the site of Guglielmo Marconi's (1874–1937) first transatlantic radio transmission. Near St. John's is **Cape Spear National Historic Park**, North America's easternmost point.

L'Anse aux Meadows National Historic Park The oldest European settlement yet discovered in North America is L'Anse aux Meadows, situated on a windswept headland at the tip of Newfoundland's Great Northern

FIGURE 5.3

The Atlantic Provinces

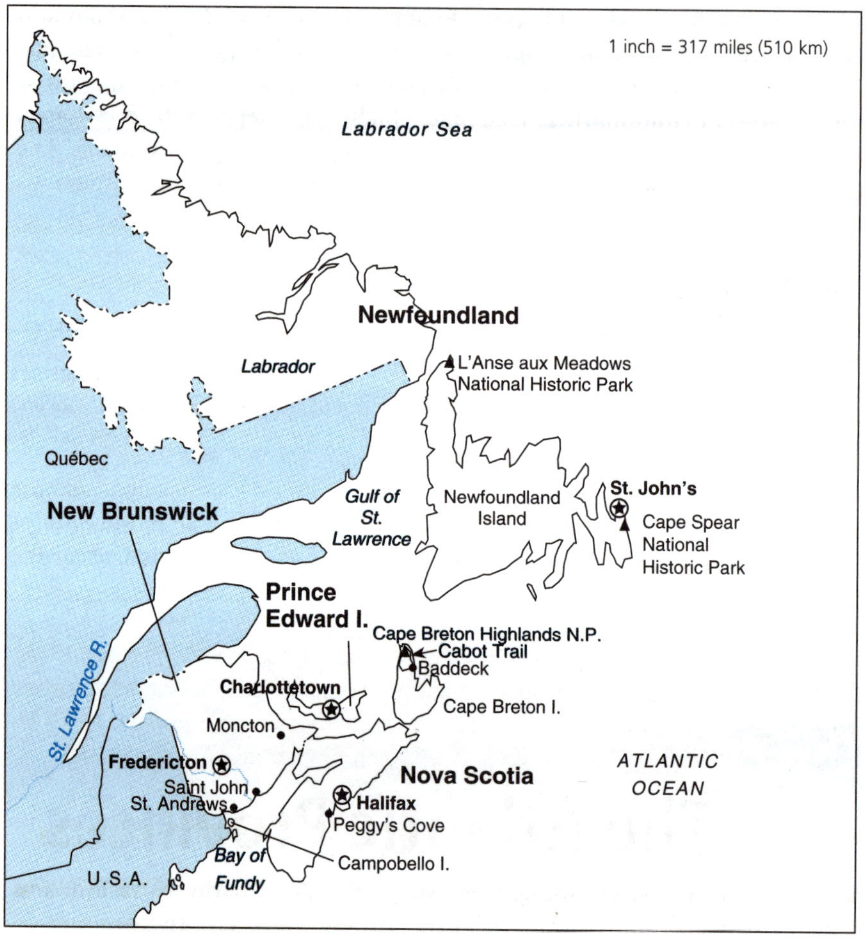

Peninsula. Six sod houses remain from a 10th-century Viking settlement. It is the only fully authenticated Norse site south or west of Greenland.

Prince Edward Island (PEI)

South of Newfoundland in the Gulf of St. Lawrence is Canada's smallest province, Prince Edward Island (PEI). Linked to mainland Canada by the Confederation Bridge, PEI has stretches of sandy beaches with a gently rolling inland plain. The water is not considered warm by Caribbean lovers, however.

Sailing, surfing, fishing, golfing, bicycling, and enjoying a relaxed way of life are PEI's principal appeals. Golfers can find excellent packages in May and October before high-season prices kick in.

Charlottetown is PEI's population center and capital. In summer, the Charlottetown Festival presents a musical version of *Anne of Green Gables*, based on the book by novelist Lucy Maud Montgomery (1874–1942), an island native. On the island's north central shore, tourists can visit the simple white Green Gables Farmhouse.

U.S. travelers can reach Nova Scotia by driving, but sailing between Yarmouth and Bar Harbor, Maine, saves approximately 725 miles (1,167 km) of highway travel.

Nova Scotia

Fishing villages dot Nova Scotia's (*NOH vuh SKOH shuh*) coastline. Most of the province is a peninsula jutting into the Atlantic, with **Cape Breton Island** to the northeast. Only a narrow strip of land and a section of the Trans-Canada Highway join Nova Scotia to the mainland province of New Brunswick.

French pioneers gave the name *Acadia* to the area. Title passed back and forth between France and Britain. In 1713 the Treaty of Utrecht awarded Nova Scotia to the British, and officialdom felt unable to trust the French settlers. The British rounded up, deported, and dispersed the French Acadians to the American colonies. Many ended up migrating to Louisiana, where their descendants are known as *Cajuns*.

Travelers come to Nova Scotia for its beauty, picturesque villages, and ethnic festivals. The peninsula features a series of interconnecting routes, each with a different view of a celebrated shore.

American Henry Wadsworth Longfellow (1807–1882) told the story of the deportation of the Acadians in "Evangeline—A Tale of Acadie," a poem that produced the province's nickname, *Land of Evangeline*.

Halifax The largest city in the four Atlantic provinces is Halifax, Nova Scotia's capital and the commercial and maritime center of Atlantic Canada. It has a waterfront casino and the second-largest natural harbor in the world after Sydney, Australia. Cruise ships visit on their way to the St. Lawrence River.

Highlights of Halifax include its waterfront shops and restaurants and the Citadel, a star-shaped stone fortress built in 1828. The Maritime Museum of the Atlantic has relics from the *Titanic*. Many of those who died when the famous ship sank are buried nearby.

Peggy's Cove Peggy's Cove faces the Atlantic at the mouth of a bay, a 45-minute drive along a winding coastal highway from Halifax. The hamlet's brightly colored houses huddle around a gap in massive granite boulders. With its lighthouse, Peggy's Cove is probably the most photographed village in Canada.

Peggy's Cove Lighthouse, Nova Scotia

Cape Breton Island and the Cabot Trail Nova Scotia's most scenic attraction is **Cape Breton Highlands National Park**. Cape Breton Island is actually two islands surrounding an inland sea connected to Nova Scotia by the Canso Causeway. Of the two islands, the western one is the more scenic.

The best-known scenic route is the **Cabot Trail**, named after the Italian explorer who landed in the area in 1497. The trail begins and ends in **Baddeck**, which is also the site of the Alexander Graham Bell National Historic Park. Bell (1847–1922), the inventor of the telephone, spent many years in Baddeck. The 187-mile (301 km) trail was voted North America's most spectacular ocean drive by the American Bus Association in 2003. It circles the northern part of the island with cliff views, charming villages, and sudden sights of sea and mountain.

Most people drive the Cabot Trail in a clockwise direction to cling to the inside of the road. Although tourists can drive the trail in a day, they shouldn't. Three or four days is a better allotment of time to try a lobster burger at one of the clam shacks, to breathe some fresh sea air, or just to sit on the porch of one of the modest resorts and relax.

ON THE SPOT

The Franklins live in Philadelphia. They had planned a two-week driving trip to eastern Canada in July, but they are having second thoughts because business constraints have limited their time to one week. They would like to see some scenery and relax. What would you suggest?

The Franklins might consider a fly-drive trip to Nova Scotia and the Cabot Trail. They can fly to Sydney airport, 40 miles (64 km) east of the trail, and pick up a rental car at the airport. To save the stress of driving, land tours are available from late May to early October from Baddeck. Two- and three-night motorcoach tours circle the Cabot Trail. Some stop at the Keltic Lodge, where guests can enjoy rose gardens, golf, and gourmet cuisine fresh from the sea. Or the Franklins might enjoy one of the boat tours of village harbors, nearby islands, and marine life, including whale watching. The weather is always uncertain in this maritime climate, so you might recommend that they bring warm sweaters and raingear.

New Brunswick

West of Nova Scotia, on the border of Maine, is New Brunswick. Both English and French are the official languages of New Brunswick, making it the only officially bilingual province in Canada.

New Brunswick is known for its natural beauty, for the traditions of the English Loyalists and French Acadian settlers, and for the tides of the **Bay of Fundy**. The upper part of the bay has the world's highest tides. The tides rise and fall in a range that is sometimes greater than 50 feet (15 m). (Their height is caused by the bay's funnel shape.) The tides flow into rivers along the coast twice a day in a wall of water called a **bore**.

Moncton From the Bay of Fundy, the bore flows inland along a river to Moncton. Here the traveler can see both the final effects of the tidal bore (commonly just a ripple) and the optical illusion of Magnetic Hill, where the road seems to be going uphill when it actually goes downhill.

Saint John, New Brunswick, is never abbreviated, presumably to avoid confusion with St. John's, Newfoundland.

Fredericton and Saint John New Brunswick's capital is the small inland city of Fredericton. The province's largest city, Saint John, is near the mouth of the Saint John River. Saint John's major attraction is Reversing Falls Rapids, where tidal effects create rapids that change direction depending on the tide.

St. Andrews This resort town near the Maine border is the access point for excursions to the Bay of Fundy islands: Grand Manan, Deer Island, and **Campobello**, which was the summer home of U.S. President Franklin D. Roosevelt.

✔ CHECK-UP

The Atlantic provinces are
- ✔ Newfoundland; its capital is St. John's.
- ✔ Prince Edward Island; its capital is Charlottetown.
- ✔ Nova Scotia; its capital is Halifax.
- ✔ New Brunswick; its capital is Fredericton, but its largest city is Saint John.

For travelers, highlights of the Atlantic provinces include
- ✔ Unspoiled scenery.
- ✔ Site of the oldest known European settlement in North America at L'Anse aux Meadows, Newfoundland.
- ✔ Golf and the Green Gables Farmhouse on Prince Edward Island.
- ✔ Cabot Trail on Cape Breton Island, Nova Scotia.
- ✔ Tides of New Brunswick's Bay of Fundy.

Québec

West of the Atlantic provinces is Québec (*kwih BEHK* or *kay BEHK*). In land area it is about twice the size of Texas. As Figure 5.4 shows, it is almost entirely surrounded by water. Most of the province is part of the Shield. At its eastern end, on the **Gaspé** (*gas PAY*) **Peninsula**, the Appalachian Mountains begin their long march down through the United States. Most of the population lives in the lowlands along the St. Lawrence River. Here the summers are warm and pleasant; the winters are long and snowy.

Explorers wrote of the "sweet water" that natives drew from maple trees. Today, Québec tree farms produce more maple syrup than the rest of the world put together.

French is the official language of Québec—a designation that deters some tourists and attracts others. The French cuisine of the province, however, is certainly an attraction. Each year tourists are drawn to Winter Carnival in Québec City and the International Jazz Festival in Montréal; pilgrims visit the province's shrines, families vacation in the wilderness, and sports fans ski or hike in the Laurentian Mountains.

The Cities

Québec City is the capital, but **Montréal** (*mahn tree AWL*) is the largest city. Their decided French flavor makes them seem more foreign to visitors than other Canadian cities. Tour operators offer trips to Montréal and Québec City throughout the year.

FIGURE 5.4 Québec

➤ PROFILE

Festivals in Québec

Québec's festivals are a big attraction. Some of the best known are

- Winter Carnival (*Carnival d'Hiver*) each February in Québec City, with elaborate ice sculptures, winter games, parades, and music.
- The International Jazz Festival in Montréal in July, featuring both international and local musicians.
- The World Film Festival each August in Montréal.

Québec City The point where the St. Charles River flows into the St. Lawrence is the site of Québec City. The name came from the Algonquian word *kebec*, "the place where the river narrows." Built in the 17th century, Canada's oldest city is one of its most beautiful. It is North America's only walled city. Cobbled lanes, old houses, and ancient churches tumble from a rocky promontory named Cap Diamont. The rock's fortifications protected the *Haute Ville*, or Upper Town. The harbor area below is known as *Basse Ville*, or Lower Town. Place Royale in Lower Town is the picturesque square where Samuel de Champlain established his settlement of New France in the early 1600s.

The city's central landmark is a castlelike hotel, the Château Frontenac, one of a series built by the Canadian Pacific Railway. It commands the city from the top of a cliff. A promenade along the cliff, the Terrasse Dufferin, provides a view of the city and river below.

Château Frontenac, Québec City, Québec

Beyond the walls of the old city, the star-shaped Citadel, a huge fort, overlooks the town. West of the Citadel is Battlefields Park, also known as the *Plains of Abraham*, where a battle changed the course of Canadian history. In 1759 British troops headed by General James Wolfe (1727–1759) defeated the French forces led by Louis Joseph, Marquis de Montcalm (1712–1759), completing the British conquest of then-known North America.

Montréal Southwest of Québec City, the St. Lawrence and Ottawa Rivers meet and create an inland port at Montréal. A superb subway system (the Métro), a logical street grid, wide boulevards, and the vehicle-free

Underground City add to the visitor's enjoyment. Montréal is—after Paris—the world's largest French-speaking city. Language laws ensure the use of French in advertising and signs of all kinds.

A caleche in Montréal, Québec

Montréal extends over a large island, but the city's central core is divided into three sections. Vieux-Montréal, the heart of the old city, runs along the St. Lawrence River; Mont Royal is the large hill that rises up behind the city center; the modern downtown lies roughly between Vieux-Montréal and Mont Royal.

The Boulevard St. Laurent divides the city into east and west sectors. In the East End, older houses have curious balconies and steep outdoor staircases. Among the city's major streets are Rue Ste. Catherine, noted for its stores and restaurants; Sherbrooke, with shops, art galleries, and hotels; and Dorchester Boulevard, a wide street known for its skyscrapers.

In the summer, activity in Vieux-Montréal centers around Place Jacques-Cartier, where café tables line the cobbled streets. Nearby is the city's oldest church, Notre-Dame-de-Bonsecours. In the 19th century, when it became the Sailors Chapel, survivors of shipwrecks carved model ships and brought them to the church. The models are hung from the church's ceiling. Other historic sites are Place d'Armes, the site of a clash between natives and missionaries, and Place Royale, the site of Fort Montréal, built in 1642.

Additional highlights of Montréal include

- Dominion Square, traditionally held to be the heart of the city.
- Underground City (*la Ville Souterraine*), inspired by Montréal's humid summers and icy winters. An ever-expanding network of passages allows people to shop, go to work, and visit museums and theaters without ever setting foot on the city's streets above.
- Place Ville-Marie, a modern office center. Here are some of the main entrances to the malls and walkways of the Underground City.
- St. Helen's Island in the St. Lawrence, home to a casino and an amusement park, La Ronde.

Casino gambling throughout Canada operates under government supervision.

Other Places to Visit

Many places worth visiting are just a short distance from Québec City or Montréal.

St. Lawrence Region and the Gaspé Peninsula Short trips from Québec City travel north along the St. Lawrence to **Montmorency Falls**, which is higher than Niagara, and to **Ste. Anne-de-Beaupré**, a major point of Catholic pilgrimage.

For those with time, a drive to the mountainous Gaspé Peninsula on the St. Lawrence's southern shore is a possibility. For scenery lovers it is one of the most attractive routes in Canada. At the end of the peninsula is the small resort of **Percé** (*peer SAY*; meaning "pierced") and Percé Rock. The rock's name comes from holes worn by waves.

The Saguenay Ships cruise from the St. Lawrence up the Saguenay (*sag uh NAY*) River to view the Saguenay Fjord, a relic of the Ice Age. From July to September whales feed where the fresh water of the Saguenay meets the salt water of the Gulf of St. Lawrence.

The Laurentians The wooded hills of the Laurentian Mountains extend across Québec. The most popular resorts are just a 30- to 60-minute drive north of Montréal. The mountains and lakes draw sports enthusiasts, especially cross-country skiers in winter. During summer the resorts offer opportunities for hiking, mountain biking, rock climbing, white-water kayaking, sailing, golfing, and fishing.

Mont Tremblant in the Laurentians is the highest skiable peak in eastern Canada. Ski season extends from mid-November to mid-April. During the dark depths of winter, the mountain can get very cold. Parking spaces at major resorts have electrical outlets for motorists, whose cars are equipped with block heaters to plug in their cars.

Skiing made its entry into North America in 1879 on the "long snowshoes" of a Norwegian immigrant. He had settled in the Laurentians, and his method of winter transportation caught on as a sport.

✔ CHECK-UP

Québec's major cities are

- ✔ Québec City, the capital of the province.
- ✔ Montréal, the largest city in the province.

Highlights for visitors to Québec province include

- ✔ Vieux-Montréal and Upper and Lower Towns of Québec City.
- ✔ Winter Carnival in Québec City in early February.
- ✔ International Jazz Festival in Montréal in July.
- ✔ French cuisine.
- ✔ Winter and summer sports in the Laurentians.
- ✔ Relaxation in the Gaspé.

Ontario

Next to Québec—in both size and location—is Ontario (*ahn TAIR ee oh*). It is Canada's southernmost province, but it extends as far north as Hudson Bay (see Figure 5.5). Near the bay the land is flat, with peat bogs and a narrow belt of permafrost. In the south, lowlands lie along the St. Lawrence River and the Great Lakes. Most of Ontario's population lives here, where the land and climate resemble the U.S. Midwest.

Ontario is Canada's dominant province, its most populous and wealthiest. It can amply supply a traveler with both urban sophistication and wilderness beauty.

The Cities

Ontario is the home of Canada's capital, **Ottawa**, as well as **Toronto**, the provincial capital and the country's largest city.

Ottawa Ottawa (*AHT uh wuh*) sits on rolling land. Attractive parks and stately government buildings add beauty to the site. The Rideau (*rih DOH*) Canal cuts through the city on its way from the Ottawa River to Lake Ontario. In winter, citizens ice-skate on the canal, claiming it to be the world's longest skating rink.

Tourists come to see Parliament Hill, the Peace Tower, and the locks of the Rideau Canal. Most of the sights cluster in the downtown grids south and east of Parliament Hill known as Upper and Lower Town. The city's shopping districts center around the Sparks Street Mall in Upper Town and Byward Market and Rideau Street in Lower Town. Canada displays its cultural heritage at the National Gallery of Canada, Canadian Museum of Civilization, National Museum of Science and Technology, and Canadian Museum of Nature.

FIGURE 5.5 Ontario

Former Queen Juliana of the Netherlands sent tulip bulbs as a gift to Ottawa. During World War II, Juliana, then a princess, lived in the city while German troops occupied her country. The Dutch government continues to send bulbs each year.

The CN Tower was built by Canadian National Railways to carry TV and radio transmissions. It is the biggest attraction on Toronto's lakefront skyline. Visitors are ferried up the tower in elevators that travel 15 miles (22 km) an hour on the outside of the building, with just a glass front between them and a free-fall.

Ottawa's festivals and fairs also attract visitors. Annual events include the *Tulip Festival* in May, when more than 3 million bulbs bloom in parks, along roadways, and on the grounds of public buildings.

Toronto The financial and communications center of Canada is Toronto (*tuh RAHN toe*). It is nestled in hills that roll down to the northern shore of Lake Ontario. UN literature calls the city the world's most ethnically diverse.

In the 17th century, the city's site was on a route used by French fur traders. Then it was a fort guarding the troublesome American border. The area was a muddy malaria-ridden swamp. Today, the mud is paved over, the mosquitoes have flown away, and the Americans are less trouble than they used to be. Toronto is a cultural center, with the St. Lawrence Centre for the Performing Arts, the Royal Ontario Museum, the Ontario Science Center, and the Art Gallery of Ontario. The city rivals New York and London as a professional theater center.

Toronto was developed on a grid pattern. Main arteries run north from the lakefront. Within the city, an underground network links the buildings to create a neighborhood of shopping malls, cinemas, and restaurants. Yonge Street is the main commercial avenue. Its intersection at Bloor Street is the city's fashion hub. The Hockey Hall of Fame at the corner of Front and Yonge Streets attracts sports fans.

Landmarks include the SkyDome stadium crouching at the feet of the CN Tower, currently the world's tallest freestanding structure. On a clear day you can glimpse Niagara Falls from the top of the tower. At its foot is a district called Harbourfront, with restaurants, boutiques, galleries, and antique stores.

Other Places to Visit

Ontario's lakes and woods offer adventure and sports, but the province is best known for its cultural and sightseeing attractions.

Festivals Ontario is home to drama festivals from April through October. The *Shaw Festival* at Niagara-on-the-Lake presents plays by George Bernard Shaw and other major playwrights. From May through October, the *Shakespearean Festival* at the Festival Theater in **Stratford**, west of Toronto, produces plays that rival England's Stratford productions.

CLOSE-UP: EASTERN CANADA

Who is a good prospect for a trip to eastern Canada? Individuals, families, senior citizens, and student groups should each find something to their taste in eastern Canada. Especially good prospects include people living in the northeastern United States and student groups, such as French clubs, who like the idea of visiting a foreign country to try their language skills but cannot afford the time or cost of international travel.

Why would they visit eastern Canada? It offers interesting cities, an opportunity to experience a different culture without going too far from home, scenic beauty, and the opportunity for outdoor activity. Its nearness to the large population of the U.S. Northeast and relatively low cost add to its attractiveness.

Where would they go? Golfers might enjoy Prince Edward Island, skiers or hikers might consider the Laurentians, and theater lovers might choose Toronto. Baseball, basketball, and hockey fans might want to see games in Toronto or Montréal. Those wanting to know about Canada's history can find interesting sites in Halifax, Acadia, Québec City, and Montréal.

If travelers have time for only a short trip, they might limit their tour to the Maritime provinces or concentrate on Montréal or Québec City. If they have time for a ten-day trip and want to sample as much as possible, they might take a motorcoach itinerary like this one.

Day 1 Fly to Toronto, Ontario. If your flight arrives in time, the afternoon is free to explore the city and arrange for evening theater tickets.

Days 2–3 Toronto–Ottawa, Ontario. Morning sightseeing tour of Toronto takes you past the CN Tower and Fort York, a reconstruction of the city's original settlement. On the drive to Ottawa, you can enjoy a short cruise through the Thousand Islands. Day 3 includes a morning tour of Ottawa, afternoon at leisure to shop or visit a museum.

Day 4 Ottawa–Montréal, Québec. A journey to the largest French city after Paris.

Days 5–6 Montréal. A morning tour visits Old Montréal, Notre Dame Basilica, and Parc Mont-Royal, acres of landscaped grounds in the center of the city. Afternoon of Day 5 and all of Day 6 are free for individual exploration.

Day 7 Montréal–Québec City. On the drive through the Laurentians, stop at a local orchard for a cider tasting.

Days 8–9 Québec City. The city tour showcases the dramatic history and timeless grace of North America's only fortified city. Day 9 is a day at leisure.

Days 10–11 Québec City–Isle aux Coudres. Travel east along the shores of the St. Lawrence, stopping en route at the Basilica of Ste. Anne-de-Beaupré and the Canyon des Chutes Ste. Anne, a majestic waterfall. A short ferry ride takes you to Isle aux Coudres, an island in the heart of the river. On Day 11, enjoy a guided tour of the island and a whale-watching cruise.

Day 12 Return to Québec. Time to go home or possibly extend for two more nights in the city.

When is the best time to visit? Winter is likely to be harsh, long, and dark so far north. May to mid-October is likely to be the best time for a trip. The travelers should know that this period is also high season and that the southernmost parts of Québec and Ontario can be hot and humid in summer. Those interested in skiing, Québec City's Winter Carnival, or professional winter sports must go when these attractions take place.

If the travelers say, "Canada is too much like home," how would you respond? Depending on the travelers' interests, you might point to the varied cultures of Québec or to natural attractions with no equal in the "lower forty-eight" states—such as the Saguenay Fjord, the tides in the Bay of Fundy, and the unspoiled wilderness of northern Québec and Newfoundland.

Think back. If you get this question often, it might be because you forgot to qualify the travelers (ask what the travelers are interested in) before you offered suggestions.

In 1859 the French tightrope walker Blondin made his way across Niagara Falls on a high wire. Others have tried going over the falls in a barrel or other contraptions; many did not survive. Today, it is illegal to try without a special permit, but in 2003 one lucky man survived a jump with no permit and no special protection whatsoever.

Niagara Falls A 90-minute drive from Toronto takes the traveler to Niagara Falls, a natural wonder on the Niagara River between Lakes Erie and Ontario and a celebrated honeymoon destination. The river forms part of the U.S.–Canadian border.

Niagara is actually two waterfalls, Horseshoe Falls in Ontario and American Falls in New York State. Eighty-five percent of Niagara's water flows over Horseshoe Falls. After the falls, the river plunges into a steep gorge and then into Whirlpool Rapids.

The falls can be experienced in several ways. For a close-up view, the little *Maid of the Mist* boats have sailed visitors to the falls' base since 1876. On land, an elevator takes people onto an observation platform or into tunnels at the base of the falls that go behind the mighty wall of water. At night, wide beams of colored light illuminate the falls. Millions of people visit annually, most between April and October.

George Boldt, builder of Boldt Castle in the Thousand Islands, was at one time the owner of the Waldorf Astoria hotel in New York City. His chef invented Thousand Islands salad dressing to honor Boldt's favorite summer vacation spot.

The Thousand Islands According to Iroquois legends, spirits battled for control of the St. Lawrence, throwing rocks at each other. The boulders that fell short landed in the narrows where the St. Lawrence empties into Lake Ontario, leaving the more than 1,700 rocks that are called the Thousand Islands. The islands are on both sides of the boundary between Canada and the United States.

Day and longer cruises on small ships sail among the islands and visit summer homes built by the rich on both sides of the river. A popular stop on the New York side is Boldt Castle on Heart Island. George Boldt sought to express his love for his wife by building a castle like those in his homeland, the Rhine Valley of Germany. When his wife died unexpectedly in 1904, the palatial summer home was left unfinished.

✔ CHECK-UP

The major cities of Ontario are
- ✔ Ottawa, the capital of Canada.
- ✔ Toronto, the capital of Ontario and the largest city in Canada.

Highlights for visitors to Ontario include
- ✔ Museums of Ottawa.
- ✔ Theater and big-city life in Toronto.
- ✔ Niagara Falls.
- ✔ Shakespearean and Shaw Festivals.
- ✔ Thousand Islands.

The Prairie Provinces

The so-called Prairie provinces are Manitoba, Saskatchewan, and Alberta (see Figure 5.6). The pioneers called the area a "sea of grass." In fact, very little land in these provinces is flat, and very little consists of grassland. The grasslands are in Saskatchewan and southern Alberta. North of them is a ribbon of land called the "wheat-growing crescent," and farther north is a zone of rolling hills and fertile farming. The land then merges with the largest zone of all—the **boreal forest**, a blanket of trees and muskeg bog that covers more than half of the region. Except for the western edge of Alberta, where the Rocky Mountains begin, these provinces are not tourist magnets, although each has its attractions.

FIGURE 5.6

The Prairie Provinces

Manitoba

Each year in mid-August **Winnepeg**, Manitoba's capital, hosts *Folklorama*, a two-week festival of Canadian culture. Visitors can view ethnic dances and handicrafts, listen to music, and try the national dishes of the many cultural groups that make Manitoba their home.

Churchill in Manitoba is called the *Polar Bear Capital of the World*. It is not muggers that people fear as they walk down its dark streets; it is *nanuk*, the polar bear. The bears can grow more than 10 feet (3 m) long and weigh more than 1,500 pounds (675 kg). They are North America's largest land carnivores. The animals come to town in June, about the time the pack ice on Hudson Bay begins to break up. Once on land, they amble around the town's outskirts, occasionally—and dangerously—wandering up the main street in search of food. They remain ashore until around November, when the hardening ice provides a platform for them to resume their more normal hunting habits.

Polar bear

Thousands of tourists come to see the bears. Churchill is accessible by air or by a two-day train trip from Winnipeg. Giant tundra buggies allow tourists to view the animals at close range in warmth and safety.

Saskatchewan

Saskatchewan (*sas KACH uh wahn*) is known as *Canada's Bread Basket*. It produces about 2 percent of the entire world's supply of wheat. Huge grain elevators, nicknamed "cathedrals of the plains," are a familiar sight as you cross the province. **Regina** (*rih JI nuh*) is the capital, but **Saskatoon** is the largest city.

Alberta

In Alberta, cattle ranches, the oil industry, and the Rocky Mountains set the province apart as the beginning of Canada's West. The Canadian Rockies begin their rise along the Great Divide, which forms the province's border with British Columbia.

ON THE SPOT

Xenia and Tom Lee and their two children Kishia and Michael (ages ten and thirteen) from Detroit plan to attend the Calgary Stampede and then spend another four days in Canada. They don't want to bother driving, but they would like a chance to see Canada's scenery and visit a city. Is this possible?

Calgary's location holds the answer. From Calgary the Lees could take the train to Vancouver, British Columbia. The train's dome cars offer magnificent views of western Canada's national parks. Kishia and Michael might enjoy the freedom to stretch their legs that train travel provides. After the train trip, the family would have time to explore Vancouver or nearby Victoria before boarding a flight home.

Lake Louise, Banff National Park, Alberta

➤ PROFILE

Skiing in Canada

Popular ski areas include

- Tremblant and Mount Ste. Anne, Québec.
- Banff/Lake Louise in Alberta.
- Whistler/Blackcomb, north of Vancouver, British Columbia.

Alberta has more land devoted to national and provincial parks than any other province. Vacationers can head north to hunt bear, caribou, deer, elk, and moose. Others can stay at deluxe guest ranches in cattle country.

Edmonton The capital of Alberta is Edmonton. It lies in a rich farm region about 325 miles (523 km) north of the U.S.–Canadian border, making it North America's northernmost major city. It has a ferocious winter climate, but a light rail rapid transit line and a citywide system of "ped-ways" (covered walkways) offer refuge. Edmonton is the home of the West Edmonton Mall, one of the world's largest shopping centers.

Calgary Alberta's largest city is Calgary (*KAL guh ree*). South of Edmonton, it sits in the foothills of the Rocky Mountains. Skyscrapers and suburbs sprawl in all directions. Calgary grew up as a cow town and continues to be a major cattle center, but oil and gas were discovered in 1914 and contributed mightily to the city's wealth.

The city is famous for its *Calgary Exhibition and Stampede,* the world's largest rodeo. For ten days each July, visitors enjoy chuck wagon races, livestock shows, and rodeo events. In winter, Calgary offers ultramodern facilities for downhill and cross-country skiing.

Banff National Park West of Edmonton and running north-south for more than 300 miles (483 km), Banff, Jasper, and Yoho National Parks combine with several smaller parks to form the Rocky Mountain World Heritage Site. Yoho is in the province of British Columbia. Banff, known as the *Jewel of the Rockies,* is the oldest (established in 1887), most famous, and arguably the most beautiful of the parks.

Banff was originally a railway settlement. When the Canadian Pacific reached Banff in 1883, the train route opened up the mountains to the public. Thirty-seven miles (60 km) from Banff town, blue, blue **Lake Louise** is another sightseeing mecca.

The railroad built castlelike hotels at both Lake Louise and Banff. Banff Springs was built after railway workers discovered hot sulfur springs bubbling from the earth. The hotel has restaurants, nightclubs, conference facilities, tennis courts, a golf course, and even a rumored ghost.

Jasper National Park Heading north, the **Icefields Parkway** links Lake Louise to Jasper National Park, the largest park in the Rockies. The road takes you past more than a hundred glaciers and dozens of waterfalls. It is the kind of scenery that turns the car's windshield into a picture postcard. The Columbia Icefield, the Northern Hemisphere's largest glacier area below the Arctic Circle, is partly in each park.

The Parkway can be driven year-round. The busy season is mid-June to September. Services and facilities are scarce. The Icefield Centre (open May through October) has an interpretive center, restaurants, gift shops, and hotel rooms. From there travelers can book Athabasca Glacier sno-coach tours. Bulbous-tired vehicles provide temperature-controlled rides on the river of ice.

Jasper was an old fur-trading post; now it is a resort town with facilities for fishing, rafting, and hiking in summer and for cross-country and downhill skiing in winter. At Jasper Park Lodge they tell of a moose invading the golf course and staying for months; no one was eager to anger the unregistered guest. Helicopter trips venture into mountain ranges with such enticing names as the Cariboos, the Bugaboos, and the Bobbie Burns.

✔ CHECK-UP

Major cities of the Prairie provinces include

- ✔ Winnipeg, the capital of Manitoba.
- ✔ Regina, the capital of Saskatchewan.
- ✔ Saskatoon, the largest city in Saskatchewan.
- ✔ Edmonton, the capital of Alberta.
- ✔ Calgary, the largest city in Alberta.

Highlights of the Prairie provinces include

- ✔ Wide-open spaces.
- ✔ Folklorama in Winnipeg.
- ✔ Polar Bear Capital, Churchill.
- ✔ Calgary Stampede.
- ✔ National parks such as Banff and Jasper.
- ✔ Columbia Icefield and Icefields Parkway in Alberta.
- ✔ Athabasca Glacier sno-coach tours.

British Columbia

Canada's Pacific province is British Columbia (BC). It is bordered to the south by the United States, to the southwest by the ocean, and to the northwest by the Alaska Panhandle (see Figure 5.7). The province includes the **Queen Charlotte Islands**, 60 miles (97 km) from the mainland, and **Vancouver Island**, 285 miles (459 km) long, on the southwest coast.

FIGURE 5.7

British Columbia

Steep forested mountains rise from BC's shore. The interior has high mountains and rugged plateaus. To the east, forests, grasslands, and lakes march to meet the Rockies.

On the coast, winters are mild and summers warm. In the interior, winters are cold with heavy snow, and summers are warm. On Vancouver Island, travelers should expect rain.

The Cities

Victoria is the capital of British Columbia, but Vancouver (*van KOO vuhr*) is the largest city.

The Indian tribes of the Pacific Northwest carved totems—symbols for a tribe, clan, or family, similar to the family crests of Europe—on wooden poles. Thunderbird Park, in Victoria, British Columbia, has a collection of historic poles.

Victoria On the southeastern tip of Vancouver Island lies Victoria. Its attractions include an English atmosphere, scenic surroundings, narrow streets, and neat gardens. Many travelers visit Victoria from Seattle on a day cruise through the **San Juan Islands**. The city's Royal British Columbia Museum is regularly ranked as one of the top ten museums in North America.

Victoria's stately Empress Hotel dates from 1905. It is another of the Canadian Pacific Railway hotels. The hotel overlooks the Parliament Buildings and the waterfront. High tea is served daily.

For flower lovers, a tour of Victoria should include the Butchart Gardens, just outside the city. Robert Pim Butchart made a fortune out of Portland cement during the late 19th century and found himself with an exhausted limestone quarry. His wife suggested turning the quarry into a garden. The result is a lovely mix of lakes, trees, and flowers.

Heading out of the city, civilization quickly disappears. On Vancouver Island's western coast, the West Coast Trail in the **Pacific Rim National Park Reserve** has been hailed by the Sierra Club as one of the most spectacular and challenging hikes on the continent.

Vancouver Unlike Victoria, Vancouver is on the mainland. Few cities can match its setting, a dazzling downtown skyline ringed by the waters of the Pacific and the snowcapped peaks of the Coast Mountains. It is the air and sea gateway between the Pacific and North America, and Canada's busiest port. The combination of protecting mountains and Pacific winds produces an unexpectedly mild climate for a city so far north. The water of the harbor never freezes. On the waterfront, Canada Place is the landmark, a building with a roof of white sails. Cruises on the Inside Passage depart from there and from other nearby docks.

Vancouver is just 25 miles (40 km) north of the Canadian–U.S. border, about a 3.5-hour drive from Seattle.

Vancouver has grown rapidly and recently. Many natives recall their fathers talking about hunting in woods now covered by houses and roads. The city is on two ridges separated by an inlet called False Creek. The intersection of Granville and Georgia Streets is the heart of downtown. Stanley Park, a spit of land projecting into the sea, is the largest urban park in North America. It has a zoo, the Vancouver Public Aquarium, beaches, a lagoon, and a collection of totem poles.

Vancouver was originally known as Gastown, after saloonkeeper "Gassy Jack" Deighton, who talked a lot while he looked after the needs of lumbermen and sailors in the 1860s. The waterfront area where Gastown began has been remade into a cobbled-street district of boutiques, bars, and restaurants.

Vancouver is filled with museums. The Vancouver Museum and the Pacific Space Center form part of a cultural center. The Museum of

Anthropology, one of the finest of its kind, is located at the University of British Columbia.

Other Places to Visit

North of Vancouver the mountains and ocean meet, freshwater lakes and saltwater inlets join, and deep forests floored with ferns become windswept isles. The area has great appeal to those seeking nature at its finest.

National Parks Better known to tourists are British Columbia's ski resorts and national parks. The province has six national parks (see Table 5.1). In **Yoho National Park** visitors can enjoy another Canadian Pacific resort and Emerald Lake—a mountain-rimmed spot for hiking, canoeing, and horseback riding.

The Inside Passage The Inside Passage along Canada's Pacific Coast is part

CLOSE-UP: WESTERN CANADA

Who is a good prospect for a trip to western Canada? Outdoor adventure lovers, families, scenery fans, and those interested in western history should find something of interest in western Canada.

Why would they visit western Canada? Its national parks offer some of the world's most spectacular scenery. Travelers can tour by ferry, rental car, train, floatplane, sno-coach, or motorcoach. Some might visit, not to experience the great outdoors but to see the modern cities of Calgary, Edmonton, and Vancouver, which offer museums, nightlife, dining, and shopping.

Where would they go? Western Canada serves up the great outdoors both to those who want to experience nature in depth and to those who simply want to gaze on its grandeur from the window of a train or motorcoach. The fun and furor of the Calgary Stampede and the possibility of a ranch stay in Alberta are lures for activity seekers. Vancouver attracts those seeking the varied cultures of the Pacific Rim before or after a cruise on the Inside Passage to Alaska.

Many would enjoy the comfort of a tour by rail from Vancouver to Toronto on this itinerary.

Days 1–2 The tour begins with two nights in Vancouver. A half-day orientation tour takes you to Gastown and the lakes and gardens of Stanley Park. You have free time to explore and visit the museums.

Day 3 You board the train early this morning and begin the journey from Vancouver to Kamloops, a city in the heart of the great forests, through some of the world's finest scenery. Economy-class service allows use of the lounge, coffee shop, and dining car; meals and beverages are extra. You need to ask what meals the tour includes. Some upgrades to first-class service include special seating in the bilevel dome coach and hot meals in the dining room. You spend the night at a hotel in Kamloops.

Days 4–5 Reboard the train early in the morning. By early afternoon you arrive in Banff, your home for the next two nights. The next day you journey by motorcoach into Banff National Park. A cable car carries you to the top of Sulphur Mountain for views of the park. The afternoon features an optional excursion to the Valley of the Ten Peaks and Lake Louise.

Day 6 A drive along the Icefields Parkway takes you from Banff to Jasper National Park. After traveling through Athabasca Valley, depart the parkway and enjoy a sno-coach ride near the glacier. Join an optional raft tour down the Athabasca River, or proceed by coach to Jasper.

Day 7 Morning is free in Jasper; then depart by train from Jasper to Toronto across the Prairie provinces.

Day 8 Your tour ends in Toronto.

When is the best time to visit? Unless travelers are interested in winter sports, the best time to visit western Canada is from late May to late September. Darkness closes in early during the winter. During the summer the days are long and, at high elevations, delightfully cool.

If the travelers say, "We aren't very interested in any kind of roughing-it experience in the outdoors," how would you respond? You might point out the amenities of the resort hotels in the national parks: restaurants, nightclubs, shops, and service.

TABLE 5.1 National Parks of Alberta and British Columbia

National Park	Location	Description
Banff	Alberta	Oldest park; includes spectacular Lake Louise
Elk	Alberta	Oasis on the plains for rare species
Glacier	British Columbia	Alpine region with more than 100 glaciers
Gwaii Haanas	British Columbia	Forest reserves on Queen Charlotte Islands (visitors need advance arrangements) with rare plant and animal life
Jasper	Alberta	Site of Athabasca Glacier, Columbia Icefield, and Jasper resorts
Kootenay	British Columbia	Scenery and hot springs
Mount Revelstoke	British Columbia	Transition area from rain forest to alpine meadows
Pacific Rim	British Columbia	On Vancouver Island; part of West Coast Trail
Waterton Lakes	Alberta	Part of Waterton-Glacier International Peace Park
Wood Buffalo	Alberta Northwest Territories	North America's largest buffalo herd and the nesting grounds of the whooping crane
Yoho	British Columbia	Rocky Mountains scenery

of a dramatic cruise ship voyage, tracing a route north from the tip of Vancouver Island to Alaska. **Prince Rupert** is the end of the true Inside Passage, but ships continue to Ketchikan, the first town in Alaska, and beyond.

✔ CHECK-UP

Major cities of British Columbia are
- ✔ Victoria, the capital of the province.
- ✔ Vancouver, the province's largest city and the nation's busiest port.

Highlights of British Columbia for visitors include
- ✔ Vancouver's waterfront.
- ✔ High tea in Victoria.
- ✔ Butchart Gardens.
- ✔ National parks.

The North

North of the 60th parallel, Canada is divided into the territories of the Yukon, Northwest Territories, and Nunavut (see Figure 5.8), an area that makes up around 40 percent of Canada's land.

The Yukon

The Yukon (*YOO kahn*) territory is north of British Columbia and east of Alaska. The territory has rich mineral deposits, magnificent scenery, and few people. It is almost entirely mountainous.

Dawson In August 1896, prospectors discovered gold in the Klondike River where it meets the Yukon River near Dawson. It is estimated that at least 100,000 people came to Dawson. By 1899, the trek was over, and the town was left to sink into its permafrost. Today, its buildings lean from the thawing and freezing action of the ground. Houses rest on wooden pads to prevent sinking and to block their heat from thawing the ground.

Discovery Days each August re-creates the rush. A cabin once home to American writer Jack London (1876–1916) is open to visitors. London joined the gold rush, and his experiences inspired him to write *Call of the Wild* (1903) and *White Fang* (1906).

Whitehorse The capital and largest city of the Yukon, Whitehorse was the staging ground for prospectors emerging from Alaska's White Pass to descend the Yukon River to the Klondike and the gold fields. The boat trip on the Yukon's dangerous rapids ended many expeditions.

Alaska Highway After the heady days of the gold rush, mining and the Yukon declined. Then, in the wake of the attack on Pearl Harbor in 1941, the fear that the Japanese might invade via Alaska prompted President Franklin Roosevelt to order a highway linking Dawson Creek, British Columbia, to Fairbanks, Alaska. The Alaska Highway opened the Yukon, although it was not fully paved until the 1970s. Each year, more than 400,000 people travel the road's 1,397 miles (2,248 km). The Yukon section is regarded as the most scenic part.

Kluane National Park The entrance to Kluane (*kloo WAN ee*) National Park in southwestern Yukon is on the Alaska Highway at Haines Junction. In the park, the St. Elias Mountains include Canada's highest peak, **Mount Logan**. Hikers should check in at the park's reception center before trying the trails. The park is known for having Canada's highest concentration of grizzly bears.

After years of being forced to look for the Northwest Passage with Henry Hudson, his crew mutinied. Hudson, his son, and seven loyal seamen were set adrift in a small boat in the bay that carries his name. They were never seen again.

Mining is the most important industry in Canada's territories, but tourism is the second-largest source of income.

The Alaska Highway was originally called the Alcan Highway. In 1996 it was granted the status of International Historic Civil Engineering Landmark, one of only sixteen projects to be so recognized to date.

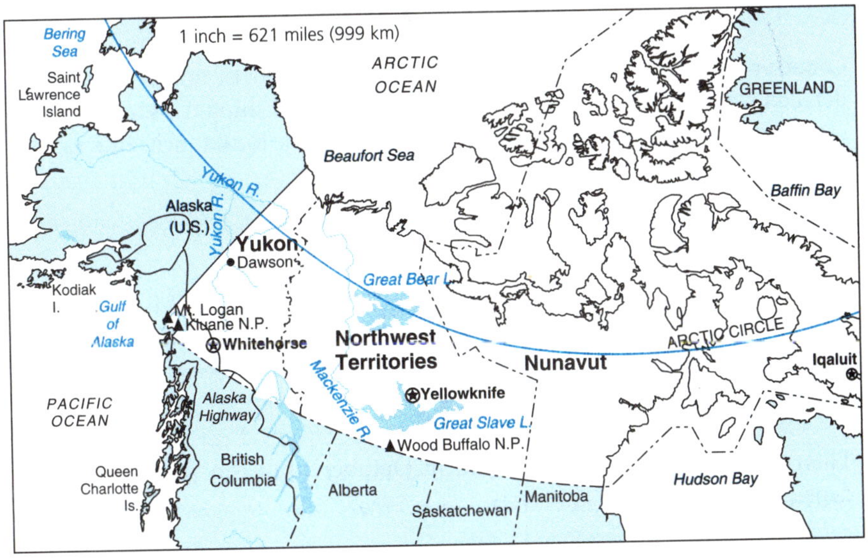

FIGURE 5.8 The North

North of Dawson, the Dempster Highway runs 448 miles (721 km) through the subarctic bush and tundra to Inuvik, above the Arctic Circle. The Eagle Plains Hotel is the only hotel on the only road to the Arctic Circle.

Northwest Territories

The Northwest Territories (NWT), lying between the Yukon and Nunavut, stretch to within 500 miles (800 km) of the North Pole. The land is crossed by the **Mackenzie River,** fed by **Great Slave Lake,** North America's deepest lake. The territories' capital, **Yellowknife,** is a gold-mining center on the shore of the lake. The city got its name from the yellow handles of the knives used to open dynamite boxes during the mining boom.

Nunavut

In 1999 Canada divided the Northwest Territories. The western part remained the Northwest Territories; the eastern part became the self-governing territory of the Inuit people. It was named *Nunavut,* meaning "our land." About half of Nunavut is north of the Arctic Circle. The territorial capital is Iqaluit.

Some Inuit continue to follow their traditional occupations—fishing, hunting, and trapping—but in general, the old Arctic life has ended. Inuit handicrafts continue to flourish with government support. Unique souvenirs include soapstone carvings picturing activities from traditional life. Inuit art is an investment. Genuine carvings have the trademark symbol of the igloo.

✔ CHECK-UP

Canada's far north has few people, but the territorial capitals are

- ✔ Whitehorse, Yukon.
- ✔ Yellowknife, Northwest Territories.
- ✔ Iqaluit, Nunavut.

Highlights of the far north for visitors include

- ✔ Unspoiled wilderness for the adventurous.
- ✔ Discovery Days in Dawson.
- ✔ Inuit culture.
- ✔ Alaska Highway.

Planning the Trip

Canada's national tourist office and the provincial tourist offices can provide detailed information about their areas. Hunting and fishing trips to wilderness areas are best arranged through guides licensed by the local tourist office.

Latitude must be kept in mind when deciding the best time to visit Canada. In summer, the days are long, particularly in the north, allowing plenty of time for outdoor activity. In winter, short days diminish the time a skier might want to spend on the slopes.

When to Go

Each Canadian season has its attractions. Fall brings colorful foliage, spring produces sweet water (maple sap), and winter is ski and ice festival season. Summer is popular with families, outdoor lovers, and those who want to visit festivals and attractions.

Canada's busiest tourist season is between May and Canadian Thanksgiving (the second weekend in October), but the best time to visit depends on the traveler's interests.

Preparing the Traveler

Travelers might appreciate the following tips:

- Canada and the United States share one of the world's longest unguarded borders, but no matter how friendly the partnership, customs and immigration procedures are in effect at gateways.
- Summer vacationers should bring along bug spray; the mosquitoes and black flies have a fierce reputation.
- The Canadian dollar and the U.S. dollar are not equal. Charge slips are written in Canadian dollars, and credit card companies convert the amount on the date the transaction is put through by the merchant.
- Meal patterns and dining hours parallel those of the United States.
- Beer is served ice-cold, but it is closer in strength to German beer than the milder American brew. Laws regulating the sale and service of alcoholic beverages vary from province to province. Generally they can be bought only at specially licensed stores. In some areas, alcohol cannot be served unless food is ordered.

Screech, the local drink of Newfoundland, originally was the dregs from casks of rum drunk by sailors when nothing else was available. It is now bottled under government supervision. Tourists can attend a "screeching-in" ceremony—a drink of the beverage accompanied by a portion of raw fish.

Transportation

From the United States, travelers from adjacent states often drive to Canada; those from more distant points fly in and continue their trip by air, water, rail, or road.

By Air Air travel is the quickest way to get from one coast to another and the only way to reach many towns in the country's interior.

By Water Canada is well served by all manner of boats and ships, particularly on its east and west coasts. In the east, ships operate from Bar Harbor and Portland, Maine, to Yarmouth, Nova Scotia. BC Ferries operates scheduled service to forty-two ports along the west coast (see Web sites in the Workbook). Reservations should be made as far in advance as possible during the summer season.

Cruise lines also operate on both coasts. On the west coast, Vancouver has regular sailings to Asia and to the Inside Passage in Alaska (in season). In the east, cruise lines sail on the St. Lawrence and Saguenay Rivers to Québec City and Montréal. Although deepwater travel must stop at Montréal, smaller ships sail on through the St. Lawrence Seaway to the Thousand Islands and Great Lakes.

North America's fastest ship, *The Cat*, operates between Bar Harbor, Maine, and Yarmouth, Nova Scotia. Travel time: 2 hours 45 minutes.

By Rail Government-owned VIA Rail Canada provides passenger rail service. Commuter rail services operate in urban areas. Toronto and Montréal have modern subway systems. (For information, contact VIA Rail.)

Unlike its neighbor to the south, Canada has maintained viable rail service ever since the 1885 completion of the coast-to-coast Canadian Pacific Railway. The route united the nation and helped save isolated British Columbia from becoming an American territory. Crossing Canada on the *Canadian* is considered one of the classic rail adventures. Trains make the trip between Vancouver and Toronto in three or four days. The train has both sleeper cars and economy cars, along with a dining car and an observation car with a bar and a lounging area. In the economy cars, people sleep in their seats. The most awe-inspiring stretch is the section crossing the Canadian Rockies between Jasper and Vancouver. Peak season is from June to mid-October.

Toronto is less than 300 miles (483 km) from Detroit and Cleveland and less than 600 miles (966 km) from New York and Boston.

By Road Travelers who drive to Canada from the United States must have a valid U.S. driver's license, car registration papers, and an insurance card or evidence of sufficient coverage to conform with local laws. Driving is on the right. Headlights must be on at all times, and seatbelts are compulsory. Speeds are posted in kilometers, and gas and oil are sold by the liter.

In its populated areas, Canada has an excellent highway system. Secondary roads are good until the traveler gets into the backwoods. As described earlier, the Cabot Trail, the Icefields Parkway, and—for the adventuresome—the Yukon section of the Alaska Highway provide especially scenic drives.

The Trans-Canada Highway runs cross-country from St. John's, Newfoundland, to Vancouver, British Columbia. The superhighway enables the motorist to drive from the Atlantic to the Pacific without a streetlight. Meandering across a continent through nine provinces, the road visits vibrant cities as well as remote forests and plains.

➤ PROFILE

Dining in Canada

Each region of Canada has its own style of cooking. A few dishes that visitors might want to sample include

- ➤ In the Atlantic provinces, *grundies*—combinations of fish and potatoes covered in cream sauce and cooked with onions and salt pork.
- ➤ The sophisticated French cuisine of the cities of Québec.
- ➤ In French-Canadian areas, a meat pie called *tourtière*, a Christmas specialty, or hearty home cooking using maple syrup in innovative ways.
- ➤ In British Columbia, king crab and salmon.
- ➤ In the territories, fish such as Arctic grayling and char as well as game such as reindeer.

Accommodations

Good lodging is not hard to find in Canada except during the busy summer months, when reservations are a must at resorts, many of which operate only in summer or in hunting and fishing season. Distinguished older properties in nostalgic surroundings include the castlelike hotels built by the railways, as well as less pretentious hotels built to entice visitors to the wilderness. Canada has no nationwide system of accommodation grading, but some provinces provide graded listings.

The Château Frontenac in Québec City was named for Count Louis de Frontenac, a 17th-century French governor who upset the local priests by encouraging the sale of brandy to the natives.

CHAPTER WRAP-UP

SUMMARY

Here is a review of the objectives with which we began the chapter.

1. **Describe the environment and people of Canada.** In area, Canada is one of the world's largest countries, but much of it is uninhabited wilderness. The Canadian Shield extends over the eastern part of the country. Canada's landscape includes forests and prairies, mountains in the west, and tundra in the north, as well as rocky coastlines on both the Pacific and Atlantic. Its climate is known for long, harsh winters. Much of the country has a subarctic climate, but southern areas have warm summers, and parts of the west coast have a mild climate.

   The people are as varied as the land, tracing their roots to the First Nations, to English and French settlers, and to 19th- and 20th-century immigrants from many nations. They have created a multicultural democracy in which the influence of these varied cultures endures.

2. **Identify Canada's provinces, territories, and most-visited sites.** The Atlantic provinces are Newfoundland, Nova Scotia, Prince Edward Island, and New Brunswick. Tourists are attracted to St. John's and L'Anse aux Meadows in Newfoundland; to the Green Gables Farmhouse on Prince Edward Island; to picturesque villages such as Peggy's Cove or the Cabot Trail in Nova Scotia; and to the tides of the Bay of Fundy in New Brunswick.

   In Québec province both Québec City and Montréal offer not only the attractions of dynamic modern cities but also the charm of centuries-old districts with a French accent. Nearby are opportunities for a tour of the Gaspé Peninsula, skiing in the Laurentians, a cruise on the St. Lawrence, and a view of the Saguenay Fjord.

The province of Ontario is the site of Canada's capital, Ottawa, and its largest city, Toronto. The museums of Ottawa and the theaters of Toronto draw many tourists. They also come to Ontario to view Niagara Falls or to cruise the Thousand Islands.

In the Prairie provinces of Manitoba, Saskatchewan, and Alberta, tourist attractions include the Folklorama festival in Winnepeg, Manitoba; the polar bears of Churchill, Manitoba; the West Edmonton Mall in Alberta; the Calgary Exhibition and Stampede in Calgary, Alberta; and the Icefields Parkway through Banff and Jasper National Parks in Alberta.

On Canada's west coast, British Columbia's attractions include the Empress Hotel and Butchart Gardens in Victoria. Stanley Park and Canada Place in Vancouver are also popular sites for visitors, as are the many parks and museums.

The territories—the Yukon, Northwest Territories, and Nunavut—are remote lands that attract adventuresome travelers.

3. **Describe Canada's main attractions, matching travelers and destinations best suited for each other.** For tourists seeking the attractions of a modern city, Toronto, Ottawa, Montréal, Québec City, or Vancouver should be satisfying destinations. Those interested in history might be drawn to the historic districts of Montréal and Québec City, to St. John's and L'Anse aux Meadows in Newfoundland, or to Discovery Days in Dawson City, Yukon.

   To sample varied cultures, travelers might go to northern Canada for its Inuit culture or to the Atlantic provinces for their Celtic and Acadian cultures. They might go to the heart of French-speaking Canada, Québec. Or they might attend Folklorama in Winnipeg, Manitoba.

   Canada also offers exceptional opportunities for outdoor family activities such as hiking, kayaking, fishing, and wildlife viewing. Cross-country skiers can find trails in the Laurentians; downhill specialists will prefer the mountains of Alberta and British Columbia.

4. **Provide or find the information needed to plan a trip to Canada.** Canada presents few obstacles to the traveler, and information is readily available. Getting to and around Canada is similar to travel in the United States. The Trans-Canada Highway stretches from coast to coast. Scenic or unusual transportation options include sno-coach tours, the train between Jasper and Vancouver, and cruises. For memorable lodging, historic hotels such as the Château Frontenac, Empress Hotel, Banff Springs, Château Lake Louise, and Emerald Lake are possibilities. Because of Canada's size and harsh winters with early darkness, trip planning requires attention to distances, seasons, and weather conditions.

QUESTIONS FOR DISCUSSION AND REVIEW

1. How does Canada compare with the United States in size? In population? Canada is larger but lesser in population

2. In what province do most of Canada's French-speaking citizens live? How do you feel the province's mandated use of the French language affects tourism? Quebec-

3. What part of Canada has the most appeal to you personally? Why? Would your favorite area appeal to a family? A couple on their honeymoon? A group of senior citizens? College students? Nature lovers?

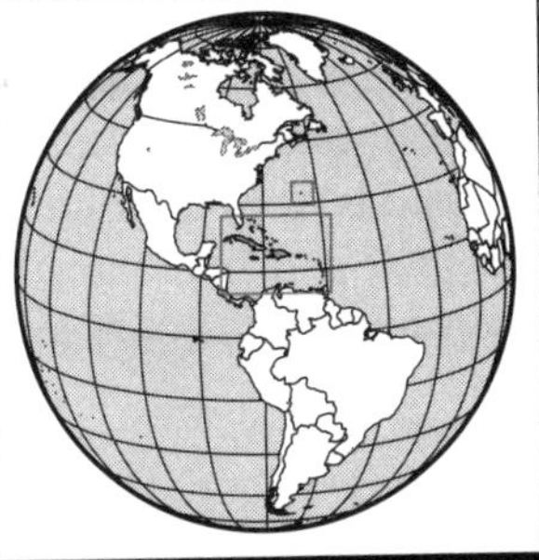

CHAPTER 6

Bermuda and the West Indies

- Bermuda
- The Bahamas
- The Greater Antilles: Cayman Islands, Jamaica, Dominican Republic, and Puerto Rico
- The Lesser Antilles: Leeward Islands and Windward Islands
- Islands off the South America Coast
- Other Destinations in the Caribbean

OBJECTIVES

When you have completed Chapter 6, you should be able to

1. Describe the environment and people of the islands.
2. Identify and locate the most-visited islands.
3. Describe the islands' attractions, matching travelers and destinations best suited for each other.
4. Provide or find the information needed to plan a trip to the islands.

Islands off the east and southeast coasts of North America lure millions of travelers each year to fun in the sun. No two islands are exactly alike even when they share a common history. Nature and events conspired to make each one different. On an air or sea approach to the islands, the deep blue of the ocean gives way to the azure blue of the island shelf and finally to the colors of sand and land. Colors remain etched in the traveler's memory long after the trip is over.

The Environment and Its People

The islands can be organized by size, formation, language, historic background, or political affiliation. See the Fact File in Appendix A for an alphabetic organization. This chapter sorts the islands by location, starting in the north and moving southward.

Both *kar uh BEE uhn* and *kuh RIHB ee uhn* are correct pronunciations for the Caribbean.

Bermuda is the island farthest north; it is alone in the Atlantic, east of North Carolina. Islands east and south of Florida are called the **West Indies**. Hundreds follow an arc from Florida to South America (see Figure 6.1). Geographically, the West Indies divide into four groups:

- A chain of islands that stretches east and southeast of Florida in the Atlantic—the **Bahamas** and the **Turks** and **Caicos**.
- A string of islands known as the **Greater Antilles**, south and southeast of Florida in the Caribbean and Atlantic. These islands are **Cuba**, the **Cayman Islands**, **Jamaica**, **Hispaniola** (shared by **Haiti** and the **Dominican Republic**), and **Puerto Rico**.
- The many small islands from Puerto Rico to South America known as the **Lesser Antilles**, which are further divided into the **Leeward** and **Windward Islands**.
- The islands off the South American coast—**Aruba, Bonaire, Curaçao** (together known as the **ABCs**), and **Trinidad** and **Tobago**. Politically and geographically, these islands are part of other groups, but their location near the South American continent sets them apart.

➤ PROFILE

Adventures in the Islands

Don't forget sunscreen and a hat when you enjoy such outdoor adventures as

- ➤ Deep-sea fishing in the Bahamas.
- ➤ Diving on the Wall in the Cayman Islands.
- ➤ Horseback riding along a beach in Jamaica.
- ➤ Sea kayaking on St. John in the USVIs.
- ➤ Yacht racing on Antigua.
- ➤ Parasailing high above the harbor in Barbados.

The Land

Of the hundreds of islands in the West Indies, only Jamaica, the Cayman Islands, and the ABCs are entirely surrounded by the Caribbean Sea. Most have shores washed by both the Caribbean and the Atlantic. The Bahamas, the Turks and Caicos, and Barbados (as well as Bermuda) are surrounded by the Atlantic Ocean.

The beaches and the landscape of an island depend on how it was formed. The islands are of three types: continental, volcanic, and coral.

Continental islands were once connected to a continent. Geologists suspect that Cuba and Hispaniola may have been part of eastern Mexico. Trinidad broke from South America. Continental islands tend to have beaches of golden sand.

Volcanic islands are mountainous islands that were formed by volcanic eruptions. **Saba** (*SAY bah*) and **Martinique** in the Lesser Antilles are examples. On some islands, wind and rain wore down the mountain peaks to

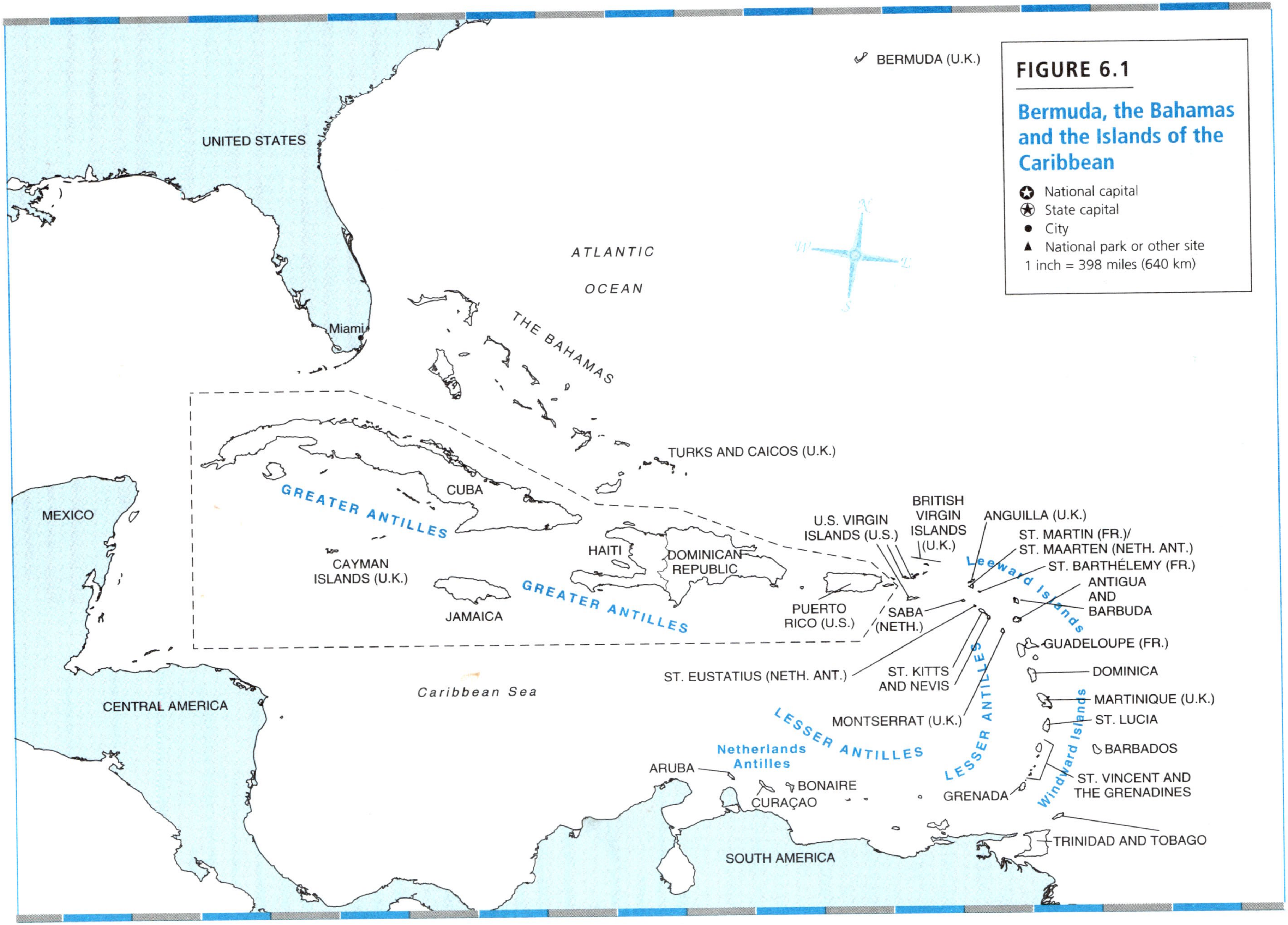

FIGURE 6.1

Bermuda, the Bahamas and the Islands of the Caribbean

- National capital
- State capital
- City
- National park or other site

1 inch = 398 miles (640 km)

form low islands, such as the Caymans. Volcanic islands have beaches of black, gray, or golden sand.

Coral islands are low islands formed in warm waters by tiny sea animals called *coral polyps*. The Bahamas and the Turks and Caicos formed in this way. Coral reefs are found mostly in warm seas, because the reef-forming corals cannot live in water colder than 65° F (18° C). Coral islands tend to have beautiful beaches of white, pink, or golden sand.

Combinations of these processes formed some islands. For example, in Bermuda coral formed on volcanic peaks.

The Climate

The climate for most of the islands changes little between winter and summer. Bermuda is one exception. Bermuda has a mild subtropical climate with seasons, although the Gulf Stream protects it from winter extremes. Summers are warm to hot; winters are mild to cool—perfect for golf and tennis, but too cold for swimming.

The Bahamas are slightly cooler than other island groups. Their weather is like south Florida's. Winter temperatures are in the 70s F (20s C) during the day and drop to the 60s at night. Rainfall is heaviest from October through January.

The trade winds blow steadily from the east across most of the Antilles and temper the tropical climate of the islands. The water's temperature varies only about ten degrees from summer to winter. Hurricane season is from June to November, but exactly where storms will strike is unpredictable.

The islands close to South America—Aruba, Bonaire, Curaçao—have a hot, windy, dry climate. These islands are off the path of most hurricanes and probably have the most dependable weather for travelers who want sunshine.

The People and Their History

People used to say that Columbus discovered America, but when Columbus arrived in 1492, someone came to greet him—thousands of someones. Columbus called these people "Indians" because he thought he had reached the East Indies. They called themselves Arawak, Carib, Lucayan, Siboney, and Taino.

Life in the islands seems serene, but the Caribbean has been a region of violence. The Arawaks were invaded by the fierce Caribs from South America, the Caribs were set upon by the Spaniards, the Spaniards fought with the British and the French, and the colonials faced slave rebellions. (For a short summary of the islands' history, see Figure 6.2.)

The Indians have died out, except for a small group of Caribs on **Dominica** in the Lesser Antilles. Most island residents are descended from black Africans who were brought to the islands in the 17th and 18th centuries as slaves. During the 19th century, the slaves gradually gained freedom.

European nations, joined by the United States, competed for power in the islands in the 19th and 20th centuries. Today, the islands are a patchwork of independent states, territories in political transition, and dependencies. The political groupings can be confusing. For example, the **Netherlands Antilles** consists of (1) the ABCs, off the coast of Venezuela, and (2) three islands east of the Virgin Islands—**Saba**, **St. Eustasius**, and **St. Maarten**.

Europeans left their mark not only on the islands' political status but also

FIGURE 6.2

Milestones of Island History

c. 1300 Carib tribes from South America invade the islands.

1492–1823 It is the age of European exploration and colonization.

1500–1800 Slave trade expands as the islands need labor for sugar cane.

1804 Haiti becomes the first independent nation in the West Indies.

1800s Revolutions weaken colonial control. Slavery is slowly abolished.

1898 After the Spanish-American War, the United States claims Puerto Rico and Cuba.

1906 Mount Pelée erupts on Martinique, killing 30,000.

1915–1934 U.S. Marines occupy Haiti.

1916–1924 U.S. Marines occupy the Dominican Republic.

1917 The United States buys the U.S. Virgin Islands from Denmark.

1945–1979 This is the era of island independence movements.

1952 Puerto Rico becomes a commonwealth.

1961 The United States breaks diplomatic relations with Cuba.

1970s Tourism becomes the economic support of the islands.

1978 All-inclusive resorts spread throughout the islands.

1983 The United States invades Grenada.

1990s Bigger and bigger ships cruise the islands.

1995 A volcano erupts on the island of Montserrat.

2004 Barbados institutes a passport requirement.

on their languages. English, Spanish, French, and Dutch are official languages on various islands. In addition, Hindi and Chinese are spoken in Trinidad, and Creole is the language of the French islands. *Papiamento*—a combination of Dutch, Spanish, Portuguese, English, African, and Indian—is spoken on several islands, including Aruba, Bonaire, and Curaçao.

Island residents often have mixed ancestry. Some have British, Dutch, French, Portuguese, or Spanish backgrounds. Some are descendants of workers brought from India to work the sugar plantations as contract laborers after slavery was abolished. The greatest number of these workers went to Trinidad, where their descendants are the dominant ethnic group.

The islands are among the world's most densely settled places, and many have grinding poverty. Despite their problems, the islands offer many wonders for vacationers. As Table 6.1 illustrates, the sun and the beaches are the primary attractions. We focus on islands that are the major tourist destinations; other islands are briefly described in the chapter's final section.

✔ CHECK-UP

Organized by location, the islands east and southeast of North America include

- ✔ Bermuda.
- ✔ The West Indies, which can be classified into four groups: (1) the Bahamas with the Turks and Caicos, (2) the Greater Antilles, (3) the Lesser Antilles, and (4) islands off the South American coast.

Features of the islands' environment include

- ✔ Continental, volcanic, and coral islands.
- ✔ White-, golden-, gray-, or black-sand beaches.
- ✔ Warm ocean water.
- ✔ Hurricane season from June to November.

The islands are notable for

- ✔ A cultural mix of African, European, and Asian influences.
- ✔ A political mix of independent countries, territories in transition, and dependencies.

A.

Bermuda

The worn-off tops of ancient volcanoes capped with coral form the substructure of Bermuda (*buhr MYOO duh*), the world's most northerly group of coral islands. They are alone in the Atlantic, about 650 miles (1,046 km) east/southeast of North Carolina. (See Figure 6.3.)

Bermuda is noted for its pink-sand beaches, gentle landscape, colorful flowers, distinctive architecture, and romantic English atmosphere. It is just 21 miles (34 km) long and a few miles wide. The best beaches and most of the hotels are on the south shore.

The landscape features pastel-colored cottages fronted by manicured lawns. Made of the islands' sandstone, the houses have white roofs. The roofs are important. Because the island has few sources of fresh water, rainwater is caught on the whitewashed roofs and stored in tanks under the houses.

Limitations on cars, on cruise ship arrivals, and on hotel construction have helped Bermuda maintain its reputation as an upscale destination. It has one of the world's highest rates of repeat visitors. Many of its guests were introduced to the island as students during spring breaks, returned on their honeymoon, came back on family vacations, and revisit whenever they can.

Table 6.1

Top Ten Interests of Travelers in the Caribbean

When asked why they chose the islands for their vacation, 90,000 tourists gave these as the top reasons. (The results total more than 100 percent because multiple answers were given.)

Interest	Percentage Who Cited
Sun/beach	48.5%
Sightseeing	28.1%
Water sports	17.3%
Scuba	14.7%
Nightlife	12.7%
Nature/outdoors	11.1%
Honeymoon	8.6%
Shopping	8.6%
Cultural activities	8.0%
Cruising	7.9%

Source: Caribbean Tourism Organization, 2004.

FIGURE 6.3 Bermuda

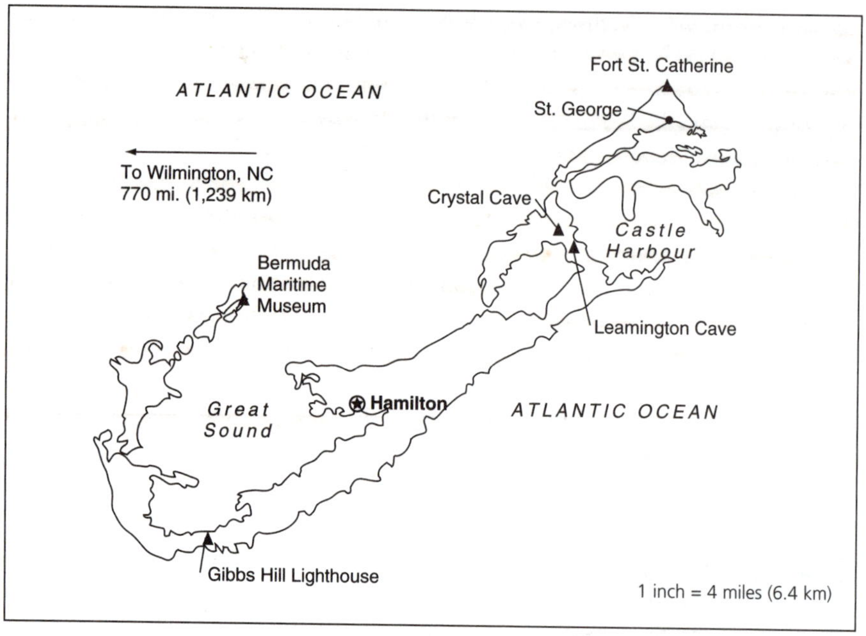

The Towns

Bermuda's capital is **Hamilton**. The airport is on the east end of the island near the town of **St. George**.

Hamilton Hamilton is in the center of the island at the end of the Great Sound (look again at Figure 6.3). In season, a limited number of cruise ships dock on Front Street. Crossing the gangway puts a passenger steps away from tantalizing shops. The town's buildings are low-lying wooden or limestone houses, adorned with arcades and balconies, or tidy cottages with roofs "exactly the white of the icing on the cake," as Samuel Clemens (Mark Twain) described them.

Hamilton is not a beach town. Visitors can take ferries to the south shore or the west end where the pink sands are ample. The historic Princess Hotel (the town's largest) has beach privileges with its sister hotel, the Southampton Princess (the island's largest). The boats stop running before midnight. The island is not known for nightlife into the wee hours. There are no casinos.

Throughout Bermuda visitors see circles of stone called *moongates*. The design was brought to Bermuda in the 1800s by a sea captain who had seen them in China. Legend has it that honeymooners should walk through the moongates and make a wish.

Front Street, Hamilton, Bermuda

St. George Bermuda's first capital, 17th-century St. George is at the eastern end of the island. Cruise ships might spend two or three nights docked in Hamilton, then move to St. George for one or two nights. St. George has pubs, restaurants, branches of Front Street shops, and **Fort St. Catherine**, which is the largest of the island's old forts.

Other Places to Visit

Bermuda has more golf courses per square mile than anywhere else in the world, and they offer spectacular scenery and challenging courses. The private Mid Ocean Club is renowned for both. Visitors from reciprocating country clubs back home can request guest privileges, but arrangements must be made in advance.

Other attractions include **Leamington** and **Crystal Caves**, forts, an aquarium, a perfume factory, **Gibbs Hill Lighthouse**, and the Swizzle Inn, which is home of the rum swizzle, a favorite island drink. On the western tip of the island, the Royal Naval Dockyard has been redeveloped into the **Bermuda Maritime Museum**, with shops and restaurants.

✔ CHECK-UP

Bermuda's towns include
- ✔ Hamilton, the capital, the largest town, and a cruise ship port.
- ✔ St. George, a port and restored 17th-century town on the east end.

Highlights for visitors to Bermuda include
- ✔ Manicured landscape.
- ✔ Pink-sand beaches.
- ✔ Water sports and golf.
- ✔ Romantic English atmosphere.

B

The Bahamas

Far to the southwest of Bermuda, the Bahamas (*buh HAH mahz*) are off Florida's coast (see Figure 6.4). The Commonwealth of the Bahamas is a chain

FIGURE 6.4

The Bahamas

1 inch = 126 miles (203 km)

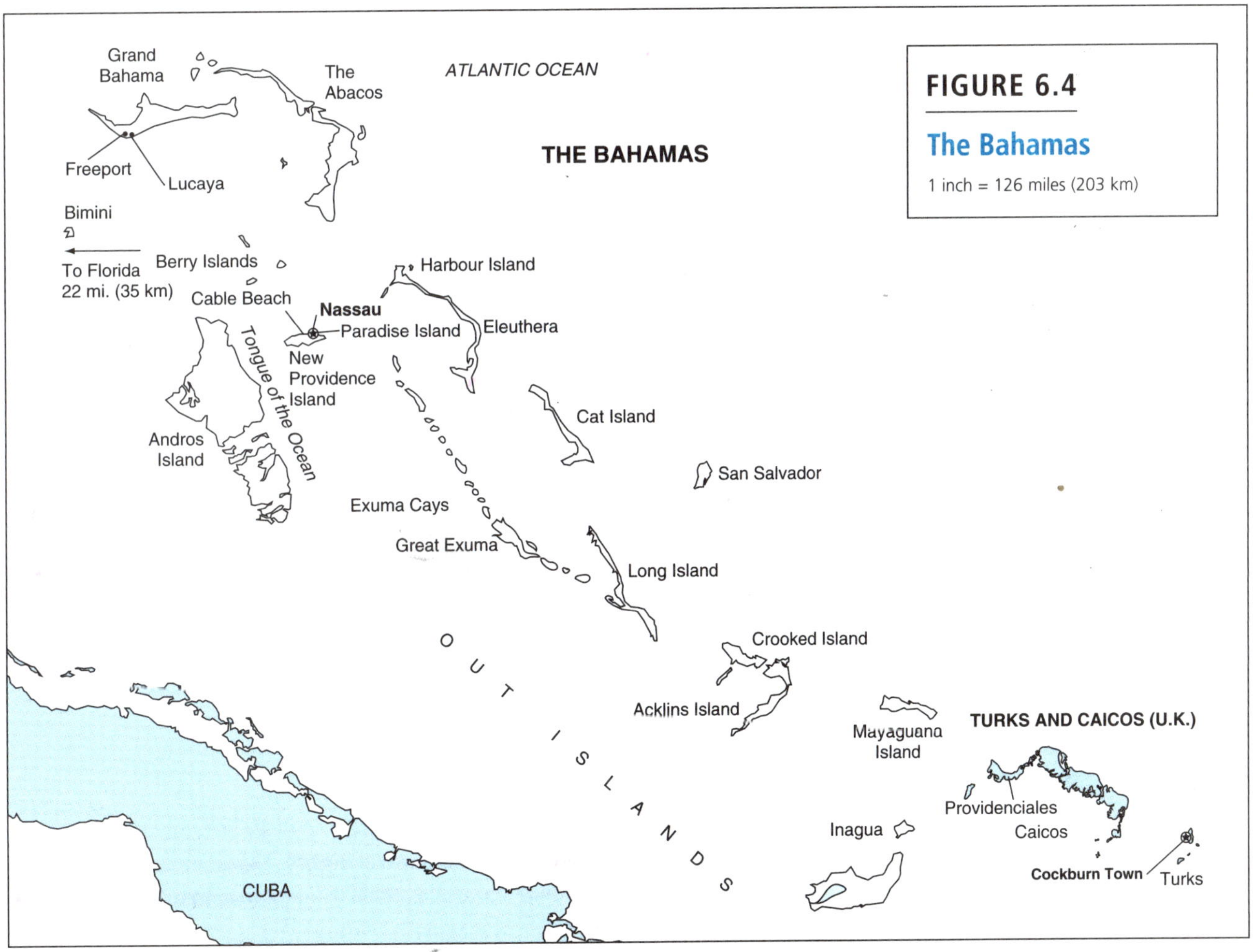

of about 2,400 cays (pronounced *keys*) and 700 flat coral islands covered with scrub and casuarina pine trees. The lush vegetation that surrounds hotels and golf courses is imported. The beautiful sand beaches and azure seas that encircle the islands are the islands' natural attractions.

Much of the archipelago is pristine and untouched, but mainstream development has reached the islands of **New Providence** and **Grand Bahama**. Three- and four-day cruises from Florida are big hits among young travelers and people with limited budgets. They seek beaches, fishing, tennis, windsurfing, and golf. Many come for the casinos and nightlife. Tourism is centered in three areas:

- **Nassau, Paradise Island,** and **Cable Beach** on New Providence.
- **Freeport/Lucaya** on Grand Bahama.
- The **Out Islands** (also called the Family Islands).

Nassau opened its first casino in 1920, the year Prohibition began in the United States. Americans would go to the Bahamas to drink and gamble.

New Providence

New Providence Island is the site of Nassau, the capital, and Paradise Island.

Nassau Nassau (*NAS aw*) is a small town on the northeast coast of New Providence. Cruise ships dock in the harbor, and passengers can walk into town. Near the docks Bahamian women at the Straw Market bargain with tourists for straw work, T-shirts, and assorted souvenirs. The persuasive ladies win the bargaining game, surely. One block inland, Bay Street offers more shops.

Paradise Island, Bahamas

Paradise Island A toll bridge and a water shuttle link Nassau and Paradise Island. (Taxi passengers are asked to pay the toll.) The small island has some of New Providence's best hotels. Guests encounter an astonishing world of water, luxury, and adventure at the Atlantis Resort. The waterscape includes marine animals, the quarter-mile Lazy River Ride (floating down a river pool in a tube), an underwater tunnel, and water slides from a six-story Mayan temple.

Cable Beach To the west of Nassau, West Bay Street follows the north coast. The road passes Fort Charlotte, the Ardastra Gardens, and an Underwater Observatory and Marine Park until it reaches the hotel area called Cable Beach, the site of more development and casinos. On the island's west end is Lyford Cay, an enclave that is home or second home to the rich and famous.

Festivals Festivals are part of the island experience. The *Goombay festival* in June, July, and August includes beach parties, sporting events, and folkloric shows. The biggest celebration for Bahamian slaves was *Junkanoo* at Christmas and New Year. Junkanoo has been commercialized, but it is still a popular island institution. Music is played on *goombay* (goat skin) drums, cowbells, bugles, horns, whistles, and conch shells. Parades and costume competitions are part of the fun.

Grand Bahama Island

Grand Bahama Island is only some 60 miles (97 km) from the coast of Florida. The island is flat, with few natural sights. Miles of sandy beaches, large hotels, casinos, golf courses, and a world-class scuba diving facility make it a favorite destination.

Charter flights and inexpensive vacation packages feature Freeport on Grand Bahama Island. After Nassau, it is the Bahamas' most popular destination. Freeport's attractions include shopping at the International Bazaar and gambling at El Casino.

Most of the island's hotels are located in Lucaya Beach on the south coast. Golf, tennis, and deep-sea fishing are popular activities. The Underwater Explorer Society (UNEXSO) maintains a diving school in Port Lucaya where swimmers can mix with dolphins that are kept in captivity while being studied.

Out Islands

Travelers to the Out Islands leave the casinos and grand hotels of Nassau and Freeport behind to see houses with gardens of tropical flowers surrounded by white picket fences. The Out Islands are known for their marina facilities and great diving. Accommodations are informal even though some are deluxe in price and amenities. From north to south, islands include **The Abacos**, **Bimini**, **Berry Islands**, **Eleuthera**, **Cat**, **Andros**, **Exuma**, **San Salvador**, **Acklins**, and **Inagua**.

Bimini, the *Big Game Fishing Capital of the World*, is the closest to Florida. On a clear night a visitor can see the glow of Miami's lights. The island was a base for smugglers who brought weapons into the United States during the Revolution, whiskey during Prohibition, and drugs recently.

Ernest Hemingway had a cottage on Bimini and used the island as background for his book *Islands in the Stream*.

Eleuthera has some very upscale resorts. People seeking the ultimate getaway should try **Harbour Island**, a tiny island approximately 1 mile (1.6 km) off the northeast tip of Eleuthera.

Andros is the largest island but probably the least known. Much of the land is uninhabited and actually consists of small islands connected by shallow canals and cays called *bights*. The Andros Barrier Reef off its eastern shore is the world's third longest. Beyond the reef the ocean floor drops steeply to a depth of more than 1 mile (1.6 km) to a place called **Tongue of the Ocean**. Divers are attracted by circles of sapphire water ringed by aquamarine shallows. These are **blue holes**—mysterious, seemingly bottomless pools that were originally dry caves on islands of limestone.

The Berry Islands are scattered to the northwest of Nassau. Cruise lines maintain private islands in the area to give their passengers a day at the beach. Except for caretakers, the islands are deserted between port calls.

Inagua (*in AH gwa*) is the most southerly island. It is a flamingo reserve and a salt farm. The saline waters where flamingos find the algae food that keeps them pink are the same waters that gave the island its prosperity as a source of salt.

✔ CHECK-UP

The major towns of the Bahamas are
- ✔ Nassau on New Providence Island.
- ✔ Freeport on Grand Bahama Island.

Highlights for visitors to the Bahamas include
- ✔ Fishing the deep seas.
- ✔ Enjoying beautiful white-sand beaches.
- ✔ Gambling and nightlife at Paradise Island, Cable Beach, Freeport, and Lucaya.
- ✔ Playing with dolphins in Port Lucaya.
- ✔ Relaxing on the Out Islands.

C

The Greater Antilles

The Greater Antilles are south of the Bahamas, as Figure 6.5 shows. All but the Cayman Islands are large and mountainous. The region's key tourist destinations are the Cayman Islands, Jamaica, the Dominican Republic, and Puerto Rico. For a brief description of the other islands, see the "Other Destinations in the Caribbean" section.

Cayman Islands

Grand Cayman, **Cayman Brac**, and **Little Cayman** make up the Cayman (*KAY muhn*) Islands. These small, flat islands are the coral-encrusted tops of a mountain range. Around them, underwater slopes descend to the **Cayman Trough**, the deepest water in the Caribbean. On average, 41 percent of the visitors to the Caymans are divers. The islands are known as the *Underwater Capital of the Caribbean*.

When Columbus found the Cayman Islands, he called them *Las Tortugas* for their abundant sea turtles. Later, Tortugas turned into *Caymanas*, the Carib word for "crocodiles." The crocodiles are no longer around, but turtles still inhabit the islands. International businesses have also made their home here. The Caymans have no income tax, no profit tax, no capital gains tax, and no estate and death taxes. Consequently, international businesses have made the Caymans a financial center, and the islands are among the Caribbean's most prosperous.

Nightlife on Grand Cayman is ample, although there are no casinos. These islands appeal to those seeking a relaxed vacation with a reasonable amount of activity. They do not have the rainfall and greenery found on other islands in the Greater Antilles. Their white-sand beaches and underwater scenery are the attractions.

Of the islands, Grand Cayman is the center of tourism. Cayman Brac and Little Cayman are largely undeveloped, catering mostly to divers and fishermen.

George Town The Caymans' capital, George Town, is on Grand Cayman. It is easy to explore. Hog Sty Bay, known less colorfully as George Town Harbor, is a busy port. A planned cruise terminal will eventually allow large ships to dock in George Town. For now, cruise passengers must be tendered.

In the center of town, the small Cayman Islands National Museum chronicles the islands' shipbuilding, turtle-hunting, and rope-making industries, as well as their history of pirates and shipwrecks. An attraction for those who do not dive is the *Atlantis Submarine* excursion. The mini-sub takes passengers below the surface so they can enjoy underwater views in air-conditioned comfort.

Each October, this British crown colony honors the buccaneers who founded the island with *Pirate Week*, consisting of parades, parties, and treasure hunts. A fishing competition, *Million Dollar Month*, is held in June.

Seven Mile Beach The center of land activity on Grand Cayman is Seven Mile Beach (actually 5.5 miles [9 km] long) on the west coast. Condos, hotels, shopping centers, and diving operations have sprouted up along the length of the inviting white sand. Facing west, the beach has a fine view of the sunset. It offers a chance of seeing the Green Flash, a tiny green strip of light that

---

Jack Nicklaus designed a golf course on Grand Cayman for the Cayman golf ball. A Cayman ball has pimples instead of dimples, and it travels only half as far as a normal ball, thus lessening the space needed for a course and shortening the time needed to play.

ON THE SPOT

The travelers have just completed their scuba (acronym for "self-contained underwater breathing apparatus") course and can't wait to try out their new skills. They want to spend as much time as possible under the water. You have suggested they go to the Caymans, islands known for their spectacular dive sites, on a package that allows for two dives a day. The last dive ends at about 1800. The couple is going with a group of friends, some of whom are leaving on a night flight home. They would like to be on the same flight as their friends. Why should you not agree to this?

Flying immediately after diving is dangerous. The unreleased nitrogen in the diver's system can cause the bends. Divers must wait a minimum of twelve hours after their last dive before getting on a plane.

FIGURE 6.5

The Greater Antilles

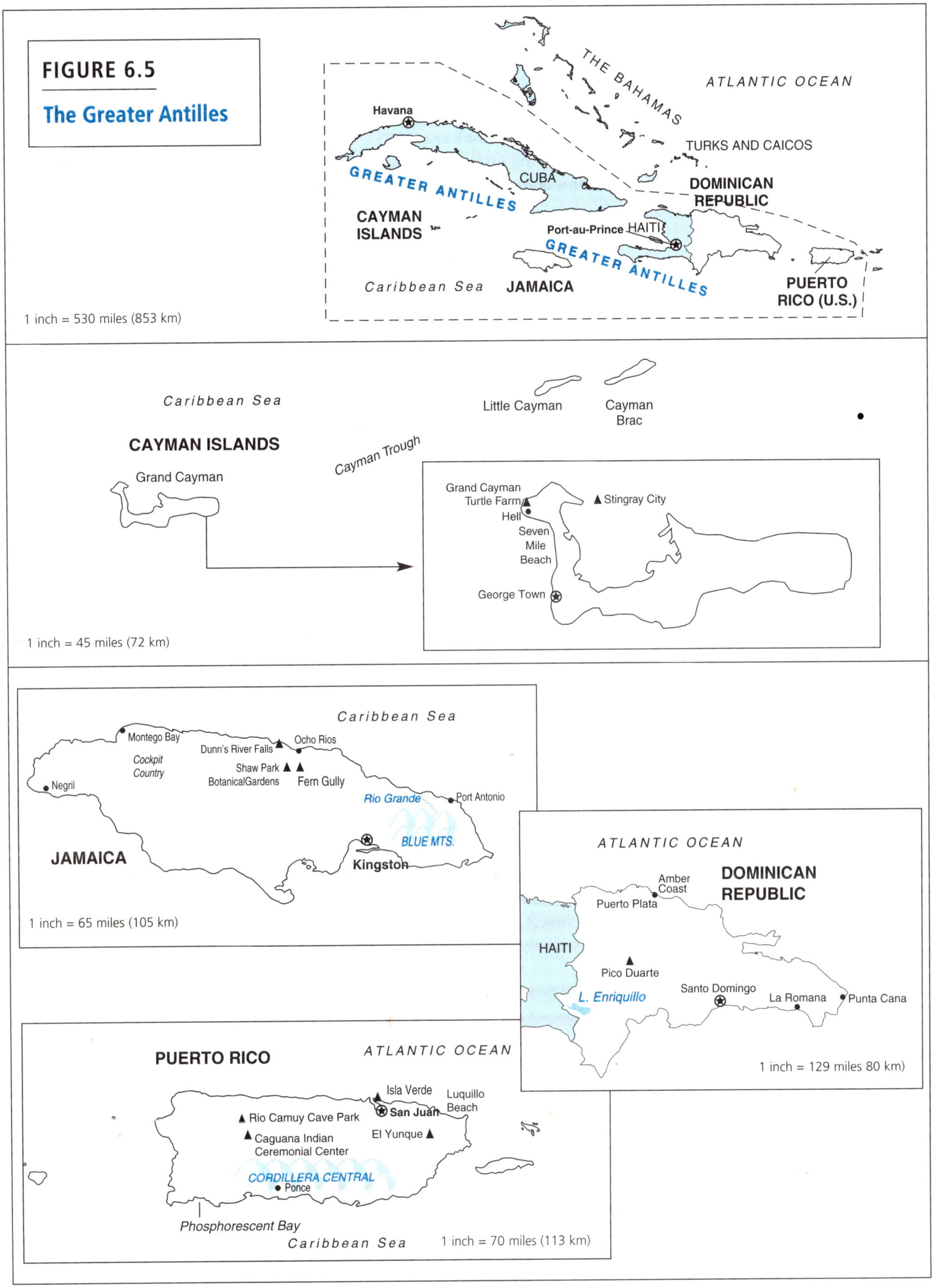

appears over the sea. It occurs only rarely, during a totally cloudless sunset at the moment the sun disappears over the horizon.

Near Seven Mile Beach, the **Grand Cayman Turtle Farm** is a breeding farm and research station. At the annual turtle release each October, visitors gather to watch turtles return to the sea. U.S. Customs bans all turtle products, so do not buy any.

From the farm, tours go to **Hell**, an area of black rock formations. Hell's major industry is selling stamps and postcards with its unique postmark.

Diving Dive sites range from shallow dives near offshore reefs to the celebrated North Wall dive off Grand Cayman, a sheer drop to the bed of the ocean. Most hotels have dive shops and offer scuba certification courses. June, July, and August are among the busiest months, the time when serious divers come to town.

In 1986 divers discovered that stingrays were gathering off the north shore of the island where boat crews cleaned their catches. The divers began visiting and feeding the rays regularly. Gradually the rays and the humans learned to get along. **Stingray City** is actually two sites: one is for divers and snorkelers; the other is a sandbar about 3 feet (0.9 m) deep for waders. The rays swim around the entire area.

Jamaica

Jamaica (*juh MAY kuh*) is the Caribbean's third largest and the most populous of the English-speaking islands. It is about 148 miles (238 km) long and 52 miles (84 km) wide. Its landscape includes beaches, waterfalls, rivers, lush tropical foliage, and the **Blue Mountains**, which rise in the island's east. Ruins of stone sugar mills dot the landscape.

Much of Jamaica is capped by limestone. When limestone erodes, streams disappear underground and break up the land, causing karst. Karst formations in northwestern Jamaica include depressions with steep sides called *cockpits* (ideal for cock fights), and the area is called **Cockpit Country**. It was once a place of refuge for escaped slaves.

Jamaica is known for its *all-inclusive resorts*—resorts at which room, meals, certain beverages, water and land sports, nightly entertainment, taxes, tips, and airport transfers are included at one prepaid price. The all-inclusives provide security and varied activity but little contact with island culture.

Jamaica has no casinos, but the resorts have ample nightlife. From east to west, **Port Antonio**, **Ocho Rios**, **Montego Bay**, and **Negril** are resort centers on the north and west coasts of the island.

Sugar mills were used to press sugar cane for rum. Sugar was the cash crop on many islands, but sugar cane cannot be moved far before it spoils. The cane was made into molasses and then fermented and distilled into rum that could be transported without spoilage. Rum remains a leading export for many islands.

Kingston Although tourists head for the beach resorts, Kingston is the island's capital. It is on the southeast coast, at the end of a large natural harbor. It was founded after an earthquake and tidal wave in 1692 destroyed nearby Port Royal, the "richest and wickedest city on earth" under the domination of Captain Henry Morgan and his pirates. Kingston is the home of *reggae*, a musical style originating in Kingston's tough urban environment.

Many Jamaicans belong to Ras Tafari, a religious and political movement known for its dreadlocks, reggae music, vegetarianism, and the belief that ganja (marijuana) is sacred. The movement became widely known thanks largely to the popularity of the late Bob Marley, who lifted reggae to an art form.

Port Antonio Once a banana-shipping port, Port Antonio is on the east end of the island surrounded by the Blue Mountains. It became an exclusive resort thanks in part to a movie star of the 1940s, Errol Flynn. He loved to sail and often came to Port Antonio. According to legend, he saw rafts carrying fruit down the Rio Grande to the port and thought the ride to the sea would be romantic. His whim started the rafting trips popular throughout the island.

The Port Antonio trips on the Rio Grande begin high in the mountains. Rafts built for two are steered and poled by a boatman.

Ocho Rios Roughly 67 miles (108 km) to the east of Montego Bay, Ocho (*OH cho*) Rios stretches along the coast. The name is a corruption of *las chorreras,* meaning "waterfalls." Ocho Rios is the port for 75 percent of the cruise ship arrivals, and its piers can handle the largest megaliners.

West of the port, **Dunn's River Falls** is a waterfall that cascades over rocks to the sea. The island's most popular excursion is climbing the falls from the bottom to the top, dunking along the way. The rocks are slippery, so footwear is a must. Guides lead participants hand in hand through the pools.

Other attractions include the **Shaw Park Botanical Gardens** and **Fern Gully,** a road running through a valley of ferns. Along the road, outdoor stalls offer everything from local crafts to fruits and refreshments.

Ian Fleming lived near Port Maria, Jamaica, in a house called *Golden Eye,* where he wrote fourteen James Bond thrillers.

Montego Bay The north coast's major international airport is at Montego (*mon TEE go*) Bay, or MoBay as the locals call it. Sam Sharpe Square is the center of town, but hotels are strung out along the coast.

The plantation great houses near Montego Bay are reminders of the days when sugar was king. Rose Hall, built in the 1770s, is the most famous. The Georgian mansion's attraction is the legend of its mistress, Annie Palmer, known as the *White Witch of Rose Hall.* An Annie Palmer did live in the house, but there is no record that she was anything other than an ordinary plantation owner's wife. The legend is a good tourist attraction, however.

Negril About 50 miles (80 km) southwest of MoBay is Negril (*nuh GRILL*), on Jamaica's westernmost point. It has fine beaches and a young and laid-back atmosphere with several clothing-optional resorts. A local law restricts building height to "no higher than a coconut tree."

3 Dominican Republic

The large island of Hispaniola (*iss pahn YOH luh*) in the Greater Antilles is home to two countries, Haiti and the Dominican Republic, separated by a rugged mountain range. The second-largest Caribbean country, the Dominican Republic occupies the eastern two-thirds of the island. (Look again at Figure 6.5.) The country has both the highest point in the West Indies, **Pico Duarte**, and the lowest, **Lake Enriquillo**. The people of the Dominican Republic speak Spanish.

The Dominican Republic has the world's second-largest reserves of amber. Experts declare that real amber comes only from pine trees that grew near the Baltic Sea millions of years ago, but the Dominican Republic's amber is in great demand.

Santo Domingo The capital, Santo Domingo, is on the south coast. The city has no beaches and is not a resort town, although it has active nightlife, casinos, and a historic center. Founded in 1496 by the brother of Christopher Columbus, the city reflects the time when the island was the center of Spain's empire.

Resort Areas Most of the country's resorts are in its southeast corner. A two-hour drive east of Santo Domingo, the area of **La Romana** is home to Casa de Campo, which *Golf* magazine called "the finest golf resort in the Caribbean." The resort also has a polo field, with matches scheduled from October to June.

On the east coast, the resort area of **Punta Cana** has white-sand beaches shaded by coconut palms. The island's north, or **Amber Coast**, is also a resort area, popular with Canadians and Europeans. It is named for one of the island's precious resources: amber. **Puerto Plata** is the north coast's largest town.

Puerto Rico

Puerto Rico (*PWAIR tuh REE koh*) is the air and cruise ship hub for the Caribbean. It is a U.S. commonwealth, not a state. Its Spanish heritage is reflected in the language and customs of the people.

The large island is green and fertile, rectangular in shape. Mountains run east to west through its center. The coast has excellent beaches and fine harbors. Rivers flow from the mountains to the sea.

Some visitors want the excitement of the capital, **San Juan** (*sahn HWAHN*). Others prefer to sit on the porch of a *parador* (a small country inn) and listen to the *coquis* (tree frogs).

El Morro Fortress

San Juan San Juan is divided into an old and a new city. Spanish colonial architecture graces *El Viejo San Juan* ("Old San Juan"), which was founded in 1521. Its bay is one of the best harbors in the West Indies. Sights include

- El Morro Fortress, dominating the harbor entrance. Its construction began in 1539.
- Casa Blanca, a house intended to be Ponce de León's home.
- La Fortaleza, the oldest governor's mansion in use in the Americas.
- El Convento, the only hotel in the old city.

Bridges and a strip of land connect the old city to the new. The area called Condado developed as a beach resort in the 1950s. The Caribe Hilton's gaming tables add to the area's reputation as a place of action. By law, all casinos are in hotels. Beyond Condado, **Isla Verde** continues the beach strip of hotels, shops, and nightclubs.

West of the city, the Dorado and Cerromar resorts have great appeal as destinations for groups and incentive travel. Both have beaches, casinos, golf courses, shops, and many amenities.

On the Island Easily reached on a day trip east of the city, **El Yunque** (*yung KAY*), "the anvil," is a mountain with the only tropical rain forest in the U.S. national forest system. Nearby **Luquillo** (*luh KEE loh*) **Beach** curves invitingly with white sand and fringing palms.

Continuing around the coast, **Ponce** (*pon TSAY*), about an hour and a half by toll road from San Juan, is the island's second-largest city. Its museum has the Caribbean's most extensive art collection.

The **Phosphorescent Bay**, on the south, has microscopic marine life that lights up when disturbed by movement. The phenomenon—especially vivid on moonless nights—is rarely found elsewhere.

West of San Juan, **Rio Camuy Cave Park** is one of the world's largest systems of caves. A short distance inland the **Caguana Indian Ceremonial Center** can be found.

✔ CHECK-UP

Islands of the Greater Antilles include

- ✔ Cayman Islands; its capital is George Town.
- ✔ Jamaica; its capital is Kingston, but its tourist center is on the north coast.
- ✔ Dominican Republic; its capital is Santo Domingo.
- ✔ Puerto Rico; its capital is San Juan.

Highlights for visitors to the Greater Antilles include

- ✔ Diving with stingrays and patting turtles in the Cayman Islands.
- ✔ Climbing Dunn's River Falls near Ocho Rios, Jamaica.
- ✔ Golfing in the Dominican Republic.
- ✔ Walking in the footsteps of the Spanish explorers in Old San Juan.

The Lesser Antilles

The Lesser Antilles are southeast of Puerto Rico, as shown in Figure 6.6. Many of the islands are independent nations; some are quite poor. This discussion moves in a north to south direction.

Leeward Islands

The Leeward Islands are sheltered from the trade winds. The chain extends from the Virgin Islands in the north to Dominica in the south.

U.S. Virgin Islands

St. Thomas, **St. Croix** (*croy*), and **St. John** constitute the U.S. Virgin Islands (USVIs). They are the easternmost part of the United States and, according to the motto on their license plates, *America's Paradise*. Denmark ruled for almost 300 years, selling the islands to the United States in 1917. Except for St. Croix, the islands are hilly to mountainous, with beautiful beaches; cactus and unusual plants grow on the hillsides. The USVIs have some of the world's best sailing waters and excellent facilities for yacht charters.

Yacht charters provide an alternative to large cruise ships and resorts. Qualified sailors can charter a yacht either bareboat (no crew) or with crew.

St. Thomas is among the West Indies' most developed islands. Hotels and condominiums cover the hillsides. Ships dock next to Havensight Mall, and taxis and vans line up to take the passengers on tours, to a beach, or to **Charlotte Amalie** (*uh MAHL yuh*) for shopping. The island's duty-free status, special U.S. Customs' exemptions, and alluring stores are a temptation few resist. Shopping is the number one activity for first-time visitors. Repeat visitors head for the beaches. Magens Bay on the north coast has won awards as "best beach" for decades.

Hint for shoppers on St. Thomas: Mondays and Saturdays—the least-busy cruise ship days—are when downtown shops are least crowded.

St. Thomas is the air and sea hub for the U.S. Virgin Islands. In an average year more than 750 ships visit, and a new pier is planned. Seaplane and ferry services connect St. Thomas to St. Croix. The sea crossing takes approximately 55 minutes.

Shopping in the U.S. Virgin Islands

St. Croix is the largest and flattest of the three USVIs. The architecture of the island's two towns, **Frederiksted** and **Christiansted**, displays their Danish heritage. From Christiansted divers can take a boat to **Buck Island Reef National Monument**, about 6 miles (10 km) offshore. Divers follow a marked trail through the underwater marine garden.

St. John is the smallest of the islands—and to many the most beautiful. Laurence Rockefeller bought St. John and gave it to the United States. He stipulated that three-fourths must remain undeveloped and designated as the **Virgin Islands National Park**. The mountains are covered with tropical vegetation. Along the north shore, white-sand beaches fringe bay after bay. The island is home to a deluxe resort, Caneel Bay, and Cinnamon and Maho Bay campgrounds.

St. John has no airport and no cruise ship dock (although ships anchor offshore and tender passengers in). To get there, visitors fly to St. Thomas and take a short boat ride to St. John.

British Virgin Islands

A sea channel called *The Narrows* separates the upscale British Virgin Islands (BVIs) from the USVIs. The British dependency has approximately sixty small islands; only fifteen are inhabited. The BVIs are hilly, and all but coral **Anegada** are volcanic.

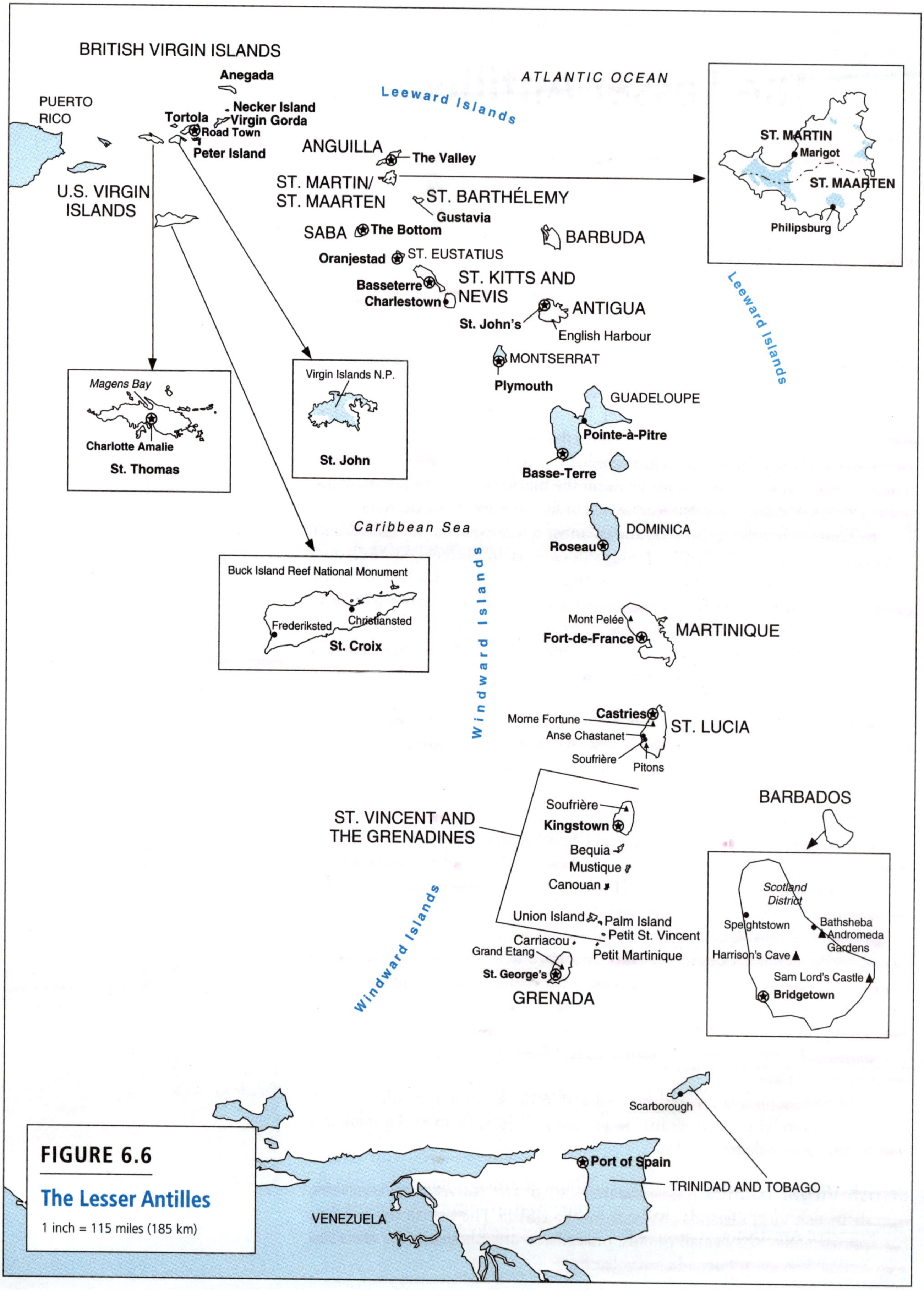

FIGURE 6.6

The Lesser Antilles

1 inch = 115 miles (185 km)

Mountainous **Tortola** ("Turtledove") is on the north side of the channel. **Road Town** on Tortola is the town and port. **Virgin Gorda** ("Fat Virgin"), the second largest of the islands, is only 10 miles (16 km) long and 2 miles (3 km) wide. It is known for The Baths, a beach whose huge round granite boulders form natural sunlit pools. Of the other islands, **Peter Island** is a deluxe resort, and private **Necker Island** can be rented by those with a fat bank account who want luxury and low-key activity.

The BVIs have been considered prime sailing grounds since the 1600s, when pirates hid out in their coves. Today, seven out of ten visitors come for a sailing vacation. Trade winds and sheltered harbors allow novices to sail in relatively flat water with plenty of safe anchorages.

Anguilla Excellent beaches, good snorkeling, sailboats for rent, stylish hotels, and fine dining have made the British dependency of Anguilla (*ang GWEE uh*) a sought-after destination among experienced and wealthy travelers. The small coral island is flat and barren. One road, appropriately named Main Road, leads to all points on the island.

Anguilla specializes in low-key high luxury. There are no glittering casinos or nightclubs, no duty-free shopping. For its size the island has more deluxe properties than any other. **The Valley** is the very small town.

St. Martin/St. Maarten St. Martin, a department of France, shares a hilly island with St. Maarten, which is part of the Netherlands Antilles. An obelisk and a *Bienvenue/Welkom* sign are the only indications of the divide. Princess Juliana Airport on the Dutch side is a hub for flights to smaller islands.

The French section has gently rolling hills, resorts, and beaches. **Marigot** is the small French town; **Philipsburg**, the Dutch town, is larger. Its streets are lined with duty-free shops. Most passengers must be tendered in, but the island is building a deepwater port.

A typical visit involves dining on the French side, visiting the casinos on the Dutch side, playing golf or tennis, shopping, and sunning on the beaches. Topless bathing is common, and there are several clothing-optional beaches. Nightlife is ample.

St. Barthélemy (St. Barts) St. Barts is a small rocky island with more than enough *anses* ("beaches"), *baies* ("bays"), and coves to explore for at least a week. The island is hilly but not mountainous. There is little rain and not much vegetation. The hills are covered with tall cacti and the St. Barts palm tree, the *latanier*, which has fronds that grow like fans.

For many years the island belonged to Sweden, its one colony in the Caribbean. **Gustavia**, the only town, is named after a Swedish king. Today, St. Barts is part of the Région de Guadeloupe, governed by France. Most natives are descendants of Norman and Breton settlers.

St. Barts has retained several old French traditions. You may see island women wearing bonnets called *quichenottes*—"kiss-me-nots." The bonnets extend forward to cover their faces, making it difficult to sneak a kiss.

The island opened to tourism just before World War II when a pioneering pilot buzzed one of the few flat places on the island, scared away the goats, and landed. Daylight airline service soon began. The runway was recently expanded, but it is still not a destination for jumbo jets.

St. Barts has no golf courses, casinos, nightclubs, high-rise hotels, all-inclusives, large cruise ships (small ships anchor offshore and tender passengers in), or poverty. Its luxury lodgings, gourmet restaurants, and chic boutiques specializing in French couture appeal to European visitors and sophisticated Americans. It is not a destination for the budget-minded.

Saba Part of the Netherlands Antilles, Saba (*SAY bah*) is the peak of an extinct volcano. The capital, **The Bottom**, is in the bottom of the volcano's crater. Mount Scenery, the island's forest-covered hill, is the highest point in the entire Kingdom of the Netherlands.

Lodging on Saba is limited to small inns and guest houses. Its airport has a runway similar in size to the deck of an aircraft carrier. Saba's only road is The Road. It was built by a local carpenter after Dutch engineers said one couldn't be built. The carpenter took correspondence courses in engineering to learn how.

Saban women make handmade lace and brew a rum-based liquor, Saba Spice.

The island appeals to the traveler who appreciates natural beauty, spectacular views, and village life. Saba is a premier scuba diving destination. Sea walls drop deep close to shore, and underwater visibility is excellent.

St. Kitts and Nevis St. Kitts and Nevis (*NEE vuhs*) stand side by side in the arc of volcanic peaks that rise out of the sea in the northern part of the Leeward Islands. The islands are separated by a channel 2 miles (3 km) wide. They have been likened in shape to a round cricket ball (Nevis) and its oval bat (St. Kitts). Both islands have a fringe of fertile plain along their coasts, lush vegetation on their mountains, historic ruins, and restored 18th-century plantation homes converted to inns. Some beaches are of black or gray volcanic sand; others have white sand.

For years St. Kitts was known as England's mother colony in the West Indies. **Basseterre** on St. Kitts is the capital and largest town on both islands. **Charlestown** is the largest town on Nevis.

The islands compete for upscale visitors. Attractions include golf courses, restaurants, deluxe hotels and condos, and a small casino (on St. Kitts). Small cruise ships visit regularly.

Antigua and Barbuda Of English background, the islands of Antigua (*an TEE guh*) and Barbuda (*bahr BOO duh*) together form an independent country. About 98 percent of the people live on Antigua. It is the largest of the Leeward Islands, an air hub for the southern islands, and also a yacht hub. The capital, **St. John's**, has a deepwater harbor where large cruise ships dock frequently.

The islands are mostly flat, formed from volcanoes worn down by wind and rain. Antigua's appeal is a coastline carved into inviting coves and white-sand beaches—365 in all, one for every day of the year, according to the tourist bureau. The north coast is the most developed, with hotels on the beaches and large villas set in hibiscus gardens. The less crowded southwest coast has black-pineapple plantations.

Antigua has small casinos and a full range of accommodations, with many all-inclusives. One sightseeing attraction is **English Harbour**, the headquarters of Lord Nelson (1758–1805), England's greatest naval hero. Because of perpetual trade winds, the Antiguan coast is ideal for sailing and racing. *Sailing Week* each spring lures sailors from around the world.

Antigua is described as the pivot in the island chain, the place where the stepping-stones from the south swing west toward Florida.

Barbuda is a flat coral island, wooded, with lovely secluded beaches and small deluxe resorts. The island is a bird sanctuary. In November bird-watchers can witness the mating dance of the frigate birds. The males inflate a bright red sac in their necks, something positively irresistible to female frigates.

The Windward Islands

The Windward Islands are in the southeast Lesser Antilles. They stretch around the eastern end of the Caribbean. The islands are so named because they are exposed to the northeast trade winds.

Martinique The northernmost of the Windwards, Martinique (*mahr tuh NEEK*) is the flagship of French culture in the Caribbean. The oval-shaped island has volcanic mountains in the north; rolling hills and sugar cane fields around the capital, **Fort-de-France**; and hills on the south peninsula. The beaches have a mix of fine black, white, or peppered sand. Hotels range from humming centers of international entertainment to tiny *auberges* ("inns") set in old gingerbread houses. The island is also a busy cruise ship port.

In 1902 St. Pierre was the most modern town on the island, but it was living on borrowed time. The town's volcano, **Mont Pelée**, had been silent since 1851. On May 6 the mountain let loose. A cloud of flames, lava, and poison gas roared down the mountain. The lava engulfed the town and poured into the sea, setting ships on fire and killing more than 30,000 people in two minutes. The only survivor was a prisoner in an underground cell, who ended his days as a fairground exhibit in America. St. Pierre has since rebuilt, although not as extensively, and it is a popular tourist attraction.

Napoleon's Josephine was born on Martinique. Locals blame her for the reinstitution of slavery, which had been abolished during the French Revolution. Her family's sugar plantation needed the cheap labor.

St. Lucia St. Lucia (*LOO sha*) is an untamed island of British background with some of the finest mountain scenery and lushest vegetation in the Caribbean. Shaped like a mango (one of the region's sweetest fruits), the island has little flatland. The western coast is the calmest side, and the one with the best beaches and the largest number of resorts. The rugged interior is a rain forest. The island's spectacular symbols are the twin peaks of **Gros Piton** and **Petit Piton**, famous for their sugar-loaf shapes.

Castries is the capital and largest city. Its docks accommodate large ships. From the city most tours go to the southwest coast to **Soufrière**, a fishing village and the oldest settlement of the island. Over the ridge behind the town is the "drive-in volcano," which is actually a smoking, smelly crater belching mud, also named Soufrière. Visitors drive to a certain point and proceed on foot with a guide.

The drive from Castries to Soufrière to see the Pitons follows a winding road along the coast and through the mountains. Often people tour one way by minivan and the other by boat. The boat trip is especially worthwhile. Near **Anse Chastanet**, the view of the Pitons is spectacular. The beaches nearby are of black volcanic sand.

Pitons of St. Lucia

St. Vincent and the Grenadines Thirty-two islands in the southern Caribbean make up the archipelago of St. Vincent and the Grenadines (*grehn uh DEENZ*). The mountainous, volcanic island of St. Vincent has 89 percent of the country's land area and 95 percent of the population. The Grenadines are coral islands that barely break the surface of the sea. Their fine white beaches are protected by offshore reefs.

St. Vincent, Guadeloupe, and St. Lucia have volcanoes with the same *name*—*Soufrière*, meaning "sulfurous."

St. Vincent was a Carib stronghold and refuge for escaped slaves. Indian arrows held off the Europeans until 1750. The islands landed in British hands in 1783. The Caribs continued to fight. In 1797 the English general threatened them with surrender or extinction. Five thousand gave up and were deported to islands off the coast of Central America.

Kingstown on St. Vincent is the capital and largest town. It is a small cruise ship port and a center for yacht charters. *Carnival* is held during late June and early July. *Nine Mornings* is a colorful tradition of street parades held during the nine days before Christmas.

St. Vincent's Botanical Gardens have a breadfruit tree from the South Pacific brought by Captain Bligh of the *Bounty*. Breadfruit starts life as a small green lollipop and swells to the size of a cannonball.

St. Vincent is dominated by its own **Soufrière**, which last erupted in 1979. The island remains relatively undeveloped, but some of the Grenadines are exclusive resorts. The best known are

- **Bequia** (*BEK wee*), the largest and northernmost of the Grenadines. Its Admiralty Bay is one of the most popular yacht anchorages in the Caribbean.

- **Canouan** (*KAN no wan*) whose idyllic beaches are protected by a coral reef, and whose luxury resort has a distinctly European flavor.
- **Mustique** (*mus TEEK*), one of the most exclusive retreats in the Caribbean, long known as a hiding place for the rich and famous, including members of the British royal family.
- **Palm Island**, a small paradise hosting day-tripping cruise passengers and one very upscale resort on its white-sand beaches.
- **Petit St. Vincent**, a cottage colony on its own island for those who really, really want to get away from it all. The staff greets you with a beverage on the dock when you arrive by boat from the airport on Union Island. When you want room service, you raise a yellow flag in front of your door.
- **Union Island**, on the south end of the Grenadines. It has low mountains and superb beaches. Yachtsmen sail from Union to some of the smaller Grenadines. Clifton Harbour is the small town.

Grenada The most southerly of the Windward Islands is Grenada (*grih NAY duh*), just 100 miles (161 km) off the Venezuelan coast. The small island is of volcanic origin and has fertile soils. A forested mountain ridge runs north-south, cut by rivers. The western coastline is rocky; the southern coast has natural harbors and beaches of white and black sand.

The outlying islands of **Carriacou** and **Petit Martinique** are part of the three-island nation of Grenada. **St. George's** is the country's capital.

In the 17th century, the French carried out a campaign of extermination on Grenada against the fierce Caribs. When defeat was certain, the last group of Caribs jumped to their death from a cliff, now known as Leapers' Hill. The island changed hands several times. After years of British rule, it became independent. In 1983 it was the site of a U.S.-led invasion.

Grenada is the *Spice Island*, the world's leading producer of nutmeg and mace. It is also a popular cruise ship stop. Tourists can see the oldest rum plant in the Western Hemisphere, beautiful beaches such as Grand Anse, and **Grand Etang Forest Reserve**, as well as plantation homes, forts, gardens, and spice shops.

■ ■ ■

The nutmeg tree is a tall-growing evergreen with a small yellow fruit. No part goes to waste. When the fruit ripens, it splits, revealing a brown nut covered with a red waxy netting. The outer flesh goes into making jams, the nut is processed to make nutmeg, and the red netting is used to make a second spice, mace.

■ ■ ■

Barbados The most easterly of the Windward Islands is Barbados (*bahr BAY dohz*). It is also one of the most prosperous islands. Just 21 miles (34 km) long by 14 miles (23 km) wide, it has a 98 percent literacy rate and an airport that can handle the largest aircraft.

The island consists of coral deposits formed around a rocky core. A fringe of coral reef has produced dazzling white beaches on its Caribbean side, where most of the resorts are located. Inland, the terrain rises to hills in the north and center. Its windward side on the Atlantic has crashing waves.

Barbados is the only former Caribbean colony that never changed hands. Its history was bound with England and the fortunes of sugar. Tourism began in the 18th century. Even George Washington slept here. About half the island's visitors arrive on cruise ships.

Barbados has a rich display of great houses, plantations, and chattel houses. Sites that attract visitors include

- **Bridgetown**, the capital, a small city on the southwest coast. Bridgetown's Victorian buildings are interspersed with modern stores and banks.
- The west coast highway leading north to **Speightstown**, lined with low-rise hotels and expensive villas on good beaches. The area was called the *St. James Coast*, then the *Gold Coast*, and then upgraded to the *Platinum Coast*—perhaps referring to the cost of a hotel room.
- The **Scotland District**, with great houses open to view. Tourists can visit St. Nicholas Abbey (1650), Drax Hall (c. 1650), and Villa Nova (1834).

■ ■ ■

Barbados's brightly painted chattel houses were small makeshift homes built on a foundation of loose stone, easy to dismantle and move. The occupants did not own the land and had to be ready to pick up and go if the plantation owner told them to move.

■ ■ ■

CLOSE-UP: A CARIBBEAN CRUISE

Who is a good prospect for a cruise? Good prospects are people celebrating special occasions, those seeking value, and those wanting a vacation experience that includes several islands. Consider honeymooners, families (reunions), gamblers, groups, travelers with special interests, singles, and companies that want to offer an incentive trip as the prize for a competition among salespeople.

Why would they take a cruise to the Caribbean? Cruises pamper their passengers with services and offer an abundance of activities as well as the allure of a sea voyage. Passengers can visit several destinations without having to pack and unpack. And because cruises are a form of all-inclusive, the cost of the trip is fairly predictable. Accommodations, meals, transportation, and entertainment are included in the price.

For families, cruises offer a chance to be together in a secure environment with something for all ages; youth programs keep children and teenagers happy while parents relax. For singles, making friends is easy in the cruise's relaxed atmosphere. People traveling as a group are likely to find that a cruise allows them to be alone or together, to meet for meals and special events, and then separate to pursue individual interests. People with interests from bingo to Wall Street, country music to baseball, can find a cruise with that interest as a theme. For gamblers, shipboard casinos just keep getting bigger and more elaborate, and for shoppers, the large ships have malls.

Caribbean cruises feature the newest ships, with such features as rock-climbing walls and ice-skating rinks, and different itineraries attract repeat passengers.

Where would they go? Most itineraries follow circles, departing and returning from the same port. Travelers have a choice of eastern, western, or southern Caribbean ports. (Figure 6.6, page 148, illustrates these choices.) Western Caribbean cruises from Miami, Fort Lauderdale, New Orleans, and Houston visit the Caymans, Cozumel (Mexico), and Jamaica. Southern Caribbean voyages from San Juan sail to St. Thomas, Barbados, St. Lucia, Martinique, and Antigua. The eastern Caribbean itinerary to the Bahamas, a private island, St. Thomas, and St. Maarten is popular with first-time cruisers.

A typical seven-night voyage leaving from Miami or Fort Lauderdale, Florida, might follow this itinerary.

Sunday Miami. Boarding after 1200; ship departs for voyage at 1700.

Monday Nassau, in port from 0900 to 1700.

Tuesday At sea.

Wednesday Philipsburg, St. Maarten, 0800 to 1800.

Thursday St. Thomas, USVI, 0900 to 1730.

Friday At sea.

Saturday Coco Cay, Bahamas, 1100 to 1800, for the private island experience.

Sunday Miami, 0830.

When is the best time to cruise? The Caribbean is year-round territory. Rates are highest during Christmas and holidays, lowest between Thanksgiving and Christmas. If weather is the concern, spring and early summer bring the calmest seas, but smooth sailing can never be guaranteed. Sunday departures are popular with honeymooners recuperating after a Saturday wedding.

If the traveler says, "I get seasick," how would you respond? Ask in what circumstances. The person who gets ill on a small boat might not have the problem on a large stable ship. The Caribbean is one of the calmest seas. If the traveler continues to have doubts, suggest a short voyage such as a three-night cruise to the Bahamas from Florida, where much of the time is spent in port. If seasickness is a real problem, don't ignore the objection; move on to another travel product.

- The east coast, with **Andromeda Gardens** and **Bathsheba**, a site popular with surfers.
- **Sam Lord's Castle**, on the windy southeast coast. The story goes that Sam lured ships to the rocks to salvage their cargo. His mansion, built in 1820, is now the centerpiece of a resort.
- **Harrison's Cave**, one of Barbados's most popular attractions. Tours of the extensive underground caverns are made by electric tram.

Barbados celebrates its culture with *Crop Over Festival* the last week in July. Dating to the 18th century, Crop Over marks the final reaping of the sugar cane.

✔ CHECK-UP

Islands with a decidedly French flavor are
- ✔ Martinique.
- ✔ St. Barts.
- ✔ St. Martin.

Countries with a British background include
- ✔ Anguilla.
- ✔ Antigua and Barbuda.
- ✔ Barbados.
- ✔ British Virgin Islands.
- ✔ Grenada.
- ✔ St. Kitts and Nevis.
- ✔ St. Lucia.
- ✔ St. Vincent and the Grenadines.

Islands in the Lesser Antilles that are part of the Netherlands Antilles are
- ✔ Saba.
- ✔ St. Maarten.

E

Islands off the South American Coast

Three islands off the South American coast—Aruba, Bonaire, and Curaçao—are very much in the mainstream of tourism. Popularly known as the ABCs, they are part of the Netherlands Antilles. In 1986 Aruba seceded from the group, but in 1994 it decided to postpone its transition to full independence. See Figure 6.7 for a map of the islands.

Aruba

As the westernmost of the ABCs, Aruba (*ah ROO buh*) is the final link in the long Antillean chain. It is a flat limestone island 20 miles (32 km) long by 6 miles (10 km) wide, with little vegetation. The island is known for its immense boulders, prickly cacti, and *watapana* (divi-divi) trees, withered trees bent horizontal by constant trade winds from the northeast. The winds keep the humidity low and pesky insects at bay. Aruba has coral reefs and white-sand beaches on its south and southwest coast. In contrast, its northeast coast is rugged and wild, with thundering waves. The hot, dry climate is perfect for tourism.

Oranjestad, the capital, is a small town with architecture reflecting Dutch and Spanish influences. Southeast of Oranjestad, the road passes Aruba's most

FIGURE 6.7

The ABC Islands

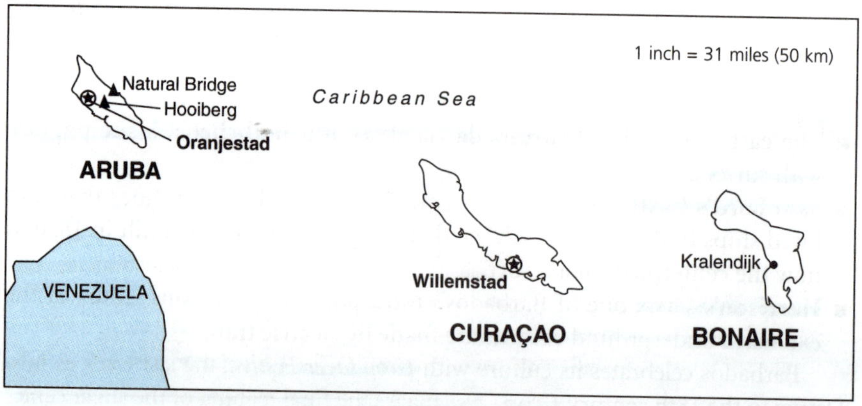

visible landmark—the **Hooiberg** (Haystack Mountain). From the top it is possible to see across the sea to Venezuela.

Aruba attracts those who enjoy activity. Queen Beatrix Airport handles the largest jets. Hotels, most of which are on the northwest coast, offer every possible service and amenity. Casino gambling is available, and nightlife is ample. Many hotels are equipped for large conventions.

On the beach in Aruba

Bonaire

Bonaire (*bun AIR*) is east of Curaçao. It is a flat coral outcropping with desertlike terrain, salt ponds, and flamingos that make the island their winter home.

Almost completely surrounded by coral reefs, Bonaire is a top-ten diving spot. Spear guns were replaced by underwater cameras in the 1970s, and the fish have become the most numerous and friendly in the Caribbean. At most hotels the dive packages include the heavy equipment that is needed for diving but is too bulky to take on a plane. A typical package includes tanks of air, weight belts and weights, transportation to the dive site, and two dives from a boat per day.

The locals say that folks "come here to dive, eat, dive, sleep, and dive." But they also come to kayak, bike, hike, snorkel, and soak in the sun. Bonaire is ideal for those who enjoy water sports but do not demand much other activity. Everyone is in bed early, building up strength for another day underwater.

The hotels are along the leeward coast in a cluster north of **Kralendijk,** the small town. The island has two casinos. Captain Don's Habitat is the nerve center for scuba divers. Its diving center is one of the Caribbean's best.

Amerigo Vespucci reached Bonaire in 1499 and named it the Arawak word for low country, *bo-nah*. The Dutch felt right at home when they arrived. They ran the island as a salt production facility.

Curaçao

Thirty-five miles (56 km) north of Venezuela, Curaçao (*koor uh SOW*) is shaped like a bow tie. It is a low island covered with strange-looking cacti. Beaches are on the island's west end, as is Mount Christoffel, the island's highest point.

The largest island and the administrative center of the Netherlands Antilles, Curaçao is an important port and trading hub. Thanks to casinos, diving, and duty-free shopping, as well as a port that can handle large cruise ships, the island is emerging as a tourist destination.

Willemstad, the capital, is Amsterdam in the tropics. Dutch ways are evident, not only in the sun-washed, gabled buildings that border its streets but also in the Indonesian food and customs brought from the Dutch East Indies. Of interest are the Queen Emma Pontoon Bridge and the Floating Market, where Venezuelan merchants come to sell their produce and spices. The town's Mikvé Israel Synagogue is the oldest in the Americas.

Curaçao liqueur is made from the skins of oranges that grow small and bitter in the barren earth of the island.

✔ CHECK-UP

The islands off the South American coast include
- ✔ Aruba; its capital and largest town is Oranjestad.
- ✔ Bonaire; its town is Kralendijk.
- ✔ Curaçao; its capital and largest town is Willemstad.

Highlights for visitors to the islands include
- ✔ Beaches, casinos, and activity of Aruba.
- ✔ Diving on Bonaire.
- ✔ Old World atmosphere of Curaçao.

ON THE SPOT

A multigeneration family (grandparents, parents, teenagers) would like to vacation together. They would like to go "someplace warm" in February during school vacation. They reject your suggestion of a cruise because the mother gets seasick even when she sees water swirling in the tub. Which island would have something for each generation?

Barbados would be a good choice. The island has sightseeing for the grandparents, beach relaxation for the parents, and plenty of water sports for the teenagers.

➤ PROFILE

Dining in the Islands

Island cuisine owes much to African influences, with contributions from India, France, and Spain. Fish is a feature of all the islands. Some foods to try:

- ➤ Ackee fruit, poisonous when green, ripe when red, and yellow when it bursts open. Ackee served at breakfast looks like scrambled eggs.
- ➤ Callaloo, a thick mud-green stew made from dasheen, okra, crab, and spices. Dasheen is a large tuber with elephant-ear leaves.
- ➤ Conch salad, conch chowder, conch fritters, and cracked conch (strips of conch deep fried) in the Bahamas.
- ➤ Flying fish and conkies in Barbados. Conkies are a mix of cornmeal, coconut, pumpkin, raisins, sweet potatoes, and spices, steamed in a banana leaf.
- ➤ Hoppin' John in Bermuda, a mix of rice, peas, onions, bacon, thyme, and chicken served with Outerbridge's Sherry Peppers Sauce.
- ➤ Jerk pit food in Jamaica, a blend of spices on meat, fish, or chicken cooked over pimento wood.
- ➤ Plantains, also called cooking bananas. Fried plantains prepared like potato chips are popular snacks.
- ➤ Fruits such as sweetsop, sugar apple, or soursop (which tastes like a cross between a citrus and a banana).

Planning the Trip

Most travelers to the islands want little more than sunscreen and a bathing suit. Many return year after year and know exactly where they want to go. Furthermore, the popularity of cruises and all-inclusive resorts simplifies the task of planning trips.

When to Go

In Bermuda, high season begins in April and ends in November. Cruises operate to Bermuda only during that time. In the West Indies, December 15 to April 14 is the traditional high season. These months are the most fashionable and the most expensive. But the Caribbean is a year-round destination. The island flora is at its height in summer, and for smooth, clear water, May, June, and July are best.

Preparing the Traveler

Puerto Rico is the only island destination where U.S. citizens have no need for documentation. Even the U.S. Virgin Islands require proof of citizenship. Most islands consider proof to be a birth certificate and a driver's license with a picture ID.

Watch out for changes in the requirements! In 2004 Barbados instituted a passport requirement. After some confusion, authorities decided cruise passengers would not need passports if their trips did not begin or end on the island.

Cruise passengers generally enjoy simplified procedures. Port taxes are paid as part of the cruise price. After passengers register their identification as they board, they can get on and off during most port calls without going through immigration procedures. They must show identification and pass through security when they reboard.

Health Some helpful hints:

- Wear shoes when walking along tropical beaches and when swimming. Many beaches are made up of coral fragments as well as sharp pieces of shell and sea-urchin spines.
- When in the sea, look but don't touch. Fish have effective protection systems, and beautiful colors are often indications of danger.
- Don't swim in still waters. *Schistosomes*, parasites that multiply in snail-infested waters, do much damage to human intestines and cause the disease *bilharzia*.
- Don't swim alone. The biggest hazard is not sharks, but drowning.
- Wear protective clothing and hats, and use a waterproof sunscreen. Be particularly careful when snorkeling. The combination of sun and cool water can be lethal.
- Don't eat the fruit of the manchineel tree that grows on the beaches. Don't shelter under one in the rain. The sap is poisonous and will blister your skin.
- Use bug spray. Mosquitoes are almost everywhere. They carry dengue fever (in the Greater Antilles) and malaria (in Hispaniola only).

Money The islands use many currencies, but unless the visitor is going to remote areas, there is little need to change money. The U.S. dollar, traveler's checks, and credit cards are widely accepted. ATMs are available in resort areas.

U.S. citizens returning directly home from the U.S. Virgin Islands from a trip of at least forty-eight hours are allowed to bring back duty-free (free of taxes) purchases totaling U.S.$1,200, subject to limitations on liquor, cigarettes, and cigars. Travelers returning from the twenty-four countries that are part of the Caribbean Basin Initiative (CBI) have special exemptions. Travelers returning from countries such as the Cayman Islands and Martinique, which are not part of the CBI, are restricted to the international duty-free allowance of U.S.$800. See the U.S. Customs Web site for the many exceptions.

Language Language in the islands is a mix. English is spoken with a lilting calypso drawl.

Customs Life is slow, and service on some islands can be unhelpful. Visitors should be prepared for high prices, a slower pace of life, and cultural differences.

Throughout the Caribbean the dress code is casual. But bathing suits, tank tops, shorts, and halters are not considered appropriate apparel for church on any island. Bermuda is the most formal island. Although Bermuda-length shorts are acceptable attire for men at dinner, they might be asked to wear a coat and tie. Travelers should check ahead for the restaurant's dress code.

Transportation

Depending on the island, the traveler can arrive by plane or ship.

By Air The islands are served by major airlines, regional partners, and charters. There are international airports on Bermuda; at Nassau and Freeport in the Bahamas; on islands of the Greater Antilles; and on St. Maarten, Antigua, Martinique, St. Lucia, Barbados, Aruba, Bonaire, and Curaçao. People who fear flying on small planes should be steered to islands with facilities capable of handling large planes.

For the return trip, passengers should allow plenty of time at the airport. Checking in, paying departure taxes (if they are not included in the ticket), clearing security, and boarding take much longer than expected.

By Water Cruising is one of the most popular ways to visit the islands. Cruises to Bermuda depart from April to November from East Coast ports. Short cruises to the Bahamas depart from Miami, Fort Lauderdale, and Cape Canaveral year-round. These ports also host cruises to the most distant islands.

Ships in the Caribbean follow eastern, western, and southern itineraries, as Figure 6.8 shows. Ships depart from almost every city that has a port. Cruises bound for the southern Caribbean depart from San Juan.

The Virgin Islands, Antigua, and St. Vincent and the Grenadines are centers for yacht charters. Interisland transport varies considerably. Nassau and the Out Islands are linked by ferry services. The Virgin Islands have ferry links. Mail boats and local ferries serve other islands.

By Road Bermuda is one of the few destinations where visitors cannot rent a car. They can rent mopeds (motor-assisted bicycles) or pedal bikes, or take horse-drawn carriages, land or water taxis, or local buses. Even though distances are not great, winding roads, heavy traffic, and a speed limit of 20

> **➤ PROFILE**
>
> ### Shopping in the Islands
>
> Cruise passengers and hotel guests enjoy shopping in St. Thomas and other duty-free ports. The islands do a brisk business in T-shirts, jewelry, perfumes, porcelains, and liquor. Some specialties:
>
> - In the Bahamas, straw goods and *batik* garments made by the Androsia company on the island of Andros.
> - In Bermuda, English woolens, china, antiques, porcelain miniature Bermuda houses, island watercolors, and jewelry featuring the Bermuda bird, the longtail.
> - In the Cayman Islands, black coral jewelry and rum cakes.
> - In the Dominican Republic, amber.
> - In Grenada, woven baskets filled with fresh spices.
> - In Jamaica, Blue Mountain coffee, Jamaican rum, straw goods, and handicrafts.
> - In St. Barts, French fashions.
> - In the Turks and Caicos, unusual stamps. Stamps from other islands are popular also.

mph (32 kph) makes getting around time-consuming. Taxis that display a small blue flag have drivers approved as guides by the Department of Tourism.

On the other islands, visitors can rent cars. On the smaller islands, sometimes the vehicle turns out to be a golf cart or a *minimoke,* which is a cross between a jeep and a golf cart. Travelers should be advised to ask about road conditions. Local licenses may be required. They are easy to get and are usually issued by the car rental firms.

Countries that are British dependencies or were once part of the British Empire drive on the left. Islands with Dutch, French, or Spanish background drive on the right. In the very Americanized USVIs, one truly foreign custom remains: motorists drive on the left.

Bermuda's buses are painted pink with a blue stripe. Bus stops are either pink or blue; the color indicates whether the bus is going toward or away from Hamilton—pink in, blue out.

Accommodations

The islands have a daunting number of hotels from which to choose. Glossy magazines, television shows featuring resorts for the rich and famous, and brochures often raise consumers' expectations. Unfortunately, budgets and expectations do not always match. Price is often the deciding factor when choosing accommodations.

The lure of the all-inclusive resort is that the price includes "everything"—lodging, food, drinks, most activities, and airport transfers. Still, most travelers will need to whip out their wallets for tips, departure taxes, some sports, and excursions. Minimum stays are usually required.

Bermuda divides its accommodations into categories: resort hotels, small hotels, cottage colonies, private clubs, housekeeping cottages, apartments, and guest houses. Most offer a meal plan, often a good buy at a destination where transportation might be difficult and prices high. Bermuda hotels offer reduced rates and special events during low season (December 15 to April 15).

In Puerto Rico, many travelers seek the experience of staying at a parador. Puerto Rican paradors are privately owned and operated by the proprietor. To be part of the official network, paradors must be located outside San Juan and have at least seven but no more than seventy-five rooms. The tourist board recommends that they also have picturesque locations and attractions such as beaches, mountains, or historical sites. Paradors target budget-conscious travelers by offering affordable rates and basic services.

In the Lesser Antilles, travelers enjoy staying at great houses and restored plantation homes. The atmosphere is easygoing, with hammocks for snoozing, lobster bakes on palm-lined beaches, and candlelit dinners in stately dining rooms.

FIGURE 6.8

Typical Cruise Ship Itineraries in the Caribbean

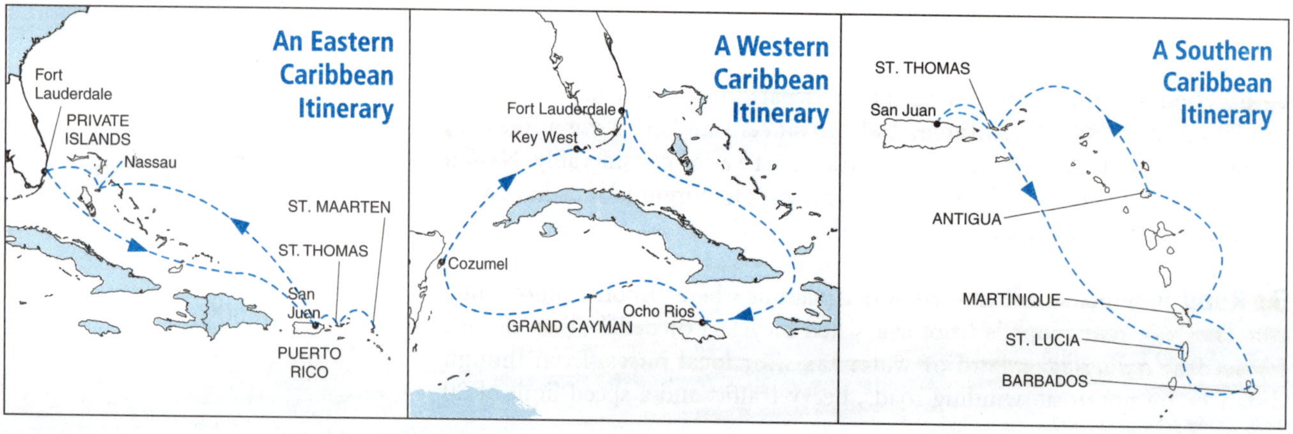

CLOSE-UP: AN ALL-INCLUSIVE

Who is a good prospect for an all-inclusive resort? An all-inclusive is a good choice for those who like a lot of activity, for families, for friends traveling together, for people who enjoy meeting people, and for sports-minded vacationers. (But all-inclusives are not a good match for people who want to experience the local life and culture.) All-inclusives have target markets. Some are for singles, others for couples only, and still others for families.

Why would they choose an all-inclusive resort? The predictability of the cost and the guarantee of a multitude of things to do are important considerations. On any island where security might be a concern, personal safety is another benefit of the all-inclusive. The grounds are usually fenced and patrolled by guards.

Where would they go? All-inclusives are found on almost all Caribbean islands. People especially seem to enjoy making just one reservation for a package vacation that includes air, accommodations, and recreation.

When is the best time to visit? The Caribbean high season is traditionally winter—from December 15 to April 14—when northern weather is at its worse, not necessarily when Caribbean weather is at its best. Singles in search of partners should visit in high season or in mid-summer, or choose a resort with a high year-round occupancy rate.

The travelers say, "We're not very sports-minded. What else is there to do?" How would you respond? All-inclusives provide activities for many interests. Ask the travelers what they like to do. Always try to mesh travelers with their special interests.

✔ CHECK-UP

Planning a trip to Bermuda and the West Indies involves
- ✔ Questioning carefully to uncover expectations.
- ✔ Meshing those expectations with budget constraints.
- ✔ Choosing between a cruise and an island stay.

Transportation choices to the islands include
- ✔ By air: jumbo jets to island-hoppers.
- ✔ By sea: cruise ships, chartered yachts, ferries, and local mail boats.
- ✔ By land: buses, vans, taxis, mopeds, minimokes, and golf carts.

OTHER DESTINATIONS IN THE CARIBBEAN

Each of the other islands in the Caribbean has its fans. We continue in a north to south direction.

TURKS AND CAICOS

The southeastern end of the Bahamas chain consists of more than forty islands known as the Turks and Caicos. (Look back at Figure 6.5.) Like the Bahamas, they are flat coral islands with beautiful beaches and dramatic scenery under the sea. In the past the islands had no facilities for large cruise ship arrivals, but plans are in the works to construct a port.

Cockburn Town on Grand Turk is the capital, but the Caicos is the larger group of islands. **Providenciales** (Provo) is the most developed for tourism. It has a casino and the world's only commercial conch farm. The conch (*konk*) is a staple of the island diet that is fast disappearing from its natural habitat.

CUBA

Cuba (*KYOO buh*) is the Caribbean's largest country, about the size of Florida. It is a beautiful island with mountains, rolling hills, grasslands, rivers, a dramatic coastline, and sandy beaches. Its capital, **Havana**, has a fine deepwater harbor.

Travel between the United States and Cuba has been restricted to Cuban Americans, journalists, researchers, and individuals with approved interests. The situation is subject to change at any time. The rules apply only to U.S. citizens.

Canadian and European visitors enjoy inexpensive package tours of Cuba. Several international hotel chains have properties at Varadero Beach east of Havana.

■ ■ ■

Labadee is a cruise ship private beach on the north coast of Haiti. It is fenced off from the rest of the island, and most passengers do not even realize they are in Haiti.

■ ■ ■

HAITI

Haiti (*HATE ee*) occupies the western third of Hispaniola in the Greater Antilles. In 1804 it became the first independent nation in the West Indies after slaves rebelled against their French rulers in a bloody revolution. Haiti has a history of producing outstanding primitive art and monumental ruins such as the Citadel and Sans Souci Palace. Political, economic, and health problems keep the country far off tourism's mainstream.

ST. EUSTATIUS (STATIA)

Once a powerful trading center, Statia (*STAY shah*) today is a quiet island, part of the Netherlands Antilles. Unlike its sister island of Saba, it has a good harbor. Although divers are lured by shipwrecks and sea life, the beaches are not the best. Because of past volcanic eruptions, Statia's sand is gray or black and hard to walk on. On the island's south end, an extinct volcano called the Quill has a lush rain forest in its crater. Island officials are preserving historic buildings and old forts and expanding the pier in hopes of attracting more cruise ships.

Oranjestad, the capital, is divided into an Upper and Lower Town. Buildings in Lower Town were abandoned when the sea moved inland. The crumbling ruins that peek out of the water make for fascinating snorkeling.

■ ■ ■

In 1776 Statia's Dutch governor saluted an unknown flag on a ship coming into the harbor. It was the first time a foreign country had recognized the flag of the United States.

■ ■ ■

MONTSERRAT

In 1995 Montserrat went from being a posh Caribbean island for the affluent to a mostly volcano-ravaged landscape; more than half the island's population was displaced. The volcano sleeps now. Volcanophiles can tour the ruined regions, spy on the still-steaming volcano, and relax on the unscathed northern part of the island. The southern half, including the capital, **Plymouth**, is caked in thick ash and mud. The island is accessible via ferry service or a helicopter ride from Antigua.

GUADELOUPE

Very French Guadeloupe (*gwah duh LOOP*) looks like a butterfly on a map. It is actually two islands—Grande-Terre and Basse-Terre—linked by a bridge. Basse-Terre is a lush, volcanic, mountainous island; Grande-Terre has the flatter sand-fringed landscape expected at beach resorts. **Basse-Terre** on Basse-Terre Island is the capital, but **Pointe-à-Pitre** on Grande-Terre is the tourist center.

Grande-Terre has the casinos and activity. Accommodations range from country inns, to a Club Med, to large hotels. Nightlife is plentiful. In the tourist hotels, staff members speak English. Outside the tourist areas, French is useful.

DOMINICA

Dominica (*dom in NEE kah*) has steep mountains, unspoiled rain forest, rushing rivers, and lush vegetation. The beaches are gray or jet black, with good offshore diving. **Roseau** (*rose OH*) on the south coast is the capital.

Dominica's piers can accommodate even the largest cruise ships. Its hotels are mainly small family-run affairs. Places of interest include Boiling Lake, Emerald Pool, and Cabrits National Park. Dominica also has the last surviving settlement of Caribs, the Indians who gave their name to the sea.

TRINIDAD AND TOBAGO

Trinidad and Tobago form one country with two islands that have different personalities. Trinidad is not a resort destination, but Tobago is.

➤ PROFILE

The Dive Industry

You might want to visit a dive travel Web site to stay on top of what's happening in the industry. Did you know that

- ➤ The United States has 3.8 million dive travelers?
- ➤ The average diver travels two to four times a year?
- ➤ Children can become certified divers at age ten?
- ➤ The most common injury divers suffer is sunburn?
- ➤ Divers need to know how to swim, but do not need to be marathon swimmers?

Source of statistics: *Travel Weekly*, July 2000.

Trinidad is about as far south as you can go in the Caribbean before you hit Venezuela. It is a big square island filled with oil refineries and sugar cane fields, with steep cloud forests and empty beaches of golden sand. Hotels see more business travelers than tourists. **Port of Spain**, the capital, is a tapestry of races, cultures, and creeds.

Columbus discovered the island, but the Spanish did not stay long. Trinidad had no gold, only pirates. The French settled the island and brought with them the tradition of Carnival, the days of merrymaking, parading, and masquerading before Lent. During one week in February, Port of Spain dances. All southern Caribbean islands celebrate Carnival, but none can match Trinidad's display. Elaborately costumed *mas* ("troupes") march to the beat of steel drums, which the locals call *pans*.

Tobago is 21 miles (34 km) to the northeast of Trinidad. It is known for its beige beaches, offshore reefs, golf courses, and wildlife. The unspoiled island is gaining popularity as a dive site. Parts of the mountainous island are heavily wooded, with the oldest protected rain forest in the Western Hemisphere. **Scarborough** is the island's town. Its airport can handle big jets, and its port can take on the megas.

The French and English planters forbade the use of skin drums in the Caribbean, wary that the drums would incite slave revolt. In the 1940s, someone in Trinidad cut a steel oil drum in two and banged the bottom with a hammer, transforming it into what Trinidadians claim is the only truly new musical instrument invented in the 20th century.

CHAPTER WRAP-UP

SUMMARY

Here is a review of the objectives with which we began the chapter.

1. **Describe the environment and people of the islands.** The islands extend from Bermuda to the coast of South America. They vary from very large (Cuba and the Dominican Republic) to tiny specks (Saba). The land was formed as chunks of a continent that broke off long ago (Trinidad), through volcanic eruptions from the ocean floor (Montserrat, Dominica, St. Lucia), from coral built by tiny sea animals (the Bahamas and the Turks and Caicos), or by combinations of these processes (Bermuda).

   An island's beaches and landscape depend on the way it was formed. Flat coral islands tend to have beautiful sandy beaches; volcanic islands have black-, gray-, or golden-sand beaches. Some islands have tropical rain forests (Puerto Rico); others have a desertlike landscape (Aruba).

   The islands' original inhabitants were Indians of various tribes. The fierce Caribs gave their name to the sea. Explorers and colonists came from Spain, England, the Netherlands, France, Denmark, and even Sweden. West Africans were brought as slaves to work the cane fields. East Indians came as contract workers after slavery was abolished. Today, the islands are a racial mix.

2. **Identify and locate the most-visited islands.** The most-visited islands are Bermuda in the Atlantic; Grand Bahama and New Providence in the Bahamas; Grand Cayman, Jamaica, the Dominican Republic, and Puerto Rico in the Greater Antilles; St. Thomas, St. Martin/St. Maarten, Antigua, Martinique, and Barbados in the Lesser Antilles; and Aruba in the islands off South America.

3. **Describe the islands' attractions, matching travelers and destinations best suited for each other.** Bermuda has great appeal for those looking for romance. Its beaches, golf and tennis facilities, shopping, choice of accommodations, and English atmosphere make the island a great choice for honeymooners and families.

   Visitors seeking small islands with deluxe accommodations, good beaches, and relaxed activity would match well with Bermuda, the Bahamas' Family Islands, Anguilla, St. John in the USVIs, the British Virgin Islands, St. Barts, St. Kitts and Nevis, Barbados, and the Grenadines.

   Although all-inclusive resorts can be found throughout the islands, Jamaica has the biggest selection. Islands with shopping, gambling, sightseeing, and water sports include Freeport and Nassau in the Bahamas, Puerto Rico, St. Maarten, and Aruba. Golf and polo are attractions on the Dominican Republic. St. Thomas (USVIs) is known for its duty-free shopping, and Barbados has plenty to do. Gambling is available on Antigua, Aruba, the Bahamas, Curaçao, the Dominican Republic, Guadeloupe, Martinique, Puerto Rico, the Turks and Caicos, and the cruise ships.

Those requesting dive facilities would match well with the Turks and Caicos, Cayman Islands, Dominica, Saba, and Bonaire. The yacht charter centers are in Antigua, the U.S. and British Virgin Islands, and St. Vincent and the Grenadines.

And just in case sunburn requires you to leave the beach for a while, Antigua, Barbados, Curaçao, the Dominican Republic, Grenada, Jamaica, Martinique, Nevis, Puerto Rico, St. Kitts, St. Vincent, and Statia have shaded historic sites.

4. **Provide or find the information needed to plan a trip to the islands.** Cruises and all-inclusive resorts are staples of island tourism and simplify planning. Special accommodations include the paradors of Puerto Rico, great houses, cottage colonies, and all-inclusives. Air and water transportation options vary from island to island. Information is readily available.

QUESTIONS FOR DISCUSSION AND REVIEW

1. Travelers to the islands often seem to think "seen one, seen them all." In what ways do the islands differ from one another?
2. How have the islands been influenced by African and colonial cultures?
3. What suggestions would you offer island tourist boards to help them counter the popularity of cruising and attract more long-stay visitors?
4. The hotel can make or break a resort vacation. What questions would you ask travelers to uncover their preferences?

1) islands differ in landscape, formation, language, political, side of road cars drive on, beaches, + history

2) affects language, food, festivals + architecture

3) competitive pricing + safety

4) where have you stayed before?

CHAPTER 7

Mexico and Central America

- Mexico
- Belize, Costa Rica, and Panama
- Other Destinations in Central America

OBJECTIVES

When you have completed Chapter 7, you should be able to

1. Describe the environment and people of Mexico and Central America.
2. Identify and locate Mexico's most-visited sites, matching travelers and destinations best suited for each other.
3. Recall and locate the most-visited sites in Belize, Costa Rica, and Panama, matching travelers and destinations best suited for each other.
4. Provide or find the information needed to plan a trip to Mexico, Belize, Costa Rica, and Panama.

South of the United States are the lands that geographers often call **Middle America.** The region includes the islands discussed in Chapter 6, **Mexico,** and the seven countries of **Central America.** (The countries are listed alphabetically in Fast Facts, Appendix A.) The region is home to beach resorts, a canyon deeper than Arizona's, North America's third-highest mountain, active volcanoes, a canal through the wilderness, rain forests, one of the world's largest cities, the earth's second-largest barrier reef, and rich archaeological sites.

The Environment and Its People

Geographically, Mexico and Central America are part of North America (see Figure 7.1). Culturally, Latin America begins once the traveler flies, drives, or sails past the U.S. border.

The Land

Mexico's northern boundary is the **Rio Bravo del Norte** (the Rio Grande). From there, the country extends southward like a V-shaped necklace. **Baja** (*BAH hah*) **California** dangles like a pendant from its northwestern corner. Baja is a thin peninsula separated from the mainland by the **Gulf of California** (also called the *Sea of Cortez*). The Gulf of California and the Pacific Ocean form Mexico's long western border; the Gulf of Mexico borders the east coast. Along the Gulf of Mexico, the coastal plain is fringed by swamps, lagoons, and sandbars; the Pacific coastal plain is narrower and drier.

Towering mountains and high plateaus cover Mexico's northern two-thirds. The **Sierra Madre Oriental** on the east and the **Sierra Madre Occidental** on the west frame a wide central plateau, the home of most of the population. At the plateau's southern edge, the beautiful **Valley of Mexico** is ringed by snowcapped volcanoes. One of these is **Orizaba** (*aw ree ZAH buh*), also called by its Indian name Citlaltépetl (*see tlah TAY peht uhl*). It is North America's third-highest mountain and is perpetually snowcapped. The valley is part of a geological rift, and occasionally the earth heaves and the volcanoes rumble.

Legend says that Hernán Cortés described the terrain of Mexico to the Spanish king by crumpling a piece of paper, throwing it on a table, and saying the land looks like that. Whether the story is true or not, crumpled paper does show Mexico's mountainous terrain.

South of the plateau, the land narrows at the **Isthmus of Tehuantepec** (*tuh WAHN tuh pehk*) before widening in the east into the **Yucatán** (*yoo kuh TAN*) **Peninsula.** The peninsula is a tableland of limestone covered by a thin layer of soil. This is karst land, a landscape that encourages the formation of pits. In the Yucatán the pits are called *cenotes*; they are natural wells formed by the erosion of subterranean limestone. The peninsula has no surface rivers.

The Yucatán is occupied not only by Mexico but also by part of **Guatemala** (*gwah tuh MAH luh*) and by **Belize** (*beh LEEZ*). To the south are the other countries of Central America: **Honduras** (*hohn DOO ruhs*), **El Salvador, Nicaragua** (*nihk uh RAH gwuh*), **Costa Rica,** and **Panama.** They occupy a narrow ribbon of land between the Pacific and the Caribbean. South of Costa Rica, the land narrows further at the **Isthmus of Panama,** which connects North and South America.

Lowlands with jungles follow both coasts of Central America. Inland, rugged mountains criss-cross the earth. More than twenty of Central America's mountains are active volcanoes. The entire region is an earthquake

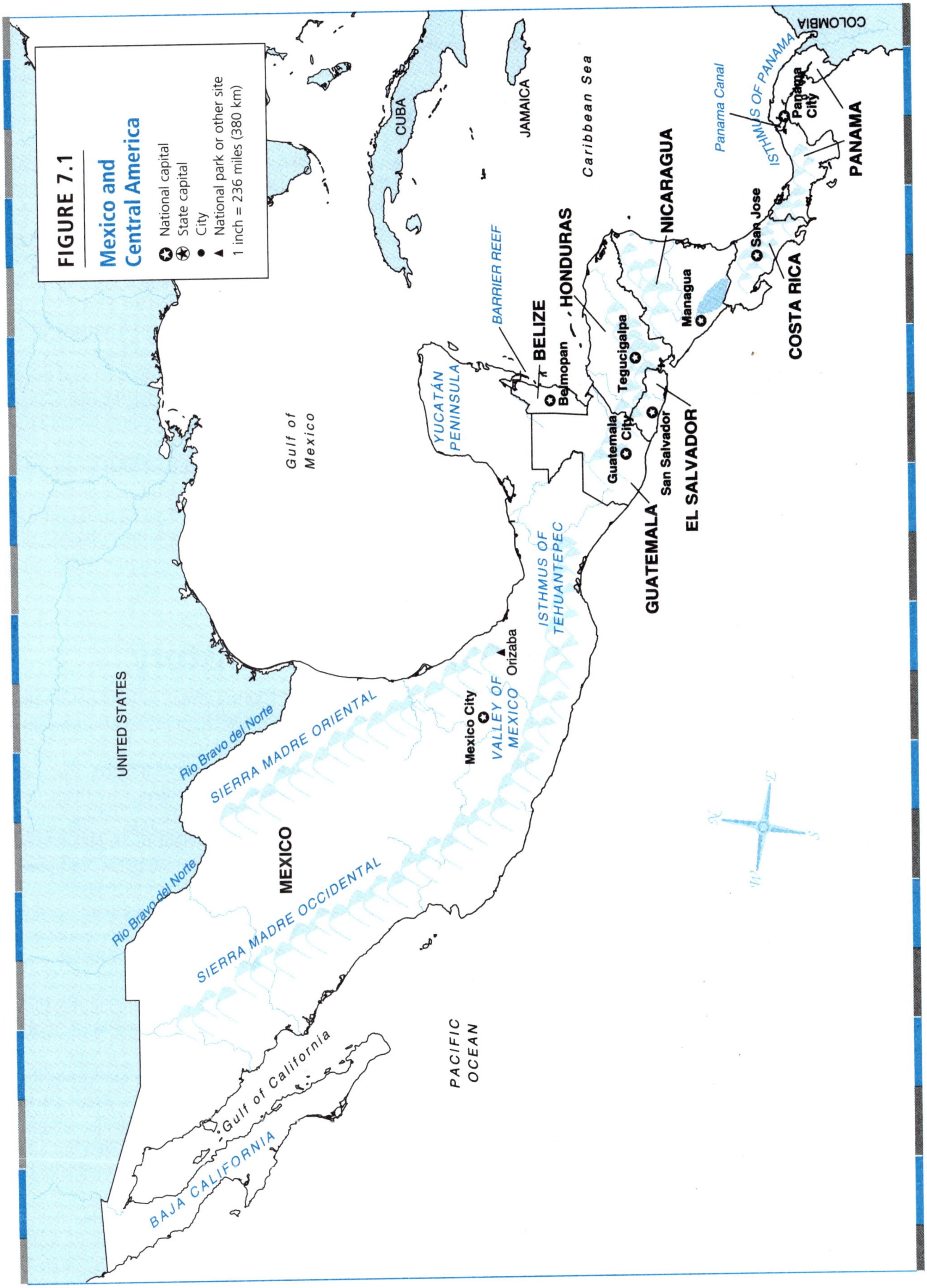

FIGURE 7.1
Mexico and Central America

zone. Although deadly to people and structures, the volcanic eruptions have produced excellent soil for growing coffee.

FIGURE 7.2

Milestones of Mexican and Central American History

1200–400 BC The Olmec culture, the progenitor of Mesoamerican civilizations, is at its height.

AD 250–900 Mayan civilization flourishes.

1300–1500 The Aztec empire is at its peak.

1492–1893 It is the age of European exploration and colonization.

1810 Catholic priest Miguel Hidalgo y Castilla launches a revolution in Mexico.

1821 Mexico and Central America declare their independence from Spain.

1823 Costa Rica, El Salvador, Guatemala, Honduras, and Nicaragua separate from Mexico and form the United Provinces of Central America.

1823 U.S. President James Monroe declares North and South America closed to European colonization.

1846–1848 The Mexican-American War takes place.

1862 Belize becomes the British colony known as British Honduras.

1863–1867 French troops occupy Mexico City, and Maximilian rules as emperor.

1890s U.S. fruit companies arrive in Honduras to grow bananas.

1914 The Panama Canal opens.

1974 Costa Rica begins its orderly succession of democratic governments.

1980s Turmoil exists in El Salvador, Honduras, Guatemala, and Nicaragua.

1981 Belize becomes an independent nation.

1989 President George H. W. Bush orders troops into Panama to overthrow Noriega.

1994 NAFTA (North American Free Trade Agreement) takes effect.

1999 The United States transfers control of the Panama Canal to Panama.

2003 Archaeologists discover one of the earliest royal Mayan graves yet at Takalik Abaj in western Guatemala.

2004 Panama announces plans to expand the canal.

The Climate

In Mexico rain, or the lack of it, has been a worry from time immemorial. Great temples were built to the rain gods. Most of Mexico has sunny weather for a large part of the year. The rainy season is from May to October. The rest of the year is not completely rainless, but the amount and frequency of rain in the winter are low.

Three important influences determine Mexico's weather. First, the cold California current that sweeps southward along the Pacific Coast lowers temperatures and reduces rainfall inland. Much of Mexico's northwest is desert or semi-desert. Second, altitude provides the plateau of Central Mexico with temperatures varying according to the height above sea level. And third, warm waters of the Caribbean and northeast trade winds give the east coast a tropical climate with a marked wet season in summer. The Gulf Coast and the Yucatán Peninsula can get unbearably hot and humid.

The Central American countries, which are situated well within the tropics, have a climate similar to Mexico's. The wet season is between May and October. The dry season is from February to April. Coastal areas on the Caribbean tend to be wetter and have a longer rainy season than those on the Pacific. The offshore waters are clearest in the spring. Hurricanes come from the east and west any time from June to November.

The People and Their History

Advanced cultures existed in Mexico and Central America long before the Spanish conquest (see Figure 7.2). Although many tribes lived in the area, the best known are the Olmec, Maya, Toltec, and Aztec.

The **Olmec** (*OHL mehk*) flourished along the Gulf of Mexico. They are known for carving colossal statues of the heads of their rulers, with thick lips, broad flat noses, and headgear resembling football helmets.

The **Maya** (*MAH yuhn*) civilization reached its height in AD 600–800 in the region that today includes southern Mexico, Guatemala, Belize, and parts of Honduras and El Salvador. The Maya were not a single people; they lived in at least fifty city-states, each with its own king and court. Their cities were lost for centuries in the dense growth of the tropical rain forest. Only in the last few decades, with the decoding of Mayan writing, has it been possible to reconstruct their history.

The **Toltec** established an empire north of Mexico City during the 10th century AD. The Toltec worshiped the feathered serpent god and made human sacrifices.

The **Aztec** had the last great empire. Life for the Aztec was linked to the sun. To guarantee the sun's existence, they offered sacrifices, particularly human hearts, and they waged war continually to provide a regular supply. The Aztec built their capital on an island at the site of Mexico City. Initially the Aztec defeated the Spaniards. The Spanish takeover became possible only after they allied themselves with an army of natives.

For 300 years Spain's territory stretched from Panama to California. Spain finally granted Mexico its independence in 1821. In 1822 Costa Rica, El Salvador, Guatemala, Honduras, and Nicaragua separated from Mexico.

Independence, however, did not free Mexico and Central America from the influence of larger foreign powers, mostly the United States.

In a region of political instability and military rule, Costa Rica is known for its stable government. After its last civil war in 1948, the army was disbanded so that military coups would be impossible. Belize also has been free from civil war. But elsewhere in the region, economic problems and periodic wars have caused widespread suffering.

The influence of Spanish control is apparent in the architecture, religion, and language of Mexico and Central America. Most of the people are Roman Catholic, and the official language is Spanish, except in Belize, where English is the official language. The population is a mix of Indian, Spanish, and *mestizo* (mixed white and Indian heritage). Large numbers of Afro–Central Americans live in Belize, Nicaragua, and Panama. Many are descendants of escaped slaves and the Carib Indians; others came from the Caribbean islands to help dig the Panama Canal. Costa Ricans are mainly of European descent.

Thousands of years ago, the Indians of what is now Mexico discovered how to grow corn. They steamed and roasted it; the Spanish introduced frying. The main cornmeal food is the *tortilla*, the bread of many Mexicans.

✔ CHECK-UP

Major physical features of Mexico and Central America include

- ✔ High mountains on both coasts of Mexico and a wide central plateau in between.
- ✔ Mexico's peninsulas: long and narrow Baja California on the west coast and the Yucatán Peninsula on the southeast coast.
- ✔ Rain forests along the east coast.
- ✔ Frequent earthquakes and erupting volcanoes.

Mexico's and Central America's culture is notable for

- ✔ Ancient cultures developed by the Olmec, Maya, Toltec, and Aztec.
- ✔ Centuries of Spanish colonial rule.
- ✔ Decades of often violent political conflict.

Mexico

Mexico is the giant of Middle America in every way: size, population, culture, and resources. Politically, Mexico is divided into thirty-one states and a Federal District (a political unit much like the District of Columbia in the United States). The United States stretches along its northern border, as Figure 7.3 shows.

Mexico, rich in reminders of ancient civilizations and Spanish-colonial atmosphere, is also a modern developing country. Ancient temples and cathedrals contrast with high-rise office buildings and contemporary beach resorts.

Ruins at Tulúm, Mexico

The Cities

About three-fourths of Mexico's population lives in urban areas. Mexico City is the world's second-largest city (Tokyo, Japan, is the largest). Border cities, particularly Tijuana (*tee WHAN uh*), Mexicali, Nogales, and Ciudad Juárez, are well known. More typical of Mexico are the large cities of Chihuahua (*chee WAW waw*), a cattle and silver-mining region in north central Mexico; Mérida, on the Yucatán; and Guadalajara (*gwahd uh luh HAHR uh*), in west central Mexico. The cultural center of the country, however, is the capital, Mexico City.

FIGURE 7.3 Mexico

Mexico City Built at an exhausting altitude (7,350 feet [2,450 m]) on a sinking lake bed, Mexico City can hardly claim an ideal site. Long ago it was the Aztec capital, constructed on an island in the middle of a lake. The Aztec extended the land with floating islands made from huge wicker baskets filled with dirt. The artificial islands eventually became rooted to the shallow lake bottom. After their conquest, the Spaniards drained the lake, and Mexico City covers the dry lakebed.

Although Mexico City is in the tropics, its high altitude gives it a mild climate. Nights are cool throughout the year. From late May until October, rain falls briefly, usually in late afternoon. The huge city is in a saucer-shaped depression. In winter, a temperature inversion causes pollution to be trapped in the bowl. When planes land at the Benito Juárez Airport, passengers feel as if they are descending into a brown sea.

Plaza de la Constitución, Mexico City

In the heart of the city, architecture from the colonial period mixes with modern buildings. The historic center has a layout common to Spanish colonial cities, with the cathedral and government buildings surrounding a public square. The official name of the square is Plaza de la Constitución ("Constitution Plaza"). But the square, as in many other cities in Mexico, is called the *zócalo.* Facing the *zócalo* are the City Hall; the Metropolitan Cathedral, Mexico's largest church; the National Palace, built on top of the ruins of Aztec emperor Montezuma's palace; and the National Pawnshop, founded as a bank for the poor in 1775.

Many of the tourist attractions are between the *zócalo* and Chapultepec (*chuh PUHL tuh pehk*) Park. The two hubs are joined by the city's major street, the Paseo de la Reforma. The attractions include

- In the park, Mexico's leading art and history museums and Chapultepec Castle. The castle houses the National Museum of History.
- Condesa, a trendy sector located near the southeastern edge of Chapultepec Park.
- Mansions along the Reforma in the Lomas de Chapultepec ("Hills of Chapultepec").
- The Zona Rosa ("Pink Zone"), south of Reforma, with shops, hotels, and restaurants.
- Alameda Park, west of the *zócalo*. The national dance company, the Ballet Folklórico, appears at the Palace of Fine Arts in the park. The top floor of the palace features murals by Mexican artists José Orozco (1883–1949) and Diego Rivera (1886–1957).

The Avenida Insurgentes (*in sur HEN tays*) leads to attractions in the southern part of the city, including the Plaza México (a bullfight ring), residential areas, the archaeological sites of Copilco and Cuicuilco, and the Floating Gardens of Xochimilco (*soh chee MEEL koh*). Lake Xochimilco was one of the lakes that filled the Valley of Mexico at the time of the Spanish conquest. On flower-bedecked barges, tourists and locals float along waterways created by the Aztec. Mariachi musicians accompany the boats.

The strolling musicians called *mariachis* include singers and players of guitars, trumpets, stringed bass, and violins. The players wear the *charro* ("cowboy") costume of a short jacket, bell-bottomed trousers with silver buttons, and the sombrero.

On the way back into the city, travelers can stop at the Dolores Olmedo Patiño Museum on the grounds of an 18th-century hacienda. It displays the works of Rivera and his wife, Frida Kahlo (1907–1954), as well as pre-Hispanic artifacts.

North of the city, the Basilica of Our Lady of Guadalupe is Mexico's most famous Catholic shrine. According to legend, the Virgin appeared at the site in 1531 to an Aztec convert. The modern basilica was built in 1976 when sinking soil put the old one in danger of collapse.

Northeast of Mexico City are some of the most striking of Mexico's ancient ruins: the huge pyramids at **Teotihuacán** (*tay oh tee wah KAHN*), known for the geometric and symbolic arrangement of its monuments. The pyramids were built by an unknown tribe about 200 BC and rediscovered by the Aztec, who called the site "the place where men became gods." The Pyramid of the Sun, the Pyramid of the Moon, and twenty temples line the Street of the Dead. The Pyramid of the Sun is similar in size to the Great Pyramid at Giza in Egypt. The Aztec used the structures for ceremonies dedicated to Quetzalcóatl—the Feathered Serpent and God of the Morning Star, the Wind, and the Arts. Montezuma thought Cortés was Quetzalcóatl and welcomed "the god" into his capital.

Guadalajara Mexico's second-largest city, Guadalajara, is the agricultural and industrial center of the western highlands. Much of what we associate with Mexican culture began in this region. In colonial times the city was reputed to be "more Spanish than Spain itself," and much of its heritage, including a 16th-century cathedral and the very ornate government palace, survives.

The city was home to the mariachis, as well as to sombreros and the *jarabe tapatío* (Mexican hat dance). Tequila was also invented there. During the annual *October Festival,* horsemanship and bullfighting can be seen at the *charreadas* (Mexican version of the rodeo). The region is noted for such crafts as leatherwork, embroidery, glass, weaving, and ceramics.

Colonial Cities North of Mexico City, Mexico has a group of towns collectively known as the Colonial Cities. **Guanajuato, Queretaro, San Miguel de Allende** (known for its wrought-iron work and metalwork), **Pátzcuaro, Morelia**, and **Dolores Hidalgo** are part of the *Independence Trail*, known as the *Bajío.* They are celebrated for their importance in Mexico's War of Independence from Spain. The cities are usually visited in a three- to five-day tour from the capital.

Puebla Southeast of Mexico City is Puebla, in a region fringed by towering volcanoes. Mexico's fourth-largest city is famous for its tilework and pottery; it is the place to buy *talavera* (handpainted ceramics with a glaze made from melted tin), which were introduced by the Spaniards in the 16th century. Puebla is also a showplace of Spanish colonial architecture, with well-preserved churches and buildings.

Cuernavaca South of Mexico City, about two hours by car or bus on the toll road, is Cuernavaca (*kwehr nuh VAHK uh*), known as the *City of Eternal Spring* for its warm, sunny climate. Tourist attractions include the Palace of Hernán Cortés and the Borda Gardens as well as spa resorts.

An American, William Spratling, came to Taxco in the 1930s, set up a silver workshop, and inspired local craftsmen to use ancient designs in modern forms.

Taxco The hillside town of Taxco (*TAHS koh*), *the Silver City*, is southwest of Cuernavaca on the road to Acapulco. Founded by Cortés to exploit Indian silver mines, the town is a community of jewelers. Shops are everywhere. The fun in Taxco is to climb up and down the narrow streets, comparing prices and bargaining, as well as watching artisans cutting, filing, and polishing silver, obsidian, and semiprecious stones.

Near Taxco are the **Grutas de Cacahuamilpa** (*kah kah wah MEEL pah*), caves as big as Mammoth Cave in Kentucky and Carlsbad Caverns in New Mexico.

Other Places to Visit

Mexico has five distinct tourism regions: in the far west, the peninsula of Baja California; on the mainland, the Pacific Coast, with its string of beautiful resorts; in the northwest, the Copper Canyon, for soft adventurers; in the southeast, the beach resorts and Mayan ruins of the Yucatán Peninsula; and finally, the archaeological mysteries of southern Mexico.

Baja California Baja California's connection to mainland Mexico is a narrow piece of land south of Arizona. Beyond the border cities of Tijuana and Mexicali, Baja offers no large cities. Only **Ensenada** (*en sen NAH duh*) and **La Paz** qualify as towns. Ensenada is popular as a destination for drive-down Californians and a port of call on cruises from Los Angeles or San Diego.

A highway extends 1,000 miles (1,609 km), the length of Baja from Tijuana to Cabo San Lucas, encouraging a thriving tourist industry along miles of sandy coastline. At the tip, a spectacular stretch of coast runs between Cabo San Lucas and San José del Cabo. The towns are jointly called **Los Cabos** ("The Capes"), and they have undergone rapid development in the past decade. Los Cabos offers excellent deep-sea fishing, diving, and whale watching (particularly from December to March), as well as beautiful resorts. The area has Mexico's largest concentration of golf courses.

The Pacific Coast For travelers who want to relax in the sun or lie under a *palapa* (a beach sun shelter), engage in water sports, do some shopping, and have a busy nightlife, the Pacific Coast of Mexico awaits.

Mazatlán is the northernmost resort in the area known as the **Mexican Riviera**. Most of the large hotels are in Mazatlán's Golden Zone, just north of downtown. In old Mazatlán, narrow streets are lined with renovated historic buildings. Nuevo Mazatlán, a bit farther north, is developing. The resort is known for its beaches, deep-sea fishing, hotels, restaurants, shops, and a harbor that accommodates large cruise ships. The town is a spring break attraction for California students. The city also boasts a massive pre-Lenten Carnival celebration each year, with parades, concerts, and street festivals.

South of Mazatlán, **Puerto Vallarta** (*vah YAR tah*) has luxury hotels and fine beaches. Tennis, deep-sea fishing, and water sports are easily available. The resort is one of Mexico's top golf destinations. It also has lively nightlife.

Puerto Vallarta

Named for the tree that grows there, **Manzanillo** (*man suh NEE yo*) was once a center of pirate activity and is now a busy port. Its diversions include sunset harbor cruises, sport fishing, and horseback riding. The deluxe resort of Las Hadas ("The Fairies") sits on a promontory on the bay. Its blend of dazzling white Moorish, Mexican, and Caribbean styles creates a fantasy village that has been featured in films.

Farther south along the coast, **Ixtapa** (*ish TA pah*) and **Zihuatanejo** (*zee wha tuh NEH ho*) are about 6 miles (10 km) apart. Developments, including an international airport, have not spoiled the area's natural beauty.

Acapulco, the *Queen of Mexican Resorts,* is just one of the west coast's beautiful resorts but is the best known. At first the city was the nearly private domain of the rich and famous; now it has millions of vacationers annually. Its famous horseshoe-shaped bay, deluxe hotels, beaches, and dry climate make it one of the world's premier resorts. High season is from the middle of December to Easter.

Acapulco is a round-the-clock town. The center of activity is the strip of restaurants and clubs on and around the broad boulevard Costera Miguel Aleman, which borders the bay. The Las Playas Peninsula, which encloses the bay, is Acapulco's oldest tourist area and where the calmest beaches are. The beaches outside the peninsula have high breakers for surfing but also a strong undertow.

Las Brisas, built in 1957, is one of the hotels that created Acapulco's fame. Bungalows, each with a small private pool, cascade down a hillside. Pink and white jeeps transport guests from their hilltop *casitas* ("little houses") to the beach.

Visitors should not miss seeing the divers at La Quebrada. Expertly judging the waves, they plunge into water 5 feet (1.5 m) deep. People watch from a small viewing area or from La Perla Nightclub at the Mirador Hotel. Tips are expected. The divers perform once in the daytime and several times at night. This dangerous tradition has expanded to other resorts along the coast.

Puerto Escondido and **Huatulco** (*wah TUL co*) are south of Acapulco. They have a good airport, luxurious hotels, and all beach and sports activities. Nearby is the Turtle Assistance Ecological Camp, where volunteers work to protect the giant sea turtles.

In the 1960s, Puerto Vallarta was a simple fishing village. It became known after the film *Night of the Iguana*, starring Richard Burton, was shot at the cove of Mismaloya. Burton and Elizabeth Taylor chose Puerto Vallarta as the setting for their love affair.

Copper Canyon Far from the glamour of the Mexican Riviera, Mexico's rugged north offers a different kind of beauty. The spectacular *Barrancas del Cobre* ("Copper Canyon") is a series of gorges in the Sierra Madre Occidental. (Look again at Figure 7.3.) Four of them are deeper than Arizona's Grand Canyon, but none are as wide.

Perhaps the most famous attraction for visitors is the thirteen-hour ride

➤ PROFILE

Cuisine of the Yucatán

Yucatán cuisine is practically unknown outside the peninsula. Specialties include

- ➤ *Achiote* chili sauce. Wow!
- ➤ *Panuchos de cazón,* shark in tortilla pockets.
- ➤ *Papadzules,* tacos stuffed with hard-cooked eggs, smothered in pumpkin sauce.
- ➤ *Poc-chuc,* pork rubbed down before grilling with a spice mixture called a *recado*.

on the *Chihuahua al Pacifico* from Chihuahua to **Los Mochis** near the Sea of Cortez, a scenic journey that climbs to a height of 8,000 feet (2,438 m). Trains stop at **Divisadero**, allowing passengers to look into the canyon and buy handicrafts from the Tarahumara Indians. Independent travelers can get off in small villages such as **Creel** and hike down to the canyon's bottom. The weather is best in spring and fall.

The Yucatán: Cancún The Yucatán Peninsula features the resorts of Cancún (*kan KOON*) and Cozumel (*KOHZ u mel*). Beaches on the Caribbean have calmer water than those on the Pacific.

In the late 1960s, trying to locate the ideal site for a beach resort, the Mexican Tourist Authority (known as Fonatur) fed a wish list into a computer. Cancún emerged from its jungle seclusion to become Mexico's and one of the world's most popular resorts. Charters that appeal to price-conscious vacationers account for about half the arrivals. College students fill the white-sand beaches during spring break.

Cancún's hotel zone is on a barrier island. The island is connected by bridges to the mainland. Hotels, shopping malls, and restaurants dot Paseo

CLOSE-UP: THE COPPER CANYON

Who is a good prospect for a trip to the Copper Canyon? Tourists who enjoy group tours and are interested in scenery, nature, and other cultures should find a Copper Canyon tour a good match. It also draws birders, hikers, and other ecotourists. The view at the Barranca del Cobre, where the Urique River has cut a chasm through the mountains, rivals that of the Grand Canyon.

Why would they visit the Copper Canyon? Travelers are increasingly interested in adventure and natural history, and the Copper Canyon satisfies those special interests. Many also want travel logistics smoothed out and do not have the time to do the research necessary for independent travel. They want to walk into (or phone) your office, tell you where they want to go, and have you make a suggestion and give a price quote within minutes. Group tours provide the answers. Tour operators control private trains and the best hotel space and food facilities in the canyon.

Where would they go? Tours to the canyon typically begin in a U.S. city where it is easy to meet and greet participants as they arrive on various flights. The Copper Canyon Railway is an engineering miracle and provides a good way to see the canyons, mesas, and peaks of the Sierra Madre. A nine-day tour to the canyon might follow this itinerary.

Day 1 Fly from home to El Paso, Texas.

Day 2 Cross the Rio Grande into Mexico by motorcoach, and journey south to Casas Grandes, a 13th-century trading center.

Days 3–4 Continue by motorcoach to Creel, where you board the *Chihuahua al Pacifico* (train) for a ride through the foothills of the Sierra Madre. Spend the next two nights at a mountain hacienda. Learn of the life, history, and culture of the Tarahumara Indians from your guide, a geologist specializing in the Copper Canyon. Hike into the countryside.

Days 5–6 Reboard the train for the ride to Divisadero, on the rim of the canyon. For the next two nights, you will stay at a hotel overlooking the canyon. Take a guided walk along the rim, or simply relax and enjoy the view.

Days 7–8 Board the train for a journey along the edge of the Septentrion Canyon. Spend the night in El Fuerte in a historic Spanish colonial mansion. Explore the town. Visit a nearby Indian village.

Day 9 Drive to Los Mochis for a flight to Phoenix, with connections home.

When is the best time to visit? Spring or fall is the best time to visit. Summers can get very hot, and winters can be cold.

The traveler asks, "What if I get sick?" How would you respond? Some people think they will become ill in Mexico. The chances are that they won't, especially if they take elementary precautions—but never promise. Repeat the safety precautions listed in the "Health" section. Serious illness is something else. Unexpected falls and sprains can happen, even to those in good health. Suggest that travelers purchase trip interruption and evacuation insurance. The cost of evacuation and transport home is very expensive. Insurance provides peace of mind.

Kukulcán, the main street. Cancún City is the commercial center on the mainland where most of the support personnel live.

Shopping, eating, and lounging in the sun are the main daytime activities. Nightlife is nonstop. Divers like the sea, which abounds with coral formations and shipwrecks. Golf and tennis are available as well as bullfights and a convention center. Although Cancún has no casinos, a jai alai fronton is open, and a sports betting parlor thrives. Local tours go to nearby Mayan sites, to the island of Cozumel, and to **Isla Mujeres** (*moo HAIR ez*), a beautiful island off the coast.

The Yucatán: Cozumel Mexico's largest inhabited island, Cozumel is 33 miles (53 km) long and 9 miles (15 km) wide. The land is mostly flat, and its interior is covered by scrub and marshy lagoons. White-sand beaches with calm waters line the island's leeward (western) side, fringed by a spectacular reef system, **Palancar Reef.** Black and red coral and huge elephant-ear and barrel sponges are among the reef's attractions.

Cozumel is a popular cruise ship port. Ships either anchor offshore and tender their passengers in or dock at the large piers south of the town. The island is a good destination for those who want sun, creature comforts, and a feeling of Mexico. Although Cozumel has lively discos and a steady influx of tourists, it lacks the crowds of Cancún.

The island's small town of San Miguel is laid out in grid fashion along the waterfront. Plaza Central is surrounded by shops offering silver, T-shirts, and handicrafts. Most of the salespeople speak English, prices are marked in dollars as well as pesos, and the shops stay open as long as a ship is anchored offshore.

For the Maya, Cozumel was a sacred island and an important trading post. As Cozumel's importance as a chicle producer diminished with the invention of synthetic chewing gum, it grew as a tourist destination. The tree cutters had uncovered Mayan ruins hidden in the forests. Soon archaeologists began visiting the island. Jacques Cousteau visited in 1961, and his reports of Palancar Reef's diving opportunities set the island on its way.

Other Attractions of the Yucatán Just a few miles south of Cancún is the newly developed **Riviera Maya**, once a commercial and religious hub for the ancient Maya. With many small resorts and spa retreats lined up along the Caribbean, the region offers easy access to archaeological sites such as Xel-Há, ecological reserves such as the Sian Ka'an Biosphere Reserve, and eco-parks such as Zcaret. Visitors can swim with dolphins, lie on the beach, and see ancient Mayan ruins all in the same day.

Xel-há (*shell HAAH*) **National Park** features caves and coves along the shore. Little islands, narrow waterways, and underground passages showcase colorful fish amid odd-shaped coral formations. No fishing, motorboating, or anything that pollutes the water is allowed. Swimmers, snorkelers, and divers can use marked areas only and are asked not to put on tanning lotions before jumping into the lagoons.

To the south, **Tulúm** (*too LOOM*) offers one of the most dramatic sites of the pre-Columbian world, the only Mayan city built on the sea. Perched atop low cliffs, the outpost commands a breathtaking view of the Caribbean. Millions visit on day trips from Cancún and on excursions from cruise ships. Seeing the ruins with a guide takes about two hours.

Inland, **Mérida** was founded on the site of a Mayan town. It has an air of faded grandeur, a legacy of its once worldwide importance as the center of henequen farms, a fiber used in the making of rope. When plastic replaced natural fiber, the town's riches dried up. A cathedral and the decaying

Cozumel was a center of activity for the chewing gum industry. For centuries, the Maya had been chewing raw sap from the zapote tree, which grows throughout Central America and on the island. In the early 1900s, the world was introduced to this sweet.

ON THE SPOT

The travelers have just received their documents for your cruise line. The cruise includes a port call at Cozumel. Included is a list of possible shore excursions. They call you with some questions about which excursions to buy. "If we take the shore excursion to Tulúm, does the bus bring us back to the ship in Cozumel?"

Maps are tools for selling as well as educating. Travelers sometimes have only a vague notion of where they are going or what physical obstacles are in the way. You might suggest (gently) that the travelers use a map to see that Tulúm is on the Yucatán mainland; Cozumel is an island. Cruise ships pause off Playa del Carmen and tender their passengers to shore for visits to the Tulúm ruins. When the last shore-excursion passenger has disembarked, the ship leaves and sails to the island of Cozumel. When the excursion is finished, passengers return to Playa del Carmen and board ferries for the 90-minute ride to Cozumel.

Males in the Yucatán wear the *guayabera*, the pleated embroidered shirt of the tropics. Women wear the white cotton *huipil* tunic, which is embroidered at the neck and hem. *Huaraches*, shoes made of woven leather strips, are part of the comfortable costume.

mansions of the planters are interesting, but Mérida is primarily a base for excursions to archaeological sites.

Uxmal (*OOSH mal*), which means "built three times" in Mayan, is to the south of Mérida. The site's surrounding vegetation is brown in winter and lush green during the rainy months of summer. Two of the most beautifully restored buildings are the Temple of the Magician and the Nunnery.

Chichén Itzá (*chee CHEHN eet SAH*), east of Mérida, is the best known, best preserved, and biggest of the Mayan ruins. The name means "mouth of the well." Between AD 900 and 1200, Chichén Itzá grew to be the most powerful Mayan city.

Chichén Itzá, Mexico

The peninsula's limestone provided the Maya with material for building and with the pits called *cenotes*. The cenotes were considered sacred to the rain god Chac. Chichén Itzá has two large cenotes, one used as a well for water, the other supposedly used for sacrifice.

Visitors can see the Pyramid of Kukulcán, a public steam bath, a huge ball court, and an observatory. Architectural features and engravings include the *chacmool*, a reclining figure with a flat surface on its stomach designed as a receptacle for the hearts of sacrificial victims, and the Kukulcán, the Mayan name for the feathered serpent deity. During the spring and autumn equinox, crowds come to see the shadows create the illusion of a serpent descending the staircase of the Pyramid of Kukulcán.

Southern Mexico: Oaxaca The mountainous rural state of Oaxaca (*wah HAH ka*) is in southern Mexico, east of Acapulco. Its capital, also called **Oaxaca**, is known as the *Jade City* due to the green color in the stone used in the construction of many of its buildings. Oaxaca is a culturally diverse city whose pre-Hispanic and colonial roots are seen in its architecture, craft traditions, Zapotec and Mixtec archaeological sites, cuisine, and festivals. Today, the city has a large student and language school population.

About 9 miles (14 km) from Oaxaca is another of Mexico's famous ancient ruins: **Monte Albán** ("White Mountain"). It was the sacred city of the Zapotec people who flourished about 2,000 years ago. Key features include a ball court, palace, monuments, and the Observatory. The site is also home to a labyrinth of tunnels and tombs.

✔ CHECK-UP

From a visitor's perspective, the major destinations of Mexico are

- ✔ Baja California.
- ✔ Pacific Coast resorts.
- ✔ Mexico City, the capital, and the pyramids.
- ✔ Colonial towns.
- ✔ Copper Canyon.
- ✔ Yucatán Peninsula, with its Mayan ruins and beach resorts.
- ✔ Archaeological sites in southern Mexico near Oaxaca.

Mexico's resort areas include

- ✔ Los Cabos, on the southern tip of Baja California.
- ✔ Mazatlán, Puerto Vallarta, Manzanillo, Ixtapa, Zihuatanejo, Acapulco, Puerto Escondido, and Huatulco, on the Mexican Riviera.
- ✔ Cancún, Cozumel, and the Riviera Maya, on the Yucatán Peninsula.

Among the major archaeological sites in Mexico are

- ✔ Teotihuacán, near Mexico City.
- ✔ Uxmal, Chichén Itzá, and Tulúm, on the Yucatán.
- ✔ Monte Albán, near Oaxaca.

Belize, Costa Rica, and Panama

As tourists crowd the best-known sites in Mexico, Central America provides interesting alternative destinations. Three countries of the region—Belize, Costa Rica, and Panama—attract a significant number of tourists (see Figure 7.4).

Belize

Mexico and Guatemala border the tiny country of Belize, in area about the size of Massachusetts. The Maya moved into Belize in about 1000 BC, and their civilization flourished here until about AD 1000. Little is known about life in Belize from that time until explorers reached the coastal area in the 1500s.

The Spanish ignored Belize. Shipwrecked British sailors established the first European settlement in 1638 and gradually gained control of the country. The colony was called *British Honduras* until 1973; it became an independent country in 1981. Although English is the official language, Spanish is gaining in use as refugees from other Central American countries move in.

Northern Belize is flat and swampy, thick with mangrove and grasses along the coast. The country's central region has large savannas. In the

Cacao trees, which flourish in the moist rain forests, were highly valued in Mexico and Central America. The beans were dried, roasted, ground, and then blended with chilis, honey, and water to produce a stimulating chocolate beverage that was enjoyed by the Mayan elite.

FIGURE 7.4

Central America

1 inch = 172 miles (277 km)

southwest the land rises to the low **Maya Mountains**. Most of the population lives near the coast. Few people settled inland, giving wildlife—including the jaguar, scarlet macaw, and other rare animals—a chance to survive.

In Belize, the 1,500-year-old pyramid of El Castillo is the country's second-tallest building. The pyramid is at the Mayan site of Xunantunich in western Belize.

Belmopan and Belize City The capital, Belmopan, was created inland in 1970 after a hurricane devastated coastal Belize City, the former capital. Belize City remains the transportation hub. Most visitors pass through quickly on their way to the cayes or the interior.

Barrier Reef and the Cayes Belize's principal tourist attraction is an unnamed barrier reef that ranks as the world's second longest; only Australia's Great Barrier Reef is longer. The ridges of the reef that run parallel to the coast are called *cayes* (pronounced *keys*); they are the small islands that are centers of the diver's life.

More than 200 islets and cayes sit either directly on or just off the 185-mile-long (298 km) reef; the two largest are **Caye Caulker** and **Ambergris Caye**. The latter is the most popular; its town of San Pedro is the reef's most important access point for snorkeling and dive sites. When not in the water, tourists putter around the island on golf carts.

Northern Belize *La Ruta Maya* ("The Route of the Maya") begins north of Belize City. The most extensively excavated of the Mayan centers and the most accessible is **Altun Ha**, about 30 miles (48 km) north of the city. The national symbol of Belize—the head of the sun god carved in jade—was found here. Another Mayan site, Lamanai, on the New River Lagoon was a large ceremonial center. Getting there involves a river safari on boats leaving from Orangewalk Town.

Northern Belize is also noted for the **Crooked Tree Wildlife Sanctuary**, administered by the Audubon Society. The sanctuary is mostly wetlands, an ideal home for birds.

Western Belize The savanna southwest of Belize City gradually gives way to the low Maya Mountains, which are covered by rain forests. The slightly higher altitude makes the humidity more bearable. San Ignacio is the district's center and the base for exploring places such as the Mayan site of **Caracol**, which claims to rival Tikal in neighboring Guatemala.

Belize has Central America's largest cave system, the **Chiquibul Caves**. The best time for exploration is from March to May, when the caves are less likely to be flooded. The Maya believed the caves were the entrances to the Underworld and used them for ceremonial acts as well as burial places.

Southern Belize For those who want to explore off the beaten track, southern Belize is the place to go. **Dangriga** is the area's largest town. Its inhabitants are descendants of the black Caribs who fled Honduras after a failed rebellion. Their arrival by dugout canoe is celebrated each November 19 as *Garifuna Settlement Day*.

Costa Rica

More than any other country, Costa Rica is linked with ecotourism and adventure travel. Its natural assets, including one of the world's best systems of reserves and national parks, make it a top attraction for travelers with these special interests. Twenty-five percent of the country is protected; choosing where to head first is a traveler's toughest choice.

The country lies between Nicaragua to the north and Panama to the east, with coasts on both the Pacific and the Caribbean. (Look again at Figure 7.4.) Mountains stretch from northwest to southeast. Many of the mountains are volcanoes, some still active. Most of the population lives in the country's coffee-growing region, the central plateau near **San José**.

Costa Rica is only slightly larger than New Hampshire and Vermont combined, but its natural diversity provides travelers with a wide variety of experiences. Travelers can experience white-water rafting on rivers that tumble off the mountains, sport fishing, horseback riding, sea kayaking, mountain biking, scuba diving, windsurfing, riding an aerial tram through the rain forest's canopy, and more.

Puntarenas is Costa Rica's principal Pacific port, but **Puerto Caldera**, a few miles south, is the port of call for cruise liners.

San José Costa Rica's capital was founded in 1737. Its architecture is a pleasant blend of traditional Spanish and modern. Built on a plateau in the agricultural heart of the country, San José is a relatively prosperous city. Hillsides covered with coffee trees surround the city. At night, bars and salsa clubs keep visitors busy.

In Costa Rican bullfights, the bull is never killed or even injured.

CLOSE-UP: COSTA RICA

Who is a good prospect for a trip to Costa Rica? The best prospect is an active traveler who is interested in nature and wants a vacation that combines either soft or hard adventure with a relaxing atmosphere. Costa Rica is not for everyone. Counselors should ask questions to identify the type of experiences travelers are looking for. Do they want to rough it a little or a lot? Find out about their comfort level. Will they be bothered by bugs and muddy trails? Do they mind rustic lodge-style accommodations? If they are looking for a Cancún-like vacation, Costa Rica is probably not the destination for them.

Why would they visit Costa Rica? Today's travelers are looking for new horizons, and Costa Rica is relatively undiscovered. Costa Rica offers tremendous natural beauty and has the infrastructure that allows the traveler to access areas of interest.

Where would they go? This active itinerary combines the best of land and sea. The use of a small cruise ship allows transportation without the hassle of packing and unpacking.

Days 1–2 Arrive in San José, Costa Rica, where you are met and transferred to your hotel for a two-night stay. Explore San José, or ride an aerial tram into the canopy of the rain forest that borders nearby Braulio Carrillo National Park.

Day 3 San José–Puerto Caldera. Travel through the countryside by van to Puerto Caldera, the Pacific port. En route, visit a coffee plantation and the Poás Volcano to view the steaming crater. At the port, board a 138-passenger ship designed for cruising in coastal waters. The ship's maneuverability and shallow draft allow easy exploration of secluded waterways beyond the reach of bigger ships.

Day 4 Onboard. A port call at Curú Wildlife Refuge on the Nicoya Peninsula. The refuge protects the howler and white-faced capuchin monkeys, armadillos, coatimundis, and deer and provides habitat for the giant conch. Swim or hike one of the many available trails.

Day 5 Onboard. Arrive at Marenco Biological Station in Corcovado National Park in the virgin rain forest of the Osa Peninsula. Marenco has been so well protected that it harbors species that are rare or absent throughout the rest of Central America.

Day 6 Onboard. Cruise the rich waters off the Pacific Coast. Onboard experts lecture on the natural and cultural history of the area.

Day 7 Disembark in Puerto Caldera, and travel to San José for the flight home.

When is the best time to visit? The coastal areas are hot and humid during most of the year. Spring is the season of least humidity and less rain.

The traveler says, "I'm not really up to all that water activity. I can't swim." How would you respond? Participants on a coastal cruise have many options. If they want to stay onboard and laze on the deck, of course that is an option. The activity on the described trip is within the ability of everyone except travelers with handicaps.

ON THE SPOT

You work for a tour operator, and the travelers call you regarding a future trip. Your qualifying questions have uncovered that they want a winter vacation to "someplace different but warm." They seem ideal candidates for a soft-adventure trip to Costa Rica. When you mention the destination, their first reaction is negative. "Why are you suggesting we visit Costa Rica? Aren't all the people poor and always shooting each other? Isn't Central America off-limits for vacations?"

Since 1974 Costa Rica has had an orderly succession of democratic governments and maintained its neutrality in international affairs. Although occasional problems occur, it is one of the most stable and prosperous of the region's countries. The travelers need reassurance, and for liability protection this is usually best when it comes from a third party. You might refer them to the State Department's travel advisories.

San José can be the base for visits to the central plateau. Nearby is the Butterfly Farm, with thousands of live butterflies in various stages of development; Café Britt, a working coffee plantation; and Sarchi, a craft center and home of an oxcart factory. A few decades ago, the usual form of country transport was by *carretas*, gaily painted wooden carts drawn by oxen. Nowadays, the carts decorate people's gardens or are converted into barbecue stands.

Parks and Biological Reserves

Northwest of San José is a cloud forest moist with mosses, palms, orchids, and bromeliads—**Volcán Poás**. It is the country's most-visited park. Its highlight is the steam-belching crater of the volcano. A ten-minute walk from the parking lot through a tunnel of ferns brings you to bright green **fumaroles**—bubbling vents in the earth's crust.

Costa Rica provides many other opportunities for experiencing nature. Examples include **Monteverde Cloud Forest Preserve** in western Costa Rica and **Tortuaguero National Park** in the northeast. Tortuaguero is an important nesting site for the green turtle, as well as a refuge for leatherback and hawksbill turtles. Monkeys, jaguars, and many other species also call Tortuaguero home.

The Pacific Coast

Costa Rica's Pacific beach resorts are popular for sport fishing and surfing. The **Nicoya Peninsula** is the site of hotel development. **Liberia** is the area's town. Its airport has daily flights from San José. By car, it is 145 miles (233 km) north of San José on the Pan-American Highway.

■ ■ ■

In 1928 travel writer Richard Halliburton swam across Panama using the Panama Canal. Charged according to size, he paid 36 cents.

■ ■ ■

Panama

Across Costa Rica's border is Panama, the *Crossroads of the World*. The narrow S-shaped country curves from west to east. (Look again at Figure 7.4.) The Caribbean Sea is to the north, and the Pacific Ocean is to the south.

A chain of rugged mountains forms Panama's spine. The highest point is in the west, **Volcán Barú**. The volcano is dormant, although hot springs around its flanks show thermal activity. The country's east is swampy.

Panama is a small country, with a land area roughly equal to South Carolina's. One-third of the country is tropical rain forest, much of it protected, including Soberanía National Park, which borders the Panama Canal. Panama also has numerous rivers and more than 1,600 islands. The country's beaches and abundant animal and plant life (there are 940 recorded bird species) attract growing numbers of ecotourists.

During colonial times, the Spaniards built a road across Panama to carry gold bound for Spain from Peru. In the 19th century, Panama was part of Gran Colombia (Colombia, Panama, and Venezuela). In 1878 the Colombian government awarded a contract to build a canal to the French diplomat Ferdinand de Lesseps, builder of the Suez Canal. Tropical diseases, particularly yellow fever and malaria, and the difficulty of digging a sea-level channel through the mountains defeated the French. President Theodore Roosevelt wanted to take over the project, but Colombia would not agree to his terms. In 1903 the United States pushed Panama to revolt against Colombia and become an independent country, thus permitting the United States to build the "Big Ditch."

The Panama Canal

Built across the narrowest point between the Atlantic and the Pacific Oceans, the Panama Canal remains one of the greatest engineering and medical achievements of the 20th century. The canal extends for 51 miles (82 km) from Limón Bay on the Atlantic to the Bay of Panama on the Pacific. The dig took ten years, at a cost of $352 million and 5,609 lives. The greatest obstacle was disease. Colonel William C. Gorgas destroyed the mosquitoes that carried yellow fever and malaria, and he eliminated the rats that brought bubonic plague. The canal opened in 1914. U.S. dominion over the canal and the land around it (the Canal Zone) ended in 1999.

Ships cross the canal twenty-four hours a day, waiting in line on both sides for their turn, a most impressive sight. The average ship takes eight to ten hours to move through the canal. A ship traveling from the Atlantic to the Pacific sails from northwest to southeast. The ship leaves the canal 27 miles (43 km) east of where it enters.

The canal has three sets of water-filled chambers called *locks:* Miraflores and Pedro Miguel Locks on the Pacific side and Gatún Locks on the Atlantic side. Like elevators, the locks raise ships from sea level up across the isthmus and then back down to sea level. (Megaships cannot use the canal because they are too large to get through the locks.) Between the locks, ships pass through an artificial lake, Gatún Lake. Crocodiles basking along the banks make for interesting viewing.

Panama Canal

The canal can be seen from an observation platform at Miraflores Locks, but the best way is from the deck of a ship making the passage. **Christóbal Colón** is the entry city on the Caribbean; the country's capital, **Panama City**, is the entry city on the Pacific. Panama City is a fast-growing metropolis situated along a wide bay. The city's elite Punta Paitilla area is crowded with high-rise condominiums and expensive stores.

Darién Gap The sparsely settled wilderness of Darién Gap links Central and South America. The region has the only break in the Pan-American Highway from North to South America. Travelers to Darién National Park are strongly advised to use an experienced guide. The area around the Colombian border is dangerous guerrilla territory.

San Blas Islands Panama's largest archipelagos are the **San Blas** and **Bocas del Toro** Islands off the Caribbean coast. The San Blas Islands are often visited by cruise ships. The largest of the islands, El Porvenir, has a small airport. The Cuna Indians who live on the islands are a self-governing tribe that the Panamanian government has encouraged to live according to their ancient ways. They have their own language, but Spanish is widely spoken.

The islands have rustic huts, palm trees, and beautiful beaches. Cuna women are known for their gold nose rings and earrings and for their colorful embroidered *molas*—hand-sewn cloths that may be worn or displayed as wall hangings.

✔ CHECK-UP

The main tourist destinations in Central America include

✔ Belize; its capital is Belmopan, but its largest city and transportation hub is Belize City.
✔ Costa Rica; its capital and largest city is San José.
✔ Panama; its capital and largest city is Panama City.

For travelers, highlights of these countries include

✔ Belize's barrier reef.
✔ Natural wonders and adventure travel possibilities of Costa Rica.
✔ Passage through the Panama Canal.

Planning the Trip

Many travelers to Middle America simply want a one-week vacation to a resort destination for fun in the sun. Mexican Pacific and Caribbean resorts have well-developed tourist facilities likely to meet their expectations.

Tour operators offer packages that include air travel, accommodations, and transfers. They focus on one-week independent or hosted vacations to the resorts and to archaeological sites in the Yucatán, the cayes of Belize, and Costa Rican adventures. Escorted tours in Mexico visit the colonial towns, the silver cities, archaeological sites, and Copper Canyon.

When to Go

The rainy season throughout the region is between May and October. Winter—December through March—is the coolest and driest time for activities such as sightseeing at archaeological sites. Mexico City is subject to smog at all times, but the situation is particularly bad in winter. High season for resort areas is from Christmas vacation through Easter. Although hurricane season is from June to November, in both Caribbean and Pacific coastal areas, the highest probability for hurricanes is from August to October.

➤ PROFILE

Divers' Delights

Some of the world's best diving spots can be found off the coasts of Mexico and Central America. Waters are generally clearest for diving from mid-February to mid-June. Sites include

- Ambergris Caye and Caye Caulker, Belize.
- Bay Islands, Honduras, which share the barrier reef with Belize.
- Cancún, with convenient offshore reefs.
- Cano and Cocos Islands, on the Pacific coast of Costa Rica.
- Palancar Reef, in Cozumel, Mexico.
- Panama Canal, with the remains of sunken trains and submerged villages in man-made Gatún Lake.
- San Blas Islands, on the coast of Panama.
- For experts, the coral reefs of the Bastimentos Island National Park off Bocas del Toro, where manatee and dozens of fish species swim.

Preparing the Traveler

Many people planning trips to this region are interested in ecotourism—traveling to see nature's wonders and leaving them in their original state. For trips involving soft or hard adventure, it is important to determine the traveler's physical condition, match the traveler with degree of difficulty, and use a reliable tour operator.

If tourists are traveling independently, recommend that they hire a guide for visits to parks, refuges, and reserves. Without a trained guide, travelers will miss much, if not most, of the wildlife.

Travelers to Mexico and Central America need to check documentation requirements and be alert to safety concerns. In addition, they should be prepared for some health hazards and cultural differences.

Health The region's most notorious health hazard is *turista* (also known as the Aztec two-step or Montezuma's Revenge), a relatively harmless combination of diarrhea and stomach upset that is no fun to have on a vacation. It almost always comes from water. Here are some guidelines that can help travelers avoid this and other hazards:

- Don't eat from street stands.
- Use bottled water, even to brush your teeth. Ask for water "with gas"; still water containers might have been refilled from a tap.
- Avoid salads and any fruit that is not personally peeled.
- If you have respiratory problems, avoid Mexico City from December through May, when air pollution is at its height.
- Use bug spray. Belize and Panama are risk areas for malaria and yellow fever.
- Consider altitude problems on mountain treks.

- Don't bumble into trouble. Before departure, ask your doctor or the Centers for Disease Control (CDC) what precautions might be needed.
- Buy trip interruption insurance that includes medical evacuation aid.

Money Travelers should take a combination of traveler's checks, credit cards, and cash. In many situations, local currency is needed.

Throughout the region most banks are open only from 0900 to 1330, Monday through Friday. Major credit cards are widely accepted at resorts and in large cities. ATMs are available but may not be operational where and when you need one. Travelers should check with their banks before they go to make sure they have compatible PINs.

Language Although Spanish is the official language in all countries of the region except Belize, English is widely spoken in the tourist areas. Some fifty Amerindian languages are also spoken. Travelers should encounter no language problems in the resorts of Cancún or the Mexican Riviera. Mexican Spanish differs from the Castilian Spanish many learn in school, but people seem very pleased when travelers attempt to say "please" or "thank you" in their language.

Customs Mexican and Central American cuisine is delicious and varied, and each region has its own dishes. For picky eaters, international cuisine is available at hotels in the larger cities and resorts. Imported alcoholic beverages are expensive. Following Latin custom, dinner is usually served from 1900 to 2300.

Casual sportswear is acceptable for daytime dress. At beach resorts, dress is informal and nowhere are men expected to wear a tie. In Mexico City, however, the Chilangos (as Mexico City residents are known) like to dress up, especially at the theater or for dinner.

The arts and crafts have played an important part in the region since the days of the ancient Indians. The skills continue to this day, offering travelers an outstanding selection for shopping pleasure. In the major tourist destinations of Mexico, diverse handicrafts are carried by Fonart stores under the auspices of the National Council for Culture and Arts.

Throughout the region bargaining is part of the culture. The typical scenario is to ask the price, counter with one that is 50 percent lower, and then work from there. Antique buyers should know that it is illegal to take pre-Columbian artifacts out of the country.

Transportation

Transportation ranges from the most modern to the most ancient. A network of airlines, superhighways, and railroads connects major cities and towns, while in the country farmers carry goods to market on their heads and backs or by burros and oxcarts.

By Air In Mexico, domestic airlines provide scheduled services to more than seventy-five airports. International airlines and charter flights also serve the cities and resorts.

San José is Costa Rica's international gateway. Regional service is available to provincial towns and villages. Panama City is Panama's gateway. Belize's only airport is at Belize City.

By Water Large and small cruise lines operate along both coasts of Mexico

> PROFILE

Food Specialties

The region's food is not like Taco Bell's! Popular foods to look for in Mexico and Central America include

- Seafood, especially grilled shrimp, in coastal cities.
- The fruit and leaves of the prickly pear, a type of cactus.
- Tortillas, called "edible plates" by the Aztec. Made of corn, they are the basic ingredient of quesadillas, tacos, enchiladas, and many other foods.
- Turkey with *mole* (*moh LAY*), a sauce of chocolate, chili, tomatoes, nuts, and spices.
- Cinnamon-flavored hot chocolate.
- For alcoholic beverages, *cerveza* (beer) and *mescal*, *pulque*, and *tequila*, the last three made from the juice of the maguey plant.

> PROFILE

Shopping Opportunities in Mexico

Shopping in craft markets is one of the pleasures of Mexico and Central America. Handicrafts are authentic expressions of the people. Items to look for include

- Coffee and brightly painted oxcarts in Costa Rica.
- Mahogany carvings in Belize.
- *Molas* in the San Blas Islands of Panama.
- Blown glass and ceramics in Guadalajara, Mexico.
- Silver in Taxco, Mexico.
- *Talavera* (handpainted tin-glazed ceramics) in Puebla, Mexico.
- Wrought-iron work and metalwork in San Miguel de Allende, Mexico.
- Black clay pottery and *alebrijes*—fanciful wood figures of animals and people—in Oaxaca, Mexico

and Central America. On the east coast, large ships visit Cozumel on western Caribbean itineraries. On the west coast, short cruises depart from Los Angeles or San Diego and turn around at Ensenada. Longer cruises include stops at Cabo and Mazatlán, turning around at Puerto Vallarta.

Acapulco can be the departure point for cruises through the Panama Canal to an east coast port. Canal crossings are also part of the more extensive itineraries that round South America in January, February, and March.

Costa Rica has expedition-style cruising on smaller ships. The cruises offer an informal lifestyle, with routes and activities that highlight natural history, water sports, and light adventure. The small ships can include stops and shore excursions that larger ships are unable to offer.

By Rail Mexico has an extensive government-owned rail network, but reservations are difficult to book outside the country, and the system needs improvement. The most popular rail trip is the Copper Canyon expedition on private trains booked through tour operators. Central American railroads are rarely used by tourists.

By Road In all countries, traffic drives on the right, distances and speeds are shown in kilometers, and gas is sold in liters. Oil company credit cards are not accepted at gas stations. Rental cars are available at airports. Rentals are usually less expensive if prearranged in the United States.

The American Automobile Association (AAA) is a good source for up-to-date information on driving conditions and car insurance needed in Mexico and Central America. Depending on the traveler's plans, a chauffeur-driven vehicle or a four-wheel-drive car might be needed.

The Mexican *autopistas* (superhighways) charge tolls. Other roads have two lanes without shoulders and are poorly lit at night; when animals are apt to wander onto the road. Driving in any city's congested traffic is difficult. Car use in Mexico City is restricted to cut down on pollution; the last digit of the license plate determines when the car can be driven. U.S. auto insurance does not apply in Mexico; people planning to drive their own cars must have Mexican insurance. In the United States, AAA offices can provide information.

Costa Rica's highways link San José and principal towns, but other roads may be primitive. Belize has less developed roads than the rest of Central America. Panama's roads are not reliable outside the Canal Zone. Anywhere in Mexico and Central America, stopping to spend the night in the car, in an RV, or on some seemingly deserted beach would be extremely ill-advised.

Accommodations

The typical tourist is happiest in at least a mid-level hotel. Health and security are concerns, and the better hotels take more precautions. A key trend is the growth of the all-inclusives, properties that provide good protection.

Mexican properties range from ultra-deluxe beach resorts to remote hideaways, restored colonial mansions, and adventure retreats. Mexico's equivalents of the B&B are called *casas de huespedes* (guest houses). Haciendas (large ranches) and monasteries from the colonial past have been converted into deluxe hotels and offer romantic places to stay. The country hotels are weekend resorts for city dwellers; they are quite popular, so reservations are necessary.

Mexico is known for its spa services. Although spas can be found throughout the country, the highest concentration is near Mexico City, partly due to the area's abundance of thermal and mineral springs.

Costa Rica's and Panama's hotels range from international standard to simple country lodges. Belize has few first-class hotels, but its small establishments give good value. There are mountain lodges in the interior and resort hotels on the coast. Only limited accommodations are available on the cayes. Divers might enjoy the live-aboard dive boat experience.

✔ CHECK-UP

Planning a trip to Mexico, Costa Rica, Belize, and Panama involves

- ✔ Keeping the weather patterns of coast and highlands in mind. In all areas, winter is the time of coolest, driest weather.
- ✔ Preparing the traveler for health and safety precautions.

Travelers seeking something different might enjoy

- ✔ Guest houses or converted haciendas and monasteries in Mexico.
- ✔ Mountain lodges or live-aboard dive boats in Belize.

OTHER DESTINATIONS IN CENTRAL AMERICA

Guatemala, Honduras, El Salvador, and Nicaragua have been wracked by political upheavals. The countries are trying to rebuild their tourism infrastructure and welcome back leisure travelers.

GUATEMALA

Guatemala is a mountainous country on the southwestern border of Mexico, with coastlines on both the Atlantic and the Pacific. It shares frontiers with Belize to the northeast and Honduras and El Salvador to the southeast. **Guatemala City** is the capital and largest city. The country is one of the most beautiful in Central America. Its attractions include

- Antigua (*ahn TEE gwuh*), a colonial city with fine examples of Spanish art and architecture and the center of the country's weaving industry and Spanish-language schools.
- Lake Atitlán, a mile-high deep-blue caldera (see the Glossary) in Guatemala's western highlands. It is framed by three volcanoes and surrounded by twelve Indian villages named for the twelve Apostles. Lake excursions include visits to picturesque Indian villages and markets.
- Chichicastenango (*chee chee kass tuh NANH go*), a colorful Quiche Indian market town and colonial outpost. In the town's 16th-century Church of Santo Tomás, Catholic and Indian rituals are practiced side by side.
- Tikal (*tee KAHL*), one of the greatest of the Mayan cities. It is near the Belize border. To reach it, visitors can fly from Guatemala City to the airport at Flores and then make a one-hour drive. More than 2,000 well-preserved structures and stone monuments are hidden by lush vegetation in the rain forest. During the walk into the jungle to the ruins, the visitor can see gorgeous greenery and perhaps be pelted by the forest's resident howler or spider monkeys.
- Takalik Abaj, a Mayan center emerging from the jungle of western Guatemala.

HONDURAS

Honduras lies between Guatemala and El Salvador to the west and Nicaragua to the southeast. **Tegucigalpa** (*teh goo see GAHL pah*) is the capital and largest city. Mountains cover more than 60 percent of the land. The northeastern part of the country, known as La Mosquitia ("The Mosquito Coast"), is heavily forested, swampy, and mostly uninhabited. The name comes from the Miskito Indians, although no one knows which came first, the Indians or the mosquitoes.

The term *banana republic* was first applied to Honduras, where U.S.-owned fruit companies took over in the 1890s to grow bananas.

Adventure seekers go to Honduras to see the Mayan ruins of **Copán**, near the Guatemala border. Travelers also fish or scuba dive around the **Bay Islands**, about 35 miles (56 km) off the northern coast in the Caribbean. The main islands—extensions of Belize's barrier reef—are Roatan, Guanaja, Utila, and the Cayos Cochinos. **Roatan** is the most developed and has dozens of resorts and hotels.

EL SALVADOR

Central America's smallest and most densely populated country is between Guatemala to the west and Honduras to the northeast. Stretching along the Pacific, El Salvador is the only Central American country without a Caribbean coastline. Its capital and largest city is **San Salvador**. The country has an assortment of off-the-beaten-path pleasures that appeal to the adventurous traveler.

NICARAGUA

Mountainous Nicaragua is between Honduras to the northwest and Costa Rica to the south. Its capital and largest city, **Managua**, is on the Pacific coastal plain. Nicaragua is the largest but most sparsely populated of the Central American countries and is only slightly larger than New York State.

CHAPTER WRAP-UP

SUMMARY

Here is a review of the objectives with which we began the chapter.

1. **Describe the environment and people of Mexico and Central America.** Geographers call the land south of the United States Middle America. The region includes Mexico and the seven countries of Central America. Mexico, the largest country of the region, consists mostly of plateaus and high mountains. Two peninsulas, mountainous Baja California and the flat Yucatán, extend from the west and east of the mainland, respectively.

   The Central American countries south of Mexico include Belize, Guatemala, Honduras, El Salvador, Nicaragua, Costa Rica, and Panama. Lowland swamps cover much of the two coasts. The Pacific Coast is drier and cooler than that of the Caribbean, but its ocean waters are rougher. The interiors are mountainous. Much of the region is prone to earthquakes and volcanic eruptions. Panama's isthmus bends eastward, with the Panama Canal cutting from northwest to southeast.

   Mexico and Central America share a broadly similar climate. Low-lying coastal regions can get hot and humid. Mountainous regions typically have springlike weather. The wet season is between May and October; the dry season is from February to May. Both coasts are subject to hurricanes anytime from June to November.

   The countries of Mexico and Central America have retained a distinctively Amerindian identity. Spanish is the official language of every country except Belize. The countries are rich in the treasures of unknown masters—the sculptors, artists, and architects of the early civilizations and the artisans and craftspeople of the present.

2. **Identify and locate Mexico's most-visited sites, matching travelers and destinations best suited for each other.** The most popular destinations in

Mexico are beach resorts such as Acapulco, Cancún, Cozumel, Los Cabos, Puerto Vallarta, Mazatlán, Ixtapa, Zihuatanejo, Huatulco, and Manzanillo. Each destination provides all the amenities, including beautiful settings, a variety of water activities, and numerous nightlife options.

Cancún, on the eastern tip of the Yucatán Peninsula, attracts tourists seeking a selection of package vacations. Cancún has plenty of activity, and nearby Cozumel Island's Palancar Reef is considered outstanding for divers.

The Pacific resorts appeal to those seeking water sports, shopping, and nightlife. Baja California has less activity and fewer people, but its resorts and fishing opportunities lure many. Train tours through the Copper Canyon provide scenery and soft adventure in a comfortable environment. The museums, architecture, fine hotels and restaurants, shopping, nightlife, and cultural attractions of Mexico City fill every need.

Those who enjoy great ruined cities, spectacular pyramids, and mysterious monuments should visit the pyramids at Teotihuacán northeast of Mexico City or the Mayan ruins in the jungle of the Yucatán Peninsula or Tulúm along the Caribbean.

3. **Recall and locate the most-visited sites in Belize, Costa Rica, and Panama, matching travelers and destinations best suited for each other.** Divers visit Belize and head to the world's second-longest barrier reef just off the coast. Ambergris Caye, with its town of San Pedro, is the center for Belize diving. Costa Rica is known for its emphasis on ecotourism. Those seeking soft- or hard-adventure trips such as birding, hiking, white-river rafting, and mountain biking should investigate Costa Rica. The slow trip through the Panama Canal draws those interested in the engineering marvel. A cruise through the canal is best for those who have a sense of history and a taste for the relaxation, security, and pampering provided by a cruise ship.

4. **Provide or find the information needed to plan a trip to Mexico, Belize, Costa Rica, and Panama.** Tour operators are good sources of information about the resort destinations. They offer independent or group packages that include air, accommodations, and transfers. Information about documentation, health concerns, flight schedules, and availability is found in industry computer systems or on the government travel sites on the Internet. It is important that adventure tours with any degree of risk be booked with experienced tour operators.

QUESTIONS FOR DISCUSSION AND REVIEW

1. What do you look for when considering a resort destination? Which of the Mexican resorts has the most appeal to you?

2. Costa Rica is in the forefront of the ecotourism movement. How can a country that wants to preserve and protect its natural resources for future generations also develop tourism?

3. Do you think other destinations in Central America besides Costa Rica, Belize, and the canal area of Panama are ready for tourists?

CHAPTER 8

South America and Antarctica

- Andean Lands: Ecuador, Peru, Bolivia, and Chile
- Argentina
- Brazil
- Other Destinations in South America and Antarctica

OBJECTIVES

When you have completed Chapter 8, you should be able to

1. Describe the environment and people of South America.
2. Identify and locate South America's countries, dependencies, and most-visited sites.
3. Describe South America's attractions, matching travelers and destinations best suited for each other.
4. Provide or find the information needed to plan a trip to South America and Antarctica.

Almost all of South America is east of Miami, Florida. The world's fourth-largest continent, it extends from the southern border of Panama and the sunny beaches of the Caribbean almost to frigid Antarctica, and it lies southeast of North America. South America is scenically splendid and culturally fascinating.

South America's 12 countries and 2 dependencies offer almost any scene a visitor could want. Fast Facts in Appendix A lists the countries alphabetically. In the past, the continent attracted sophisticated travelers. But thanks to safety concerns in other countries, the cost of travel to Europe, and education about the continent's attractions, travel to the "other America" is booming.

The Environment and Its People

South America is a region of mountains, jungles, ancient civilizations, and natives in bowler hats. It has one of the world's driest deserts, the tallest volcano, the longest mountain chain, the largest rain forest, the highest navigable lake, the highest waterfall, and a river with more water than the Mississippi, Nile, and Yangtze combined. The continent offers rural villages and sophisticated cities as well as archaeological mysteries.

The Land

South America is almost surrounded by water (see Figure 8.1). It borders land only in the north at the Isthmus of Panama, where Central America joins Colombia. At the southernmost tip of the triangular continent is an archipelago called Tierra del Fuego ("Land of Fire"), which is less than 700 miles (1,126 km) from the continent of Antarctica. The Strait of Magellan separates Tierra del Fuego from the mainland. Cape Horn is at the archipelago's southern tip.

In 1520 Ferdinand Magellan named Tierra del Fuego ("Land of Fire") when he sighted large fires blazing along the shore. The Indians who lived on the islands wore no clothes and kept fires burning to keep warm.

South America's west coast lies along the Pacific Ocean. Colombia, **Ecuador, Peru,** and **Chile** border the Pacific. South America's two landlocked countries, **Bolivia** and **Paraguay**, are in the continent's center. On the Atlantic, **Brazil** occupies almost half the continent. **Venezuela, Guyana, Suriname**, and the French dependency of **French Guiana** are on the north coast along the Caribbean. **Uruguay** and **Argentina** border the Atlantic on the southeast coast. The British dependency of the **Falkland Islands** is isolated in the South Atlantic off Argentina. (Other islands are described in Table 8.1.)

TABLE 8.1 Some Major Islands off the South American Coast

Island	Country	Location	Characterization
Easter Island	Chile	Isolated in the South Pacific	Unique destination
Falkland Islands (Malvinas)	Great Britain	Atlantic, off Argentina	British territory
Galápagos Islands	Ecuador	Pacific	Nature lover's delight
Îles de Salut (Safety Islands)	France	Caribbean	Former penal islands
Juan Fernández Islands	Chile	Pacific	Fit for Robinson Crusoe
Marajó	Brazil	Mouth of the Amazon	In flat, swampy river delta
Tierra del Fuego group	Argentina and Chile	Strait of Magellan	Archipelago at southern tip of South America

FIGURE 8.1

South America

- National capital
- State capital
- City
- National park or other site

1 inch = 671 miles (1,080 km)

FIGURE 8.2

Milestones of South American History

8000 BC There is evidence of Mapuche tribes in the Chilean coastal valleys.

AD 1400–1500 It is the height of the Inca empire.

1494 A papal grant known as the Treaty of Tordesillas divides the Americas into Spanish and Portuguese zones of influence.

1500 On his way to India, Pedro Alvares Cabral finds Brazil and claims it for Portugal.

1531–1535 The conquest of Peru by Spaniard Francisco Pizarro takes place.

1743 French naturalist de la Condamine explores the Amazon.

1819–1825 Simón Bolívar, known as *El Libertador* ("The Liberator"), leads Colombia, Venezuela, Peru, and Bolivia to independence.

1822 Brazil becomes an independent empire under Dom Pedro I, son of the Portuguese king.

1835 English naturalist Charles Darwin visits the Galápagos Islands on a surveying expedition.

1911 Norwegian Roald Amundsen reaches the South Pole.

1911 American explorer Hiram Bingham finds the ruins of Machu Picchu.

1939 North American scientist Paul Kosok flies over strange markings in the Peruvian desert near the town of Nazca.

1969 The *Lindblad Explorer* sails on the first Antarctic cruise.

1982 Argentina invades the Falkland Islands. Britain protects its claim.

2004 More than eighty cruise ships sail around the Horn.

Despite its long coastline, South America has few natural harbors or bays. The best Atlantic harbor is at Rio de Janeiro, Brazil. Although located inland on the wide Río de la Plata, Buenos Aires in Argentina and Montevideo in Uruguay are also major ports. The Pacific's best port is Guayaquil, Ecuador.

South America's Pacific Coast has resorts, but the waters are too rough and too cold to entice international visitors. Venezuela and Colombia, however, have beautiful sandy beaches on their Caribbean coasts, and Brazil, Uruguay, and Argentina have popular beach resorts on the Atlantic. Like North America, South America has high mountains in the west, central plains with mighty rivers, and lower mountains in the east. The western mountains, the **Andes** (*AN deez*), are the earth's longest mountain system. The range, which is prone to earthquakes and volcanic eruptions, is narrow in the north, broadens into a high plateau in the center, and narrows again in the south. **Aconcagua** (*ah kawng KAH gwah*), the highest peak in the Western Hemisphere (at 22,831 feet [6,959 m]), is in Argentina on the border with Chile.

East of the Andes in the north is South America's second dominant geographic feature: **Amazonia**, the Amazon River basin. The Amazon has been described as the "lungs of the world" because of its vast capacity to produce oxygen. It is home to as much as 30 percent of the planet's animal and plant species and is an important source of medicines. In volume, the **Amazon** is the world's largest river. Fed by a thousand tributaries, the river breaks into many channels as it meanders to the Atlantic. Other major river systems are

- The **Orinoco River**, which flows through Venezuela to the Caribbean.
- The **São Francisco River**, which crosses Brazil to empty into the Atlantic.
- The **Paraná** and **Uruguay Rivers**, which form the **Río de la Plata**. The rivers provide inland water routes for Argentina, Bolivia, Brazil, Paraguay, and Uruguay.

On the Atlantic side of the Andes, flat or rolling plains cover about three-fifths of the land. In the northeast, French Guiana, Suriname, and Guyana meet the Atlantic with swampy coastal plains. In Colombia and Venezuela, the plains are rolling grasslands called the **llanos** (*YAAN ohz*). To the south, Amazonia's tropical rain forest is part of a plain (*selva*) that covers the greater part of Brazil and parts of Colombia, Ecuador, Peru, and Bolivia.

Plains also extend through the center of the continent. The **Gran Chaco** (*grahn CHAH koh*) is a region of swamps, thorny brush jungles, and grassy plains in northern Argentina, western Paraguay, and southern Bolivia. The **Pampas** (*PAHM puhs*) is the fertile plain of Argentina. **Patagonia** is the cold, high desert region covering the southernmost provinces of Argentina and part of Chile.

South America's terrain has hindered its development. But disadvantages for development are to tourism's advantage. Vast areas of the continent remain unspoiled.

The Climate

South America's climate ranges from tropical to polar. Heat and humidity characterize the rain forests of the Amazon basin, while icy cold air surrounds the Andean peaks.

Latitude and elevation account for much of the climatic variation. The equator crosses South America about 400 miles (644 km) north of the continent's widest point. The climate is tropical both north and south of the equator at low elevations. At high elevations, the temperature can be chilly. South of the equator the seasons are reversed, and the climate slowly changes as the traveler goes south toward the continent's tip.

Ocean currents also shape the continent's climate. The cold **Humboldt Current** (also called the Peru Current) cools the west coast and reduces the rainfall. It helps to create one of the earth's driest places, Chile's **Atacama** (*aht uh KAM uh*) **Desert**.

The People and Their History

Except for Brazil and the small countries on the northeast coast, most of South America was explored and colonized by Spain (see Figure 8.2). Before they knew the extent of the continent, Spanish and Portuguese ambassadors met in 1494 in Spain to divide territory at a line in the mid-Atlantic. The treaty enabled Portugal to claim Brazil after its discovery by Cabral in 1500.

When Spanish *conquistadores* ("conquerors") first visited the northern coast, dozens of tribes inhabited the region. The tribes might have been left alone except that some people wore jewelry of gold and pearls. The Spaniards wanted to know where the gold came from, and by exploration and exploitation they proceeded to find out.

The arrival of Europeans brought an end to a series of South American native cultures that dated back more than 2,000 years. These civilizations are known as *pre-Columbian* (before Columbus). Spanish and Portuguese colonial rule was followed by wars of independence and unsteady progress. Immigration and the importation of slaves and laborers brought Spaniards, Portuguese, Italians, Germans, Africans, and East Indians to various countries. The extent to which the cultures intermingled differed from place to place. Thus South American society reflects a rich mix of traditions.

> **➤ PROFILE**
>
> ### Flora and Fauna of Amazonia
>
> Travel to the Amazon rain forest might include views of
>
> - ➤ Air plants, such as bromeliads, mosses, and orchids.
> - ➤ Lianas (woody vines), which wind themselves around trees.
> - ➤ Mammals, such as the bat, anteater, jaguar, monkey, sloth, and tapir.
> - ➤ More than 1,500 species of birds, including parrots and toucans.
> - ➤ Reptiles, such as the cayman and the anaconda.
> - ➤ The giant Brazil nut tree, which grows 150 feet (46 m) tall, as well as the cedrela, cordia, kapok, mahogany, rosewood, and rubber trees.
> - ➤ The largest rodent, the capybara, which can weigh as much as 100 pounds (45 kg).
> - ➤ Some 30 million insect species.
> - ➤ Some 3,000 species of fish.

✔ CHECK-UP

Major physical features of South America include

- ✔ Andes Mountains.
- ✔ Rain forest of Amazonia.
- ✔ Central plains: the llanos, the selva, the Gran Chaco, and the Pampas.
- ✔ Its barren southern tip, Patagonia.
- ✔ Highest mountain in the Western Hemisphere—Aconcagua.
- ✔ Climate ranging from tropical to polar.

South America's culture is notable for

- ✔ Its pre-Columbian civilizations.
- ✔ Its ethnic mix.

Andean Lands

About AD 1200, a people called the Inca founded a kingdom in southern Peru. Their capital was **Cuzco** (*KOOS koh*). The Inca were architects, road builders, and astronomers. They were also lawmakers and warriors, but they did not have a form of writing, so information about their culture is limited. By the early 1500s, Inca rule extended northward from Peru into parts of present-day Colombia and Ecuador and southward through Bolivia (see Figure 8.3), with occasional forays into Chile and Argentina.

At the height of their power, the Inca rulers united the empire by

FIGURE 8.3

Andean Lands

imposing the Quechua (*KETCH wah*) language on their subjects and by building a network of roads through mountains, jungles, and rivers. Although the Inca used neither the wheel nor the horse, their roads included tunnels and suspension bridges that hung precariously over canyons. The great royal highway, or *Inca Road*, ran from the Ecuador–Colombia border to Santiago, Chile. Nearby villages and towns maintained the road and kept inns (called *tambos*), placed conveniently every 15 miles (24 km). The road exists today. Most parts can be traveled only on foot. The most-used section, from Cuzco to **Machu Picchu** (*MAH choo PEEK choo*), is known as the *Inca Trail*.

When the ruthless conquistador Francisco Pizarro (1475–1541) landed in 1532, he found the Inca recovering from a civil war. By a trick, Pizarro captured the Inca winner, Atahualpa (c. 1500–1533), and demanded a ransom for his release. As soon as the demand was filled, Pizarro had Atahualpa strangled. The Inca empire fell apart, but Inca culture continues. Ecuador, Peru, and Bolivia owe their place in tourism to their Inca past.

Andean music uses instruments and songs played long before the Spaniards came. Clothing styles such as the *poncho* (a cloaklike blanket with a slit in the middle for the head) and elaborate woven textiles reflect the heritage.

Ecuador

The Inca left no monumental ruins in Ecuador (*EHK wuh dawr*), one of the smallest South American countries. It lies on the Pacific Coast astride the equator. The country is a charming surprise. It offers variety within a small area and the added attraction of the exotic **Galápagos** (*guh LAH puh gohs*) **Islands**.

Like other countries on South America's west coast, Ecuador is divided into three geographic regions: the Amazon basin, with its tropical rain forest, in the east (*Oriente*); the mountains (*Sierra*) in the center; and the coastal region (*Costa*) in the west.

Each region has its own climate, terrain, and customs. The sparsely populated Oriente has some really wild territory with exotic animals such as pumas and jaguars, but the modern world's encroachment threatens the way of life of local native communities.

The Sierra is a land of high mountains prone to earthquakes. Two parallel ranges of the Andes, the Western and Eastern Cordilleras, run north to south. The fertile valley between them, called the **Avenue of the Volcanoes**, is a patchwork of fields and towns. The valley is lined on both sides by volcanoes, many snowcapped but active. One, **Cotopaxi**, is the world's tallest active volcano. When the volcanoes are behaving, the mountains offer numerous climbing possibilities.

Panama hats are actually made in Ecuador. The hats got their name when Panama became the hats' shipping center in the 1800s.

ON THE SPOT

Mr. and Mrs. Portál come to you to book a trip to South America. This is the first time you have met the couple. How would you begin your work?

Questioning is the first step. Questions about where the Portáls have traveled before, what level of accommodations they prefer, what level of physical activity they want, and what they are looking for in the trip will let them know that you care about their needs. It will also avoid wasting time making suggestions that are of little interest to the couple. In this case, questions reveal that the Portáls are experienced travelers, have been to South America before, are prepared to spend what it takes, are flexible in their time, are used to a high standard of living, and know and enjoy nature. See the Close-Up on page 195 for a possible trip.

Quito The capital of Ecuador, Quito (*KEE toe*), in the Avenue of the Volcanoes, is a place of great natural beauty about 15 miles (24 km) south of the equator and 2 miles (3 km) above sea level. It is the second-highest capital in South America. (La Paz, Bolivia, is the highest.)

Called the *Florence of South America*, old Quito has cobbled plazas, whitewashed buildings, and gold-encrusted churches that rub shoulders with modern skyscrapers. The government tries to preserve the past, but an earthquake in 1987 did much damage to the old buildings. Poverty and street crime live side by side with the gilt of Spanish churches.

Visitors to Quito can travel a few miles north of the city on a day excursion to reach the *Middle of the World* (La Mitad del Mundo) monument and have their picture taken while "hemisphere straddling" (one foot on each side of the equator). The monument marks the location of the equatorial line.

Otavalo Also north of Quito is the home of the industrious Otavalo Indians.

Early birds will want to arrive at the Otavalo market at dawn for the best bargains and certainly get there before the day-trippers arrive on buses from Quito around 10 AM. Some travelers arrive the night before to enjoy a stay at a colonial inn.

The oldest and best-known Indian market in South America takes place every Saturday morning in Otavalo. Textiles, Panama hats, ceramics, and crafts are for sale, and bargaining is a must.

Riobamba and Guayaquil The market town of Riobamba, four hours south of Quito, is the starting point for a rail ride, the Riobamba Express, that follows the Avenue of the Volcanoes. Travelers have a choice of antique refitted trains or more modern cars. The trip offers dramatic views of Cotopaxi and Mount Chimborazo as the train travels south to Guayaquil (*wy ah KEEL*), which is Ecuador's largest city and South America's principal Pacific seaport. The industrial city's attractions are limited. Most travelers pass through quickly on their way to a ship or plane for the Galápagos.

The Galápagos In 1535 Bishop Fray Tomás de Berlanga of Panama was on his way to Peru. His ship was becalmed, drifting without water for three days. At last the bishop and his crew sighted some islands and landed. They named the islands Galápagos from the Spanish word *galápago*, meaning "saddle," because the shell of the giant tortoises found there resembled the saddles of the day.

The islands are peaks of volcanoes, some rising 5,000 feet (1,500 m) out of the ocean. Their terrain ranges from barren to rain forest. The fifteen large islands and many small ones and their friendly animal inhabitants continue to enchant nature buffs and adventurers (see Figure 8.4).

The Galápagos have been home to pirates, whalers, sealers, prisoners, and (during World War II) a U.S. Air Force base. In 1835 a ship named *The Beagle* arrived, and the islands' most famous visitor, young Charles Darwin (1809–1882), came ashore. He made many of the observations on which he based his theories of evolution. In 1954 the Galápagos were declared a province of Ecuador, in 1968 they became Galápagos National Park, and in 1978 UNESCO declared the Galápagos to be "the universal natural heritage of humanity."

Four of the islands (**Santa Cruz**, **Floreana**, **San Cristóbal**, and **Isabela**) have permanent residents. The capital, **Puerto Baquerizo**, is on San Cristóbal. The government strictly limits the number of visitors and the amount of time they can spend on the islands, and it charges a fee for entrance. The commercial airport is on the island of **Baltra**. Limited flights (lasting an hour and a half) arrive from Quito and Guayaquil each day. From Baltra, the visitor takes a combination of ferry and bus to **Puerto Ayora**, on Santa Cruz.

Although it is possible to stay on the Galápagos, most travelers arrive by

FIGURE 8.4

The Galápagos

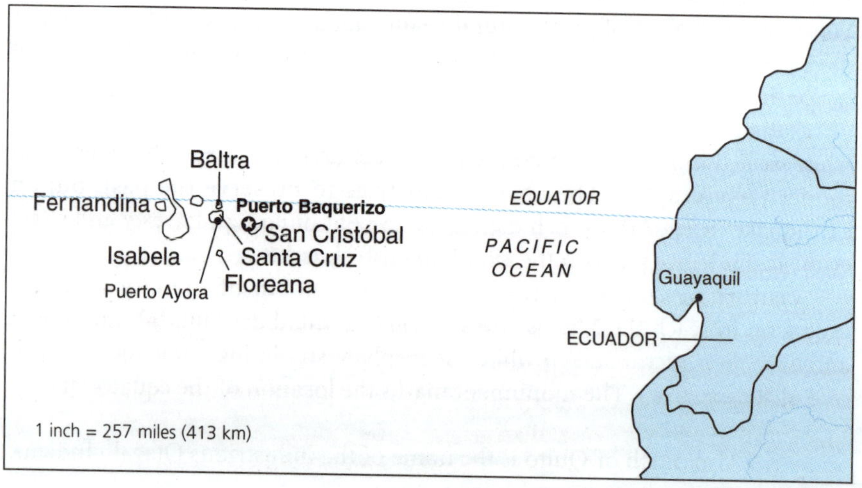

CLOSE-UP: THE GALAPAGOS

Who is a good prospect for a trip to the Galápagos? The destination appeals to experienced travelers, those who have been to South America, those who enjoy the oddities of nature, and those who have the time and money for the trip.

Why would they visit the Galápagos? They can view what may be the planet's single richest sanctuary for land and aquatic wildlife. The Galápagos were never connected to the mainland. The unique wildlife includes marine iguanas, giant tortoises, flamingos, penguins, blue-footed boobies, sea lions, and thirteen species of Darwin's finch.

Where would they go? You might suggest a tour led by a marine biologist. For nine days they could experience the islands in secure comfort. Here is a possible itinerary.

Day 1 Fly to Quito, Ecuador. On arrival, you are met and transfer to your hotel.

Day 2 Quito. A morning walking tour introduces the town's historic treasures. Afternoon free for rest, shopping, or a visit to the Museo Guayasamín to see its collection of regional art.

Day 3 Quito–Baltra. Fly to Baltra to board a yachtlike vessel designed for Galápagos travel—small enough for exploration but large enough to provide amenities. Cruising to Isla Seymour, you see blue-footed boobies, frigate birds, marine iguanas, and sea lions. In the evening, enjoy a sunset cocktail party onboard.

Day 4 Transfer to small boats, and travel to Gardiner Bay to see the sea lions. At Punta Suarez, walk through a nesting colony of masked boobies. Then continue to the site of the world's only known breeding colony of the waved albatross.

Day 5 Snorkeling is possible at Devil's Crown, a sunken volcanic crater.

Day 6 Visit the Charles Darwin Research Station to learn about conservation efforts.

Day 7 Observe the penguins on Isabela, the largest of the Galápagos. View lava fields, distant volcanoes, and Darwin's Lake.

Day 8 Baltra–Quito. Fly back to Quito. The evening includes a farewell dinner.

Day 9 Transfer to the airport for the flight home.

When is the best time to go? High season is from June to August and from early December to late January. Cooled by the Humboldt Current, the temperature is pleasant. The showers during the rainy season—from February to May—are short. The sea is normally cold, being at its warmest during the rainy season.

The travelers say, "It's such a long trip." How would you respond? Remind them of the uniqueness of the destination and its value as an experience.

and stay on their ships. To protect the fragile ecosystem, vessels must drop anchor at a certain distance from the islands. Visitors are brought to land in small boats called *pangas*. From the *pangas*, people must either walk or wade to the islands.

The volcanic rocks of the Galápagos can be sharp, so sturdy shoes of some sort are recommended.

2 Peru

South of Ecuador is Peru (*puh ROO*), South America's third-largest country, three times the size of California. In the southeast, **Lake Titicaca** (*tee tee KAH kah*), the world's highest navigable lake, forms part of Peru's border with Bolivia. (Look again at Figure 8.3.)

Like Ecuador, Peru has three natural zones: Amazon rain forest in the east, Andes highlands in the middle, and the Pacific Coast. The Andes and the Amazon jungle create imposing barriers to travel. The coast is dry desert. As a result, ancient temples and adobe buildings, earth designs, and underground tombs have survived remarkably well for centuries.

Before they spread their empire, the Inca lived in the Cuzco area. Today, more Indians live in Peru than in any other South American country. They make up nearly half the country's population.

Peru is the classic South American destination. If a traveler could go nowhere else on the continent, a visit to Peru would satisfy desires to see lost empires, cities of gold, mysterious line drawings in the desert, and mountainous beauty.

Plaza de Armas, Lima

Lima Lima (*LEE mah*), the *City of Kings*, is Peru's capital and largest city. The city is on an open plain about 10 miles (16 km) from the Pacific. Earthquakes are common, and winter from May to October is a time of gray skies and a dreary wet fog known as *garúa.*

Most travelers to Peru begin their journeys in Lima. It has some of the country's finest colonial architecture, most impressive museums, and good hotels, as well as being the hub for the country's domestic flights. The city's Spanish colonial and modern architecture is surrounded by shantytowns called *pueblos jóvenes* ("new towns"). The Plaza de Armas is the city center.

Sipán and Chan Chan On the coast north of Lima, excavations at **Sipán** have unearthed treasures, including glittering masks of gold and copper, that were created by the Moche, a culture that developed long before the time of the Inca. When the Moche kingdom collapsed in the 7th century, another northern tribe, the Chimú, ascended to power and soon controlled the Peruvian coast. Their most important remnant is the city of **Chan Chan**, Peru's largest pre-Columbian city. The Chimú fell to the Inca around 1400.

Small cups of *mate de coca*, a tea of coca leaves, are handed out at the airport in Cuzco to help new arrivals counteract side effects of the altitude.

Cuzco On a high plain called the *altiplano* southeast of Lima lies Cuzco, the *City of the Sun*. It was the center of the Inca empire. Today, Cuzco is the archaeological capital of the Americas, the center of South American tourism. Most visitors should rest the first day (or more) in town and eat lightly to allow for the effects of high altitude (11,024 feet [3,360 m]).

Colonial Cuzco offers panoramic vistas, shopping, Spanish plazas, churches, Inca fortresses, and fascinating museums. The Sacred Valley is about a 40-minute walk (uphill) from town; cabs are available. The Valley has half a dozen Inca ruins, including Sacsahuamán (*sahc sy wah MAHN*), an immense Inca fortress. Its parade ground, rock walls, and massive throne took about 20,000 Inca subjects eighty years to build.

Machu Picchu In 1911 Hiram Bingham—a Yale professor and later a U.S. senator—literally stumbled on the ruins of Machu Picchu, the *Lost City of the Incas.* It is called the greatest archaeological site in the Americas. Machu Picchu was the last refuge of the Inca. Only the remains of women and children have been found there. It remained hidden for centuries and was inaccessible until the 1940s.

Machu Picchu

The city is located high above the Urubamba River on a mountain known as the Machu Picchu ("Old Peak"). It is surrounded by terraced fields, all of whose soil was carried up on men's backs. Stones for the buildings were cut and assembled with amazing precision. The city is divided into sections starting with a cemetery, the jail, small houses, palaces, and temples. High up is the astronomical observatory and the *Intiwatana*, a curiously shaped stone block that might have been a solar clock. Some claim that to the sun-worshiping Inca it was the "hitching post to the sun."

Travelers get to Machu Picchu from Cuzco by helicopter,

CLOSE-UP: PERU

Who is a good prospect for a trip to Peru? Adventurers and romantics, people interested in history, culture, and archaeology, and those in good enough physical shape to enjoy the high-altitude visit.

Why would they visit Peru? To see a classic South American destination with a combination of ruins of lost empires, magnificent scenery, and vibrant Indian culture.

Where would they go? You might suggest a small group tour with a lot of outdoor activity.

Day 1 Overnight flight to Lima. Explore the city.

Day 2 Fly to Arequipa, beautifully situated in a valley at the foot of El Misti volcano. Tour the city.

Days 3–4 Depart for a two-day overland trip to the Colca Canyon, thought to be the deepest in the world, with the crystalline waters of the Colca River snaking along its bottom.

Day 5 Depart by train for Cuzco, with its mix of Inca and Spanish colonial architecture. In the afternoon, hike up to the impressive Sacsahuamán Fortress.

Day 6 An excursion to the Sacred Valley of the Inca. Walk by the cultivated terraces to the Inca Astronomic Observatory.

Days 7–8 Board the train for Machu Picchu. Stay at a hotel at the site for the night. Spend the next day exploring the ruins. Return to Cuzco late in the afternoon.

Day 9 Fly to Puerto Maldonado and cruise up the Tambopata River to the Posada Amazonas Lodge in the Eselja Indian community.

Day 10 Depart at dawn. Travel by canoe along the edge of Tres-Chimbadas Lake to see giant otters, turtles, and strange birds.

Day 11 Fly back to Lima. Perhaps a farewell dinner with new friends at a colonial mansion.

Day 12 Transfer to the airport for the flight home.

When is the best time to go? The best time to visit the highlands—and for most people, the best time to visit Peru generally—is between May and September, when views of the mountains are clearest. Although the days are warm, the nights can be cold. During the rest of the year, the weather is warmer but wetter, and the Andes are often obscured.

The travelers ask, "Isn't the country in political turmoil?" How would you respond? To reassure travelers and protect yourself from liability, suggest they check the U.S. State Department's travel advisories, as described in Chapter 1 of the Workbook.

by train, on a combination bus and train ride, or on a three- to five-day hike. A local train takes hikers to the start of the grueling 27-mile (43 km) Inca Trail. As the road zigzags up the mountains, it passes fascinating Inca fortresses with secret rooms and complex stonework. Only fit trekkers should attempt this high-altitude route over difficult terrain.

The Nazca lines are called **geoglyphs**, which are marks in rock that give evidence of past geological events. The definition is stretched a bit to include human markings.

The Nazca Lines Another work of ancient people, the Nazca, can be seen south of Lima on Peru's desert coast. The Nazca were a southern Peruvian people about whom little is known; they disappeared before the Spanish conquest. Over a 31-mile (50 km) area, drawings of animals, geometric figures, and birds—ranging up to 1,000 feet (300 m) in size—are scratched onto the desert.

At one time, people believed the Nazca lines were an irrigation system. In 1939 Paul Kosok, a specialist in irrigation, was flying a small plane over the area when he realized that the lines had nothing to do with water. Maria Reiche, his translator, developed the most widely accepted theory about the drawings. She believed that "the work was done so that the gods could see it, and from above, help the ancient Peruvians with their farming, fishing, and other activities."

Visitors take a one-hour flight to Nazca from Lima and then board small planes to fly over the drawings. Lunch and a stop in the archaeological museum in Nazca are usually included in the excursion.

Amazon Basin An increasing number of travelers are visiting an area that takes up more than half of Peru's landmass in the northeast: the Amazon basin. The city of **Iquitos** (*ee KEY toes*) is the embarkation point for cruises down the river to the Amazon's mouth. While waiting for their ships, travelers can stay in lodges built on stilts along the river's edge.

Colca Valley Five hours by road from *La Ciudad Blanca* ("The White City") of **Arequipa**, the green rolling Colca Valley lies beneath Misti volcano. The valley is speckled with small terraced villages inhabited by natives who live, farm, and dress today as they have for centuries. The Colca River canyon is twice as deep as Colorado's Grand Canyon. The valley and canyon offer scenery, wildlife watching (including vicuñas and condors), hiking trails, prehistoric cave paintings, and country inns.

3 Bolivia

When the Spanish conquistadores arrived in Bolivia (*boh LIHV ee uh*), they found silver and established the famous mine at **Potosí**. It became the most important and populous city on the continent. But the silver boom passed. Despite natural resources, Bolivia became one of South America's poorest countries, plagued by political instability. Although Bolivia is a leading producer of tin and the coca leaf, rugged terrain and geographic isolation have hampered its development.

The population of landlocked Bolivia is concentrated on a high plateau in the west, sandwiched between two lofty ranges of the Andes. To the east, the terrain varies, with forests in the northeast whose rivers feed into the Amazon basin near the Brazilian border, savanna country in the center, and the semiarid Chaco in the southeast.

Two-thirds of the people are full-blooded Indian, and many speak only their native Quechua or Aymara. Travelers to country markets will see women with layered dresses, odd bowler hats, and plaited hair. The outfits were first worn by decree of an 18th-century Spanish king.

The llama is used in the mountains as a pack animal. Despite its smiling face, it has some nasty habits. When it thinks it has worked enough, it stubbornly sits down and refuses to move. When angry or under attack, it spits bad-smelling saliva in its enemy's face.

La Paz Bolivia has two capitals: **Sucre** (*SOO kray*), the legal capital, and La Paz, the actual capital and largest city. The country has a near monopoly on things called "the world's highest." At 12,000 feet (3,658 m), La Paz is the world's loftiest capital. It sits in an immense brown bowl flanked by the peaks of the Andes. Most people approach La Paz on a plane, and some are struck immediately by the nausea and dizziness of *soroche*—altitude sickness. The city of more than a million has a high-rise center surrounded by low brick buildings. Attractions include a coca museum and an open-air witches' market.

La Paz is a popular starting point for trekking excursions, many of which follow ancient Inca routes. Mountain bikers come to the city for the *Road of Death*, a bike ride that drops nearly 12,000 feet (3,658 m) to the valley floor in less than 40 miles (64 km). Customized adventure tours focus on trekking, mountaineering, ecotourism, and wildlife and jungle tours.

The Indians of Lake Titicaca used the lake's rush and totoro plants to make unique boats and floating islands.

Lake Titicaca West of La Paz, Lake Titicaca, the world's highest navigable lake, is on the boundary of Peru. The lake is 110 miles (177 km) long and about 45 miles (72 km) wide, and its waters are cold year-round. Most of the surrounding mountains are snow-covered. Steamers cross the lake from Puno, Peru, to **Guaqui**, Bolivia, the lake's most important port. Boats tour the lake's various islands, which have ruins of Indian civilizations that existed before the Spanish conquest.

Chile

In the ancient Indian Aymara language, Chile (*CHIHL ee* or *CHEE lay*) means "the place where the land finishes." The country stretches from Peru south to the tip of the continent. Squeezed between the Andes and the Pacific, Chile averages only 120 miles (193 km) in width but is 2,600 miles (4,183 km) long. Chile's island possessions include the **Juan Fernández Islands**, where the shipwreck ordeal of Alexander Selkirk inspired Daniel Defoe's *Robinson Crusoe*, and **Easter Island**.

The Andes form Chile's eastern border with Bolivia and Argentina. In some places mountains take up one-third to one-half of the land. From north to south, Chile has four topographical areas. First, in the north is the Atacama Desert, which stretches from the Peruvian border to roughly the **Copiapo** area (look again at Figure 8.3). Second, south of the desert is the **Central Valley**, an area of fertile farms and vineyards where most of the population is concentrated. This region is the site of the national capital, **Santiago**; the busy port of **Valparaíso**; and the elegant resort of **Viña del Mar**. The third region is the **Lake District**, which extends from **Concepción** south to **Puerto Montt**. South of Puerto Montt is the fourth area, the realm of the condor: the **Archipelago**. It is a region of fjords, glaciers, and beauty that extends to the tip of the continent.

Trips to see the geoglyph at Pintados leave from Iquique in northern Chile. The geoglyph is an enormous picture of a man, the *Giant of the Atacama*. No one is sure how the lines were created or why they are there.

The Atacama Northern Chile's landscape is dotted with ghost towns and copper mines. In 1971 the Atacama Desert received rain for the first time in 400 years. Winds that blow across the cold Humboldt Current bring cool, cloudy weather and frequent fogs. The desert is the world's chief source of nitrates.

Santiago Santiago (*san tee AH goh*) is Chile's capital. It is a huge modern city with skyscrapers, traffic, pedestrian-only streets, subways, luxury hotels, and fine restaurants. The city's major focal points are the Plaza de Armas, graced by the Cathedral, Town Hall, and La Moneda, which is the national palace.

The Andes rise immediately to the east of the city. Surrounded by mountains on all sides, the smog of the bustling metropolis builds up. Along with Mexico City, Santiago is one of the world's most polluted cities.

Valparaíso and Viña del Mar These coastal cities are 75 miles (121 km) west of Santiago via a modern superhighway. Busy Valparaíso ("Valley of Paradise") has a jumble of old and modern buildings and colorful hillside houses. Cable cars connect the upper and lower towns. From the port, cruise ships depart or arrive from their voyages around the Horn. Disembarking passengers must trek to Santiago to catch their flights home.

Viña del Mar ("Vineyard of the Sea") ranks as one of South America's most elegant seaside resorts. It has a casino, luxury hotels, elegant condominiums, and striking seaside vistas. As at other resorts on South America's Pacific Coast, the surf is powerful, the undercurrents strong, and the water chilly.

Portillo Northeast of Santiago, the ski resort of Portillo (*port TEE yo*) is set in the heart of the southern Andes. On a clear day visitors can glimpse Mount Aconcagua 25 miles (40 km) away on Chile's border with Argentina. The resort is far above the timberline in a moonlike landscape reached by an ever-winding road. A legendary 9-mile (14 km) ski run starts at the statue of Christ of the Andes. The huge statue marks the settlement of a boundary dispute between Argentina and Chile. An abundance of natural snow can be enjoyed from June to September.

The Wine Valleys Chile's principal vineyards are in the Central Valley in the provinces near Santiago, where several beautiful valleys produce the grapes. Travelers to the region can fill their days with tastings, visits to local markets, and a stop at La Sebastiana, the home of Chile's revered Nobel Prize–winning poet, Pablo Neruda (1904–1973).

The Lake District South of the Bío-Bío River, snowcapped volcanoes—some still active—rise on the slopes of the Andes in the Lake District. It is a land of beauty, a seemingly endless succession of lush alpine valleys surrounded by Andean hills. Within the region are the Petrohue Waterfall, the Osorno Volcano, and the resorts of Villarica and Lake Llanquihue, the fourth-largest lake in South America. Puerto Varas, on Lake Llanquihue, resembles parts of Germany or Austria.

Puerto Montt, which is at the end of the Pan-American Highway, is the entry by ship to the Lake District. The handicraft market near the dock offers boldly patterned woolen goods as well as the broad-brimmed hats of the Chilean cowboy, the *huaso* (*WHAH so*).

The Archipelago While Chile's northern desert is one of the driest places on earth, parts of the Archipelago are among the wettest. Ships cruise through a region called the **Inside Passage**, which leads south to the Beagle Channel and around Cape Horn. The spectacular route goes through glacial valleys and fjords and past huge icebergs.

Cape Horn is the southernmost point of the archipelago of Tierra del Fuego, which is divided between Chile and Argentina. It is a wild windswept region broken into thousands of islands. **Punta Arenas** ("Sandy Point") is Chile's only major settlement on Tierra del Fuego and the country's (and the world's) southernmost city. It was a port for ships rounding South America en route to California during the mid-19th-century Gold Rush. Today, Punta Arenas is a port for cruises through the glaciers, a stop for round-the-continent voyages, and a port for ships sailing to Antarctica. The best times to visit are December to March, and even then clear skies are rare and disappear within minutes.

Moai on Easter Island

Easter Island Chile owns several small islands far out in the Pacific, including Easter Island (Rapa Nui), famed for its giant stone faces. The island is about 2,300 miles (3,701 km) west of the continent, one of the world's most isolated destinations. The first European to see the island, a Dutch explorer, arrived on Easter Sunday, 1722—hence the island's name. Early settlers called it the "Navel of the World." Getting there involves a five-hour flight from Santiago.

No one is sure who the first inhabitants were or when they built the more than 600 statues called *moai* (*MOH eye*) scattered around the island. Most are from 11 to 20 feet (3.4 to 6 m) tall; some rise as high as 40 feet (12 m). Islanders used stone picks to carve the statues from the island's volcanic *tufa* ("rock"). They placed their statues on raised pedestals called *ahu* and balanced huge red stone cylinders on the statues' heads.

✔ CHECK-UP

The Andean countries include

- ✔ Ecuador; its capital is Quito, but its largest city is Guayaquil.
- ✔ Peru; its capital and largest city is Lima.
- ✔ Bolivia; its capitals are Sucre and La Paz, and its largest city is La Paz.
- ✔ Chile; its capital and largest city is Santiago.

Typically the Andean lands have three natural zones:

- ✔ To the east, the rain forests of Amazonia, except in Chile, where the east meets the mountains.
- ✔ In the center, the Andes highlands.
- ✔ To the west, dry lands along the Pacific—except Bolivia, which has no coastline.

For travelers, highlights of the Andean lands include

- ✔ Ecuador's Avenue of the Volcanoes.
- ✔ Exotic Galápagos Islands.
- ✔ Center of ancient civilizations, Machu Picchu in Peru.
- ✔ South America's highest navigable lake, Lake Titicaca.
- ✔ Glacier cruises through Chile's Archipelago.
- ✔ Chile's Easter Island.

B

Argentina

East of Chile is Argentina (*ahr juhn TEE nuh*), South America's second-largest country (see Figure 8.5). It is shaped like a long, narrow triangle. Its climate ranges from the heat of the Gran Chaco in the north, through the pleasant climate of the central Pampas, to the sub-Antarctic cold of the southern region known as **Patagonia**. More than two-thirds of the population and most of the cities are on the Pampas, the fertile plain that extends from the

FIGURE 8.5

Argentina

The Falkland Islands are in the South Atlantic Ocean east of Argentina. Argentina, which calls them the *Islas Malvinas*, wanted the islands for itself and in 1982 invaded. Britain won the war. Locals describe the altercation as "two bald men fighting over a comb."

Atlantic Ocean to the Andes. The southwest, with a string of beautiful lakes framed by the Andes, is often compared to Switzerland.

Most Argentines are of Spanish, Italian, or German ancestry, and the country has a decidedly European atmosphere. The Spanish came for silver and gold, but the land lacked mineral riches. The Pampas' fertile soil proved to be more valuable than any minerals. During the late 1800s, Argentina grew wealthy from the export of meat and grain to Europe. In the 1920s, it was one of the world's wealthiest nations, solidly middle class. The Depression of the 1930s and a series of military dictatorships shattered the economy. Unprecedented rates of joblessness and poverty in the 1990s plunged the country into crisis. Argentina has begun a slow climb back to prosperity and political stability.

Argentina is the home of the tango, ski resorts, excellent beef, fine wines, waterfalls, modern cities, and penguin colonies. Travelers can swim in February, ski in August, and tango anytime.

The Cities

Argentina's appeal starts with the attractions of sophisticated **Buenos Aires** (*bway nohs EYE rays*), the capital and largest city.

Buenos Aires, Argentina

Buenos Aires One of the world's largest cities, Buenos Aires sprawls over the flat plain beside the wide Río de la Plata, 150 miles (241 km) upriver from the Atlantic. Although inland, it is a major port. With more than one-third of the country's inhabitants living in or around Buenos Aires, the city is the political, economic, and cultural center of Argentina and the country's gateway.

Buenos Aires' architecture is a mix of styles. Modern high-rises sit next to ornate buildings from days long gone. Internet cafés, malls, and McDonalds line the streets, which are laid out in a grid, although some streets transverse the grid diagonally. The city is dotted with squares, the Plaza de Mayo being the most historic. The presidential palace, La Casa Rosada ("The Pink House"), is on the plaza. The symbol of the city, the Obelisk, is on Avenida 9 de Julio (the world's widest avenue), as is the Teatro Colón, one of the world's largest opera houses.

Buenos Aires' identity is in its *barrios* ("neighborhoods"), each with its own character and history. Perhaps the most vibrant ones are La Boca ("The Mouth") and San Telmo. The blue-collar community of La Boca is where waves of mostly Italian immigrants settled during the late 1800s; brightly colored houses line the pedestrian walkways. La Boca is home to the country's most popular soccer team and its stadium. San Telmo's streets are lined with antique shops, restaurants, and tango halls. On Sundays, San Telmo's Dorrego Square turns into an outdoor bazaar of crafts, clothing, and antiques.

The passionate tango is the dance of Argentina, and San Telmo is considered its home. Travelers might be treated to a spontaneous display as couples tango in the streets. A visit to a tango nightclub is a must.

Day trips from Buenos Aires visit the Pampas—an unending sea of grass—for an *asado* ("barbecue") and riding display at one of the cattle and horse *estancias* ("ranches"). Some visitors stay at a ranch for a few days, perhaps to observe polo pony training.

Tigre Just north of Buenos Aires is Tigre, a base for exploring the delta of the Paraná River. The delta is a maze of canals, tributaries, and rivers lined with weekend houses. Boat trips on the waterways are pleasant excursions.

➤ PROFILE

Shopping Opportunities in Buenos Aires

Buenos Aires' shopping area is near Calle Florida. The most expensive shops are located in the Recoleta area. The dedicated shopper will find

- Jewelry fashioned from rhodocrosite, a rose-colored gemstone.
- Leather goods, including jackets, shoes, bags, and accessories.
- Maté gourds with silver straws—souvenirs of the gaucho life.
- Sheepskin products.
- Tango music on CDs and tapes.

Other Places to Visit

A typical tour of Argentina visits the capital, perhaps adds a few days of relaxation at a beach resort, and then flies over to a national park or Patagonia.

Beach Resorts **Mar del Plata** is Argentina's most popular beach resort. It is south of Buenos Aires, about forty minutes by air or four hours by car. Deep-sea fishing and water sports are popular diversions. Most resorts have casinos. Necochea reputedly has the world's largest casino.

Iguazú Falls One of South America's famous sights is Iguazú (*ee gwa ZOO*) Falls, the most spectacular waterfalls in the Western Hemisphere. (It is spelled *Iguazú* in Spanish-speaking Argentina and *Iguaçu* in Portuguese-speaking Brazil.) Taller than Niagara and twice as wide, the falls' cascades spread nearly 2 miles (3 km). The whole system can be seen only from the air. The falls are on the border with Brazil and Paraguay and are part of Argentina's national park system. The Argentine side has catwalks to observation points at the brink of the falls.

The most comfortable time for viewing is June through August—when the region is dry and at its coolest. The water is crystal clear then, but the flow is less dramatic. Also, July is local vacation month, and the place is packed with people. The flow of water over the falls is greatest from January to March, but then the weather is hot and humid.

The Andes The Andes region has national parks with abundant wildlife and opportunities for hunting and fishing. Argentina shares Aconcagua with Chile, but most of it is in Argentina. As one of the classic *Seven Summits* (composed of the tallest peak on each continent), Aconcagua is a sought-after goal for mountaineers.

The town of **San Carlos de Bariloche** is on the shore of an Andean lake just south of Nahuel Haupi National Park, near the Chilean border. Bariloche looks like the Germany of its earliest settlers. Many buildings are designed like chalets, and its streets are full of chocolate shops and restaurants offering fondue. Ski season is May to September. In summer, the town lures hikers, fishing enthusiasts, and mountain bikers.

Outside the United States and Canada, mountain guiding services are controlled by the UIAGM (the French acronym for the International Association of Mountain Guides). It accredits individual guides. Certification standards require extensive formal training and testing.

Patagonia Patagonia occupies more than one-quarter of Argentina but has less than 3 percent of the population. The region is virtually barren except around the river valleys, where grapes and other fruits are grown. Welsh-speaking farmers raise sheep. Tourists go to **Peninsula Valdéz** to watch sea lions, penguins, and—during September and October—whales mating offshore.

Southern Patagonia is the home of **Glaciers National Park**. **Calafate** is the stepping-off point to the huge blue glaciers wedged in the forest-covered countryside.

The name *Patagonia* refers to the local tradition of wearing bulky shoes to keep the feet warm. The Spanish word *patagones* means "big feet."

Tierra del Fuego The islands of Tierra del Fuego are staging points for Antarctic expeditions, and both Chile and Argentina claim large sections. In Argentina, **Ushuaia** claims to be the world's southernmost town. The port's steep streets overlook the whirling green **Beagle Channel** (named for Charles Darwin's ship).

Ushuaia's many scenic attractions include the Tierra del Fuego National Park to the west of town. It is the world's southernmost national park. Large colonies of penguins, sea lions, and sea elephants can be seen along the park's coast. A narrow-gauge railway operates as a tourist train through the park.

Cape Horn People round the rocky island of Cape Horn in the Drake Passage, the waters south of the island. Weather conditions are usually not nice. It is normally choppy because it marks the point at which the Atlantic and Pacific Oceans meet. People cruising the area have a fifty-fifty chance of a peaceful voyage. A carved marble monument on the Horn commemorates the mariners who have suffered the journey. It includes a sculpture of the great albatross, an appropriate expression of the wild freedom that Cape Horn symbolizes.

✔ CHECK-UP

Buenos Aires is
- ✔ Capital of Argentina and its largest city.
- ✔ Known for its European atmosphere.
- ✔ Home of the tango.

Outdoor attractions of Argentina include
- ✔ Iguazú Falls from the Argentine side.
- ✔ Skiing in July and August in Bariloche.
- ✔ Glaciers National Park in Patagonia.
- ✔ Tierra del Fuego National Park.

C

Brazil

Brazil (*bruh ZIHL*) is the continent's largest country, in area almost the size of the continental United States. It borders every country in South America except Chile and Ecuador (see Figure 8.6). The landscape is relatively flat. The Amazon River basin covers one-third of the land. South of the Amazon is a tableland, the **Mato Grosso**. The east coast has beautiful beaches.

The equator passes through Brazil's north. All but the southernmost part of the country is in the tropics, and most of the country has warm to hot weather year-round.

While Francisco de Orellana (c. 1490–1546) was exploring a Brazilian river in 1542, his expedition was attacked by what appeared to be female warriors. The Spaniards called their attackers Amazons after the female warriors in Greek mythology. The name was later given to the river and surrounding area.

People lived in what is now Brazil long before the Portuguese explorers arrived. The colonists established sugar cane plantations and enslaved the natives to work the fields. As the Indians died from European diseases, African slaves were brought in as replacements. Between 1820 and 1939, huge numbers of people immigrated to Brazil from Europe, the Middle East, and Asia.

Since it achieved independence in 1822, Brazil has had its share of military dictators, corrupt politicians, and economic problems. Two percent of the people are extremely rich. The middle class is growing, but a large percentage of the people are very poor. Amazonia beckons as a possible engine for economic growth. Exploitation of the Amazon's resources, however, threatens both the rain forest and the native Amazonians.

The Cities

Brazilian cities look much like those of the United States and Canada, with impressive skyscrapers, traffic jams on expressways, and elegant stores and restaurants. High-rise apartment buildings on broad avenues contrast with the old houses that line narrow, winding streets. **Rio de Janeiro** (*REE oh day zhun NAIR oh*) is the center of trade, transportation, and tourism.

Rio de Janeiro The Portuguese who came to Rio in 1502 believed that its beautiful bay was the mouth of a great river, and they named the place *January*

FIGURE 8.6

Brazil

River. The bay is ringed by rocky islands and beautiful beaches, of which Copacabana and Ipanema are the most famous. Most days, the broad white strands, coconut vendors, and beautiful bodies make the beaches a powerful lure, but sometimes the crowds, street crime, and hawkers diminish the appeal.

A ridge of mountains divides Rio. The southern half has most of the sights and luxury hotels. Wherever the slopes are too steep for normal housing, the beachfront suburbs have *favelas*—shantytowns of the poor—as their backdrop.

Rio's landmark, Sugar Loaf, provides a spectacular view of the city. A gondola/cable car system takes tourists up and back. Corcovado ("Hunchback") Mountain (2,310 feet [704 m]) provides an even better view. The statue of Christ the Redeemer on its summit stands above the city with its arms outstretched in blessing.

Poor or rich, the Brazilian people are seen at their talented best when they celebrate at *Carnival*. Its street parades, opulent costumes, and music became a tradition in the 1930s when the neighborhoods started adding choreography and theme songs. Samba became the festival's signature music. Each year a theme is chosen, and sambas are composed and costumes designed to reflect the theme. Months of preparation go into brief moments of glory during the five frantic days before Ash Wednesday. The centerpiece of the event is the Carnival Parade, the grand spectacle of Rio's samba schools. The schools dance their way through the Sambadrome (a viewing stadium).

Carnival in Rio de Janeiro, Brazil

Brasília Until 1960, Rio was Brazil's capital. To bring people to the west, the government built a city in the wilderness and made it the nation's capital.

Brasília (*bruh ZEAL yuh*) is 600 miles (960 km) inland. Brazilian architect Oscar Niemeyer designed its major buildings in the shape of an airplane. The wings are formed by high-rise residential blocks and the plane's body by government offices. Brasília attracts tours of architects, real estate developers, and city planners.

São Paulo São Paulo (*sown PAU loh*), located almost exactly on the Tropic of Capricorn, is Brazil's and South America's largest city, as well as one of the world's largest cities. It is the center of Brazil's coffee and telecommunications industries. Big, busy, and modern, it is of more interest to the business traveler than the leisure tourist. Its pleasures are entirely human made. Popular diversions are dining at fine restaurants or visiting the Museum of Art.

Best buys in Brazil are precious and semiprecious stones. Gold sold throughout the continent is generally 18 carat, but it is always safest to check the mark.

Salvador Much of the food, religion, dance, and music that characterize Brazil originated in the coastal city of Salvador, which is also known as **Bahia**. Here the Catholic Portuguese culture was blended with that of the West African slaves. The city is built on two levels and has more than a hundred 17th- and 18th-century buildings. Carnival in Salvador is as lively or livelier than the one in Rio.

Surfers congregate on the Amazon at São Domingos do Capim every March around the full moon and the equinox to chase the river's endless wave, known as a *pororoca* ("mighty noise" in the Tupi Indian language). Long before the wave can be seen, it can be heard. A ride on a *pororoca* lasts 34 minutes and 10 seconds—but surfers must watch for not only debris stirred up by the wave but also alligators, piranhas, snakes, and leopards.

Other Places to Visit

Outside the cities, taking a tour by plane or a combination tour/cruise is the most convenient way to travel. Tours are available for every interest, in every size, and with a range of prices.

The Amazon Most tourists see the Amazon from the deck of a ship. Small ships cruise the upper Amazon between Iquitos, Peru, and Manaus, Brazil. Passengers often leave their larger ship to board zodiaks (small rubber boats) that take them up tributaries to view wildlife and occasionally meet the natives.

Halfway down the river, the ships steam past the place where the café-au-lait–colored Amazon and the tea-colored Tapajós meet at the "wedding of the waters." To the west of Manaus, the Amazon weds the Río Negro, adding dark water from the forested north. In each case, the waters flow together for miles before mingling colors.

From the Atlantic, oceangoing ships enter the Amazon by way of the Pará River on the southern side of **Marajó Island**, where, 90 miles (145 km) from the sea, **Belém** is the port. An unusually high ocean tide occasionally creates a bore that can measure up to 15 feet (4.6 m) high and rush upstream at speeds of 20 miles (32 km) per hour.

The largest city on the river (with a population of more than a million people) is the port of **Manaus** (*muh NAUSS*). When rubber became valuable (thanks to the invention of the rubber tire), the rubber barons earned the city a reputation for extravagance and decadence. Manaus was known as the *Paris of the Tropics*. Its opera house, Teatro Amazonas, is a monument to those glory days. Manaus is a destination for cruise ships sailing up the Amazon, taking travelers into Brazil's green heartland.

Iguaçu Falls

Iguaçu Falls Day excursions from Rio bring people to Iguaçu Falls, near the border of Brazil, Argentina, and Paraguay. The Brazilian side has the best view, but the falls are most accessible on the Argentine side.

✔ CHECK-UP

Key cities of Brazil, South America's largest country, are

- ✔ Rio de Janeiro, the center of tourism.
- ✔ Brasília, the capital.
- ✔ São Paulo, the largest city in South America.
- ✔ Salvador, where much of Brazil's culinary, religious, dance, and music culture originated.
- ✔ Manaus, the Amazon's inland port.

For travelers, highlights of Brazil include

- ✔ Carnival in Rio.
- ✔ Cruises on the Amazon.
- ✔ Iguaçu Falls.

Planning the Trip

South America is usually a once-in-a-lifetime trip. Countries such as Peru, Chile, Argentina, and Brazil have a good tourism infrastructure; but travelers still benefit from regional tours led by experienced guides. Tour operators provide real value for trips to South America. Some tour companies operate multicountry tours of considerable depth; however, most operators concentrate on a specific area or event.

When to Go

Thanks to South America's size and its variety of climates and altitudes, travelers have many choices about when to visit. The tropics surrounding the equator have no particular season. To the south, the reversal of seasons between hemispheres makes the resorts of Argentina and Chile an appealing destination for winter sports enthusiasts during July and August. In Andean lands along the coast, December to April are the warmest months, and it seldom rains. The wettest months are June through August. In the highlands, the driest months are June through October.

ON THE SPOT

You receive a phone call from Mr. and Mrs. Hiram Gates. Your questions reveal that they are in their early thirties, enjoy active sports, and haven't traveled much because they were so busy starting an Internet company, which is prospering. Now they want to see some of the world and have an adventure. What do you suggest?

More than 60 percent of travel business is done by phone. By phone you lose the clues you get from physical appearance. But you have found the answer to a most important question: price. The clients' business is prospering. Good. Now you can sell value more than price. The Gateses sound like prospects for Machu Picchu or the Amazon.

Preparing the Traveler

Several countries require passports, visas, and entrance and exit taxes. Travelers should be sure that they understand the documentation rules. Political situations require the traveler to keep up with State Department warnings. Travelers who plan extensive touring in the countryside should check with their doctors and the Centers for Disease Control if they have health concerns.

Health In remote areas, malaria and yellow fever are present, and travelers may need inoculations. Swimming in the continent's rivers and lakes requires caution. Many are infested with stingrays, electric eels, crocodiles, and parasites that affect the skin.

Cities such as Bogotá, Quito, Cuzco, and La Paz are at high elevations, and altitude sickness (*soroche*) is common. *Soroche* can affect anyone, young or old, even those in top physical shape. Dizziness, headaches, loss of appetite, and vomiting are the major symptoms. For many people *soroche* is mild; for others, especially obese people with heart problems, high blood pressure, or asthma, it can be fatal. To adapt as easily as possible, travelers should try to eat lightly for two days before their trip, drink a cup or two of coca tea on arrival, and take it easy for a day or so. People need time to acclimate before attempting strenuous exercise. The cure for *soroche* is descent to lower altitudes.

Money Each country has its own currency and exchange rate. Banks, money exchange houses, hotels, and travel agencies are authorized to exchange money. Exchange rates fluctuate daily. Using an ATM is a good option. In many tourist centers, U.S. dollars are accepted.

Language Language can pose a challenge across much of the continent. Spanish is spoken in most countries, but Portuguese is the mother tongue in Brazil. Native dialects are common in the countries west of the Andes. In the cities, most hotel and restaurant employees speak enough English to communicate. But in remote areas, very few people speak more than a few words of English.

Customs Meal patterns and dining hours differ from those of North America. Most international-chain hotels offer a buffet breakfast. Lunch is around 1400 and in many places is the main meal of the day. Dinner is taken late, between 2100 and 0100.

➤ PROFILE

South American Cuisine

Food preparation reflects the continent's Portuguese, Spanish, French, Dutch, and African heritage. All the countries use red beans, potatoes, rice, and, above all, corn. The following are some specialties:

- Beef in Argentina. The *parrillada* is a restaurant specializing in grilled meats.
- Sea bass in Chile, fresh from the Pacific.
- Excellent Chilean wines.
- *Feijoada*, the national dish of Brazil, made with rice, black beans, meat, and manioc.
- Fruits such as the chirimoya, lucuma, mamey, níspero, and sapodilla. The naranjilla from Ecuador has a taste somewhere between citrus and peach.
- Highly spiced soups. Bolivian soups include creamy peanut soup with vegetables and pumpkin stew served with corn, melted cheese, and fava beans.
- *Maté*, the national beverage of Paraguay and Argentina, a tea brewed from the dried leaves of a holly tree.
- *Pisco*, a potent drink made from fermented grapes.

Transportation

Airline routes link the major cities and towns. Air travel is the best way to see as much as possible in a limited time. Each country has its national airlines; international carriers also provide service. Reservations are important because most routes are heavily booked.

Driving is on the right. An inter-American or international driver's permit (IDP) is required in addition to, not in place of, a person's home driver's license. Most car rental firms will not permit their cars to cross borders.

Andean Lands The adventurous traveler who wants to drive the Pan-American Highway should do a lot of research before attempting the trip. Road conditions vary from excellent to impassable. Police and military checks along certain sections are routine. Travel by air is often not only the most convenient choice but also a beautiful one.

PeruRail, in partnership with Orient Express, operates train service to Machu Picchu using renovated cars that provide luxury services. The scenic three-and-a-half-hour train ride from Cuzco is the favorite way to go, but a helicopter ride takes only half an hour, flying through the Sacred Valley. PeruRail also operates train service from Machu Picchu south to Lake Titicaca and then west to the Colca Canyon, a truly spectacular route.

In Chile, the Pan-American Highway snakes its way through the northern half of the country and almost makes it to the southern coast. To connect this remote region with the rest of the country, a highway called the *Carretera Austral* is being built. Brochures praise the Carretera Austral as "a beautiful road studded with rivers, waterfalls, forest, lakes, glaciers, and the occasional hamlet." The description is accurate, but the highway is mostly unpaved, shoulders are nonexistent, and single-lane bridges span streams and rivers. Drivers must be sure that they have a spare tire, a jack, jumper cables, and enough food in case they are stuck far from the nearest town. What the Carretera Austral offers adventurous travelers is a chance to see a part of the world where few have ventured.

Argentina Air travel is the most efficient way to get around Argentina.

Argentina's domestic rail network is extensive but unreliable. Car rentals are available. Major roads are quite good. Tolls are imposed on the *autopistas* (superhighways).

Brazil Unless the traveler has unlimited time, travel around Brazil should be by air. The country has more than 1,500 airports. Amazonia has only recently been connected to the Brazilian highway system.

Cruises South America offers good cruising possibilities, including

- Southern Caribbean or Panama Canal cruises with port calls at Cartagena, Colombia.
- Cruises around the continent.
- Segments of the around-the-continent cruise, perhaps leaving from Rio or Buenos Aires, stopping at the Falkland Islands, sailing around Cape Horn (weather permitting) through Chile's fjords and glaciers, and debarking in Valparaíso, Chile.
- Cruises through Chile's Archipelago.
- Antarctic expedition cruises, perhaps leaving from Ushuaia, Argentina, or Punta Arenas, Chile.
- Galápagos Islands cruises.
- Amazon River cruises.

Accommodations

In the cities, international chains have first-class and deluxe hotels. Budget hotels usually leave much to be desired. The quality of accommodations outside the cities varies considerably. Travelers can stay at luxurious converted *estancias* or spend the night at a 16th-century colonial plantation reincarnated as a first-class country inn.

In several countries, hotels are classified by the star system, the highest and most luxurious being a five-star property. Reservations are important. Tour operators control space in hotels and resorts, a real benefit at times such as Carnival in Rio, when demand is high.

✔ CHECK-UP

Planning a trip to South America requires close attention to
- ✔ Altitude as well as climate variations.
- ✔ Scarcity of accommodations and need for reservations.
- ✔ Documentation and health concerns.

For most travelers to South America, a trip involves
- ✔ Air transportation from city to city.
- ✔ Use of tour operators.

OTHER DESTINATIONS IN SOUTH AMERICA AND ANTARCTICA

South American tourism centers on the Andean lands, Argentina, and Brazil. The countries off the tourist path include five countries along the Caribbean (see Figure 8.1)—Colombia, Venezuela, Guyana, Suriname, and French Guiana—as well as two southern countries, Paraguay and Uruguay.

COLOMBIA

The connecting point between the Americas is Colombia (*kuh LUHM bee uh*), the only South American country with a coastline along both the Atlantic and Pacific Oceans. The Andes cover about one-third of the country. Colombia has natural and cultural attractions, but civil war has raged for decades.

Bogotá (*boh guh TAH*) is the capital and largest city. **Cartagena** (*kar tah HAY nah*), a port on Colombia's north coast, continues to attract tourists. When pirates harassed the Spanish Main, Cartagena's forts guarded the gold looted from the Indians. Today, *Ciudad Vieja* ("Old Town") is a World Heritage Site, and new Cartagena is a resort with hotels and wide sandy beaches. Modern pirates come by cruise ship.

The emerald is a brittle green gemstone. The value of the emerald lies in its color and freedom from flaws. Colombia is the source of the world's finest emeralds.

VENEZUELA

Of the South American countries on the Caribbean, Venezuela is the one most involved in tourism. It is a leading producer of petroleum and has both natural and cultural wonders. Its climate varies with elevation.

Caracas (*kuh RAH kuhs*) is the capital and largest city. It is the high-rise, crowded, traffic-clogged heart of the country. On the coast east of Caracas, a succession of beautiful palm-fringed and mountain-framed beaches attracts European tourists.

In the south, Venezuela's Gran Sabana is an ancient plateau. Its rock formations have sheer walls and *tepuí* (*te poo ee*), or flat-topped mountains. The Sabana is home to Canaima National Park, the site of **Angel Falls**, the world's highest waterfall, nineteen times higher than Niagara. Day excursions from Caracas offer an aerial view from a plane that circles two or three times. Travelers must hope that the clouds lift long enough to allow a glimpse of the falls.

Tiny Canaima is the service center for tourists interested in seeing the falls on land. The excursion requires a canoe trip on tea-colored rivers, overnights in a hammock, and an hour's trek through jungle to the base of the falls.

Angel Falls are named for Jimmy Angel, a U.S. Air Force pilot from World War I who drifted to Venezuela. A man who hired him to fly into the Gran Sabana found gold but did not tell Angel its source. In 1935, while looking, Angel landed on top of a mesa. His plane bogged down, and he and those with him had to walk out. On their way, they spotted the falls.

THE NORTHEAST COAST

The Atlantic Coast between Venezuela and Brazil is a hot, humid region, most of it covered by tropical rain forest. The countries are destinations for the curious who want to see every place on earth.

Guyana South America's only English-speaking country is Guyana (*gy AN uh*). **Georgetown** is the capital and largest city. Parts of Guyana's interior have never been explored. Rivers lead inland to exotic rain forests, home to more than 700 species of birds. One of the most spectacular sights is Kaieteur Falls, which is five times the height of Niagara.

The arapaima, the world's largest freshwater fish, also calls Guyana home. It can reach up to 10 feet (3 m) in length.

Suriname In 1667 the Dutch exchanged a territory they did not want—the state of New York—for Suriname (*sur ree NAHM*), the smallest country in South America. Throughout the 18th and 19th centuries, Suriname was a plantation colony dependent on sugar and slave labor. The Netherlands ruled until 1975. For years political instability discouraged development.

Most of the population lives in **Paramaribo**, the capital, largest city, and chief port. Tropical rain forests cover 85 percent of the country. Adventurous travelers can see howler monkeys, jaguars, boa constrictors, bats, ocelots, and toucans. They can paddle through the lush Marowijne region aboard dugout canoes or explore the Kasikasima Mountains.

French Guiana French Guiana (*gee AH nuh*) is an overseas department of France. **Cayenne** is the capital and largest city. The country is 90 percent impenetrable forest. It is the site of a research center of the French National Space Agency. Off the coast are the three *Îles de Salut* ("Isles of Health"), which France used as penal colonies. Cruise ships visit notorious Devil's Island, where most prisoners were kept.

PARAGUAY

Paraguay (*PAHR uh gway*) is a landlocked country south of the equator, with neither beaches nor Andes. It is part of the Chaco, a vast plain. Special interest tours visit to see the country's agriculture, dairy farming, hunting, fishing, and birding.

Asunción (*ah soon SYAWN*) is the country's capital and largest city. South of the city, travelers can visit the remains of missions called *reducciones* ("reductions"). Jesuit missionaries established the *reducciones* in 1588 to convert the friendly Guaraní Indians. The missions' choral and instrumental groups were said to have rivaled those of Europe. The settlements prospered, but other colonists wanted to use the Guaraní as slaves. The colonists got their way. When the king, Charles III, expelled the Jesuits from all Spanish territory in 1767, the missions soon fell apart. The beautiful harp music so typical of Paraguay has endured, fortunately.

Nadutí (Guaraní for "cobweb") lace is a Paraguayan handicraft used to decorate tablecloths and handkerchiefs. Motifs are taken from the fauna and flora of Paraguay.

URUGUAY

One of the smallest of the continent's countries, Uruguay (*YUR uh gway* or *oo roo GWY*) is on the southeastern coast. It is blessed with rich farmlands and with beautiful beaches.

About half of the country's population lives in the port of **Montevideo** (*mahn tuh vih DAY oh*), the capital and largest city. It is in many ways a smaller, more modest, and less spectacular version of its neighboring Argentine capital. Both cities sprawl beside the Río de la Plata; both received Spanish and Italian immigrants in the late 19th century; both became wealthy as exporters of wheat, cattle, and sheep products; both have a largely homogeneous white population; and both have experienced economic and political problems in the past decades.

Most visitors come to Uruguay on a day excursion from Buenos Aires. Uruguay's beaches appeal to South American and European tourists. Punta del Este is a chic resort with fine beaches, pine woods, stately homes, and gourmet cuisine.

ANTARCTICA

Antarctica (*ant AHRK tih kuh*) is the "bottom of the world," the ice-buried continent that covers and surrounds the South Pole. It belongs to no country, but seven nations (Argentina, Australia, Chile, France, Great Britain, Norway, and New Zealand) claim territory. In addition, Belgium, Japan, Russia, South Africa, and the United States have scientific stations there but do not claim land. The McMurdo Station is the largest community. About 1,000 scientists, pilots, and other specialists are summer residents (during the Northern Hemisphere's winter). Fewer than 200 people stay in Antarctica's winter.

Antarctica is an expensive destination with unreliable weather. Unless visitors are going for approved scientific research, travelers must be part of a tour.

Late November or December is the warmest season. An Antarctic cruise is a lottery. Ocean waters in the area can be rough. Ships may be unable to enter a bay or zodiacs to make a landing. But should the traveler win, the experience is unforgettable.

Roald Amundsen of Norway and Robert Scott of Britain both wanted to be the first to reach the South Pole. Amundsen made it and returned to base safely, but Scott and his four assistants died on the return.

CHAPTER WRAP-UP

SUMMARY

Here is a review of the objectives with which we began the chapter.

1. **Describe the environment and people of South America.** South America extends from the border of Panama and the sunny beaches of the Caribbean to frigid Antarctica. The Andes Mountains, the longest mountain chain on land,

stretch from Cape Horn to Panama. Many active volcanoes dot the range. To the Andes' east, tropical rain forests cover a huge portion of northern South America. A vast river system, the Amazon, flows through the rain forest. In volume, the Amazon is the world's largest river.

West of the Andes on the Pacific, the climate tends to be dry; to the east, it is tropical or temperate, depending on latitude. In the high altitudes of the Andes, it can get very cold, even on the equator.

The original inhabitants of South America were Indians of various tribes. The Inca had reached a high level of civilization when the Spanish conquistadores arrived. In Brazil, the first colonists were the Portuguese. They settled and colonized, bringing in West Africans as slaves to work the cane fields. Waves of immigration swept the continent in the late 1800s. Today, the continent has a mix of ethnic groups and cultures.

2. **Identify and locate South America's countries, dependencies, and most-visited sites.** The twelve countries are Argentina, Bolivia, Brazil, Chile, Colombia, Ecuador, Guyana, Paraguay, Peru, Suriname, Uruguay, and Venezuela. The dependencies are French Guiana and the Falklands. Travelers are most likely to want to see the Andean lands (including the Galápagos); Chile and the glaciers; Argentina and its city of Buenos Aires and the Pampas; and Brazil, with Rio and the Amazon rain forest.

3. **Describe South America's attractions, matching travelers and destinations best suited for each other.** For travelers seeking the shops and nightlife of a city, Rio, Santiago, and Buenos Aires provide all the amenities. Those interested in history and culture will want to see the colonial treasures of Quito, Ecuador; or the Nazca lines in Peru; or archaeological finds at Sipán, Chan Chan, Cuzco, and Machu Picchu in Peru; or the mix of Portuguese and West African culture in Salvador, Brazil. Travelers with a sense of adventure are delighted with visits to the Galápagos, the Amazon rain forest, or Chile's Archipelago or with a cruise around Cape Horn.

4. **Provide or find the information needed to plan a trip to South America and Antarctica.** A South American trip requires close attention to documentation as well as health and safety concerns. Accommodations at popular resorts are scarce in season. Logistical information is available from industry resources. The U.S. State Department and the Centers for Disease Control (CDC) have useful Web sites.

QUESTIONS FOR DISCUSSION AND REVIEW

1. Compare the landscape of the South American countries. List some geographic factors that influenced the development of cities.
2. Tours to South America sometimes require a spirit of adventure. What questions would you ask to separate the adventurous from the mainstream traveler?
3. Do you think people should visit the rain forest? If so, what do you think they should do to protect the fragile ecosystems?

1) Altitude is one factor that influenced the development of the West Coast cities. - The Amazonia Rain forest hinders access to the interior. The fertile pampas of Argentina contributed to that country's prosperity.

CHAPTER 9

The British Isles

- England
- Scotland
- Wales and Northern Ireland
- Republic of Ireland

OBJECTIVES

When you have completed Chapter 9, you should be able to

1. Describe the environment and people of the British Isles.
2. Identify and locate the most-visited sites of the United Kingdom.
3. Describe the attractions of the Republic of Ireland.
4. Provide or find the information needed to plan a trip to the British Isles.

In 1990, when French and British construction workers met beneath the English Channel, Britain became linked to continental Europe for the first time in 7,000 years. When the last Ice Age ended, about seven millennia ago, the melting ice flooded the low-lying lands at the edge of the continent, creating the English Channel, the North Sea, and Europe's largest group of offshore islands, the **British Isles**. They are one of Europe's most popular destinations.

The Environment and Its People

The **English Channel**, the **Strait of Dover**, the **North Sea**, and the **Atlantic Ocean** surround the British Isles (see Figure 9.1). Politically, the British Isles are divided into two countries: (1) the **United Kingdom of Great Britain and Northern Ireland** and its dependencies and (2) the **Republic of Ireland**. The United Kingdom (U.K.) has four political divisions: **England, Wales**, and **Scotland**, which are on the island of **Great Britain**, and **Northern Ireland**, located on the northeast corner of the island of **Ireland**. Each division of the United Kingdom has its own culture, language, and political history. The **Republic of Ireland** is an independent country that occupies five-sixths of the island of Ireland.

➤ PROFILE

Festivals and Special Events in the British Isles

Festivals devoted to the arts, literature, sports, harvests, and animals fill the calendar year-round. The following are just a few:

- Edinburgh Festival, the world's largest festival of art, music, and theater, held for three weeks in August/September.
- Glyndebourne, an opera festival held in summer in Kent, England.
- Henley Regatta, held on the banks of the Thames in Oxfordshire, England, in July.
- Royal Highland Games in September in Braemar, Scotland.
- Irish Grand National horse race, held near Dublin in April.
- Royal National Eisteddfod, held in August in a different place in Wales each year.
- St. Patrick's Week in Ireland in March.
- Trooping of the Color, the monarch's birthday celebration, held each June in London.
- Tennis matches at Wimbledon, a suburb of London, held each June and July.

The Land

No volcanoes explode, no earthquakes rumble, and no giant mountains tower in the British Isles, but the land has great diversity.

England England has three main regions—the **Lowlands**, the **Southwest Peninsula**, and the **Pennine Hills**. The Lowlands include the **Cotswold Hills** in the southwest. England's longest river, the **Thames** (*tehmz*), rises in the Cotswolds and flows east into the heart of London and out to the North Sea. Most of the land north of the Thames and up to an area in central England called the **Midlands** is low and flat. South of the Thames, long, low lines of chalk and limestone hills, called **scarplands**, cross the land. Along the English Channel the scarplands form the White Cliffs of Dover.

The Southwest Peninsula ends with the westernmost point in England, **Land's End**, and the southernmost point in the British Isles, **Lizard Point**. Near much of the coast, the peninsula ends in cliffs that tower above the sea.

The Pennine (*PEH nine*) Hills are England's main mountain system, often called the *backbone of England*. Not very high, they begin in central England and run north to the Scottish border. Their deep U-shaped valleys are called *dales*. In the northwest, near the Scottish border, is the **Lake District**, with gentle mountain scenery.

Travelers usually want to catch a glimpse of the moors, which have been featured in romantic novels and films. **Moors** are large areas of open land covered by grass, a layer of peat, or low-growing scrubs such as heather. They are found in both the northeast and the southwest of England and in parts of Scotland.

Wales Wales is the broad peninsula to the west of England bordered by the **Irish Sea** to the north, **St. George's Channel** to the west, and the **Bristol Channel** to the south. The **Cambrian Mountains** fill most of the country's center.

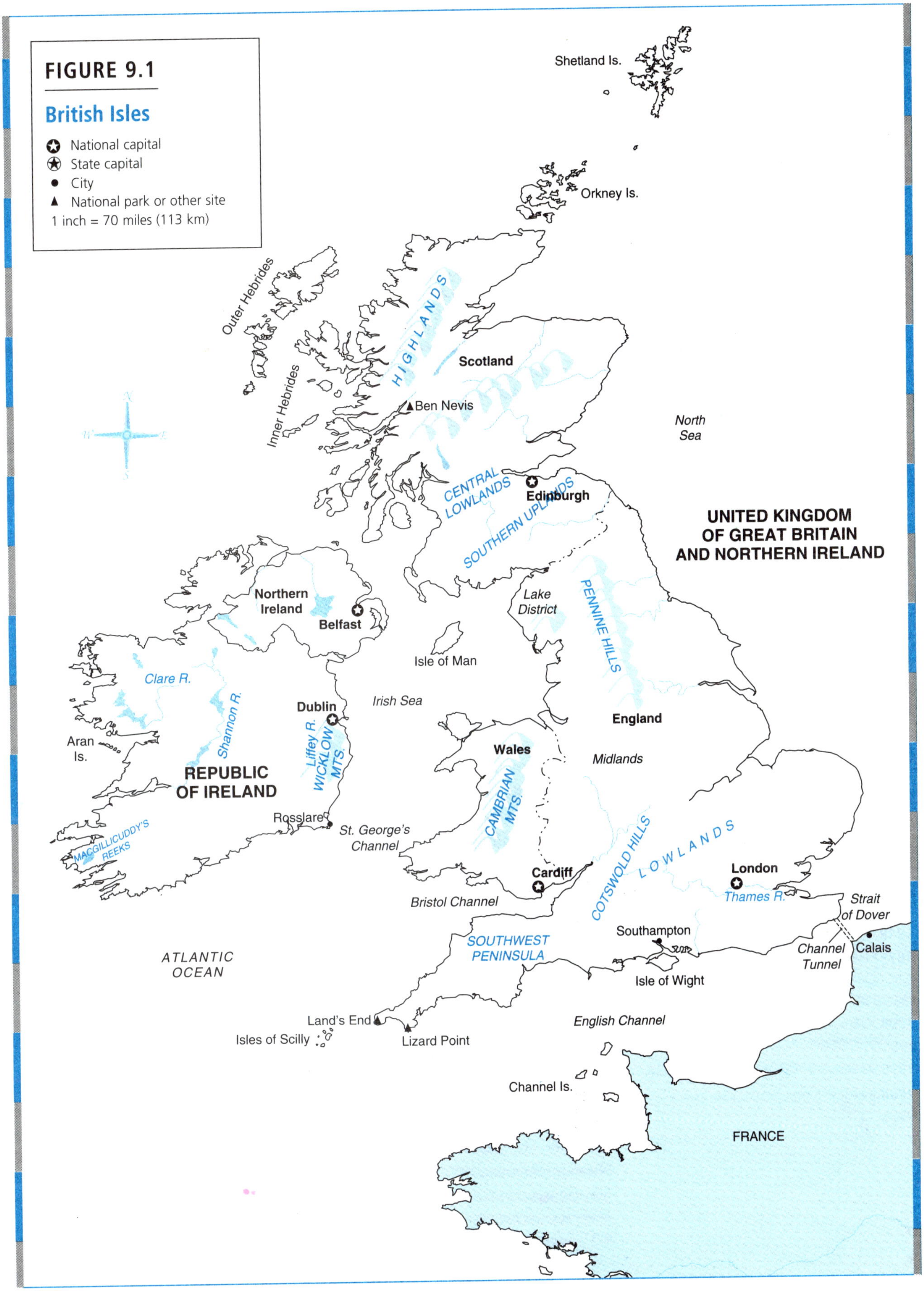

FIGURE 9.1

British Isles

FIGURE 9.2

Milestones of British History

c. 2000 BC Stonehenge is built.

55 BC Julius Caesar heads first Roman invasion.

AD 119 Hadrian's wall is built to keep the Picts and Scots out of England.

432 St. Patrick brings Christianity to Ireland.

980–1016 Vikings invade Ireland and Great Britain.

1066 William, Duke of Normandy, invades and conquers England.

1536 Henry VIII unites England and Wales.

1558–1603 The reign of Queen Elizabeth I is known as the Golden Age.

1585 William Shakespeare begins his career in London.

1588 The Spanish Armada is defeated.

1665–1666 The Great Plague of London is followed by the Great Fire.

1700s The Industrial Revolution begins in Great Britain.

1707 England, Wales, and Scotland unite to form the Kingdom of Great Britain.

1801 Ireland becomes part of the United Kingdom.

1837–1901 The British Empire reaches its height.

1845–1848 The potato blight devastates Ireland.

1921 Ireland becomes the Irish Free State.

1939–1945 During World War II, the Blitz by the German Luftwaffe changes the face of London.

1947 Edinburgh Festival begins; Welsh Eisteddfod is reestablished.

1949 Ireland declares itself a republic.

1973 United Kingdom joins the European Community (now called the European Union).

1994 Railroad tunnel opens under the English Channel.

1999 Wales and Scotland begin self-rule.

2004 London retires its double-decker buses.

Scotland Scotland is the northernmost part of Great Britain. It is bordered by the Atlantic Ocean on the west and north and by the North Sea on the east. It accounts for less than one-tenth of the United Kingdom's population, but it takes up 37 percent of the land. Its west coast is broken by long, narrow bays called **firths**.

Scotland has hundreds of islands (see Table 9.1) and three physical regions: the **Highlands**, the **Central Lowlands**, and the **Southern Uplands.** Most of the population lives in the Central Lowlands. The rugged, barren Highlands cover the northern two-thirds of Scotland. They have two kinds of valleys—steep, narrow **glens** and broad, rolling **straths**—as well as **lochs** (lakes).

Ireland Across the Irish Sea, the island of Ireland is shared by Northern Ireland and the Republic of Ireland. Mountains rim the island. The largest are the **Wicklow Mountains** in the east and **Macgillicuddy's Reeks** in the southwest. The western coastline is known for dramatic cliffs. In the far southwest, three broad peninsulas (the Beara, the Iveragh, and the Dingle) meet the Atlantic Ocean.

The interior of Ireland is a low-lying plain with hills and ridges. Small lakes, known as *loughs* (*lahks*), are common. Peat bogs, which the Irish call "turf," cover about 16 percent of the land. Most are located in the central and western parts of the country. The main rivers—the **Liffey**, the **Clare**, and the **Shannon** (the longest river in the British Isles)—are broad and slow moving.

The Climate

The British Isles feature cool, damp summers and cold, damp winters. The operative word is *damp*. The visitor in any season should dress in layers, expect rain, and bring an umbrella. Rapid changes of weather are common. In recent years, tropical storms, winter blizzards, and even summer heat waves have struck the islands.

There are strong regional variations. Western Scotland has heavy snow in the mountains. Wales tends to be wetter than England, with even less sunshine. The moisture, combined with minerals in the soil, produces the rich greenery for which Wales is known. Southern England has the country's highest summer temperatures and the widest range of temperatures.

Ireland has a mild, wet climate. Temperatures average about 41° F (5° C) in winter and about 59° F (15° C) in summer. The island is farther north than New England, but the North Atlantic Current of the Gulf Stream creates a temperate climate. Plenty of rainfall—"Irish mist," as the locals like to call it—keeps the grass green. Atlantic winds bring rain on two days out of three. There is little snow, except in the mountains.

The People and Their History

Britain's recorded history begins with the Roman invasion and occupation of Wales and England from the 1st to the 5th century. During the 8th and 9th centuries, the northeast and east of England came under Viking rule. In 1066 a Norman duke known as William the Conqueror (1027–1087) won the Battle of Hastings and with it the English throne. The Normans were the last to invade; no conquering foreigners have landed on the English mainland since (see Figure 9.2). In the 12th century, the Norman king of England conquered Ireland.

Famous rulers include Henry VIII (1491–1547), husband of the six wives, who broke from the Catholic Church in 1533 and formed the Church of England. Under his daughter Elizabeth I (1533–1603), England enjoyed a Golden Age of prosperity, literature, and exploration.

Over the next centuries, British rule spread. In the 16th and 17th centuries, England confiscated lands in the northeast of Ireland and settled "plantations" of Protestants from England and Scotland, a policy that produced Northern Ireland's Protestant majority. In 1707 England, Scotland, and Wales united as the Kingdom of Great Britain. During the reign of Queen Victoria (1819–1901), the British Empire covered one-fourth of the world's land surface.

By 1931, Britain began loosening control over its empire, granting independence to, for example, Australia, Canada, New Zealand, Newfoundland, and South Africa. These countries became members of the Commonwealth, also known as the British Commonwealth. It consists of the United Kingdom and independent countries that were once part of the British Empire. Immigration to Great Britain from Commonwealth countries—notably the West Indies, India, and Pakistan—has created a multiracial and multicultural society.

The 20th century also saw great changes in relationships among the political divisions of the British Isles. The Republic of Ireland won independence in 1921, but Northern Ireland elected to remain part of the United Kingdom. Thus the island divided into two parts: the Republic of Ireland, which is predominantly Roman Catholic, and Northern Ireland, which is 58 percent Protestant. Conflict in Northern Ireland increased between the Protestant majority, who wanted to remain in the United Kingdom, and the Catholic minority, who sought union with the Republic of Ireland. Representatives of Great Britain, Northern Ireland, and the Republic of Ireland have been working to resolve problems.

Meanwhile, Scotland, Wales, and Northern Ireland are moving toward greater independence from London, with more control over their own affairs, in a process called *devolution.* In 1999 Scotland elected its own parliament, and Wales opened the Welsh National Assembly.

TABLE 9.1

Islands off the British Isles

Island	Government
Aran Islands	Republic of Ireland
Channel Islands	Dependencies
Hebrides	U.K./Scotland
Isle of Man	Independent
Isle of Wight	U.K./England
Isles of Scilly	U.K./England
Orkney Islands	U.K./Scotland
Shetland Islands	U.K./Scotland

✔ CHECK-UP

Major physical features of the British Isles include

✔ Landscape's diversity.

✔ Moors, downs, scarplands, cliffs, dales, firths, glens, lochs, and peat bogs.

✔ Pennines, the backbone of England.

✔ Lochs of the Scottish Highlands.

✔ Ireland's green valleys and the cliffs of its dramatic west coast.

✔ Changeable weather.

The British Isles include

✔ Two main islands: Great Britain and Ireland.

✔ Two independent countries: the United Kingdom of Great Britain and Northern Ireland (which includes England, Scotland, Wales, and Northern Ireland) and the Republic of Ireland.

England

England is the largest of the four divisions that make up the United Kingdom (see Figure 9.3). No other country possesses a richer variety of historic buildings and small treasures, and none has taken more trouble to preserve the best for the traveler's view. From London, with its theaters, stores, and museums, to the quaint villages of the countryside, there is plenty to see and do.

The Cities

England's history is especially visible in the capital of the United Kingdom, **London.** The city also provides many other enticements.

London London sprawls across the south of England. The city has everything: palaces, pageantry, parks, museums, theaters, opera, concerts, ballet, shops, clubs, casinos, and a river. From the start, the Thames has been London's gateway, deep enough for oceangoing vessels to reach the city.

London covers an area on both sides of a north-south bend in the Thames and divides into three sections: (1) the City, the oldest part of London and its financial center; (2) the West End, the center of government and nightlife and home to some exclusive residential areas as well as the best-known shopping streets, such as Oxford, Regent, and Bond; and (3) the South Bank, the site of a large cultural center and office complexes. The City and the West End are on the north side of the Thames. The South Bank is across the river.

Trafalgar Square, dedicated to Admiral Lord Nelson, is a good place to start sightseeing. The City is to the east, shops are to the west, the entertainment district lies to the north, and the government buildings of Westminster are to the south along the river. Throughout London, blue porcelain plaques mark buildings where famous people lived or historic events happened.

➤ PROFILE

Shopping in London

A shopping trip to London is a lesson in the finer things in life. The royal coat of arms displayed above a doorway indicates that royalty patronizes the shop. Visitors might want to shop in

- Burlington Arcade, whose little shops line a covered walkway.
- Fortnum and Mason's, featuring exotic groceries and afternoon tea.
- Harrods, the department store with everything. Seek out its food halls.
- Mayfair, for really up-upscale shopping.
- Oxford Street, with a branch of every British chain store.
- Portobello Road, a haven for antiques on Friday and Saturday mornings.
- Regent Street, to visit Liberty's. The building alone is worth a visit.
- Savile Row, a center for men's bespoke tailoring—custom-made suits.
- Sloane Street, home to many designers.

FIGURE 9.3 England

Casino gambling is permitted only at private clubs in London. Temporary memberships are available through hotels and tour operators.

Things to see in London include

- St. Paul's Cathedral in the City. Built between 1675 and 1710 as the first Protestant cathedral, it was the crowning achievement of architect Sir Christopher Wren. It hosted Queen Victoria's Diamond Jubilee in 1897, Winston Churchill's funeral in 1965, and the wedding of Prince Charles and Diana in 1981. Encircling the great dome is the famous Whispering Gallery.
- Tower of London, built by William the Conqueror on the Thames in the 11th century and used as a palace, fortress, and prison. The Crown Jewels are on display, the Yeoman Warders (popularly called *Beefeaters*) wear costumes designed in Henry VIII's reign, and ravens perch on the walls. It is said that if the ravens leave, the Tower will fall and England will lose her greatness. The birds are well fed.
- Whitehall, the broad avenue that runs south from Trafalgar Square to the Houses of Parliament. It passes No. 10 Downing Street, the prime minister's residence, on its way to Westminster Abbey, where royalty is crowned and famous Britons are buried. The tombs of Queen Elizabeth I and Mary, Queen of Scots, are in the Abbey.
- Houses of Parliament and Big Ben, located beside the Thames River. Big Ben is the bell in the clock tower of the Houses of Parliament. It was named after Sir Benjamin Hall, the commissioner of works at the time of its installation.
- Piccadilly Circus, an intersection of six busy streets. Piccadilly is the center of London's entertainment area. The area extends east to the Strand, a street that links the City and the West End, and north into Soho, a district of restaurants, pubs, and nightclubs. Many of London's finest shops are north and west of Piccadilly.
- Buckingham Palace, the monarch's London home. The royal standard flies if she or he is in residence. The changing of the guards is a top tourist attraction (normally held at 1130 daily; on alternate days in winter). The State Rooms and the Royal Mews are open to visitors during the summer months.
- Russell Square, the intellectual and scholastic heart of London and the site of many budget-class hotels.
- Royal Albert Hall, the home of the Henry Wood Promenade concerts (the *Proms*) from July to September and other concerts throughout the year.
- Parks that once formed part of royal estates, still owned by the British monarch and now set aside for public use. Central London's parks include St. James's Park bordering the Mall, the route for royal parades; Hyde Park, famous for Speaker's Corner and nearby Marble Arch; and Regent's Park, with the London Zoo.
- South Bank Arts Complex, the site of the National Theatre, the Royal Festival Hall, the Hayward Gallery, and the National Film Theatre. Here also is the reconstruction of Shakespeare's Globe Theater as well as Tate Modern, a museum with art from the 1900s to the present. The original Tate has been renamed Tate Britain and features the classics.
- Docklands, the largest urban renewal project in Europe. This chic area on the revitalized waterfront has restaurants and museums where dilapidated warehouses once stood. Once again, London begins on the banks of the Thames.

London can be the base for trips by rail or motorcoach. Excursions are available on the Thames. Boats travel upstream to Hampton Court Palace or downstream to **Greenwich**, the home of the Greenwich meridian, the line responsible for setting the world clock on zero degrees latitude.

Other Cities London is England's largest metropolitan area. Six other large

Looming over London from the South Bank is the *London Eye*, a ferris wheel that is one of London's tallest structures. Round trips in the wheel's thirty-two air-conditioned or heated passenger capsules carry up to twenty-five people and last thirty minutes.

Big Ben, London, England

➤ PROFILE

London Museums

London's museums include

- ➤ The British Museum, "Mankind's Attic," home to the Elgin Marbles from the Parthenon in Athens; the Rosetta Stone, used to decipher Egyptian hieroglyphics; and a copy of the Magna Carta.
- ➤ The Queen's Gallery at Buckingham Palace, with selections from the royal collection.
- ➤ The Tate Britain, the original classic collection.
- ➤ The Tate Modern, a collection of 20th-century art.
- ➤ The Victoria and Albert Museum, the world's largest collection of the decorative arts.
- ➤ The National Gallery.

The National Trust of England, the National Trust of Scotland, the Welsh Heritage Foundation, and the National Trust of Ireland are charities set up to acquire and preserve places of historic interest and natural beauty for the enjoyment of the visiting public.

cities are Manchester, Liverpool, Sheffield, Newcastle, Birmingham, and Leeds. Except for the port of **Liverpool**, they are not tourist attractions.

In the 1980s, Liverpool's city council embarked on a renewal project to restore the old dock area. The Albert Dock is the centerpiece of the restoration. Here a top attraction is the *Beatles Story,* which has a replica of the Cavern Club, where the group made its name. The Grand National horse race takes place at Liverpool's Aintree Racecourse each year.

Other Places to Visit

VisitBritain divides England into touring regions based around historic counties; this section describes only a few of the highlights.

The West Country: Somerset, Devon, and Cornwall The character of England's southwest sets it apart from the rest of the country, partly because of its geographic isolation, partly because of its Celtic history, and partly because of its association with the legends of King Arthur and the Knights of the Round Table. The southwest is exceptionally beautiful, and there are still unspoiled stretches of coast and wild, lonely places on the moors. The area includes the counties of Somerset, Devon, and Cornwall. This is the *West Country,* Britain's popular holiday region.

The pub is so much a part of the culture and social life of the British Isles that many small towns boast a dozen or more establishments. Licensing (opening and closing) hours vary.

The old port of **Bristol** is on the north coast at the beginning of the peninsula. From there, John Cabot set off for Newfoundland in 1497. Robert Louis Stevenson supposedly used the city's Llandoger Trow pub as a model for Long John Silver's inn in *Treasure Island.*

Another West Country entry port is southeast of Bristol at **Bath**. Bath owes its fame to the Romans, who enjoyed the hot mineral springs, and to 18th-century developers, who made it a fashionable resort. The dandy Richard "Beau" Nash (1674–1762) brought society's elite to Bath, where he set standards for proper dress. Among the sights to see is the Royal Crescent, built in the 1770s. It is a sweep of thirty impressive town houses, said to be the first group ever built in a crescent shape.

Cornwall, the county at England's southwest tip, is steeped in legend, with tales of shipwrecks, smugglers, and strange happenings in the subterranean world of the tin miners. At the peninsula's end, the granite mass of Land's End tumbles into the sea.

The Poldark novels, the books by Winston Graham on which the PBS TV series was based, tell the story of the Cornish tin mines. The Poldark mine, which has been worked since Roman times, is now an underground museum.

On Cornwall's south shore, palm trees grow in sheltered coves. **Penzance** has long been the premier town of western Cornwall, thanks to its commanding site on Mount's Bay. The town was a tin-shipping port for the Roman Empire and a passenger terminal for emigrants bound for the New World. It is now a popular holiday resort.

On Cornwall's north coast, rugged cliffs defy the Atlantic. The birthplace of the legendary (and mythical) King Arthur is said to be here at **Tintagel Castle**. Even though the ruins date from long after his time, the location overlooking the sea is magical and makes it easy to believe in Camelot. Walks along the Cornish Coastal Path to view the ruins make the site one of the most romantic in England.

Inland, south of Tintagel, the traveler finds stately homes and gardens and ancient **Bodmin Moor**, which has granite **tors** (rock piles) and tricky marshes. On the Launceton Road is Jamaica Inn, the setting for one of Daphne du Maurier's classic romances.

Plymouth, to the east on the Cornwall–Devon border, is a relic of the Age of Exploration. Here Sir Francis Drake casually finished a game of bowls before he set off to defeat the Spanish Armada in 1588. From here in 1620 the Pilgrims set sail for the New World. Devon's south coast resorts of Torquay, Brixham, and Paignton are collectively known as the *English Riviera*. The beaches are rocky and the water is cold, but people flock to the resorts.

Directly inland from Plymouth is **Dartmoor National Park**, an expanse of forest and moorland that protects the West Country wilderness area. Wild ponies roam freely, and the park has miles of public footpaths and hiking trails. Humans have lived on the moor for centuries in caves, abbeys, castles, and some of the prettiest villages in England. In Sir Arthur Conan Doyle's *Hound of the Baskervilles*, Sherlock Holmes encountered the beast on Dartmoor.

Hardy Country: Dorset and Wiltshire To the east, Dorset and Wiltshire are rich in natural beauty and ancient monuments. Dorset's market towns were immortalized in the novels of Thomas Hardy (1840–1928) as the fictional Wessex.

Some of England's great stately homes and gardens, including Longleat, Wilton, Lacock Abbey, Corsham, and Stourhead, are in Wiltshire. Longleat is a very grand Elizabethan mansion, famous for the lions roaming its grounds.

Also in Wiltshire is **Salisbury**. Its "new" cathedral was built between 1220 and 1258 with "as many windows as days in the year, as many pillars as hours, and as many gates as moons." The cathedral's spire is England's tallest.

Salisbury Cathedral, England

North of the city on the Salisbury Plain is the collection of standing stones called **Stonehenge**. It is the most famous of the more than 900 stone circles in the British Isles. American writer Ralph Waldo Emerson (1803–1882) described Stonehenge as looking like "a group of brown dwarfs on the wide expanse." The mysterious monuments were built some 3,500 years ago for unknown purposes. It remains a matter of wonder that prehistoric man could have quarried, transported, shaped, and raised such rocks. Stonehenge is normally fenced off to protect it from the crowds.

The **Isle of Wight** is off the coast near **Portsmouth**. Queen Victoria and Prince Albert made the small island their summer home. Osborne House was the queen's favorite residence, and it has been left much as it was in her lifetime. The island's multicolored sands can be carried away in bottles as souvenirs.

Queen Victoria's bathing machine is on view at Osborne, on the Isle of Wight. It resembles an outhouse on wheels. The queen stayed in her machine until it was wheeled into the sea for a discreet dip.

Back on the mainland, **Southampton** is the port from which great ocean liners sailed for America and from which modern ships depart today.

The Southeast The counties of West and East Sussex, Surrey, and Kent are in England's southeast corner, south of the Thames between London and the Channel. **Brighton** is known for its pier and its antique shops, but most of all for the onion domes and minarets of the Royal Pavilion, built for George IV (1762–1830). Architect John Nash remodeled the seaside home in 1822. George escaped there with his mistress, later his secret wife, Marie Fitzherbert. The pavilion was the setting for the king's lavish parties. It is Indian in style outside, oriental within, and one of the world's decorative wonders. Brighton grew when sea bathing became a fad. The elite deserted spa towns such as Bath in favor of England's first seaside resort.

To the east, the Kent coast is 21 miles (34 km) from France. As the nearest point to the continent, this was the way of invaders: Romans, Angles, Saxons, and Normans. Towers and castles were built to withstand later attempts by France and Spain.

Among the region's attractions is **Hever Castle**, the home of Anne Boleyn (1507–1536), second wife of Henry VIII and mother of Queen Elizabeth I. The castle contains mementos of Anne, including the prayer book she carried to her execution. Nearby is **Chartwell**, Winston Churchill's home.

➤ PROFILE

Stately Homes

According to the Historic Houses Association, England's most-visited stately homes are

- ➤ Blenheim Palace, in Oxfordshire, Sir Winston Churchill's (1874–1965) birthplace.
- ➤ Buckingham Palace, the monarch's London residence.
- ➤ Chatsworth House, in the Peak District.
- ➤ Hampton Court Palace, in suburban London, built by Henry VIII's archbishop and Lord Chancellor, Thomas Wolsey.
- ➤ Leeds Castle, in Kent, the castle of the queens of medieval England.
- ➤ Warwick Castle, near Stratford, one of England's most popular historic attractions.
- ➤ Windsor Castle, in the London suburb of Windsor, the sovereign's residence since its construction by William the Conqueror and the world's largest occupied castle.

Along the coast facing the Strait of Dover are towns known as the **Cinque Ports**, built to repel Danish invaders. The original five towns were Dover, Sandwich, Romney, Hastings, and Hythe. Other towns such as **Rye** share the romantic past. The sea has retreated from Rye. The land lies flat across the great expanse of Romney Marsh, a strange haunted place and a favorite hiding place of smugglers. Travelers can stay at the 15th-century Mermaid Inn in Rye, sleep in a four-poster bed, and listen for the ghost that is said to haunt the halls.

Dover remains an important port. Its castle has a labyrinth of tunnels that served as the nerve center for the evacuation of Dunkirk and the Battle of Britain in World War II. It was the busiest passenger port in the world until the Channel Tunnel (Chunnel) opened. Some of the unused ferry docks have been converted to cruise ship piers.

North of Dover is **Canterbury** and Canterbury Cathedral, the mother church of the Anglican faith. The Conqueror's Castle, the cathedral, and its Thomas à Becket Shrine have been magnets for pilgrims for centuries and the inspiration of Geoffrey Chaucer's *Canterbury Tales* (1400).

Central England Central England stretches from the Welsh border to the east coast. It features the university towns of **Cambridge** and **Oxford**, both of which are home to famous institutions of higher learning. Oxford, the oldest, started to develop during the 1100s.

Farther west, wool and stone gave the Cotswold Hills their distinctive character. Medieval merchants, rich from the fleece of sheep, built great manor houses and noble churches. Little villages with thatched-roof houses grew along the rushing streams that powered the mills that produced woolen cloth. The gold color of Cotswold stone bound all into a harmonious whole.

The *Cotswold Way* is a series of walking paths that follows the hills from Bath to **Chipping Campden**, a small village. **Broadway** is the Cotswolds' show village. There the Lygon Arms, built in the 16th century, continues to be a popular inn and restaurant.

Other attractions of central England include

- **Stratford-upon-Avon**, birthplace of William Shakespeare (1564–1616), where he spent his final years with his wife, Anne Hathaway, and was buried. The Royal Shakespeare Company performs at the Royal Shakespeare Theater, while works by his contemporaries are staged across the river at the Swan. Nearby, at The Other Place, modern productions are performed. The season is from March to September, and tickets should be bought as far in advance as possible.
- **Ironbridge Gorge** in Shropshire, the 18th century's Silicon Valley. A series of museums re-creates the working and living conditions of the Industrial Revolution.
- Blenheim Palace, a huge home given to John Churchill in 1704 by a grateful country for his military successes. In 1874 one of the palace's 200 rooms echoed to the first cries of the infant Winston Churchill.
- The Potteries, sites tied to England's famous porcelain and pottery factories. The Wedgwood Visitor Centre in **Stoke-on-Trent** displays pieces from the company's beginnings in 1754. Other potteries in the area are Royal Doulton and Spode.

A popular English snack is fried fish and chips (French fried potatoes). In the old days it was served wrapped in newspaper and eaten with vinegar or mayonnaise.

The Lake District The Lake District in northwest England covers a small area, but as the poet William Wordsworth (1770–1850) said, "I do not know of any tract of country in which, within so narrow a compass, may be found an equal variety in the influences of light and shadow upon the sublime or beautiful features of landscape." The lakes provided inspiration for poets and writers, including children's author Beatrix Potter (1866–1943). Her home is open to view. Attractions include **Lake Windermere**, the largest of the district's sixteen lakes, and **Scafell Pike**, the highest point in England.

Yorkshire The lands of northeast England are wide-open spaces, littered with ruins of a turbulent past, but they shelter picture-book villages, bustling towns, and the historic city of **York**. York is a city of Roman walls, medieval streets, a pub or tea shop every few yards, and the stately bulk of York Minster, England's largest cathedral.

The Romans and the Vikings had bases in York. An archaeological dig in 1976 turned up a treasure chest of Viking artifacts. Travelers can wander through ancient alleyways such as the Shambles, the former butchers' quarters. Now antiques and souvenirs instead of carcasses are on display.

York can be the center for excursions. To the west is **Haworth**, a bustling industrial town that was the home of the Brontës, the famous literary family. Each year more than 700,000 visitors tramp the steep cobbled streets of the town to see the parsonage where Charlotte, Emily, Anne, and Branwell grew up.

City walls of York

CLOSE-UP: ENGLAND

Who are good prospects for a trip to England? Senior citizens and baby boomers account for about 60 percent of the present market. Many are repeat visitors with great knowledge of the country. "Sinks" (singles) and "dinks" (double income, no kids) are also prospects. England can satisfy almost any special interest group, except those who want to lie on a warm, sunny beach.

Why would they visit England? North Americans visit for history and culture. In addition, London's theater and quality shops are powerful draws.

Where would they go? You might suggest an escorted tour to southern England and the West Country. Here is a typical eight-day itinerary.

Day 1 Board an overnight transatlantic flight.

Day 2 Early-morning arrival in London. You are met at the airport by an escort and transferred to the hotel. Afternoon at leisure to nap or start independent sightseeing.

Day 3 London. Morning sightseeing to Royal Albert Hall, the Houses of Parliament and Big Ben, and Westminster Abbey. Visit St. Paul's Cathedral, and see the changing of the guard at Buckingham Palace (if held). Free time in the afternoon for independent activities or an optional excursion to either Windsor Castle or the Tower of London to see the Crown Jewels. At night, an optional dinner followed by a cruise on the Thames River.

Day 4 London–Stratford. Depart London at 0800 on your motorcoach for a day of sightseeing. Stop at Henry VIII's Hampton Court Palace; drive to Oxford to see the famous university. Arrive in Stratford-upon-Avon in time for a walking tour of Shakespeare's birthplace. Optional theater tickets to a play at night.

Day 5 Stratford–Bath. Enjoy the scenery of the Cotswold Hills as you motor to Wales for a drive through the beautiful Wye Valley and see the romantic ruins of Tintern Abbey. Continue to Bath. Explore the town on your own. Evening at leisure.

Day 6 Bath–Brighton. Visit Stonehenge on your drive across Salisbury Plain. See Salisbury's cathedral before driving on to the seaside resort of Brighton. Here have a walking tour of the exotic Royal Pavilion. Evening at leisure.

Day 7 Brighton–London. On your way back to the city, enjoy a visit to Leeds Castle. Return to London in the early afternoon. Optional tickets to a West End show at night.

Day 8 Board your homebound flight.

When is the best time to visit? It depends on the traveler's interest. England is a year-round destination. Theater, museum, and shopping tours are very popular in the winter. Trips into the countryside are best in spring, summer, and fall. Avoid August if possible; this is when most Europeans are on vacation and crowds are thickest.

The traveler says, "I've heard that England is very expensive." How would you respond? Traveling at the deluxe or even the first-class level can be costly, especially in the cities. But there are many ways to cut costs. The most common is by staying outside the city center and using the public transportation system to visit the sights. When in the country, staying at a B&B also helps control costs. Restaurants post their menus and prices outside their doors, allowing travelers to choose places within their budget.

For insight into the 18th century at its most magnificent, a drive northeast of York leads to Castle Howard, a stately home featured in the BBC's 1981 adaptation of Evelyn Waugh's *Brideshead Revisited.* Farther north are the **North York Moors**, England's largest expanse of heather moorland.

Northumbria Close to Scotland, in an area known as the Borders, the Roman emperor Hadrian built a wall in AD 122 to keep out the wild Celtic tribes of Scotland. Built of mud and stone, **Hadrian's wall** stretches from Solway Firth in the west to the Tyne River in the east (near Newcastle). The area is now a national park.

Island Dependencies

As the mainland overflows with visitors, travelers are visiting destinations that were previously ignored.

The Isle of Man is the home of the Manx cat, the only breed of cat without a tail. Legend says the cat lost its tail when it was late boarding Noah's Ark and the closing door cut off the appendage.

The Isle of Man The Isle of Man had settlers as early as 2000 BC. It lies in the Irish Sea, equidistant from Scotland, Ireland, and England. Celts were among the first visitors, and their language, Manx, remained the everyday speech of the people until the 19th century. Today, the Isle of Man has its own laws and a governor appointed by the Crown.

The small island's rocky coastline encloses a central highland. It is regarded by many as the road-racing capital of the world. The island's varied terrain, sometimes mountainous and with sharp bends, adds to the challenge and excitement of the motorbike and car races.

The Channel Islands Victor Hugo called the Channel Islands "pieces of France that fell into the sea and were gathered up by England." The self-governing islands are just off the French coast. The islands were the only part of British soil occupied by German troops in World War II.

Best known as tax havens, the bank-laden islands export distinctive cattle, and tourism is an important business. Holidaymakers like the slightly French atmosphere combined with the familiar English language.

The islands are Alderney, Guernsey, Jersey, Herm, and Sark. Alderney's only town resembles a Normandy village; Guernsey displays its links with the sea; Jersey has two proud castles; and tiny Sark is a feudal remnant, ruled by a hereditary seigneur.

✔ CHECK-UP

For travelers, highlights of England include

- ✔ London, the United Kingdom's capital and largest city, a treasure trove of sightseeing, theater, museums, and shopping.
- ✔ Countryside of castles, manor houses, stately homes, and thatched-roof cottages.
- ✔ History at every turn in the road.

Key places to see outside of London include

- ✔ West Country, with its tin mines, romantic moorland, and rocky beaches, as well as Bristol, Bath, Tintagel Castle, and Plymouth.
- ✔ Hardy Country, for Salisbury Cathedral and Stonehenge.
- ✔ Southeast England, with Brighton, Canterbury, and the Cinque Ports.
- ✔ Central England, home to Cambridge and Oxford Universities, the Cotswolds, Shakespeare's Stratford-upon-Avon, and palaces and manor homes.
- ✔ Lake District, featuring rural beauty and England's highest hills.
- ✔ Yorkshire, for the Brontës' moors and the city of York, with England's largest cathedral.
- ✔ Northumbria, where Hadrian's wall tried to contain the wild Celtic tribes of Scotland.

Scotland

The Tweed River, the Cheviot Hills, and the Solway Firth form England's border with Scotland (see Figure 9.4). North of the border, the Southern Uplands consist of rolling moors, broken in places by rocky cliffs. The Clyde, Forth, and Tay Rivers cross the valleys of the Central Lowlands. The Highlands form one of the last great wildernesses of Europe—endless stretches of wild country, mountains, glens, and moorlands probed by the long fingers of sea lochs. Two mountain ranges, the **Northwest Highlands** and the **Grampian Mountains**, rise in the region. A deep valley called **Glen Mor**, or the Great Glen, separates the ranges.

The Cities

Most of the people live in the Central Lowlands, where there is flatter and more fertile land. Cities of the region include **Glasgow**, Scotland's largest city, and **Edinburgh**, the capital.

Edinburgh Edinburgh (*EH duhn buh roh*) stands on a hill south of the Firth of Forth. It has been a long time since Edinburgh was known as *Auld Reekie* for its choking smoke-laden air, but on a typical cloudy day, the city's gray granite buildings remind a visitor of the city's smoggy past. The city straddles

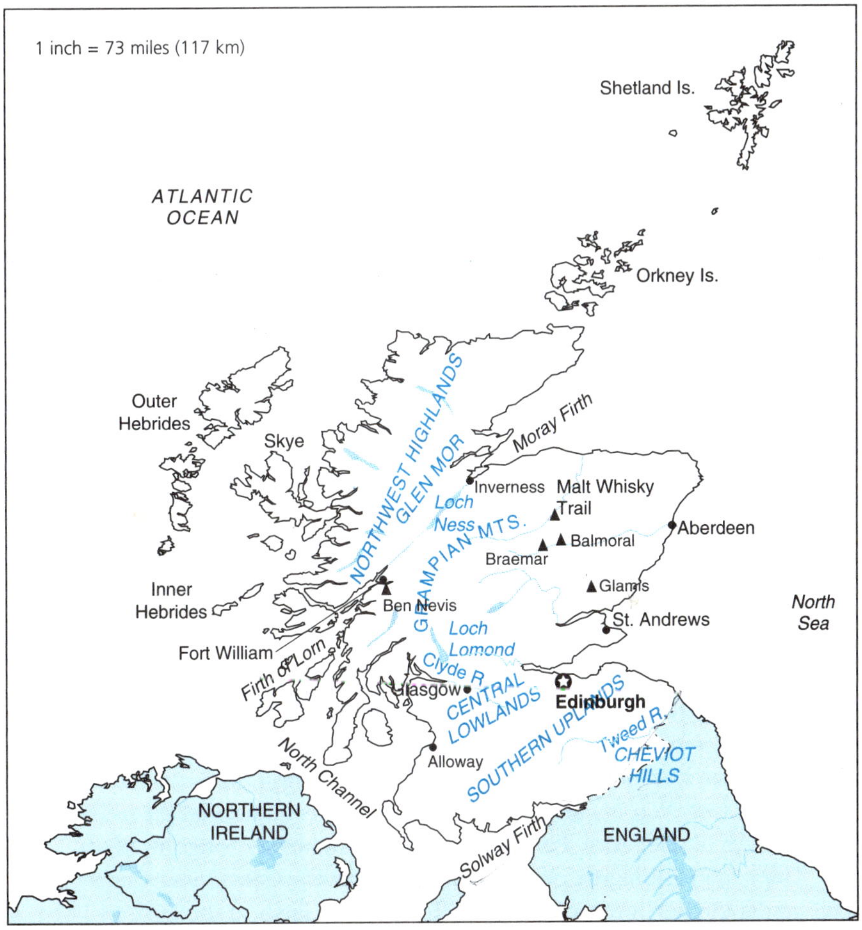

FIGURE 9.4 Scotland

Royal Mile, Edinburgh, Scotland

a deep gorge. On the ravine's south side is Old Town, the original city center; opposite it is New Town, which has elegant 18th-century architecture and the main shopping area, centered on Princess Street.

Old Town is dominated by 12th-century Edinburgh Castle, perched atop a rocky outcrop. From the castle, the Royal Mile leads down the hill to the Palace of Holyroodhouse, the monarch's official home in the city. Mary, Queen of Scots (1542–1587), lived there for six years. Shoppers looking for crafts, antiques, textiles, and art find stores scattered throughout Old Town. They can visit the royal kilt maker, Kinlock Anderson, and have an ancestral design whipped up for wearing.

Edinburgh's other attractions range from museums to pubs and discotheques. The National Gallery of Scotland is one of the best of the world's smaller museums.

The annual *Edinburgh International Festival of the Arts* is the world's largest drama and music festival. For three weeks in late August and early September, theater companies, dance groups, opera companies, orchestras, puppeteers, and visual artists take over the concert halls, theaters, and churches of Edinburgh in a grand celebration. The festival season kicks off with the spectacular Military Tattoo staged outside the castle.

Glasgow Southwest of Edinburgh is Glasgow (*GLAS goh*), Scotland's largest and liveliest city and Britain's great industrial center. Oil discoveries in the North Sea have stimulated support industries. The city straddles the Clyde River. It is home to the Scottish Opera, the Scottish Ballet, the Royal Scottish National Orchestra, and many theater companies. The Art Gallery and Museum is second only to London's original Tate Gallery in numbers of visitors. The Glasgow Science Center features interactive attractions and a revolving tower.

Attractions near Glasgow include **Alloway**, the birthplace of Scotland's national poet, Robert Burns (1759–1796). The *Burns Heritage Trail* features houses and inns associated with his life. Back in Glasgow, tourists are treated to "Burns Nights." A kilted Highlander pipes in the first course of haggis, bashed neaps (mashed turnips), and tatties (potatoes). All of this is washed down with Scotland's water of life, single malt whisky. As midnight approaches, everyone sings a rousing chorus of "Auld Lang Syne."

Authentic haggis is made from the heart, liver, and lungs of sheep combined with oatmeal, suet, onions, and seasonings, boiled in the skin of an animal's stomach. Less authentic alternatives are available.

Other Places to Visit

St. Andrews Scotland is considered the birthplace of golf. The Royal and Ancient Golf Club of St. Andrews, north of Edinburgh on the coast, claims to be the place where golf started. The British Open Championship is held there in July. Golfers who wish to play the Old Course at St. Andrews should contact the club at least eight weeks before their visit to apply to play. The courses are "links courses," which means they have tough seaside dunes lightly covered by rough grass.

The Golf Club of St. Andrews was issued a license in 1552 that gave it permission to "play golf, futeball, and do schuteing." The course lies within the curve of a bay. The slightest variation in the wind can make the difference between being trapped or getting a straightforward shot to the green.

Scottish Highlands Roads and rails run north to the Highlands along the bonnie, bonnie banks of **Loch Lomond**, Britain's largest freshwater lake. Across the loch is Ben Lomond, the first of Scotland's 277 mountains that rise to more than 3,000 feet (900 m) and challenge climbers. Britain's highest peak is **Ben Nevis**, south of Glen Mor. **Fort William** is the Highlands' tourism center.

The lakes running through Glen Mor form the Caledonian Canal, which cuts across the northwest of Scotland from Moray Firth to the Firth of Lorn. A trip from Fort William up the canal toward **Inverness,** the United Kingdom's northernmost city, leads to **Loch Ness,** the reputed home of the famous monster. Scientific expeditions have failed to produce any solid evidence for Nessie's existence, but the monster is a great tourist attraction. Nearby is the site of the Battle of Culloden, where in 1746 the English crushed Bonnie Prince Charlie.

Many travelers come to Scotland to fish for trout and salmon. The lochs of the Highlands feed the Tay River, considered to be one of the kingdom's best fishing rivers. Throughout the British Isles fishing rights belong to the owner of a stream's property. Most hotels and inns have rights for their guests, but serious fishermen should clear details in advance.

The Scottish people have long been famous for their close-knit *clans* (groups of related families), colorful kilts, and skills as fierce warriors. The clans have lost much of their importance, kilts are worn mainly for ceremonial occasions, and no war has been fought in Scotland for more than 200 years. Still, traditions linger on.

Each clan has its own *tartan*—a plaid design—for its kilts. (Only clan members should wear a tartan.) Other traditions include bagpipe music and the Highland Games. Held from June to September, the Games feature dancing and massed pipe bands as well as athletic events such as throwing the hammer and tossing the caber (a tree trunk).

A properly dressed Scottish Highland male wears a tartan kilt (a knee-length pleated skirt), a plaid (a blanketlike shawl fastened with a brooch at the shoulder), a *sporran* (a pocketbook made of hair or fur that hangs in front of the kilt), a *doublet* (jacket), and a *bonnet* (hat).

Scottish Castles The area to the west of the North Sea port city of **Aberdeen** has the greatest concentration of castles of all styles and ages, from **Braemar Castle,** stronghold of the earls of Mar, to Victorian mock-medieval **Balmoral,** the residence of the royal family. The house and grounds at Balmoral are open from May through July, unless closed for some royal reason.

To the south, near Dundee, is **Glamis Castle,** childhood home of the late Queen Mother. It is reputed to be the most haunted stately home in Great Britain.

Castle at Eilean Donan, Scotland

The Malt Whisky Trail The Scots have been making whisky since the 1400s, and it is one of the country's major exports. The *Malt Whisky Trail* through the Spey Valley in the Grampian Mountains is a road tour that takes in an area where there are a great number of distilleries, most of which welcome visitors.

Outer Islands Discovering Scotland's outer islands is an exciting vagabond adventure. These islands are the **Orkneys** and the **Shetlands** (home of Shetland ponies) off the north coast and the **Inner** and **Outer Hebrides** off the west coast.

The Hebrides are a group of 500 islands, 100 of which are inhabited. The green and misty isles evoke a past of clans and crofters and prehistoric movers of stones. Iona is Scotland's Holy Island and the burial place of many kings and chiefs. The lobster-shaped island of **Skye** is the largest and most visited. Ferry services operate between the mainland and the islands, but schedules should be checked as services are seasonal and infrequent during the winter.

✔ CHECK-UP

Scotland includes
- ✔ Edinburgh, the capital.
- ✔ Glasgow, the largest city.
- ✔ Fort William, center for Highland touring.

Scotland's attractions include
- ✔ Edinburgh's annual International Festival.
- ✔ Golf at St. Andrews.
- ✔ Exploration of the Highlands and possibly finding the Loch Ness monster.
- ✔ Highland Games.
- ✔ Misty offshore islands.

FIGURE 9.5

Wales and Northern Ireland

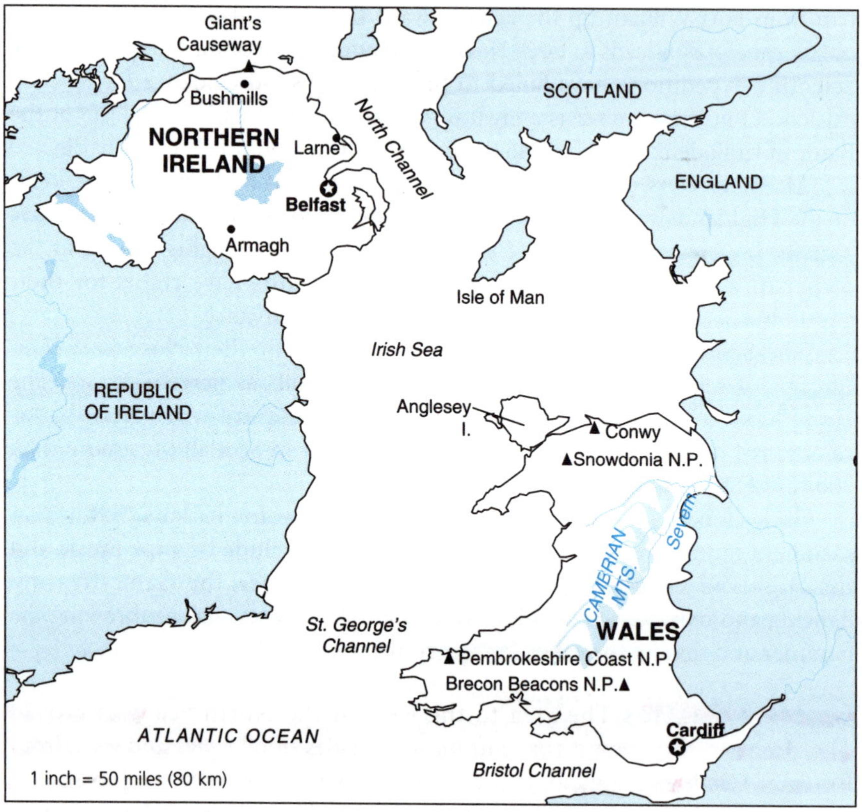

Wales and Northern Ireland

Britain and Scotland overshadow the other countries of the United Kingdom—Wales and Northern Ireland—in size and population (see Figure 9.5). Both political units are undergoing change. National identity among the Welsh has strengthened, and Wales has moved toward greater self-government. In Northern Ireland, precarious progress has been made toward ending the long-standing conflict known as the "Troubles."

Wales

A Welsh symbol is the leek, an onionlike herb.

The Welsh name for Wales is Cymru (*KUM ree*). The sign at the border greets you in two languages—"Welcome to Wales: Croeso I Cymru"—as has been the rule for signs everywhere in Wales since 1973. It is the first visible evidence that the visitor is in a part of Britain where the culture has remained distinctly different even though the sovereign's oldest son has been called Prince of Wales since the 14th century.

The mountainous land that points to the Irish Sea is rugged, with crumbling castles and fast-flowing rivers stocked with trout and salmon. A large island, **Anglesey**, lies off its northwest coast.

Wales is a land of music and poetry. A rich tradition of choral music developed in the 1700s, especially among the miners. The *eisteddfod* (*eye*

STEHTH vahd), a popular Welsh tradition, is a festival of poetry and music in which performers compete. Performances by male choirs are a highlight. Annual *eisteddfods* are held throughout the land. The largest is the Royal National Eisteddfod, which is hosted alternately in northern and southern Wales.

Cardiff The capital and largest city of Wales is Cardiff (*KAHR dihf*), a seaport on the south coast facing the Bristol Channel. It served the coal and iron industries of the Industrial Revolution. Cardiff Castle brings together the strands of the city's history. The train trip to Cardiff from London takes approximately two hours.

Welsh Castles Wales has some 300 castles to explore. Most are either old native structures or castles built by Edward I (1239–1307) after his successful campaigns against the Welsh. Edward's famous four are Conwy, Beaumaris, Caernarfon, and Harlech.

Conwy, one of the best-preserved medieval fortified towns in Europe, is on the north coast near Anglesey Island. Beaumaris, with its moat, is on the eastern end of Anglesey. Caernarfon is on the mainland. The castle's exterior walls and three towers are intact, though most of the interior is in ruins. Caernarfon is also a town, the largest in the area, and a resort popular with yachtsmen. Harlech was prominent in the War of Roses, when its siege inspired the famous marching song "Men of Harlech."

Welsh villages have some long names. For example, one of the longest is Llanfairpwllgwyngyllgogerychwyrndrobwi llllantysiliogogogoch, which translates to "St. Mary's Church by the white aspens over the whirlpool and St. Tysilio's Church by the red cave." Pronouncing it is even more difficult than spelling it!

National Parks One-fifth of Wales is covered by national parks—including the rugged mountain peaks and lakes of **Snowdonia** in the north, the flat-topped plateaus of the **Brecon Beacons** in the south, and the sandy bays and sea-carved inlets of **Pembrokeshire Coast National Park** along the southwest coast. The parks provide space for walking, mountain biking, rock climbing, and white-water rafting.

Northern Ireland

Slightly larger than Connecticut, Northern Ireland consists of six counties—Antrim, Down, Armagh, Fermanagh, Tyrone, and Londonderry—in the northeast corner of Ireland. (Look again at Figure 9.5.) It is a lovely land. Among its attractions are top-ranked golf courses, spectacular scenery, and personal ties for Irish Americans.

Ulster is Northern Ireland plus the counties of Cavan, Donegal, and Monaghan in the Republic of Ireland. The term is often used (incorrectly) as an unofficial name for Northern Ireland.

Belfast The capital of Northern Ireland, Belfast grew in the 19th century around the shipbuilding, rope-making, tobacco, and linen industries. The city is home to one-third of the country's population. Its highlights include the City Hall, Linen Hall Library, Lagan Lookout, and Ulster Museum. The museum display has gold from the Spanish Armada.

The "unsinkable" *Titanic* was built in Belfast, Northern Ireland. It struck an iceberg on its maiden voyage from Southampton, England, to New York in 1912.

The Antrim Coast Road The glens of Antrim and the northeast coast from **Larne** to **Bushmills** contain some of Northern Ireland's most beautiful scenery. Travelers can experience it by taking the Coast Road, which was completed in the 1830s. Prehistoric relics, mounds, castles, and churches along the road recall the country's long history of war, settlement, and religious conflict.

One of the drive's highlights is a stop at the **Giant's Causeway**. The causeway is a formation of pillars of basalt rock formed about 60 million years ago by the cooling of lava. The pillars form stepping-stones into the sea.

Irish whiskey is spelled with an e, Scotch whisky without an e.

Colorful legend explains the Giant's Causeway this way. Giant Finn MacCool built a road across the sea from Ireland to Scotland to reach a giantess he loved who lived on a Scottish isle. Unfortunately, she had another giant boyfriend, Finn Gall, whom MacCool would have to fight. MacCool went home to take a nap first. When Gall crossed over to peek at his rival, someone told him the sleeping giant was MacCool's baby son. Gall was so scared that he rushed home, destroying the sea road as he went.

A few miles from the causeway is the village of Bushmills, home to the world's oldest legal whiskey distillery, licensed in 1608. There probably is no better way to end a journey in Northern Ireland than to take a tour of the distillery and sample its product.

✔ CHECK-UP

Attractions of Wales include

- ✔ Cardiff, its capital and largest city.
- ✔ Mountains and fast-flowing rivers.
- ✔ Music and poetry at an *eisteddfod*.
- ✔ Castles.

Northern Ireland's best-known sites are

- ✔ Belfast, the capital and largest city.
- ✔ Giant's Causeway.

The Republic of Ireland

The *Emerald Isle* welcomes more visitors annually than it has residents. (See Figure 9.6 for a map of the country.) Prosperity has changed the ancient land. The growth of high-tech business has been coupled with increased sophistication about catering to travelers.

Thankfully, some things have not changed. Rain and sunshine continue to mingle almost every day, often every hour, and you can still go for a walk on a cool morning and smell the peat fires.

The Cities

The visitor must venture down Ireland's back roads to discover that hospitality is still among the greatest of Irish virtues. But the traveler can also find pleasures in the cities.

Limerick Many travelers first glimpse Ireland at Shannon Airport, on the west coast near Limerick—a city known for its lace and Georgian architecture. Medieval banquets at nearby Bunratty and Knappogue Castles introduce overseas visitors to Irish culture.

Dublin Ireland's capital and largest city is also an airport gateway. Dublin rests in the valley of the Liffey River with the Wicklow Mountains sheltering it on the south. The river divides Dublin into north and south. Dublin is rich in 18th-century architecture and theater.

Sights to see in Dublin include

- Dublin Castle, the stronghold of British rule until the 1920s.

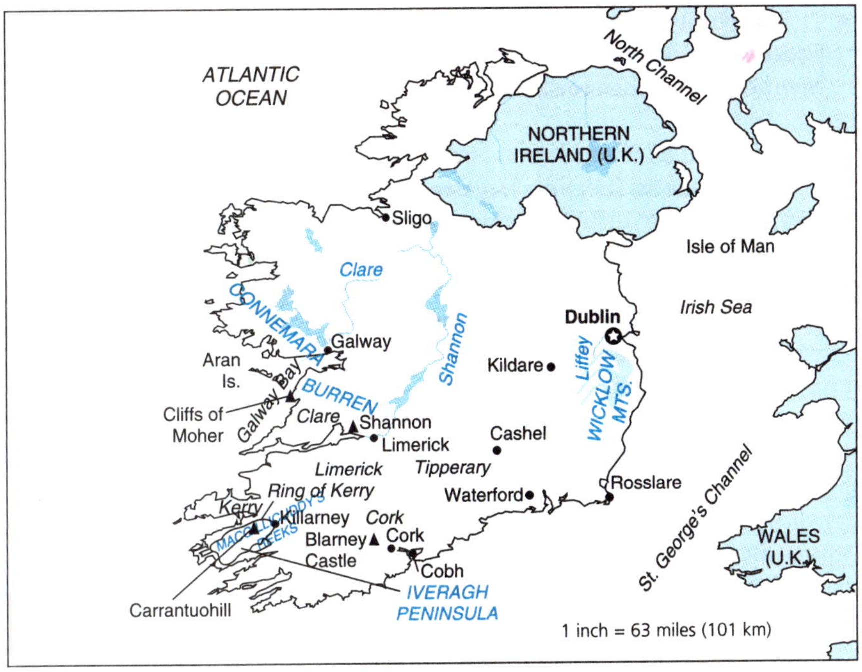

FIGURE 9.6

The Republic of Ireland

- St. Patrick's Cathedral, the Protestant cathedral where Jonathan Swift (1667–1745), the author of *Gulliver's Travels*, was dean.
- The Liberties, one of Dublin's oldest quarters and the center of the antiques trade.
- Trinity College, built by Queen Elizabeth I. The college's library displays the 8th-century Book of Kells, a beautifully illustrated version of the Bible.
- Merrion and Fitzwilliam Squares, Georgian architectural landmarks. The style flourished between 1714 and 1820.
- James Joyce Cultural Center, in an 18th-century town house.
- Abbey Theatre, Ireland's national theater.
- Grafton Street, a pedestrian-only shopping area.
- Guinness Brewery, Ireland's all-dominating brewery. Founded in 1759, it is the most popular tourist destination in Dublin.
- Jury's or Doyle's Irish Cabaret, for an evening of Irish dancing, music, and song.
- An Irish pub, of course.

The counties that surround Dublin were part of the Pale, the area most strongly influenced by English rule. The stately homes of former Anglo-Irish landlords dot the landscape, and many welcome overnight paying guests.

Other Places to Visit

Most tours begin at Shannon or Dublin and circle the country. The Republic of Ireland's counties attract travelers of Irish heritage seeking their roots.

The Southeast Picturesque farmlands, small towns, and ancient ruins characterize the southeast. Tours might include stops at

- **Kildare**, a market town southwest of Dublin, the heart of Ireland's horse-racing industry and home of the National Stud and Horse Museum.
- **Waterford**, on the southeast coast, for tours of the Waterford crystal factory.

Waterford glass is cut glass. Apprentices must produce a bowl displaying every important cut before they are promoted. The apprentice bowl is a popular purchase at the factory's gift shop.

- The market town of **Cashel**, inland in County Tipperary. On the Rock of Cashel stands a 12th-century cross near the spot where St. Patrick is said to have held aloft a shamrock to illustrate the Trinity, giving Ireland its emblem.

The Southwest Cork, Kerry, and Limerick are the counties of Ireland's southwest. Cork is Ireland's largest county. Its coastline has magnificent scenery, especially in the southwest, where rocky peninsulas jut into the Atlantic Ocean. Attractions include **Cobh**, the port from which millions of emigrants sailed to America. **Cork** is the business and shopping center of the region and Ireland's second-largest city.

Just to the northwest of Cork is **Blarney Castle**. Queen Elizabeth I wanted Lord Blarney to will his castle to the Crown. He kept refusing her with eloquent excuses. The queen reportedly exclaimed, "This is all Blarney. What he says he rarely means." Visitors come to kiss the Blarney Stone, set in the battlements of the castle. Potential kissers climb steep steps, wait their turns, lay down on their backs on an old blanket, are suspended in space by two strong men, lean backward, and aim a kiss at the granite stone. Kissers can buy a certificate guaranteeing they have kissed the Blarney Stone and are "sent forth with the gift of eloquence that the stone bestows."

CLOSE-UP: THE REPUBLIC OF IRELAND

Who is a good prospect for a trip to the Republic of Ireland? Prospects include North Americans of Irish ancestry, Catholic priests who lead pilgrimages to religious shrines, theater lovers who want to attend Dublin's plays, and golfers. The mist creates lush greens, but a rain poncho is a golfer's necessity.

Why would they visit the Republic of Ireland? The immigrant experience is recent in many American families, and many people go to Ireland to see where their families came from. Religion is also a magnet. The Roman Catholic Church plays a major role in Irish social life. Almost every city has a Catholic cathedral with extensive parish rolls for those seeking ancestral information.

Where would they go? An introduction to Ireland might include the following eight-day tour.

Day 1 An overnight flight.

Day 2 Arrive in Dublin. At 1500, meet your tour director and companions for an orienting drive through the city. See O'Connell Street and elegant Georgian squares on your way to St. Patrick's Cathedral. Visit Trinity College to see the Book of Kells. Tonight's welcome dinner ends with delicious Irish coffee.

Day 3 Dublin–Limerick. Drive through horse-racing country this morning to visit the Irish National Stud and Horse Museum at Kildare; then go south to the Rock of Cashel, where St. Patrick preached, and on to Limerick. Tonight's optional outing is a medieval banquet at Knappogue Castle.

Day 4 Limerick–Killarney. A west coast excursion begins with the Cliffs of Moher and their breathtaking views. In the afternoon, visit a farm and enjoy a traditional tea in a thatched-roof farmhouse.

Day 5 Killarney. An all-day drive around the Ring of Kerry.

Day 6 Killarney–Waterford. Cross County Cork to Blarney and a chance to kiss the stone. In the afternoon, proceed to Waterford for a tour of the crystal factory.

Day 7 Waterford–Dublin. Visit the handweaving mill at Avoca, cross the Wicklow Mountains, and stop at Glendalough to see the ruins of a center of early Irish Christianity. Tonight's optional outing is a traditional Irish dinner and cabaret show to celebrate your trip to Ireland.

Day 8 Board your homebound flight.

When is the best time to visit? Spring is the driest time of year and May is the sunniest month, but summer remains the most popular time to visit, when the days are long (daylight lasts until after 2200 in late June and July) and the countryside is green and beautiful.

The travelers say, "We've heard it rains a lot in Ireland. Why do we want to go there?" How would you respond? The fickle Irish weather is what makes the island so gloriously green, but yes, it does rain a lot. You should never promise good weather where the odds favor rain. Always find out the travelers' interests and tastes early so you can match them to an appropriate destination. These travelers sound more like prospects for a beach vacation.

Killarney's **Ring of Kerry** is Ireland's most popular scenic drive, a mix of scenic countryside and picturesque villages. The route makes a circuit of the **Iveragh Peninsula** on the southwest coast. Because tour buses travel the Ring counterclockwise, independent travelers should go clockwise to avoid as much traffic as possible. In the midst of the Ring is Macgillicuddy's Reeks, the mountain range molded by glaciers. Here too is **Carrantuohill** (*kar RAHN tuo hill*), Ireland's highest mountain.

At the base of the peninsula, **Killarney** is the tourist center. Killarney National Park, Ireland's first national park, was founded in 1932. Muckross House in the park is a Victorian mansion open to the public. Its gardens are noted for the rhododendrons and azaleas that grow like weeds in the damp climate. Motor vehicles are not allowed, so people visit by two-wheeled horse-drawn jaunting carts.

Great Britain's National Health Service does *not* offer free treatment to travelers. Most U.S. health insurance plans and Medicare programs for seniors do not cover U.S. citizens when they travel outside the country. Travelers should check their coverage with their insurance providers before departure.

The West While other parts of Ireland were influenced by Norman, Scottish, or English settlers, the western and northwestern counties (Clare, Galway, Mayo, Sligo, Leitrim, and Donegal) escaped settlement. These counties are the most Gaelic parts of Ireland. Remnants from prehistoric times include stone forts and *dolmens* (Stone Age burial chambers). The area's castles range from the immaculate to the dilapidated.

The west has some of Ireland's most unusual, even eerie, scenery. The **Burren** is a barren windswept region on the south side of Galway Bay in County Clare. The area has more than seventy megalithic tombs, along with wells, cairns, and stone forts, indicating that the area was inhabited during the Stone Age. English troops stationed there in the 1600s claimed that "there was no wood to hang a man, no water to drown him, and no earth to bury him." The **Cliffs of Moher**, also along Clare's coast, are one of Ireland's most-visited attractions. They are limestone stacks rising from the sea.

The mountains of Connemara

Galway, the west's largest city, is a youthful university town. To the west of the city lie the rugged coast and mountains of **Connemara**, loved by painters and writers. Connemara is known for its ponies, descendants of the horses that swam to shore from the sinking ships of the Spanish Armada.

Sligo is a market town on the Atlantic Coast. The poet William Butler Yeats (1865–1939) spent his boyhood summers there. Later, when Yeats was living in London, he recalled those summers in his poems.

Off the west coast of Ireland, forming a natural breakwater across Galway Bay, are the three **Aran Islands** (Inishmore, Inishmaan, and Inisheer). These "ancient islands of the saints" are populated by Gaelic-speaking fishermen and farmers. Potatoes grow on fields that were created by laying seaweed and sand on the islands' bare rocks. Inishmaan attracted John Millington Synge (1871–1909), who was inspired there to write *The Playboy of the Western World*. Tourists arrive by ferry or light aircraft. Inishmore is the largest of the islands and the one most visited.

Hand-knitted sweaters with distinctive patterns originally made for fishermen are popular Aran Island purchases.

✔ CHECK-UP

Key cities of the Republic of Ireland include

- ✔ Dublin, the capital and largest city.
- ✔ Limerick, the gateway city near Shannon Airport.
- ✔ Cork, Ireland's second-largest city.

For travelers, highlights of the Republic of Ireland include

- ✔ Dublin theater.
- ✔ West coast scenery.
- ✔ The Blarney Stone.

Planning the Trip

Historic and cultural ties combined with a common language make the British Isles a good choice for North American travelers on their first trip abroad. The endless variety of things to do brings people back again and again.

When to Go

Perhaps as a result of their unpredictable weather, the British Isles have more indoor attractions than outdoor ones. The destinations can be recommended year-round, with more than enough to do in any season.

Popular times to tour are in April and May or in September and October. In spring, the moors are covered with beautiful yellow gorse, and in fall the land is blanketed with purple heather. Summer is also a popular time for visits.

Preparing the Traveler

Passes are bargains for sightseeing-minded independent travelers. Many can be ordered from VisitBritain, booked through a Web site, or bought at the British Visitor Center in London. The Great Britain Heritage Pass allows admission to more than 600 of Britain's historic properties, and the London Visitor's Travelcard helps tourists negotiate the city's subway and bus networks.

Money Traveler's checks and credit cards are widely accepted, and ATMs are plentiful. Small B&Bs, restaurants, and stores are unlikely to accept credit cards; therefore, local money is necessary. Banks, hotels, and exchange bureaus change money.

At present, the United Kingdom has its own currency and does not use the euro, the common currency of the European Union, although it is a member of the organization. Ireland uses the euro.

When leaving, foreign visitors can get a refund of the value-added tax (VAT), which ranges from 12 to 21 percent of the purchase price of many goods. VAT is not refundable on lodging, car rental, meals, or other forms of personal service. Many rules affect the refunds, so travelers who plan extensive purchases should check ahead.

Language Great Britain has numerous dialects, overlaid with class, town, and country variations. According to writer George Bernard Shaw, "It is impossible for an Englishman to open his mouth without making another Englishman despise him." With Asian and West Indian immigrants added to the variety of speech patterns, consensus about what constitutes proper speech remains elusive.

Wales is the only one of the four divisions of Great Britain with an active language of its own, but only around 20 percent of the people speak Welsh. Irish (also known as Gaelic) is the official national language of the Republic of Ireland. In reality, English is spoken widely. Irish-speaking communities are found in rural areas along the west coast and on some of the offshore islands.

Customs Mealtimes and pub opening hours create confusion. In general, breakfast is served between 0730 and 0900, and lunch between 1200 and 1400 (in the north the latter meal is called "dinner"). Tea, often a meal in itself, is served between 1600 and 1730. Dinner or supper is served between 1930 and 2130, sometimes earlier in the country. High tea, at about 1800, replaces dinner in some areas, especially Scotland. In large cities, pre- and after-theater suppers are available. After the meal in many country hotels, guests leave the dining room and go to the parlor to linger over coffee and conversation.

Transportation

Most flights from North America arrive in the British Isles in the early morning. Passengers continue their exploration by plane, train, rental car, or motorcoach.

By Air Travelers to the British Isles can choose either a U.S. carrier, the flag carrier of the destination country, or a carrier from a third country for their international flight. National carriers used to be government-owned and -operated, but today, most are private companies with code-sharing agreements with other airlines. British Airways, a private company, has one of the world's most comprehensive international air networks. Aer Lingus is the airline of the Republic of Ireland.

A flight from New York's JFK to Shannon, Ireland, takes approximately five and a half hours; to London's airports, about an hour longer.

By Water Between April and early December, subject to change, Cunard Line's *Queen Mary 2* sails between New York City and Southampton. At present it is the only ship making scheduled ocean crossings. Cunard offers programs whereby passengers can cruise one way and fly the other. In spring and fall, transatlantic passage is possible on lines making repositioning cruises.

The British Isles have miles of rivers and canals suitable for cruising. Travelers might sail down the Thames in a luxury yacht, squeeze through a Midlands canal in a classic "narrowboat," explore Scotland's Caledonian Canal aboard a sailing vessel, or meander along Ireland's Shannon River on a barge.

Sea services cross the English Channel between British and continental ports. From England to the Continent, the shortest route is from Dover to Calais, France, which takes about 90 minutes by ferry and 30 minutes by hovercraft (vehicles that ride over water on a cushion of air). The principal ferry routes from Great Britain to Ireland are from Wales to Dublin or Rosslare.

By Rail The Industrial Revolution gave rise to the railroad, and Great Britain was among the first countries to benefit from train travel. London's rail terminals were built on what were then the outskirts of the city, and it was proposed that, as far as possible, railroad lines within the city would be underground. Thus in 1863 London's Metropolitan Railway became the first passenger-carrying underground railway.

Outside the city, the United Kingdom's BritRail system has its own rail passes and does not participate in Europe's Eurailpass. Many money-saving rail passes are available. Rail Europe's Web site provides information.

The Channel Tunnel is a railway tunnel beneath the English Channel, of which 23 miles (37 km) are underwater. Cars do not drive through; they are put on a train. The Chunnel has three types of trains: high-speed passenger-only trains; shuttle trains for automobiles, trucks, buses, and their passengers;

➤ PROFILE

Dining in the British Isles

Travelers might like to try these traditional meals:

- ➤ A country breakfast of sausages, grilled tomatoes, eggs, cereal, dry toast, and strong tea.
- ➤ A pub lunch. *Pub* is short for "public house," a bar established by a brewery to sell its products. Pubs usually sell light lunches, but many are full-service restaurants.
- ➤ An afternoon tea accompanied by cakes or small sandwiches.
- ➤ A cream tea, a specialty of England's West Country. Scones heaped with clotted cream are served with jam or fresh strawberries.
- ➤ Cornish pasties, the mainstay of Cornish miners. Pasties (pronounced *PASS tees*) are turnovers filled with seasoned meat or fish.
- ➤ A dinner of roast beef or lamb and Yorkshire pudding. Restaurants that specialize in roasts are called *carveries*.
- ➤ Welsh rarebit (cheese on toast), leek soup, and laver bread made with seaweed in Wales.
- ➤ *Cullen skink* (fish soup), *partan bree* (crab with rice and cream), and black bun (fruitcake on a pastry base) in Scotland.
- ➤ Bacon and dairy products in Ireland. Specialties include colcannon (a mix of potatoes and cabbage), soda bread, and a soufflé made with carrageen (a variety of seaweed).

The *Queen Mary 2* entered service in 2004. It is more than twice as long as the Washington Monument is high and is as tall as a twenty-three-story building. The vessel's fourteen decks can house 2,620 passengers served by 1,253 crew members.

and freight trains. The English entrance is near Folkstone in Kent. The actual trip through the tunnel takes about 20 minutes.

Eurostar provides passenger-only trains linking London, Paris, and Brussels through the Chunnel. Passengers board the train at London's Waterloo station. The completion of a section of high-speed track in 2003 cut Eurostar's travel time between Paris and London (now a journey of 2 hours, 30 minutes) and between London and Brussels (2 hours, 20 minutes).

The Republic of Ireland participates in the Eurailpass system, but its rail system has shrunk in recent years. *Coras Iompair Eireann* (CIE) operates both Ireland's rail system and its more extensive, less expensive bus system.

By Road Driving in the British Isles offers challenges for North American tourists. The change to driving on the left is not easy. The driver's seat is on the right side of the car. Most cars have stick shifts to save expensive fuel. Drivers must shift gears with the left hand rather than the right. Congestion and parking are problems in city centers. Rental firms require drivers to be at least twenty-five years old, although some cover younger drivers at an increased rate. There is also a maximum age, usually seventy or seventy-five. See Table 9.2 for some translations of driving terms between American and British English.

Because motor vehicles drive on the left, people must remember to LOOK RIGHT when walking across the street. Each season, some tourists forget and are struck by a car.

London's public transport network takes travelers to virtually any part of the city and probably negates the need for a car there. Travelers who do need cars should pick up their vehicles away from the city so that they can practice "thinking left" before they hit major traffic.

The motorways (expressways) provide quick connections throughout Great Britain. They are designed for high speed rather than scenic travel and are numbered M1, M2, and so on. Maps also show trunk roads (A category) that link major towns and cities as well as scenic but slow rural roads (B category). Roundabouts (traffic circles or rotaries) are entered and exited from the left. Country roads are often bounded on both sides by rock walls. For comfortable sightseeing, travelers should not plan a journey of more than 100 miles (161 km) in a day.

Many of Ireland's National Primary Routes (designated on maps by the letter *N*) are two-lane. If people plan to rent a car in the Irish Republic and visit Northern Ireland (or vice versa), they should inform the car rental firm and check that insurance applies when they cross the border.

TABLE 9.2

Variations on Driving Terms

American	British
The Boot for overparking	Wheel clamping
Detour	Deviation
Divided highway	Dual carriageway
Expressway	Motorway
Gas	Petrol
Hood	Bonnet
Men working	Roadworks
No passing	No overtaking
Overpass	Flyover
Traffic circle or rotary	Roundabout
Traffic lane	Carriageway
Truck	Lorry
Yield	Give way

Accommodations

British chain hotels and familiar international brands meet a reliable standard. Hotel rates may or may not include breakfast. It pays to ask exactly what the rate includes and get room prices quoted in the local currency. The traveler pays the exchange rate on the date of departure. Many older hotels, even in London, are not air-conditioned. The early-morning arrival time of most flights from North America presents difficulties: hotels may not have rooms available for the jet-lagged traveler who arrives before noon.

Country house hotels and renovated castles offer a unique combination of luxury and history. The gentry invite guests to stop for an overnight and an elaborate meal cooked by the chef, but guests must pay for the privilege.

Guest houses and B&Bs are found throughout the country. They are classified by a diamond rating system. The traditional B&B was a spare room for rent in someone's home, with a bathroom down the hall and potluck as to whether the hostess would cook anything for breakfast other than fried bread in lard. That has changed to meet modern demands. Travelers can now find lists of B&Bs with four- or five-diamond ratings.

CHAPTER WRAP-UP

SUMMARY

Here is a review of the objectives with which we began the chapter.

1. **Describe the environment and people of the British Isles.** The British Isles are gentle, settled lands. England's landscape is mostly rolling and rarely flat. The moors of England and Scotland have a stark beauty. Wales is a land of rugged mountains with great appeal to outdoor lovers. Scotland has a dramatic landscape, with lakes and rushing streams in its Highlands. Ireland is a green, green land, a central plain rimmed by low mountains, lush with evergreens. Where Ireland's west coast meets the Atlantic, dramatic cliffs face the ocean's gales.

   In 1999 both Wales and Scotland began self-government, although remaining part of the United Kingdom. Northern Ireland is slowly working its way toward independence. The Republic of Ireland is a fully independent country.

2. **Identify and locate the most-visited sites of the United Kingdom.** The capital cities of London and Edinburgh attract millions of visitors each year, both repeaters and first timers. In England, attractions include Bristol, Bath, the ruins of Tintagel, Plymouth, and the tin mines, beaches, and moors of the West Country; Salisbury and Stonehenge in Hardy Country; resorts and historic sites such as Canterbury in the southeast; the university towns and Cotswold Hills of central England; the beauty of the Lake District; and York and the moors in Yorkshire. Mountains and lakes lure those who love the outdoors to Wales and Scotland. Golfers are drawn to the course at St. Andrews, Scotland, and curiosity seekers want to know if there really is a monster in Loch Ness. Belfast and the Giant's Causeway are the key attractions of Northern Ireland.

3. **Describe the attractions of the Republic of Ireland.** The most-visited sites are the capital city of Dublin, Blarney Castle, the Waterford factory, the Ring of Kerry, and the Killarney area.

4. **Provide or find the information needed to plan a trip to the British Isles.** The British Isles are year-round destinations, and they present few obstacles to North American travelers. The British and Irish Tourist Authorities provide exceptionally good service when you need to go beyond standard reference sources for information. Choosing among the many options may be the most time-consuming part of planning the trip.

QUESTIONS FOR DISCUSSION AND REVIEW

1. Can you think of anyone for whom the British Isles would *not* be a good destination?

2. VisitBritain is marketing Great Britain as a destination for the future, not just a museum of old attractions. What do you think VisitBritain should do to attract the next generation of travelers?

CHAPTER 10

Northern Europe

- Benelux: Belgium, the Netherlands, and Luxembourg
- Germany
- Switzerland, Liechtenstein, and Austria
- Nordic Europe: Denmark, Norway, Sweden, Finland, and Iceland

OBJECTIVES

When you have completed Chapter 10, you should be able to

1. Describe the environment and people of northern Europe.
2. Locate each country's principal gateway and major cities.
3. Describe the key attractions that the region offers travelers.
4. Provide or find the information needed to plan a trip to northern Europe.

Natural and created landscapes, excellent travel services, and historic sites combine to make Europe one of the world's most popular destinations. The Continent's political ideas, scientific discoveries, religious beliefs, and cultural attractions have influenced the world.

The countries of the Continent can be classified in many ways. This chapter defines northern Europe as consisting of twelve countries: the three countries of the Benelux (**Belgium**, the **Netherlands**, and **Luxembourg**), **Germany**, **Switzerland**, **Liechtenstein**, **Austria**, and the countries of Nordic Europe (**Denmark**, **Sweden**, **Norway**, **Finland**, and **Iceland**). Chapters 11 and 12 explore eastern and southern Europe. See the Fact File in Appendix A for an alphabetic listing of Europe's countries.

The Environment and Its People

Northern Europe includes many of the world's major cities as well as some of Europe's largest countries. At the region's southern edge is Europe's largest mountain system, the **Alps** (see Figure 10.1). At its eastern edge is the **Oder** (*OH duhr*) **River** and low mountains that mark Germany's frontier.

The sea is key to much of the region. The **North Sea** is the wide arm of the Atlantic that lies between Great Britain and northern Europe. The **Baltic Sea** extends into northern Europe and links Sweden, Finland, and eastern Europe with the North Sea.

The Land

Northern Europe's coastline curves in and out in a series of large and small peninsulas, principally the **Scandinavian Peninsula** and the **Jutland Peninsula**.

The **Kjølen Mountains** form the spine of the Scandinavian Peninsula and separate Norway on the west from Sweden on the east. The peninsula is a land of high mountains and immense plateaus with many lakes and forests. During the Ice Age, glaciers carved Norway's west coast into a zigzag of steep-walled valleys. As the ice receded, the ocean waters rose and partly filled the valleys, creating long, narrow inlets called *fjords* (*fee AWRDZ*) and a maze of islands.

Finland is to the east of Scandinavia. It is surrounded to the north and east by Russia, Sweden, and Norway; to the south by the **Gulf of Finland**; and to the west by the **Gulf of Bothnia** and the Baltic. Apart from a small hilly area in the northwest, Finland is a heavily forested lowland dotted with many lakes.

One-third of Finland as well as the north of Norway and Sweden lies inside the Arctic Circle in a region called the *Land of the Midnight Sun*. There, for periods during the summer, the sun shines twenty-four hours a day. Above the Arctic Circle the wilderness is called **Lapland**.

South of the Scandinavian Peninsula, Denmark's flat Jutland Peninsula borders Germany. To the west of Germany are the Benelux countries—Belgium, the Netherlands, and Luxembourg. Near the sea the land of Belgium and the Netherlands is flat, but it rises inland to low mountains in the south near Luxembourg.

From the Benelux countries the **Great European Plain** extends eastward to Russia in a gigantic arc across northern Germany, Denmark, and southern

➤ PROFILE

Special Events in Northern Europe

Among the most popular festivals and events in northern Europe are the following:

- ➤ Bayreuth Festival, dedicated to Wagner's music, in late July and August in Germany.
- ➤ Garden Festival at Keukenhof, Holland, from March through May.
- ➤ Hans Christian Andersen Festival in Odense, Denmark, in July and August.
- ➤ Helsinki Festival in Finland from June through September.
- ➤ International Music Festival in Vienna, Austria, in May and June.
- ➤ Nobel Peace Prize, awarded in Oslo, Norway, in December.
- ➤ Nobel Prizes in physics, chemistry, medicine, and literature, awarded in Stockholm, Sweden, on December 10.
- ➤ Oktoberfest in Munich, Germany, in September.
- ➤ Salzburg Festival in Austria in late July and August.
- ➤ Viking Festival in Denmark in June and July.

FIGURE 10.1

Northern Europe

Sweden. South of the plain the land rises to low mountains and plateaus that extend through central Europe. The peaks of the **Harz Mountains** of central Germany rise more than 3,000 feet (910 m).

Europe's greatest mountain system, the Alps (or more formally, the Alpine Mountain System), dominates the south. The mountains begin near the Mediterranean Sea in France and extend in a curve eastward through northern Italy, Switzerland, Liechtenstein, southern Germany, and Austria. The broadest part of the system reaches across Switzerland, a country renowned for its spectacular scenery.

Throughout northern Europe great rivers provide routes for trade as well as waterways for tourists. The Rhine, Rhône, Ticino, and Inn Rivers begin in Switzerland, which is often called the *Fountain of Europe*. Commercially, the **Rhine** is Europe's most important river. It flows from the Alps through Switzerland, along the Austrian, German, and French borders, and through Germany and the Netherlands to the North Sea. The **Danube** (*DAN yoob*) **River** begins in southwest Germany and flows east to the Black Sea.

FIGURE 10.2

Milestones of Northern European History

300s–400s Germanic tribes rove throughout northern Europe.

700s–1100s Vikings plunder much of the Continent.

800s–1400s Castles provide security in the feudal age.

1291 Three Swiss cantons sign a defense agreement that marks the start of the Swiss Confederation.

1300s Hanseatic League of trade associations from towns along the North and Baltic Seas devise a system of maritime and commercial laws.

1517 Martin Luther nails his theses to a church door in Wittenberg, starting the Protestant Reformation.

1600s The Netherlands becomes a major sea power and develops a great colonial empire, providing opportunities for the middle class.

1814–1815 After the Napoleonic Wars, the Congress of Vienna arranges peace settlements and remaps the Continent.

1914–1918 World War I takes place; Denmark, Sweden, and Switzerland remain neutral.

1939–1945 World War II takes place; Sweden and Switzerland remain neutral.

1945 The Yalta Conference divides Germany and Austria into four zones of occupation.

1990 East and West Germany reunite.

1993 The European Union (EU) is formed.

2000 Denmark and Sweden are linked by a bridge and tunnel system.

2002 The euro becomes the official currency of EU countries.

The Climate

The north of Norway, Sweden, and Finland has severe winters resembling those of Alaska. South of the Arctic Circle, northern Europe has a four-season climate. Summers are warm, with plentiful precipitation. Winters are cold, with varying amounts of snow. Rain falls year-round.

Europe generally has milder weather than North America at the same latitude. For example, although Berlin, Germany, and Calgary, Canada, are at the same latitude, January temperatures in Berlin average about 15° F (8° C) higher than those in Calgary. The milder climate is caused by winds that blow from the Atlantic Ocean and are warmed by the North Atlantic Current, which is the remnant of the Gulf Stream. The winds affect northern Europe because no mountain barrier is large enough to block them.

In the mountains of Germany, Switzerland, and Austria, altitude causes a variety of climatic conditions. Atlantic air blocked by the mountains often settles over low areas, producing dampness and fog. Fog sometimes covers the entire Swiss Plateau like a sea of clouds. Snow covers the ground at least six months a year. The higher peaks of the Alps are snow-covered throughout the year. Warm, dry winds, called **foehns**, often blow downward along the mountain slopes, melting the snow and causing avalanches.

The People and Their History

The Roman Empire extended its rule into northern Europe as far north as the Danube and into areas west of the Rhine. When Rome fell in the fifth century AD, small kingdoms replaced the strong central government. The Vikings of the north went their own way. As pirates and warriors, they terrorized coastal Europe from the late 700s to about 1100 (see Figure 10.2). The Viking kingdoms would eventually become Denmark, Norway, and Sweden.

Castles played a central role in providing security against the Vikings and later marauders. When the lords of the castles were able to secure local peace, merchants could travel the land and sea roads, and towns grew along their trade routes. By the 1300s, northern European merchants formed a powerful association, the Hanseatic League, that controlled trade around the Baltic and North Seas.

The introduction of gunpowder from Asia in the 1300s undercut the power of the castles and their lords. Stone castles could not withstand cannons. Cities became more important. The 1300s also brought a greater disruption: the Black Death, an epidemic of plague that killed about one-fourth of the population.

The Roman Catholic Church had become the most powerful force on the Continent, not only in religious matters but also in politics, learning, and the arts. In the 1500s, however, the Reformation led to the growth of Protestantism, while the ideals of the Renaissance spread throughout most of Europe.

The 1600s were the golden age of the Netherlands. The country became the leading sea power and developed a great colonial empire. Its new wealth contributed to the growth of the cities and the middle class.

The Industrial Revolution spread throughout northern Europe in the 1800s. As the need for raw materials and sales outlets grew, European powers looked to colonial expansion. World War I was partly a result of their competition for colonies and economic power. World War II soon followed.

From the late 1940s through the 1980s, while the United States and the Soviet Union competed for influence, western Europe's countries banded together into various organizations. Most influential was the European Community, which worked to eliminate obstacles to the free movement of goods, services, workers, and capital among its members. The European Community soon became the **European Union (EU)**.

Today, the EU is an organization of countries that promotes political and economic cooperation among its members (see Table 10.1). Its capital is in **Brussels, Belgium**. In 2002 the EU introduced a single currency—the euro—for its member countries, although not all countries are using it. The easing of border controls and the use of a single currency are of great help to travelers.

TABLE 10.1

Members of the European Union

Austria	Latvia
Belgium	Lithuania
Cyprus	Luxembourg
Czech Republic	Malta
Denmark	The Netherlands
Estonia	Poland
Finland	Portugal
France	Slovakia
Germany	Slovenia
Greece	Spain
Hungary	Sweden
Ireland	The United Kingdom
Italy	

✔ CHECK-UP

Major physical features of northern Europe include

- ✔ Irregular coastline featuring the peninsulas of Scandinavia and Jutland.
- ✔ Great European Plain, which stretches from the Benelux to Russia.
- ✔ Flat land in Denmark and along the North Sea in Belgium and the Netherlands.
- ✔ Rolling hills and low mountains in the central uplands.
- ✔ Alpine Mountain System.

The culture of northern Europe is notable for

- ✔ Fragmentation after the fall of Rome.
- ✔ Powerful cities and the emergence of a strong middle class as early as the 17th century.
- ✔ Easing of border barriers and the introduction of a common currency through the European Union.

Benelux

Benelux is the name of the economic union formed in 1948 by Belgium, the Netherlands, and Luxembourg. (The name is made up of the first letters in each country's name.) The countries play an important part in the European Union, are lively tourist destinations, and contribute mightily to the Continent's cultural life.

Belgium and the Netherlands are also known as the *Low Countries*. Flat as well as low, they offer little resistance to winds, and since the 15th century windmills have been used to drain the land for farming. Figure 10.3 shows a map of the region.

Belgium

The small, densely populated kingdom of Belgium has a short coastline on the North Sea and is bounded by the Netherlands to the north, Germany to the east, Luxembourg at its southeastern corner, and France to the south. In area it is about the size of Maryland. Belgium is a treasure worth exploring.

Sandy beaches along Belgium's coast are lined with resorts. Behind the dunes is flat land reclaimed from the sea. Here grow the poppies made famous in John McCrae's poem "In Flanders Fields." The land rises gently to a fertile plateau. In the southeast, the flat-topped mountains of the **Ardennes** (*ar DEN*) are cut by the Meuse River and its tributaries. The country's highest points are near the German border.

Belgium has two main ethnic groups. The Dutch-speaking *Flemings*, the

FIGURE 10.3 Benelux

larger group, live in the north; the French-speaking *Walloons* live in the south. Almost all the industrial centers are in the Flemish area. Highway signs and maps list place-names in both languages. In this book Flemish names are given first, with their French counterparts in parentheses.

Points of interest in Belgium are rarely more than an hour apart. Roads and rail services connect all corners of the country. Visitors will see a country rich in both commerce and culture. Feudal lords built Belgium's castles, but merchants and craftsmen were responsible for the guild houses and sculpture-adorned town halls of **Brussels**, **Antwerpen**, **Gent**, and **Brugge**. The land of Brueghel, van Eyck, Rubens, Van Dyck, Ensor, and Magritte is also the place to see the artists' best work.

A hint for leisure travelers: Hotels in Brussels offer special rates when business and government officials are likely to leave town on weekends and in summer.

Brussels The capital of the European Union and the headquarters of NATO, Brussels attracts high-powered visitors. Luxury hotels and fine restaurants accommodate their demands. The city is heart-shaped, with the oldest section, called the *lower city*, in the center.

The lower city includes the Grand' Place, often called the most beautiful medieval square in Europe. Elaborately decorated buildings constructed during the 1600s border the square. The Grand' Place comes alive during local festivals such as the *Ommegang*, a pageant held the first Tuesday and Thursday in July that re-creates Holy Roman Emperor Charles V's reception in the city in 1549, and the Christmas Market, which features stalls representing many nations.

Near the Grand' Place is a must-see tourist attraction: a fountain with a small bronze statue of a little boy relieving himself. Everyone from Louis XV of France to the Boy Scouts of America has donated clothes to the Manneken Pis.

Brussels is a treasure house of architecture. The city was the home of the Art Nouveau movement of the 1880s, a movement that marked the beginning of modern architecture. Undulating lines suggesting waves, flames, vines, flower stems, and tresses of hair were favorite motifs.

The city's major and minor museums have collections of old and new masters. For those with a sweet tooth, tours visit Brussels's chocolate museum and factories. The *Chocolate Passion Festival* is held around Valentine's weekend each year.

Day tours from Brussels visit parks, forests, castles, and **Waterloo**, the site of Napoleon's final defeat, about 12 miles (19 km) south of the city.

Antwerpen (Antwerp) The center of Dutch-speaking Flanders, Antwerpen is about a 40-minute drive north of Brussels. Despite being 55 miles (88 km) up the Scheldt River from the sea, it is one of the world's largest ports. Its diamond-cutting industry has been established for more than 500 years and carries out 70 percent of the world's diamond dealing. Antwerpen's attractions include three outstanding museums: the Plantin-Moretus (with a copy of the Gutenberg Bible), the Royal Museum of Fine Arts (with works by Rubens), and the home of Peter Paul Rubens (1577–1640). His masterpiece, a triptych called *Descent from the Cross*, is housed in the Gothic Cathedral of Our Lady.

Brugge (Bruges) West of Antwerpen, a few miles from the North Sea, is Europe's lace-making capital, Brugge. It is often called the *City of Bridges*. During the 13th and 14th centuries, Brugge was a leading member of the Hanseatic League. Its link to the sea silted up in the 15th century. This caused the city to decline as a trading center but helped to preserve its medieval buildings and canals.

ON THE SPOT

Florence and Dan Burgundy are going to Brussels, Belgium, where Dan is scheduled to present a seminar before an agency of the European Union. Florence is wondering if you have any touring suggestions to keep her busy while Dan is at the meeting.

In talking to Florence, you discover that she has never traveled by herself and is somewhat nervous about tackling a foreign city on her own. Her interests include art, architecture, and antiques. You might suggest that she begin by taking a half-day city tour. Areas worth future exploration are the Ilot Sacré, the picturesque area of narrow streets to the northeast of the Grand' Place, and the Sablon, known for its antique shops (on Sundays it becomes an outdoor antique market).

Brugge, Belgium

One remnant of medieval times is the *beguinage*, a religious community for women (also found in the Netherlands). During the Middle Ages, women entered beguinages either because they had been left on their own when their men went on the Crusades or because they wanted a life devoted to religion but were unwilling to take full vows as nuns. The communities were active until the early part of the 20th century.

Gent (Ghent) Sister city and ancient rival to Brugge, **Gent** is a medieval town known as the *City of Flowers*. Like Brugge, Gent is built on a series of canals. The city's priceless art includes van Eyck's *Adoration of the Mystic Lamb*. Many historic buildings are lit at night from May through October, making an evening walk a memorable experience.

Ardennes The Ardennes, a French-speaking area in the country's southeast corner, is Belgium's vacationland. This heavily wooded plateau is punctuated by flat-topped peaks and cut by deep chasms and valleys. The grottos at **Fond de Quarreaux**, auto racing, and the casino at **Spa** are some of the region's attractions.

From Waterloo to World War II, Belgium in general and the Ardennes in particular have been in the line of fire. The village of **Bastogne** was the site of the last major German offensive of World War II—the Battle of the Bulge. Memorials testify to the sacrifices made in the battle.

Spa is a Belgian town with mineral springs that has given its name to similar establishments around the world.

The Netherlands

The Netherlands is bordered by the North Sea to the north and west, by Germany to the east, and by Belgium to the south. In area it is only a little larger than the states of Connecticut and Massachusetts combined, but it is one of the most densely populated countries in Europe (see the Fact File in Appendix A). Strictly speaking, the name **Holland** refers to only two of the country's provinces—North Holland and South Holland—but the name is commonly used to refer to the whole country.

The Netherlands is part of a flat, low coastal region. The only relief from flat land comes in the far southeast, where a range of hills rises. Because more than half of the country is below sea level, the Dutch must carry on a continuous battle against the sea. Since the 11th century, they have built dikes and drains to control flooding and gain new land. The most spectacular reclamation was the Zuider Zee (*sider ZAY*) project, which began in 1920 and took almost fifty years to complete. The Zuider Zee was part of the North Sea before a dike transformed it into a freshwater lake and *polders* (new land behind a dike). Wind farms (groups of windmills) pump the water out of the reclaimed land into canals, where the water can run safely out to sea.

"God created the world, but the Dutch made Holland," according to a Dutch saying.

Three major rivers—the **Scheldt, Maas** (**Meuse** in Belgium), and **Rhine**—cross the country and make the Netherlands an important commercial center. Much of the water traffic converges on **Rotterdam**, the world's largest port. Heavily bombed in World War II, the city is largely of modern design.

Amsterdam No place in the Netherlands is more than 170 miles (274 km) from Amsterdam, the country's capital, commercial center, largest city, and second-largest port. Amsterdam is the capital of European counterculture. Its relaxed atmosphere (cafés openly sell soft drugs) attracts large numbers of youthful visitors.

The city is built on piles sunk in sand and mud along the banks of the

Amstel River. The old city was built mostly from 1650 to 1720. It is laid out in the shape of an opened fan, with the base along the harbor and the framework made up of three large horseshoe-shaped canals. The canals are connected by hundreds of smaller waterways. The Central Railway Station is in the middle of the horseshoe. Everything within the circle is called the Centrum. The main street, the Damrak, leads from the station to Dam Square, the city center.

The city has some 6,800 architecturally significant houses and buildings dating from the 16th century. The Dutch built tall, narrow gabled houses along the canals, with many windows and beams by which they hoisted goods into upper stories. Families lived on the middle floors, the ground floor served as a workshop, and the attic was a storeplace. The prosperous merchants graced their walls with paintings. They especially liked paintings that idealized their daily lives. Rembrandt van Rijn (1606–1669) was among the artists who moved to the city to satisfy the demand.

Amsterdam has more than forty museums. Its compact size makes sightseeing easy. The best way to get oriented is to take a canal cruise aboard a boat with a glass roof. The city's attractions include

- Dam Square, with the World War II National Monument, a tall obelisk that is a memorial to the country's liberation. Also on the Dam are the Koninklijk Paleis ("Royal Palace") and the Nieuwe Kerk ("New Church"), begun in 1408.
- Rijksmuseum ("State Museum"). Visitors can see Rembrandt's huge painting, *Night Watch*—which many say is the greatest painting of all time—and a selection of Vermeers.
- Van Gogh Museum, a display of the artist's paintings as well as other works of his period.
- Diamond-cutting workshops. The city's famed tolerance attracted Jews expelled from Portugal in the 1500s, and they made Amsterdam a center of the gem trade.
- Anne Frank House, Amsterdam's most popular museum. When Germany invaded the Netherlands in 1940, Anne Frank, a young Jewish girl, hid in an attic for two years until she was discovered and transported to a concentration camp, where she died. Her diary vividly describes the horror of those times.
- *Bruin cafés,* or "brown bars," named for their nicotine-stained walls. These pubs serve snack-type meals.
- *Rosse Buurt* ("Red-Light District"). In the windows at canal level, women (and some men) wait for their customers. They are registered, regulated, taxed, and represented by a union. The famous area can be shocking, but in the day it is generally safe.

North of Amsterdam The land north of Amsterdam is a region of polders, windmills, wooden shoes, and cheese. Day tours visit Volendam and the Alkmaar Cheese Market.

Volendam is on the banks of the **Ijsselmeer** (*EYE sell mere*), the former Zuider Zee. Volendam is known for its costumes, especially the winged lace caps of the women, and for its small port with little wooden houses.

At **Alkmaar** a cheese market is held every Friday morning from mid-April to mid-September. Balls of Edam and Gouda cheese are heaped in piles for wholesale buyers to inspect, sample, and haggle over. Costumed porters haul the cheese to the truck or boat of the buyer.

Bulb Fields Just behind a dune barrier that extends from Alkmaar south to

Tulipomania occurred in Holland in the 1630s when people developed a passion for beautiful bulbs. Prices soared. A single bulb was sold at auction for more than $5,000 in today's dollars. When the boom burst, speculators were ruined.

The Dutch say about their cities, "Rotterdam is the place to make money, Amsterdam the place to spend it, and The Hague the place to talk about it."

the Hook of Holland are the Dutch bulb fields. Ribbed like corduroy, the bulb fields become bright-colored stripes in April and May as tulips come into bloom. Flowers are picked in the evening and auctioned the next morning. At **Aalsmeer** (between Lisse and Amsterdam) 11 million flowers and 1 million plants are sold every day. **Haarlem** is the center of the growing region. South of Haarlem, the world's largest flower display is at **Keukenhof** ("Kitchen Garden") from March through May. The garden includes bulbs and flowering shrubs in a parklike setting.

The Hague Although Amsterdam is the Netherlands' capital, The Hague (*haygh*) is the seat of government and the official residence of the country's monarch. (It is always referred to as "The" Hague.) It is 27 miles (44 km) south of Amsterdam. A dignified place, The Hague is home to parliament and the Peace Palace, and it is the site of the International Court of Justice. It was at the city's Hotel des Indes that famous spy Mata Hari practiced her wiles when the hotel was used as Allied headquarters during World War I.

Just a short tram ride away is **Scheveningen**, a resort on the North Sea. It has wide sandy beaches and the Kurhaus, a huge hotel with restaurants, bars, and a casino. Nearby is **Madurodam**, a Dutch city in miniature. It reproduces well-known buildings from throughout the country at 1/25th their actual size. Also nearby is **Delft**, a compact old town. Its narrow canal-lined streets contrast with a spacious open square with a Gothic church and Renaissance town hall. The town has given its name to the famous blue-and-white pottery and tiles known as delftware.

Windmills Today, only a few original windmills remain. The best place to see them is **Kinderdijk**, near Rotterdam, though they are occasionally part of the landscape in the polder lands north of Amsterdam. Some have been moved and reassembled in open-air museums at **Zaanse Schans** (north of Amsterdam) and **Arnhem** (near the German border).

Luxembourg

The Grand Duchy of Luxembourg, in area smaller than Rhode Island, is bounded by Belgium in the west and France in the south. Three rivers—the Our, Sure, and Moselle—separate it from Germany in the east. Part of the Holy Roman Empire since the 10th century, Luxembourg became an independent duchy in 1354, one of hundreds of such states in medieval Europe. It is the only one to survive today as an independent country.

The hills of Luxembourg are studded with castles and vineyards. It continues to be an agricultural country, but its prosperity depends on international finance. Its residents have the highest per capita income in Europe. Drawn by tax advantages, many financial institutions, including the European Bank, have their headquarters here.

Luxembourg City, the capital and largest city, is dominated by its ancient fortress. The fortifications and the Old Town make for terrific exploring.

The heart of the city is the Place d'Armes. Almost everything the visitor would want to see is within a few blocks of this central point: the palace of the ruling family, the cathedral, and the rambling National Museum. Nearby is the Chemin de la Corniche, sometimes called the *City's Balcony*. It is a promenade built on the ramparts of the old town walls. Next to Castle Bridge lie the ruins of the old fortress and the entrance to the Casemates of Bock, tunnels dug in the mid-18th century to link the city's fortifications.

Travelers can drive to almost any place in the duchy within an hour. The northern highlands were the hunting grounds of emperors and kings. Castles dot the hills; rivers pour off the slopes. Luxembourg claims to have the world's densest network of walking paths. The trails of this storybook land lead to snug country inns with gastronomic delights.

✔ CHECK-UP

The Benelux includes

- ✔ Belgium; Brussels is the capital and largest city and the capital of the European Union.
- ✔ The Netherlands; its capital and largest city is Amsterdam, but The Hague is the seat of government.
- ✔ Luxembourg; its capital and largest city is Luxembourg City.

For travelers, highlights of the Benelux are·

- ✔ Belgium's Grand' Place in Brussels, the medieval cities of Brugge and Gent, and the diamond-cutting center of Antwerpen.
- ✔ The Netherlands' canals, diamonds, cheese, museums, tulips, and windmills.
- ✔ Luxembourg's castles, casemates, and walking trails.

Germany

Landlocked, except for stretches of coast along the North and Baltic seas, Germany has borders with nine European countries (see Figure 10.4). Situated at the crossroads of Europe, the country has been a power since the 8th century, but Germany remained a patchwork of rival kingdoms until the late 19th century when it united as one country. The price of nationalism was high. At the end of World War II, Germany lay in ruins, divided between the East and the West. It was split into two countries until the collapse of communism made reunification possible in 1990.

A *ratskeller* is a restaurant in the basement of a town's *rathaus* ("town hall"). Go there for good, moderately priced food in a traditional setting.

Politically, Germany is divided into states (*Bundesländer*). Geographically, its northern and southern regions differ markedly. Northern Germany is part of the North European Plain. A network of rivers drains the plain into the Baltic. The central part of Germany is a highland area with rugged peaks in the Harz Mountains and fertile valleys. The southern part of the country is mountainous and heavily forested.

Lake Constance forms part of Germany's southern border with Switzerland. The Rhine River, which flows from the lake, forms the border with France in the southwest. In this region the rounded peaks of the **Black Forest** look across to their French counterparts, the Vosges. Germany's most dramatic scenery is in the state of **Bavaria**, in the far southeast on the border with Austria. The area contains numerous alpine peaks, including the **Zugspitze**, Germany's highest mountain.

The Cities

Travelers to Germany can now enjoy famous eastern cities that were difficult to visit when they were part of East Germany. These include **Dresden**, which was destroyed overnight in 1945 by American bombs but lovingly rebuilt; **Leipzig**, where Johann Sebastian Bach (1685–1750) spent most of his musical life; **Meissen**, which is famous for exquisite porcelain; and **Potsdam**, which was once the residence of the Prussian kings. Central Germany includes **Frankfurt**, the financial capital of the country, but not a tourism center. Two cities that do attract tourists are **Berlin**, the reborn heart of Germany, and **Munich** (in the southeast).

Bradenburg Gate, Berlin, Germany

Berlin Berlin (*buhr LIN*) is once again the capital of Germany. It bustles with shops, restaurants, museums, and nightlife. At the end of World War II, the city lay in ruins. The Allies divided the city into four sectors. The Russian sector became East Berlin. The Berlin Wall went up in 1961. In 1989 the wall came tumbling down. Slowly the sectors came together.

Berlin is one of the largest and most spread-out European cities. Things to do include the following:

- Start at Alexanderplatz, once the center of 1920s Berlin and now reemerging as the focal point of the unified city.
- Stroll down *Unter den Linden* ("Under the Lime Trees"), which was built in 1788 as the main thoroughfare of the Prussian empire. At its far end is the Brandenburg Gate, once the symbol of a Germany divided between East and West.
- Visit the Berlin Wall Museum at Checkpoint Charlie, the former crossing point from East to West Berlin.

FIGURE 10.4 Germany

- Go to *Museumsinsel* ("Museum Island"), an island lying between two arms of the Spree River. Outstanding museums include the Pergamon, which houses sculpture and architecture from the Classical world.
- Stay at the Hotel Adlon, which was considered Europe's premier hotel until its destruction during World War II. It has been rebuilt on its former site.
- See the Reichstag, the parliament building gutted by fire in 1933 under suspicious circumstances. The restored structure reopened in 1999, retaining walls that show bullet holes and graffiti scrawled by Russian soldiers when the battle for control of the city raged within the building.
- Shop on the Kurfürstendamm ("Ku'damm," as Berliners call it), one of Europe's busiest streets.
- Reflect at the Kaiser Wilhelm Memorial Church, another symbol of old Berlin. The shell of the tower is all that remains of the church dedicated to Kaiser Wilhelm I (1797–1888).
- Enjoy the culture. The Berlin Philharmonic and the Berlin Opera are acclaimed. Jazz clubs, cabarets, and seasonal events offer plenty to do in the evenings. In the fall, the annual Jazz Fest draws international stars. *Kneipen* ("pubs") feature live music.

ON THE SPOT

Ms. Bergman is a nervous traveler. She anticipates every possible problem and wants you to provide her with reassurance. Her latest question is, "What about security in European airports? I hear the security checkers there are not as thorough as the ones in my home airport."

Security precautions in northern Europe meet international standards. Unfortunately, total safety cannot be guaranteed anywhere in the world. Steer Ms. Bergman to State Department Web sites to avoid any liability problems.

Munich City of beer and baroque and capital of the state of Bavaria, Munich is the place to visit for its relaxed charm. It is also a gateway for excursions into the Bavarian Alps. It is Germany's third-largest city. It keeps some of the character of the Wittelsbachs, the princely family that ruled Bavaria from 1180 to 1918. Munich was also the birthplace of Adolf Hitler's Nazi movement in the 1920s.

Marienplatz is the city's heart. Here is where people meet, to sit out at the café tables or inside the beer halls. The city's oldest and largest beer cellar is the Hofbrauhaus, founded in 1589.

Munich, which calls itself the *Beer Capital of the World*, holds a festival each year that draws millions. *Oktoberfest* happens mainly in September, not October. The fest's activities are at Theresienwiese ("Theresa's Meadow"), where local breweries sponsor gigantic tents that can hold up to 6,000 drinkers.

Munich sights include

- Alte Pinakothek, a treasure trove of classic art.
- Deutsches Museum, one of the world's most important showcases of science and technology.
- Schloss Nymphenburg ("Nymphenburg Palace"), the summer home of the Wittelsbachs.
- Dachau (*DAH kow*), organized in 1933 as the first concentration camp. It became the model for other Nazi death camps.

In southern Germany, the tradition of elaborate pre-Lenten parties called *Fasching* began in the 16th century. It is a time of merrymaking, with fancy-dress balls and people wearing masks. The celebrations start in early January and last until the beginning of Lent.

Other Places to Visit

The German countryside is as varied as its cities. Germany's National Tourist Office (GNTO) has produced information about approximately 150 travel routes through the country, each with a particular cultural or scenic theme, such as the Wine Route, the Glass Route, the German Clock Route, the Classic Route, and the Fairy Tale Road (Märchenstrasse), which passes through towns associated with the stories of the Brothers Grimm. Among the most popular routes are the Castle Road and the Romantic Road.

You can find a list of the routes developed by the GNTO and detailed itineraries on Germany's Web site (www.cometogermany.com). Some of the routes date back to 1927.

The Castle Road Going east from Mannheim (near **Heidelberg**) to Prague in the Czech Republic, the Castle Road is 606 miles (975 km) lined by fortresses, ruins, and monasteries as well as castles. Many of the castles offer overnight stays.

The university city of Heidelberg near the start of the route is a popular stop. The city is on the Neckar River at the edge of the mountains in Germany's south. Heidelberg has a ruined 13th-century castle and associations with the musical *Student Prince*. Over the years the student tavern *Sum Roten Ochsen* ("The Red Ox") has drawn beer drinkers from Mark Twain to Bismarck.

The Romantic Road The Romantische Strasse ("Romantic Road"), which visits places that were important in medieval times, stretches for 220 miles (354 km) between **Würzburg** in the center of Germany to **Füssen** in the foothills of the Bavarian Alps. The journey by private car might take about a week, depending on how many stopovers are selected. Traffic is very heavy on weekends and during the summer.

Frankfurt's international airport is a convenient gateway to the Rhine River and the Romantic Road.

Every town on the road has its special charms and its drawbacks. **Rothenburg**, for example, is a perfect museum town, but it is often overwhelmed with tourists. After the coach tours depart, independent travelers might enjoy a night at the celebrated *Eisenhut* ("Iron Hat"). The luxury hotel is made of four medieval patrician houses joined together.

Two attractions at the road's end near Füssen are the castles of **Hohenschwangau** and **Neuschwanstein**. Hohenschwangau was built in the 12th century and remodeled by Prince Maximilian of Bavaria. Its interior walls feature paintings of the German legends used by composer Richard Wagner for his operas. Wagner often stayed there and was greatly admired by "Mad King" Ludwig II (1845–1886), Maximilian's son.

Neuschwanstein, Germany

Neuschwanstein Castle was the indulgence of King Ludwig. Built between 1886 and 1889 high on a rock, it overlooks mountains near the Austrian border. The unfortunate king enjoyed only 102 days in his castle. Mental illness and eventual suicide by drowning ended his reign. Ludwig's lavish expenditures created great public debt, but his fairy-tale castles are among Germany's most popular tourist attractions (and income producers) today. Two of Ludwig's other castles—Linderhof and Herrenchiemsee—are nearby and of equal interest.

The Bavarian Alps In addition to castles, the alpine area south of Munich has many other attractions. Southwest of Munich is the small mountain town of **Oberammergau** (*oh buhr AH muhr gow*), famous for its production of the *Passion Play*. The production began in 1634 when the town's citizens took a vow to give thanks after they were spared from the plague. The play is performed only one year out of ten (next in the year 2010). Performances last all day, with a break for lunch. Tickets are sold out years in advance. The best chance to get them is to book a tour that includes the play. A visit to Oberammergau is ideal even without the play.

Neuschwanstein Castle was the model for Sleeping Beauty's castle in Walt Disney theme parks.

Garmisch-Partenkirchen are twin towns at the foot of the Bavarian Alps. They form one of Germany's leading winter sports resorts. From the town, a cogwheel train goes to the top of the Zugspitze for a view of three countries.

About 75 miles (121 km) southeast of Munich, near the Austrian border, is the alpine resort town of **Berchtesgaden**. Hitler's retreat, the *Eagle's Nest*, sits on a mountain above the town. It was here, in September 1938, that he met British Prime Minister Neville Chamberlain to discuss peace "in our time."

The Rhine In Germany's west the Rhine River winds northward through a spectacular valley. Steeply terraced vineyards along the river produce delicious white wine. The area is home to famous legends and for centuries has inspired poets, novelists, and composers.

The most scenic part of the river is the stretch between **Mainz** and **Cologne**. To view the Rhine by car, the best route is along the west bank, the site of most of the castles. Small roads have been linked to form a route called the *Rheingoldstrasse* ("Golden Road of the Rhine"). Signposts display a castle and a glass of wine. Count on heavy traffic. Ferries cross the river, excursion boats ply day routes, and longer cruises leave from Basel, Switzerland, to end in Amsterdam, the Netherlands (and the reverse).

Koblenz sits at the meeting of the Rhine and Moselle Rivers, a place known as *Das Deutsche Eck* ("The German Corner"). The Moselle, which runs west to the ancient Roman town of **Trier**, flows through a region of vineyards, ancient villages, and castles.

A *burg* is a fortified medieval structure, today often in ruins. A *schloss* is more like a palace. Many have been converted to hotels.

South of Koblenz, vineyards cover all arable land. Towns such as **Rüdesheim** and **Bingen** are familiar to wine lovers. Near Bingen is the Mäuseturm ("Mouse Tower") on an island in the middle of the Rhine. The tower was named for the wicked bishop who was chased by an irate populace to the tower, where he was eaten by mice.

At the heart of the area is the famed **Lorelei**, a high cliff on the right bank of the river near the town of Saint Goarshausen. The river there is swift and dangerous. Legend says the echo heard at the spot is the voice of a beautiful siren luring boatmen to their death.

The Black Forest The term *Black Forest* (*Schwarzwald*) describes the southwest corner of Germany. It is bounded by the French border to the west, by the German cities of **Karlsruhe** and **Stuttgart** to the north and **Freiburg** to the south, and by the western end of Lake Constance to the east. The region is an area of evergreen forests dotted with fairy-tale towns where the cuckoo clock has been developed into an art form.

If a town's name has the word *bad* in it, it means it has a spa.

Only two centuries ago the Black Forest was one of Europe's wildest stretches of countryside. But then the hot springs enjoyed by the Romans were rediscovered, and the small villages became spas. In the 1800s, it was fashionable for the upper classes to spend a few weeks each year at a spa "taking the waters." **Baden-Baden**, with its casino, became one of the most famous resorts. Black Forest ham and Black Forest cake keep the Black Forest name in the public eye.

✔ CHECK-UP

For travelers, Germany's principal cities include
- ✔ Berlin, Germany's capital.
- ✔ Newly accessible cities of former East Germany.
- ✔ Munich, city of beer and the baroque.

Travelers to the country might enjoy
- ✔ Cruising on the Rhine.
- ✔ Taking the waters in Baden-Baden in the Black Forest.
- ✔ Traveling along the Romantic Road between Würzburg and Füssen.
- ✔ Visiting Munich's Oktoberfest.
- ✔ Viewing King Ludwig's fairy-tale castles in Bavaria.

Switzerland, Liechtenstein, Austria

The German language is but one of many characteristics that Switzerland, Liechtenstein, and Austria share with Germany. Like Germany, they are among the most prosperous and attractive countries on the Continent. They have alpine scenery, medieval towns, art-filled museums, and *gemütlichkeit* ("comfort, coziness, friendliness"). Tie up these goodies with the shining ribbon of the Danube and ornament the package with elegant hotels and good food, and you have Europe's *central region*—a gift to travelers. Figure 10.5 is a map of the region.

Switzerland

Switzerland is a landlocked country in the heart of Europe, in area about twice the size of New Jersey. In no other country do mountains so dominate the landscape. The **Jura Mountains** are in the northwest. Various ranges of the Alps begin in the south; the highest peaks are along the Italian border. Between the mountains, a plateau stretches from **Lake Geneva** in the southwest to Lake Constance in the northeast.

A country made up of separate cantons, the Swiss nation preserves a remarkable sense of unity. It is also famed for its independence. While wars raged in Europe, Switzerland remained neutral. It has not joined the EU or adopted the euro as its currency.

The country has four languages. German is spoken by about 64 percent of the people, and German speakers live in the central, northern, and eastern cantons. French speakers live in the west, and Italian speakers live in the southern canton of Ticino. The fourth language, *Romansh,* a descendant of Latin, is spoken by less than 1 percent of the population.

Switzerland is one of the most prosperous countries in the world. Its location, combined with its political stability and tradition of confidentiality, has made it a center of international finance. It has little flat area for farming, but its Swiss cheese, chocolate, and watches are famous.

In North America, ski areas tend to be high on the mountain. In Europe, you ski all the way down the mountain, which makes for longer runs and less crowding.

Switzerland is a mecca for skiers. The season runs from late December through April, although summer skiing is possible on the high glaciers. Old villages at the center of the resorts provide wonderful après-ski experiences.

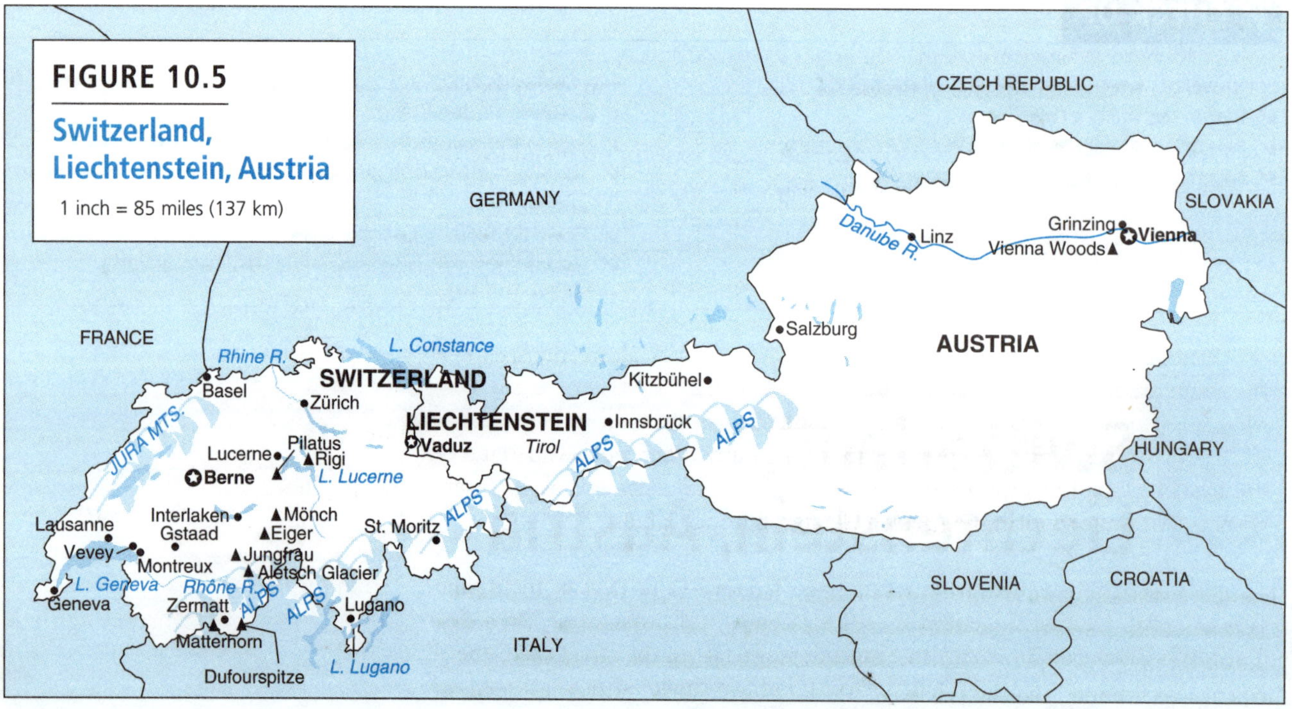

FIGURE 10.5

Switzerland, Liechtenstein, Austria

1 inch = 85 miles (137 km)

Berne Switzerland's capital, Berne (*bairn*), is a small city with medieval charm. Legend says that in the 15th century the local duke named the town after the first animal he killed while hunting. Bears appear on the town's coat of arms, stone bears are on the city's fountains, and real bears are in the town's Bear Pit.

Berne is also known for its Clock Tower, which was part of the original city gate. At four minutes to the hour, a group of mechanical figures parades out of the clock. Father Time beats time while a knight hammers out the hours.

Zürich German-speaking Zürich (*ZUR ihk*) is Switzerland's largest city, and its airport is the country's international gateway. The banking center is set on its own lake on the banks of the Limmat River. The *Bahnhofstrasse* ("Railroad Station Street"), the main street, is lined with elegant shops selling Swiss watches and luxury items. Several churches, museums, and the Old Quarter of town are worth a visit.

Zürich is a place where people enjoy life. The glistening lake, the scent of lime trees in the spring, swans on the river, and sidewalk cafés add to the traveler's pleasure.

Basel On the border with Germany and France, Basel (*BAH zuhl*) is second in size and economic importance to Zürich. It is a river port at the highest point of navigation on the Rhine. The longer Rhine cruises originate or terminate here. Exceptionally rich in museums and art galleries, Basel is the site of Switzerland's oldest university.

Lucerne South of Zürich, Lucerne (*Luzern* in German) is a very popular tourist center. The city straddles the Reuss River as it empties into Lake Lucerne. For generations the city's beautiful lake, promenades, elegant shopping streets, well-run hotels, and mountain vistas have attracted visitors. Lucerne's landmarks include

- The Chapel Bridge. The original 14th-century covered bridge was destroyed in a fire but has been rebuilt.
- The Lion Monument. A dying lion carved on the hillside symbolizes the heroism of Swiss Guards who died defending Louis XVI at the Tuileries in Paris in 1792.
- The Richard Wagner Museum. Wagner (1813–1883) composed some of his greatest music in this mansion beside the lake, about half a mile from the city.

Central Switzerland Resorts Lucerne is a good base for excursions to the cableways and cog railways of the great peaks of **Pilatus** and **Rigi** in central Switzerland. The mountain resorts have snow sports in winter and mountaineering and hang gliding in summer. Summer activities are accompanied by the tuneful music of the bells worn by cows in the high meadows. (The word *alp* means a "high-country pasture.")

Interlaken lies on the valley floor between the lakes of Thun and Brienz. To the south are peaks of the Bernese Alps, most famously the **Eiger** ("Ogre"), the **Mönch** ("Monk"), and the **Jungfrau** ("Maiden")—names that have launched a million postcards. This area, perhaps more than any other, put Switzerland on the tourist map. The mountains are part of a circular ridge enclosing several glaciers that unite to form the **Aletsch Glacier,** Europe's largest.

Geneva At the westernmost tip of Lake Geneva (Lac Léman in French, Genfer See in German), Geneva is the most French of Swiss cities. On a clear day, Mont Blanc (*mohn blahn*) in France is visible from the city. Lake Geneva, with its Jet d'Eau ("Water Jet"), is the focal point of the town.

John Calvin (1509–1564) made Geneva the "Rome of the Protestants." Calvin became virtual dictator at one point, even burning people at the stake who did not agree with him.

The Swiss Alps were climbed for the first time in the mid-1800s, when mountaineering became a sport. Professional guides help people scale the highest peaks. Each year more than 2,000 people climb to the top of the Matterhorn.

Matterhorn, Switzerland

The combination of Swiss efficiency and French grace gives Geneva a chic polish. It is the headquarters of the World Health Organization, the International Red Cross, the International Air Transport Association (IATA), and other international organizations. Geneva has many luxurious hotels, shops selling French fashion, interesting museums, and fine restaurants.

Southwestern Resorts Along the north shore of Lake Geneva are the resort towns of **Lausanne, Vevey,** and **Montreux**. Lausanne is the home of the Swiss Hotel School. Vevey is a wine-producing area. Montreux is known for its mild climate and International Jazz Festival.

Just east of Montreux is the 11th-century Castle of Chillon, its dungeons made famous in Byron's poem "The Prisoner of Chillon." **Gstaad**, one of the most exclusive winter and summer resorts, is also east of Montreux. It is known for visitors who own or rent private chalets.

Zermatt is a car-free resort north of the Italian border. It is ringed by the Pennine Alps—among them Monte Rosa, with its peak, the **Dufourspitze**, the highest point in Switzerland. Its height is overshadowed by the horn shape of one of the world's legendary mountains, the **Matterhorn**. The Swiss–Italian border runs along the mountain's summit.

The *Haute Route* ("High Road") between Zermatt, Switzerland, and Chamonix, France, is one of the most spectacular and challenging hikes in the Alps. The nine-day hike is rated moderate to strenuous by adventure tour companies. Along the route are ten of the twelve highest peaks in Europe, including the Matterhorn and Monte Rosa.

Southeastern Resorts Famous resorts in Switzerland's southeast include Davos, Klosters, Pontresina, Arosa, and **St. Moritz**. St. Moritz has thermal baths—one of which has been used for 3,000 years—and is noted for its winter sports and summer mountaineering. The region can be explored by train or Swiss Postal Buses.

Ticino is the Italian-speaking canton south of the Alps near the border. The climate is subtropical and the atmosphere Mediterranean. The largest city, **Lugano**, is a health and holiday resort on Lake Lugano.

Liechtenstein

The very small country of Liechtenstein (*LIK tuhn stiyn*) is on the east bank of the upper Rhine, sandwiched between Austria to the east and Switzerland to the west and south. Liechtenstein measures about 16 miles (25 km) from north to south and is 4 miles (6 km) wide. Once marshy, it was drained in the 1930s for agriculture. To the east, the foothills of the Alps rise to snowcapped peaks.

Liechtenstein uses Swiss currency and belongs to the Swiss customs union, but it is a fully independent state, known for its decorative postage stamps. It also has a cuisine of its own: rich old-style Austrian-French food in all its buttery glory.

Vaduz is the capital. Once a small market town, Vaduz is now an international finance center due to its liberal taxation laws. Royalty still lives in the 18th-century fortress overlooking the town, parts of which date to the 12th century. It is not open to the public, but you can climb up for the view from the terrace. The thing to do is go to the tourist information office to have your passport stamped with the Liechtenstein crown, buy some beautiful stamps, and send a postcard or two.

Austria

East of Liechtenstein, the area that is now Austria has at various times been an outpost of the Roman Empire, the eastern frontier of Charlemagne's Holy Roman Empire, a part of the kingdom of the Habsburg family (whose members occupied European thrones from the 1200s to the early 1900s), the center of the Austro-Hungarian empire, an independent republic (in 1918), and the eastern point of Germany's Third Reich. Mountainous and landlocked, Austria is bordered by eight countries, as Figure 10.6 shows. The Alps cover two-thirds of the land, stretching from west to east in several ranges. The great Danube (twice as long as the Rhine) meanders eastward across northern Austria.

Music is king in this land of Mozart and the Strauss family. Composers from other countries, including Beethoven and Brahms, studied and worked in Austria under royal patronage. Numerous homes of the great composers survive to be seen, and music festivals are part of the Austrian scene.

This small country is about the size of Maine. The magnificent alpine scenery, together with the cosmopolitan atmosphere and cultural attractions of its cities, makes Austria a major attraction for tourists.

Vienna Austria's largest city and capital is Vienna. It is built on the south bank of the Danube at the head of a narrow fertile plain between the Alps and the Carpathian Mountains.

During the 17th century, a baroque building boom created a legacy of palaces and mansions unequaled in Europe. The Viennese coffeehouse may be another gift from that century. In 1683 the Turks retreated from the city, abandoning a load of coffee beans. Whether this windfall really triggered the opening of the city's first coffeehouse is disputed, but there is no doubt that the Viennese love coffee. Like the pubs of Great Britain, coffeehouses in Vienna bind the community in ways that have no counterpart in North America.

The Danube Canal crosses the city from northwest to southeast. The canal and boulevards make up the horseshoe-shaped Ringstrasse ("Ring Street"), with the canal at the open end. The *Innere Stadt* ("Interior Town"), the ancient heart of the city, and Vienna's most significant buildings are within the Ring. City sightseeing includes

- Hofburg, the Imperial Palace and residence of members of the Habsburg dynasty.
- Hofburgkapelle, the oldest portion of the original palace. The Vienna Boys' Choir performs in the chapel on Sundays and holidays from September to June.
- Spanish Riding School, also part of the Hofburg. Here, beneath elegant chandeliers, the white Lipizzaner stallions perform to the music of Mozart. Tickets must be reserved in advance. The horses are on vacation during July and August.
- Kunsthistorisches Museum, with works by Brueghel, Rubens, Titian, Rembrandt, and Vermeer.
- Home of Sigmund Freud (1856–1939), father of psychoanalysis.
- Kärtner Strasse, the main shopping street, which is closed to vehicular traffic.
- St. Stephen's Cathedral. The diamond-patterned glazed-tile roof dominates the skyline of Vienna. Visitors can take an elevator to the tower's top for a splendid view of the city.
- Staatsoper. The State Opera House was almost destroyed in World War II and has been carefully reconstructed. The season is from September through June. Just behind the opera is the Hotel Sacher, famous for its dessert lover's dream, the *Sachertorte*.

St. Stephen's Cathedral, Vienna, Austria

The Sachertorte is a multilayered cake, filled or spread with apricot jam and then covered with chocolate icing; it is traditionally served with whipped cream. It was created in 1814 by Franz Sacher, chief pastry cook at the Hotel Sacher in Vienna.

Innsbrück, Austria

Vienna's suburbs house the Belvedere, the former summer residence of the Prince of Savoy, and the Schönbrunn Palace, a 1,200-room summer house for the Habsburgs. The famed **Vienna Woods** lie to the west and south of the city.

Nearly as important to Vienna as its coffeehouses are the villages on the outskirts of the city, where rustic restaurants called *heurige* sell new wine, heralded by green boughs above the doors. As the greenery ages, so does the wine. **Grinzing** and Heiligenstadt are destinations for supper and a taste of the grape.

Salzburg West of Vienna, Salzburg is a baroque jewel nestled under its Hohensalzburg Fortress. The castle was begun in 1077. A funicular (incline railway) takes visitors from town to castle. Salzburg is the city where Wolfgang Amadeus Mozart (1756–1791) was born, an event celebrated each year by the great summer music festival. His home is now a small museum.

Familiar to many as the site of *The Sound of Music* film, the Salzburg area is what tourists look for when visiting Austria, and the area does not disappoint.

Tirol Austria's alpine region is in the narrow arm of land between Switzerland and Italy, an area known as the Tirol. **Innsbrück** is the major city. The Alps provide an awe-inspiring backdrop for the green domes and red roofs of the picturesque town. Its medieval Old Quarter, which is closed to cars, features shops in Gothic arcades and the Goldenes Dachl ("Golden Roof"), a three-story balcony topped with gold-plated tiles. Twice host of the Winter Olympics, Innsbrück has extensive sports facilities.

Kitzbühel, one of the best-known alpine resorts, is located midway between Innsbrück and Salzburg. Not just a ski village, it is a small town enclosed within old walls and full of tempting shops and cafés. In summer, golf, tennis, hiking, and horseback riding are in season.

✔ CHECK-UP

The central region of northern Europe includes
- ✔ Switzerland; its capital is Bern, but its largest city is Zürich.
- ✔ Liechtenstein; its capital and only city is Vaduz.
- ✔ Austria; its capital and largest city is Vienna.

For travelers, highlights of the central region include
- ✔ Ski resorts, mountain climbing, or hiking in Switzerland.
- ✔ Stamps in Liechtenstein.
- ✔ Cruises on the Danube.
- ✔ Music near Salzburg.
- ✔ Wine, coffeehouses, and song in Vienna.
- ✔ Winter sports in Innsbrück and Kitzbühel.

Nordic Europe

Five countries make up Nordic Europe: Denmark, Norway, Sweden, Finland, and Iceland (see Figure 10.6). Great distances separate the countries, but historically they have had close ties. Norway, Sweden, and Denmark united in 1397. Sweden broke away in 1523, but Norway remained under Danish rule until 1905. The area is often called "Scandinavia," but Scandinavia refers only to the mountainous peninsula that includes the countries of Norway and Sweden. The residents call the region the Norden and themselves the Norse.

Denmark

The kingdom of Denmark lies between the North Sea and the entrance to the Baltic. It is the smallest of the Norden, about the size of Connecticut, Rhode Island, and Massachusetts combined. Denmark consists of a western peninsula called **Jutland** (*Jylland* in Danish) and an eastern archipelago. The southern part of Jutland is shared with Germany. The major islands of the archipelago are **Fünen** (Fyn) and **Zealand** (Sjaelland). To the east in the Baltic, the island of **Bornholm** is known for its round fortified medieval churches.

Other islands far away also belong to Denmark. The **Faroe Islands** are a small group north of Scotland. **Greenland** is the world's biggest island.

Dunes, lagoons, and sandbars shelter Denmark's west coast from North Sea storms. Denmark is a land of green pastures, blue lakes, and white coastal beaches. The carefully tended farms make up about three-fourths of the country. The roofs of most houses are made of red or blue tiles or thatch. Storks, which the Danes believe bring good luck, build nests on some rooftops. Castles and windmills rise above the land.

Denmark enjoys a high standard of living, education, and culture. The country's extensive social services ensure that the cities have virtually no slums or substandard housing. Both English and German are taught in Danish schools. The country is known for its butter, cheese, bacon, and ham and for its beautifully designed manufactured goods, including furniture, porcelain, and silverware.

FIGURE 10.6 Nordic Europe

A story about the Lur Blowers statue says that the musicians will play beautiful music if a pure maiden walks by. The statue has been in place since 1914, and not a peep has been heard.

In 2000 Denmark and Sweden were linked by a 10-mile (16 km) bridge and tunnel system known as the Öresund link. Three bridges and one tunnel connect Malmö, Sweden, to the Copenhagen airport, slashing travel time between the countries.

Headlights must be on both day and night when driving in any of the countries of Nordic Europe.

Copenhagen Zealand's eastern coast is the site of Denmark's capital and the largest city in the Nordic countries, Copenhagen. The heart of Copenhagen is the Radhuspladsen, as the Danes call their town hall square. City tours depart from the Lur Blowers statue in the square. Tours visit

- Amalianborg Palace, consisting of four identical 18th-century rococo mansions. The changing of the guard takes place at noon in good weather.
- Nyhavn, the harbor area.
- *The Little Mermaid* (*Den Lille Havefrue*). The life-size statue sits on a harbor rock and looks longingly out to sea.
- Stock Exchange, one of the city's most graceful buildings. Its tall wooden spire is fashioned like the carved tails of four dragons.

The capital's famous pedestrian-only street begins from the Radhuspladsen. Narrow Strøget (*STROY et*) winds its way to the city's other main square, Kongens Nytorv, changing names several times. Travelers can satisfy shopping needs along the way.

A summer evening in the Tivoli Gardens is a Copenhagen treat. Tivoli is a combination garden, restaurant area, cultural center, and amusement park in the heart of the city. At dusk thousands of lights illuminate the gardens.

Less than an hour's drive from Copenhagen is Fredensborg Palace, the royal summer residence, and Frederiksborg Castle, which serves as a national historic museum of paintings, furnishings, and tapestries.

Tours from Copenhagen lead north to the castle of Kronborg, near **Elsinore** on the tip of Zealand. The moated castle was built in the 15th century on the end of a promontory that commands the narrowest part of the **Skagerrak** (*SKAG uh rak*), the strait separating Denmark and Sweden. The castle was the setting for Shakespeare's *Hamlet*. Shakespeare never visited the place.

Odense Denmark's third-largest town, Odense, is on the island of Fünen. Most visitors come to the city because it was the birthplace of Hans Christian Andersen (1805–1875), the author of many of the world's best-loved fairy tales, including "The Little Mermaid." Several museums display mementos of his life.

Norway

North of Denmark, Norway's long, narrow landmass wraps around the western part of Sweden and the north of Finland and shares a border with the northwest of Russia. Its northern tip, an area called the **North Cape**, juts into the Arctic Ocean, making it the most northerly part of Europe.

Norway's more than 13,000 miles (20,917 km) of coast are punctuated by deep fjords. The highest mountains and the most spectacular fjords are in the wider southern half of the country. Glacial erosion has flattened some mountains, creating immense plateaus, such as the **Hardangervidda** in south central Norway. Toward the west coast is the Jostedal Ice Field, with its flowing glaciers.

About 150,000 islands lie off the coast. Some are only rocky reefs called *skerries*, which shield the coastal waters from stormy seas. The **Lofotens** are the largest island group. The Maelstrom Current sweeps between the two outermost Lofotens, sometimes forming dangerous whirlpools.

Norway's spectacular landscape supports a relatively small population. The country's most-visited areas are Oslo, Bergen, and the western fjords.

Oslo Oslo, the capital and largest city, is in the southeast near the Swedish border. It covers a great area, but only a portion of the city is developed. The rest, known as the *Oslomarka*, is a recreation area. No other capital in Europe has more ski resorts and hiking trails within its city limits. An elevator takes tourists to the top of the Holmenkollen Ski Jump in west Oslo for a view from the takeoff point of the jump. Most visitors gain new admiration for ski jumpers.

Town Hall, the city landmark, is lavishly decorated inside and out by Norway's leading artists. The king of Norway presents the Nobel Peace Prize in the Town Hall. Oslo's other attractions include

- Edvard Munch (1863–1944) Museum, with works of Norway's most famous painter.
- Fram Museum, displaying the ship used by Roald Amundsen (1872–1928) for Arctic expeditions.
- Kon-Tiki Museum, with the balsa raft used by Thor Heyerdahl (1914–2002) in his 1947 expedition to Polynesia.
- Vigeland Sculpture Park, dedicated to the art of Gustav Vigeland (1869–1943). He used granite and bronze to carve figures that depict the human life cycle from cradle to grave.
- Viking Ship Museum, with 9th-century ships and objects from the Viking era.

Alfred Nobel (1833–1896) was an inventor, engineer, industrialist, and, most of all, a pacifist. The irony is that he invented dynamite.

Bergen When it opened in 1909, the train line known as the Bergensbanen was considered an amazing engineering feat. A journey on the train from Oslo to Bergen (*BEAR gn*) still amazes. The high spot of the trip, awesome in any season, comes above the timberline. The terrain is so hostile that you can sense the struggle it must have been to build and maintain this iron link from east to west. Snowdrifts linger into June.

Norway's second city is very much an overgrown fishing village. Bergen's prized medieval buildings along the harbor are of wood. It lies on the shore of its own fjord, with seven majestic mountains forming a perfect backdrop. Freighters, ferries, cruise liners, and visiting yachts share the harbor. Bergen is the embarkation point for the Norwegian Coastal Voyage, the mail boat route from Bergen north to **Kirkenes** and the **North Cape**.

A city excursion visits Troldhaugen ("Hill of Troll"), composer Edvard Grieg's (1843–1907) home, and Fantoft Stavekirke, one of the wooden stave churches. The churches are the most famous examples of medieval Norwegian architecture. Their distinguishing feature is the use of vertical planks, or "staves," either anchored in the ground or connected to a base. The interiors of some churches look like an upside-down ship's hull. Carved gables have dragons' heads that resemble the prow of a Viking ship. Some thirty stave churches have survived, all in southern Norway.

A stave church in Norway

Fjord Country Bergen is in the center of fjord country, which extends from **Stavanger** in the south to **Kristiansund** in the north; less spectacular fjords continue all along the coast. The Norwegian fjords equal the Swiss Alps as one of Europe's natural wonders. The longest, **Sogne Fjord**, extends inland for more than 100 miles (161 km). The **Hardanger Fjord** is known for beautiful fruit trees that blossom in the spring. The **Geiranger Fjord** is thought by many to be the most beautiful. The Seven Sisters waterfall tumbles down the mountainside into the fjord. Cruise ship passengers in the fjord marvel at the walls of rock and the tiny farms clinging to ledges high up on the mountainsides.

Sweden

Sweden occupies the eastern part of the Scandinavian Peninsula. It is roughly the size of California, but the land is thinly populated. Its people enjoy a high standard of living and a highly developed welfare system.

Sweden is a land of lakes, swift rivers, flower-filled meadows, and rocky offshore islands. Northeast Sweden has low plateaus that drop away to a coastal plain along the Gulf of Bothnia but rise to the **Kjølen Mountains** along the Norwegian border. The mountains and plateaus of the north account for two-thirds of the country's landmass; they are thickly forested and rich in minerals.

Central Sweden stretches between **Stockholm** in the east and the country's second-largest city, **Göteborg** (*YUH tuh bawrg*), in the southwest. Four large lakes cover much of this region, the most heavily populated part of the country. South of the lakes is a rich plain.

Stockholm Sweden's capital and largest city is splashed across a string of

CLOSE-UP: THE NORDIC COUNTRIES

Who is a good prospect for a trip to Nordic Europe? Individuals, couples, or groups with Nordic heritage would enjoy a return to their roots. Those who love scenery and the challenge of soft or hard adventure will find plenty to satisfy their wants. Timid travelers will feel comfortable in countries where health and safety standards are high.

Why would they visit the Nordic countries? They offer familiar cultures and dramatic landscapes, and it is easy to get around. English is the second language spoken by many.

Where would they go? Visitors might choose a coastal cruise or a land-based trip. An itinerary to the cities of three Nordic countries might include the following.

Day 1 Overnight flight.

Day 2 Arrive in Copenhagen, Denmark.

Day 3 Copenhagen. Guided tour of the city. Optional tour to the castles of North Zealand in the afternoon. In the evening, enjoy a meal and entertainment in the Tivoli Gardens.

Day 4 Copenhagen–Arhus. Morning drive over the world's longest suspension bridge to Fünen. Visit Hans Christian Andersen's home at Odense. Then go to Jutland. Arrive in Arhus in time for shopping and exploring.

Day 5 Arhus–Göteborg. From the tip of Denmark, board a ferry for a three-hour ride across the Kattegat to Göteborg, Sweden.

Day 6 Göteborg–Stockholm. While crossing Sweden, you see pastoral scenes and major industrial centers.

Day 7 Stockholm. Tour the city. Afternoon at leisure for shopping or an optional excursion.

Day 8 Stockholm–Karlstad. Along the way, visit Gripsholm Castle; then go west through the Lake District. Overnight in Karlstad on Lake Vänern.

Day 9 Karlstad–Lillehammer, Norway. Take a scenic drive across the border.

Day 10 Lillehammer–Laerdal. Spend a day in the mountains and forests. Stop at a stave church.

Day 11 Laerdal–Bergen. Embark at Laerdal for a two-hour cruise on the Sogne Fjord. Land at Gudvangen, and motor past spectacular waterfalls to arrive in Bergen by noon. Afternoon tour of the town and the home of Edvard Grieg, Norway's famous composer.

Day 12 Bergen–Telemark. Morning free in Bergen. Afternoon drive along the Hardanger Fjord, then into the mountains where skiing was invented.

Day 13 Telemark–Oslo. Enjoy beautiful scenery on the way to Norway's capital.

Day 14 Oslo. Tour the city. Visit Frogner Park to see Gustav Vigeland's famous sculptures.

Day 15 On your way home.

When is the best time to visit? The tourist season runs from May to September and peaks in July and August, when the weather is warmest. May and September offer the advantage of generally clear skies and smaller crowds. With the midnight sun, midnight may seem more like twilight, and dawn comes early. The weather can be fickle, and rain gear and waterproof shoes are recommended even in the summer.

The travelers say, "We went to Alaska last summer. Isn't this the same?" How would you respond? The latitude may be the same, but the culture is very different. Alaska is the frontier; Nordic Europe is part of an old civilization. Alaska's landscape has few people and little development. Nordic Europe has towns, castles, people, fine dining and accommodations, shopping, culture, and history.

islands that drain into the Baltic, an area referred to as the *Archipelago*. Bridges connect the fourteen islands that form Stockholm, known as the *City between the Bridges*.

The heart of Stockholm is Gamla Stan ("Old Town"), a cluster of old buildings and narrow cobbled streets. The main streets are traffic free and lined with boutiques and antique shops. It is the site of the huge Royal Palace. The palace has more than 600 rooms. The royal family spends most of its time in Drottningholm Palace, in a suburb of the city. Parts of both palaces are open to the public.

The Town Hall is the landmark and emblem of Stockholm. Each November the Nobel Prize banquet is held in the hall.

Gotland is the largest island in the Baltic. Once a Viking stronghold, this Swedish island has ninety-two churches, all built before 1350.

Dalarna Northwest of Stockholm to the Norwegian frontier is one of Sweden's vacation regions, **Dalarna**. The area is popular for cross-country skiing. Brightly colored wooden horses are the traditional local craft.

Glass Country Sweden's glass country is in an area of lakes and forests near **Växjö**, in the southeast. Because the forests offered an unlimited supply of wood for firing furnaces, the glass industry started here. The Swedish glass companies, including Orrefors and Kosta Boda, open their plants to the public.

Göta Canal The Göta (*YUH tuh*) Canal flows across southern Sweden, linking Göteborg to Stockholm. The canal was dug by soldiers in the 18th century. Ships traverse the route on four-day cruises via a series of canals and lakes and even a stretch of inland sea. Canal-side towpaths serve as bicycle paths, which allow passengers to get off and ride along. Cruises operate from mid-May to the beginning of September. Early booking is advisable. It is a slow trip, not for the hyperactive.

Finland

Except for the small section of Norway that cuts it off from the Arctic Ocean, Finland is the most northerly country in continental Europe. (Look again at Figure 10.6.) Finland borders northern Sweden to the west and Russia to the east. In the south, the Gulf of Finland separates it from Estonia.

The Finnish name for the country, *Suomi*, means "land of lakes and marshes." Lakes cover one-tenth of the country, and they are linked by extensive river systems. Most of the country is forested, chiefly with pine, spruce, and other evergreens. In the north, the barren tundra is rich in berry-producing plants, especially the unique cloudberries.

Finland's culture and language are distinct from the other Nordic countries. For long periods it was ruled by either Sweden or Russia, but neither was able to subdue the Finnish spirit. The arts—particularly the music of Jean Sibelius (1865–1957) and the folk epic *Kalevala*, compiled by Elias Lönnrot (1802–1884)—played an important part in establishing a distinctive identity. Finnish design skills, particularly in glasswork and bright Marimekko fabrics, are famous.

The Finnish sauna has been used to get warm, keep clean, give birth, smoke meats, and gather the community. After the steam bath, bathers cool off by taking a cold shower or jumping in a lake.

Helsinki On the south coast, Helsinki, *Daughter of the Baltic*, is a clean city with wide boulevards. The old town was destroyed by fire several times, and each time totally rebuilt. As a result, the city is very modern. Most of its sights can be seen in a half-day tour.

Kuappatori, the Market Square, is located near the harbor. Within walking distance can be found the Presidential Palace and the Uspenski Cathedral. The Temppeliaukio Church, known as the Rock Church, is carved out of rock in the side of a hill. From the street or air, only the copper dome is visible.

Lapland The area of Norway, Sweden, and Finland north of the Arctic Circle is called **Lapland**. It has no formal boundaries. Traditionally, it was inhabited by the Lapp people who followed the reindeer herds, but today Lapps make up only about 10 percent of the population. The Lapps call themselves the *Sami*.

Rovaniemi is the capital of Finnish Lapland. It is just a few miles south of the Arctic Circle. Visiting Santa Claus Village and obtaining *Crossing the Line* certificates are popular tourist excursions.

Iceland

Iceland is an island just south of the Arctic Circle in the North Atlantic; in size it is slightly smaller than Kentucky. Its culture derives from 9th-century Viking settlers. The country and its people have grown up in a harsh, volcanically active environment. It is the only place on earth where you can see the tectonic plates of both Europe and North America. Earth tremors are frequent.

Glaciers cover one-tenth of the land. The largest is **Vatnajökull**, in the southeast. Only 1 percent of the country is forested.

Iceland is sometimes called the *Land of Ice and Fire* because large glaciers lie next to steaming hot springs. Hot springs are common—most notably at **Geysir** (after which all shooting springs are named), in the southwest. Similar springs gave the capital and largest city its name—**Reykjavik** (*RAY kyuh veek*), or "Smoky Bay."

Most of Iceland's people live in the narrow coastal plain near Reykjavik. Outside the city the Blue Lagoon is one of the country's most popular attractions. It is a natural pool of mineral-rich geothermal water located in the middle of a lava field. The warm waters (approximately 90° F [35° C] year-round) are known for their beneficial effect on the skin.

Iceland is only a short distance from the East Coast of North America, and Reykjavik stages major international conferences. Day-trippers can ride horses to the mountains, fish, hike, view volcanoes, or experience a hot-spring dip. Tours feature Iceland's national wonders, including glaciers, waterfalls, lava fields, and volcanoes, with accommodations provided sleeping-bag-style in huts.

✔ CHECK-UP

Nordic Europe includes

- ✔ Denmark; its capital and largest city is Copenhagen.
- ✔ Norway; its capital and largest city is Oslo.
- ✔ Sweden; its capital and largest city is Stockholm.
- ✔ Finland; its capital and largest city is Helsinki.
- ✔ Iceland; its capital and largest city is Reykjavik.

For travelers, highlights of Nordic Europe include

- ✔ Evening in Tivoli Gardens in Copenhagen.
- ✔ Oslo and the Viking ships.
- ✔ Bergen and the Norway fjords.
- ✔ Sweden's Archipelago or a slow cruise on the Göta Canal.
- ✔ Travel through the lakes and forests of unspoiled Finland.
- ✔ Steaming hot springs of Iceland.

Planning the Trip

Few obstacles face the traveler to northern Europe. Travelers are diverse in age and interests and likely to have high expectations. They want top-notch service, a chance for meaningful cultural exchanges, and fulfillment of their special interests. Meeting their needs requires deep involvement in the destination.

When to Go

Although summer is peak travel season, the Benelux, Germany, Austria, and Switzerland are year-round destinations, offering something unique in every season and plenty of indoor activities. For most travelers, Nordic Europe is a destination for the summer months, when the temperatures are mild and the days long. In winter, tourist attractions in these countries reduce their hours or shut down.

Preparing the Traveler

To help travelers get the most out of their trips, check with each country's tourist office for the availability of sightseeing passes. Certain passes give visitors free or reduced-price admission to museums and attractions.

Visitors entering a country that is a member of the European Union (EU) have to show passports only once. After that, going from one EU country to another is as easy as passing from one U.S. state or Canadian province to another.

Health standards in northern Europe are very high and health problems of little concern to travelers.

Money The euro is the currency of most European Union countries, but several have opted not to adopt the euro as yet. See the Fact File (Appendix A) for a review of each country's currency.

Travelers should plan to exchange the bulk of their funds in Europe, where the exchange rate is usually better than at home. If they need cash immediately on arrival (say, for a taxi to the hotel), most gateway airports have currency exchange facilities or ATMs open at all hours. Banks usually offer better exchange rates than hotels or exchange shops that say "cambio, wechsel, change," although banks also impose a fee.

Credit cards are accepted throughout northern Europe, and ATMs are widely available.

Language Northern European languages have many local variations. Although English is a popular second language, it is always helpful to know a bit of the country's language, at least a few common words and phrases. There is no shortage of phrase books and dictionaries.

Customs Other differences can be challenging for the first-time visitor. The 24-hour clock is used to express time, Celsius to express temperature, and the metric system to express weights and measures. The electrical current is 220–240 volts instead of the 110–120-volt system used in North America.

➤ **PROFILE**

Famous Potteries, Porcelains, and Crystals of Northern Europe

Factories that once made crystal and china for royalty now attract the traveler. For beautiful design, see

- ➤ Arabia china and Iittala glass in Finland.
- ➤ Orrefors, Kosta Boda, and other glass companies in Sweden.
- ➤ Delft and Makkum in the Netherlands.
- ➤ Meissen, Rosenthal, and Nymphenburg porcelain in Germany.
- ➤ Royal Copenhagen porcelain in Denmark.
- ➤ Val-St-Lambert crystal in Belgium.

➤ **PROFILE**

Shopping Opportunities in Northern Europe

In northern Europe, you might look for

- ➤ Bulbs and cheese in Holland.
- ➤ Diamonds in Amsterdam and Antwerpen.
- ➤ Georg Jensen silver in Denmark.
- ➤ Lace and chocolates in Belgium.
- ➤ Modern design in the Nordic countries.
- ➤ Precision instruments, such as cameras and binoculars, in Germany.
- ➤ Soviet Army uniform articles in Berlin.
- ➤ Swedish crystal.
- ➤ Watches, scissors, music boxes, and Swiss Army knives in Switzerland.

➤ PROFILE

Cuisine of Northern Europe

Travelers might enjoy trying

- In Holland, *rijsttafel* (rice with spicy side dishes and sauces, originally from Indonesia), *broodjes* (sandwiches), and herring served raw with a garnish of onions and pickles.
- In Belgium, *carbonnades* (stews made with beer); also handmade chocolates filled with fresh cream.
- In Germany, *wurst* (sausage) and *schnitzel* (breaded veal cutlet).
- In Switzerland, cheese. Try *fondue* made from cheeses combined with white wine and kirsch, served at the table in a pot with bread cubes for dipping; or *raclette*, toasted cheese served with potatoes, pickles, and onions.
- In Scandinavia, *smörgåsbord*. The buffet starts with cold dishes (smoked fish or reindeer), moves on to hot foods, and ends with fruit and cheeses.
- In Denmark, *smørrebrød* (open-faced sandwiches) and flaky Danish pastries.
- In Finland and Sweden, cloudberries, relatives of the raspberry that grow only above the Arctic Circle.

TABLE 10.2

International Airport Gateway Cities

Country	Principal Gateway
Austria	Vienna (VIE)
Belgium	Brussels (BRU)
Denmark	Copenhagen (CPN)
Finland	Helsinki (HEL)
Germany	Berlin (THF), Frankfurt (FRA) Munich (MUC)
Iceland	Reykjavik (REK)
Luxembourg	Luxembourg City (LUX)
The Netherlands	Amsterdam (AMS)
Norway	Oslo (OSL)
Sweden	Stockholm (STO)
Switzerland	Zürich (ZHR)

Dining traditions and meal hours are similar to those in North America. Breakfast ranges from a roll and coffee to a full buffet, especially tempting in the Nordic countries, where lavish buffets include eggs, meats, fish, pickles, and a huge assortment of breads.

The usual drink is beer, wine, or mineral water. Beverages such as iced tea are generally not available, but soft drinks such as colas are. In the coffeehouses, whipped cream piled on top of tempting pastries is simply irresistible.

Transportation

Northern Europe has one of the world's best transportation systems. Networks of airlines, canals, highways, railroads, and rivers criss-cross the region.

By Air Table 10.2 lists cities that are the major international air gateways of northern Europe. European airlines fly throughout the Continent and the world. The airlines of Denmark, Norway, and Sweden form the Scandinavian Airlines System (SAS). Finnair is the airline of Finland, and Icelandic of Iceland.

The Benelux is served by the Netherlands' Royal Dutch Airlines (KLM). It merged with Air France in 2004. Other mergers are on the horizon.

The central region has Germany's Lufthansa and Switzerland's Swiss International Air Lines. Austrian Airlines runs domestic and international flights from its headquarters near Vienna.

By Water Canals expand the options for travel in northern Europe. The Kiel Canal in northern Germany connects the Baltic with the North Sea, shortening the trip around Denmark for ships cruising from England to Russia. The Main-Danube Canal connects the major rivers of central Europe. Regularly scheduled boat services operate on most rivers, lakes, and coastal waters.

Northern European cruising areas are along the Norwegian coast to the North Cape and in the Baltic. The season lasts from late May to late September. The Norwegian Coastal Voyages and Baltic ferries operate year-round.

For more than 100 years, the Norwegian Coastal Voyage has been captivating travelers who like informal scenic adventures. The ships sail along the *Hurtigruten*, Norway's marine highway. Ships depart every day from Bergen and sail to Kirkenes and back, covering thirty-four ports each way. The round-trip voyage takes twelve days, but the voyage can also be taken as a seven-day northbound trip or a six-day southbound passage. Shore excursions include visits to Tromsø's Polar Museum, the Lofoten Islands, and the reindeer lands of the North Cape.

A network of ferries serves ports in the Baltic. European ferries can be big. They carry cars, tour buses, and freight along with 2,000 or so passengers. Onboard are restaurants, bars, duty-free shops, casinos, and several classes of overnight accommodations.

Ships sail from Easter to late October on the Rhine and Moselle Rivers. The river ships accommodate from 130 to 210 passengers and stop along the way and each night so passengers can take in local attractions.

A Danube cruise between Vienna and Linz, or on to Passau, Germany, travels through some of the most romantic and scenic parts of Austria. The voyage from Vienna to Passau takes two days. Short excursions are available.

In the summertime, more than 100 ships ply the Swiss lakes. Free or reduced-rate services are available for rail-pass holders.

By Rail Europeans rely on trains for their city-to-city travel, and the trains are modern and comfortable. In addition to simple one-way tickets, there are about a dozen pass options, the most well known being the Eurailpass. Choices range from multiday to weeklong and monthlong passes. Students and those over age sixty-five qualify for discounts. Passes must be purchased in North America prior to departure. Rail Europe is the official Eurailpass representative in the United States. A pass entitles travelers to board a train, but they must also have reservations (at additional cost) for seats on popular trains and for sleeping accommodations on overnight trains. Rail passes also include discounts on steamers sailing on Lake Constance and on a number of Eurobus routes.

InterCity (*IC*) passenger trains serve large and medium-size cities; *EuroCity* (*EC*) trains connect countries. Stations are located conveniently in city centers. Many cities—such as Amsterdam, Brussels, Frankfurt, and Zürich—have rail service from the airport to their city rail stations.

Some tips for travelers:

- Rail schedules are displayed in the 24-hour clock.

CLOSE-UP: A RIVER CRUISE FROM VIENNA TO AMSTERDAM

Who is a good prospect for a river cruise? Individuals, couples, and groups looking for something new would enjoy this in-depth exploration of the legendary rivers. Mature travelers are good prospects.

Why would they take this cruise itinerary? The voyage was not possible before the Main-Danube Canal opened in 1992. Many experienced travelers will find this a new attraction. It offers a chance to relax while seeing several countries and beautiful scenery. There is no need to pack and unpack daily as on independent or motorcoach tours.

Where would they go? Thanks to the canal, it is possible to travel from Vienna to Amsterdam by ship. A typical journey might include the following itinerary.

Day 1 Overnight flight to Vienna.

Day 2 Arrival and greeting by a tour representative, who helps you transfer to your ship. Sailing time is 1700.

Day 3 Travel through the Wachau region to the ornate Benedictine abbey at Melk, the inspiration for Umberto Eco's novel *The Name of the Rose*.

Day 4 Passau, the meeting place of the Danube, Inn, and Ilz Rivers, and the market town of Romans and emperors. Take a walking tour through the city.

Day 5 Regensburg, Germany's largest and best-preserved medieval city.

Day 6 Kelheim. Transfer to a small ship for a scenic trip through the Danube Gorge.

Day 7 Nuremberg. The walled city is the site of 13th-century buildings.

Day 8 Main-Danube Canal. Sail the canal to Bamberg, a city dating from 902.

Day 9 Würzburg. Visit fortresses and museums. At night the ship hosts wine tasting and a lesson in German vintages.

Day 10 Wertheim, the meeting place of the Main and Tauber Rivers.

Day 11 Aschafenburg–Heidelberg. A motorcoach tour takes you to the university city. You rejoin the ship in Mainz.

Day 12 Mainz–Rüdesheim. In the evening, visit the city's Drosselgasse wine alley.

Day 13 Koblenz. The meeting of the Rhine and Moselle is the site of Festung Ehrenbreitstein, Germany's largest fortress.

Day 14 Cologne. Enjoy shopping and nightlife in a big city.

Day 15 Amsterdam. The boat is your hotel for city exploring. Farewell dinner.

Day 16 On your way home.

When is the best time to cruise? The season runs from late April to October, when the weather is best. Hundreds of folk festivals take place during this period. Summers are usually sunny and mild, although you should be prepared for cloudy and wet days.

The travelers object, "Won't it be frustrating floating by interesting towns when we want to stop and explore?" How would you respond? River cruises are designed with overnight or daytime stops at the most interesting towns and attractions.

- Accommodations should be reserved as far in advance as possible.
- Written communication shrinks the language barrier. Write out your destination and questions before dealing with the ticket seller.
- Seating is either first- or second-class. First-class costs more but has more space.
- Verify your train's departure station. Brussels has three, and even Switzerland's little Interlaken has two.
- Clip luggage to the train's overhead rack to foil thieves if you leave your seat.
- Prices of sleeping accommodations are not included in rail passes.
- Budget travelers on overnight trains might consider a *couchette,* a berth in a sleeping compartment shared by three to five people and monitored by an attendant.
- Plan on carrying your own luggage. Porters are extremely rare.

By Road A network of excellent highways serves most of Europe. Travel is on the right. Rental cars come with standard shift unless automatic is specifically requested (at a surcharge). Models are smaller than American cars, and air-conditioning is rare. Cell phone use is prohibited while driving in several countries. Gas is sold in liters, and prices tend to be about four times those found in the United States.

Perhaps the best-known highways are the German superhighways called *autobahns.* On about one-third of the autobahns, speed limits are posted. On the rest, authorities recommend that drivers keep to about 81 miles (130 km) per hour, but many drivers ignore that advice. The left lane is designated for high-speed traffic. If you are in that lane and moving too slowly, drivers tailgate and flash their lights when they want to pass. Move over!

In the Alps, roads wind considerably, and hazardous weather closes some roads in winter. For some tunnels through mountain passes, trains transport cars while the passengers remain inside (rather like going through a very long car wash).

Most countries have bike paths in both rural and urban areas. Tourists can rent bikes by the hour, day, week, or longer at train stations or bicycle shops in a rent-here/leave-it-there arrangement.

Drivers in foreign countries need maps printed in the local language. While whizzing by on the autobahn, you might easily miss the turnoff to Munich if you did not know its German name, *München*.

Accommodations

Northern Europe has modern hotels and superior deluxe properties, but tourists may be more excited by the prospect of a stay at a castle, fortress, or manor house. Few people can afford to live in the family castle anymore. Their loss is the traveler's gain.

In German-speaking countries, there are numerous *gasthöfe* or *gasthäuser* (country inns); pensions or *fremdenheime* (guest houses); and, at the lowest end of the scale, *zimmer* (rooms in private houses). Most hotels have restaurants, but those describing themselves as *garni* provide only breakfast. Among the most delightful places to stay and eat are the aptly named Romantik Hotels and Restaurants. All are in historic buildings and are personally run by the owners.

Special accommodations of the Nordic countries include inns called *kro* in the Danish countryside. Many are located in centuries-old buildings that range from rustic and unpretentious to divinely elegant. Norway's *rorbuer,* originally built for fishermen, are rented to tourists who want a unique getaway to fish, bird-watch, or merely relax in an out-of-the-way locale. Finland's accommodations include vacation villages similar to condominiums.

Iceland has a variety of farm/stay accommodations. Some properties are modest homes with shared baths; others are more modern. Almost all offer sweeping views, home-cooked meals, and lots of time for relaxing, walking, fishing, or horseback riding.

CHAPTER WRAP-UP

SUMMARY

Here is a review of the objectives with which we began the chapter.

1. **Describe the environment and people of northern Europe.** Northern Europe is blessed with natural and created attractions. The sea is central to the region. It helped form the irregular coastline around the Scandinavian and Jutland Peninsulas and the fjords of the west coast of Norway. In the Lowlands, the enterprising Dutch have reclaimed land from the sea. Rivers such as the mighty Rhine have made Rotterdam an important port. Alone in the Atlantic, the volcanically active environment of Iceland has produced unmatched geological attractions.

   The Great European Plain crosses northern Europe in a band that extends from the Benelux countries eastward to Russia and that includes Denmark and the south of Sweden. The plain rises in the south to the Alpine Mountain System, which dominates southern Germany, Switzerland, Liechtenstein, and Austria.

   Except for the part of Norway, Sweden, and Finland north of the Arctic Circle, northern Europe has a warmer climate than other continents at the same latitude. The area has four seasons. The alpine countries have heavy snow in winter, and the higher peaks are snow-covered all year.

   The history of the people of northern Europe is long and varied. It extends from the Roman Empire to the present-day European Union.

2. **Locate each country's principal gateway and major cities.** In the Netherlands the gateway is Amsterdam. The Hague, however, is the seat of the Netherlands' government. In Belgium, Brussels is the gateway as well as the capital of the EU. It offers the beautiful medieval Grand' Place as well as a sophisticated atmosphere. Other Belgian cities—particularly Antwerpen, Gent, and Brugge—immerse the traveler in medieval Europe with their guild houses and town halls. In Luxembourg, Luxembourg City is the gateway and the site of fascinating fortifications.

   Germany has three gateways: Frankfurt, Munich, and Berlin. Their lively atmosphere and museums attract many tourists.

   Switzerland's gateway is Zürich. Berne, Basel, Lucerne, and Geneva are also well known to tourists, in part because of their convenience as a base for cruises on the Rhine or for travel to mountain resorts. Austria's gateway is Vienna, also the site of palaces, coffeehouses, and the Spanish Riding School.

   In Nordic Europe, gateways are Copenhagen, Denmark; Oslo, Norway; Stockholm, Sweden; Helsinki, Finland; and Reykjavik, Iceland. Copenhagen is the region's largest city. Its Tivoli Gardens are known for summertime evening entertainment.

3. **Describe the key attractions that the region offers travelers.** Travelers are drawn by ancestral ties, historic sites, museums, and activities that match their special interests. Belgium has sophisticated cities such as Brussels and an alluring countryside. Windmills, canals, museums, and springtime floral displays attract tourists to the Netherlands. Luxembourg is a compact country dotted with castles and vineyards.

   Germany's delights include a cruise on the Rhine, a visit to the resorts of the

Black Forest, travel on the Romantic Road, or outdoor recreation in the Bavarian Alps. King Ludwig's castles are a plus.

Switzerland, Liechtenstein, and Austria have the best in winter sports facilities plus charming alpine surroundings. In summer, outdoor offerings include music festivals, golf, tennis, hiking, hang gliding, and mountaineering. Each offers museums, a range of accommodations, fine dining, shopping, and plenty of evening activities.

The Nordic countries' scenery includes the gentle landscape of Denmark, the beautiful fjords of the west coast of Norway, the mountains and meadows of Sweden, the forests and lakes of Finland, and the dramatic geysers and volcanoes of Iceland.

4. Provide or find the information needed to plan a trip to northern Europe. Northern Europe has few travel obstacles, and information is readily available. Cruising options—including cruises along the Norwegian coast and the Baltic as well as river cruises—should be kept in mind. Castles, fortresses, and manor houses are available as accommodations. Other choices include gasthäuser in Germany as well as the Romantik Hotels. Denmark offers kro; Norway, rorbuer; and Iceland, farm/stays.

QUESTIONS FOR DISCUSSION AND REVIEW

1. Food for thought: Ralph Waldo Emerson wrote, "We come to Europe to be Americanized." What do you think Emerson meant by that?

2. How has the natural environment of northern Europe affected the leisure activities of its population?

3. What natural features have helped and hindered the development of land transportation systems in northern Europe?

4. How will the development of a united Europe affect tourism?

2) Winters have short days & frigid weather conditions - good for skiing & indoor cultural activities. Summers have long days - good for outdoor activity

3) Rivers provided communication links. The mountainous terrain was not good for agriculture but was good for industrial developments.

4) border crossings easier. One currency.

Exam

CHAPTER 11

Eastern Europe

- The Baltic Region: Poland, Estonia, Latvia, and Lithuania
- The Heart of Europe: Czech Republic and Hungary
- The Russian Federation
- Other Destinations in Eastern Europe

OBJECTIVES

When you have completed Chapter 11, you should be able to

1. Describe the environment and people of eastern Europe.
2. Identify eastern Europe's most-visited attractions.
3. Provide or find the information needed to plan a trip to eastern Europe.

No landform clearly marks off eastern Europe. The division between east and west has been based less on geography than on culture and on who managed to conquer what piece of real estate. After World War II, the division between east and west was based on which were communist countries and which were not.

Then, in 1989, the Berlin Wall came down. Within months, Russia's empire crumbled. Estonia, Latvia, Lithuania, Ukraine, and Belarus—which had been part of the Soviet Union—became independent countries. In 2004 eight eastern European countries (Czech Republic, Estonia, Hungary, Latvia, Lithuania, Poland, Slovakia, and Slovenia) entered the European Union.

Although the collapse of communism was swift, the development of tourism has been slow. In most of eastern Europe, tourism is a fairly young industry. Visitors should not expect that travel in the region will be as smooth and easy as in western Europe.

The Environment and Its People

Figure 11.1 shows a map of eastern Europe. The region is enclosed in the south by the **Black Sea** and the **Caucasus** (*KAW kuh suhs*) **Mountains**. In the east, the **Ural** (*YUR uhl*) **Mountains**, the **Ural River**, and the **Caspian** (*KAS pee uhn*) **Sea** form the arbitrary division between Europe and Asia.

The Baltic Sea is in the region's northwest. Bordering it are the Baltic States (**Estonia**, **Latvia**, **Lithuania**), **Poland**, and a small piece of the **Russian Federation**. In the central region east of Austria and Germany are five landlocked countries: the **Czech Republic**, **Slovakia**, **Hungary**, **Belarus**, and **Moldova**. **Bulgaria**, **Romania**, and **Ukraine** border the Black Sea. The gigantic Russian Federation stretches from the Black and Caspian Seas in the south to the Barents Sea in the north, extending east into Asia to the Pacific.

It is no longer correct to say "the Ukraine." The use of *the* implies that the country is a province rather than an independent country.

The Land

Eastern Europe is known more for its land than its coastline. The Great European Plain continues almost without interruption to Siberia, Russia's immense territory in northern Asia. For centuries invaders flowed over the prairies (known as steppes), with no major landforms to block the way.

In the south is the Alpine Mountain System. It includes the **Balkans** of Bulgaria and the **Carpathians** (*kar PAY theons*) of northern Slovakia, southern Poland, western Ukraine, and Romania. The Caucasus Mountains in the southeast extend from the Black Sea to the Caspian. The range's chief peak is **Mount Elbrus**, at 18,510 feet (5,642 m), Europe's highest mountain.

Eastern Europe also includes some impressive bodies of water. In the southeast, the Caspian Sea is the world's largest inland body of water. It is a great salt lake below sea level and has no tides and no natural outlets. In contrast, the Black Sea to the west is connected to the Mediterranean through the Bosporus (*BAHS puhr uhs*) Strait, the Sea of Marmara, and the Dardanelles Strait.

The region also boasts Europe's longest river, the **Volga** (*VOHL guh*), which begins southeast of St. Petersburg in Russia and flows south to the

FIGURE 11.1

Eastern Europe

The rivers that flow into the Caspian Sea produce most of the annual Russian harvest of sturgeon, whose precious eggs become caviar.

FIGURE 11.2

Milestones of Eastern European History

BC Slavic tribes and Magyars roam throughout the region.

AD 395 The Christian Church splits into the Roman Catholic Church and the Eastern Orthodox Church.

1147 A village is established on the site of modern Moscow.

1200s–1400s The Mongols conquer Russia and invade Hungary and Poland.

1500s Ivan the Terrible (1530–1584), the first Russia ruler to use the title *tsar* formally, reigns.

1680s–1725 Peter the Great introduces Western customs, culture, and technical achievements to Russia.

1700s Russia becomes a world power ruled by Catherine the Great.

1867 The dual monarchy of Austria-Hungary is established.

1917 The Russian Revolution takes place.

1918 Czechoslovakia is created from part of Austria-Hungary after World War I.

1939 Germany invades Poland to begin World War II. Bulgaria, Hungary, and Romania join the Axis.

1945–1990 Soviet-led dictatorships control Eastern Europe.

1986 Chernobyl nuclear reactor in Ukraine explodes.

1991 The Soviet Union formally dissolves. Satellite republics become independent nations.

1993 Czechoslovakia divides into the Slovak Republic and the Czech Republic.

2004 Czech Republic, Estonia, Latvia, Lithuania, Hungary, Poland, the Slovak Republic, and Slovenia join the European Union.

Caspian Sea. Another important river, the **Don**, flows to the Black Sea. The Volga-Don Canal links the Caspian and Black Seas.

The Climate

Countries in the heart of Europe have cold winters, with snow and frequent fog. The most unpleasant winter weather comes when bitterly cold winds blow from Russia. In countries in the south, spring and early summer are generally the wettest time of year. Much of the summer is pleasantly warm.

In the Baltic region, winter cold is greatest toward the east and in the southern mountains; the coast has slightly milder winters and cooler summers. Precipitation is distributed year-round. Snow covers the ground for much of the winter.

Russia's climate is less varied than its vast size might suggest, but conditions do vary with latitude and elevation. The dominant feature is the extreme winter cold. The harsh Russian winter helped defeat invaders such as Napoleon and Hitler, and it affects almost all aspects of Russian life. Anyone proposing to visit Russia between late October and April should take boots and appropriate winter clothing. Surprisingly, Russia's summers are warm, even hot. The transition between winter and summer comes quickly.

The People and Their History

Many groups have battled back and forth to gain control of eastern Europe. Countries did not exist in their present form until the 20th century (see Figure 11.2). See the Fact File in Appendix A for information about the countries today.

Important characteristics of the region are rooted in the events of AD 395, when Christianity split into two branches—Eastern Orthodox and Roman Catholic. Roman Catholic missionaries introduced the Roman alphabet in the western part of the region; Orthodox missionaries taught the Cyrillic alphabet in the east. The Roman Catholic Church claimed authority over monarchs; the eastern churches taught Orthodox Christians to obey their rulers. As a result, the Russian nobility was able to increase its power over the people, and class structure became firmly entrenched.

In the 1200s, Mongol horsemen came out of the east. The Mongols cut parts of the region off from Western influences. Poland, the Czech Republic, and Hungary maintained contact with western Europe, but Russia was isolated from the spirit of the Reformation and Renaissance.

During the 1500s and 1600s, the Ottoman Turks moved in from the south. They ruled parts of southeastern Europe for about 300 years. They were Muslims, and they spread Islam throughout their land, including parts of Russia. Russia dealt the Ottomans a series of defeats during the late 1700s, and little by little, the Ottomans lost their empire.

By the 19th century, Russia had a vast empire, but the authoritarian rule of the tsars and disruptions caused by wars fed revolutionary stirrings. Unrest during World War I forced Tsar Nicholas II (1868–1918) to abdicate; he was later executed by revolutionaries. The Bolsheviks, led by Lenin (1870–1924), withdrew Russia from World War I and set up a communist government, the Union of Soviet Socialist Republics.

After World War II, as the eastern European countries were liberated from German occupation, the Soviet Union helped communists take control of their governments. The Baltic States were absorbed into the Soviet Union.

Others became satellite nations, dominated by the Soviet Union although nominally independent.

Tourism during these years was tightly regulated. The state owned the airlines, ground transportation, hotels, and restaurants, and it employed the tour guides. Independent travel was restricted. For security reasons, even maps were difficult to obtain. Palaces and historic sites fell into disrepair. All this changed with the dissolution of the Soviet Union in 1991.

✔ CHECK-UP

Major features of the environment of eastern Europe include

- ✔ Great European Plain.
- ✔ Ural Mountains, separating Europe and Asia.
- ✔ Caspian Sea, Caucasus Mountains, and Black Sea in the south.
- ✔ Europe's highest mountain, Mount Elbrus.
- ✔ Europe's longest river, the Volga.

Eastern Europe is noted for

- ✔ Centuries of invasions and warfare.
- ✔ Diverse religions and alphabets.
- ✔ History of authoritarian rule.
- ✔ Tourism once stifled by state-controlled restrictions but now slowly regaining ground.

The Baltic Region

Poland, Estonia, Latvia, and Lithuania, which border the Baltic Sea, appeal to people who have traveled extensively and want to see new and different territory. Figure 11.3 shows a map of the area.

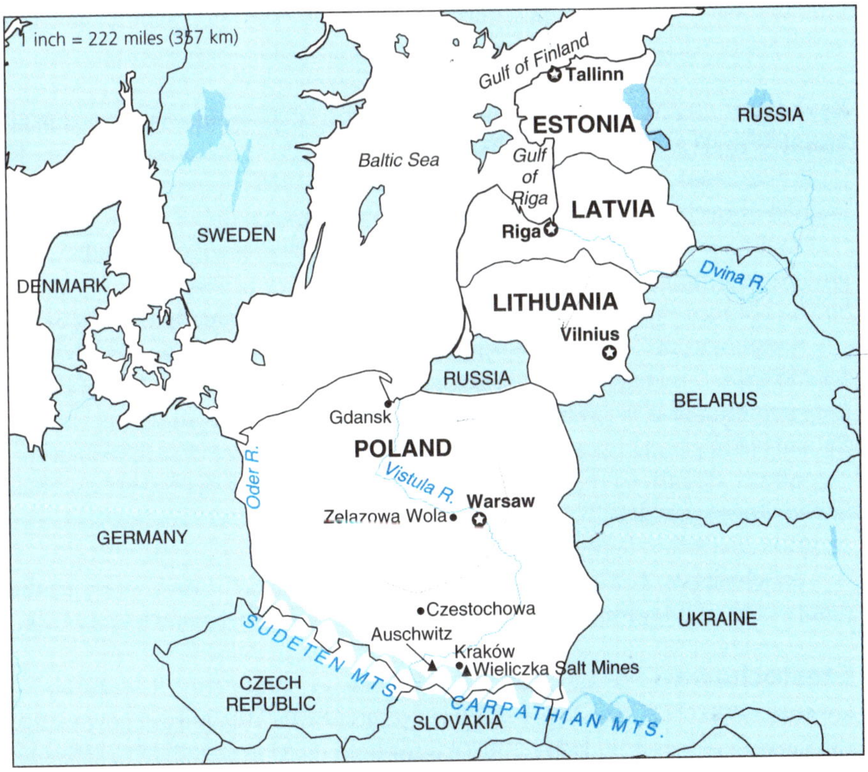

FIGURE 11.3

The Baltic Region

Poland

Poland's north coast is on the Baltic Sea, and it has land borders with seven countries: Germany, the Czech Republic, Slovakia, Ukraine, Belarus, Lithuania, and Russia.

In size Poland is smaller than the state of New Mexico. Except for the mountains, Poland is low-lying. Many rivers drain the land; the most significant is the **Vistula** (*VIHS choo luh*), which flows through Warsaw to the Baltic. It empties into the sea near **Gdansk**, an industrial city that gave birth to Solidarity, the trade union movement of the 1980s that marked a first step in the unraveling of the Soviet Union.

Wilanow Palace, Warsaw, Poland

Warsaw Poland's capital and largest city is Warsaw. At the end of World War II, it was in ruins. Polish architects were determined to re-create the oldest part of the city. Architectural studies and the work of Bernardo Bellotto (1720–1780), an artist who had painted detailed cityscapes, allowed them to achieve their goal.

Skyscrapers and modern stores surround Warsaw's Old Town, with its façades rebuilt in 17th- and 18th-century designs and its interiors constructed with modern conveniences. Warsaw's attractions include

- Wilanow Palace, in Old Town. Its paintings, furniture, and Museum of Posters display Poland's excellence in the graphic arts, especially in poster design.
- Cathedral of St. John, a 14th-century church in Gothic style.
- Lazienki Palace, built in the 18th century as a royal residence, now restored with a monument to a Polish famous son, composer Frédéric Chopin (1810–1849).
- Marie Curie Museum, dedicated to the woman who conducted pioneering studies in radioactivity (her term) with Pierre Curie. Madame Curie (1867–1934) died of leukemia; some papers in her laboratory are still believed to be radioactive.

Frédéric Chopin was born in **Zelazowa Wola**, a tiny village west of Warsaw, and lived there for twenty years before leaving for Paris and international fame. On Sunday mornings during the summer, pianists perform in the parlor where Chopin composed his waltzes, polonaises, and mazurkas.

Kraków Unlike Warsaw, Kraków (*KRAK ow*) was spared destruction during World War II. A city with a turbulent history, Kraków has some of Poland's most treasured architecture and art. Since the 1970s, car traffic has been banned from the city's core to protect its architecture from pollution.

Kraków's Market Square is dominated by the *Sukiennice* ("Cloth Hall"). The ground floor functions as a market; upstairs is a gallery of Polish art. At Market Square's eastern end, the Gothic spires of St. Mary's Church reach to the heavens.

Overlooking the city is the Royal Palace on Wawel Hill, home of Polish kings for 500 years. It is Poland's most important historic site, the first in a line of castles and ruins known as the *Trail of the Eagle's Nests*. The cathedral on Wawel Hill was the seat held by Archbishop Karol Wojtyla until his election as Pope John Paul II.

About 10 miles (16 km) from Kraków, the **Wieliczka Salt Mines** are among Europe's oldest. Beginning in the 17th century, miners sculpted statues of saints, kings, and heroes out of the rock salt.

Auschwitz is west of Kraków. Some 4 million people were killed at the notorious concentration camp. The site has been made into a national museum.

Czestochowa Between Warsaw and Kraków, the hilltop monastery of Czestochowa (*chess toe COW wah*) has dominated its Warta River town since the monastery was founded in 1382. Pilgrims come to see the Black Madonna, an icon of the Virgin Mary said to have been painted by St. Luke. At 0600 and 1530 each day, the Madonna is unveiled to the roll of drums and trumpets.

Every hour on the hour, a bugle call from the spire of the Church of the Virgin Mary in Kraków fades after four short notes, just as it did in the 13th century. The city lookout was attempting to blow a warning that the Mongols were about to attack when an arrow pierced his throat.

Baltic States

The Baltic States of Estonia, Latvia, and Lithuania were seized by the Soviet Union in 1940 and made Soviet republics. In 1991 each broke free. Although the region does not have famous attractions, its peace and quiet may be just what some travelers are looking for.

Estonia The most northerly, smallest, least densely populated, and most westernized of the three Baltic States is Estonia (*es STOH nee uh*). It is bordered by the Baltic Sea, Russia, and Latvia. Farmland covers about 40 percent of the country, forest about 30 percent, swamp 20 percent, and cities 10 percent.

Tallinn (*TAHL lyn*) is the capital and largest city. It is across the Gulf of Finland from Helsinki, a four-hour trip by hydrofoil. Once an important city of the Hanseatic League, Tallinn is a medieval enclave with red roofs, pointed towers, and onion-bulb steeples. The Town Hall, built in the 14th and 15th centuries, dominates the town center. Toompea Castle overlooks the town.

German and Polish domination from the Middle Ages on suppressed the country's literary tradition. In its place, folk music played an important part in maintaining Estonian culture. Villages have their own choirs, many of a professional standard. Every five years a song festival in Tallinn attracts thousands of singers and hundreds of thousands of listeners.

Latvia South of Estonia, Latvia (*LAT vee uh*) is another country of low hills, lakes, swamps, and forests, in area slightly larger than West Virginia. Its beaches are popular local vacation areas, although the Baltic water is cold.

The river highway of the Baltic States has been the **Dvina** (*dvee NAH*), which rises west of Moscow, passes through Latvia, and flows into the sea at **Riga** (*REE gah*), the capital. "Its banks are silver and its bed is gold," said Ivan the Terrible. Ivan failed to control Latvia, but over the years others—including the Germans, Poles, Lithuanians, Swedes, and Soviets—were more successful. Riga is Latvia's largest city. It is rich in history and culture, with buildings of Gothic, baroque, classical, and Art Nouveau style. (Table 11.1 describes these styles.)

Lithuania Lithuania (*lih thoo AY nee uh*) is the largest and southernmost of the Baltic States. Like its neighbors, the country is flat or gently rolling, with lakes and rivers.

In the 12th century, Lithuania was a large and powerful country, but by 1386 it seemed likely to become part of Russia, while nearby Poland was in danger of being gobbled up by the Habsburg empire. To avert this, politicians decided to merge the countries. They arranged the marriage of Prince Jogaila of Lithuania to eleven-year-old Princess Jadviga of Poland. He was three times her age, known for murdering a number of relatives, and pagan, but that hardly mattered. As part of the deal to gain Poland, Jogaila had to become a Christian and convert Lithuania. Jadviga hated her husband and died childless at twenty-four, but Christianity flourished.

Vilnius (*VIHL nee uhs*) is Lithuania's capital and largest city. It is inland in the far southeast corner of the country. Vilnius has one of the region's best-preserved old towns. Its most striking feature is the Upper Castle and the Tower of Gedimnas, named for the prince who supposedly founded the town in response to a howling wolf that appeared to him in a dream.

ON THE SPOT

Mr. and Mrs. Pilsudski eagerly booked their tour to the Baltic States a year in advance. Since then, they have been reading about the region and have come up with many questions. Their latest is quite appropriate: "Since we booked this tour so far in advance, what happens if the dollar falls before departure and prices rise? Will the tour operator charge more?"

Look for tours that guarantee that prices will not change. A price guarantee is a benefit to the traveler. Tours without guarantees are subject to price increases due to currency fluctuations and energy surcharges.

TABLE 11.1

Catalog of Common Architectural and Decorative Styles

Style	Period	Characteristics
Art Deco	1920–1930	Geometric shapes, smooth lines, streamlined forms
Art Nouveau	1890–1910	Nongeometric curves influenced by forms found in nature
Baroque	1500s–1800s	Ornate decoration and large-scale curving forms
Byzantine	300s–1400s	Chuches with plain exteriors, elaborately decorated interiors, and large central domes
Classical	500 BC–AD 300s	Style of architecture of ancient Greece and Rome
Gothic	1000s–1400s	Pointed arches, flying buttresses, stone vaults, and stained-glass windows
Neoclassical	Mid-1700s	Based on a renewed interest in ancient Greece and Rome
Rococo	1700–1780	Extravagant art and decoration; the final phase of baroque
Romanesque	800–1100	Round arches and vaulted ceilings

✔ CHECK-UP

The Baltic region includes
- ✔ Poland; its capital and largest city is Warsaw.
- ✔ Estonia; its capital and largest city is Tallinn.
- ✔ Latvia; its capital and largest city is Riga.
- ✔ Lithuania; its capital and largest city is Vilnius.

For travelers, highlights of the Baltic region include
- ✔ Warsaw's Old Town.
- ✔ Kraków's Market Square.
- ✔ Black Madonna of Czestochowa.
- ✔ Song festivals in Estonia.
- ✔ Beautiful Riga in Latvia.
- ✔ Rural Lithuania and the Old Town of Vilnius.

Czech Republic and Hungary

Two of the brightest spots of central European tourism are the Czech Republic and Hungary. Both have plenty of places to see and things to do. Their travel infrastructure is years ahead of that of neighboring countries, and they strongly promote tourism.

Czech Republic

The Czech Republic occupies the land of the ancient kingdoms of Bohemia and Moravia. It is bordered by Slovakia, Poland, Germany, and Austria (see Figure 11.4). In area the country is about the size of Maine. Its scenery includes the **High Tatras**, which are among the most spectacular mountains

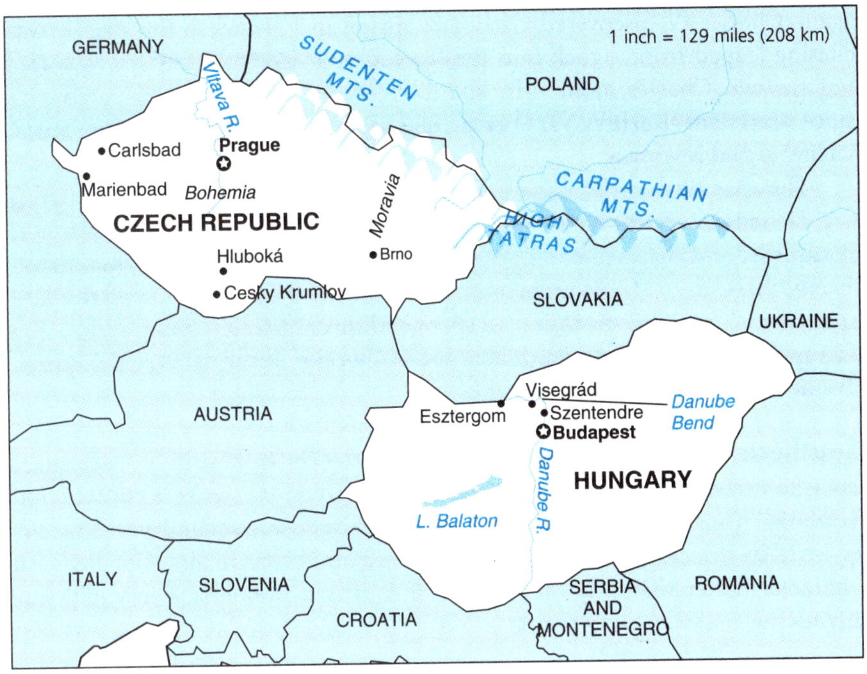

FIGURE 11.4

Czech Republic and Hungary

in Europe. The tourist areas are the plateau of **Bohemia** in the west and the lowlands of **Moravia** in the east.

"Good King Wenceslas" is the patron saint of the Czech Republic. He helped convert Bohemia to Christianity but was murdered by his heathen brother.

Prague The capital, Prague (*prahg*), is the country's largest city and a top attraction. It is a center of culture and learning and was a favorite city of the Habsburg emperors.

Prague is built on seven hills bisected by the **Vltava** (Moldau) **River**. Sometimes it is called *Prague the Golden*; sometimes *Prague, the City of 100 Spires*. The German poet Goethe called it the "prettiest gem in the stone crown of the world." It is a living architectural museum, a mix of Romanesque, Gothic, classical, baroque, rococo, neoclassical, and Art Nouveau architectural styles (look again at Table 11.1).

Old Town, the historic center of Prague, is on the right bank of the Vltava. A tour of Prague might start at Old Town Square, where the astronomical clock chimes each hour as twelve tiny Apostles march around the face, followed by the grim figure of death tolling the bell. The clock's ornate face shows three sets of time: Central European Time, Old Bohemian Time, and Babylonian Time.

Old Town Square, Prague, Czech Republic

Many buildings in Old Town are national monuments. The Royal Way was the processional route for the Habsburgs' coronation ceremonies. A pedestrian route on the way leads from Old Town Square to Charles Bridge, the city's most familiar monument. Built in 1357, it was the only connection between the two halves of Prague for 400 years. Charles Bridge links the city even today, although motor traffic is no longer allowed on the bridge.

Visitors cross the river to climb to Prague Castle. The castle's spires can be seen from virtually anywhere in Prague. It is more of a complex than a castle. Its most famous attraction is St. Vitus Cathedral, the country's largest church. The castle complex is the seat of government as well as the center of the city's religious and cultural life.

The Spas In western Bohemia, elegant resorts built around natural hot springs, once the playground of European aristocracy, are attracting visitors

Marienbad, Czech Republic

again. Charles IV discovered Carlsbad's spring in 1347 when the stag he was chasing leaped from a rock into the Sprudel, the oldest of Carlsbad's twelve hot springs. Charles named the spa for himself, and it has prospered ever since. **Carlsbad (Karlovy Vary)** is the largest spa, but **Marienbad (Mariánské Lázne)** is better known.

The spas offer carbonic, alkaline, saline, ferrous, and mineral gas waters for disorders of the digestive and nervous systems, painful vertebral syndrome, and diseases of the respiratory tract, kidneys, and urinary tract. The health claims of European spas always surprise Americans, who think of spas as someplace to go to be pampered while shedding a few pounds. The European full spa treatment takes several weeks. Ibsen, Chopin, Kipling, Twain, and Goethe went to Marienbad.

In Marienbad, the seventy-three-year-old poet Goethe fell in love with seventeen-year-old Ulrike and sought her hand. When her mother discreetly moved the family away, Goethe wrote his "Elegy of Marienbad," one of the most passionate of his love poems.

Southern Bohemia Its lakes and woods have made southern Bohemia a favorite holiday area. Attractions include the towns of **Cesky Krumlov** and **Hluboká**. Their castles are adorned with the round towers and pointed caps so loved by directors of horror films. Cesky Krumlov has retained its medieval character better than any other town in southern Bohemia. Every alleyway invites the visitor to tarry awhile.

Brno Situated in the southeast, Brno (*BUR noh*) was once the capital of the kingdom of Moravia. It guarded the trade routes to the Baltic and Black Seas.

In 1805 three armies faced each other in the Battle of Austerlitz, just east of town. Napoleon's French forces defeated the regiments of Austria and Russia, opening the way for Napoleon to rule central Europe. Each year on December 2, thousands take part in a reenactment of the *Battle of the Three Emperors.*

North of Brno is a karst region, a landscape of romantic gorges and caves carved out of the limestone by underground rivers.

Hungary

People have lived in Hungary for thousands of years. In size, the country is smaller than Pennsylvania. On its borders are Slovakia, Austria, Slovenia, Croatia, Serbia and Montenegro, Romania, and Ukraine, as Figure 11.4 shows.

Western Hungary has hills and low mountains, but most of eastern Hungary is a flat plain. The plains are called the *puszta* ("barren or deserted"), a place where traditionally dressed cowboys continue to herd horses (and tourists). Horseback riding is a popular activity across the wide-open spaces.

Lake Balaton, central Europe's largest lake, lies among the gently rolling hills of western Hungary. Its north shore is noted for wineries and spas. The scenic surroundings make the lake one of Hungary's most popular vacation spots.

Budapest is a lively city at night. Bars and pubs have sprung up throughout the city. Most casinos offer gambling in hard currencies only.

Budapest Budapest, Hungary's capital and largest city, is bisected by the Danube River. **Buda**, on the river's south side, is the older, more graceful section, with cobbled streets and medieval buildings situated on the hills overlooking the water. **Pest** is on the flatlands of the river's north side and is packed with an array of hotels, restaurants, and shopping areas. Attractions of the city include

- In Buda, Castle Hill (Várhegy), a long, narrow plateau crowned by the Budavári Palota ("Buda Castle Palace"). The palace, first inhabited in the 13th century, is home to the Ludwig Museum, the Hungarian National Gallery, and the Budapest History Museum.

CLOSE-UP: THE CZECH REPUBLIC AND HUNGARY

Who is a good prospect for a trip to the Czech Republic and Hungary? The region appeals to travelers with roots in the region who want to see their ancestral homeland, to those with interest in the architecture and cultural attractions of Prague and Budapest, and to those with special interest in the history of the region.

Why would they visit central Europe? It combines the mystique of the romantic East with the creature comforts of the West. The tourism infrastructure is comfortably in place.

Where would they go? You might recommend a tour with stops in some of the region's most interesting destinations. A typical escorted tour might cover the following territory.

Day 1 Depart for Warsaw, Poland.

Day 2 A tour representative meets you at the airport and escorts you to the hotel. After an afternoon to relax, gather with your group for dinner and the escort's briefing.

Day 3 Warsaw. Tour the city with a local guide. Dine at the home of a Polish family.

Day 4 Warsaw. A day at leisure or an optional tour. Chopin piano recital at night.

Day 5 Warsaw–Czestochowa–Kraków. Motorcoach to Poland's holiest shrine. Arrive in Kraków by early afternoon. Dinner includes folk music.

Day 6 Kraków. Morning tour of the city. Optional afternoon tour to Auschwitz.

Day 7 Kraków. Day free to relax or explore. An optional afternoon tour goes to the Wieliczka Salt Mines, an underground art gallery.

Day 8 Kraków–Prague. Travel through vineyards and valleys, with a lunch stop in the city of Brno, an area inhabited in prehistoric times. Prague by nightfall.

Day 9 Prague. Morning tour of Old and New Town (which is actually 600 years old). Evening includes a Vltava River dinner cruise.

Days 10–12 Prague. Days free with optional tours to nearby castles.

Day 13 Prague–Budapest. Motorcoach to Hungary, with a lunch stop in the Slovak capital of Bratislava.

Days 14–16 Budapest. Morning city tour on Day 14. Full-day tour to the Danube Bend by boat and motorcoach on Day 15. Day 16 at leisure for last-minute shopping. Farewell dinner.

Day 17 Transfer to airport for flight home.

When is the best time to go? The tourist season is from May through September. Major cultural events take place during the fall. The early spring is often wet and windy.

The travelers ask, "What are all these optionals?" How would you respond? Optionals allow tour operators to keep prices as low as possible. Final documents usually provide a list of optionals and their prices so that tour participants can plan which ones they want and budget accordingly.

- Fishermen's Bastion, built in 1905 and named after the guild of fishermen responsible for defending the Royal Palace during the Middle Ages. Its seven turrets represent the seven Magyar tribes who founded the country.
- Matthias Church, a 13th-century church next to the very modern Budapest Hilton. The hotel's sensitive design incorporates the ruins of the church.
- Chain Bridge, the most beautiful of the Danube's bridges. It was built twice: once in the 19th century and again after it was destroyed in World War II.
- In Pest, Parliament Buildings, which dominate the banks of the Danube.
- Opera House. Composer Franz Liszt (1811–1886) was the first president.
- St. Stephen's Basilica, a massive basilica built in the 19th century, one of Pest's chief landmarks.

Gerbeaud is a Budapest coffeehouse dating from 1858 that astounds visitors with its scrumptious confections. The seven-layer chocolate cake or the cherry strudel? Yum!

The Danube The Danube (*Duna* to Hungarians) forms part of the border between Hungary and Slovakia. Travelers can travel on the river by jetfoil, hovercraft, or slow boat. North of where it divides Buda from Pest, the wide river twists through a narrow valley that many consider the loveliest stretch of the river. The *Duna Kanyar* ("Danube Bend") is between **Esztergom** and **Visegrád**. Much of Hungarian history took place in the area, and historical, cultural, and architectural treasures have been preserved. **Szentendre** is the tourist center. Only 12 miles (19 km) from Budapest, it is linked to the city by commuter rail service.

✔ CHECK-UP

The major cities of the Czech Republic and Hungary include
- ✔ Prague, the Czech Republic's capital and largest city.
- ✔ Budapest, the capital and largest city of Hungary.

Highlights of the region include
- ✔ Old Town of Prague.
- ✔ Spas of Carlsbad and Marienbad.
- ✔ Castles in Bohemia.
- ✔ Buda on the hill and Pest on the flatlands, divided by the Danube River.
- ✔ Lake Balaton, Hungary's busy summer resort.
- ✔ Danube Bend north of Budapest.

Russian Federation

Sprawling across the easternmost part of northern Europe and occupying the whole of northern Asia, the Russian Federation is the world's largest country (see Figure 11.5). The land is so vast that someone can be dining in St. Petersburg (formerly Petrograd, formerly Leningrad, and originally St. Petersburg) near the Finnish border at the same time someone is having breakfast in Vladivostok (*vlad uh VAHS tahk*) in the far east. Russia has coastlines along the Arctic Ocean, Pacific Ocean, Sea of Japan, Sea of Okhotsk, Caspian Sea, Black Sea, and Gulf of Finland. Its mainland has borders with twelve other countries.

Siberia, the vast region in northern Asia, makes up about 75 percent of the land but has only about 20 percent of the people. Russia has Europe's highest mountain, Elbrus; its longest river, the Volga; and in Asia, the world's deepest lake, **Baikal** (*by KAHL*). Despite its gigantic dimensions, most of the landscape is quite monotonous. The Ural Mountains that separate Europe from Asia are worn-down rounded hills.

Peter Carl Fabergé (1846–1920) won fame for his designs of decorative objects made from gold, silver, and Russian gemstones. His most famous pieces are jeweled eggs that were made for the tsars.

Between the 9th and 16th centuries, the country was under constant invasion from east and west. In turn, the Russians took land from the invaders. The tsars ruled from their *kremlin* (generic name for "fortress") in Moscow. In 1713 Peter I (the Great) moved the capital to St. Petersburg, where it remained until 1918, when the Bolsheviks made Moscow the capital again.

The Cities

Sir Winston Churchill, trying to describe Russia in 1939, wrote that the country was "a riddle wrapped in a mystery inside an enigma." Travelers seeking to solve the riddle usually begin their journey in the cities of **Moscow** and **St. Petersburg**.

Moscow The Moscow River, for which the metropolis was named, flows through Russia's capital and largest city. Day cruises on the river are popular.

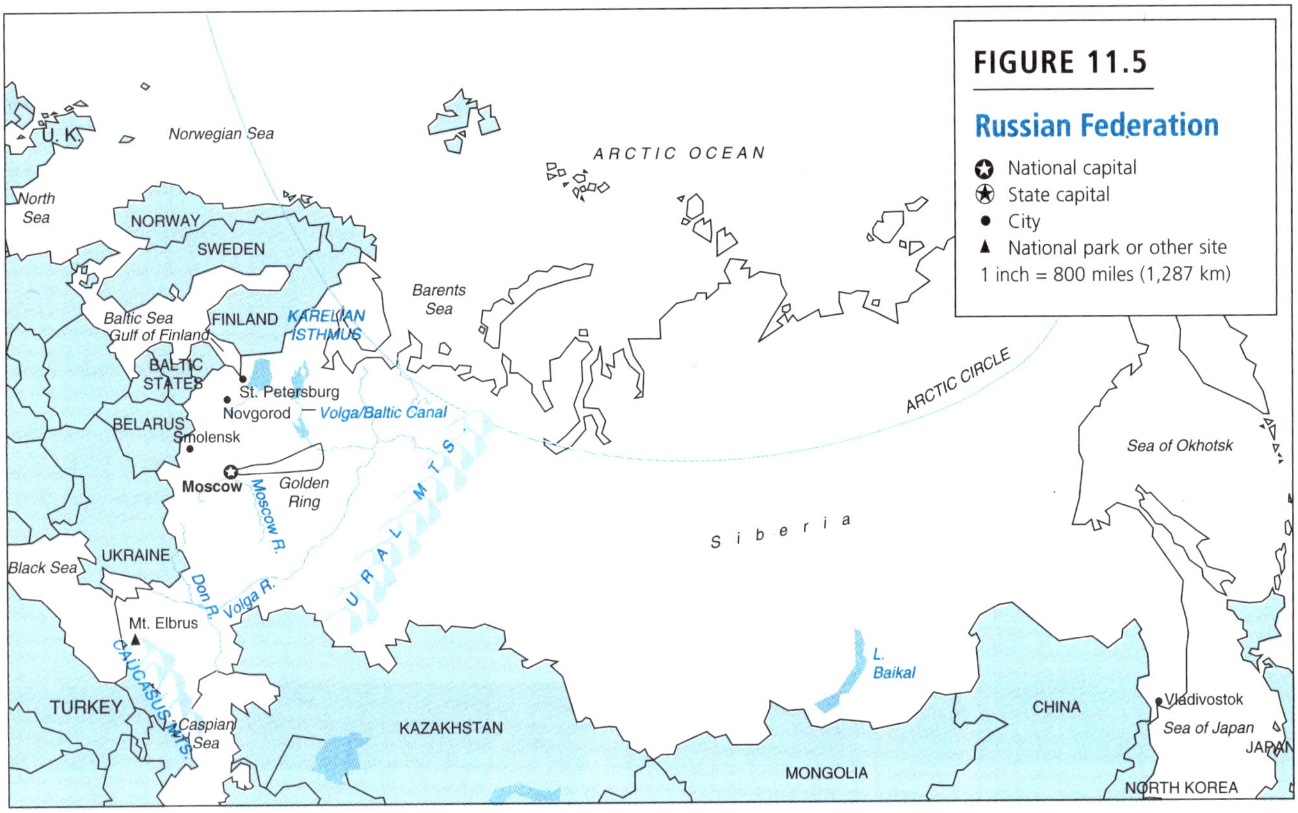

FIGURE 11.5

Russian Federation

Moscow is not particularly attractive. The ugly concrete blocks of Stalin's era create a depressing sprawl. But dotted about the faceless city are odd gems—onion-domed churches and ancient monasteries.

Moscow's wheel-like shape dates to the time when rings of fortifications were built to protect the city from attack. Wide boulevards form the spokes of the wheel. They cross boulevards that make up the wheel's inner and outer rims. Forests and parks called the Green Belt are part of the outer rim.

Travelers visiting the city for the first time will probably want to join a city tour. A typical place to start is Red Square. The square was laid out in the 15th century as a marketplace and has been the scene of numerous parades and demonstrations. It is framed by four structures—the Kremlin, St. Basil's Cathedral, Lenin's Mausoleum, and GUM department store.

The Kremlin dates back to the founding of the city in 1147. Today, it is a collection of palaces, churches, and armories used by the government. Exhibits include royal weaponry, armor, carriages, thrones, and some Fabergé eggs. The Troitskaya Bridge is the main entrance for visitors.

St. Basil's Cathedral, with its wildly colored onion-shaped domes, is undoubtedly one of Russia's most famous images. It supposedly was commissioned by Ivan the Terrible and built between 1555 and 1560. It blends eleven religious buildings into one incredible whole. Legend says that when the cathedral was finished, Ivan had the architect blinded so that he could not create anything else of comparable splendor.

The Lenin Mausoleum contains the embalmed body of the founder of the Russian Communist Party and leader of the 1917 Russian Revolution. Although there is talk of burying Lenin's body, his mausoleum remains open to the public.

Opposite the Kremlin on the east side of Red Square is GUM, the country's largest department store. The acronym comes from Russian words

Under the Soviets, Red Square was used for huge military parades held each May Day and on the anniversary of the October Revolution.

meaning "State Department Store." It was once state owned but was privatized after the breakup of the Soviet Union.

Moscow's business, commercial, and administrative district is north and east of the Kremlin. Other attractions include

- Bolshoi Opera and Ballet, among the world's best. The Bolshoi's theater is closed in July and August.
- Metro, or subway, a tourist attraction in itself. Its stations are a mix of marble columns and platforms, cut-glass chandeliers, paintings, stained glass, statues, and escalators that are longer and quicker than most people have ever experienced.
- Arbat Street, a pedestrian zone with crafts and artists' stalls and street performers.

Art enthusiasts will find much to fill their time. The collections of the Tretyakov Gallery and the Pushkin Museum include works by Kandinsky and other famous artists. Performances at the Moscow Circus are also popular attractions.

St. Petersburg Russia's second-largest city and the country's largest port, St.

CLOSE-UP: RUSSIA

Who is a good prospect for a trip to Russia? Russia appeals to experienced travelers who want to go everywhere and try everything. Cultural groups enjoy trips to the museums and palaces of St. Petersburg as well as ballet or opera performances in St. Petersburg or Moscow. Travelers who are interested in history, art, and architecture and groups who want friendship exchanges are also prospects. University professors specializing in the region are often interested in leading a tour.

Why would they visit Russia? People have heard a lot about the largest country in the world and want to see it for themselves. They want to understand the changes taking place and see how they are affecting the people.

Where would they go? For those with time and budget limitations, the following tour is a possibility.

Day 1 Overnight flight to Helsinki, Finland.

Day 2 Arrive in Helsinki. Afternoon at leisure.

Day 3 Helsinki–St. Petersburg. By motorcoach, travel the coast to the Russian border. After completing frontier formalities, stop for lunch. In the afternoon, cross the Karelian Isthmus (the land bridge between the Gulf of Finland and Lake Ladoga) on the way to St. Petersburg.

Day 4 St. Petersburg. City tour in the morning; afternoon at the Catherine Palace.

Day 5 St. Petersburg–Novgorod. Take a morning tour of the Hermitage Museum in the Winter Palace complex. In the afternoon, drive to Novgorod, a staging post on the trade route between the Baltic and the Black Sea.

Day 6 Novgorod–Moscow. Travel through the countryside on the way to the sprawling capital.

Day 7 Moscow. In the morning, take a walking tour of Red Square; then an afternoon coach tour of the city. Evening entertainment in season.

Day 8 Moscow–Smolensk. Morning at leisure in Moscow. After lunch, travel westward, tracing the road of Napoleon's retreating army in the cruel winter of 1812. Overnight in Smolensk, a town established in the 9th century.

Day 9 Smolensk–Minsk. Drive through the White Russian plains to Minsk, capital of Belarus, a city largely rebuilt after World War II.

Day 10 Minsk–Warsaw. Westward to the Polish border for an afternoon arrival, followed by a tour of the Polish capital.

Day 11 Warsaw. Board the flight home.

When is the best time to go? The optimum months for travel are June through September.

The travelers say, "We want to explore on our own and try the Moscow Metro, but we don't know how to deal with the unfamiliar alphabet. What can we do?" How would you respond? If the travelers are on a tour, the language barrier is minimal, and the Metro might even be a scheduled sightseeing stop. Independent travelers can find help at their hotel. They should ask someone who speaks English to write the Metro stops in the Cyrillic alphabet so that they can familiarize themselves with the signs, and they should carry the hotel's name and address in writing in case they want to catch a cab home.

Petersburg draws millions of visitors. Finland lies only 100 miles (161 km) to the north. St. Petersburg has very short periods of daylight in winter, and for about three weeks in June, it has "white nights," during which the sky is never dark.

Built by Tsar Peter the Great in 1703 on the Baltic Sea, St. Petersburg has seen more than its share of history. With an empty site to work with, Peter's European architects had unlimited space. The result was a city that could stand comparison with the world's finest. It has a relatively low skyline, in part because the city is built on marshland but also because Peter decreed that no structure should be taller than the spires of the Cathedral of Saints Peter and Paul. One famous street, the Nevsky Prospekt, is filled with the mansions of a long-gone aristocracy.

The city straddles forty-two islands at the mouth of the Neva River. Granite embankments built in the time of Catherine the Great (1729–1796) contain the rivers, canals, and streams that separate the islands, but flooding occurs when gales drive in from the Baltic. Bridges join the islands.

The Hermitage Museum, one of the world's largest, has more than 3 million works of art. Housed in the Winter Palace, which once was the residence of the tsars, the Hermitage showcases paintings by artists such as Rubens, Rembrandt, and Leonardo da Vinci. Only with the revolution did the public get an inside look. The museum's rooms are so beautiful that they almost upstage the art collection. The Malachite Room, made almost entirely from the green stone mined in the Ural Mountains, is a masterpiece in itself. The museum is not air-conditioned, and the viewing halls can get very hot during the crowded summer season.

Hermitage, St. Petersburg, Russia

The Mariinsky Theater (called the Kirov during the Soviet era) is worth seeing for its beautiful decorations alone. Some of Russia's best-known operas and ballets, including Tchaikovsky's *Sleeping Beauty*, were first performed here. Dancers such as Anna Pavlova (1882–1931) and Vaslav Nijinsky (1890–1950) made their debut at the Mariinsky.

A visit to St. Petersburg is not complete without a visit to one or more of the suburban palaces collectively known as the Summer Palaces. Petrodvorets, the Catherine Palace at Pushkin (Tsarskoe Selo), and Pavlovsk are the most geared for tourism. Petrodvorets, the tsars' summer home, is the best known. It is southwest of the city on the Gulf of Finland, accessible by hydrofoil from the Winter Palace embankment. The buildings were badly damaged during World War II but have been carefully restored.

Other Places to Visit

Because of Russia's vastness, the typical traveler's limited time, and the lack of accommodations in many areas, most people limit their tours to the major cities. Travelers who venture into the countryside see a different side of Russia.

Several towns of historical, architectural, and spiritual significance make up the **Golden Ring**, a route northeast of Moscow. The ring's route passes Trinity-St. Sergius, a seat of the Orthodox Church founded by Ivan the Terrible in 1559. The monastery's blue domes are decorated with gold stars.

Since many of the kremlins, monasteries, cathedrals, and fortresses were built on riverbanks, taking a cruise is a pleasant way to see the region. It is possible to cruise in comfort from Moscow to St. Petersburg and explore some of the villages that make up the Golden Ring. Ships sail on a combination of the Moscow Canal, Volga River, Rybinsk Reservoir, Volga/Baltic Canal, Lake Onega, Svir River, Lake Ladoga, and Neva River. Some ships voyage from Moscow to the Caspian Sea on the Volga.

➤ PROFILE

Russian Monasteries

Before communist rule, monasteries of the Russian Orthodox Church were religious retreats and extensions of royal power and control. Some famous ones include

- *Solovyetsky Monastery*, Russia's most northerly and largest, for centuries a refuge for holy men and a prison for political dissenters. The Solovyetsky Islands were called the "Gulag Archipelago" by writer Alexander Solzhenitsyn.
- *Trinity Monastery*, the monastery on the Golden Ring dedicated to St. Sergius, the patron saint of Russia. It is one of Russia's most famous religious buildings.
- *Ipateyev Monastery*, outside Moscow. It enjoyed the patronage of the Godunov family, whose vault lies under the church, and later that of the Romanovs.

✔ CHECK-UP

Russia's major cities include
- ✔ Moscow, the capital and largest city.
- ✔ St. Petersburg, on the Baltic.

Highlights of Russia include
- ✔ Kremlin and Red Square in Moscow.
- ✔ St. Basil's Cathedral, with its onion-shaped domes.
- ✔ Bolshoi Ballet and Opera.
- ✔ Golden Ring, northeast of Moscow.

Planning the Trip

In the old days, travel within the (then) Soviet Union was the monopoly of Intourist—a travel agency, transport company, and hotel chain combined—and to some extent of Aeroflot, the Soviet airline. Satellite countries such as Poland, Hungary, and Czechoslovakia had their own versions of state-managed tourism organizations as well as their own national airlines. Today, the core of Intourist remains as a privatized Russian travel company with branches that cater to independent travelers and special interest tours. Elsewhere in eastern Europe, much of the travel infrastructure has been privatized.

ON THE SPOT

Anastasia Luwin has a business trip to London and leaves in about three weeks. This will be her first trip overseas, and she is very excited. She has an extra week of vacation and is thinking of trying to see her grandparents' birthplace in Poland. What would you say to her?

You might want to do some diplomatic counseling. Does Ms. Luwin know what she is getting into? Does she have time to get the necessary visa? Does she understand the costs involved? Does she realize that of the seven days, two would involve travel? Time must be allowed for the trip to the airport, for international check-in and security precautions, for a flight from London to Warsaw of approximately two and a half hours, for passport and customs procedures, and for travel to her grandparents' town. You do not want to discourage her enthusiasm, but you should prepare her. Qualifying is the most important part of the counseling experience.

When to Go

High season for travel in eastern Europe is from the end of May to late September. The cities are year-round destinations, but the countryside is best seen in summer.

Preparing the Traveler

A trip to eastern Europe can be the trip of a lifetime. Most logistical difficulties arise when the independent traveler wants to explore. Details are best put in the hands of experienced tour operators. Documentation requirements must be checked carefully. Visitors must carry ID at all times. In the Russian Federation, visas of various kinds (tourist, business, private, or transit) are required.

Health The farther off the beaten path travelers go, the greater the need for health precautions. For minor difficulties, visitors should ask the management at their hotel for help. For major problems, they should seek help outside the country. Trip interruption insurance is recommended for all travelers. If they must seek treatment and hope to be reimbursed by their health insurance at home, they should obtain payment receipts and a certificate of the exchange rate at the time of treatment.

Money Travelers should keep up-to-date on currency exchange procedures in their destination before departure as rules are subject to change. New EU members must continue to use their national currencies until adjustments in their economies and national budgets are completed.

ATMs have only recently appeared in some areas, and travelers should not count on being able to find one. Traveler's checks may be subject to additional exchange charges. Credit cards are accepted at the larger hotels, stores, and restaurants, but again travelers should not rely on them. In remote areas, cash is the medium of exchange. It is wise to use money belts and to take other precautions for security.

Language Broadly speaking, the languages of eastern Europe are Slavonic (Russian, Polish, Czech, Ukrainian, Belarussian, and Bulgarian), Indo-European (Latvian and Lithuanian), or Finno-Ugrian (Estonian and Hungarian). They are generally written in Cyrillic script, which was loosely based on the Greek alphabet. The strings of consonants without vowels are difficult to convey in the Latin alphabet. Visitors should expect communication difficulties in all but hotels and shops that cater to foreign visitors.

Customs Each country has its own social conventions, but throughout the region it is customary to shake hands when greeting someone. (Even teenagers do so.) Public displays of affection are common. Tipping is an accepted practice.

Food varies with the time of year and the city. The cuisine is based on Austro-Hungarian dishes, and pork is very popular. Breakfast often features cold meats, boiled eggs, and bread served with tea or coffee. In summer, breakfast might include cucumbers and tomatoes with yogurt. Fruit is served in pieces, not as juice. Breads, especially dark rye, are good.

Transportation

By Air The capital city is usually the gateway for each country. National and international airlines operate flights to the gateways. Which airline serves which city changes as airlines merge, share routes, or face financial problems. Facilities vary considerably. See Table 11.2 for a list of national airlines.

By Water Moscow is the hub of Russian river tourism, and the waterway between Moscow and St. Petersburg allows a seven-day cruise link between the present and former capitals. Several companies offer cruises on comfortable boats. Cruises on the Volga River and the Golden Ring are popular routes.

Danube cruises sail from Vienna to the Black Sea or westward to Germany. Ferries connect the Baltic States and Poland to Germany, Sweden, and Finland. Cruise lines visit St. Petersburg, the Baltic States, and Poland.

By Rail Eastern European railway systems are extensive. Russian Federation rail is important because of the region's poor road system, but only a few long-distance routes are open to tourists. The railroads have two classes of service, first and second. Reservations are essential, and on most routes first-class travel is advised. Security can be a problem.

The *Trans-Siberian Express*, one of the world's most famous train journeys, is the route for those who want to see the interior of Russia. The journey from Moscow to **Vladivostok** on the Pacific Coast crosses taiga, steppe, desert, and mountains. The world's longest continuous train trip takes ten days and crosses seven time zones. Travelers have a choice of three slightly different routes, plus the option of including Mongolia and ending up (or beginning) in Beijing. Bed linen and towels are provided in "soft class"

➤ **PROFILE**

Shopping Opportunities in Eastern Europe

Best buys in eastern Europe include handicrafts and curios, but the region has other shopping opportunities:

- Amber of high quality in the Baltic States.
- Bohemian crystal in the Czech Republic.
- Dolls in regional costumes.
- Fur hats, handpainted boxes, and *matryushkas* (nesting dolls) in Russia.
- Hand-embroidered items in all countries.
- Handicrafts in Poland.
- Herend porcelain in Hungary.
- Painted Easter eggs in virtually every country.

➤ **PROFILE**

Drinks of Eastern Europe

Specialties in eastern Europe include

- Latvia's Black Balsam, a thick black alcoholic liquid that includes ginger, oak bark, bitter orange peel, and cognac.
- Czech Republic's Pilsner beer. Its brewery was founded in 1295. Beer is popular everywhere.
- Vodka, the national drink of Russia and Poland, drunk chilled.

TABLE 11.2

National Airlines of Eastern Europe

Country	Airline (Code)
Czech Republic	Czech Airlines (OK)
Estonia	Estonian Air (OV)
Hungary	Malév (MA)
Latvia	No national airline
Lithuania	Lithuanian Airlines (TE)
Poland	Lot Polish Airlines (LO)
Russian Federation	Aeroflot (SU)

(first-class) berths, and each carriage has a toilet and wash basin. An attendant serves tea from a samovar, and trains have restaurant cars.

Gypsies live in all parts of the world, but the largest number live in eastern Europe. Gypsy wagons roam the roads of eastern Europe.

By Road In countries of eastern Europe, driving is on the right. The Czech Republic, Poland, and Hungary have been relatively accessible for years, but challenges mount in the remote areas. Motoring information can be obtained from motoring organizations such as AAA. Chauffeured cars are available in major cities. Most roads are two-lane. Drivers should check insurance rules and road conditions carefully and obtain maps in the language of the country. In Russia, gas stations may be far apart; it is advisable to fill up at every opportunity.

Accommodations

Reservations are essential for independent travelers. Many hotels are reserved for groups or business travelers. Accommodations range from the state-run hotels from the 1960s to international chains with modern deluxe properties. Hungary and the Czech Republic have a good selection of hotels. Russia has approximately 2,500 hotels, of which about 100 specialize in accommodating foreign guests. Throughout the region there are new hotels that meet international standards.

✔ CHECK-UP

Planning a trip to eastern Europe

- ✔ Should involve the use of specialized travel companies.
- ✔ Requires flexibility on the part of the traveler.

Trips to eastern Europe require special attention to

- ✔ Currency exchange rules and regulations.
- ✔ Need for hotel reservations.

OTHER DESTINATIONS IN EASTERN EUROPE

Figure 11.6 shows a map of other countries in eastern Europe that welcome tourists. They are interesting destinations, physically attractive, with unique attractions. However, language barriers and scarce amenities in many areas continue to deter the traveler.

BELARUS

Belarus (*behl uh ROOS*) stretches from the borders of Poland to Russia, an area about the size of Idaho. Ukraine lies to the south, Lithuania and Latvia to the northwest. **Minsk** is the capital and largest city. Often referred to as *White Russia* (a literal translation of its name), the country has a long history of domination by neighboring powers.

One-third of the land is covered by forests, a remnant of the primeval wood that once covered much of Europe. Wide plains, picturesque villages, ancient castles and monasteries, scenic landscapes, and thousands of lakes await the visitor.

Yogurt was invented in Bulgaria. The bacillus that turns fresh milk into yogurt is named *lactobacillus bulgaricus*.

BULGARIA

Bulgaria (*buhl GAIR ee uh*) is on the east of the Balkan Peninsula with a coastline along the Black Sea. In the north, the Danube forms most of the border between Bulgaria and Romania. As Figure 11.6 shows, Bulgaria also shares borders with Serbia and Montenegro (formerly Yugoslavia), Macedonia, Turkey, and Greece.

FIGURE 11.6

Other Countries of Eastern Europe

More than 10 million tourists come to Bulgaria each year, attracted to the Black Sea's beaches. The Greeks called the sea *Pontos Euximos*—the "Hospitable Sea"—but the Turks, who feared its storms, renamed it the Black Sea. Bulgaria's coast has golden dunes, mineral springs, and antique ruins. **Varna** is the major town.

Sofia (*so FEE ah*), the capital and largest city, has architecture that strongly reflects Turkish and Russian influences. The Alexander Nevsky Cathedral was designed in the 1800s by the architect of Moscow's GUM.

Nestled between the Balkan Mountains and the Sredna Gora range just east of Sofia is the *Valley of the Roses*. It is the source of more than 80 percent of the world's supply of the rose attar used in making perfume.

MOLDOVA

Moldova (*mawl DOH vuh*) is only slightly larger than Vermont. The landlocked country borders Romania to the west and is otherwise surrounded by Ukraine. Romanians continue to think of Moldova as their long-lost province of Bessarabia. **Chisinau** (*kee shee NUH*) is the capital and largest city.

ROMANIA

Except for its east coast on the Black Sea, Romania is surrounded by Moldova, Hungary, Ukraine, Serbia and Montenegro, and Bulgaria. The Carpathian Mountains curve through the center of the country, dividing the uplands of **Transylvania** from the Danube Plain. The southern part of the range, the Transylvanian Alps, contains the highest peaks and the most rugged scenery. **Bucharest** (*BOO kuh rehst*) is the capital and largest city.

Anyone who knows anything about Romania knows (from Bram Stoker's novel *Dracula*) that it was among the "lofty steppes . . . the jagged rocks and pointed crags" of Transylvania that Count Dracula lured his prey to ruin. What they might not know is that the model for the thirsty vampire count was Vlad Tepes, a 15th-century prince. He destroyed his enemies by impaling them on spikes or by having them boiled, roasted, strangled, or buried alive. His friends called him Vlad the Impaler.

➤ PROFILE

Cuisine of Eastern Europe

The Western palate tends to consider eastern European food heavy, but travelers might like to try

- ➤ Braised goose stuffed with apples and plums, a Baltic specialty.
- ➤ Bulgarian kebabs served with a *pitka* (hot roll) and *chubritsa* (a mix of salt and spices).
- ➤ Caviar in Russia.
- ➤ In Hungary, *gulyas* (goulash), a thick stew flavored by paprika and topped with sour cream. Noodles, potatoes, and *galuska* (soft, chewy dumplings) are popular side dishes.
- ➤ *Mamaliga*, mashed cornmeal, served in Romania and Moldova.
- ➤ Polish *kielbasa* (sausages), accompanied by *pierogi* (filled dumplings) and a salad of marinated beets, cabbage, and carrots. *Paczki* (doughnuts) are filled with rose-petal jam.
- ➤ Roast pork, dumplings, and cabbage in Prague.

A painted church, Romania

Vlad's 14th-century Bran Castle is known as **Dracula's Castle**, a purely fictional attraction, but a tourism winner.

Romania's architectural treasures, the *painted churches*, are tucked beneath the birch- and fir-clad hills in the northwest. Built in the 15th and 16th centuries, the churches are vividly painted inside and out with Bible stories for congregations that could not read. They have retained much of their color despite the winds, rains, and snows of centuries. The churches are approached from the town of **Sucevita**.

SLOVAK REPUBLIC (SLOVAKIA)

Slovakia is at the center of Europe. The 1993 "Velvet Divorce" from the Czech Republic gave the country independence for the first time in more than a thousand years. **Bratislava** (*BRAH tih slah vuh*) is the capital and largest city.

Slovakia is ruggedly mountainous, with extensive forests. Its hiking trails lure those who enjoy the outdoors. Ski resorts in the Tatra Mountains and spas attract tourists. Painted wooden houses and other forms of folk architecture are found in many regions.

UKRAINE

Ukraine (*yoo CRANE*) has a southern coastline on the Black Sea and on the almost landlocked Sea of Azov. Russia and six other countries circle its borders (see Figure 11.6). It is Europe's second-largest country; only Russia has more land. Formerly referred to as "the granary of the Soviet Union," Ukraine has vast steppes, mile after mile of rolling farmland broken only by the Carpathian Mountains in the far southwest. It is the land of the Cossacks. The name comes from the Turkish *kazac*, which means horseman, outlaw, or free man, depending on its context. The **Dnieper** (*KNEE purr*) **River** flows through the heart of the country and empties into the Black Sea. The **Crimea** (*kry MEE un*), a peninsula about the size of Vermont, extends into the Black Sea in the south.

Kiev (*key EHV*) is the capital and largest city, home of chicken Kiev and borscht (beet soup) and one of eastern Europe's largest cities. It was the cradle of Russian civilization, the place where the Rus State was founded in the 8th and 9th centuries and the city from which the Orthodox faith spread throughout eastern Europe. The Mongols from Asia invaded in the 1200s, and Kiev lost its place as a world leader.

Kiev's most significant attractions are St. Sophia's Cathedral, modeled after the one in Istanbul, and the Golden Gate of Yaroslav the Wise, the last remnant of the 10th-century wall built to defend the city. The Monastery of the Caves, from 1037, was the focal point of the Orthodox Church.

A day's travel south from Kiev by road leads to **Odessa** (*oh DEHS uh*) and the Black Sea, the last part through mudflats. The mud is reputedly a cure for all ills, and many come to the city to take mud baths. Tunnels twist for miles under Odessa. They were a refuge for criminals, revolutionaries, and World War II Resistance fighters.

The Crimea has been a resort for privileged Russians for centuries. **Yalta** (*YAWL tuh*) is a port for ships sailing the Black Sea. Nearby is the *dacha* (country house) used by Russian leaders as well as the palace at Livadia that was the summer home of Nicholas II and the site of the 1945 Yalta Conference in which Roosevelt, Churchill, and Stalin remapped postwar Europe.

In 1223 the Golden Horde of Batu, a grandson of Genghis Khan, invaded Kiev. The prince was taken prisoner, a predicament for the captors, who did not shed the blood of a ruler except in battle. The Mongols stretched him out beneath a platform of boards and sat on him while they had dinner. The prince suffocated and died, but no one shed his blood.

As a symbol of fertility, the egg was held in high esteem by Europe's breadbasket country, Ukraine, and people there began the art of decorating eggs, known as *pysanky*.

CHAPTER WRAP-UP

SUMMARY

Here is a review of the objectives with which we began the chapter.

1. Describe the environment and people of eastern Europe. Eastern Europe ends at the Ural Mountains, the Ural River, and the Caspian Sea. In the south, the Alpine mountain system extends eastward. Russia has Europe's highest mountain, Elbrus, and longest river, the Volga. Lake Baikal, the world's deepest lake, is in Russia's Siberia.

Most of the region has extremely cold and snowy winters, but the southeast has a milder winter. Summer temperatures can be hot.

Hundreds of ethnic backgrounds, languages, and cultures are represented in eastern Europe. The eastern part of the region uses the Roman alphabet and practices the Roman Catholic religion, but Russia uses the Cyrillic alphabet, and Eastern Orthodoxy and Islam are its principal religions.

2. **Describe eastern Europe's most-visited tourist attractions.** The restored city center of Warsaw and the medieval city of Kraków, Poland, are attractions, along with Old Towns of Tallinn, Estonia; Riga, Latvia; and Vilnius, Lithuania. Prague in the Czech Republic and Budapest in Hungary are among eastern Europe's most-visited cities. In Russia, tourism centers on Moscow and St. Petersburg. Art museums such as the Hermitage in St. Petersburg and architectural sites such as the Kremlin in Moscow are the principal draws. Travelers enjoy cruises on the Volga River and tours of Dracula's Castle in Romania.

3. **Provide or find the information needed to plan a trip to eastern Europe.** A trip to eastern Europe can be difficult for the independent traveler. The tourist on an escorted tour benefits from the up-to-date knowledge of an experienced tour operator.

QUESTIONS FOR DISCUSSION AND REVIEW

1. How would you begin to qualify a potential traveler to eastern Europe? What questions would you ask?

2. At its height, the Soviet Union controlled all aspects of tourism. Today, most foreign governments have tourist boards that market their destinations and provide information to potential travelers. The United States has no official organization. Do you think government should get involved in tourism? If so, to what extent?

CHAPTER 12

Southern Europe

- The Iberian Peninsula: Portugal, Spain, Gibraltar, and Andorra
- France
- Italy
- Greece
- Other Destinations in Southern Europe

OBJECTIVES

When you have completed Chapter 12, you should be able to

1. Describe the geography and people of southern Europe.
2. Identify and locate southern Europe's most-visited attractions, matching travelers and destinations best suited for each other.
3. Recall areas of special interest touring.
4. Provide or find the information needed to plan a trip to southern Europe.

Southern Europe includes the popular destinations of Portugal, Spain, France, Italy, and Greece. These countries have some of the Continent's most glittering cities and finest hotels and restaurants, as well as historic and cultural attractions. But no place on earth owes as much of its popularity to geography as does southern Europe. At almost every turn, physical beauty comes running to meet you. The region's nearness to the sea and its mountains, valleys, rivers, and vegetation make southern Europe the dream vacation of millions of travelers.

The Environment and Its People

The shores of the **Mediterranean** (*mehd uh tuh RAY nee uhn*) have attracted travelers since ancient times. **Spain**, **France**, and **Italy** border the sea, as Figure 12.1 shows. **Portugal** and **Greece** have coasts on nearby waters. This chapter explores these destinations as well as several smaller countries. See the Fact File in Appendix A for an alphabetical list of European countries.

The Land

Peninsulas, islands, mountains, and plateaus are the landforms of southern Europe. The region has three large peninsulas: the Iberian (*eye BEER ee un*), the Italian, and the Balkan. The largest, the Iberian Peninsula, extends into both the Atlantic Ocean and the Mediterranean Sea, which are joined by the Strait of Gibraltar (*juh BRAWL tuhr*) at the peninsula's southern tip. To the east are the Italian and Balkan Peninsulas. They divide the Mediterranean into the smaller Ligurian, Tyrrhenian (*tih REE nee uhn*), Adriatic, Ionian, and Aegean Seas. (Look again at Figure 12.1.) Islands in these seas lured ancient explorers as they now attract modern travelers (see Table 12.1).

Portugal and Spain share the Iberian Peninsula. Both have southern coasts that are well known to tourists: in Portugal, the **Algarve** along the Atlantic; in Spain, the **Costa del Sol** ("Sunshine Coast") along the Mediterranean. The center of the Iberian Peninsula is a large dry plateau broken by hills and low mountains. The **Sierra Nevada** range rises in the southeast and the **Pyrenees** (*PIHR uh neez*) in the northeast.

The Pyrenees form a barrier between Spain and France. France's geography combines the landscape of northern and southern Europe. In the northwest, the peninsulas of **Normandy** and **Brittany** jut into the Atlantic. In eastern, central, and southern France, the land rises in hills and mountains. In the south, the **Riviera** (*rihv ee AIR uh*) is the narrow strip of land along the Mediterranean from Toulon, France, to La Spezia, Italy. The Alps begin in southeastern France near the Mediterranean; their arc northward forms the border with Italy. The highest alpine peak, **Mont Blanc**, rises 15,771 feet (4,807 m) between France, Italy, and Switzerland.

The Italian Peninsula belongs to Italy. The Alps create a wall across the country's north. South of the Alps are the Po Valley and fertile plains. Farther south, the **Apennine** (*AP uh nyne*) **Mountains** form Italy's spine. Southern Italy has two of the world's most famous volcanoes: **Mount Etna**, on the eastern coast of the island of Sicily, and **Vesuvius** (*vuh SOO vee uhs*), near Naples.

➤ PROFILE

Museums of Southern Europe

Art lovers won't want to miss the museums of southern Europe, including

- ➤ D'Orsay Museum in Paris, France, known for 19th- and 20th-century art.
- ➤ Gulbenkian in Lisbon, Portugal, a varied private collection.
- ➤ Louvre in Paris, France, the world's largest museum.
- ➤ National Archaeological Museum in Athens, Greece, for ancient art and sculpture.
- ➤ Prado in Madrid, Spain, with royal collections.
- ➤ Uffizi Gallery in Florence, Italy, located in a Renaissance palace.
- ➤ Vatican Museum in Vatican City, known for the Sistine Chapel.

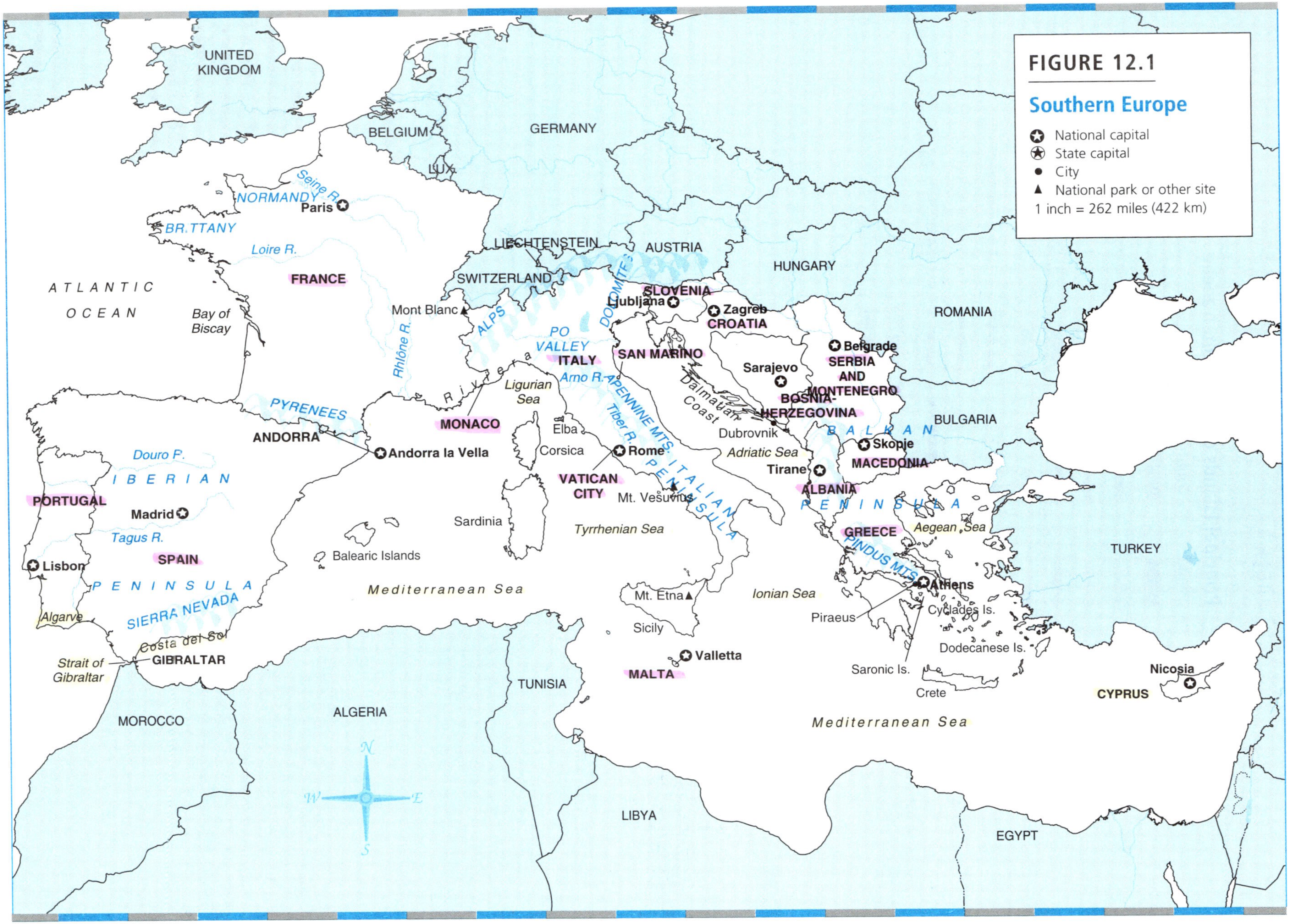
FIGURE 12.1
Southern Europe
National capital
State capital
City
National park or other site
1 inch = 262 miles (422 km)
UNITED KINGDOM
BELGIUM
LUX
GERMANY
NORMANDY
Seine R.
Paris
BRITTANY
Loire R.
FRANCE
LIECHTENSTEIN
AUSTRIA
HUNGARY
ROMANIA
SWITZERLAND
ATLANTIC OCEAN
Bay of Biscay
Mont Blanc
ALPS
DOLOMITES
SLOVENIA
Ljubljana
Zagreb
CROATIA
PO VALLEY
ITALY
SAN MARINO
Rhône R.
Riviera
Ligurian Sea
Arno R.
Sarajevo
Belgrade
SERBIA AND MONTENEGRO
BOSNIA-HERZEGOVINA
Dalmatian Coast
Dubrovnik
BULGARIA
PYRENEES
ANDORRA
Andorra la Vella
MONACO
Elba
Corsica
Rome
Tiber R.
APENNINE MTS.
Adriatic Sea
BALKAN PENINSULA
Skopje
MACEDONIA
Douro R.
IBERIAN PENINSULA
PORTUGAL
Madrid
Tagus R.
SPAIN
Lisbon
Algarve
SIERRA NEVADA
Costa del Sol
GIBRALTAR
Strait of Gibraltar
VATICAN CITY
Mt. Vesuvius
ITALIAN PENINSULA
Tirane
ALBANIA
Sardinia
Tyrrhenian Sea
GREECE
Aegean Sea
PINDUS MTS.
Athens
Balearic Islands
Mediterranean Sea
Mt. Etna
Ionian Sea
Cyclades Is.
Piraeus
Sicily
Valletta
MALTA
Dodecanese Is.
Saronic Is.
Crete
TURKEY
Nicosia
CYPRUS
TUNISIA
MOROCCO
ALGERIA
N
W
E
S
LIBYA
EGYPT
Mediterranean Sea

TABLE 12.1

Principal Islands of the Mediterranean

Island	Country	Group	Attractions or Characteristics
Corfu	Greece	Ionic	Green landscape
Corsica	France	None	Napoleon's home
Crete	Greece	None	Palace of Knossos
Cyprus	Independent	None	Divided land
Elba	Italy	None	Napoleon's first retreat
Ibiza	Spain	Balearic	Jet-set appeal
Majorca	Spain	Balearic	Busy and built-up
Malta	Independent	None	Beautiful harbor
Mykonos	Greece	Cyclades	Windmills
Rhodes	Greece	Cyclades	Largest of the group
Santorini	Greece	Cyclades	Volcanic caldera
Sardinia	Italy	None	Costa Smeralda
Sicily	Italy	None	Mediterranean's largest island

The Balkan Peninsula is occupied by many countries, including Croatia, Albania, Bosnia-Herzegovina (*hurt suh goh VEE nuh*), Macedonia, Serbia and Montenegro, Bulgaria (discussed in Chapter 11), and the mainland of **Greece**. *Balkan* is a Turkish word meaning "mountain," and mountains cover much of the peninsula. A branch of the Alps called the **Pindus Mountains** extends along the Adriatic Sea to Greece.

Greece is a land of peninsulas and island archipelagos formed by mountain ranges that were flooded by the rising levels of the Mediterranean. Its coastline is deeply indented with bays and inlets.

The Climate

The lands bordering the Mediterranean have moist, mild winters and hot, dry summers. A winter vacation anywhere along the Mediterranean should not be recommended to anyone wanting warm-water conditions. The average water temperature drops below 40° F (4° C) in winter.

Olives have grown in the Mediterranean region for at least 6,000 years. Olive trees, with their twisted trunks and leaves that change from green to silver in sunlight, have inspired poetry, paintings, and philosophy. Spain is the top producer, followed by Italy and Greece.

Atlantic winds and hot, dry air blown from the Sahara affect Portugal and Spain. Their northern Atlantic coasts have cool, wet winters and warm, humid summers. Their south coasts have mild winters and dry, hot summers. Spain's dry central plateau has cold winters (with snow) and extremely hot summers.

In France, summer along the Mediterranean coast is generally settled, sunny, and warm. Away from the coast, France has a four-season climate similar to that of the northeast United States, with precipitation in any season. The Alps have much snow in winter. The **mistral**—a cold, dry wind—funnels down from the Alps to the Mediterranean coast in winter.

Italy is often called "sunny Italy," but this description is only partly true. Spring, summer, and fall are generally sunny, but winter is rainy and cloudy. The upper slopes of the mountains get plenty of snow, but the Alps protect northern Italy from intense cold. Snow falls even as far south as Rome. In spring, the hot **sirocco** wind from Africa brings stifling conditions to southern Italy. The north gets rain, but dryness increases to the south.

Greece has cold, wet winters and hot, dry summers. The climate varies sharply between the mountainous interior and the coastal regions. Snow falls in the mountains, but rarely in the islands. A persistent northerly wind, known as the **etesian**, blows in the Aegean, sometimes reaching near-gale force.

The People and Their History

Between 3000 and 1500 BC, the island of Crete was the center of one of Europe's earliest civilizations—the Minoan. By the 1600s BC, its influence passed to Mycenae on the mainland of Greece, which in turn was overrun. The Greek city-states originated at this time as villages joined for defense. In the 5th century BC, Greek civilization reached its peak (see Figure 12.2). Its achievements in government, science, philosophy, and the arts continue to influence our lives.

By the 3rd century BC, Greece succumbed to the power of Rome. The Romans ruled southern Europe for more than 700 years. Their language, Latin, became the basis of French, Italian, Spanish, and other Romance languages. Barbarian invasions from the north divided the Roman Empire into many kingdoms. Italy would not be a united country again for centuries. Greece became part of the Byzantine empire, ruled from Constantinople (now Istanbul), which later fell to the Ottoman empire. For centuries, Greece developed outside the European mainstream.

Elsewhere in Europe, the Roman Catholic Church was the primary force in the Middle Ages. Medieval cathedrals trained and employed gifted craftsmen and served as centers of public life. The Gothic churches were filled with sculptures and their walls lined with paintings or tapestries illuminated by stained-glass windows.

On the Iberian Peninsula, however, the church's influence was challenged by the Moors, who invaded from Africa about AD 711. They conquered almost all of the peninsula except the far north. The Moors constructed fine buildings, including mosques and fortified palaces called *alcázars*. But by the mid-1200s, the Christian kingdoms of Spain's north—Aragon, Navarre, and Castile—gained power. In 1469 Ferdinand of Aragon married Isabella of Castile, and their combined forces pushed the Moors from Spain.

Meanwhile, the Renaissance had begun in what is now Italy during the 1300s, bringing a renewed interest in learning and a curiosity about the world. Exploration in the 1500s brought wealth to Portugal, Spain, and France.

From the 1500s to the 1700s, the power of kings grew steadily. France became one of the strongest countries on the Continent. Louis XIV (1638–1715) of France, the *Sun King*, was an absolute monarch. The construction of his palace at Versailles and wars drained the treasury. By the late 1700s, the stage was set for the French Revolution. In its wake Napoleon Bonaparte (1769–1821) rose to power and led France in wars across the Continent.

In the 1800s, Napoleon was defeated, Portugal lost her colony of Brazil, Spain lost her empire in the Americas, the Kingdom of Italy was formed, and Greece fought for independence from the Ottoman empire. Southern Europe was victim to one power struggle after another.

World Wars I and II began as boundary disputes between European countries before engulfing the world. Currently most of Europe's boundaries are accepted, with some exceptions. The breakup of Yugoslavia resulted in ethnic wars that sought to redraw borders. The division of Cyprus into Greek

FIGURE 12.2

Milestones of Southern European History

3000–1200 BC Minoan and Mycenaean cultures develop.

477–431 This is the Golden Age of Greece.

300 BC–AD 476 This is the height of the Roman Empire.

718 Moors conquer most of the Iberian Peninsula.

1300s–1500s The Renaissance takes place in Italy.

1456–1822 Greece is part of the Ottoman empire.

1492 Moors are expelled from Granada, their last center in Spain.

1556–1598 The Spanish empire reaches its height under Philip II.

1643–1715 Louis XIV rules France.

1789–1799 The French Revolution is followed by Napoleon's rule.

1815 Napoleon is defeated at Waterloo.

1861 The Kingdom of Italy forms.

1900 The *Guide Michelin*, the first guide to European restaurants, is published.

1936–1939 Spanish Civil War brings Franco to power.

1939–1945 In World War II, France and Greece are occupied by Germany, Italy is part of the Axis, Spain and Portugal remain neutral.

1940 Four boys discover drawings on the walls of the Lascaux Cave in southwestern France.

1975 Greece becomes a republic.

1992 Slovenia, Croatia, Bosnia-Herzegovina, and Macedonia split from Yugoslavia.

2004 The Olympic Games come home to Greece.

and Turkish areas has created friction. Spain's claim to British-held Gibraltar is another issue. Language-based separatist movements—some involving armed conflict—exist in the Basque and Catalan regions of Spain, in Corsica (France), and in Kosovo (Serbia).

Southern Europeans today are a varied group. An influx of immigrants from former African colonies and eastern Europe has added to the ethnic mix. Although most of this region's countries are members of the European Union, travelers will find sharp regional differences in languages, customs, and culinary tastes.

✔ CHECK-UP

Major physical features of southern Europe include

- ✔ Mediterranean Sea and its divisions: the Ligurian, Tyrrhenian, Adriatic, Ionian, and Aegean Seas.
- ✔ Three peninsulas: the Iberian, the Italian, and the Balkan.
- ✔ Pyrenees and the Alps.
- ✔ Two famous volcanoes: Mount Etna and Mount Vesuvius.
- ✔ Influence of the sea on the climate.

The culture of southern Europe includes

- ✔ Ancient Roman and Greek civilizations.
- ✔ Moorish influence in the Iberian Peninsula.
- ✔ Renaissance, born in Italy.
- ✔ Legacy of monarchs, as seen in art and architecture.

The Iberian Peninsula

The Iberian Peninsula has enormous historical interest, architectural wealth, intriguing medieval towns, splendid scenery, relaxing resorts, and fascinating cities. Portugal and Spain occupy most of the peninsula, but tiny **Gibraltar** and **Andorra** also attract tourists (see Figure 12.3).

Portugal

Located at the western edge of the Iberian Peninsula, Portugal has a long Atlantic coastline on the west and a shorter one on the south. Spain surrounds it on the other two sides. The **Tagus** (*TAY guhs*) **River** flows west from Spain and divides Portugal into a wetter northern region and a more arid southern region.

Close to the size of Maine, Portugal is large enough to have variety, but its attractions can be reached in a conveniently short time. One of those attractions is a distinctive architectural style called *Manueline.* It developed when the riches of Portugal's colonies were flowing into the country, and it was named after the king of the period, Manuel I (1469–1521). The style uses designs with nautical motifs, foreign fruits, flowers, and strange animals. On interior and exterior walls, shining blue-and-white tiles called *azulejos,* originating from the Moorish era, complement the buildings. Manueline designs are found throughout the country.

The Portuguese *fado* ("fate" or "destiny") parallels American blues. Songs are sung by a man or woman accompanied by a guitar. Most fados deal with such themes as unrequited love.

Lisbon The Tagus enters the Atlantic at one of Europe's most important harbors, Lisbon, which is also Portugal's capital, its largest city, and a popular

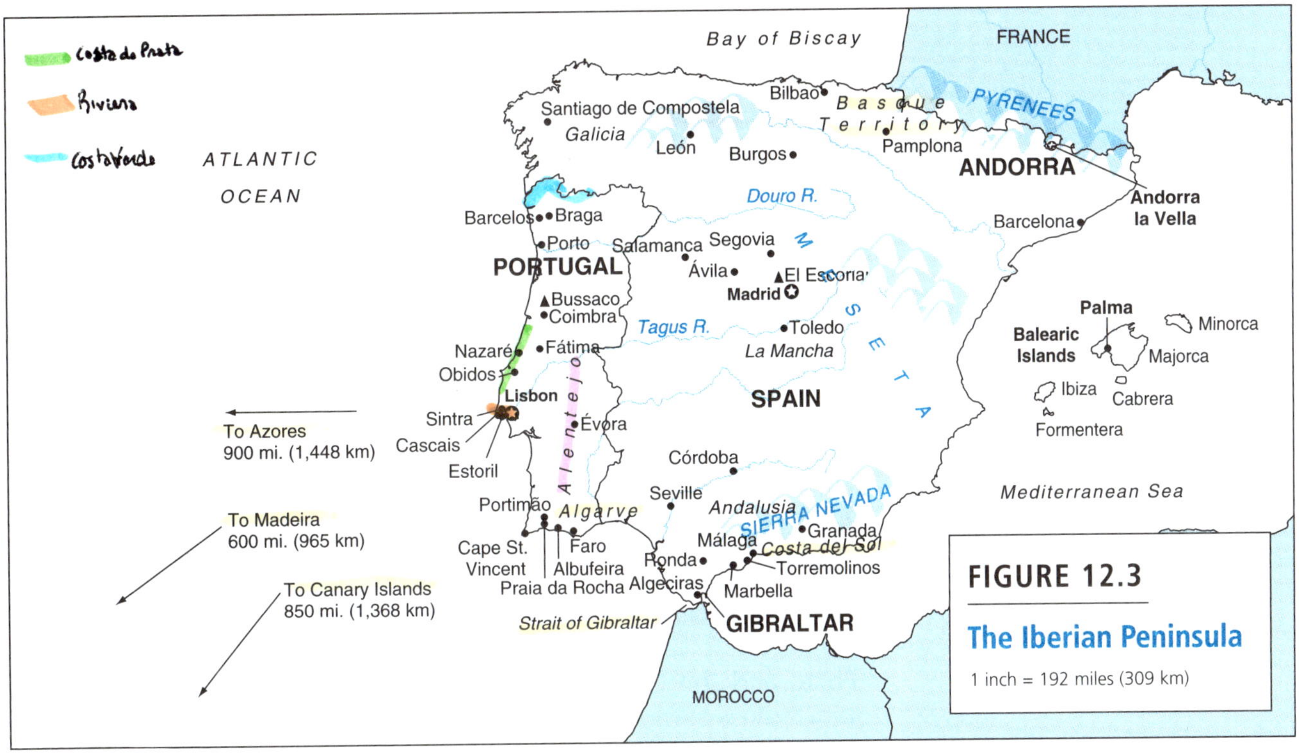

FIGURE 12.3

The Iberian Peninsula

1 inch = 192 miles (309 km)

port for cruise ships. The Ponte 25 de Abril Bridge—one of the longest single-span suspension bridges—crosses the Tagus and dominates the skyline.

Lisbon is built on low hills. In 1775 a massive earthquake and tsunami devastated the city. Only the old Moorish quarter, the Alfama, survived. St. George's Castle overlooks the city from the top of a hill in the quarter. A walk from the castle down through the Alfama takes the visitor back into medieval times. The business district along the waterfront, known as the Baixa, was rebuilt with straight, wide avenues and sidewalks made of black and white mosaic. Streets bear colorful names such as the *Rua do Açúcar* ("Street of Sugar").

Monastery of Jerónimos, Lisbon, Portugal

Rossio Square is a good place to begin exploring the city. Here the tourist can sit sipping strong unblended coffee from the former Portuguese provinces in Africa while plotting the day's sightseeing. Highlights include

- Avenida da Liberdade, Lisbon's main avenue, a handsome street dating from 1880, with trees, cafés, and shops bordered by some of the best hotels.
- Gulbenkian Museum and Art Center, a private art collection that was a gift to Portugal.
- Coach Musuem, a collection of antique coaches, considered the finest of its type.
- Monument of the Discoveries, dedicated to Prince Henry the Navigator (1391–1460).
- Tower of Belém, a masterpiece of Manueline architecture overlooking the river. The tower looks like a huge chess piece and is often used as a symbol of the country.
- Monastery of Jerónimos, another example of Manueline architecture. It combines Flamboyant Gothic and Moorish influences.

Costa Lisboa West of Lisbon is a string of beach resorts, including **Estoril** and **Cascais**. This is the Portuguese Riviera, long a home to exiled European royalty and the setting for many World War II spy movies. The deluxe Palácio Hotel in Estoril was legendary as a center of espionage.

Sintra, once the summer retreat of the Portuguese kings, nestles in the mountains 40 miles (64 km) from Lisbon. Its narrow lanes wind past decaying royal villas and country estates. Two stops should be on every itinerary: the National Palace, which has two funnel-shaped chimney towers that form Sintra's most distinctive landmark, and the Peña Palace, which would fit in well in Disneyland.

Coimbra and the Costa de Prata Stretching north of Lisbon along the Atlantic is the region known as the Costa de Prata. Attractions are **Obidos**, a tiny whitewashed medieval town, and **Nazaré**, a much-photographed fishing village.

Fátima is east of Nazaré. It is the center of pilgrimages celebrating the reported appearance in 1917 of the Virgin Mary to three shepherd children. The shrine is especially popular on May 13, the anniversary of the first vision.

Coimbra, Portugal's third-largest city, is a university town. North of Coimbra is the palace of **Bussaco**, an architectural fantasy set in a forest arboretum with exotic trees brought home by explorers centuries ago. The building was created as a summer pleasure palace for the Portuguese king. When royalty fled in 1910, the king's cook persuaded the government to let him run the palace as a hotel.

Porto and the Costa Verde Portugal's northwest corner along the border with Spain is the region known as the Costa Verde ("Green Coast"). Porto, the country's second-largest city, gave the name *port* to its fortified wine and to the left-hand side of ships sailing south. The vines are grown along the length of the **Douro River** up to the border with Spain. Visitors can taste the wines at old port lodges along the river.

Braga is near the border of Spain. Nearly everywhere you look, there is a church, a palace, or a fountain. To Braga's west is **Barcelos**, a sprawling river town that is home to the Barcelos cock, the most characteristic souvenir of Portugal. Its legend began when a man was sentenced to hang. Appealing to the judge, who was eating a chicken dinner at the time, the condemned man said that to prove his innocence, the rooster on the judge's plate would get up and crow. Of course it did!

Temple at Évora, Portugal

Évora and the Alentejo Plains stretch south and east of Lisbon in Portugal's largest province, Alentejo (*allen TAY shoe*). The plains cover one-third of Portugal, but the province is inhabited by only 10 percent of the country's population. It was the center of the Roman Iberian Empire. The Romans left us Évora and its 2nd-century Temple of Diana. Castle ruins and walled cities abound throughout the province, which is known for its cork oaks and olive trees.

Before plastic was invented, cork had no equal as a strong, lightweight material. It was used for life preservers and floats on fishing nets and only now is being replaced as a stopper for wine bottles. The cork oak tree is stripped once every five years. After stripping, the new bark turns bright red, embarrassed to lose its clothes.

Faro and the Algarve A range of mountains separates the Alentejo from the Algarve, the province that runs along Portugal's south coast. Often called the *Garden of Portugal*, the Algarve stretches along the Atlantic from **Cape St. Vincent**, the westernmost point of Europe, to the Spanish border. Almond and citrus trees dot the landscape. A 30-minute flight from Lisbon brings travelers to **Faro**, the Algarve's capital.

Travelers should seek the smaller towns along the coast, although finding a sleepy village these days is difficult. **Albufeira** and **Portimão** are busy with resorts, shops, and active nightlife. **Praia da Rocha** is less developed and known for its creamy beaches.

Sports can be pursued year-round in the Algarve, and golf courses beckon. In winter, retirees from all nations rent time-share condominiums;

the sea is too cold for swimming, however. A rental car is needed as attractions are widely spread.

The Azores and Madeira Portugal's self-governing regions in the Atlantic are the nine volcanic islands of the Azores and the volcanic archipelago of Madeira.

In the Azores, most of the population lives on the largest island, São Miguel, or on neighboring Santa Maria. The landscape is spectacularly beautiful, with many crater lakes. The mild Atlantic climate produces almost no rain during the summer months when European vacationers come for long periods.

Madeira is off the coast of Africa. The main island, also called Madeira, is steep and mountainous, with deep valleys and lush vegetation, but no beaches. The only flat land is on the south coast near the capital, Funchal, a port call for ships making repositioning cruises across the Atlantic. The island was "discovered" by winter-weary Britons in the 19th century. The famous Reid's Palace Hotel has accommodated such visitors as Winston Churchill and George Bernard Shaw. A network of walking paths encourages hikes along the *levadas*—a web of irrigation channels that carry water from the mountaintops to the fields and towns below.

Riders of the toboggan run in Funchal, Madeira, sit in wicker chairs mounted on wooden runners. Two men control the chairs on their long, noisy, and swift descent down the slippery cobblestones of the city. It is not a trip for the faint of heart.

Spain

East and north of Portugal is Spain. It occupies the bulk of the **Iberian Peninsula** and has coastlines along the Atlantic, the Bay of Biscay, and the Mediterranean. (Look again at Figure 12.3.) The Pyrenees form its northern border with France. Most of the country consists of mountains and the **Meseta**—the high, dry plateau of central Spain.

The late 16th century began a gray time in Spain's long history. In 1588 Phillip II (1527–1598) sent his invincible Armada to invade England; its destruction by the British cost Spain its supremacy. Spain never again played a major role in European politics. A civil war during the late 1930s was followed by decades of dictatorship under Francisco Franco. After his death in 1975, Spain became a parliamentary monarchy.

Each year millions visit Spain's sunny beaches, its rocky Atlantic Coast, and the castles and churches of its historic cities. They also enjoy the **Balearic Islands** in the Mediterranean and the **Canary Islands** off the coast of Africa.

Most visitors to Spain want to see *flamenco*, originally a dance performed by gypsies. The performer makes up heel-clicking, foot-stomping steps according to his or her mood. The guitars follow the dancer.

Madrid Spain's capital and largest city, Madrid is on the high, dry plateau in the country's center. *Puerta del Sol* ("Door of the Sun") is the city's core and the square from which all Spanish roads are measured. From this spacious plaza, streets branch out like the spokes of a wheel.

Anchoring Madrid's attractions is a trio of museums: the Reina Sofía Center, the Thyssen-Bornemisza Museum, and the Prado. All are within a 10-minute walk of each other on the *Paseo del Arte* ("Art Walk"). The most visited is the Prado, famous for its collection of Spanish and European masterpieces. The Reina Sofía houses a collection of 20th-century art including Picasso's *Guernica*, and the Thyssen-Bornemisza contains a collection of European art.

Other attractions include

- Palacio Real ("Royal Palace"), commissioned in the early 18th century. Its 2,800 rooms compete for opulence. The current monarchs rarely stay in the palace.

At the bullfights, the cheap seats are in the sun; the more expensive ones are in the shade.

- Parque del Retiro, which is filled with street musicians, gypsy fortune-tellers, and sidewalk painters on weekends.
- Plaza Mayor, a public square that through the centuries has been host to everything from the burning of heretics to royal marriages.
- Las Ventas, a bullring with seats for 22,500 people. *Corridas* ("bullfights") are held from March to October. They begin at 5 PM, when some of the heat has gone from the day.

Outside Madrid in the mountain village of San Lorenzo is the **Monasterio de San Lorenzo de El Escorial**, Spain's largest building. Built by Philip II, the most powerful ruler of his time, it is part palace, part monastery, part mausoleum of kings. A few miles away is Franco's tomb, *Valle de los Caidos* ("Valley of the Fallen").

Central Spain The former kingdoms of León and Old Castile—which led the fight for the recapture of Spain from the Moors—are in central Spain. Their attractions are the cities of

- **Ávila** (*AH vee lah*), enclosed by walls built in the 11th century.
- **Burgos** and **León**, ancient Castilian capitals with glorious cathedrals.
- **Salamanca**, with splendid architecture and a 13th-century university.
- **Segovia**, with a functioning Roman aqueduct, 14th-century Alcázar, and cathedral.
- **Toledo**, the city that inspired the painter El Greco (1541–1614). It has a wealth of Roman remains and fine Moorish and medieval architecture.

Galicia Northwestern Spain is the region known as Galicia. **Santiago de Compostela** in Galicia has been the goal of pilgrims since the Middle Ages. Soaring above Santiago's rooftops are the baroque towers of the cathedral—the pilgrims' destination. Believers come to visit a tomb said to be that of St. James the Apostle, the patron saint of Spain. Millions of pilgrims still walk what is thought of as the Way of St. James, which goes to Santiago from Roncesvalles in France through the Pyrenees to Pamplona, Burgos, and León. In the 12th century, one of the first tourist guides was written by a French cleric about the journey. The guide is preserved in the cathedral.

The plaza in front of the cathedral is also home to the Hotel Reyes Católicos, one of the most luxurious of the Spanish *paradores* (historic sites transformed into government-owned hotels).

Basque Territory The western end of the Pyrenees, on both sides of the border between France and Spain, is the home of the Basques. They appear to be descendants of some of the first people to live in Europe. The Basques have fought for years to preserve their culture and language.

Bilbao (*bil BOU*) is the regional capital, Spain's fourth-largest city. The opening of a Guggenheim Museum in Bilbao designed by Frank Gehry increased tourism to the region 40 percent. The dazzling titanium and stone-covered building is one of the most-talked-about contemporary museums.

Pamplona is a Basque city near the western end of the Pyrenees. At the Festival of San Fermín, bulls run through the streets on their way to the bullring. Each July thousands test their courage by running in front of the bulls.

Barcelona In the northeast corner of Spain is Barcelona, the capital of Catalonia and Spain's second-largest city. It is the principal cruise port of the western Mediterranean.

Las Ramblas, the city's main street, is an avenue that was formed by covering over a series of ravines. Cafés, bookstalls, street artists, and flower and bird markets are just some of the attractions of this fashionable street.

Barcelona is popularly symbolized by one building—the incomplete church of La Sagrada Familia ("The Holy Family"), designed by architect Antoni Gaudí (1852–1926). Gaudí is noted for his use of masonry and tile, Art Nouveau with a twist.

Barcelona has claim to another great artist: Pablo Picasso (1881–1973), who studied there. A collection of his works is on exhibit at the Museo Picasso.

In Barcelona, street signs are in Catalan first and Spanish second. Most Spaniards speak Castilian Spanish, which is the official language of the country, but Catalan, Galician, and Basque are the official languages of particular regions.

Southern Spain To the south of Madrid, the region of **La Mancha** is an arid treeless plateau. It is Spain's principal grape-growing district. In about 1580, windmills were introduced there from the Low Countries. The windmills became celebrated when the hero of *Don Quixote* tilted at them with his lance, mistaking their sails for the arms of a giant. Hundreds of windmills were built, but only a few remain.

Across the plateau, roads lead south—often through wild and barren country—to **Andalusia**, which includes Spain's eight most southerly provinces. Here the Spanish raise their fiercest bulls and train their matadors. Flamenco performers with clicking castanets dance to the music of the guitar. Whitewashed villages dot the countryside, and vineyards and olive groves thrive. The Moors' influence can be seen in the blend of Moorish and Christian architecture known as *mudéjar*. Andalusia, Spain's most popular tourism region, includes the cities of Seville, Granada, and Córdoba.

Church of La Sagrada Familia, Barcelona, Spain

Seville was the port for treasure ships from the New World. It is equally renowned for the pageantry of *Semana Santa* ("Holy Week") and the exuberance of the *Feria de Abril* ("April Fair"). Its cathedral took 104 years to build and incorporates the graceful Moorish Giralda Tower from the 12th century. In Seville, the Alcázar is a great Moorish palace, and the Plaza del Toros a famous bullfighting ring.

Granada has the harsh peaks of the Sierra Nevada looming behind it. On a hot, dry hilltop stands the Alhambra, the palace-fortress of the last Moorish rulers of Spain. Inside its thick protective walls is a world of cool, airy courtyards, trickling fountains, and lush gardens. One of the most famous of Spain's government-run inns, the Parador de San Francisco, is located in a former Moorish palace next to the Alhambra. A long waiting list attests to the hotel's popularity.

In 1812 Napoleon's troops tried to blow up Granada's Alhambra. Fortunately, they failed.

Córdoba's cathedral was an Islamic mosque until the Christians captured the city in 1236. Much of the Moorish atmosphere remains.

Costa del Sol The densely populated Costa del Sol extends along the Mediterranean coast to Gibraltar. The region's big city, **Málaga**, is near the resorts of **Marbella** and **Torremolinos**. The area has beaches, golf courses, shopping, casinos, nightclubs, and luxury resorts. The coast is built up, and visitors can find fish and chips and sausage and sauerkraut as well as McDonald's. Ferries run from **Algeciras** to Tangier and Ceuta on the North African coast, as well as to the Canary Islands.

Excursions go inland to the "White Towns" tucked within the pastoral and isolated mountains. The towns' whitewashed buildings can be seen for miles. **Ronda** is the largest and in many ways the most picturesque.

Balearic Islands The Balearic (*bal ee AR ick*) Islands are in the Mediterranean off the east coast of Spain. They include **Majorca** (*muh JOR kuh*), **Minorca**, **Cabrera**, **Formentera**, and **Ibiza** (*ee BEE sah*). **Palma** on Majorca is the capital and only large city.

The islands have rich and varied landscapes. Winters are mild, and summers are generally hot; most rain falls in spring and autumn.

Canary Islands The volcanic Canary Islands are in the Atlantic off the northwest coast of Africa. Santa Cruz on Tenerife and Las Palmas on Gran Canaria are the sea and air gateways. The Pico de Teide, on Tenerife, is Spain's highest mountain. Its summit is snow-covered from November to April, although the island's beachside weather is generally warm and dry.

Gibraltar

Legend has it that as long as Gibraltar's apes stay, the rock will remain British.

Gibraltar is a rocky peninsula on the southern shore of Spain. It is a small self-governing British colony. Spain has never ceased to lay claim to the land, but so far Gibraltarians have voted to remain British.

The land consists of a single steep rock shaped like an arrowhead. A sandy isthmus joins the Rock of Gibraltar to Spain. Not as solid as advertised, the Rock has caves, roads, and tunnels.

Tourism is served by a small airport near the Spanish border and by cruise ships making port calls. Cable cars take visitors to the top of the Rock. Halfway up, the cars stop at the Apes' Den, where tourists can see the fabled Barbary apes, a breed of tailless monkeys, the only simians living wild in Europe.

CLOSE-UP: SPAIN

Who is a good prospect for a trip to Spain? History and architecture lovers will find much to enjoy in the country. In winter, the Costa del Sol promotes its apartments and condos to retired travelers who want a pleasant climate. People with ancestral roots in Spain are also prospects. And for those with sports interests, the Costa del Sol is known for excellent golf. The springlike weather is great for tennis.

Why would they visit Spain? The Moors left the country with an architectural legacy of castles and monuments. Spain's exploration of the New World provided the wealth that enabled the country to build impressive cathedrals and palaces and populated the Americas with people of Hispanic heritage. Winter visitors enjoy off-season rates at the Costa del Sol's resorts.

Where would they go? Spain is a very large country. Most tours are restricted to certain regions. An introductory tour might include the following itinerary.

Day 1 Overnight flight to Madrid.

Day 2 Mid-morning arrival. Possible afternoon trip to the Royal Palace.

Day 3 Madrid. Take a guided tour of the city with a visit to the Prado Museum, and possibly an afternoon tour to El Escorial and the Valley of the Fallen. Optional visit to a bullring to see a *corrida*.

Day 4 Madrid–Seville. Motor south through the landscape of Don Quixote's La Mancha. To Seville by nightfall.

Day 5 Seville. A local guide joins the tour to explain the city's highlights. Visit the cathedral with Columbus's tomb. Optional flamenco show at night.

Day 6 Seville–Torremolinos. Travel by motorcoach through the scenic mountains to the Costa del Sol.

Day 7 Torremolinos. A day at leisure or an optional tour to Gibraltar.

Day 8 Torremolinos–Granada. Travel away from the sea and into the mountains to see the Alhambra, a fantasy of lace in stone.

Day 9 Granada–Toledo–Madrid. Head north to the high plateau and back to Madrid. A stop in Toledo on the way allows time for a visit to a damascene steel workshop.

Day 10 Home again.

When is the best time to go? Spring and fall are the most pleasant times for a visit, although those who want to stay on the beach would prefer summer.

The travelers say, "The brochure says we'll be staying in paradores. That doesn't sound promising. Aren't they owned by the government?" How would you respond? The government's control of the paradores allows the preservation of significant historic sites that would otherwise be left to decay. Individual paradores are run like privately owned hotels. Some are luxury properties; others are more modest.

Andorra

High in the eastern Pyrenees, between France and Spain, is tiny Andorra (*an DAWR uh*), a country governed according to a system that dates from feudal times. In 1278 an agreement divided Andorra between Spain and France. Apart from a short period after the French Revolution, it has remained as a co-principality to the present day. The heads of state are the president of France and the bishop of Urgell.

Andorra's land covers little more than half the area of New York City. The only large town is the capital, **Andorra la Vella**. The landscape is extremely rugged, with high peaks towering above deep valleys and gorges that were carved out by glaciers. It is usually visited on multicountry tours passing from France to Spain or by day excursions from Barcelona. Tourists come to ski in winter and walk in the mountains in summer. Andorra has no airport or rail service.

✔ CHECK-UP

The Iberian Peninsula includes

- ✔ Portugal; its capital and largest city is Lisbon.
- ✔ Spain; its capital and largest city is Madrid.
- ✔ Gibraltar.
- ✔ Andorra; its capital and only city is Andorra la Vella.

For travelers, highlights of the Iberian Peninsula include

- ✔ Azulejos and Manueline architecture in Portugal.
- ✔ Shrine at Fátima in Portugal. (Virgin Mary appearance)
- ✔ Resorts of the Costa del Sol and the Algarve. NW Portugal
- ✔ Prado Museum in Madrid.
- ✔ Castles in Castile. (Central Spain)
- ✔ Gaudí's architecture in Barcelona.
- ✔ Moorish architecture at its best in Granada. Southern Spain
- ✔ Running with the bulls in Pamplona. in the Basque Region

France

The republic of France is the third-largest country in Europe; only Russia and Ukraine have more land. France has long stretches of coastline on the English Channel, the Bay of Biscay, and the Mediterranean. As Figure 12.4 shows, the Alps rise at its borders with Switzerland and Italy, and the Pyrenees separate it from Spain. France also shares borders with Belgium, Luxembourg, and Germany. The island of Corsica in the Mediterranean is also part of France.

Famed for its sophistication and style, each of France's regions has colorful traditions and a strong identity. The sophistication of Paris, the fairy-tale châteaux of the Loire Valley, the elegant resorts of the Côte d'Azur, the flower-filled landscape of Provence, and the vineyards of Bordeaux, Burgundy, and Épernay are but a few of the gems to be found.

The Cities

France offers the tourist a choice of cities such as Bordeaux, Nice, and Reims. None, of course, can match **Paris**, France's capital and international gateway, a city of dreams and discoveries.

Creating Paris The region surrounding Paris is known today as it was in medieval times as the *Île de France.* It was so named because it is surrounded by the waters of the rivers **Seine** (*sayn*), Marne, and Oise. Around 300 BC the Parisi tribe set up fishing huts on what is now the Île de la Cité ("Island of the City") in the middle of the Seine. The settlement spread to the river's left bank after the Romans occupied Gaul and founded a town. During the 12th and 13th centuries, the Louvre (*LOO vruh*) Palace was built (originally as a fortress) as well as the Cathedral of Notre Dame and the Sorbonne, and Paris became a crowded medieval city of narrow and winding streets.

In season, excursion boats (called *bateaux-mouches*) ply the Seine in Paris. At night, passengers can enjoy dinner and music while cruising past illuminated monuments.

In the 16th century, the Tuileries Gardens were built in front of the Louvre, which by then was the residence of the king. Cultural life flourished until Louis XIV, feeling restricted by the narrow streets, moved his court to Versailles (*vehr SY* or *vehr SAYLZ*). The Champs-Élysées was Louis' processional route between the Louvre and Versailles.

After the French Revolution, Napoleon wanted to make Paris the world's most beautiful city. He built bridges, opened new avenues, and raised monuments in honor of his victories. But it was not until the 1850s, when

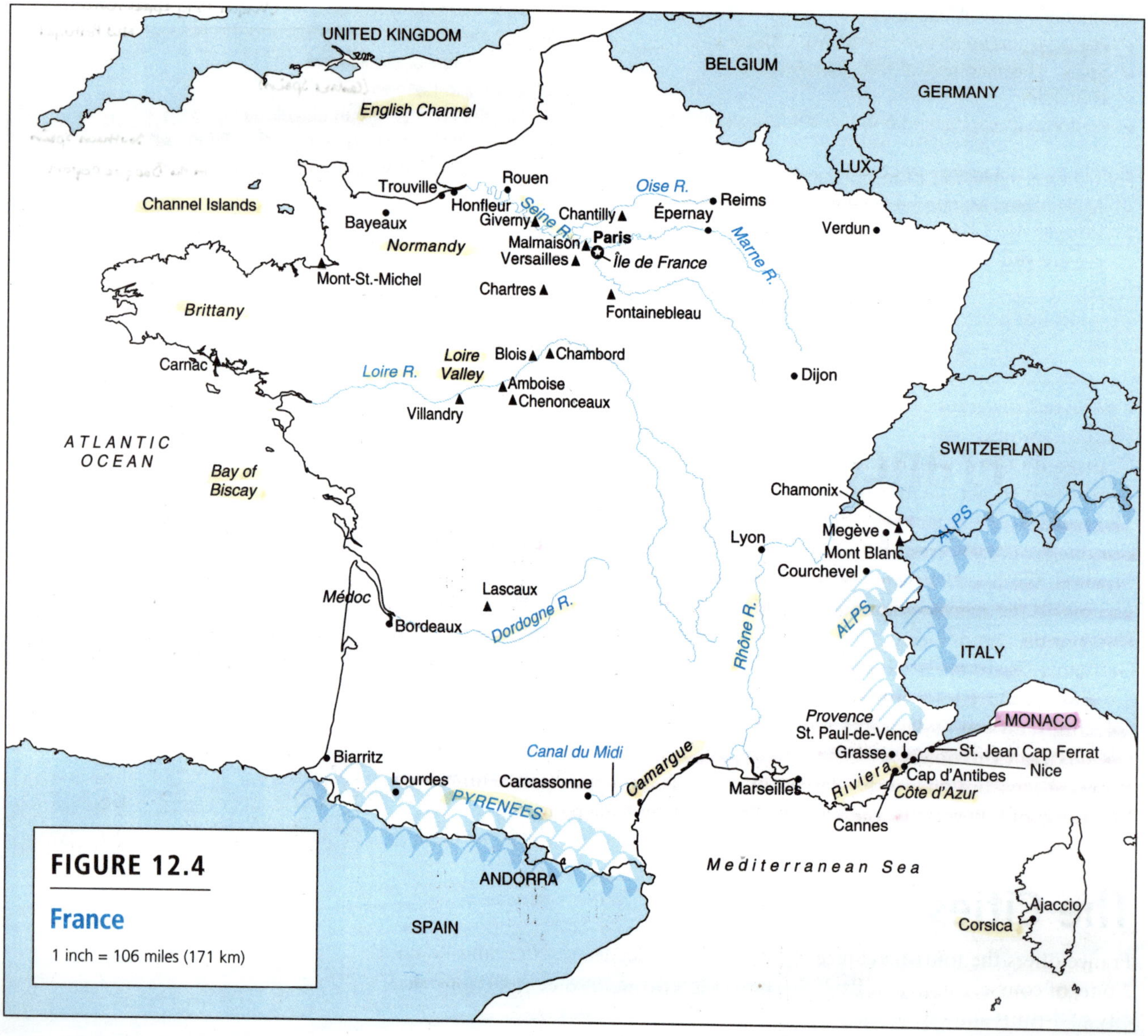

FIGURE 12.4

France

1 inch = 106 miles (171 km)

Georges-Eugène Haussmann took control, that the city was transformed to the beauty it is today.

Haussmann created a new city essentially by placing a ruler on a city map, making straight lines through crowded areas, and demolishing everything that stood in his way. Forty-three percent of the city's houses were torn down to make way for the new boulevards. New public parks had restaurants and even a racetrack. Rail stations and a glittering opera house were added. Although not popular at the time, Haussmann's achievements today are considered extraordinary. They include the Rue de Rivoli, the radiating roads around the Place de l'Étoile ("Square of the Star"), and the Avenue de l'Opéra.

The city continues to be restored and embellished. Since the 1970s, the French have built a commercial center west of the old city called La Défense. The Champs-Élysées continues to be one of the world's grandest boulevards. The vista from the Louvre—looking through the gardens of the Tuileries past the Place de la Concorde up the gentle slope to the Arc de Triomphe ("Arch of Triumph")—is truly impressive. Beyond the Arc, the road continues along the Avenue de la Grande-Armée (Napoleon's army) to the Bois de Boulogne and the Pont de Neuilly. Modern touches are the glass pyramid in front of the Louvre (designed by architect I. M. Pei) and the Grand Arch at La Défense, one of Paris's monumental buildings of the 1980s. The Champs-Élysées represents more than 300 years of design.

Paris is split into administrative districts called *arrondissements*. Addresses indicate in which arrondissement a place is located. Numbers up to nine designate the oldest districts of the city.

Touring Paris The embankments of the Seine are a perfect place to begin a walk. Here booksellers open their metal boxes to display old prints, maps, and books, and houseboats moored along the bank display their potted plants.

On the **Left Bank** (*Rive Gauche*)—the section of the city south of the Seine—are such landmarks as

- Eiffel Tower, the symbol of Paris. Originally it was built as a temporary exhibit but is now considered one of the culminating achievements of 19th-century civil engineering. Lines are long for the elevators to the top. For those who want to keep in shape, there are 1,625 steps.
- Hôtel des Invalides, Napoleon's tomb.
- Luxembourg Gardens, the prettiest of the city's large parks.
- Musée d'Orsay, which was converted from an old railway station. It is dedicated to art created from 1848 to 1914. If you see no other, see the d'Orsay.
- St.-Germain-des-Prés, the oldest church in Paris. The surrounding streets are crammed with tiny galleries and antique shops. At night, the cafés buzz to music and conversation.
- Sorbonne, one of Europe's oldest universities.

On the **Right Bank** (*Rive Droit*) are

- Arc de Triomphe, a memorial to Napoleon. It stands at the top of the Champs-Élysées. A flame of remembrance is lit each evening at the Arc's Tomb to an Unknown Soldier.
- Louvre Museum, the world's largest art museum, a former palace built over a period of 700 years by the kings of France. After the French Revolution, it became the national gallery, home of the *Mona Lisa* and the *Winged Victory* statue.
- Montmartre, on a dramatic rise above the city. Site of the Sacré Coeur Basilica and many nightclubs, the area was formerly home to the artistic community (now touristy).
- Fashion houses and major department stores. Browsing along the Boulevard Haussmann, the Rue de la Paix, and the Faubourg St. Honoré is

Eiffel Tower, Paris, France

a shopper's delight. The department stores Au Printemps, Au Bon Marché, and Galeries Lafayette are Paris institutions.

On the Île de la Cité in the middle of the river are

- Cathedral of Notre Dame, a "symphony in stone," according to Victor Hugo.
- Sainte-Chapelle, a small chapel built by Louis IX, a vision of shimmering stained glass.
- Conciergerie, the former city prison.

To many, Paris is its nightlife. Clubs and jazz bars are abundant. The cancan is still a regular feature at the famous cabaret Moulin Rouge. Its wild early days were immortalized by Henri de Toulouse-Lautrec (1864–1902) in his posters and paintings. *Paris by Night* tours include visits to the Folies Bergères and the Lido as well as the Moulin Rouge. Although the clubs are mainly for tourists, most visitors enjoy their evening.

Paris remains the ultimate gourmet destination. Good food and wine are an important part of everyday living. Fauchon, established in 1886, is the food store to visit when you want to plan a picnic with gourmet fixings and expense is no consideration.

Day tours from Paris lead to the **Château de Versailles**. Here Louis XIV dazzled everyone with the opulence of his court. Other nearby attractions are **Fontainebleau** (*FAHN tihn bloh*), near the old artists' village of Barbizon, southeast of Paris; **Chantilly**, famous for lace, a château, and a racetrack; **Giverny**, with Monet's garden; and **Malmaison**, home of Napoleon's Josephine. Soaring above the cornfields to the southwest and visible from miles around is the spire of the Gothic cathedral at **Chartres** (*SHAHR truh*). Chartres Cathedral is one of the finest examples of French Gothic architecture in a country renowned for its great Gothic churches. The cathedral was the first to use flying buttresses to hold up its walls. The inside is lit by the glorious "Chartres blue" stained-glass windows.

The Regions of France

From Paris the typical circular tour proceeds west to the Normandy and Brittany peninsulas and then south to visit the Loire Valley. It continues south to Bordeaux and then eastward to Provence and the Côte d'Azur. The next turn might be north to the ski resorts in the Alps or to the champagne district near Reims.

Normandy and Brittany The Normandy coast has cliffs, sandy beaches, and rocky coves with picturesque villages and resort towns. The ports of **Honfleur** and **Trouville** hosted most of the Impressionist painters during the late 1800s. The region is famous for its cider, cheeses, and Calvados, an apple-flavored brandy.

Normandy's past was not always peaceful. The Bayeux (*bay YOO*) Tapestry is a work of embroidery that tells the story of the Norman conquest of England and also provides a record of the ships, weapons, clothes, and way of life of the Middle Ages. Joan of Arc was burned at the stake in **Rouen**, and 3 million men invaded the Normandy beaches on June 6, 1944—D-Day. Few visitors can leave the area unmoved.

Mont-Saint-Michel is unique in its setting, the wealth of its history, and the beauty of its architecture. The tiny island rises out of the sea where Normandy joins Brittany. According to legend, the archangel Michael commanded the bishop of Avranches to build a chapel to honor his memory.

➤ PROFILE

Food Shops of France

Here is a brief guide to French food shops and what you are likely to find when you search for picnic provisions:

- ➤ *Boucherie*, the classic butcher's shop.
- ➤ *Boucherie chevaline*, the horse butcher, recognized by a horse head over the door.
- ➤ *Boulangerie*, the baker's shop, for the long loaf, the *baguette*.
- ➤ *Charcuterie*, a butcher's shop specializing in cold cuts.
- ➤ *Confiserie*, the confectioner's.
- ➤ *Fromagerie*, devoted entirely to cheese.
- ➤ *Hypermarket*, a super-supermarket.
- ➤ *Pâtisserie*, for pastries, cakes, and ice cream.
- ➤ *Poissonnerie*, the fishmonger.

ON THE SPOT

Mr. and Mrs. Monceau are looking forward to their escorted tour of France. They have read every line of the brochure and have a few questions. Mrs. Monceau calls to ask, "I see the brochure says we will visit the Eiffel Tower. Does that mean we will get to go to the top?"

A good question. *View* means just a drive-by. *Visit* means a stop and entry, but how long and how much the visit includes is rarely clear. Does this visit allow time to go to the top? Such a special feature would probably be promoted, but when the traveler asks and you do not know, find out.

The result has become a place of pilgrimage, a tiny isle topped by the spires of a Benedictine abbey. A causeway connects the island to the mainland. At the island's base, walls enclose a village of houses, shops, and restaurants. In summer, the narrow streets are crammed with people.

Before the causeway was built, quicksand and tides racing faster than a galloping horse claimed the lives of many pilgrims. Today, because of the causeway, the bay has silted up, and the spectacular tides no longer occur regularly. Most of the time Mont-Saint-Michel is surrounded only by mud. The French government hopes to preserve the island's setting by replacing the causeway with a footbridge to let the water flow through.

In Brittany, the traveler finds a land of legend. Its ancient megaliths parallel those of Stonehenge in age and magnitude. In **Carnac**, the megaliths stand in clusters and attract endless summer visitors. The countryside is celebrated for elegant manor houses and a good choice of *gîtes* ("farmhouses") available for rent.

La Mère Poulard ("Mother Chicken") is a restaurant and small inn within the walls of Mont-Saint-Michel. Built in 1875, it is famous for its omelets.

Loire Valley Northwest France includes the winding Loire River Valley southwest of Paris. It is the site of the magnificent houses called *châteaux* (*shat TOE*) that were the high point of French Renaissance architecture. The region boasts more than 3,000 buildings of various periods, including Chambord, Chenonceaux, Villandry, Blois, and Amboise. Some of the smaller, less publicized estates, such as Azay-le-Rideau, Villesavin, Loches, and Issoudon, are just as enjoyable, and sometimes less crowded.

The Loire (*luh WAHR*), France's longest river, runs westward to empty into the Bay of Biscay. Visitors can float down the river on a luxury barge, eat gourmet meals while aboard, and take excursions to points of interest. Several firms specialize in hot-air balloon trips over the countryside.

Château de Saumur on the Loire, France

The Atlantic Coast South to the Spanish border, France's Atlantic Coast contains havens of spectacular beauty. **Bordeaux** (*bor DOE*) is the port of distribution for some of France's finest wine.

North of Bordeaux, on the left bank of the Garonne River, is a strip of land called the **Médoc**. Nowhere on earth is more perfectly suited to the art of wine making than this small piece of land. The locals say that the vines of the Médoc thrive "with a sea view and their feet in the gravel." The museum of one vineyard, Château Mouton-Rothschild, displays wine labels designed by such artists as Cocteau, Braque, Dalí, Chagall, and Henry Moore.

The seaside resort of **Biarritz** has enjoyed a reputation for luxury since the nobility discovered its charms in the 19th century. The deluxe Hôtel du Palais was built by Napoleon III for his wife, Empress Eugénie.

Inland, attractions include

- The valley of the Dordogne River, which has caves that were home to prehistoric man. Although the cave with the most exceptional paintings, **Lascaux**, is closed to the public, others are open.
- The town of **Lourdes** (*loordz*), on the fringes of the Pyrenees, where pilgrims seek miracles at the shrine of St. Bernadette.
- The walled city of **Carcassonne** (*karh kah SAWN*), Europe's largest medieval fortress and one of its best preserved.
- The **Canal du Midi**, popular for barge tours, from Béziers near the coast to Carcassonne and beyond.

The Riviera and Provence The region between the Rhône (*rohn*) River and the Italian border along the Mediterranean is part of the larger province of Provence, which extends far inland. The coast is not all resort. The Rhône empties into the sea near **Marseilles**, and its delta region west of the city is a barren expanse of marshland called the **Camargue**. The French Riviera, one of the world's most beautiful resorts, begins to the east.

The **Côte d'Azur** (*koht da ZHOOR*) is the eastern end of the French Riviera. Côte d'Azur means "azure coast," and the name has become almost interchangeable with Riviera. The first wave of tourists came in the 1800s when English and Russian aristocrats would visit during the winter. The Alps shield the area from cold north winds, but it can be damp and rainy in winter. This didn't matter to the well-clothed Victorians. Not until 1936, when France passed the first paid-vacation law and the summer suntan became an emblem of success, did the middle class begin flocking to the area. But even in summer visitors should not expect Caribbean-type weather and sandy beaches. Beaches are rocky unless the hotels have imported sand.

Waterfront at Nice, France

Nice (*nees*), capital of the Côte d'Azur, stands in a position of great beauty. Its beautiful Promenade des Anglais, which hugs the seashore for several miles, was built in 1820 by an Englishman who lived in Nice during the winter months. The Négresco Hotel is as elegant a place to stay as possible.

Cannes (*cahn*) is another beautiful seaside city. Its Film Festival draws international attention each May. The Hotel Carlton is unofficial headquarters for the stars.

St. Paul-de-Vence is a hilltop village inland from Nice. Matisse, Picasso, and Georges Roualt all stayed in Vence. What drew them to the Côte d'Azur was not just the blue sea but also the medieval villages within easy reach among the hills beyond. Vence is enclosed by ramparts and has gorgeous views, galleries, restaurants, shops, and the Maeght Foundation, a fine small museum.

Grasse (*grahs*) is also in the hills behind the coast. It is the center of the French perfume industry. Tours include a visit to one of the factories.

Between Nice and Monaco are the three Corniche roads. *Corniche* means a "road carried across the precipitous face of a height as if it were a shelf." The roads provide some of the most spectacular views in France.

The French *concierge* was the person who handled the mail and performed the functions of a janitor and doorkeeper at the entrance to a building. The hotel concierge today is the person who smoothes the way for the traveler, arranges tickets and restaurant reservations, gives advice, and does a little bit of everything.

Rhône-Alps

The Alps and the Rhône River form the link between the north and south of France. The Rhône runs west from Lake Geneva before heading south to the Mediterranean. The *Route des Grandes Alpes* is the most famous and spectacular of the many roads through the mountains. Linking Lake Geneva with the Riviera, it offers wonderful views.

The resorts of **Chamonix** (*shah mo NEE*), **Megève**, and **Courchevel** draw devotees of winter sports. Courchevel has 310 miles (499 km) of ski runs linking nine resorts. The gateway to the ski resorts is through Geneva, Switzerland, or **Lyon** (*lee OHN*), France.

Monks perfected the blends and techniques that put sparkle into still wine. Dom Pérignon himself worked as a cellar-master.

Champagne Country

The region where wine is king and the grape is a symbol of wealth begins near **Dijon**, famed for its mustard. Northeast France includes the vineyards of **Épernay** and **Reims** (*reemz*). Champagne can be made officially only in this region. It is so far north and so cool that the grapes barely get ripe by conventional standards. But Champagne's harsh climate and chalky limestone soils are ideal for making sparkling wines. Attempts to duplicate the magic invariably fall short of the originals. A tourism trail is marked throughout the region with signs indicating *La Route Touristique du Champagne*. Vineyard cellars are open to visitors. Miles of galleries are hollowed out of the chalk, and perfectly aligned rows of bottles carry the famous names of *Moët et Chandon, Veuve Cliquot,* and *Taittinger.*

The region's most famous Gothic cathedral is at Reims, about 98 miles (158 km) northeast of Paris. Traditionally it was the coronation church of the French kings. The area has suffered the repeated devastation of war and invasion. The trenches of **Verdun** and the complex of the Maginot Line are memorials to the conflicts of the 20th century.

Corsica The fourth-largest island in the Mediterranean, Corsica is the most mountainous of them all. It is located about 100 miles (161 km) southeast of mainland France. **Ajaccio** (*ah JAHK oh*) is the capital and largest city.

Although the beaches are nothing great, in July and August Corsica is jammed with vacationers. The island continues to celebrate the memory of its most famous son, Napoleon. The Maison Bonaparte National Museum, the Bonaparte family funeral chapel, and statues and squares pay homage to the little general.

✔ CHECK-UP

The most-visited cities of France are

- ✔ Paris, the capital and largest city.
- ✔ Bordeaux, the center of fine wine production.
- ✔ Nice, the capital of the Riviera.
- ✔ Reims, where French kings were crowned and champagne now rules.

For travelers, highlights of France are

- ✔ Barge and balloons trips through the countryside.
- ✔ French cuisine and wine.
- ✔ Loire Valley and the châteaux.
- ✔ Mont-Saint-Michel, the rocky island between Brittany and Normandy.
- ✔ Paris, Paris, Paris.
- ✔ Provence and the French Riviera.

Italy

In south central Europe, Italy is a mountainous peninsula that juts into the Mediterranean (see Figure 12.5). Shaped roughly like a long high-heeled boot, it is bordered (from west to east) by France, Switzerland, Austria, and Slovenia. At the southwestern tip of the peninsula (the boot's toe), the narrow Strait of Messina separates Italy's mainland from **Sicily**, the Mediterranean's largest island. Sitting just south of the French island of Corsica is the island of **Sardinia**. About seventy other small islands, scattered mainly around Sicily and Sardinia, make up the rest of Italy.

The **Po River** flows from west to east across the widest part of the country, the Plain of Lombardy. This lowland region is in Italy's north but south of the Alps. The area is heavily industrialized and populous. From the plain the Apennines stretch southward the length of the country, extending into Sicily.

Italy has delights everywhere. For centuries Italy was a collection of feuding city-states, and each of the formerly independent states boasts a distinctive character. The cities are fascinating, the landscape is spectacular, and the past has left a legacy of art and architecture. Within Italy's borders are two independent countries: the tiny **Republic of San Marino** in north central Italy and **Vatican City**, located completely within the city of Rome.

The Cities

For the first-time visitor, Rome, Florence, and Venice are must-sees, with maybe a stop in Assisi or Pisa along the way. But Italy offers so much more. One gateway to the riches is the *Eternal City*—Rome.

Rome In the city of emperors and popes, even the ancient past seems like yesterday. Rome includes a Roman city, a Renaissance city, and an ordinary, crowded, noisy modern one. Inhabitants take the past casually, living in apartments overlooking great plazas, driving their Fiats wildly over Roman paving stones on the Via Appia, and going to the opera in the 1,800-year-old Baths of Caracalla.

Rome's earliest settlement was probably a shepherds' village on a hill close to the **Tiber River**. The mound, called the Palatine Hill, was one of seven hills that lay on the eastern side of a swampy valley.

Italy's capital was the hub of the mighty Roman Empire. But the sacking of Rome by the Visigoths in AD 410 fragmented the country, and Rome lost its importance and soon disintegrated into a sad city.

During the Renaissance, Pope Nicolas V (reigned 1447–1455) saw the rebuilding of the city as a way of passing on the Christian faith. During the 1500s and 1600s, various popes appointed the finest painters and sculptors, including Michelangelo, to design and decorate the buildings.

When Victor Emmanuel II became king of a reunified Italy in 1861, he ended the power of the pope and made Rome the country's capital. During World War

FIGURE 12.5 Italy

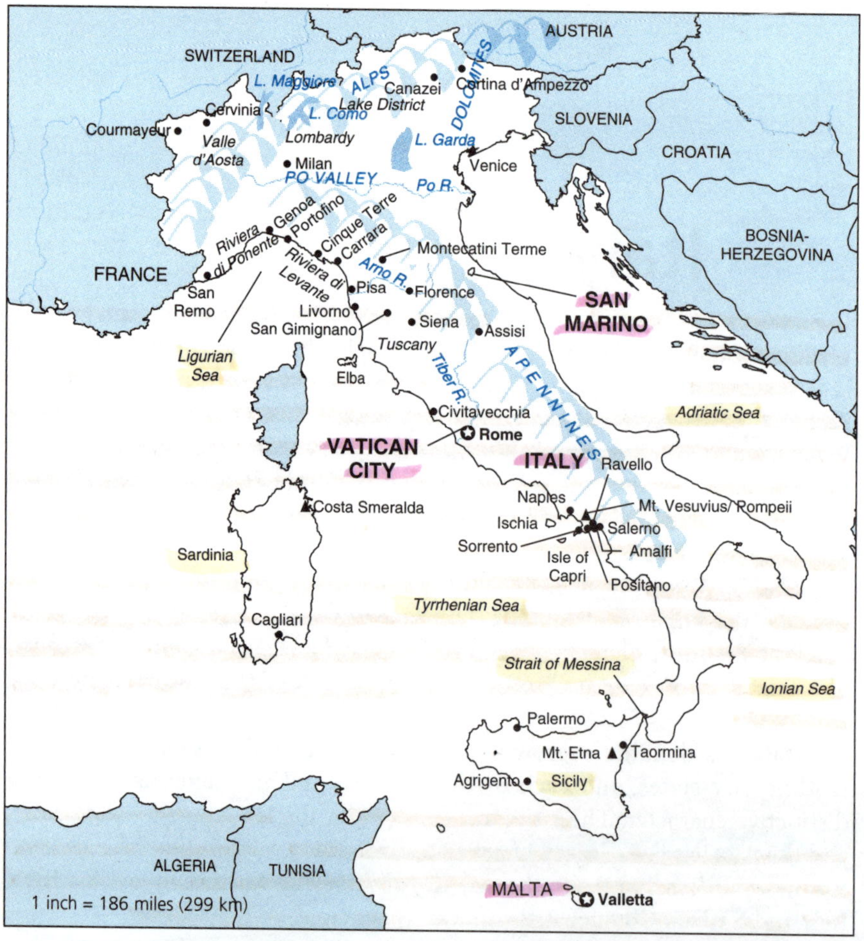

II, Rome was declared an "open city" and avoided bombing by the Allies, thus escaping the damage endured by many European capitals. A referendum in 1946 abolished the monarchy and established a democratic republic.

A few of Rome's attractions are

- Baths of Caracalla, suitable for 1,600 bathers at a time. It is used now in summer as a setting for music performances.
- Catacombs, south of Rome on the Appian Way, tombs steeped in the history of Christianity.
- Roman Forum, the center of ancient Roman life.
- Pantheon, a 2nd-century Roman temple built to honor the gods.
- Colosseum, perhaps the city's most enduring monument, dedicated in AD 80.
- Piazza del Campidoglio, designed by Michelangelo for the Capitoline Hill.
- Piazza di Spagna (literally, "Spanish Plaza," but known to tourists as the "Spanish Steps") and Trinità dei Monti, a square in the center of Rome's shopping district. The ship-shaped monument in the piazza was designed in the 16th century, possibly by Bernini. Poet John Keats's house is beside the steps. The deluxe Hassler Hotel sits at the top of the steps. Its rooftop restaurant provides a wonderful view of Rome's seven hills.
- Piazza Navona, a long oval famed for Bernini's *Fountain of the Four Rivers* in its center and for the luscious chocolate dessert *tartufo* sold at Tre Scalini café. In ancient Rome, the piazza was used for horse races and flooded for naval battles.
- Piazza Venezia, the geographic center of the city, surrounded by palaces and overshadowed by the "wedding cake"—which is what Italians call the huge white marble memorial to Victor Emmanuel II.
- Trevi Fountain, an 18th-century baroque fountain where travelers must throw two coins over their shoulders. The first brings them back to Rome; the second fulfills a wish.

The Eternal City's monuments, churches, and palaces stand as reminders of past glories. The city also has fine hotels, excellent restaurants, and quality shopping. Unfortunately, the city's attractions have brought problems, including acute traffic congestion. Motor traffic is now banned in much of the city center.

Although Rome is no longer anywhere near the sea, **Civitavecchia** is called the port of Rome, a stop for cruise ships. Cruise passengers are bused into Rome for city excursions.

As people say when frustrated with so much to see and so little time, "Rome—a lifetime is not enough."

Colosseum, Rome, Italy

Vatican City Although completely surrounded by the city of Rome, Vatican City is an independent state, the smallest in the world. It is on the west bank of the Tiber River, its medieval walls cutting it off from the city except at St. Peter's Square. Within its walls the pope has absolute power.

St. Peter's Basilica (built 1506–1626) is the home of the Catholic Church, its principal shrine, and one of the world's architectural masterpieces. The Vatican Museum's works of art include the frescoes on the walls and ceiling of the Sistine Chapel. Artists that contributed to the building of St. Peter's include Raphael, Michelangelo, and Bernini.

Admission to the pope's weekly general audience is a simple procedure, but private audiences are almost impossible to obtain. Most people see the pope when he makes an appearance on his balcony overlooking the square in front of the basilica.

The difference between a basilica (e.g., St. Peter's in Rome) and a cathedral (e.g., Notre Dame in Paris) has mostly to do with architecture. A basilica was originally a Roman hall of justice. Its plan was adopted as the basis of Christian church design. Cathedral architecture began in the 13th century when engineering developments such as the flying buttress permitted soaring walls with openings for stained-glass windows.

North of Rome

A tour north of Rome is like a journey through a patchwork of little countries, each proudly distinct from its neighbors.

> PROFILE

Food Specialties of Italy

Cooking (or eating!) tours are popular special interests. Sometimes on a biking tour, a chef rides along to guide participants through open markets. Tuscany is where Italian cooking was born. Some regional specialties include

- In the Alps: vermouth and *grissini* (bread sticks).
- In Venice: *polenta*, a form of semolina made from corn.
- In Genoa: *pesto*, a sauce made from basil leaves, pine nuts, olive oil, and garlic.
- In Rome: *saltimbocca alla romana*, veal rolled around ham, sautéed, and sprinkled with Marsala wine.
- In Sicily: *cassata*, an ice cream cake with candied fruits, and pasta with fresh tomato-based sauces.

Also, note that *alla milanese* means with butter; *alla bolognese*, with meat sauce (Bologna is a meat-producing region); *alla fiorentina*, with olive oil and spinach.

Leaning Tower of Pisa, Italy

Assisi Assisi is a hill town in central Italy crowned with a cathedral and surrounded by ramparts. It is built of pink stone and spreads like a fan on the slope of a low mountain. Its narrow streets are lined with shops displaying the local pottery.

Assisi was the home of St. Francis (1182–1226), saint of simplicity and founder of the Franciscan order. Among his followers was a woman named Clare, who founded the Order of Poor Clares. The town is dedicated to their memories.

Florence Northwest of Assisi is Florence (*Firenze*), the capital of the region of **Tuscany** (*Toscana*). The abiding image of Florence is that of Il Duomo—the magnificent ribbed dome of the cathedral of Santa Maria del Fiore, which rises above the city's terracotta roofs.

Florence developed along the banks of the **Arno River**. The Ponte Vecchio ("Old Bridge"), which was built across the river during the 1340s, is the only one of Florence's bridges that survived World War II. The first tenants of the bridge's shops were butchers and tanners, who used water from the river in their work. In 1593 a duke evicted the butchers and installed goldsmiths and jewelers, whose successors occupy the tiny shops to this day.

During the 15th and 16th centuries, Florence attracted poets, artists, architects, musicians, and scientists to enjoy the patronage of the powerful banking families, headed by the Medici. Such artists and scientists as Botticelli, Brunelleschi, Leonardo da Vinci, Michelangelo, and Galileo enjoyed their patronage. The city is truly a world treasure struggling to maintain its heritage. Although no major buildings were lost in the wars, damage was done by the Arno flood of 1966 and by a terrorist bomb in 1993, which destroyed part of the great Uffizi Museum. Michelangelo's priceless statue of David is protected from the elements in another museum, the Galleria dell'Accademia. To help preserve the city's grandeur, cars have been banned from the central area.

Tuscany In addition to Florence's treasures, Tuscany is home to the Leaning Tower of **Pisa**, the spas of **Montecatini Terme**, the horse races in **Siena**, the marble of **Carrara**, the beautiful tower houses of **San Gimignano**, vineyards (the home of Chianti wine), and the port of **Livorno**. Rides through the countryside lead to such places as the walled village of Montereggioni, mentioned in Dante's *Inferno*.

San Marino Some 62 miles (100 km) northeast of Florence is the most serene republic of San Marino, one of the smallest countries in Europe. It is perched on the western slope of Monte Titano. Walls guard it, only one road enters it, and the narrow winding streets are mostly closed to traffic. Its isolated terrain has preserved this ancient state from predatory neighbors. The Rocco Fortress on top of the hill offers magnificent views.

Venice The *Queen of the Adriatic*, Venice is a living museum. The city is built on a series of islets in the center of a saltwater lagoon. Islands in the lagoon include Murano, famous for glass making; Burano, known for its lace; and Torcello, with an old Romanesque church. The only forms of transport in town are motorboats (*motoscafi*), water buses (*vaporetti*), and very expensive *gondole*.

St. Mark's Square, with its basilica, Campanile ("Bell Tower"), cafés, and yes, pigeons, is one of the world's great outdoor spaces. Between the square and the lagoon, the Doge's Palace is connected to a prison by the Bridge of Sighs. Prisoners walked across the bridge on their way to execution, sighing perhaps at their last glimpse of the world.

To many, Venice is the most entrancing of cities; others are saddened by its crumbling stone and smelly canals. Work is underway to save Venice. Mobile dikes are being built to block the entrance to Venice's lagoon against winter floods. Tunnels are being constructed to link some of the islands, making travel among them easier. Cynics can go to Hemingway's favorite, Harry's Bar, just off St. Mark's Square to savor a *Bellini* (champagne and peach juice) and brood over the perils of pollution and progress.

Doge's Palace, Venice, Italy

Milan Milan is the capital of **Lombardy** and the center of Italian fashion. Its Duomo is a marvel of green-veined marble. Leonardo da Vinci's fresco of *Il Cenacolo* ("The Last Supper") is in the Convent of Santa Maria delle Grazie. Special permission is now needed to view the fresco.

Opera was born in Italy in the early 1600s, and Milan's La Scala is possibly the world's most famous opera house. The opera season runs from December through April or May. Tickets are expensive and hard to get.

Lombardy is also home to much of Italy's Lake District. The great northern lakes lie in a series of long, deep valleys running down onto the plains from the Alps. Two of the most spectacular lakes are **Maggiore** (*muh JOHR ee*) and **Como**. Another lake, **Garda**, is to the east; it is the largest lake in Italy.

Ski Regions Northwest of Milan, near the Swiss border, is Italy's most mountainous region, the **Valle d'Aosta**. The area has numerous ski resorts, most notably **Courmayeur** and **Cervinia**.

To the east, the rugged **Dolomites**, a range of the Alps, make a scenic detour worthwhile in any season. The Dolomites look like towers, castles, or pinnacles in the sky. An ideal way to tour the region is to follow the *Dolomite Road* between the ski resorts of **Cortina d'Ampezzo** and **Canazei**.

The Italian Riviera A narrow strip of coastline sandwiched between sea and mountains curves in an east-west arch from the French border to Tuscany. Known as the Italian Riviera, the region has two sections divided by the large port of **Genoa**.

The **Riviera di Levante** ("Riviera to the East") boasts the exclusive resort of **Portofino** and the **Cinque Terre** ("Five Lands"), where hikers can village-hop along a seaside trail called the *Sentiero Azzuro* ("Blue Trail"), which links the five villages. These medieval fishing villages were accessible only by mule tracks or by water until recently, but new rail routes and hiking paths have improved access. The area retains its special customs, culture, and great coastline beauty.

The **Riviera di Ponente** ("Riviera to the West") has the better beaches and more hotels. **San Remo** is a large, lively resort near the French border.

South of Rome

Italy's south—the region called the *Mezzogiorno* ("Midday")—is a contrast to the north. Excursions to Pompeii, the Isle of Capri, and the Amalfi Drive occupy most tours south of Rome, but independent travelers will find much more to see.

Naples Its location on the Bay of Naples has made Naples an important port for naval operations, cruise lines, and oceangoing ferries. Mount Vesuvius looms over the city. A toll road leads most of the way up to the summit. At the mountain's southern base are the ruins of **Pompeii**. In AD 79 the volcano's most famous eruption destroyed Pompeii as well as the cities of Stabiae and

Herculaneum. The volcanic ash that buried the cities also preserved them, as if frozen in time. More than two-thirds of Pompeii has been excavated. The decoration in some of the villas is amazingly intact, with wall paintings ranging from the heroic to the erotic.

Capri and Ischia Daily excursion boats depart from Naples for the Isle of Capri and Ischia (*ees KEY ah*) in the Bay of Naples. On a visit in 29 BC, Caesar Augustus liked Capri so much that he bought the island. His successor, Tiberius, built villas and started rumors (never proven) of secret orgies. Today, the tiny whitewashed houses and flower-filled squares look like a stage setting. Funiculars and cable cars carry visitors to the island's mountain peaks.

The Blue Grotto is one of Capri's special sights. Weather permitting, visitors board a large motorboat that takes them to the entrance of the grotto. There they transfer to a small rowboat. Those who make it this far are asked to keep their heads down. When the wave is right, the boatman grabs a chain and pulls the small boat through a narrow passageway into the grotto. The grotto's dazzling blue light and crystal waters have made it one of the world's most admired attractions.

Ischia is the largest island in the Bay of Naples. It has good beaches, scenic beauty, archaeological attractions, thermal springs with medicinal qualities, and mud considered to be of great value.

Amalfi Coast The peninsula south of Naples is one of the most popular regions of Italy. Sheer cliffs rise from the deep-blue waters of the Mediterranean, and everywhere hills and sea dominate the view. **Sorrento** is on the north side of the peninsula. It is a tour center with many fine hotels. Ferries sail to Capri from its port.

The Amalfi Drive begins at Sorrento and continues to **Salerno**. The hairpin road is carved into rocky walls above the beautiful sea. The road is so narrow in some places that drivers must fold back their outside mirrors so they can pass each other. Motorcoach access is limited.

Positano, **Amalfi**, and **Ravello** are resorts on the Amalfi coast. With Positano as a base, travelers can hike the *Pathway of the Gods*, a most spectacular walk.

Sicily Sicily is the Mediterranean's largest island. **Palermo** is the regional capital. Sicily is notorious for its earthquakes, mudslides, and association with the Mafia. It is also famous for its Greek temples, *gelato* ("ice cream"), and Europe's largest active volcano, Mount Etna.

Etna is in the northeast of the island. The volcano has been credited with some 150 significant eruptions, several quite recently. When it is dormant, Etna can be climbed, hiked, and toured, except to the area of active lava flow.

In the shadow of the volcano, few resorts can match **Taormina**'s site on a lofty terrace above the sea. Its streets are lined with cafés and boutiques, and its Greek theater dates from the 3rd century. A cable car runs from the town to the rocky beaches, hotels, and restaurants along the shore. In the town, the Hotel San Domenico, a luxurious property with views of Mount Etna, was built as a Dominican monastery in 1430. Dining in the main restaurant is a culinary event.

The outstanding archaeological site of the southwest coast is the Valley of the Temples in **Agrigento**. Honey-colored ruins left by the Greeks crown a ridge overlooking the sea. At the height of power, Agrigento attracted poets such as Pindar.

Sardinia The Mediterranean's second-largest island is Sardinia. Its dramatic landscape of mountains, rocks, and *macchia* ("heathland") is dotted with *nuraghe,* cone-shaped stone fortresses dating from earliest times. **Cagliari** is the regional capital.

A consortium presided over by Prince Karim, the Aga Khan, developed palatial hotels and marinas in the northeast corner of Sardinia on one of the world's most exquisite coasts, known as the **Costa Smeralda** ("Emerald Coast"). Luxury hotels beckon super-rich and world-famous travelers to this exclusive retreat.

✔ CHECK-UP

The most-visited cities of Italy are

- ✔ Florence, home of the Renaissance.
- ✔ Milan, center of fashion and industry.
- ✔ Pisa, known for its leaning tower.
- ✔ Rome, the capital and largest city.
- ✔ Sorrento, for rest and relaxation.
- ✔ Venice, Queen of the Adriatic.

For travelers, highlights of Italy are

- ✔ Rome and Vatican City.
- ✔ Florence and the Tuscan countryside.
- ✔ Canals of Venice.
- ✔ Italian Riviera and the Cinque Terre.
- ✔ Amalfi coast and the Isle of Capri.
- ✔ Ruins of Pompeii.
- ✔ Resorts of Sardinia and Sicily.

Greece

For history buffs and museum lovers, and for those who enjoy sailing the seas or lying on a sun-drenched beach, Greece is an ideal destination. East of Italy, mainland Greece occupies the southernmost part of the Balkan Peninsula (see Figure 12.6). Its western shores are washed by the Ionian Sea; on the east, the Aegean Sea lies between Greece and Turkey. In the north, Greece shares borders with Albania, Macedonia, Bulgaria, and Turkey.

Long arms of the sea reach into the coasts of Greece's mainland, forming peninsulas. Nearly three-quarters of the land is mountainous and uninhabited. A Greek legend says that God sifted the earth through a strainer while making the world. He made one country after another with the good soil and threw away the stones left in the strainer. The stones became Greece.

In addition to the mainland, Greece consists of more than 1,500 islands dotted all over the Aegean and the Ionian Seas. Only about one-tenth of the islands are inhabited. South of the mainland in the Mediterranean is the large island of **Crete**.

Isolated geographically and culturally from most of Europe, Greece has struggled since the days of ancient Rome to maintain its independence. From 1460 to 1827, Greece was a Turkish province. Political strife extended well into the 20th century.

Athens

Almost half of the Greek population lives in the Greater Athens area. The city is a sprawling metropolis that is noisy and prone to traffic jams and the notorious *nefos* ("smog"). The infrastructure built for the 2004 Olympic Games—new and improved highways, an extended Metro system, and a tramline to the southern suburbs—has made getting around the city easier than in the past.

Acropolis, Athens, Greece

The capital clusters around the Acropolis, the rocky hill that dominates the city. The statesman Pericles (495–429 BC) wanted Athens to be the center of art and literature and the world's most beautiful city. Of the temples he built on the Acropolis, the most magnificent is the Parthenon, dedicated to Athene, the goddess of wisdom. Regarded as the most perfect of all buildings, it has no straight lines—every part, even the pavement, is slightly curved to enhance its proportions.

The life of modern Athens centers around three squares: Syntagma, Omonoia, and Monastiraki. Syntagma, or Constitution Square, is the administrative center. Hotels, office buildings, and the Parliament Building (formerly the Royal Palace) face the square. A special corps of Greek soldiers, the *evzones*, guards the Tomb of the Unknown Soldier and Parliament. On Syntagma is the Hotel Grande Bretagne, a city landmark with magnificent views of the Acropolis. The structure opened as a hotel in 1872 in a former palace. The interior was recently gutted and rebuilt.

The *acropolis* was the religious and military center of a city-state in ancient Greece and was often sited on a hill for defense reasons. The most famous acropolis is the Acropolis of Athens.

Omonoia Square is northwest of Syntagma. The area between the two squares is Athens's chief shopping area. Monastiraki Square is south of Omonoia in the heart of the old market district. Small shops, stalls, and street vendors surround Monastiraki. To the southeast is the Plaka, a district with winding alleys, cafés, shops, and nightclubs.

The National Archaeological Museum presents an impressive overview of Greek art through the centuries. High points include the gold artifacts found at Mycenae and examples of classical sculpture.

FIGURE 12.6 Greece

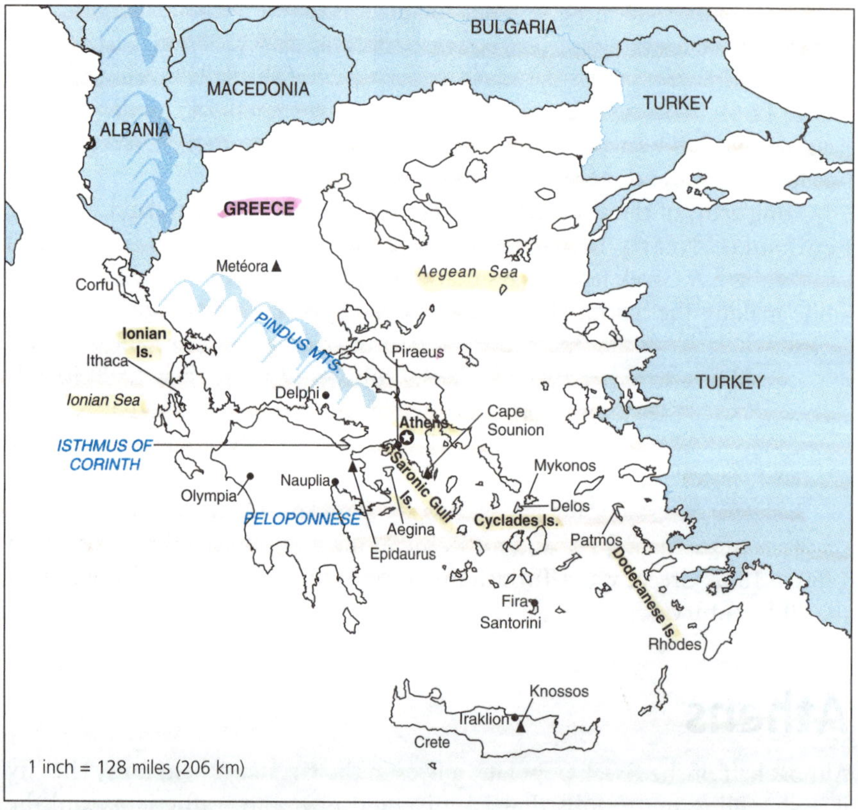

A short drive (about one and a half hours) from the city along the Saronic Gulf coast takes travelers to **Cape Sounion** and the Temple of Poseidon, an ideal location for a temple to the god of the sea. Its white marble columns have been a landmark for ancient and modern mariners. Lord Byron carved his name on one of the columns in 1810, setting a bad example of graffiti.

Other Places to Visit

A first-time trip to Greece needs at least two weeks. The tourist should spend two to three days in Athens, then head north to Metéora and Delphi on the mainland, circle down to the Peloponnese, and return to Athens to board a ship for a cruise of the islands.

Metéora, Greece

Metéora North of Athens (about four or five hours by car) on the mainland, the fantastic monasteries of Metéora (*may TAY oar ah*) should not be missed. From the valley floor, towers of rock rise almost perpendicularly. In the 14th century, Byzantine monks built twenty-four monasteries on top of the rocks. Supplies and people were hauled up in nets. Only five buildings remain. In the 1920s, stairs were carved to make the monasteries accessible, and a religious revival has seen the return of monks and nuns.

Delphi In the mainland's southwest are the ancient ruins of Delphi. According to legend, when Zeus released two eagles from opposite ends of the earth, their paths crossed in the sky above Delphi, establishing the site as the center of the world. People visited Delphi to consult the god on what to do in both public and private life. For a fee, people could hear the ambiguous words of the god, spoken through a priestess called the Oracle.

The Peloponnese The highway from Athens to the Peloponnese Peninsula crosses the **Isthmus of Corinth**. The Corinth Canal provides the shortest route from the eastern Mediterranean to the Adriatic and Italy. Today's megaships cannot use the 75-foot-wide (23 m) canal, but small ships squeeze through regularly.

A few miles to the south is **Epidaurus**, the best preserved of the ancient Greek theaters, and it is still used today. Its remarkable acoustics amaze visitors. Even a whisper on stage can be heard clearly in the outermost tier of seats.

Nauplia, last of the Peloponnese sites accessible from Athens on day trips, is a city nestled by the sea. Its lovely site is a popular tour stop and a cruise ship port.

Olympia is on the west coast of the peninsula. It was the athletic and religious center of the ancient world and the inspiration for the modern games. The flame of Altis, used to light the torch carried to the Olympic Games, still burns.

Bouzoukias is music played on a bouzouki guitar. Sometimes the music moves the audience to break plates or throw flowers. Today, those who break plates must pay for the privilege.

The Islands

Over the centuries the sea brought settlers and invaders to the Greek islands and provided the inhabitants with their way of life. It now brings millions of visitors each summer. Some destinations (such as Corfu, Crete, Mykonos, and Rhodes) have airports; to get to other islands, travelers take ferries from **Piraeus** (*pie RAY us*), the port of Athens.

Ionian Islands West of the mainland, the Ionian Islands are different from most of the Greek islands. They are lush and green; in contrast, the islands in the Aegean are desertlike. **Corfu** has secluded coves and stretches of coast given over totally to resorts. **Ithaca** was Ulysses' home in the epic poem *The Odyssey.*

Saronic Gulf Islands Because of their proximity to Athens and convenient ferry and hydrofoil services from Piraeus, the Saronic Gulf Islands receive many visitors. The most visited are Aegina, Poros, Hydra, and Andros.

Cyclades The classic whitewashed houses and blue-framed doorways of the Cyclades are the image of Greece. They are in the south Aegean. **Delos**, the nucleus of the group, was once a sacred island, considered the birthplace of Apollo. Other popular islands are Mykonos and Santorini.

Mykonos is a chic resort, a dry and barren island with sandy beaches and active nightlife, thick with sun worshipers throughout the summer. Mykonos town is a tangle of cube-shaped houses and a maze of narrow lanes lined with interesting shops. Three 16th-century windmills overlook the harbor.

Santorini is widely believed to be the lost kingdom of Atlantis. The island's white villages cling to cliffs above black-sand beaches. Its volcano erupted in 1450 BC, forming the island's present crescent shape. The town of **Fira** overlooks the collapsed caldera left by the eruption. From the docks the town can be reached by foot, on muleback, or by cable car.

CLOSE-UP: GREECE

Who is a good prospect for a trip to Greece? Those interested in ancient history, particularly the classics, will enjoy mainland Greece. The islands appeal to romantics and resort lovers. Some may enjoy just sipping a glass of ouzo in a café by the water's edge on Mykonos while watching the yachts sail into the harbor.

Why would they come to Greece? To see the ruins, hear the legends, gaze at the deep-blue sea, and explore the land that influenced the culture of the Western world.

Where would they go? A journey through Greece on a small group tour might be accompanied by a classical historian and follow this itinerary.

Day 1 Overnight flight to Athens.

Day 2 Arrive in Athens in the late morning. Afternoon for rest or exploration. Meet the group and your escort at dinner.

Day 3 Athens. Climb to the top of the Acropolis before the sun heats up the pathway. Optional afternoon tour to Cape Sounion.

Day 4 Athens–Corinth–Nauplia. In the morning, visit the National Archaeological Museum to view ancient history. In the afternoon, depart in small vans to Nauplia, on the way crossing the Corinth Canal.

Day 5 Nauplia. Optional visit to the ruins of Mycenae.

Day 6 Delphi. Travel north up the Peloponnese to Delphi, the home of the Oracle. Do you have a question?

Day 7 Motor back to Athens and its port of Piraeus. Board your elegant two-masted ship with a capacity for thirty-three guests. Your tour has reserved all cabins for this exclusive voyage.

Days 8–12 Sail the sea of the ancient Greeks. Visit Santorini, Naxos, Delos, Mykonos, and Rhodes. Your ship is just the right size to enter the harbors.

Day 13 Sail past Cape Sounion at the tip of the Attica Peninsula on your way back to Piraeus.

When is the best time to go? Late spring or early fall is usually best. The crowds are sparser, and the weather still holds.

The traveler says, "Seeing ancient ruins and hearing a lot of stuff based on mythology seem kind of boring to me. You know I like beach vacations to an all-inclusive with lots to do. What can I do in Greece that is like that?" How would you respond? Greece has options for those who prefer something other than exploring the Classical world. You might suggest a few days in Athens to shop and to sample the nightlife of the Plaka then on to one of the islands to sit in the sun, relax, meet people, and dance all night.

Dodecanese In the southeast Aegean near Turkey are the Dodecanese, including the island of **Rhodes**. The Colossus of Rhodes—one of the Seven Wonders of the Ancient World—once spanned the harbor. The walled city is perfect for leisurely walking.

Kos, Patmos, Kalimnos, and Simi are other islands in this group. On Patmos, St. John the Evangelist supposedly wrote the Book of Revelation in the Cave of the Apocalypse. The monastery dedicated to him dominates the island.

Crete The largest of the Greek islands, Crete belongs to no island grouping. Just outside the capital of **Iraklion** is the ruin of the great **Palace of Knossos**, one of Europe's most outstanding archaeological sites. The palace is proof of the once-thriving Minoan culture. Built against a hill and buried under mounds of earth, the palace was uncovered in 1900. Images of bulls adorn its walls.

✔ CHECK-UP

The most-visited areas of Greece are
- ✔ Athens, the capital and largest city.
- ✔ Peloponnese, with its ancient ruins.
- ✔ Greek islands.

For travelers, highlights of Greece are
- ✔ Acropolis in Athens.
- ✔ Monasteries perched on rock pinnacles at Metéora.
- ✔ Delphi.
- ✔ Ruins at Mycenae.
- ✔ Site of the first Olympic Games at Olympia.
- ✔ Palace of Knossos on Crete.
- ✔ Ouzo at sunset on the terrace of a café on Santorini.
- ✔ Cruise on the deep-blue waters of the eastern Mediterranean.

Planning the Trip

Southern Europe is a much-visited destination, and experienced travelers on return trips often have special interests and know where they want to go. They might want to visit southern Europe's archaeological sites, battlefields, castles, cooking schools, festivals, gardens, museums, shrines, spas, and so on.

When to Go

Summer is the most popular season for travel to southern Europe, but for travelers who have the time, spring and autumn are the best seasons to visit. Here are some specifics to consider:

- Europeans have four- to six-week vacations and tend to spend August at the beach or in the country, leaving the cities a little less crowded (although many shops and restaurants are closed).
- Paris and Rome are year-round attractions, but winters can be cold and wet.
- In winter, the French and Italian rivieras and the Greek islands are cold and damp.
- The Algarve and the Costa del Sol have mild, sunny winters that appeal to golfers and tennis players, but they are not destinations for travelers who crave Caribbean warm water.

■ Summer is the best season for cruising; the Mediterranean can get rough off-season.

➤ PROFILE

Shopping in Southern Europe

Shopping ranges from high fashion in Paris and Milan to handicrafts and souvenirs from roadside stands:

- ➤ Portugal's buys include items made from cork, gold and silver filigree work, handmade embroideries from Madeira, carpets from Arraiolos, and ceramic tiles.
- ➤ Spanish craftworkers produce ceramics, Toledo's damascene steel, Córdoba's embossed leather, Seville's silk shawls, and Granada's lace mantillas.
- ➤ French products are fashion and art in Paris, truffles from Périgord, mustards from Dijon, and herbs, fabrics, and perfumes from Provence.
- ➤ Italy features leather, gold, pottery, silk, inlaid wood, coral, paper goods, and items made from marble and alabaster.
- ➤ Greece specializes in gold jewelry, pottery, Flokáti carpets, and worry beads.
- ➤ San Marino, Monaco, Andorra, and Vatican City sell unique postage stamps.

■ ■ ■

Italian "bars" are where one goes for coffee. Table service costs more, so you often see people taking their coffee standing up.

■ ■ ■

■ ■ ■

Greek tavernas welcome guests to their kitchens to see what's cooking and make their choices.

■ ■ ■

Preparing the Traveler

Travelers to southern Europe have few problems with documentation, health standards, or medical procedures. Depending on their experience, they may appreciate tips about handling money, language, or customs.

Money Changing money in southern Europe poses few special problems. Most members of the European Union (EU) discussed in this chapter use the euro. (See the Fact File in Appendix A for more information.) Ample exchange facilities and ATMs are available. Some hotels, restaurants, and shops do not accept credit cards. Taxes are added to almost every purchase.

Language Although English is widely spoken in the tourist centers, it helps to learn to say "please" and "thank you." Fortunately (except in Greece), the Roman alphabet is used, and many English words come from Latin. Independent travelers need phrase books.

Customs Southern Europeans are used to the strange ways of tourists and generally can accommodate polite requests. When in doubt about what to do, observe the natives and follow suit.

Many people of the region live in small apartments, and central air-conditioning is rare. To escape their quarters, they walk in the evening, meeting for coffee, ice cream, or socializing. Outdoor cafés are everywhere.

The region places great importance on food. Olive oil is the staple cooking oil, garlic is used extensively, and wine or mineral water—with or without "gas" (carbonation)—is the drink that accompanies a meal. Iced water or tea is rare. Coffee is stronger than the American variety. Breakfast is usually coffee and a roll, lunch may be hearty (although that tradition is changing), and dinner tends to be after 1900 or later (2100 or later in Spain). The siesta tradition of closing shops from 1300 to 1400 continues in rural towns but has disappeared in the cities.

Many restaurants offer *prix-fixe* ("fixed price") dining. All establishments must post their offerings and prices outside. Asking for the "menu" is like asking for the fixed price meal. The *carte* is the term for a listing of the day's food. A *restaurant* traditionally serves a three-course meal (first, main, and dessert). In France, *bistros* serve lighter fare; *brasseries* are ideal places for quick one-dish meals; and sidewalk stands sell *crêpes* (pancakes wrapped around a choice of fillings) for quick snacks. In Italy, the *tavola calda* ("hot table") provides a quick self-service meal. *Gelato* ("ice cream") stands offer a wonderful selection.

Transportation

In southern Europe, you can travel by air, automobile, balloon, barge, bike, foot, horse, motorcoach, skis, train, or yacht.

By Air The airlines compete fiercely for international traffic. Both North American–based carriers and international airlines service the countries, many as code-sharing partners. The capital cities are the major international gateways, although the larger countries—Spain, France, and Italy—have more than one gateway.

By Water With miles of coastline and hundreds of islands, the sea plays an important part in transportation. Year-round car and passenger ferries serve the islands. The Mediterranean cruise season begins around Easter and continues through October.

Typical one-week cruises depart from Barcelona, Spain, for the western area or from Piraeus, Greece (see Figure 12.7), for the east. There is a wide range of ship sizes and itineraries.

By Rail Advantages of rail travel include

- Comfort and the ability to move around.
- Scenery, which is actually visible.
- Stations close to city centers and tourist attractions.
- Frequent service between major cities.
- On-time trains.
- Connections made reliably within minutes.
- Luxury overnight services with roomlike accommodations.
- First-class seats, which are less crowded than second-class. (Most rail passes available to Americans are first-class.)
- Few cancellations. Only severe weather conditions change train schedules.
- Less harm to the environment than most other means of transportation.

High-speed trains operate in Spain, France, and Italy. "High speed" means that they clock at least 125 miles (201 km) per hour. France boasts the world's fastest trains, the *trains à grande vitesse* (TGVs), which run at 150 miles (241 km) per hour or more.

Portugal's railroad network covers just about everywhere the independent traveler wants to go. Greece's network is limited to the mainland, and the system is fairly skeletal by European standards.

Although most trains are just transportation from one place to another, the *Orient Express* is a destination in itself. It is a nostalgic ride back to the past, with private passenger compartments, white-glove service, and gourmet cuisine. The 1883 Orient Express traveled from Paris to Istanbul, but the train today runs trips from Paris to such destinations as Venice, Florence, Rome, Vienna, Prague, and Monte Carlo. Spain also operates luxury trains on scenic routes.

By Road Car rentals are readily available. Driving is on the right in all countries except Malta and Gibraltar. Drivers need their licenses plus an international driver's permit (IDP) or a translation of their English-language license. Gas is expensive and sold in liters; distances are expressed in kilometers. The word *gasoleo* (Spanish) or *gasolio* (Italian) does not mean gas! It is diesel fuel. Using it by mistake could cause real problems. Road signs in Greece are in both the Roman and Greek alphabets.

Driving in the major cities is difficult. Many streets are pedestrian only, and finding parking is a problem. The best advice for city transportation is to ditch the car and take local services.

The Spanish *autopistas*, French *autoroutes*, and Italian *autostradas* connect major cities. Some are free; others have steep tolls. Drivers go fast.

Accommodations

The area offers unique accommodations in addition to standard hotels. Unfortunately, the outstanding deluxe properties come with a price.

In Portugal, the state-owned *pousadas* may be castles, monasteries, or convents. Some are new but are designed to blend in with their surroundings.

> **PROFILE**
>
> ### Potteries, Porcelains, and Crystal of Southern Europe
>
> Among the well-known names are
>
> - Vista Alegra in Portugal.
> - Lladró in Spain.
> - Lalique crystal, Limoges porcelain, Crystal d'Arques, and pottery from Quimper and Vallauris in France.
> - Murano glass in Venice and Capodimonte porcelain near Naples.

> **ON THE SPOT**
>
> "I'd like to ride on the Orient Express from Paris, but after seeing the brochure photos of passengers in beautiful clothes wearing tuxedos and formal gowns at night, I'm not sure I'd feel comfortable. Would an ordinary passenger be snubbed onboard?"
>
> As Orient Express's literature notes, "You can never be over-dressed on the Orient Express." However, on the train there are just as many unremarkable wash-and-wear travel dresses and plain suits as evening gowns and tuxedos. Jeans and shorts are about the only thing not worn. The train has no closets and no drawers, so if you bring that ball gown, it has to hang from a hook behind the compartment's door.

Estalgens are similar to *pousadas* but are privately owned and operated. *Quintas* are old farmhouses or private estates converted to accommodations.

A wonderful way to absorb Spain's atmosphere is to stay at a *parador*. The Paradores de Turismo is a government-run chain of three- to five-star hotels located in castles, former convents, medieval fortresses, and some modern properties. Each operates its own restaurant specializing in regional cuisine.

Hotels throughout most of Europe are officially rated with stars, and the outcome is posted by the door. A *pension* is a small guest house, usually providing breakfast. The *Relais et Château* hotels are luxury properties located in old mansions or palaces, always beautifully situated and offering outstanding service and food.

In France, the *Logis et Auberges de France* ("Lodgings and Inns of France") are more moderately priced independent hotels. The *Gîtes* (*ZJEET*) *de France* are rural rentals offered by private individuals but regulated and rated by the government. The first *gîte* opened in 1951; now there are more than 42,000 throughout France and its territories. The *gîtes* rate their properties with ears of corn.

Italian hotels have their rates fixed by the Provincial Tourist Boards, which rate properties with one to five stars. The term *pensioni*, which described small hotels, is no longer used. Hotels of that type are rated from one to three stars. Renting a villa in Italy's Tuscan hills is the dream of many. Tourist boards can provide lists of firms that specialize in international rentals.

Accommodations in Greece are best described as standard and only occasionally inspired. The Greek equivalent of the B&B is the *domatia*, a rented room.

Author E. M. Forster wanted *A Room with a View* in his novel, but that's sometimes not the best choice in a busy city. The back of a hotel might be quieter.

✔ CHECK-UP

Planning a trip to southern Europe involves

- ✔ Matching travelers and their special interests to the best choice of destination.
- ✔ Choosing between air and rail transportation on the Continent.
- ✔ Planning the best time to travel to avoid crowds and find the good weather.

Accommodations in southern Europe might be in

- ✔ A big-name chain hotel anywhere.
- ✔ A *pousada* in Portugal.
- ✔ A parador in Spain.
- ✔ The Ritz, a château, a pension, or a *gîte* in France.
- ✔ A villa in Tuscany.

OTHER DESTINATIONS IN SOUTHERN EUROPE

Hardly anyplace in southern Europe is off the beaten path. You can be crawling through a cave in the hills of Sicily and encounter someone from your hometown. The small countries are just as alluring as the large ones.

MONACO

Tiny Monaco (*MAHN uh koh*) is surrounded by France on three sides and the Mediterranean on the fourth. The principality of Monaco has four distinct districts, of which Monte Carlo is the best known. The country is densely populated. Its location, excellent climate, and tax advantages have made Monaco a popular destination.

Monaco is wedged into an amphitheater at the foot of a mountain; its daring skyscrapers cascade down the hills. The old town center of Monaco-ville is set on a rocky promontory. The principal attraction is the royal palace, which is the home of the Grimaldi family, the oldest ruling house in Europe.

Many have tried in vain to break the bank at Monaco's Monte Carlo. The first casino was built in 1856 to give the ruling prince an income. The present structure was built between 1878 and 1910. Monégasques are not allowed to gamble in the casino.

Monaco's other attractions include the Oceanographic Museum and Aquarium; the Grand Prix Formula I car race, which is held each May; and the International Tennis World championships, held in April.

MALTA

The independent country of Malta is an arid archipelago made up of three islands in the Mediterranean between Sicily and North Africa. Golden fields, rocky coasts, and the clear blue water of the sea dominate the landscape. **Valletta**, on the island of Malta, is the capital, largest city, and port.

Located at the center of trading routes, Malta has assimilated the cultures of many invaders across the ages. The Apostle Paul is said to have been shipwrecked there in AD 58 and to have converted the inhabitants to Christianity. The islands were leased to the Knights of Malta in the 16th century by Charles I of Spain. The Knights built Valletta into a giant fortress, surrounded by huge stone walls. Virtually every building is built of the same smooth stone, and approaching the Grand Harbor by sea is one of the special experiences of cruising.

In 1814 the island of Malta became a British colony. During World War II, it suffered relentless German bombardment and blockade. The islanders' bravery earned the entire population the British George Cross. Full independence was granted in 1946. In 2004 the country joined the EU.

Modern hotels dot Malta's beaches, and the island is a busy cruise ship port and a popular destination for Europeans. The Maltese language is a difficult Arabic dialect that uses lots of *X*'s. Fortunately, English is widely spoken.

Author Somerset Maugham wrote, "Monte Carlo is a sunny place for shady people."

The Knights of Malta were founded in the 11th century as a hospital service for the Crusaders. According to legend, Charles I leased Malta to the Knights for an annual rent of one Maltese falcon.

BALKAN COUNTRIES

Albania, **Croatia**, **Bosnia-Herzegovina**, **Macedonia**, **Slovenia**, and **Serbia and Montenegro** are part of the Balkans. In the 1990s, civil wars in the region virtually wiped out the tourist trade. Croatia's beautiful walled city of **Dubrovnik**—a cruise ship stop—is the star of the rugged Dalmatian Coast. Fourteenth-century convents guard its gates.

CYPRUS

Geographically, Cyprus (*SY pruhs*), the easternmost island in the Mediterranean, is part of Asia, but it is a vacation destination for Europeans. Politically, Cyprus is split between its Greek south—a holiday island—and the Turkish-dominated north, which is much poorer. In 1960 Cyprus became an independent republic. In 1974 Turkey invaded, seizing the northern part of the island. Reunification has been attempted on and off for years. **Nicosia** is the capital and largest city. In 2004 the Greek part of the island joined the EU.

CHAPTER WRAP-UP

SUMMARY

Here is a review of the objectives with which we began the chapter.

1. **Describe the geography and people of southern Europe.** Peninsulas,

mountains, islands, and plateaus are the geographic features of southern Europe. The landscape includes three major peninsulas—the Iberian, the Italian, and the Baltic—and thousands of islands, most lying in the eastern Mediterranean and belonging to Greece. Italy's Sicily is the sea's largest island.

The Iberian Peninsula is dominated by Spain and Portugal. France is the region's largest country. Its landscape includes the Normandy and Brittany Peninsulas in the west and mountains in the east. The Alps form a wall across the top of Italy, and the Apennines run down the Italian Peninsula's spine. The mountainous countries of the Balkan Peninsula separate Greece from the rest of southern Europe. Greece is a dry land with long fingers of land stretching out into the sea. Its islands in the Ionian Sea have green vegetation; those in the Aegean are desertlike.

History has shaped the lives of the people, and travelers should expect regional differences in languages, customs, and culinary tastes. Early civilizations such as the Minoan, Mycenaean, Greek, and Roman left strong legacies. Greece became part of eastern empires and developed outside the European mainstream. Centuries of civil and international wars wreaked havoc in southern Europe. Outside the Balkan states, however, the past sixty years have been a time of peace and prosperity.

2. **Identify and locate southern Europe's most-visited attractions, matching travelers and destinations best suited for each other.** Travelers to southern Europe are attracted by historic sites, bustling cities, attractive shopping, and wonderful food.

   Portugal's attractions include the city of Lisbon and the coast resorts to the west of the city. Resorts of the Algarve attract long-stay visitors.

   Spain's attractions are the Prado Museum in Madrid, the castles of Castile, the Moorish legacy of Granada and Seville, and the beach resorts of the Costa del Sol.

   France is one of the world's premier destinations. Paris, the Loire Valley, Brittany and Normandy, the Riviera, and ski resorts are top attractions, but the country offers endless riches.

   In Italy, Rome and Vatican City lure millions. From there travelers move north to Assisi, Florence, the hill towns of Tuscany, Milan, the Italian Riviera and the Cinque Terre, the Lake District, and Venice or south to the Amalfi coast, Pompeii, and the Isle of Capri.

   Greece has three principal tourist areas: Athens, the mythology-soaked ruins of the Peloponnese, and the Greek islands.

3. **Recall areas of special interest touring.** Shoppers would enjoy Paris, Rome, Florence, and Milan. Resort lovers flock to the beaches of the Algarve, the Costa del Sol, the French and Italian Rivieras, and the Greek islands. A history buff would be satisfied almost anywhere. Opera fans would like Paris, Rome, and Milan. Religious interests would be satisfied by Rome, Santiago de Compostela in Spain's Galicia, and the shrines of Fátima in Portugal and Lourdes in France.

4. **Provide or find the information needed to plan a trip to southern Europe.** Logistical information about transportation and accommodations is available through standard industry sources. The Web provides the added data that contribute to successful travel.

QUESTIONS FOR DISCUSSION AND REVIEW

1. What were the main themes of art and architecture during the Middle Ages?

2. How do the leisure activities of Europeans differ from those of North Americans?

3. Why do people travel less by air in Europe than they do in North America?

CHAPTER 13

Africa and the Middle East

- Morocco
- Egypt
- The Safari Lands: Kenya, Tanzania, Zambia, Botswana, Namibia, and South Africa
- Israel
- Turkey
- Other Destinations in Africa and the Middle East

OBJECTIVES

When you have completed Chapter 13, you should be able to

1. List the geographic features that make Africa and the Middle East attractive tourist destinations.
2. Describe the appeal of Africa, matching travelers and destinations best suited for each other.
3. Summarize the appeal of the Middle East.
4. Provide or find the information needed to plan a trip to Africa and the Middle East.

Africa and the Middle East are regions so vast and so rich in contrasts that a lifetime of traveling could scarcely skim the surface of their diversity. For hundreds of years the land below the Sahara was unknown territory. Mapmakers would draw only outlines and had to fill in their maps with pictures of monstrous men and beasts. Today, Africa's plains have been surveyed, its mountains climbed, its rivers harnessed, and its minerals exploited. The age of exploration is long past.

The story of the Middle East is better known. Two of the world's first great civilizations—those of Sumer and Egypt—developed there around 3500 BC. Three religions—Judaism, Christianity, and Islam—were born in the region. Shrines have attracted pilgrims and warriors throughout the centuries. Political conflict, however, limits tourism.

Tourism flourishes best in regions of peace and stability. The physical and cultural geography of Africa and the Middle East offers much to the traveler, but its political geography requires careful monitoring. This chapter discusses those countries that are most important to tourism. In Africa, tourism from North America is centered in the North African countries of **Morocco** and **Egypt** and the Safari Lands of east and southern Africa: **Kenya, Tanzania, Zambia, Botswana, Namibia**, and **South Africa**. Tourism to the Middle East centers on two countries in the eastern Mediterranean: **Israel** and **Turkey**. Other destinations are discussed in the chapter's supplemental section. See the Fact File in Appendix A for an alphabetical list of the countries.

The Environment and Its People

The second-largest continent, Africa has forty-seven independent countries on the mainland plus six island countries and two dependencies off its east and west coasts (see Table 13.1). On cultural and climatic grounds, the continent can be divided broadly into Africa north of the **Sahara** (*suh HAHR uh*), the world's largest hot desert, and Africa south of the Sahara. The countries of the arid north are climatically and culturally akin to the Middle East.

The *Middle East* is defined in numerous ways. Geographically, the label refers to Israel, Syria, Lebanon, and Jordan plus the six countries of the **Arabian Peninsula** (Saudi Arabia, Bahrain, Qatar, United Arab Emirates, Oman, and Yemen) and four countries of Asia (Iraq, Kuwait, Turkey, and Iran). Politically, the Middle East includes these countries plus the North African countries of Morocco, Algeria, Tunisia, Libya, and Egypt. This chapter uses the geographic definition.

The Land

Africa is nearly bisected by the equator. Alone among the continents it has land in all four hemispheres. It is separated from Europe by the Mediterranean Sea and from Asia by the **Red Sea** and the **Suez Canal**, as Figure 13.1 shows. The Atlantic Ocean bounds it to the west and the **Indian Ocean** to the east.

The Middle East is in the Northern and Eastern Hemispheres. Its water borders include the **Black** and Mediterranean Seas to the north and the

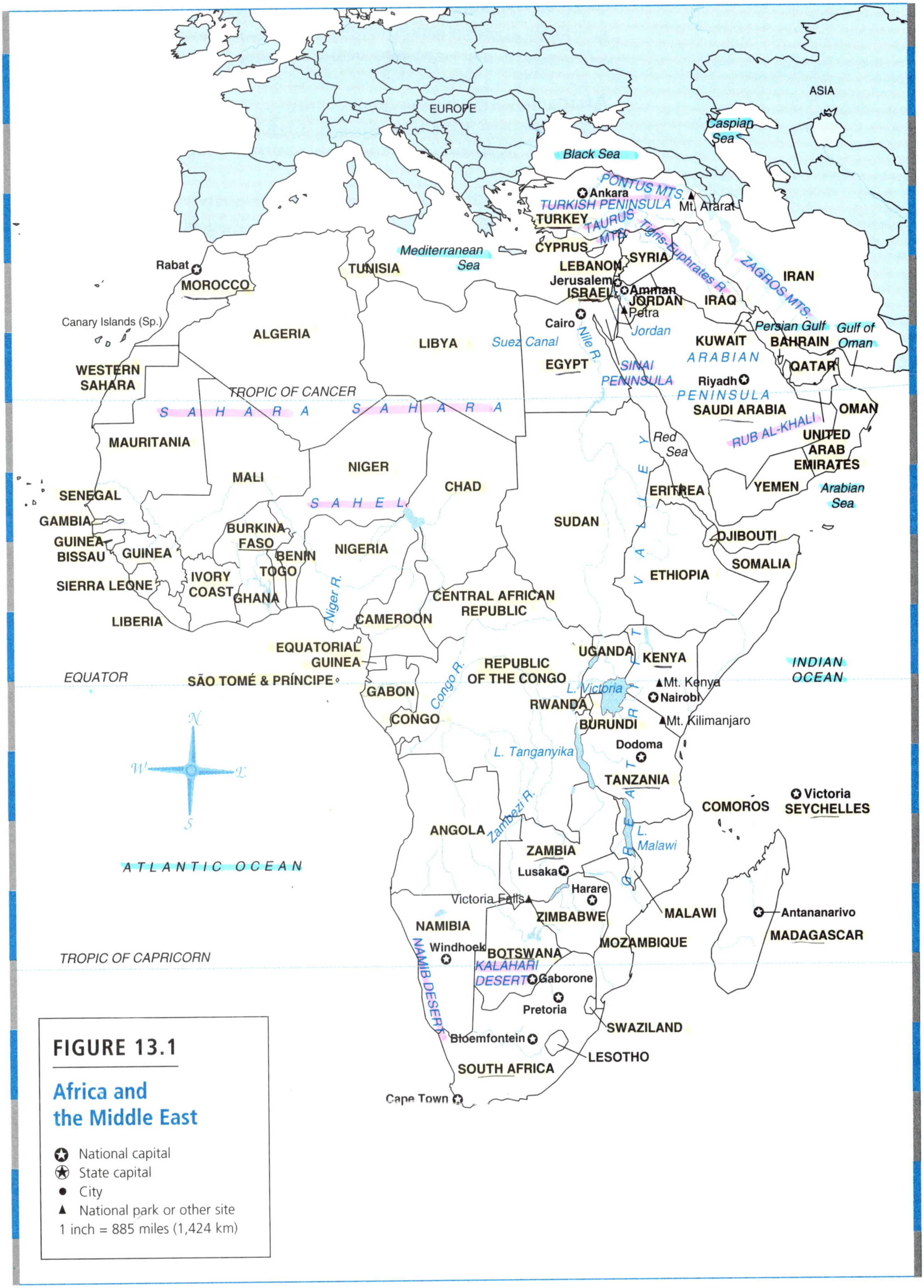

FIGURE 13.1

Africa and the Middle East

- ✪ National capital
- ★ State capital
- ● City
- ▲ National park or other site

1 inch = 885 miles (1,424 km)

Indian Ocean, **Arabian Sea**, and **Gulf of Oman** to the south. The Suez Canal and the Red Sea lie between the Arabian Peninsula and Africa; the **Persian Gulf** separates the Arabian Peninsula from Iran.

Africa The African continent is an immense plateau, broken by a few mountain ranges and bordered in some areas by a narrow coastal plain. Four of the world's greatest rivers are in Africa—the **Nile, Congo, Niger**, and **Zambezi** (*zam BEE zee*)—but they do not permit much commerce because they are studded with rapids and waterfalls. The world's longest river—the Nile—flows north to the Mediterranean from its headwaters south of **Lake Victoria**.

The Sahara covers about 25 percent of Africa. South of the Sahara is a large region of dry grassland called the **Sahel** (*sah HEHL*), from an Arab word that means "changing." Because of climatic changes and overgrazing, the Sahara is advancing into the Sahel at an estimated 3 miles (5 km) a year.

Much of Africa below the Sahel is tropical rain forest, second in size only to that of the Amazon basin. The Congo River flows west through the region to empty into the Atlantic.

Farther south, the African plateau is mostly flat or rolling grassland with widely scattered trees, an area called the **savanna**. But southern Africa also has deserts, swamps, and forests. The **Namib** (*nuh MIHB*) **Desert** borders the Atlantic Coast of southwestern Africa; the **Kalahari** (*kah luh HAHR ee*) **Desert** lies inland from the Namib.

Geology has given eastern Africa some special attractions. The region has Africa's tallest peaks—mighty **Kilimanjaro** (*kihl uh muhn JAHR oh*) in Tanzania (19,340 feet [5,895 m]) and **Mount Kenya** (17,057 feet [5,199 m]) in Kenya. Although they rise near the equator, both mountains have glaciers, but climate changes are causing the ice to melt.

Eastern Africa also features one of the continent's most striking landforms: the **Great Rift Valley**. When a series of rifts, or breaks, in the earth's surface opened long ago, lava poured out, forming peaks and valleys. The Great Rift Valley begins in the Middle East in Syria and extends south to

People use the name *Timbuktu* to refer to an extremely distant place. It is actually a town in Mali in western Africa. It was a salt-trading post for Saharan camel caravan routes.

The term *sahara* comes from an Arabic word that means "desert." So never say "Sahara Desert"; that would be like saying "desert desert."

The *Horn of Africa* is the eastern protrusion of the continent that includes Somalia, Ethiopia, and Djibouti.

TABLE 13.1

Islands/Countries/Dependencies off the African Coast

Country	Location	Characteristics
Cape Verde	Atlantic, west of Senegal	Rugged volcanic islands
Comoros	Indian Ocean	Volcanic archipelago
Madagascar	Indian Ocean	World's fourth-largest island; rare animal and plant life
Mauritius	Indian Ocean	Volcanic islands east of Madagascar
Réunion	Indian Ocean	Volcanic island; department of France
St. Helena Group	Atlantic Ocean	British dependency; Bonaparte's place of exile
São Tomé and Príncipe	Atlantic, west of Gabon	Extinct volcanoes
Seychelles	Indian Ocean	90 granite and coral islands with beautiful beaches

Mozambique (*moh zahm BEEK*). South of the equator the Great Rift Valley cuts through the savannas. Scattered along the valley are Africa's largest lakes: Lake Malawi (*mah LAH wee*), Lake Tanganyika (*tang guhn YEE kuh*), and the sealike Lake Victoria. At the southern edge of the valley, the spectacular **Victoria Falls** are on the Zambezi River.

Middle East The northern and southern extremities of the Middle East are two great peninsulas: the **Turkish Peninsula**, which is between the Black Sea and the Mediterranean, and the Arabian Peninsula, which is bordered by the Red Sea, the Arabian Sea, and the Persian Gulf.

The region includes some of the world's most spectacular mountains. In Turkey, two ranges run from west to east—the **Pontus Mountains** in the north and the **Taurus Mountains** in the south. They meet in the tangle of the Armenian Knot, whose greatest peak is **Mount Ararat**. From the knot, mountains stretch across northern Iran to merge with the high ranges of Afghanistan. The most spectacular of these, the Hindu Kush, rises to more than 24,600 feet (7,500 m) and forms the western extremity of the Himalaya of central Asia.

Mount Ararat's snow-covered peak rises above a stark, uninhabited desert. The mountain was supposedly the final resting place of Noah's Ark; however, no traces of the ark have been found, despite many searches.

The southern part of the Middle East is a plateau with large deserts. The **Rub al-Khali**, known as the "Empty Quarter," stretches across southern Saudi (*SAW dee*) Arabia. The **Tigris-Euphrates** (*yoo FRAY teez*) River system begins in the mountains of Turkey and flows through Syria and Iraq. In Iraq, the rivers meet and form a river called the Shatt al Arab, which empties into the Persian Gulf.

The Climate

The availability of water was a powerful determinant of human settlement in Africa and the Middle East. Great civilizations developed in river valleys, and the stories of how the desert nomads learned to cope in the heat without water continue to fascinate.

Climate zones on either side of the equator mirror one another. As you go either north or south of the equator, the climate changes slowly from tropical to semitropical, to semiarid, to desert, and finally to the temperate climates that are found along both the north and the south coasts of Africa.

Morocco enjoys a temperate climate with hot summers and mild, wet winters. However, toward the south and the interior, the climate becomes increasingly arid and extreme. Rainfall is uneven, and drought is common.

Egypt has little rain except along the Mediterranean. The average winter temperature in Cairo is 46° F (8° C). In summer, it is 96° F (36° C)—and even hotter in the desert. Between March and June, a hot wind, the **khamsin**, may blow, carrying sand and producing a yellow fog.

The climate of the Safari Lands is equatorial, and temperatures change little throughout the year. The warm, wet season (from November to April) is characterized by high humidity and heavy rain. The dry season is cool, with frosts in the mountains. Altitude tends to cancel out the effect of latitude. Climatically, South Africa has as much variety as half a dozen separate countries.

Israel has hot, dry summers and mild, wet winters. But in areas of the Middle East that are away from the cooling influence of the Mediterranean, the climate is harsh, with some of the earth's hottest places. In the Rub al-Khali, for example, temperatures have soared as high as 130° F (55° C) in the shade. Central Turkey has searing heat in summer and freezing cold in winter, but coastal areas are milder.

FIGURE 13.2

Milestones in the History of Africa and the Middle East

c. 4000 BC The Sahara begins to turn into a desert.

c. 3000 Sumerian civilization flourishes between the Tigris and Euphrates Rivers. Egyptian civilization rises in the Nile Valley.

c. 2900 The Great Pyramid of Giza in Egypt is built.

AD 1400s The Portuguese explore Africa's west coast.

1453–1922 The Ottoman empire reigns.

1652 The Dutch found Cape Town.

1700s Europeans explore the African interior.

1884 Berlin Conference draws the boundaries of Europe's African colonies.

1917 Britain supports Jewish homeland in Palestine and issues the Balfour Declaration.

1923 Republic of Turkey is proclaimed, with Ankara as the capital.

1947 The United Nations divides Palestine into Jewish and Arab states.

1950s–1960s European colonies in Africa become independent countries.

1990 President deKlerk calls for an end to apartheid in South Africa.

1991 The first Iraq War takes place.

2003 The second Iraq War begins.

2005 Iraq holds free elections.

The People and Their History

Africa has been called the "birthplace of the human race." Humanity also has ancient roots in the Middle East (see Figure 13.2). People lived in the region as early as 25,000 BC. Experts believe that farming began in the Middle East around 8000 BC and spread westward to Africa. The Sahara was grassland then, but by about 1500 BC, the Sahara had become a desert and a barrier to the movement of people between northern Africa and the rest of the continent.

The fertile soil of the Nile Valley supported the Egyptian civilization. Egypt reached the height of its power about 1400 BC, but foreign invaders soon came for its riches. In 331 BC Alexander the Great conquered the Middle East and the north coast of Africa and united it into one empire. Next came Rome, which conquered Egypt in 30 BC.

Islam was the next major force in the region. The Prophet Muhammad (AD 570?–632) united the fierce tribes of the deserts. By 711, Arab Muslim rule extended from Spain in the west to Iran in the east. By the 1100s, the Ottoman Turks, who were also Muslims, ruled Turkey and the Arab lands of the Middle East. The area was a Turkish stronghold until the 19th century.

South of the Sahara, Africa had powerful kingdoms, but little is known of their history. During the late 1400s and 1500s, Europeans established trading posts. Gold and slaves became the most valuable exports. In 1884 European powers that had been busily colonizing the continent met in Berlin to draw the boundaries of their possessions. The Berlin Conference created African countries with no consideration of the cultures of the inhabitants and their languages, religions, or economic practices.

In the 20th century, the countries of Africa and the Middle East slowly regained their independence. World War I was critical for the Arab states. The Turks joined with Germany against Great Britain, France, Italy, and Russia. Arabs who hoped to win independence supported the Allies. After the war, the League of Nations divided the Arab lands between Britain and France. The 1940s through the 1960s were years of turmoil, as Arab states grappled for independence and Israel struggled to become a country. African colonies gained independence between 1950 and 1989.

The path since independence has been difficult for the region. Violent conflicts continue in much of the Middle East. Meanwhile, civil war, tribal conflict, famines, and the AIDS epidemic have wracked Africa.

✔ CHECK-UP

Major physical features of Africa include

- ✔ Sahara (classified as the world's largest desert), Kalahari and Namib Deserts.
- ✔ World's longest river, the Nile.
- ✔ Sahel, which separates the Sahara Desert from the rain forests.
- ✔ Great Rift Valley, extending from Syria in southwest Asia south to Mozambique in southeast Africa.
- ✔ Snowcapped mountains on the equator.
- ✔ Climatic zones that mirror each other on either side of the equator.

Major physical features of the Middle East include

- ✔ Two great peninsulas, the Turkish and the Arabian.
- ✔ Rub al-Khali.
- ✔ Some of the world's highest mountains.
- ✔ Extreme heat on the Arabian Peninsula.

The region's culture is notable for

- ✔ High level of its early civilizations.
- ✔ Centuries of colonial rule.
- ✔ Continuing conflict.

Morocco

Strategically placed at the western entrance to the Mediterranean Sea, Morocco (*muh RAHK oh*) is but a step away from Europe and yet is unmistakably different. The Arabs call it *al-Maghrib*, the "land of the west," the Atlantic fortress of Islam. From 1085 its rulers played an important part in the Muslim domination of Spain. Morocco today is a conservative state that maintains links with both Arab countries and the West.

Larger in size than California, Morocco has high, rugged mountains, the arid Sahara, and green fields near the coast. The **Atlas Mountains** (see Figure 13.3) run southwest to northeast. To the north and west are fertile coastal plains along the Atlantic; to the south, the Sahara takes over, with scattered oases. In the far south, the region called **Western Sahara** is under Moroccan control, although its status is a matter for dispute.

The Cities

Most tourists visit the four imperial cities: Rabat, Marrakesh, Meknès, and Fez. Each was at one time the capital of a Moroccan empire.

In the 17th and 18th centuries, the Barbary Coast (Tunisia, Algeria, and Morocco) was home to pirates. The most famous were based in Rabat and Salé in Morocco.

Rabat The French had great influence on Morocco, and this is most apparent in Rabat (*rah BAHT*), the capital, which has European-style cafés and broad avenues. Attractions include nearby beaches; the Tour Hassan, the minaret of a vast uncompleted 12th-century mosque; the Muhammad V Mausoleum; the Royal Palace; and the National Museum of Handicrafts.

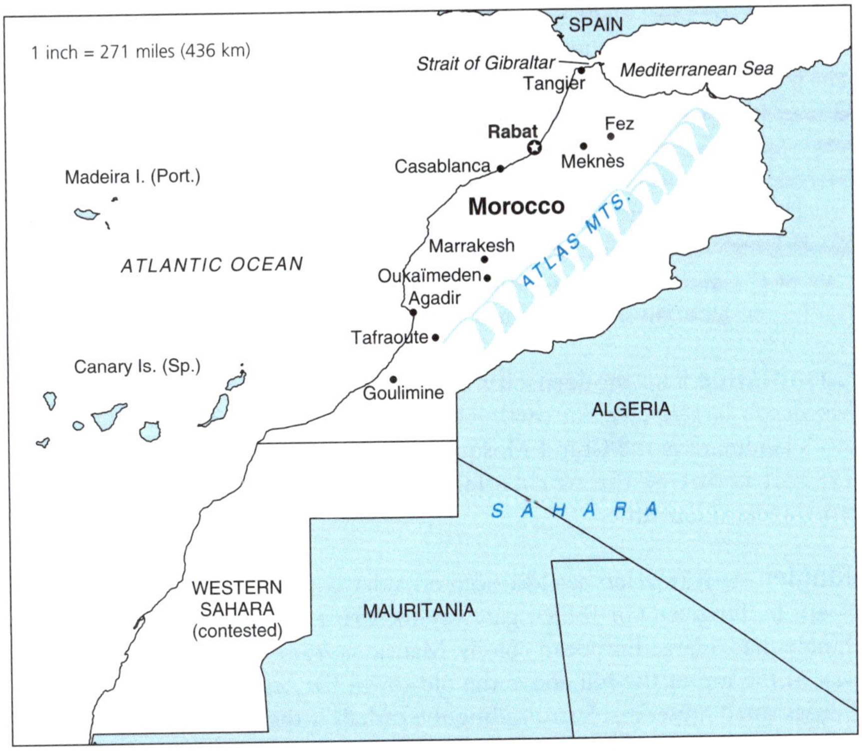

FIGURE 13.3 Morocco

Marrakesh, Morocco

Marrakesh Founded in 1062, the *Red City* of Marrakesh (*mar uh KEHSH*) has been the country's southern stronghold. Approached on a clear day from the west, the brown foothills give way to a broad plain dominated by what seems to be a mirage: the snowcapped peaks of the mountains floating above a band of clouds behind the city. The city gained its nickname from the color of its walls and buildings made of reddish clay.

The Djemaa el-Fna ("Place of the Dead") Square, a huge open square, is the heart of Marrakesh. Here snake charmers, fire and glass eaters, acrobats, fortune-tellers, and jugglers vie for your attention. The water seller's costume and gleaming copper cups are attractive, but somehow his water bag—a hairy goatskin tightly sewn with a tube coming from one of the legs—does little to inspire confidence in the purity of his product. The women are veiled. Medicine men practice on the sidewalks. Scribes write wills and bills. A merchant hawks a tray of false teeth. Care to try on a set? Activities continue long into the night.

The Mamounia Hotel, frequented by the rich and famous, was once a palace. Built in the 1920s, it is set in a garden just inside the walls of the old city.

Meknès While Louis XIV of France was building Versailles, King Moulay Ismail of Morocco chose Meknès (*MEK nez*) as his capital and set about building a city to rival Paris. He surrounded his palace with 16 miles (25 km) of walls with twenty *bâbs* ("gates").

Meknès is two cities: the old imperial city and *medina* (the old section) are on the west side of the valley; the modern town is on the slopes of the Oumer Rbia. The Bâb el-Mansour serves as the gate to the old city.

The medina greets you with a thousand sights, sounds, and smells—including the odors of sweet incense, fruit, new wood, grilling meats, and (not such a treat) mule droppings. Tiny shops await buyers. Men and boys sew away at *jellabas* (long hooded robes) and caftans. For refreshment, boys sell roasted chickpeas in paper cones.

Fez, Morocco

Fez Fez is the most ancient and impressive of the imperial cities. Built in the 8th century, it was on the trade route from the Sahara to the Mediterranean. The jewel of Fez is the Karaouine Mosque, which was built in the 9th century. One of Islam's oldest and most prestigious universities survives and prospers here. The great medina is so difficult to explore without getting lost that a licensed guide is absolutely essential.

Those who want to immerse themselves in atmosphere should stay at the Palais Jamai Hotel, a former palace (built in 1879) set in a beautiful garden within the walls of the medina. The spacious rooms are decorated in traditional Moorish style, with heavy ornate furniture.

Casablanca The modern city of Casablanca (*kas uh BLANG kuh*) is Morocco's largest city. An earthquake in 1755 destroyed the old city. The city's landmark is the Grand Mosque of Hassan II, which was completed in 1993. It is one of the world's largest mosques, able to house 80,000 worshipers at one time.

Tangier Many travelers see Morocco on a day trip by ferry from Algeciras in Spain to Tangier (*tan JEER*), gateway to Africa. During the 19th century, Tangier had a large European colony. Mansions from the period overlook the sea. At the top of the hill above the old town, the *casbah* ("fort" or "castle") houses small museums. Surrounding the casbah is the medina, with the city's *souks* ("marketplaces").

Other Places to Visit

Southern Morocco is rich in spectacular scenery and dotted with small oasis-villages. **Agadir** is a coastal resort town. Southeast of Agadir, the pink casbahs of **Tafraoute** perch on spurs of rock, their façades painted with strange designs in white or ochre. **Goulimine** is the site of the Blue Men's souk each weekend. It is named for the Tuareg (*TWAH rehg*), the largest group of nomads in the Sahara, who are sometimes called the "Blue Men of the Desert" because their indigo-dyed robes leave a blue color on their skin.

✔ CHECK-UP

Morocco's most-visited cities include

- ✔ Tangier, a city for day-trippers from Spain.
- ✔ Rabat, the capital.
- ✔ Casablanca, the largest city.
- ✔ Marrakesh, the Red City at the feet of the High Atlas.
- ✔ Meknès, with a ruined palace and a medina of note.
- ✔ Fez, the oldest of the imperial cities.

Egypt

Egypt is called the *Gift of the Nile* because the river's waters have been the lifeblood of the country. The Nile enters the country from Sudan. It fills huge **Lake Nasser**—which was formed by the Aswan High Dam—then bends eastward before flowing north (see Figure 13.4). At Cairo, the river fans out into a broad delta before entering the Mediterranean. The area north of Cairo is known as **Lower Egypt**; the area south of Cairo is called **Upper Egypt**.

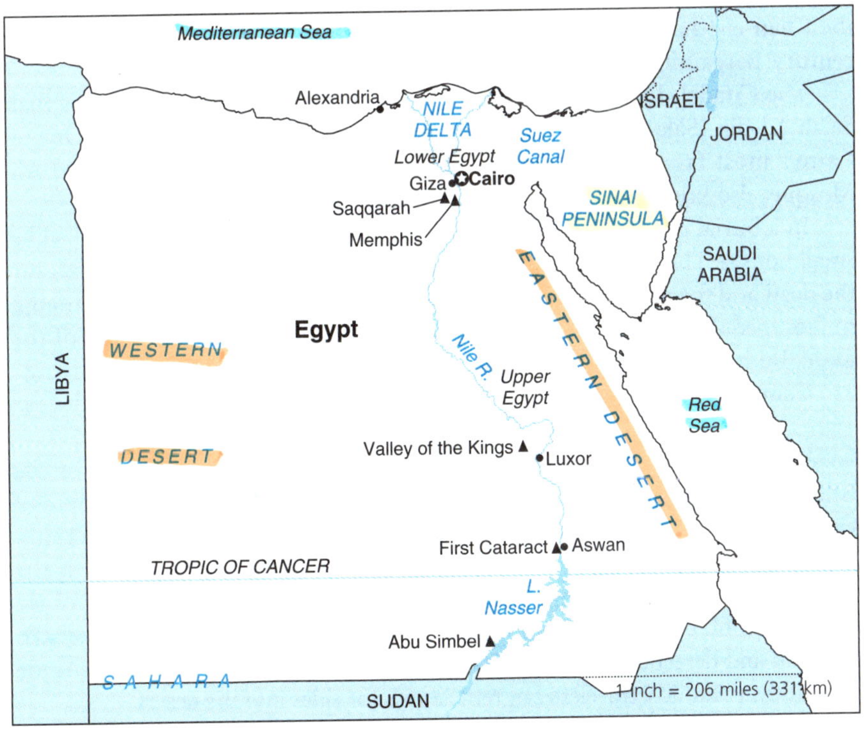

FIGURE 13.4 Egypt

West of the Nile, the **Western** (or Libyan) **Desert** extends to the Libyan border. Scattered across the desert are isolated oases where date palms grow. Between the Nile and the Red Sea is the **Eastern** (or Arabian) **Desert**. At the north tip of the Red Sea, the triangular plateau of the **Sinai Peninsula** links Egypt and Israel. Egypt's highest peak is in Sinai's mountainous south.

Egyptian civilization began in the Nile Valley. The worship of gods and god-kings in ancient Egypt produced great monuments. In time, the country was subjected to foreign masters, yet along the banks of the river, the *fellahin* ("country people") preserved their way of life, impervious to change.

The people working the fields today seem to have stepped straight from the wall paintings of the pharaohs' tombs. The men often wear the *galabiyah*, a long robe that falls to the ankles. The women wear long dresses of brightly colored cotton and often carry shawls or veils to cover their heads and faces.

The Cities

Egypt's cities combine the architecture of conquerors with modern buildings, but outside the cities about half the population lives in mud-brick villages. **Cairo** (*KY roh*) is the capital and Africa's largest city.

In ancient Egypt, a *cartouche* was an oval frame with the inscribed name or symbol of a ruler in it. A cartouche with the tourist's name in hieroglyphics (picture writing) has become a popular souvenir.

Cairo Egypt's capital is about 100 miles (161 km) south of the Mediterranean. It is a noisy traffic- and people-jammed city. A forest of minarets proclaims its Islamic affinity, but beneath them lives a mixed population of Arabs, Turks, Africans, and Europeans.

A walk around Tahrir Square provides an immersion in Egyptian culture. One attraction is the Egyptian Museum. Its superb collection of treasures includes the contents of the tomb of Tutankhamen (King Tut), incredible riches from a minor king.

Islamic Cairo is on the east bank of the Nile. The area has more than 300 mosques. Officials called *muezzins* announce prayer time by loudspeaker from atop the minarets five times a day. Bazaars (outdoor shopping areas) fill almost all the available street space. For tourists, the most popular bazaar is the Khan-el-Khalili, a maze of winding alleyways that dates back to the 13th century. Bargaining is a must.

The Citadel dominates the area. An inscription over the gate states that Salah Ad-din (Saladin), the Crusaders' foe, began the building in 1176. One of Cairo's most famous landmarks is within the Citadel, the Muhammad Ali Mosque, also known as the Alabaster Mosque.

In a burial ground near the Citadel, dignitaries were buried in tombs like small houses. The houses were places for the family to stay during the feast for the dead and for prayers. Because of Cairo's severe overcrowding, more than 2 million people now live inside the memorials in what is called the City of the Dead. Built as a home for the dead, the cemetery is now a home for the living.

Cairo's nightclubs feature belly dancers. Many hotels have casinos and discos.

Pyramid at Giza, Egypt

Giza Ancient wonders bring tourists to Giza (*GEE zuh*), a suburb of Cairo on the Nile's west bank. It is the site of the most famous pyramids: the Great Pyramid of Cheops and the pyramids of his son Chephren and of his grandson, Mycerinus. The tombs were built from about 2575 to 2130 BC. The Great Pyramid is the world's largest single building, one of the Seven Wonders of the Ancient World (see the Profile). Those who do not mind tons of rock overhead can enter the pyramid and descend the long, narrow passageway to the burial chamber. At the base of the pyramids, travelers can rent camels for rides into the desert.

The Sphinx was originally no more than a piece of rock that stuck up above the limestone plateau that surrounds the pyramids. At some point, a head, possibly that of a lion, was carved into it. Unfortunately, the sands of time, target practice by Napoleon's riflemen, and Cairo's air pollution have taken their toll on the statue.

The Mena House Hotel, which opened in 1869, is within walking distance of the pyramids. From its patios the views of the monuments are spectacular.

Memphis Little remains of Memphis, the city southwest of Cairo that was the first capital of ancient Egypt. Nearby **Saqqarah** (*sah KAR ruh*) was home to Old Kingdom tombs; it was royalty's burial place before Giza's pyramids were built. The first tombs were flat houselike structures, called *mastabas*. The Step Pyramid, built for King Zoser (who lived from 2667 to 2648 BC), has six mastabas on top of each other like steps. Also in Saqqarah is the Serapeum, in which the bodies of sacred bulls, embalmed like human beings, were placed in sarcophagi.

Alexandria Egypt's port and second-largest city is Alexandria. It was founded by Alexander the Great in 332 BC. Today, it is a Mediterranean beach resort. While scouring the murky waters off the port in 2000, explorers found two long-lost cities—Herakleion and Menouthis—as well as the wreckage of Napoleon's flagship, which was destroyed by Britain's Admiral Nelson in the Battle of the Nile in 1798.

Luxor Egypt's most important tourist destination is Luxor (*LUX oar*). The city is on the east bank of the Nile about 405 miles (652 km) south of Cairo. This was the site of ancient Thebes (*theebz*), the empire's capital. Temples and palaces were built on a colossal scale. Many regard the remains of the Temple of Luxor as the most important site in Egypt.

Across the river from Luxor on the Nile's west bank is the **Valley of the Kings**—a rocky, narrow gorge that was used as a cemetery by the pharaohs between 1550 and 1100 BC. The tombs are corridors and rooms cut into the rock of the hillside. Painted scenes and hieroglyphic texts cover the walls. More than sixty tombs have been discovered, the largest in 1995. Archaeologists are still digging.

Ferries transport tourists across the Nile from Luxor to see the valley as well as the Mortuary Temple of Rameses II, the Colossi of Memnon, the Temple of Queen Hatshepsut, and the Village of the Necropolis Workers.

Aswan The winter resort of Aswan (*AS wahn*) is south of Luxor near the Nile's **first cataract**. Elephantine Island in the river was the original site of the town. *Feluccas* (boats with a triangular sail) traveling to the gardens of Plantation Island (once known as Kitchener's Island) float past the Mausoleum of the Aga Khan and the ruins of a Coptic monastery. The Old Cataract Hotel, built in 1899 on the Nile's banks, was featured in Agatha Christie's mystery novel *Death on the Nile* and was also used in the film version.

Other Places to Visit

A Nile cruise to or from Upper Egypt's Aswan and Luxor is the centerpiece of any Egyptian journey. Travelers can cruise from Cairo to Aswan, but most fly or take the train to Luxor and begin the voyage there. Four-night, five-day cruises stop at temples in Esna, Edfu, and Kom Ombo for sightseeing.

The temple of **Abu Simbel** (*ahb oo SIHM buhl*) is about 168 miles

➤ PROFILE

Seven Wonders of the Ancient World

Ancient Greeks and Romans made up lists of notable objects that travelers should see. Of the world they knew, five of the seven wonders were in the Middle East, close to the Mediterranean Sea:

- Colossus of Rhodes, a huge bronze statue on the Greek island.
- Hanging Gardens of Babylon, near Baghdad.
- Mausoleum at Halicarnassus in Turkey, a marble tomb.
- Statue of Zeus at Olympia, Greece.
- Temple of Artemis at Ephesus, Turkey. The ruins are still on view.
- Pharos (Lighthouse) of Alexandria, Egypt. It was toppled by an earthquake in 224 BC.
- Pyramids of Egypt at Giza, the only surviving ancient wonder.

Hatshepsut was a female pharaoh. She had herself represented as a man on monuments. Her memorial temple, Deir el-Bahri, is one of the most beautiful of those on Luxor's west bank.

Abu Simbel, Egypt

(270 km) south of Aswan. It was carved in a mountainside beside the Nile about 1200 BC and contains seated figures of Ramses II and his wife, Queen Nefertari. When the Aswan High Dam was being built in the 1960s, the temple's site was due to be flooded by the waters of Lake Nasser. UNESCO made a heroic effort to save the temple. It was cut into blocks and moved to higher ground; the mountainside was replaced by a concrete dome covered in rock to look exactly like the mountain. The temple is at its original position, just higher up the embankment. When the first rays of the sun reach into the temple's interior on February 22 and October 22—thought to be the anniversaries of Ramses' birth and coronation—they shine on murals of the pharaoh and his fellow gods.

Most visitors fly to Abu Simbel on day trips from Aswan because there are few accommodations in the area and few ships proceed this far. Bad weather can affect the flight.

✔ CHECK-UP

Cairo's attractions include

- ✔ Egyptian Museum.
- ✔ Khan-el-Khalili.
- ✔ City of the Dead.
- ✔ Muhammad Ali Mosque.

Egypt's major archaeological sites include

- ✔ Pyramids at Giza.
- ✔ Step Pyramid at Saqqarah.
- ✔ Temples of Luxor.
- ✔ Valley of the Kings on the west bank at Luxor.
- ✔ Abu Simbel.

The Safari Lands

The word *safari* means "a journey" in Kiswahili, the common language of East Africa. The word entered all languages in the 1800s as hunters came to Africa in search of game and adventure. Today, film is the method of hunting, but the adventure of safari endures.

Game is found in many African countries. The best facilities for viewing, however, are in the east and south—in Kenya, Tanzania, Zambia, Botswana, Namibia, and South Africa. Figure 13.5 shows a map of the countries.

Based on the transportation used, there are two types of safaris: *land safaris*, which use specially equipped minibuses, and *wing safaris*, which use planes as well as minibuses. Deluxe operators never put more than six passengers in a nine-passenger vehicle so that everyone not only gets a window seat but also has easy access to the roof hatch. Wing safaris eliminate tedious drives, allow travelers more time in each game area, and are less tiring, but they cost more.

On safari, a typical day involves two game drives, one in the early morning and one in the late afternoon, when wildlife is the most active. Game drives last usually between three and four hours and provide ample opportunities to observe and photograph the animals in their natural habitats and social groups.

Safari van and elephants

Kenya

U.S. State Department travel warnings issued in 2004 have caused heavy financial losses for Kenya (*KEHN yuh* or *KEEN yuh*). The warnings followed an incident in which terrorists launched a missile at a commercial aircraft. The State Department advises citizens to defer visits to any country where "terrorism poses a continuing threat." Consequently, Kenya, once the premier destination for safaris, joined Afghanistan, Iraq, and Bosnia as places the U.S. government recommends that its citizens avoid.

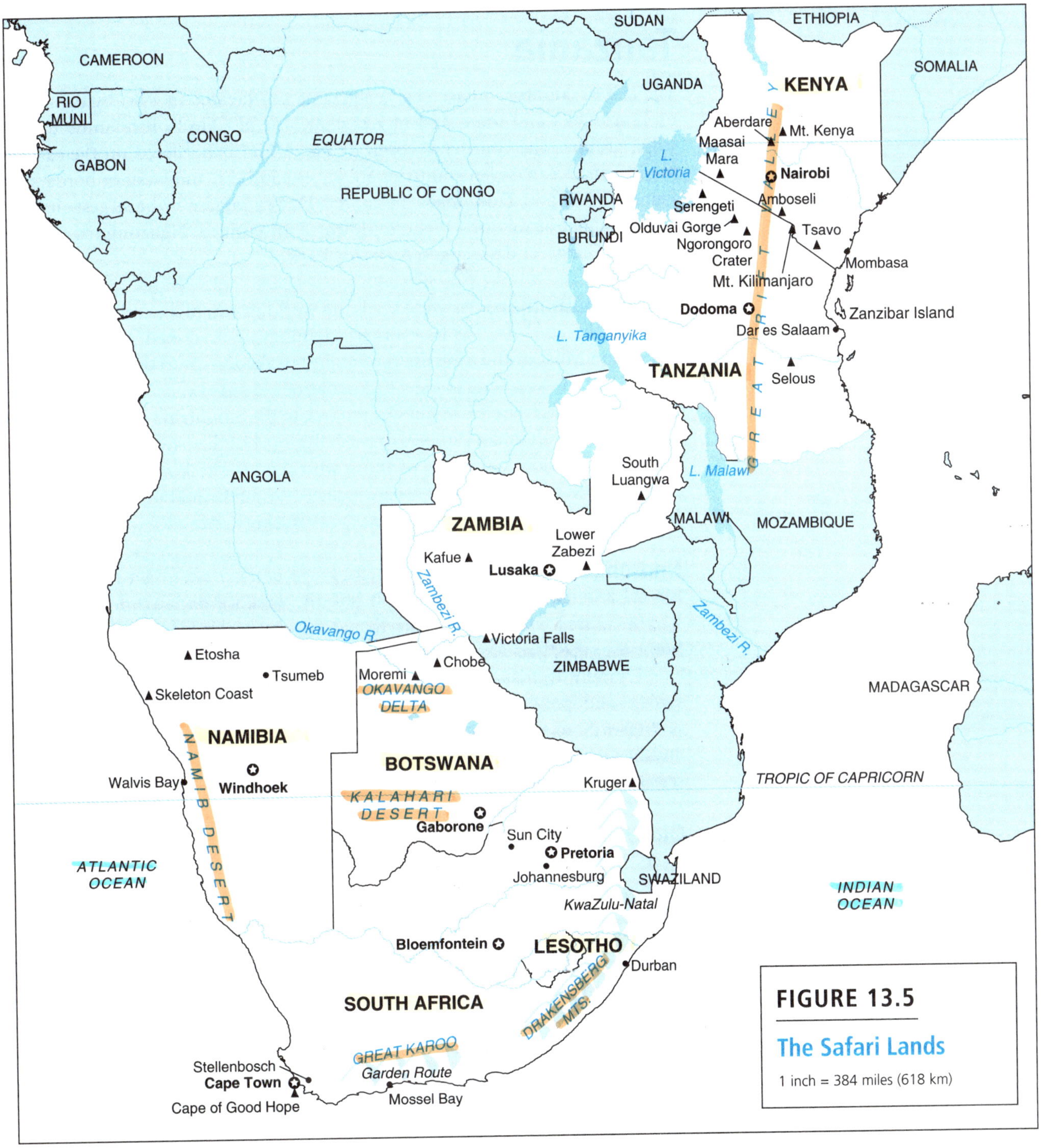

FIGURE 13.5

The Safari Lands

1 inch = 384 miles (618 km)

Nairobi (*ny ROH bee*), one of Africa's largest cities, is the traditional gateway. It is on a high plateau in south central Kenya. Nairobi National Park is within the city, adjacent to the airport. The park is home to lions, gazelles, gnus, zebras, and other wild animals. Nearby is the farmhouse of Karen Blixen (author of *Out of Africa*).

To see the "big five"—elephant, lion, leopard, buffalo, and rhino—is the goal of game viewers in Africa.

Kenya's many national parks include **Aberdare**, **Amboseli**, **Maasai Mara**, and **Tsavo**. Along with its rich tribal cultures and abundant opportunities for active adventures, the parks have long made Kenya popular. The country is noted for the variety of its safaris—including wildlife, cultural, scenic, adventure, birding, beach, and sports safaris.

Tanzania

The largest country in East Africa, Tanzania was created in 1964 by the union of Tanganyika and the island of Zanzibar (*Isle of Cloves*). It is home to 125 tribal groups. The country is south of Kenya and is bordered on the east by the Indian Ocean; seven countries are on its southern and western borders, as Figure 13.5 shows. **Dodoma** is the capital; **Dar es Salaam** is the largest city.

Principal attractions include **Mount Kilimanjaro**, **Ngorongoro Crater**, **Olduvai Gorge**, and **Serengeti National Park.**

Mount Kilimanjaro "As wide as all the world, great, high, and unbelievably white in the sun." That is how Ernest Hemingway described Africa's highest mountain. Most of the time the mountain's peaks are covered in clouds; from the ground the best time to view Kilimanjaro is at sunrise.

Adventurous travelers might want to trek to the mountain's summit. They do not have to be mountain climbers to reach the top, but they should be in excellent physical condition. Only half of those who start the trek make it to the top. During the five-day trek, climbers are escorted by guides and porters and stay in huts at night. Peak climbing periods are January, February, and September.

Ngorongoro Crater The Ngorongoro (*gor ohn gor oh*; forget the *n*) Crater is a volcano that caved in on itself. It is to the west of Kilimanjaro. The world's largest **caldera**, it measures more than 12 miles (19 km) across. The crater is home to more than 30,000 animals.

Typically, tourists depart for the interior of the crater in four-wheel-drive vehicles and spend the day exploring. The steep, winding descent down the inner wall takes 30 to 40 minutes. Wildlife cannot be seen until you get to the bottom and begin to travel the various roads among grasslands, lakes, swamps, and streams. The best time to visit is during the dry season from June to October.

Olduvai Gorge West of the crater is Olduvai Gorge, which consists of five layers on top of black lava that flowed for millions of years. Here, humanity's ancestors left clues to the story of human evolution. Some of the bones and artifacts discovered are more than a million years old.

Serengeti National Park West of the gorge and just across the border from Kenya's Maasai Mara reserve is Serengeti National Park, noted for its lions and herds of antelopes and zebras. The terrain is greatly varied.

Selous Game Reserve In south Tanzania, the Selous Game Reserve covers a land area larger than Switzerland, making it one of the biggest parks in the world. It has a massive elephant population as well as lions and other game.

Zambia

While political unrest in Zimbabwe has, for the time being, removed that country from most itineraries, neighboring Zambia (*ZAM bee uh*) hopes to gain tourists. Zambia is a landlocked country in south central Africa,

CLOSE-UP: A SAFARI

Who is a good prospect for a safari? Anyone with an interest in the outdoors and wildlife would enjoy a safari. The traditional safari is operated in minivans, ideal for senior citizens and those who have minor walking disabilities. Being in good physical shape is a requirement only for those who want a trekking safari.

Where would they go? Any of the Safari Lands mentioned in the chapter would make a good destination. Qualify the travelers to find out their interests before you make any suggestions. The average and most acceptable length of a safari, including travel from and back to North America, is about fourteen days. Here is an itinerary for Botswana.

Day 1 Fly across the Atlantic.

Day 2 Land in Europe in the morning and connect to a flight to Sir Seretse Khama International Airport in Gaborone. Arrive in the evening. You are met and transferred to your hotel.

Day 3 Day free to relax and recover from jet lag or to take a local tour. Perhaps go to the National Museum, with natural history and ethnological exhibitions. Shoppers can browse the craft shops and markets, where pottery, basketwork, leatherwork, and handwoven objects are on display.

Day 4 Start north. Stop in Serowe, one of Botswana's largest villages and the birthplace of the country's first president. Near Serowe, visit Thathaganyana Hill, home to the ruins of an 11th-century settlement. Visit the small Khama Rhino Sanctuary; almost all of the country's rhinos are gathered here to protect them from poachers. You'll also find 28 other animal species and 150 bird species. On to Francistown for the night.

Day 5 Francistown, the usual stopping-off point for visitors on the way to Chobe National Park. The area has been inhabited for about 80,000 years. Gold was discovered nearby in 1867

Days 6–7 Drive to Chobe National Park, in the northeast corner of Africa where Botswana, Zambia, Namibia, and Zimbabwe come together. The park is home to the world's largest elephant population. The Chobe River is the park's water supply. Sunset boat rides float you past yawning hippos, herds of elephants, and many birds. The floodplains are filled with buffalo. Spend the night in a luxurious thatched-roof bungalow with a view overlooking the park and river.

Day 8 To Maun, on the southern edge of the Okavango Delta. It is a sprawling little town. From Maun board a charter flight to a permanent safari camp located on the edge of Makgadikgadi salt pans in the middle of the Kalahari Desert. The camp's tents are furnished with iron beds and Persian carpets. A Bushman tracker escorts guests on walks to view the desert and wildlife.

Days 9–12 Okavango Delta. The delta region covers about 5,600 square miles (15,000 sq. km). Grass flats, low tree-covered ridges, and a network of narrow waterways make up the landscape. Transport is by dugout canoe or elephant. The waters are clear, and crocodiles, hippos, and birds can be seen as well as zebras, giraffes, and elephants. During your visit you will stay in a luxury-style tent and have three gourmet meals per day served on linen with silver under a giant fig tree.

Day 13 The group is escorted to the airport for the flight to Europe for connections the next day to North America.

When is the best time to go? In the Safari Lands, the rainy season is from April to the middle of June; winter is from June through September; another short rainy season occurs from October through November; and summer is from November through April.

If possible, pick the time of year to visit based on the traveler's interests rather than the weather. In the wet season, there is ample food and water available, so the animals are spread out across the game reserves. As a result, the safari vehicles have to cover a lot of ground in search of them. In the dry season, it is easier to spot the animals because they cluster around the few remaining water holes and salt licks.

The traveler says, "I don't really want to stay in a tent." How would you respond? Generally, tented camps cost more than the deluxe lodges and provide better accommodations. In Botswana, some lodges are permanent structures, but the majority are tented. Most tents have proper beds, private baths, and many amenities. Service in a tented camp is also generally better than in a lodge. And on a tented safari, the absence of walls separating guests from the outdoors brings a greater sense of the wilderness experience.

ON THE SPOT

Mr. and Mrs. Livingstone have booked an African safari. They have asked you what clothes they should bring and how to pack for the trip. How would you respond?

Dress on safari is casual. Travelers need something dressier only for the cities or for a layover in Europe. People should pack lightly and have a canvas bag in their large suitcase. Once they are in Africa, they should repack their casual clothes in the canvas bag. They can leave their large suitcases in the porter's locker in the city hotel. On chartered or small planes, luggage is severely restricted. Travelers should bring earth-tone clothing, especially for game drives, when everything gets dusty. If they plan to take any game walks, comfortable hiking shoes are a must. Everyone should bring a wide-brim hat that covers the face; baseball hats leave the ears and neck too exposed to the sun.

stretching from Victoria Falls in the south to Lake Tanganyika in the north. A piece of the Republic of the Congo in the north almost divides the country in two. **Lusaka** (*loo SAH kuh*) is the capital and largest city.

Most of Zambia is covered by *bush*—a mix of woodland and savanna. The Zambezi River forms much of the southern border. The country has long provided outstanding game viewing in places such as **South Luangwa**, **Kafue**, and **Lower Zambezi National Parks**. Wildlife includes giraffes, elephants, leopards, and lions.

Zambia's top attraction is Victoria Falls, the curtain of water that straddles the Zambia–Zimbabwe border. As the river threads its way to the Indian Ocean, it drops suddenly into a deep, narrow chasm. The mist and spray created can be seen for a great distance. The local people named the falls *Mosi oa Tunya* ("Smoke That Thunders"). The river is ranked a Class 5 for its rapids. Canoe trips range from half a day to five days. In addition to bungee jumping off the bridge linking Zambia and Zimbabwe, adventurers can abseil (rappel) down the gorge or high-wire across it.

Botswana

North of South Africa is the landlocked country of Botswana (*baht SWAHN uh*), one of the most desirable safari destinations. A series of best-selling detective novels by Alexander McCall Smith that are set in Botswana has raised awareness of this quiet gem. It stands out among African countries because of its political calm and stability. It is also the world's single-largest producer of gem-quality diamonds. **Gaborone** (*gahb uh ROH nee*), which is in the southeast near the South African border, is the capital and largest city. Roughly the size of Texas, Botswana is part of a huge plateau. The land is hilly in the east and flat or gently rolling elsewhere. The Kalahari Desert spreads across the central part of the country. The desert has been home to the Bushmen (or San) people for 25,000 years; they are one of the last surviving hunter-gatherer societies.

Elephants at watering hole

In the north, the Okavango River forms a huge inland delta, the **Okavango**. Described as the "river that never finds the sea," the Okavango begins near the Atlantic Coast in Angola. Instead of flowing west, the logical route to the sea, the river flows eastward. When it meets the Kalahari, the river breaks into channels, swamps, lakes, and lagoons, forming a delta in a sea of sand. Thick grasses that thrive in the water make much of the delta impenetrable except by dugout canoe (*makaro*), which is the local people's traditional form of transportation. Most of the land is carved into giant private concessions with luxury lodges and camps. The only part of the delta that is officially protected is **Moremi National Park** in the east.

Chobe National Park is another popular destination. Chobe boasts the world's highest elephant population, approximately 90,000 of the great beasts.

Luxury and comfort are the order of the day at the safari camps throughout the country. Some lodges are permanent, but the majority are tented. In Botswana, game viewers use not only vehicles but also elephants, canoes, and motorboats. Wildlife viewing is best in the dry winter months (late May to August) when the animals huddle around water sources.

Namibia

West of Botswana, Namibia (*nuh MIHB ee uh*) is also bordered by Angola, Zambia, South Africa, and, on the west, the South Atlantic Ocean. **Walvis Bay** is the Atlantic port. **Windhoek** (*VINT huk*), the capital and largest city, is in the center of the country. Windhoek's architecture reflects its past as a German colony.

The Namib Desert on the coast is one of the world's oldest and driest deserts. When the rain comes, water is trapped under the sand, which wildlife, including elephants, must dig through to drink.

The northern part of the desert is called the **Skeleton Coast**. Here, the cold Benguela Current flowing from Antarctica meets the dry, hot air of the desert. Where they meet, an incredible strip of fog descends each night. The Skeleton Coast was the coast of death for unfortunate explorers whose boats wrecked in the fog. Diamonds and other precious stones hide among the pebbles littering the beaches. The Skeleton Coast Park is a true wilderness area, the domain of jackals, hyenas, desert elephants, and lions.

Etosha National Park, northwest of Windhoek, is one of the world's largest game parks. The center of the park is Etosha Pan, a huge salt pan more than 12 million years old. For a few days each year after the rains, the pan fills with water, and flamingos and pelicans descend by the thousands. All of Africa's "big five" are found in Namibia, along with antelopes, giraffes, and zebras. Although visitors can reach the park by car (six hours from Windhoek), the majority fly from Windhoek to **Tsumeb**.

South Africa

South Africa lies at the southern tip of the continent, with the Indian Ocean to the east and the South Atlantic Ocean to the west. It is also bordered by Namibia, Botswana, Zimbabwe, Mozambique, and Swaziland. (Look again at Figure 13.5.) Its Southern Hemisphere location lets visitors swap winter for summer. In land area, South Africa is about three times the size of Texas. Enclosed within its borders is the small kingdom of **Lesotho**.

South Africa has three main geographic regions. First, the vast plateau of the interior slopes north and west to form part of the Kalahari basin. Second, the Great Escarpment, which includes the **Drakensberg Mountains**, rims the plateau. Third, a strip of fertile land runs along the coastal plain.

The Dutch settled Cape Town in the 1600s, calling themselves "Afrikaners" or "Boers." In 1806 the Cape Province became British, and new settlers arrived. The Boers and the British battled each other, with the British emerging victorious. Blacks and whites also clashed. In 1948 the whites established *apartheid* ("separateness"), a policy that enforced strict separation of blacks, whites, Asians, and "coloreds." Apartheid laws were not repealed until 1991. South Africa started life without apartheid in 1994 with Nelson Mandela as its first black president.

The major cities are along the Cape's south and east coasts. The most popular international gateways are **Johannesburg** and **Cape Town**. Cape Town is the legislative capital, **Pretoria** the administrative capital, and **Bloemfontein** the judicial capital.

Cape Town Lying in a natural amphitheater at the foot of Table Mountain is Cape Town, which is often wreathed in a summer cloud known as the "tablecloth." The mountain forms an unforgettable background, as majestic now as in the 16th century, when Sir Francis Drake described the Cape Peninsula as the "fairest cape we saw in the whole circumference of the earth." Visitors can go to the mountaintop via cable car, or they can hike a variety of trails that range in difficulty.

The restoration of the Victoria & Alfred Waterfront has made the harbor an attraction. From the waterfront, a ferry goes to Robben Island, the nature reserve best known as the place where Nelson Mandela was imprisoned.

The **Cape of Good Hope** juts southward from Cape Town. Semitropical plants, ostrich farms, and the rugged terrain make it one of earth's most beautiful places.

The Winelands The area north of Cape Town includes vineyards and old Cape Dutch villages. South Africa's major wine-producing regions have signposted wine routes; the Stellenbosch Wine Route is one of the best known. Founded in 1679, **Stellenbosch** is considered the heartland of the Afrikaners. Many of the wine estates are open to visitors.

Garden Route East from Cape Town lies the *Garden Route*, one of the world's most beautiful drives. The highway passes resorts, long-established towns with elegant Cape Dutch buildings, and vineyards. **Mossel Bay** was one of the first harbors visited by Portuguese sailors, and the town has a museum charting the maritime history of the coast. Peak season for visitors is from November to March.

South Africa's mines yield 28 percent of the world's gold.

Johannesburg Inland, Jo'burg is the largest African city south of the Sahara. Gold Reef City is an attraction that highlights South Africa's legendary gold mines. Also popular are excursions to Soweto to visit the homes of Nelson Mandela and Bishop Desmond Tutu, another leader in the fight to end apartheid.

From Johannesburg most tours include an extension to Victoria Falls in neighboring Zimbabwe or a visit to **Sun City** Resort, the "Las Vegas of Africa."

Durban Southeast of Johannesburg, Durban faces the Indian Ocean. It is South Africa's third-largest city and has a mix of cultures, including a large Indian community. It has long been a favorite with beachgoers. Swimming is possible year-round.

Durban is the gateway to the province of **KwaZulu-Natal**, a warren of hills and valleys about one and a half to two hours north of Durban. The province is home to about 7 million Zulus. This is where King Shaka defeated his tribal enemies during the early 1800s, and here are the battlefields of the Zulu, Boer, and British wars of the 1830s. Several Zulu sites have been developed for tourists. Most tours include a visit to a *kraal* ("homestead").

Wildlife Safaris South Africa's wildlife sanctuaries include nature parks, private game reserves, and national game reserves. Nature parks are noted more for their scenic beauty and hiking trails than for wildlife.

Kruger National Park is a national game reserve, probably South Africa's most important attraction. It is along the border with Mozambique and is roughly the size of Massachusetts. The park has 137 species of mammals, 500 species of birds, and more than 100 kinds of reptiles. June through October is the prime time for game watching.

A dozen private game reserves share the park's perimeter. Upscale Kapama and Sabi Sand provide game viewing in opulent surroundings.

✔ CHECK-UP

The Safari Lands include

- ✔ Kenya; its capital and East Africa's largest city is Nairobi.
- ✔ Tanzania; its capital is Dodoma.
- ✔ Zambia; its capital is Lusaka.
- ✔ Botswana; its capital and largest city is Gaborone.
- ✔ Namibia; its capital is Windhoek.
- ✔ South Africa, with three capitals.

Highlights of game viewing in the Safari Lands include

- ✔ Tanzania's Ngorongoro Crater and Mount Kilimanjaro.
- ✔ Victoria Falls in Zambia.
- ✔ Botswana's Okavango Delta.
- ✔ Namibia's Etosha Pan.
- ✔ South Africa's Kruger National Park.

Israel

The small state of Israel (about the size of New Jersey) was established by the United Nations as a Jewish homeland in Palestine in 1948. Jews have historical ties to the region that date back more than 3,000 years. However, their claim to the land conflicts with that of the Palestinian Arabs, whose historical ties are no less ancient.

The country occupies a narrow stretch of land at the southeastern corner of the Mediterranean (see Figure 13.6). In the north, a region of hills is called Galilee. In the center is the urban sprawl of Jerusalem and Tel Aviv. The south

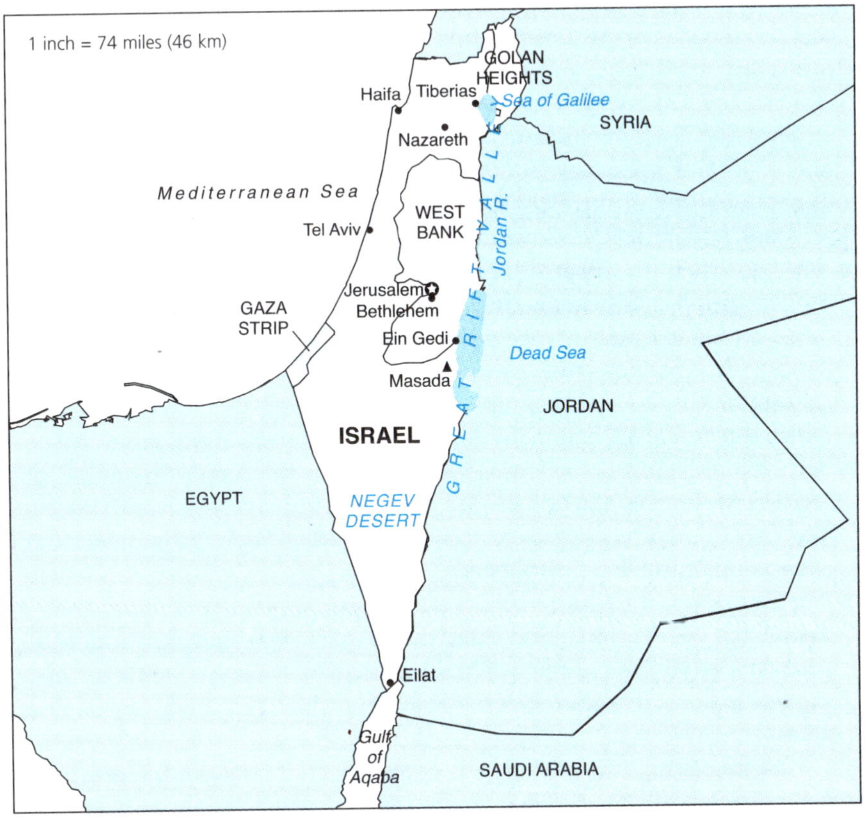

FIGURE 13.6 Israel

is dominated by the **Negev** (*NEH gehv*) **Desert**, which ends at the **Gulf of Aqaba** (*AK ah bah*), Israel's opening on the Red Sea. The **Jordan River** flows from Lebanon to the **Sea of Galilee** south to the **Dead Sea**, which is Asia's lowest point, at 1,299 feet (396 m) below sea level. The Sea of Galilee is the country's main reservoir of fresh water.

Israel's northern half is temperate and fertile; the south is arid and barren. The country is virtually self-supporting in food thanks to modern farming and irrigation methods used at the *kibbutz* ("collective settlement") or *moshav* ("cooperative village"). Hard work has made parts of the desert bloom.

The *kibbutzim* are agricultural collectives but are also geared, especially in border areas, for defense in time of war. A stay at a kibbutz (*kih BOOTS*) is an interesting travel experience.

The Cities

Despite threats of terrorism, travelers of different faiths continue to go to Israel in search of religious inspiration. **Jerusalem** is the capital and largest city, **Haifa** is the major port, but **Tel Aviv** has Ben Gurion Airport, the international gateway.

Tel Aviv

Modern Tel Aviv is Israel's cultural capital and economic powerhouse. From its beachfront high-rise hotels, visitors can reach tourist sites throughout the small country. The drive from Tel Aviv to Jerusalem, for example, takes about 45 minutes. Dizengoff Street is the city's main thoroughfare.

Old Jaffa is part of Tel Aviv in geography, but centuries away in atmosphere. It is one of the world's oldest cities, the port from which the biblical Jonah sailed to meet his whale. Jaffa today is an artists' colony with shops, restaurants, and nightclubs.

Dome of the Rock, Jerusalem, Israel

Jerusalem

Jerusalem lies on hilly, rocky land in the Judean Hills. The city owes its character to the ethnic groups of its past: Jews, Arabs, Armenians, Turks, British, Greeks, and Romans. Today, the city is divided into three sections: the Old City, West Jerusalem, and East Jerusalem.

The Old City is the historic heart of town. It has four neighborhoods: the Armenian, Christian, Jewish, and Muslim quarters. The Temple Mount occupies one-fifth of the Old City and is sacred to three religions. Shrines on the Mount and in the Old City include

- For Muslims: the silver-domed El-Aksa Mosque, the largest and most important place of Islamic prayer after Mecca and Medina. Nearby is the Dome of the Rock, whose golden cupola is the city's most famous landmark. The large rock under the dome is sacred to both Jewish and Muslim faiths. It is said to mark the place of Abraham's intended sacrifice of his son and of Muhammad's flight to heaven on a winged horse.
- For Jews: the Western or Wailing Wall, which is the supporting wall of the Temple Mount and the holiest place of prayer in the Jewish world. Pilgrims place written prayers in the crevices of the Wailing Wall. Tradition demands separation of worshipers by gender.
- For Christians: the Church of the Holy Sepulchre (the traditional tomb of Jesus), the Garden of Gethsemane, the Via Dolorosa, and the room of the Last Supper. As the most holy Christian site, Jerusalem is a center for many denominations; the Church of the Holy Sepulchre is controlled by no fewer than six.

Airport-style security checks at the Wailing Wall leave you in no doubt as to the importance of the site.

West Jerusalem is the modern part of the city, with fashionable shops, hotels, restaurants, and tall office buildings. In the Israeli Museum, the Shrine of the Book is home to a number of Dead Sea scrolls from the 1st century BC.

East Jerusalem also has many restaurants and shops. It is where most of Jerusalem's Arabs live.

Bethlehem South of Jerusalem is the "little town of Bethlehem." The heart of Bethlehem is Manger Square, where the Church of the Nativity is shared by the Greek Orthodox, Catholic, and Armenian churches. Bethlehem was long the wished-for destination for Christians on Christmas Eve, but visits in the area have been suspended because of political tensions.

Other Places to Visit

Israel offers a cornucopia of experiences for visitors.

Galilee In the north, Galilee is Israel's most fertile region. The area is associated with Jesus, and the Sea of Galilee is a site for Christian pilgrims. Around the lake, the Church of the Multiplication of the Loaves and Fishes and the Mount of the Beatitudes are pilgrims' goals.

Tiberias is the only settlement of any size on the lake. It is a modern

CLOSE-UP: ISRAEL

Who is a good prospect for a trip to Israel? The country has special appeal to members of Jewish, Christian, and Muslim faiths. Agricultural groups have a special interest in seeing how the desert was made to bloom. Independent travelers with archaeological interests are also prospects.

Why would they visit Israel? Israel offers the attractions of religion, history, archaeology, and culture. But to many, going to Israel is not just a vacation; it is the high point of their lives. Family celebrations of a Jewish coming-of-age ceremony are popular. Techniques used at the kibbutzim are of interest to farmers, and the underwater world of the Red Sea near Eilat is an attraction for divers.

Where would they go? The most popular venue for a boy's bar mitzvah is in Jerusalem at the Western Wall. Family groups who come for a girl's bat mitzvah generally choose between the southern wall of the Temple Mount (around the corner from the Western Wall) and the ruins of the synagogue at Masada.

A tour of Israel might follow this itinerary.

Day 1 Overnight flight to Ben Gurion Airport in Tel Aviv.

Day 2 Arrive in the late morning; be met and transferred to your hotel. In the evening, meet your traveling companions at a welcome party hosted by your tour director.

Day 3 Tel Aviv–Haifa. Take a walk in the port of Jaffa. Then travel north to Caesarea to visit its crusader fortress. Drive through vineyards and apricot groves and the fertile Jezreel Valley on your way to Haifa.

Day 4 Haifa–Kibbutz Ginosar. In Haifa, visit the Bahai Shrine, the center of the Bahai faith. Then travel to Acre, the capital of the crusader kingdom. Spend an afternoon in the Galilee on your way to a lakeside kibbutz. In the evening, you are invited to a lecture on kibbutz life.

Days 5–8 Jerusalem. The next days include tours of the sacred shrines of the Old City and a day at leisure. Day 8 includes an excursion to Masada, with a cable car ride to the top and a visit to the Dead Sea, with time for a float.

Day 9 Morning at leisure; then back to Tel Aviv with stops along the way.

Day 10 Homeward bound.

When is the best time to go? Peak season is Christmas, Easter, and other religious holidays. Low season is summer because of the heat. To avoid crowds and have the best weather, a late fall or early spring trip might be best.

The traveler says, "It's not safe, is it?" How would you respond? When a terrorist incident occurs and shows up immediately on television, travelers are wise to inquire about their safety. You should refer the traveler to multiple information sources, and let the traveler make the final decision of whether or not to go.

resort with a long and important Jewish heritage, one of Israel's four holy Jewish cities, along with Jerusalem, Hebron, and Safed.

Nazareth is a dusty Christian/Arab town with sprawling modern developments and ornate churches. The center of attention is the Basilica of the Annunciation, on the traditional site of the Virgin Mary's house.

Dead Sea A visit to Israel would not be complete without a trip to the Dead Sea, which forms part of the border between the countries of Israel and Jordan. The sea is fed by the Jordan River and flash floods, but because the land is so low, the water has no outlet. In the desert's heat the water evaporates, leaving behind strangely shaped salt formations and water with a mineral content some 30 percent more concentrated than ordinary water. No animal, fish, or plant life can live in these waters, but the human body floats like a cork on the surface.

Ein Gedi is an oasis on the shore of the sea. The mineral-rich water has spawned spa facilities and resorts. Coach tours stop at the spa at Ein Gedi to allow tourists a swim in the sea. Men should not shave before a dip. Salt in any cuts hurts. Wade in, sit back, stretch out your legs, and float! Then have a roll in the mud, a tradition rumored to be part of the Queen of Sheba's and Cleopatra's beauty routines. Once you leave the sea and mud, shower quickly to get rid of the sticky film coating skin and hair.

Masada The cliffs of *Masada* ("Fortress") soar above the Dead Sea and are totally isolated from the surrounding mountains. On top is a broad plateau.

King Herod built a fortress here, stocking it with food and fitting it with cisterns to ensure plentiful water. In AD 73 a group of 967 Jewish rebels seized the fortress and proceeded to hold off a Roman force of some 10,000 soldiers for several years. When defeat was inevitable, the Jews took their lives rather than surrender to the Romans. Israeli army recruits come here to be sworn in with the words, "Masada shall not fall again."

It is a national tradition to walk up the Snake Path—a hot and tiring route that takes 30 to 60 minutes, depending on a hiker's fitness. Most tourists take the cable car.

In Israel, hotels and restaurants serve kosher foods prepared according to Jewish dietary laws. Its best-known rule is that meat and dairy products must not be served together. Pork and shellfish are also out of bounds.

Eilat Once an isolated military base, Eilat (*ee LOT*) grew to become an international beach resort. Eilat is on an arm of the Red Sea but has a very Mediterranean feel. It enjoys yearlong sunshine, superb underwater sports, plenty of nightlife, and good hotels. The greatest attractions are under the sea, where travelers can dive or snorkel among brilliantly colored coral and fish. Jacques Cousteau described diving in the Red Sea as seeing a "corridor of marvels." The sea is famed for its marine life and the clarity of its water. Live-aboard dive boats take divers to pristine reefs and dramatic wrecks.

✔ CHECK-UP

Israel's important cities are

- ✔ Jerusalem, the capital and most important religious shrine.
- ✔ Tel Aviv, the modern city on the Mediterranean closest to the international airport.

Highlights include

- ✔ Monuments sacred to three of the world's major religions in Jerusalem.
- ✔ The Galilee, with sites sacred to Christians.
- ✔ Dead Sea, the lowest point in Asia.
- ✔ Masada, Israel's most spectacular archaeological site.
- ✔ Eilat, the country's vacation capital.

Turkey

Turkey bridges Europe and Asia across the narrow straits of the **Bosporus** (*BAHS puhr uhs*) and the **Dardanelles** (*dahr duh NEHLZ*), which link the Black Sea through the **Sea of Marmara** to the Mediterranean. The country has coastlines on the Black, Mediterranean, and Aegean Seas (see Figure 13.7) and is bordered by Greece, Bulgaria, Georgia, Armenia, Iran, Iraq, and Syria.

European Turkey (ancient Thrace) is mainly rolling grasslands. Asian Turkey (also called Asia Minor or Anatolia) is a plateau ringed by mountains. The highest peaks rise in the east. The country endures frequent earthquakes and has geysers and other volcanic phenomena.

For 1,000 years Turkey was the hub of the Byzantine empire; then for nearly 500 years it was the center of the Ottoman empire. Its alliance with Germany in World War I brought the Ottoman empire to an end. Mustafa Kemal (1881–1938), a powerful general who took the name Atatürk, became president in 1923 and is considered the father of modern Turkey. To westernize his country, he separated religion and the state, abolished polygamy, banned men from wearing the fez (the brimless felt hat), and discouraged women from using the veil. He sent everyone under age forty to classes to learn the Latin alphabet.

For the adventurous traveler, Turkey offers high mountains and rugged scenery. For the historically inclined, Turkey has Hittite, Greek, and Roman remains, as well as examples of Byzantine art. For relaxation, Turkey offers the beautiful Mediterranean and Aegean coasts.

In 1915 Allied troops landed on the Gallipoli Peninsula on the Dardanelles and fought one of the bloodiest battles of World War I against the Turks and Germans. The Allies suffered 250,000 casualties before they withdrew.

The Cities

Turkey's urban life is centered in two cities: **Istanbul**, the largest city, and **Ankara**, the capital.

Istanbul The only city in the world to span two continents, Istanbul is

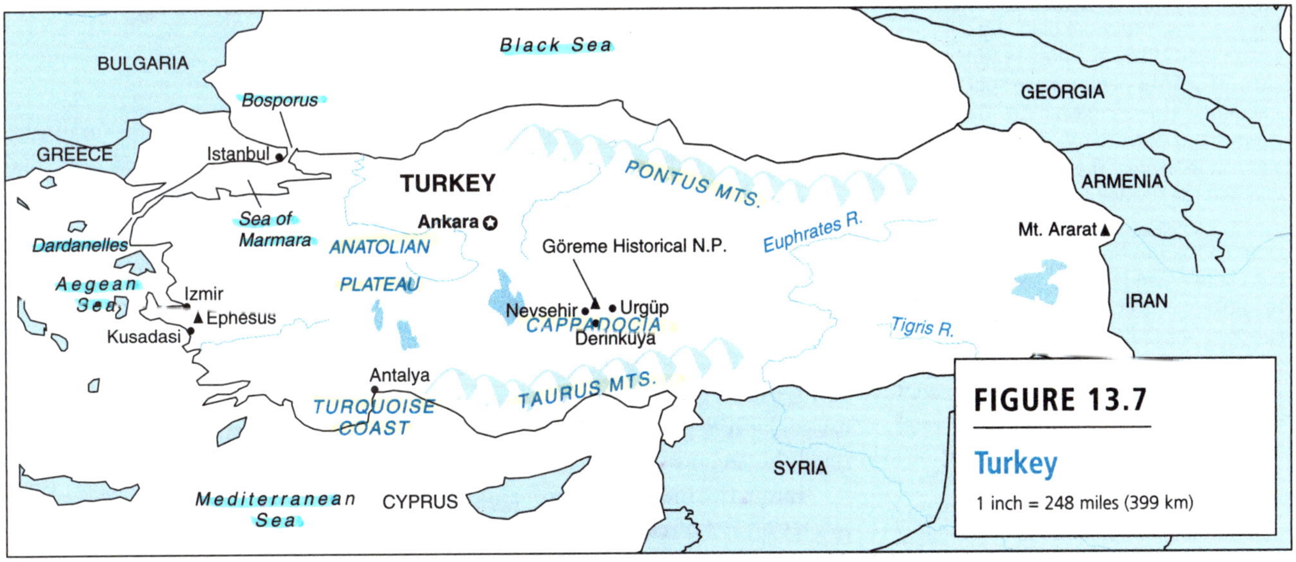

FIGURE 13.7
Turkey
1 inch = 248 miles (399 km)

divided by the Bosporus and the Golden Horn (an arm of the Bosporus) into three parts. The Asian part contains the so-called modern section of the city, which dates back only to the 13th century. European Istanbul has two parts, one of which is Stambul, the original center of the city. Most of the city's tourist sights are in Stambul.

Topkapi Palace is Istanbul's most popular attraction. Begun in 1462 and built on a promontory overlooking the Bosporus, it is a vast complex. The star attractions are the Pavilion of the Holy Mantle, the Treasury, and the Harem. The Pavilion contains the mantle of the Prophet Muhammad, hairs from his beard, and a tooth. The Treasury displays the emerald-encrusted Topkapi Dagger, the Spoonmaker's Diamond (the fifth-largest diamond in the world), and bejeweled thrones. The Harem is accessible on a tour that shows 20 of the 300 rooms. It was the sultan's private quarters and effectively a prison for his concubines.

Blue Mosque, Istanbul, Turkey

Among Istanbul's other major attractions are

- Hagia Sophia, once the greatest church in Christendom. It was turned into a mosque in 1453 and converted to a museum in 1935. The dome and ceiling are covered in gold mosaic. Probably few buildings are so overwhelming in their sheer beauty.
- Blue Mosque, Istanbul's principal place of worship. More than 20,000 blue tiles cover the walls (hence its name). Non-Muslim visitors are allowed in Turkish mosques, although they are cordoned off from the sanctuary.
- Grand Bazaar (Kapali Çarsi), the world's biggest covered bazaar. The market has some 4,000 shops on sixty-six streets, all surrounded by a wall. The shops are grouped according to guilds, with carpets in one area, jewelry in another, and so on.
- Galeta Tower, built in 1343 as part of the city's fortifications. It was used as a jail for Christian slaves and then as a fire station; currently, it houses a nightclub.

Tourist boats sail the Bosporus regularly. Taking a short cruise is a good way to see the old wooden pavilions and palaces that line the shores.

Ankara Atatürk chose Ankara as Turkey's new capital to symbolize a break with the Ottoman past. It was a primitive settlement with mud-brick houses. Today, it is a city of millions with little for the tourist except the Museum of Anatolian Civilizations.

ON THE SPOT

Mr. and Mrs. Yimaz are planning a vacation in Turkey, the home of their ancestors. Their parents have spoken frequently of the Turkish bath. They are curious and want to try one. They ask if you can recommend one. How would you find the answer?

Contact the Turkish Tourism Bureau. The bath recommended most frequently is the 300-year-old Cagaloglu *Hamam* in Istanbul. The Turkish bath, or *hamam*, dates from classical times. It had a dual function: for bathing and for socializing. Bathing is strictly segregated. You change in private cubicles and then go to the *hararet*, or steam room. You can wash yourself or have an attendant scrub you down. Finally, you can have a massage.

Other Places to Visit

Outside the cities, life for most Turks follows traditional ways. The small café in a town or village is the place where men meet to drink tea and talk. The café reflects the male-dominated society. Seeing a waitress is uncommon. Women are tolerated in mosques but are expected to say their prayers in separate areas or at home. For travelers, both the Aegean coast and the Anatolian Plateau have special attractions.

Aegean Coast From Istanbul one of the most rewarding trips is south along the Aegean coast. Two-story whitewashed houses sit like sugar cubes on rocky hillsides, their doors and window frames painted cobalt blue to repel the "evil eye."

Izmir (formerly Smyrna) is the region's largest city, but the region's prime attraction is **Ephesus** (*EHF ih suhs*). Unmatched by any archaeological site in terms of sheer size, Ephesus is the best preserved and most visited of Turkey's ancient cities. Its marble-paved main street, grooved by chariot wheels, leads past the Great Theater and the two-story Celsus Library (built in AD 135). Travelers need a minimum of three hours, a hat, and a water bottle to appreciate the city. Most tours begin at the top gate and head downhill along the main street, leaving the highlights for last.

Nearby is the bustling town of **Kusadasi** (*koo SHAD eh see*), a port that allows cruise ship passengers access to Ephesus. Strolling its streets one sees restaurants offering fish and chips and "English breakfasts."

Turkish delight (*loukoum*) is a candy made of sugar, honey, syrup, and flour. It is flavored, colored, and decorated with nuts. It has a rubbery consistency and is served as large cubes covered in confectioners' sugar.

The Turquoise Coast The Turks call their share of the Mediterranean on the southwest coast the *Akdeniz*, or "White Sea." Those familiar with its clear blue waters and spectacular vistas punctuated with coves, castles, and cities of the ancient world prefer to call it the *Turquoise Coast*. The area has rapidly developed as a major sun-and-sea paradise for European vacationers. Airports are at Dalaman, **Antalya**, and Adana.

Cappadocia The expression "Turkish delight" takes on a new meaning in Cappadocia, a region southeast of Ankara in the center of Turkey. It is a geological wonderland. The region is dominated by Mount Argaeus, Turkey's third-highest mountain. Long ago its volcanic eruptions covered the plateau with ash. The soft rock, called *tufa*, was transformed by erosion into a landscape of cones and columns.

The finest formations are in the *Valley of the Fairy Chimneys*. People have cut homes into the tufa since at least 400 BC. Some homes are still inhabited, but most have been evacuated due to the persistent threat of rock falls.

From Ankara it is a four-hour drive to Cappadocia's main towns of **Nevsehir** and **Urgüp**. The **Göreme Historical National Park** is probably the region's biggest attraction, with more than thirty rock churches open to the public. At **Derinkuya**, visitors find underground cities to depths of six and seven stories. Tunnels connect a honeycomb of apartments, kitchens, wineries, chapels, stables, and rooms estimated to have accommodated a population of 30,000.

Cappadocia, Turkey

✔ CHECK-UP

Sights to see in Istanbul include
- ✔ Hagia Sophia.
- ✔ Blue Mosque.
- ✔ Topkapi Palace.
- ✔ Grand Bazaar.

Travel within Turkey should include visits to
- ✔ Cappadocia, a geological wonderland.
- ✔ Ephesus, the best preserved of Turkey's ancient cities.
- ✔ Turquoise Coast.

Planning the Trip

The tourism industry faces challenges in Africa and the Middle East. Droughts in Africa's northeast, the ever-growing Sahara, earthquake activity in Turkey, terrorism, and war have greatly added to the region's problems. Promotional materials rarely mention any negatives. Travelers must be alert to conditions and watch the State Department travel advisories.

The experience of the tour or safari operator is crucial to the success of trips to this region. It is well worth the work it takes to research the operator. Tourists will probably have questions about how to prepare, what to bring, and what to expect, as well as general questions about the region. Tour and safari operators are excellent sources of information about their specialties.

When to Go

Morocco, Egypt, Israel, and Turkey can be very hot during the summer months. Inland Turkey can be very cold in winter. Below the equator, the seasons are reversed.

In the Safari Lands, destinations in the higher altitudes can be pleasant year-round, no matter how close they are to the equator. Visitors can enjoy South Africa during any month of the year. In peak summer season (the Northern Hemisphere's winter), however, its national parks and private game reserves can be hot and uncomfortable.

Preparing the Traveler

Whether going on safari or exploring Morocco, Egypt, Israel, or Turkey, travelers need to be prepared for cultures that are very different from those at home.

Health When seeking information on health concerns in Africa, you should try to find a doctor qualified in tropical medicine or contact the Centers for Disease Control in Atlanta. The people who own the hotels, lodges, and safari camps tend to be careful about sanitation because health problems would put them out of business. Nevertheless, tourists must take precautions. In most areas, they should stick to bottled water and avoid peeled fruits and vegetables.

Malaria is a problem. Some doctors recommend medications or vaccinations for malaria, yellow fever, and cholera and suggest that travelers update their polio and tetanus shots as well. Shots must be recorded on a vaccination certificate, which should be carried with the passport. Bilharzia (a parasite found in a certain species of snail) infests the waterways in Africa. No one should walk barefoot along rivers or streams or swim in lakes or rivers, especially the Nile.

To combat safari dust, travelers should have scarves for nose and mouth, wet wipes for hands and face, and disposable contact lenses for those who wear them. Air pollution in Cairo and Istanbul causes respiratory problems. Stomach woes and colds are common ailments.

Money Credit cards and traveler's checks are accepted in major cities, but outside the cities, visitors can have difficulties with both. ATM use varies. Bargaining is the rule in the souks and markets. The guideline is to pay no more than one-third to one-half the asking price. Pay with cash, and take purchases with you if at all possible. Credit cards can be overcharged, and inferior items may be substituted for quality buys.

On safari, travelers should make sure they have local currency before they start. Safaris are all-inclusive, but tips to drivers and guides are extras. Optional charges vary from tour to tour. They may include charges for extra meals, beverages, mineral water, balloon rides, visits to local tribes, purchases, and additional game drives.

Language The region has many languages and several alphabets. English

➤ PROFILE

Shopping in Africa and the Middle East

For shoppers, treasures of Africa and the Middle East include

- In Morocco: saffron, leatherwork, pottery, and tea caddies made of beaten copper and tin.
- In Egypt: a cartouche, copper, brass, oriental rugs, perfumes, glass, and papyrus paintings.
- In the Safari Lands: carvings of ebony, batiks, jewelry, beadwork, and baskets.
- In Israel: arts and crafts, and religious jewelry.
- In Turkey: handpainted boxes made of camel bone, carpets, tiles, leather jackets, and the blue beads worn by many to protect against the evil eye.

cannot be counted on outside tourist areas. Hebrew and Arabic scripts are difficult to decipher. Turkish is one of the more difficult languages, but fortunately Atatürk introduced the Roman alphabet.

Customs The Middle East is a difficult place for solo women travelers. The best way to avoid problems is to dress conservatively and avoid eye contact. Respect all holy sites, cover bare legs and arms, and be wary of photographing people without their permission.

In Israel, the days that stores are open may be confusing. The Jewish Shabat ("Sabbath") starts at sunset on Friday, lasts until sunset on Saturday, and is strictly observed. In Orthodox quarters, all work and even such minor activities as smoking or pushing the button in a self-service elevator are banned. The Muslim holy day is from Thursday sunset to Friday sunset.

Transportation

Most trips to African and Middle Eastern destinations arrive and depart from the same airport and follow a circular route within each country.

By Air Casablanca is the main arrival point in Morocco, Cairo in Egypt, Johannesburg in South Africa, Tel Aviv in Israel, and Istanbul in Turkey. All are served by international, national, and domestic airlines.

By Water Cruises in the eastern Mediterranean visit Istanbul and Kusadasi in Turkey. Some lines offer combination cruise/safaris along Africa's east coast. The Nile cruise is a must for anyone visiting Egypt.

By Rail For the most part, the region has little rail service of use to tourists. The train trip from Cairo to Luxor along the Nile is one exception. First-class travel is quite comfortable. Food is brought to your compartment.

South Africa is another exception. There, the Blue Train is called the "Five-Star Hotel on Wheels." The twenty-five-hour journey from Pretoria to Cape Town is one of the great rail journeys. Rovos Rail offers luxury steam safaris to the eastern Transvaal.

By Road Driving in the region is generally fast and aggressive. Towns of any size are congested and confusing. Car rental in the region is available, but travelers might consider alternatives such as hiring a car with driver. In Morocco, Egypt, Israel, and Turkey, traffic drives on the right. In the Safari Lands, driving is on the left.

In Israel, public transport either stops or is greatly reduced on holy days. *Sheruts* are shared taxis, holding up to seven people, that ply routes both in and between cities. Often they operate when there is no bus service because of a religious holiday.

Accommodations

Hotels in Morocco, Egypt, Israel, and Turkey are similar to those in any country geared to international tourism, and large international chains are well represented.

Travelers on safari can enjoy everything from lodges and elegant tented camps to unique tree hotels. The concept of building a hotel at tree level began

➤ PROFILE

Cuisine of Africa

International cuisine is widely available in hotels and big-city restaurants. Here are some local specialties:

- In Morocco: *couscous* made of semolina; *tajine*, fish or meat and vegetables boiled slowly in an earthenware bowl; *pastilla*, a sweet, layered pastry dish made with pigeon, almonds, and saffron; and sweet mint tea served in a glass stuffed with mint leaves.
- In Egypt: *foul* (pronounced "fool"), chickpeas puréed with sesame seed. Meat is usually grilled lamb.
- In South Africa: *bredie*, a dish of lamb and vegetables; *bobotie*, a curried meat dish; and *potjiekos*, a stew served at *braais* (barbecues).
- In other Safari Lands: *sambusa*, a deep-fried pastry filled with meat. Game is available at some reserves.

➤ PROFILE

Cuisine of the Middle East

Try these specialties:

- In Israel: falafel, hummus, tahini, shishlik, and kebabs, as well as foods from other parts of the world where Jews settled. Kosher food is widely available.
- In Turkey: lamb, shish kebab, dolma, *karniyarik* (eggplant stuffed with meat), *ayran* (a yogurt drink), and strong coffee in small cups, sugared, often with cardamom added for flavoring. *Raki* (brandy flavored with anise) is the national drink.

in Kenya with Treetops; the Ark and Mountain Lodge soon followed. Tree lodges are skillfully built around water holes where the animals come to drink. Guests can sit on the decks and watch the animals in comfort and safety.

Both land and wing safaris offer accommodations at lodges or tented camps. Land safaris that use informal lodges are the least expensive type of safari and are usually confined to one park. The use of tented camps increases the cost of a safari. Wing safaris that use domestic air or charter flights, minibuses, and exclusive tented camps are the most expensive type of safari, but they also provide the best way to experience the African bush.

In Israel, those seeking the unique might stay at a kibbutz or at the historic King David Hotel in Jerusalem. The grandest hotel in Istanbul is the Çiragan Palace, a restored 19th-century Ottoman palace on the edge of the Bosporus.

✔ CHECK-UP

Travelers to Africa and the Middle East must be concerned with

- ✔ Using health precautions.
- ✔ Understanding language and alphabet differences.
- ✔ Carrying cash when credit cards and traveler's checks are not useful.
- ✔ Observing local standards of conduct.
- ✔ Driving on the correct side of the road.

OTHER DESTINATIONS IN AFRICA AND THE MIDDLE EAST

The Iraq War and terrorism have affected destinations in this chapter. (Look again at the map of the region shown in Figure 13.1.) This section discusses destinations in Africa and the Middle East that have geographic and cultural attractions that someday will restore them to tourism's mainstream.

ZIMBABWE

Zimbabwe (*zim BAHB way*) is a Safari Land in southeastern Africa between the Zambezi River, which forms its northern border with Zambia, and the Limpopo River, which forms the border with South Africa. It is approximately the size of California. **Harare** (*huh RAH ray*) is the capital and largest city. Political unrest makes this a destination to be checked out carefully.

Great Zimbabwe was the center of an extensive trading empire from the 9th to the 17th century. Its wealth was based on gold. The stone walls of its ruins remind us of its power.

THE AFRICAN ISLANDS

Madagascar, the world's fourth-largest island, lies in the Indian Ocean southeast of the African mainland. **Antananarivo** (*ahn tuh nah nuh REE voh*) is the capital and largest city. The country's attractions are its unique animals and plants, most of which exist nowhere else on earth. Bandits operate in certain highland regions, and the terrain and climate make surface travel difficult if not impossible for much of the year.

The **Seychelles** (*say SHELLS*) are about ninety islands in the Indian Ocean northeast of Madagascar. The largest island is Mahé. **Victoria** on Mahé is the country's capital, chief port, and only town. The climate is hot and humid, but that makes little difference to the many visitors who come for the island's beautiful beaches and water sports. English and French are the official languages.

JORDAN

Jordan is an Arab kingdom on the east bank of the Jordan River in the heart of the

Middle East. Most travelers begin their journey in **Amman** (*ahm MAHN*), the modern capital.

From Amman visitors are within easy driving distance of any tourist destination in the country. Foremost is the rose-red city of **Petra** (*Wadi Moussa* in Arabic). Petra was built by people who settled here more than 2,000 years ago and dominated the trade routes of the ancient world. Perfectly preserved in a secret valley and not rediscovered until the early 19th century, Petra is a place of magic. At the visitor center near the entrance gates, you can rent a horse to take you into the site à la Indiana Jones.

In the south near the Red Sea and the town of Aqabah is Wadi Rum. "Godlike," is how T. E. Lawrence (better known as Lawrence of Arabia) described this vast, starkly beautiful desert. Jordan's other attractions include Kerak, the 12th-century crusader castle, and Jerash, a well-preserved Roman city.

King Abdul Aziz Airport in Jeddah, Saudi Arabia, covers an area larger than Manhattan. It handles the pilgrims who visit Mecca.

SAUDI ARABIA

Saudi Arabia holds a place of special honor in the Muslim world. **Mecca** and **Medina**, the two holiest cities of Islam, are there. Muslims visit these cities on annual religious pilgrimages. Non-Muslims may not enter the holy cities. **Riyadh** in the east is the capital and largest city.

CHAPTER WRAP-UP

SUMMARY

Here is a review of the objectives with which we began the chapter.

1. **List the geographic features that make Africa and the Middle East attractive tourist destinations.** Nature's displays in Africa and the Middle East range from the dry to the wet. Of the former, examples are the Sahara in North Africa, the Kalahari in Botswana, the Namib in Namibia, and the deserts of the Middle East. How water tames the desert can be seen in Israel, where modern techniques have caused the desert to bloom, and along the Nile in Egypt, where land along the river glows green against the sands of the desert. Other water attractions are the beaches of Morocco; the rain forests of central Africa; Victoria Falls on the Zambezi between Zambia and Zimbabwe; the Okavango Delta in Botswana; the Sea of Galilee, Jordan River, and Dead Sea in Israel; and the Turquoise Coast of Turkey.

   The land's attractions include the sweeping savannas and snowcapped mountains on the equator in Africa and the strange landscape of Cappadocia in Turkey. Excavations in the Great Rift Valley have provided some of the earliest evidence of human existence.

2. **Describe the appeal of Africa, matching travelers and destinations best suited for each other.** Morocco and Egypt appeal to those seeking something different, those with an interest in history, and also those who still want their creature comforts. The Safari Lands are for people who want to see animals in their natural settings and to experience soft or hard adventure.

3. **Summarize the appeal of the Middle East.** Since the beginning of time, Israel and Turkey have been part of the history of civilization, and history is one of the area's greatest appeals. Travel to Israel has great emotional appeal to Christians, Jews, and Muslims, especially to those traveling in a group with members of their church, synagogue, or mosque.

4. Provide or find the information needed to plan a trip to Africa and the Middle East. This is a region requiring special attention to documentation requirements, health needs, and political updates. Necessary information is available from the U.S. State Department, the Centers for Disease Control, various tourist boards, tour and safari operators, industry trade sources, and the Internet.

QUESTIONS FOR DISCUSSION AND REVIEW

1. What is the most common type of climate found in Africa and the Middle East?
2. What are the must-sees of an East African safari?
3. How can women traveling alone protect themselves in Middle Eastern countries?

1) tropical around the equator to temperate north + south of the [illegible]. Elevation plays a big part.

2) The "Big Five" - elephant, lion, leopard, buffalo, + rhino

3) dress moderately, avoid eye contact, respect holy sites, + keep a low profile.

Exam

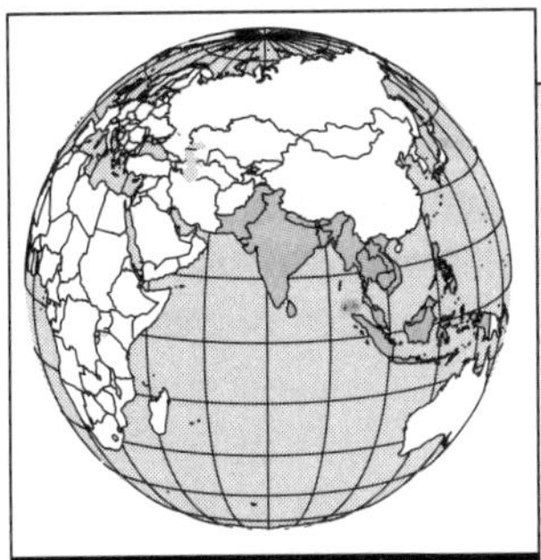

CHAPTER 14

Asia

- India
- Thailand and Singapore
- China
- Japan
- Other Destinations in Asia

OBJECTIVES

When you have completed Chapter 14, you should be able to

1. Describe the environment and people of Asia.
2. Identify the most-visited attractions, matching travelers and destinations best suited for each other.
3. Recall factors limiting tourism to Asia.
4. Provide or find the information needed to plan a trip to Asia.

Asia, the largest continent, covers about one-third of the world's land surface (see Figure 14.1). Of the Asian countries, those most likely to attract travelers are India, Thailand, Singapore, China, and Japan. They offer important business opportunities; outstanding art, architecture, and natural beauty; and a chance to learn about cultures far different from those of North America. These countries are the focus of this chapter, but first we take a broader look at Asia.

The Environment and Its People

Geographically, Asia includes certain countries of the Middle East (discussed in Chapter 13), part of Russia (Chapter 11), and the former Soviet republics of **Armenia, Azerbaijan, Kazakhstan, Kyrgyzstan, Tajikistan, Turkmenistan,** and **Uzbekistan** in central Asia. The rest of Asia can be divided into three regions, each with its own characteristics: South, Southeast, and East Asia. See Appendix A for the Fact File about each country.

South Asia includes **India, Pakistan, Bangladesh,** and **Sri Lanka** (*shree LAHNG kuh*). It also includes **Bhutan** (*boo TAHN*) in the Himalaya, mountainous **Nepal** (*nay PAHL*), war-torn **Afghanistan**, and the coral island archipelago of the **Maldives** (*MAL dyvz*). To the north, the **Himalaya** (*hih muh LAY uh* or *hih MAHL yuh*)—the world's youngest and highest mountain system—separates southern from central and northern Asia.

Southeast of India is the region known as Southeast Asia. Across the **Bay of Bengal**, a long curving peninsula extends into the **South China Sea**. The eastern half of the peninsula (known as Indochina) includes **Cambodia, Laos** (*LAH ohs*), and **Vietnam**. The peninsula's long western half contains **Myanmar** (*MYAHN mahr*; formerly Burma), **Thailand** (*TY land*), and **Malaysia** (*muh LAY zhuh*). Islands at the end of the peninsula make up **Singapore**. To the south and east, Southeast Asia extends to the island countries of **Brunei** (*BROO nay*), **Indonesia**, and the **Philippines**.

East Asia includes the lands south of Russia and east of the Himalaya. The region is vast in size but includes only a small number of countries: **China, Japan, South Korea, North Korea, Taiwan,** and **Mongolia**. About one-fourth of all the people in the world live here. East Asia covers about 15 percent of the Asian continent, and China by far covers the vast majority of East Asia.

Plate tectonics continuously push the peaks of the Himalaya even higher.

The Land

A glance at the map of Asia (look again at Figure 14.1) shows that its mountains flow in a different direction from those of North America. In North America, the mountains run from north to south; in Asia, they run from east to west. It is the most mountainous of all the continents and has the highest point on earth, **Mount Everest**, which is located in the Himalaya north of India.

South Asia Geographically, South Asia is divided into three parts. The Himalaya in the north form a barrier between India and China. At the foot of the mountains, the land changes into a huge plain drained by three great rivers—the **Indus**, the **Ganga** (formerly the Ganges), and the

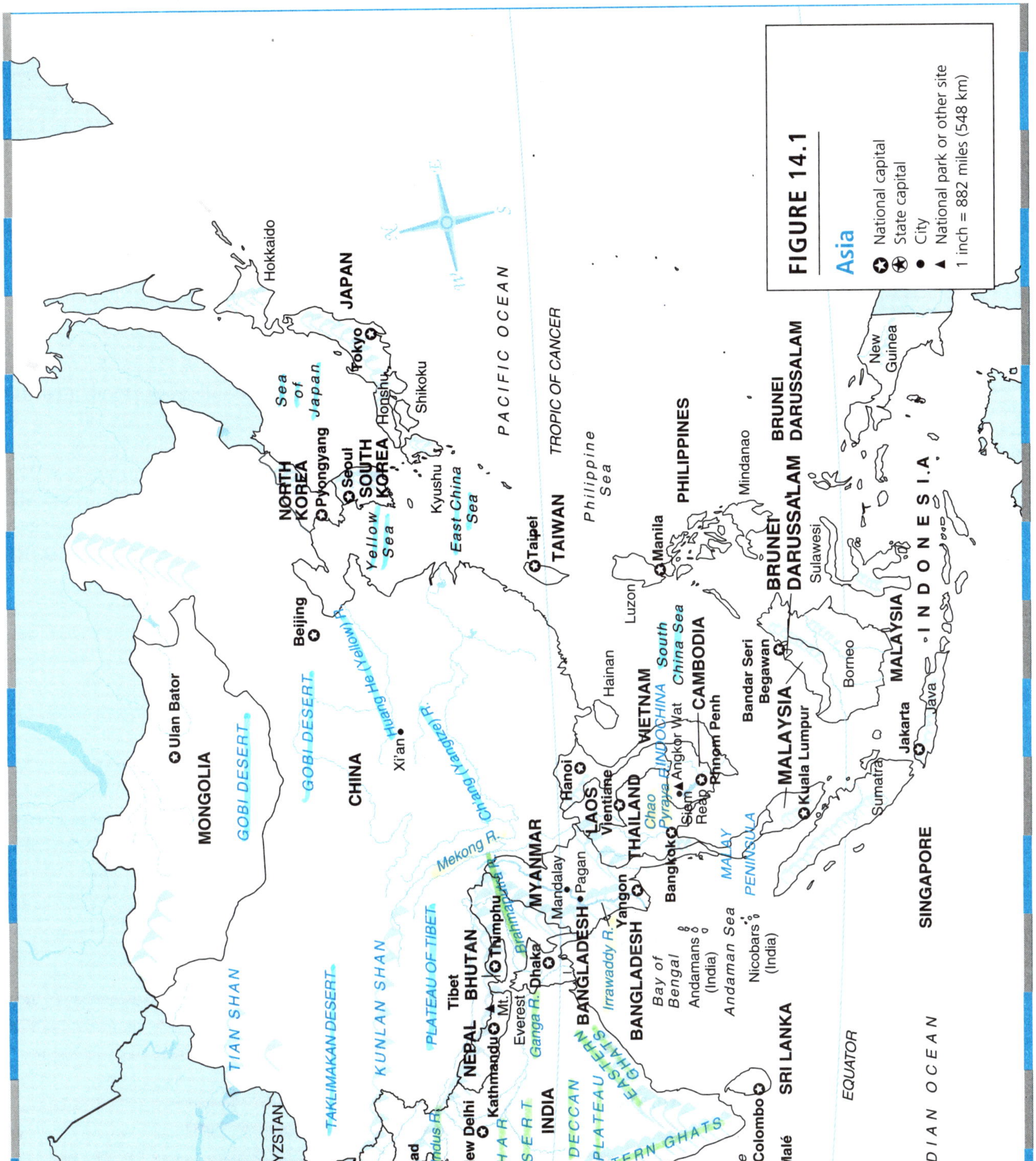

FIGURE 14.1
Asia

Brahmaputra—and their tributaries. South of this great plain, the **Deccan Plateau** lies between two rugged mountain ranges, the **Eastern** and **Western Ghats** (*gatz*), which border the coasts and meet at the southern tip of the Indian peninsula.

Southeast Asia Southeast Asia has jungle-clad mountains; dense and humid forests; vast plantations of teak, rubber, and oil palm trees; and miles of golden beaches. Each of the mainland countries has a major river valley: the **Irrawaddy** (Ayeyarwady) in Myanmar, the **Chao Phraya** (*CHOW pruh yuh*) in Thailand, and the **Mekong**, which rises in the mountains of Tibet and flows to Laos, along the border with Thailand, and through Cambodia and Vietnam before emptying into the South China Sea.

Most of Southeast Asia's volcanoes are on the so-called **Ring of Fire**, which runs along Asia's east coast from the Kamchatka Peninsula in Russia south to Indonesia. Volcanic eruptions formed mountainous islands that rise steeply from the sea.

In 1883 Krakatoa, an island volcano in the strait between Java and Sumatra, exploded, killing 36,000 people. The sound of the explosion, the most violent ever recorded, was heard nearly 3,000 miles (4,827 km) away.

East Asia In East Asia, deserts follow the mountains from the west. The **Taklimakan Desert** of western China and the **Gobi** of China and Mongolia form huge wastelands. South of the deserts, southwest China has the highest plateau on earth, the plateau of Tibet, averaging 13,000 feet (3,962 m) in altitude. In eastern China, the north and south are very different: northeastern China is dry and brown; southeastern China is green.

China's rivers rise in the Himalaya and flow east into the Pacific Ocean. These include the **Huang He** (*hoo AHNG HE*), sometimes called the *Yellow River*, and the **Ch'ang** (*chang*), called the *Yangtze* in the West. More than 3,915 miles (6,303 km) long, the Ch'ang is Asia's longest, the world's third-longest, and China's most important river.

The Sea of Japan, Yellow Sea, East China Sea, and South China Sea border East Asia. The mountainous **Korean Peninsula** separates the Sea of Japan from the Yellow Sea. East of Korea, between the Sea of Japan and the Pacific Ocean, is Japan. It consists of four major islands and about 3,900 smaller ones. All of the main islands are noted for their rugged terrain.

The Climate

The climate of Asia is as extreme as its landscape. The chief feature is the **monsoon**, during which the prevailing winds change direction, bringing rain to the region. Monsoons cause both wet and dry seasons, especially in the tropics.

Monsoons The monsoon blows from the northeast from November to March; it blows from the southwest from April to October (see Figure 14.2). It is following the path of the **intertropical convergence zone** (ITCZ), the place where the trade winds of the Northern and Southern Hemispheres meet. In summer, when the ITCZ is north of the equator, the Southern Hemisphere's trade winds cross the equator. As the moisture-laden ocean air moves inland, it is heated by the warm Asian landmass. This causes the air to rise, shed its moisture as rain, and be replaced by cooler air. It takes awhile for the winds to move across the region, so not every destination gets the monsoon at the same time. For reasons unknown, the monsoon may arrive late or not at all.

As autumn approaches, the ITCZ moves south again. By January, it sits south of the equator, causing the winds in the Southern Hemisphere to shift direction. Then they deliver rain to Indonesia and the north coast of Australia.

India India's climatic conditions range from the eternal snows of the Himalaya to the heat of the plains. The monsoon begins to set in along the western coast of India toward the end of May, bringing welcome relief as it moves across the country through June and July and withdraws by late September.

Thailand Thailand has a generally tropical climate with three seasons: hot, rainy, and cool. The hot season (March to mid-June) has temperatures from 80 to 95° F (27–35° C); in the rainy monsoon season (June to October), temperatures range from 75 to 90° F (24–32° C); the cool season (November to February) has temperatures from 65 to 90° F (18–32° C) but with less humidity.

China Extremes are the hallmark of the climates across vast China. Both Tibet and northern China have long, cold winters. The southeast and south are pleasantly warm and dry during the winter, but hot and humid during the summer, when the monsoon brings rain. The southeastern coast is tropical. Cyclones and typhoons often ravage the coast during the fall.

Japan Japan is on approximately the same latitude as North America, and its regional climates are similar to those of the eastern United States. Seasonal monsoons bring cold air and heavy snow to northern Japan in winter. Summer monsoons bring hot, humid weather to central and southern Japan. The rainy seasons are from mid-June to early July and from September to October. Typhoons may strike in late summer and fall.

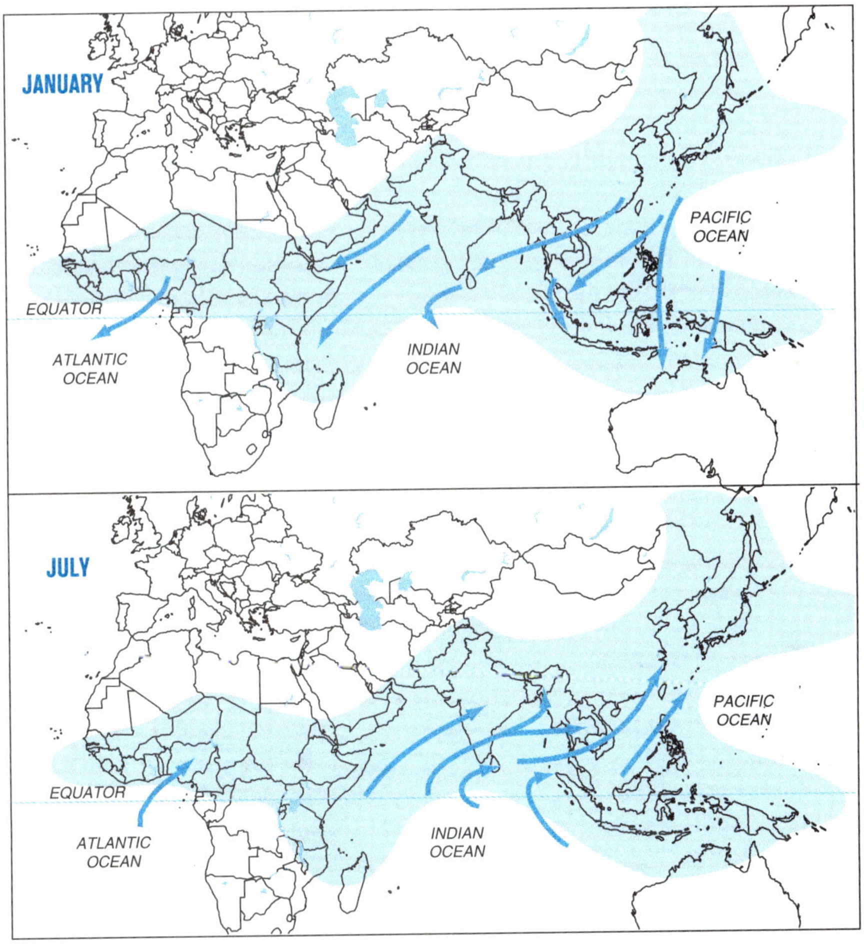

FIGURE 14.2

Monsoons

The arrows indicate the direction of the winds; the shading shows the extent of the monsoon's effect.

Source: National Geographic Society, 1995.

FIGURE 14.3

Milestones in the History of Asia

4500 BC Advanced civilizations flourish in India.

400s BC Construction starts on the Great Wall of China.

AD 1275–1292 Marco Polo visits China.

1526–1857 The Mughal empire is in India.

1600s–1700s The Dutch, English, and French form powerful trading companies.

1639 Japan closes its doors to European influence.

1819 Sir Stamford Raffles establishes a trading post in Singapore.

1842 The Treaty of Nanjing gives Hong Kong to Britain and opens five Chinese ports to British trade.

1853 Admiral Perry forces Japan to reopen its doors to the West.

1883 Krakatoa erupts in the Sunda Strait between Java and Sumatra.

1912 The Chinese overthrow the emperor.

1920 Mohandas K. Gandhi begins a campaign of nonviolent disobedience against the British in India.

1929 Brunei discovers oil.

1937 Burma (Myanmar) separates from India.

1947 India gains independence. Pakistan is formed as a separate nation.

1949 The People's Republic of China is established. Taiwan splits from communist China.

1950–1953 The Korean War takes place.

1954 The Geneva Accords create Cambodia, Laos, and North and South Vietnam.

1957 The Federation of Malaysia becomes an independent country. Singapore, Sarawak, and Sabah join Malaysia, but Singapore withdraws in 1965.

1964–1973 The Vietnam War disrupts Southeast Asia.

1971 East Pakistan becomes the country called Bangladesh.

1979 China and the United States reestablish diplomatic relations.

1997 Britain returns Hong Kong to China.

2002 Terrorism erupts on Bali.

2004 Shanghai operates the first commercial magnetic levitation trains.

The People and Their History

People have lived in Asia since ancient times (see Figure 14.3). India was the site of one of the world's oldest civilizations. In 1500 BC, nomadic tribes called Aryans invaded India and spread their rule. The Aryans developed the practices that formed the basis of Indian culture, including the caste system. *Caste* is the assignment of a person's social class from birth with no possibility of change. India had as many as 3,000 castes, each with its own customs and rituals. In modern India, caste has little legal significance, but it continues to influence society.

In AD 1526 people from central Asia established the Mughal (*MOO guhl*; also called Mogul) empire in India. The Mughal emperors were Muslims who ruled a largely Hindu country, thus setting the stage for later conflict. Life in Mughal India set a standard of magnificence, and the architecture of the period is one of India's principal attractions.

The British were the next outsiders to rule India. European navigators had opened routes to the riches of Asia in the late 1400s, and the British became the principal traders with India as the Mughals lost power and the country splintered into states. By 1849 Britain dominated the country. The 1900s brought decades of political conflict. By 1920 Mohandas K. Gandhi (1869–1948) was leading an independence movement based on nonviolent civil disobedience.

In 1947 India gained independence from Britain, but Muslim leaders demanded that a new country be carved out of the land for Muslims. To end the violence between Hindus and Muslims, Indian and British leaders agreed to divide the country into India and Pakistan. The eastern portion of Pakistan later broke away to become Bangladesh.

In Southeast Asia, Thailand (once known as *Siam*) is the only country that remained free of European rule. During the colonial period, the Portuguese controlled the Indian Ocean; the Spanish began trading in the Philippines; the Dutch captured parts of Indonesia; and the British ruled Malaysia and Singapore. Meanwhile, the French gained control of Laos, Cambodia, and Vietnam. After World War II, Southeast Asian countries won independence from the European powers. Communism gained a strong foothold in the region. Ethnic tension, civil wars, and border disputes, as well as the U.S. war in Vietnam, marked the last half of the 20th century.

Colonialism and communism were also major players in the modern history of mighty China. China's technologies as well as its arts have fascinated the world from the time of Marco Polo. For hundreds of years, the flow of learning was from East to West. In the late 1700s, the British began selling a product that changed the balance of trade—opium. China entered a long period of instability, with concessions to colonial powers and civil wars. The communists won control in 1949. Politically, China remains communist, although it has experimented with many economic reforms since 1978.

Throughout history, China has dominated East Asia, but Japan has also been a powerful force. Japan was both isolated and unified for centuries. In 1639 Japan closed its doors to the world. Ships from the Netherlands and China were allowed to trade, but only at the port of Nagasaki. In 1853 U.S. Commodore Matthew Perry arrived at Tokyo Bay and, with the help of his warships, opened relations. Within a few years, Japan's feudal systems were abolished under Emperor Meiji (1852–1912) and Western ideas introduced.

In the 20th century, Japan developed into an industrial and military power. In 1910 Japan annexed Korea; in 1931 it invaded China; and in 1941 it attacked Pearl Harbor, Hawaii. World War II ended in August 1945 when the

United States dropped the first atomic bomb on Hiroshima, followed by another at Nagasaki. After the war, the United States occupied Japan from 1945 to 1952.

Throughout Asia, religion plays an important role. Hinduism is the dominant religion of India and Nepal. Several forms of Buddhism are strong in Thailand, Cambodia, Laos, Myanmar, and Sri Lanka. Islam is followed in Pakistan, Bangladesh, Malaysia, Brunei, and Indonesia, as well as in parts of India. Singapore has a mix of religions. China is officially atheist. In Japan, Shinto and Buddhism are observed.

Throughout the area travelers see Buddhist monasteries called *wats,* compounds where saffron-robed monks live and pray. Within a wat is the *bot,* the temple that houses an image of Buddha. Other sacred objects are housed in *chedis,* which are tall, pointed spires atop bell-shaped bases, and in *prangs,* which are thick stone columns with rounded tops.

A *stupa* is a circular mound of earth covered with bricks and plaster. Buddhist relics are buried in the mound. Most stupas are topped with a small spire or a stylized umbrella. Parasols were a royal symbol, and they were placed on stupas to signify Buddha's universal dominion.

✔ CHECK-UP

Notable physical features of Asia include

- ✔ Mighty Himalaya north of the Indian subcontinent.
- ✔ Mountains, jungles, and beaches in Thailand, Malaysia, and Indonesia.
- ✔ Small, mostly flat islands of Singapore.
- ✔ Active volcanoes along the Ring of Fire.
- ✔ China's immense and diverse land.
- ✔ Earth's highest plateau in Tibet.

Asia's culture is noted for

- ✔ Long history of civilization.
- ✔ European invasion and cultural intervention.
- ✔ Centuries of political conflict.
- ✔ China's contributions to technology.
- ✔ Japan's isolation and subsequent development into an industrial power.
- ✔ Importance of religion in everyday life.

India

As Figure 14.4 shows, India is one of the world's most clearly defined geographic regions. It looks somewhat like a triangle. Two sides are bordered by water (Table 14.1 describes the islands off the coast). Across the north, the Himalaya extend in a curve from Afghanistan eastward.

India is the world's largest democracy and one of Asia's oldest and most successful countries. It is also the world's second most populous country after China, with a great variety of people, several major religious groupings, and 700 languages. About 80 percent of the people are Hindus, and 12 percent are

TABLE 14.1 Islands off the Coast of Asia

Islands	Number	Location	Political Affinity	Description
Andamans	204	Bay of Bengal	India	Lush forests, coral reefs popular with divers
Laccadives	14	Arabian Sea	India	Tiny coral islands, no tourism
Maldives	1,200	Southwest of Sri Lanka	Independent	Coral island resorts
Nicobars	19	Bay of Bengal	India	Previously used as a penal colony
Sri Lanka	1	Southeast of India	Independent	Beautiful country

FIGURE 14.4 India

Muslim. Christians, Sikhs, Buddhists, and Jains divide the remaining 8 percent. Towns whose names end with *pur* have a Hindu background; those ending with *abad* began as Muslim.

The Cities

Throughout the country cities are changing their Anglo-Indian names back to the original Indian; here the Anglo-Indian names are given in parentheses. The largest city is Mumbai (Bombay), which is in western India. Other major cities are **Delhi,** the capital, in the north; **Chennai** (Madras) in the south; **Kolkata** (Calcutta) in the east; and **Varanasi** (Benares) in central India.

Delhi India's capital is situated on the banks of the Yamuna River in an area filled with ancient sites and monuments. Delhi itself has two distinct parts, New and Old Delhi.

New Delhi was built in 1931 to serve the British colonial administration and provide comfortable living quarters for its rulers. New Delhi is a city of skyscrapers, gleaming domes, and Victorian houses. It centers around Rajpath Avenue, which leads to the Rashtrapati Bhawan, the former British viceroy's palace, now the residence of India's president.

Old Delhi is a walled Muslim city built around the Red Fort, which was constructed between 1636 and 1658. Streets are narrow and bustling. Places of interest include the Jama Masjid, India's largest mosque, and the Qutab Minar's soaring tower.

Agra India's most popular sightseeing destination is Agra (*AHG ruh*), a four-and-a-half-hour car ride south of Delhi and the site of the Taj Mahal ("Crown Palace"). It was built from 1631 to 1653 by the Mughal emperor Shah Jahan to house the body of his wife *Mumtaz Mahal* ("Chosen of the Palace"). Of the several hundred women in his harem, she was his love. She bore him fourteen children and died in childbirth at the age of thirty-nine.

The Taj Mahal is a complex of buildings within a walled rectangle. The famous mausoleum stands on a platform with a slender minaret (prayer tower) at each corner. All the buildings are strictly symmetrical. Originally the Taj Mahal was inlaid with precious and semiprecious stones, but most were stolen during the 18th century. Passages from the Koran and floral patterns decorate the exterior. The bodies of Shah Jahan and his wife lie in a vault in a central room. The building is closed after dark.

In addition to the Taj Mahal, Shah Jahan commissioned the Pearl Mosque in the Agra Fort and the Peacock Throne. The emperor was deposed by his son in 1658 and kept prisoner in a fort within sight of the Taj Mahal until his death.

Taj Mahal, Agra, India

Jaipur The *Pink City*, Jaipur, is southwest of Agra. In 1876 the city was painted pink, the traditional color of hospitality, to welcome the Prince of Wales (later King Edward VII), and it has been pink ever since. The Amber Palace, just outside the city, is particularly beautiful, as is the *Hawa Mahal* ("Palace of the Winds"), within the city walls. The Hawa Mahal is a façade of 953 screened windows where ladies of the harem could view the outside world without being seen. Next to the Taj Mahal, it is probably India's most photographed sight.

The cow is sacred to Hindus and has the right of way everywhere, whether it walks through the center of the biggest city or reclines across an expressway.

Mumbai (Bombay) Rudyard Kipling (1865–1936) was born in Mumbai and wrote in his "Ballad of East and West" that "never the twain shall meet." Perhaps they never will, but this is the city where the British tried their best to make it happen.

Mumbai has a superb natural harbor on the Arabian Sea, modern high-rise buildings, and crowded slums. It is India's most important commercial and industrial city. The Victorian-style Taj Mahal Hotel has been a luxury landmark since 1903. Traces of the British raj ("rule") linger throughout the city.

Mumbai is noted for its Victorian buildings, although today it is better known as the home of "Bollywood," the Indian film industry. The city grew in importance after the Suez Canal was opened in 1869 and Mumbai became India's port of entry. An arch at the waterfront known as the Gateway to India commemorates the 1911 visit of King George V and Queen Mary.

Travelers can visit ancient religious sites near Mumbai. An hour's ride by motor launch from the Gateway takes the traveler to Gharapuri (Elephanta Island) to see Hindu cave temples from the 7th century. Northeast of Mumbai, the hill town of **Aurangabad** is the starting point for visits to the temples of Ajanta and Ellora. The thirty Buddhist cave temples at **Ajanta** date from 200 BC to AD 650. Some were decorated with painted frescos. They were untouched for more than 1,000 years until they were rediscovered by British soldiers on a tiger hunt. The thirty-four rock cut caves at **Ellora** contain religious stories and are Hindu, Buddhist, and Jain in origin.

Chennai (Madras) Chennai is a huge tropical city where sleek new office buildings coexist with palm-thatched huts, wandering livestock, and brightly painted Hindu shrines. It is India's main southeastern port and the most convenient gateway for people wishing to explore the region. The city is bustling with activity. New jobs from outsourcing have given a lift to a generation of educated young people. The south is the part of India least visited by tourists, but it reflects Indian heritage in its purest form. Chennai is home to the classic style of Indian dance and a center of temple sculpture art.

Kolkata (Calcutta) India's largest city and the port for trade with Southeast Asia is Kolkata. It is on the Hooghly River on the Bay of Bengal. On a very hot day in 1756, Kolkata's Indian ruler seized the British garrison for violations of local trading laws. He held the prisoners in a hot, poorly ventilated cell, later called the *Black Hole of Calcutta.* By morning, most had died. The incident brought Robert Clive's crushing reprisal at Plassey and eventually the consolidation of the British Empire in India.

Kolkata today is one of India's most crowded cities. Wealthy citizens live in pleasant neighborhoods with wide streets and modern houses, but the majority of the people live in slums called *bustees.* Thousands sleep in the streets.

Varanasi (Benares) In the center of India, between Delhi and Kolkata, the city of Varanasi is comparable to Rome, Jerusalem, and Mecca. Aged and infirm Hindus come here to die, for nothing is more blessed than to die in Varanasi and thus be released from the eternal cycle of rebirth. Varanasi is on the holy Ganga, the river that the god Shiva poured down on the plains from his home in the Himalaya. Muslim conquerors destroyed the city over and over, but it was always rebuilt.

A morbidly fascinating sight is the series of *ghats*—stoned-stepped river embankments. People swim, bathe, drink, wash clothes, and brush their teeth at sunrise and sunset in the polluted water. Cremations take place on the ghats, and the ashes of the dead are thrown into the river.

Other Places to Visit

The most-visited parts of India are in the north and west. Attractions in the north include Delhi, the Taj Mahal, and mountain treks. The west is the land of the *maharajahs*—rulers of the ancient states—and their palaces and gardens. Today, the palaces might be museums or hotels or might stand idle, a romantic reminder of the past.

Darjeeling, in northeast India, is the headquarters of the Indian Mountaineering Institute as well as the birthplace of Tenzing Norgay. Since Norgay and Edmund Hillary became the first people to reach Mount Everest's summit in 1953, the peak has been reached about 2,200 times.

Kashmir The disputed northern territory of Kashmir is at the root of antagonism between India and Pakistan. India controls two-thirds of this Himalayan region, the only Indian state that is predominantly Muslim. The area is very volatile and very beautiful. Travelers are advised to consult government warnings before planning a visit.

The gateway to the region is **Jammu**. The cool climate of **Srinagar**, the ancient capital, provides welcome relief from the heat of the plains. When the British controlled Kashmir, they lived in elaborate houseboats on a lake because the maharajah had forbidden Europeans to own land. Srinagar is a base for treks into the mountains.

Goa Tucked away between the hills of the Western Ghats and the Arabian Sea, Goa is about halfway down the west coast of the Indian peninsula. Strung along its coastline are beautiful sandy beaches. The Portuguese colonists brought their Catholic religion and lifestyles to the predominantly Hindu society of Goa. It was absorbed into the Indian Union in 1961 and has developed into a resort, mostly for the affluent. **Panaji** is the capital.

Wildlife Tours India has many national parks and hundreds of wildlife sanctuaries. Each region has something special to offer, but visitors will not find the large herds seen on the open African plains. India's terrain is such that animals are solitary and elusive, hiding in the vegetation. The ever-increasing human population has turned India's once-great jungles into ever-growing villages. Two of India's most impressive animals, the Bengal tiger and the Asiatic elephant, are still found, but their population has shrunk drastically.

✔ CHECK-UP

Major physical features of India include
- ✔ Mighty Himalaya in the north.
- ✔ Central plains. Western • Eastern Ghats
- ✔ Ganga River.
- ✔ Southern Deccan Plateau.

Key Indian cities include
- ✔ Delhi, the capital, in northern India.
- ✔ Mumbai in western India, India's major commercial city.
- ✔ Chennai, gateway for those visiting southern India.
- ✔ Kolkata in eastern India.
- ✔ Holy city of Varanasi in central India.

For travelers, highlights of India include
- ✔ Taj Mahal in Agra.
- ✔ Palace of the Winds in Jaipur.
- ✔ Buddhist rock-cut temples at Ajanta.
- ✔ Sacred Ganga River in Varanasi.
- ✔ Trekking in the Himalaya.
- ✔ Wildlife tours seeking the elusive tiger.

Thailand and Singapore

Roughly the size of France, Thailand is on the Malay Peninsula bordered by Myanmar, Laos, Cambodia, and Malaysia (see Figure 14.5). Its long tail is bordered by the Gulf of Thailand on the east, the Andaman Sea on the west, and Malaysia to the south. Farther south, at the tip of the peninsula, about fifty-eight islands make up the tiny country of Singapore.

Thailand

Thailand has no deserts or dry plateaus. It has the southernmost extension of the Himalaya in the north, emerald green plains dotted with rice fields and villages on stilts in the center, and miles of beautiful beaches backed by mountains and jungles in the south. Treks, resorts, and river cruises are available.

Thailand's modernization has transformed the country. Fortunately, the past is preserved in the form of temples, palaces, and cultural presentations. **Bangkok** (*BANG kahk*) is the capital and largest city.

The plays and movies variously called *The King and I* are based on the journals of an English governess whom King Mongkit (1804–1864) of Thailand hired to teach his children. Most Thai people consider the musical to be a distortion of history.

Bangkok The city that the Thais call *Krung Thep*, the "City of Angels," is a sprawling metropolis, increasingly westernized in appearance and notorious for its traffic jams. An overhead railway that enables visitors to glide over the crowded city below helps immeasurably. The city's image as a place of waterways and temples is only partially accurate. Many canals (called *klongs*) have been filled in. Apart from the commercialized Floating Market, it is necessary to travel a long way up the Chao Phraya River to see traditional waterfront life.

FIGURE 14.5

Thailand and Singapore

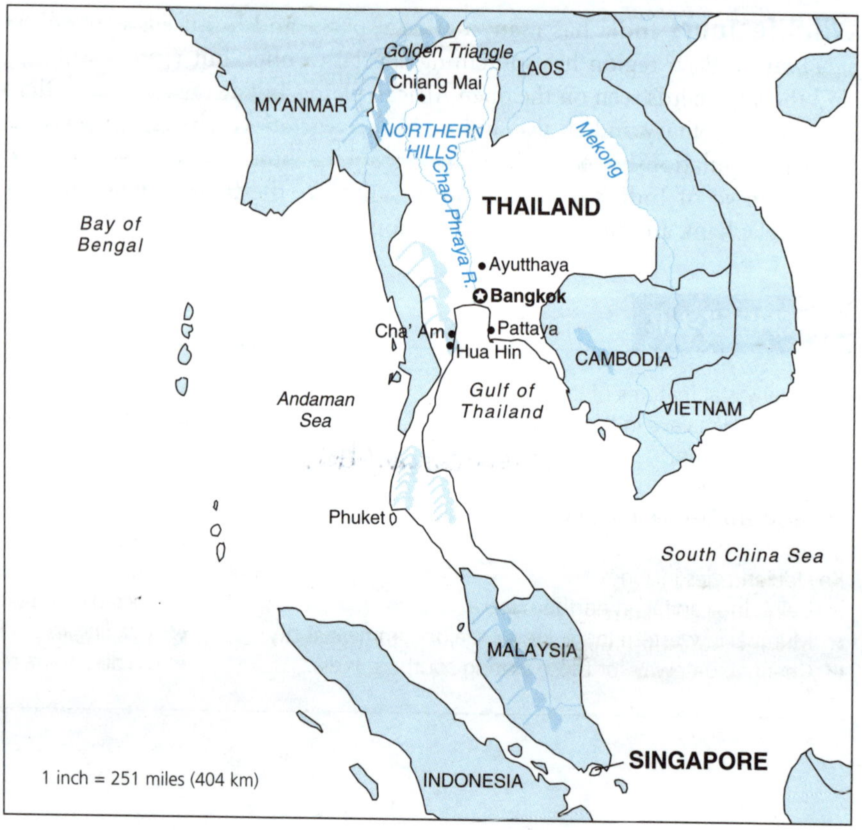

The ornate Grand Palace is Bangkok's major landmark, but it is no longer the walled residence of the king. Wat Phra Kaeo, a temple complex, houses the Emerald Buddha, which is a small statue made of solid jade—not emeralds—dressed in clothes of the season.

Grand Palace, Bangkok, Thailand

Within the city, Buddhist temples and shrines seem to be everywhere. Wat Pho has more than thirty buildings, of which the Temple of the Reclining Buddha is the largest. The statue is enormous, its feet inlaid with mother-of-pearl designs depicting the 108 signs by which believers feel a living Buddha can be recognized. Other sights include the Lak Muany (the city stone), the Erawan Shrine, the National Museum, and the Jim Thompson House, which contains a priceless collection of Thai antiques. Thompson was the American who introduced Thai silk to the world. He disappeared mysteriously in 1968.

For the most part, Bangkok's buildings are low, a backdrop to the frantic traffic, spicy food smells, and the colors of silks. Newer sections that invite shoppers include areas along Rama I Road and the Mahboonkrong Shopping Center, which has four floors of shops. At night the neon lights come on and people emerge to shop, eat, and play. Restaurants offer superb cuisine and evenings of classical dance. Some travelers prefer the infamous Patpong, a short street known for its strip bars and massage parlors.

Chiang Mai Located in the mountainous north, the *Rose of the Northern Hills* is Thailand's second-largest city. For generations Chiang Mai (*chee AHNG mye*) has been prized as a place to escape from the sticky humidity of Bangkok. People used to come by elephant; now tourists come by air, rail, and road. Chiang Mai is the center for excursions to the region's ancient temples; its teak forests, with working elephants, caves, and waterfalls; and its hill tribes.

Chiang Mai workshops create the art objects for which northern Thailand is famed: wood carvings, gold and lacquer objects, ceramics, celadon pottery, and woven silk. At Borsang, the *Umbrella Village*, women make umbrellas from bamboo, oiled paper, or silk and paint them with bright designs.

From Chiang Mai active travelers can trek in the **Golden Triangle**, a region known for its production of opium. The largest part of the Triangle is in Myanmar, but the area also includes parts of Thailand, Laos, and China. Reliable trek operators know the territory and can steer trekkers clear of possible trouble zones. Most treks last four to five days and include such experiences as an elephant ride and river rafting.

Resorts South of Bangkok, beach resorts have developed on both coasts of the narrow Kra Isthmus. The waters are warm and inviting. The sands are golden. There are spas (usually affiliated with hotels) and yoga centers. Glitzy, self-contained hotels loom over the best beaches.

The resort centers include **Phuket** (*poo KET*), an island in the Andaman Sea attached by a causeway to the mainland; **Hua Hin**; **Cha' Am**; and **Pattaya**. Pattaya is often called the *Thai Riviera*. Its well-developed environs offer luxury hotels, restaurants, golf courses, dive shops, fishing, other water sports, and evening entertainment. The resorts' special interest programs include biking, hiking, canoeing, and elephant trekking, as well as Thai cooking.

Chao Phraya Cruises One way to experience Thailand beyond the cities and resorts is to take a cruise on the Chao Phraya River, Thailand's equivalent of Egypt's Nile. The river flows south to the Gulf of Thailand. It passes three

➤ PROFILE

Trekking

India, Nepal, and Thailand are destinations for trekking holidays, ranging from easy excursions the to long challenges of snowy peaks. Preparations should include

- Equipment: the trek company provides a tent and sleeping bag; the trekker needs an umbrella (which doubles as a walking stick), hat, and sunglasses.
- Clothing: windproof jacket, down jacket, trousers, shirts, wool sweater, underwear (for high altitudes), gloves.
- Footwear: one or two pairs of comfortable trekking boots and at least three pairs of woolen socks.
- A first-aid kit, especially for stomach relief.
- Permits: the trek company should provide all that are needed.
- Consideration of the high altitude: trekkers must allow time to adjust before attempting strenuous walks.

CLOSE-UP: THAILAND

Who is a good prospect for a trip to Thailand? Thailand is popular with those seeking something different but not wanting to go too far off the beaten path. Because of distance and cost, travelers from the West Coast of North America are more likely to visit than those from the East Coast.

Why would they visit? Travelers come to see the exotic culture, to laze on the beautiful beaches, to shop, or to trek in the hills around Chiang Mai. Curiosity is a powerful motivation for travel to an exotic land.

Where would they go? A two-week vacation in Thailand might follow this itinerary.

Day 1 Depart for Bangkok.

Days 2–6 Bangkok. You are met at the airport and transferred to your hotel. After a half-day city tour on Day 3, the next three days are yours to plan. Your hotel is in the heart of the city, where you can take taxis and *tuk tuks* (motorized carts). You might decide on taking a cruise upstream, or shopping for Thai silk or jewelry, or seeing a performance of Thai kick-boxing, known as *muay thai*. This traditional sport can be seen every day of the year at stadiums in Bangkok. The matches are preceded by elaborate ceremonies and accompanied by lively music.

Day 7 Fly to Chiang Mai. Enjoy a walking tour of the 700-year-old city.

Days 8–13 Chiang Mai is the center for excursions to ancient temples, to teak forests to see working elephants, and to caves and waterfalls. From Chiang Mai you might join a trek into the mountain villages of the Golden Triangle, where Thailand, Laos, and Myanmar meet. Treks usually last three or four days. Picking a reliable guide is vital to ensure a safe trek as the region is mostly unpoliced and the origination area of much of the world's opium.

Day 14 Fly to Bangkok before returning home. Or perhaps extend your trip with a week at a Thai beach resort.

When is the best time to visit? For the most pleasant weather, a visit to Thailand should be scheduled between November and February.

The travelers say, "I want to buy some jewelry while I'm there. How do I know I won't be cheated?" How would you respond? Refer them to tourist bureaus in Bangkok. The bureaus are careful not to recommend unreliable stores and can be helpful if something goes wrong. Also, recommend that the travelers use a charge card for purchases. This gives them time to have the purchase appraised at home before the bill comes due.

capitals—**Ayutthaya** (founded in the 14th century), Thon Buri (an 18th-century capital), and Bangkok—as well as villages that continue to practice farming, arts, and crafts in traditional ways.

Singapore

The name *Singapore* is used to refer to the country, the main island, and Singapore City, which is the government center. The country is flat, with some low hills and muddy mangrove swamps. It has one of the world's highest standards of living. Unemployment, poor housing, and illiteracy have been almost wiped out. Most of the population lives on the main island of Singapore.

When frequent travelers are polled for their choice of best airport and best international airline, Singapore's Changi Airport and Singapore Airlines are consistent winners.

Singapore was an important trading post as far back as the 12th century, but it was virtually abandoned for centuries. Early in the 19th century, Sir Stamford Raffles (1781–1826), an official of the East India Company, catapulted the city into prominence as a port for ships sailing between Asia and Europe. Raffles drew up detailed plans for the city's development, carefully assigning areas to each ethnic group—Europeans, Chinese, Arabs, Indians, and Malays—and specifying the size of the houses and the width of the streets.

Raffles would love the orderliness of Singapore today. Rules abound, and travelers should be aware of them. Laws relating to jaywalking and littering are strictly enforced.

Legend has it that in 1902 the last tiger to be killed in Singapore was pursued to the Raffles Hotel, where it was shot under the bar in the billiard room.

The best way to experience the city's diversity is on foot. The traditional architecture, customs, and cuisine of the various ethnic areas are in fascinating contrast to the luxury shopping arcades of Orchard Road and Raffles City. The city is a sleek, modern metropolis and a world financial center. It has the best port facilities in Southeast Asia. A number of international operators use Singapore as a base for cruises throughout Southeast Asia. Roads and rail link the country to neighboring Malaysia.

In the heart of the city, skyscrapers dwarf Singapore's gracious colonial buildings. What remains of old Singapore is a large flat green space called the Padang ("Plain"). The historic district encircles the Padang. At the end of World War II, Lord Louis Mountbatten accepted the Japanese surrender at the city hall in 1945. St. Andrew's Cathedral (1862) sits on its own large green, a site designated by Raffles himself.

No trip to Singapore would be complete without a visit to the Raffles Hotel. It is as much a tourist attraction as it is a luxury hotel. A Singapore Sling in the Long Bar is de rigueur. The Writers' Bar provided inspiration for, among others, Noel Coward, Somerset Maugham, and Joseph Conrad.

✔ CHECK-UP

The major cities and resorts of Thailand are

- ✔ Bangkok, the capital and largest city.
- ✔ Chiang Mai, the second-largest city and the center for excursions to the hill tribes.
- ✔ Phuket, Thailand's largest island and a highly developed beach resort.
- ✔ Pattaya, also a busy resort area.

Cultural highlights of Thailand include

- ✔ Bangkok's Grand Palace, with the Temple of the Emerald Buddha.
- ✔ Craft workshops near Chiang Mai.
- ✔ Cruise on the Chao Phraya River past traditional villages and farms.

Singapore is noted for

- ✔ High standard of living.
- ✔ Dense population.
- ✔ Discipline and order.
- ✔ Raffles Hotel.

China

China is bordered to the north by Russia and Mongolia and to the east by North Korea, the Yellow Sea, the East China Sea, and the South China Sea, as Figure 14.6 shows. Twelve countries lie on its southern and western borders.

China has mountains and deserts in the west and plains in the east. The eastern region of central China is where two-thirds of the country's people live. This was the cradle of Chinese civilization. Very different regions lie on either side of an imaginary line running eastward from the city of Xi'an (*SHE ahn*) to the sea. North of the line, the rather inhospitable land is generally brown and dusty. South of the line, the land is green, crossed by rivers, creeks, and canals. This is the China of rice paddies, terraced hillsides, water buffaloes, and farmers in broad-brimmed hats.

Many dialects are spoken in this vast country, but the official language is Mandarin Chinese. The written language uses characters, not an alphabet. In the mid-1950s, the government introduced *pinyin,* a system of writing Chinese that uses the Roman alphabet, and directed that names used in foreign-language publications be written in pinyin. The chapter gives the names of cities in the pinyin spelling but also gives the spelling by which they have traditionally been known.

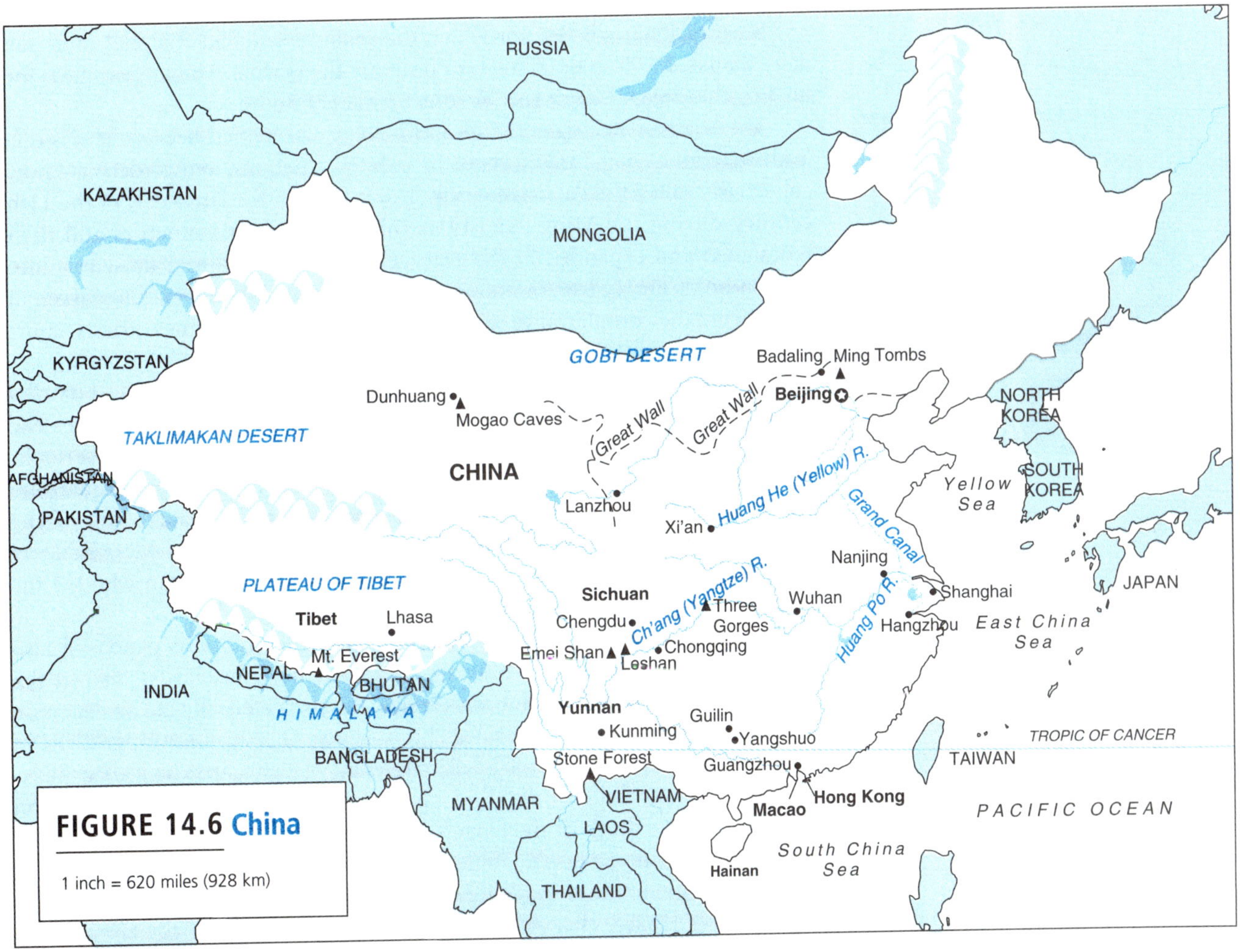

FIGURE 14.6 China

1 inch = 620 miles (928 km)

China's attractions are so varied and so far apart that a first trip can be little more than a preview. Altogether there are twenty-six provinces, each with its own dialect and regional characteristics. Even if time and money permit a tour of more than three weeks, travelers will probably have to choose between areas of the country.

The Cities

China has more than thirty-nine cities with a population of 1 million or more. Being in one of these giant cities is an unforgettable experience. To walk out of the hotel is to wade into a sea of humanity. There are waves of jingling bicycles, people doing slow-motion calisthenics, and street stalls where Chinese snacks are prepared, sold, and consumed. First-time travelers, especially those who can spend only two weeks in China, tend to visit the cities of **Beijing**, **Shanghai**, and **Guangzhou**.

Beijing (Peking) China's capital is in the northeast, just south of Inner Mongolia. Beijing (*bay jihng*) is the country's political and cultural center. Its royal gardens, temples, palaces, and modern buildings, combined with fine restaurants, good hotels, and plenty of shopping, make the city an important hub. But nowhere are China's extremes more uncomfortable than in Beijing. It swelters during the summer months, is raked by winds from Siberia and Mongolia in winter, and is carpeted by yellow dust blown from the Gobi Desert during the spring.

Most of Beijing is flat, for which the millions who ride bicycles must say daily thanks. Modern hotel towers dominate the skyline. The preparations for hosting the 2008 Olympics are driving a building boom.

Forbidden City, Beijing, China

The heart of Beijing is the Forbidden City, so named because it was off-limits to commoners for 500 years. Its palaces, pavilions, and gardens are now collectively called the Palace Museum. It was built in the latter part of the 13th century during the Ming dynasty as the palace of the emperors and then redesigned and expanded in the 15th century. Preserved as a museum since 1950, it holds nearly 1 million objects. Visitors can use a self-guiding tape that helps bring the complex alive with tales of eunuchs, concubines, priests, court intrigues, and royal excesses.

The Imperial City surrounds the Forbidden City. Its roofs, curved like the crests of waves, were not allowed to rise above the height of the palace. The Gate of Heavenly Peace at the southern edge of the Imperial City overlooks Tiananmen Square, called the biggest plaza on earth. Bordering the square are the Great Hall of the People (Parliament Building), the Museum of the Revolution, the Historical Museum, and the Chairman Mao Zedong Memorial Hall, which contains the embalmed body of the man who led the People's Republic for its first twenty-seven years.

Chinese rulers, like the Egyptian pharaohs, were buried with treasures, images of favorite servants and animals, and, in the early years of the Ming dynasty (1368–1644), members of the household who were forced to commit suicide.

China's largest zoo is in northwest Beijing. Known for its pandas, it also houses Manchurian tigers, Tibetan yaks, and snow leopards. Also in the northwest is the rambling Summer Palace. Beached eternally at the edge of a lake is the Marble Boat, which was built by the Dowager Empress Ci Xi in 1888 with money that had been intended for the building of a navy. Originally a concubine of the third rank, Ci Xi placed herself on the Dragon Throne after the death of the emperor and ruled in an unscrupulous way for fifty years in the name of her child, Pu Yin, the last emperor.

Excursions north of Beijing go to both the **Ming Tombs**, the last resting place of the dynasty that ruled from AD 1368 to 1644, and the **Great Wall**,

China's oldest and most spectacular monument. The Great Wall was begun in the 3rd century BC when rulers erected barriers against each other as well as against the northern tribes. Sections of the wall wind across the mountains of north China for an estimated 3,930 miles (6,288 km). The most continuous section extends from the northeast coast to the Gobi Desert. Originally troops were stationed in 25,000 watchtowers. What travelers see today was built in the 15th and 16th centuries. Parts are very steep, and stairs have been installed in areas open to the public. Helicopter tours are available.

The wall's popularity has taken a toll, bringing graffiti, car fumes, and trash. Now the wall is on the World Monuments Fund's list of the world's 100 most endangered sites. In 2002 the Beijing principality made laws to protect the wall.

A popular spot for viewing the Great Wall is about 47 miles (75 km) north of Beijing, at **Badaling**. It turns into a tourist carnival from 10:00 AM to 3:00 PM. The avalanche of visitors streams past countless stalls selling souvenirs before taking the steep climb up the wall for a breathtaking view.

Shanghai Far to the south of Beijing on the sea—approximately two hours by air or twenty hours by train—is China's largest city, Shanghai (*SHANG hi*). Once notorious as a port where men were "shanghaied" to be sailors, it had deteriorated badly. But this great trading city, once known as the *Paris of the East*, is busily reinventing itself. The Jin Mao Tower—a silvery pagoda whose name signifies "great wealth"—rises over the financial district of Pudong. Skyscrapers are sprouting everywhere. The world's tallest building is due to be completed in 2007. Freeways speed travelers through tunnels under the river and high above bustling streets. Banks and trading houses have been refurbished. More than 120,000 cultural relics—paintings, sculpture, calligraphy, furniture, ceramics, and jewelry—that trace 5,000 years of Chinese history are displayed in the Shanghai Museum. Elegantly dressed crowds flock to the French-designed opera house across the street from People's Square, where only four decades ago Red Guards denounced the "poisonous weeds" of Western culture.

The Bund is the promenade along the river. Tourists flock to Nanjing Road for its bargains or to the upscale boutiques along Huai Hai Road. The city's turnaround has resulted in the building of new luxury hotels that cater to international business.

Nanjing (Nanking) One of China's most beautiful cities, Nanjing is 155 miles (250 km) west of Shanghai. It became important under the Ming, whose emperors had their seat of government in the "southern capital," a literal translation of the name *Nanjing*.

Sights to see are the tomb of the first Ming emperor; the Sun Yatsen Mausoleum, built after the death of the founder of the Republic in 1925; and the Nanjing Museum. The museum's most important exhibit is a 2,000-year-old shroud made from 2,600 green jade squares sewn together with silver wire.

Guangzhou (Canton) Located in the far south near the Tropic of Cancer—three hours by air or thirty-seven hours by train from Beijing—Guangzhou (*gwahng joh*) is at the head of the Pearl River delta just north of Hong Kong. Guangzhou has long been a center of handicraft industries. The city's workers are famous for their ivory and jade carvings, lacquerware, and porcelain. But for decades its chief reason for being was as China's window on the West, the closest city to Hong Kong's radio and TV signals. Things to see in the city include museums, temples, and the Cantonese Opera.

➤ PROFILE

Chinese Art

Through the centuries, Chinese craftsmen developed the arts of

- Bronze making. Vessels made of bronze were used in religious rites starting about 2000 BC.
- Calligraphy, or fine handwriting. In China, literacy was a sacred or at least a scholarly preserve.
- Ceramics. Chinese artisans made both porcelain (unknown abroad for centuries) and celadon (with a translucent pale-green glaze).
- Jade carving. Objects ranged from the burial suits of the Han emperors to screens, wine jars, vases, and items of jewelry.
- Music, using the five-tone scale, with melody being the most important element.
- Sculpture. Monumental sculptures in stone and relief were inspired by Buddhism.
- Painting. Sophisticated designs were painted on pottery as early as 5000 BC and later on silk.
- Gardens, designed to create a feeling of peace.

Dim sum is a Cantonese smorgasbord of tidbits stuffed in flour wrappers or buns and steamed or fried as dumplings. It is a brunch or lunchtime favorite and a good way to sample specialties. Dishes are chosen from trays or trolleys brought to the table. The bill is totaled from the empty dishes.

The Northwest Provinces

Our overview of attractions outside the major cities begins in the northwest provinces but southwest of Beijing—about two hours by air or twenty-two hours by train. Here, the region at the bend of the Huang He (Yellow) River is regarded as the cradle of Chinese civilization. For eleven dynasties from the 11th century BC on, **Xi'an** was the country's capital.

Terracotta warriors, Xi'an, China

Terracotta Warriors After Beijing, Xi'an is China's most popular tourist attraction, the home of the Terracotta Warriors. In 1974 farm workers digging wells near Xi'an began unearthing large pottery fragments, and archaeologists hurried to the site. The tomb of the ancient emperor Qin Shi Huangdi (259–210 BC) was nearby, and they had high expectations. Their hopes were more than fulfilled. The site contained an army of life-size terracotta figurines of Chinese warriors, complete with horses and the remnants of wooden chariots and weapons. Some have been restored and are exhibited in a hall built above the excavation site. Each of the more than 6,000 soldiers has a different face.

The Silk Road Xi'an was the easternmost city of the fabled Silk Road, which first linked East and West in the 2nd century BC and was the route Marco Polo traveled in the 13th century. The highway was a path for the spread of Buddhism into East Asia and later for the growth of Islam. Monasteries, grottos, stupas, minarets, and other ruins dating back centuries can be seen along the way. The ancient road starts in Xi'an, reaches the oasis of **Lanzhou**, and stretches along the edge of deserts and mountains before dividing into winter and summer routes at the oasis of **Dunhuang**.

Mogao Caves Southeast of Dunhuang are the 492 grottos of the Mogao Caves. The caves, hewn from a desert cliff, are covered in murals telling the story of Buddhism. Begun in the 4th century, they were created over the next thousand years. The caves have brightly colored pictures and more than 2,000 painted sculptures, realistic and fantastic. Of the several hundred grottos still intact, only a few are open to the public. These are kept locked so that visits must be preplanned and supervised.

The Central Provinces

Southwest of Xi'an, almost in the center of the country, is Sichuan Province, China's most populous province. It lies at the foot of the Tibetan plateau and is mostly a plain surrounded by high mountains to the north, east, and west. Around the edges of terraced fields are the mulberry trees that supply food for the silkworm industry. The mountain forests are home to the giant panda, which has been pushed into ever-higher mountain regions.

Chengdu The capital of Sichuan Province is Chengdu. It is the base for visiting the religious sites of Emei Shan and Leshan. **Emei Shan**, 99 miles (160 km) southwest of town, is one of the four sacred mountains to which Buddhist pilgrims and trekkers flock each year. **Leshan** displays the giant Stone Buddha, the tallest statue in China. Monks in the 8th century spent ninety years carving the seated figure out of a cliff.

Three Gorges Southeast of Chengdu, **Chongqing** is the largest city in

CLOSE-UP: CHINA

Who is a good prospect for a trip to China? Getting to China means crossing more than mere oceans and time zones. It is another world, culturally, linguistically, and ideologically. China is a destination for the curious traveler, one with the time for a fascinating excursion to the world's oldest civilization and the stamina for a busy itinerary. Chinese Americans will enjoy a visit to the land of their ancestors.

Why would they visit China? Realists go to China for business or education; romantics, to fulfill a dream or satisfy wanderlust. They may visit to experience the very diversity of the country: in the morning, the sweeping roofs of a historic temple; in the afternoon, classic mountain scenery; in the evening, an acrobatic performance or folk music. Or perhaps they want to sample classic recipes prepared with genuine ingredients in the time-honored manner. China offers something for every taste.

Where would they go? China's immense size calls for the longest tour possible; much time is spent waiting around at airports for travel between cities. Jet lag will probably cloud the visitor's first few days. The country is rarely combined with any other destination because there is so much to see in China alone. A fourteen-night escorted tour to the Realm of the Dragon might follow this itinerary.

Day 1 Overnight flight to Beijing.

Day 2 You are met at the airport and transferred to your hotel. In the evening, meet your fellow travelers at dinner.

Day 3 Beijing. See the Forbidden City, Tiananmen Square, and the Mao Zedong Mausoleum. In the evening, enjoy a traditional Peking duck dinner at a local restaurant.

Day 4 Beijing. A day of sightseeing to the Great Wall and the Ming Tombs.

Day 5 Beijing. A full day with a visit to the Summer Palace. In the evening, enjoy a performance of the Beijing Opera.

Day 6 Beijing–Xi'an. Fly to the ancient Tang dynasty capital, and enjoy an afternoon visit to the city's symbol, the Big Wild Goose Pagoda.

Day 7 Xi'an. Visit the legendary Terracotta Warriors of the emperor Qin Shi Huangdi.

Day 8 Xi'an–Nanjing. Enjoy a free morning before your afternoon flight to Nanjing.

Day 9 Nanjing. The morning tour visits the mausoleum of Sun Yatsen, founder of modern China.

Day 10 Nanjing. Visit the Temples of Confucius; then see the caves carved in the mountains that are shrines to Buddha.

Day 11 Nanjing–Shanghai. Depart early this morning for a scenic rail journey through rural China to Shanghai. A sightseeing drive introduces the great port city.

Day 12 Shanghai. A trip to the Temple of the Jade Buddha, followed by a visit to the Yuyuan Garden and a drive along the Bund, Shanghai's waterfront promenade.

Day 13 Depart for home.

When is the best time to visit? Spring or fall is the peak time for travel. At that time reservations are a must for all popular destinations.

The traveler says, "I have stomach problems and have to be careful what I eat. What will I do?" How would you respond? City hotels have coffee shops featuring Western food when too much Chinese food takes its toll. But remember, rice, a staple of Chinese cuisine, is part of anyone's bland diet.

Sichuan. It is a port on the Ch'ang and a popular starting point for river cruises. Only the Nile and the Amazon are longer than the Yangtze.

The river flows through nine provinces, but the section between Chongqing and **Wuhan** holds the most interest for tourists. It takes about three days to cruise from Chongqing to Wuhan and as many as five days in the reverse direction against the tide. The most scenic area is between Baidi and Nanjin Pass.

Unfortunately, it is not the beauty of the Three Gorges that is bringing record numbers of people to the river. In 1994 the government began building the world's largest dam downstream of the gorges. When the dam is completed in 2009, the Yangtze will be changed from a river to a long lake. The homes of more than 1 million people will be inundated, and many historic sites will be submerged.

The Southern Provinces

Southern China

Breakneck development is evident in China's south at **Guangzhou** (Canton), a subtropical city on the south coast. Slower-paced pleasures can be savored to the west, around the city of **Guilin** (*gway LIN*) and in the Stone Forest.

Guilin Region The beautiful region around the city of Guilin is located to the northwest of Guangzhou. For more than 2,000 years the area has been a magnet for poets and painters, monks and missionaries. It offers the classic scenery of Chinese scroll paintings—where "the river forms a green silk belt, the mountains are like blue jade hairpins," as the Tang dynasty poet Han Yu described it. Strange toothlike mountains rise like towers from the plain. These karst formations dominate the town and surrounding countryside. Among them winds the Li River.

The four-hour boat trip from Guilin on the Li is an exceptional experience. Boats leave in the early morning and travel downriver. Along the way you pass Bat Hill, Dragons Playing Water, Five Tigers Catch a Goat, and Painting Brush Peak—names growing more fanciful with each turn of the river. **Yangshuo** is the southern end of the cruise. From Yangshuo, there is a bus back to Guilin (about two hours).

Stone Forest Near the borders of Vietnam, Laos, and Myanmar southwest of Guilin, bizarrely shaped rock needles form the "trees" of the **Stone Forest** (Shilin). This karst formation goes back about 200 million years. The forest is southeast of **Kunming**, the capital of Yunnan Province. Kunming is known as the *City of Eternal Spring* because of its pleasant alpine climate.

Tibet (Xizang)

Tibet has been part of China since the 1950s, but for centuries it was an independent country isolated from the world by mountains. Around AD 650, monks from India introduced Buddhism into Tibet. It was combined with local beliefs to form Lamaism. Between 900 and 1400, several sects developed; the most powerful was called the Yellow Hat because its monks wore yellow robes. The leader became known as the Dalai Lama. From the mid-1600s to 1950, the Dalai Lama was the supreme political and spiritual ruler of Tibet. When the Chinese invaded in 1950, they removed the lamas from power, and the Dalai Lama went into exile.

Potala Palace, Lhasa, Tibet

Tibet opened to tourists in 1980. Although it is possible to visit Tibet as an independent traveler (provided a permit is obtained), it is much easier to go as part of a tour. The scenery is spectacular and the culture unique. The capital is **Lhasa** (*LAH suh*), the world's second-highest capital, after La Paz, Bolivia. At an altitude of 12,000 feet (3,658 m), travelers may experience health problems.

Lhasa has been not only the capital but also the holy city of Tibet with few interruptions since the 7th century. Traditionally, pilgrims who enter Lhasa perform three circuits of the town in a clockwise direction. The greater the number of circuits, the greater is the religious merit acquired.

Lhasa's Potala Palace occupies a dramatic position high on a hill overlooking the city. It was the home of the Dalai Lama and is one of the world's largest buildings. Made of wood, earth, and stone, the thirteen-story structure has approximately 1,000 rooms. No nails were used in its construction. A climb of many steps to the building is rewarded by sights of dungeons, torture chambers, bejeweled Buddhas, treasure hoards, 10,000 chapels (some with decorations of human bones), and Buddhist frescos.

Hong Kong

In China's southeast corner, Hong Kong (Xianggang) combines British colonial influence, traditional Chinese style, and hi-tech high-rises. Rickshaws are long gone, but Hong Kong is still a place where visitors can buy custom-tailored suits, shop till they drop at quaint outdoor markets or glitzy indoor malls, or gaze at tall buildings with laundry hung out to dry because the Chinese think the practice brings good luck. English is widely spoken, and Western ways are understood.

Hong Kong begins as a peninsula extending from the Chinese mainland with two sections: the New Territories in the north and Kowloon Peninsula in the south. Across Victoria Harbor south of Kowloon is Hong Kong Island. An additional 235 small islands float in the bay. The Star Ferries (which sail every five minutes), three tunnels, and an underwater subway connect the two sides of the city. The seven-minute voyage aboard the ferry offers million-dollar views of the harbor.

The British acquired Hong Kong Island after they defeated the Chinese in the First Opium War (1841), and they gained Kowloon Peninsula after the Second Opium War (1860). In 1898 the New Territories were added on a ninety-nine-year lease. In 1997 the lease was up, and the British handed the area back to China.

Kowloon Side On the Kowloon side, hotels are located on Nathan Road, Hong Kong's *Golden Mile*. An evening stroll up the road takes you to the Temple Street night market. The narrow side streets are choked with hawkers selling everything from hot food (want squid on a stick?) to bizarre Asian medicines. The New World shopping center and deluxe hotels are on the waterfront. Farther west, the Ocean Terminal, Ocean Center, and Ocean Galleries form Harbor City, Asia's largest shopping center. Nearby are the ferry terminals to Macao. Passenger ships dock at Ocean Terminal, one of Asia's largest piers.

Hong Kong Side Hong Kong is a world financial center, and Victoria Peak is its most prestigious residential address. Towering luxury apartment buildings and attractive houses line the steep sides of the mountain. A tram ride to the Peak provides a fine view.

On the south side of the island, people still live on *sampans* (flat-bottomed boats) on Aberdeen Bay. The bay boasts the world's largest floating restaurants. When it comes time to escape the city, visitors might want to see Lantau Island, the biggest island in the territory. It is still largely undeveloped, though one part is home to the new airport and a Disney park is planned for another bay. Situated high in the mountains in Precious Lotus Monastery, its Big Buddha statue is visible for miles.

ON THE SPOT

Mr. Lee has a two-week business trip scheduled to Hong Kong. He will have a two-day weekend free in the middle of the trip and wants to do some sightseeing. He would like to fly up to Beijing on his weekend. He knows how busy Chinese airlines can be and wants to make the arrangements before he leaves for Hong Kong. What do you think?

Would this hurried trip serve Mr. Lee's best interests? Research would tell you that the flight between Hong Kong and Beijing takes approximately three and a half hours. Mr. Lee will also need time to get to the airport, check in, and travel from the airport to a hotel in Beijing (at least 40 minutes by taxi). Most of Mr. Lee's weekend would be wasted in travel. You might suggest instead that he take a weekend excursion to nearby Guangzhou, which he can reach by train from Hong Kong. He might save Beijing for his trip's end when he has more time.

Macao

Macao (*muh KOW*) is a former Portuguese territory about 40 miles (64 km) from Hong Kong. It was returned to China in December 1999.

Nearly 40 percent of Macao's income comes from gambling at booming state-sanctioned casinos and horse and dog tracks. The casino, shaped like a stack of chips, is one of the first sights to greet visitors coming by sea.

✔ CHECK-UP

China's key tourist areas include
- ✔ Beijing, the capital.
- ✔ Shanghai, the country's largest city and an important port.
- ✔ Central provinces, featuring Xi'an, Chongqing, and Chengdu.
- ✔ Southern provinces, with Guangzhou, Guilin, and Kunming.
- ✔ Tibet and its capital, Lhasa.

Tourist attractions include
- ✔ Beijing's Forbidden City.
- ✔ Ming Tombs and the Great Wall near Beijing.
- ✔ Army of Terracotta Warriors at Xi'an.
- ✔ Dunhuang on the Silk Road and the grottos of the Mogao Caves.
- ✔ Cruising through the Yangtze's Three Gorges.
- ✔ Stone Forest near Kunming.
- ✔ Tibet's Potola Palace, one of the world's largest buildings.
- ✔ Hong Kong, the bridge between East and West.

Japan

As the legend goes, the tears of a goddess formed the Japanese islands. Where each tear fell into the waters of the Pacific, an island arose (see Figure 14.7).

Mainly mountainous, with intensively cultivated coastal plains, the archipelago of Japan lies off the Asian coast close to Korea, Russia, and China. Four large islands, so closely grouped that bridges and a tunnel connect them, make up 98 percent of the territory. From north to south they are **Hokkaido** (*hah KY doh*), **Honshu** (*HAHN shoo*), **Shikoku** (*shi KOH koo*), and **Kyushu** (*kee OO shoo*). They occupy a highly unstable zone on the earth's crust, and earthquakes and volcanic eruptions are frequent. **Mount Fuji** (12,388 feet [3,776 m]), Japan's highest mountain, is a dormant volcanic cone.

Japanese traditions include a deep respect for beauty: Shinto teaches love of nature's beauty; Zen Buddhism is famous for its emphasis on beauty in even simple things. Long ago, Japanese monks made art forms of everyday functions, including bathing, *ikebana* ("flower arranging"), gardening, and the tea ceremony. The Japanese flair for style is also evident in its cuisine. How food looks is as important as how it tastes, even in the humblest ramen shops, where a bowl of noodles might be artfully adorned. Although the presentation is elegant, consumption is not: ramen, soba, and udon noodles are to be eaten with lots of loud slurping to show appreciation.

The Cities

Rising from the ruins of World War II, the homogeneous society of Japan created dynamic business organizations and produced the astonishing growth of Japanese cities. The key cities of **Tokyo**, **Kyoto**, and **Osaka** are all on the island of Honshu, where the Japanese Alps provide spectacular scenery.

Tokyo The business center of Japan, Tokyo is also the home of the emperor and the government. One of the world's largest cities, Tokyo can easily overwhelm the jet-lagged first-time visitor. Buildings got their numbers based on the order in which they were built, not on any geographic system.

The city plan was designed in feudal times when Tokyo was a small fishing village called Edo. The streets were arranged in an interlocking maze around Edo castle to keep invaders from finding their way to the center. Edo became the headquarters of the Tokugawa clan of *shoguns* ("warlords") of Japan. It was renamed Tokyo (meaning "eastern capital") when Emperor Meiji (1852–1912) took power from the shoguns and became the ruler in 1869.

Edo's castle became the Imperial Palace. The palace stands amid parklike grounds near the city's center. Stone walls and a series of moats separate it from the city's hubbub. The grounds are open to the public, although the buildings are not.

Tokyo twice has risen from the ruins. In 1923 it was devastated by an earthquake, and in 1945 it was severely damaged in the firestorms caused by Allied bombings. Tokyo has satellite cities and is divided into distinct districts. Of interest to the traveler are

- Ginza, an expensive shopping and business district. Mitsukoshi is one of Tokyo's premier department stores.
- Shinjuku, with Tokyo's tallest skyscrapers, a hub for electronic entertainments (video games and pachinko halls) as well as nightclubs and theaters. Each day more than 2 million passengers pass through Shinjuku's subway station.

Japanese restaurants have plastic or wax food models of the various dishes in their windows. If necessary, bring the waiter to the window and point to what you want.

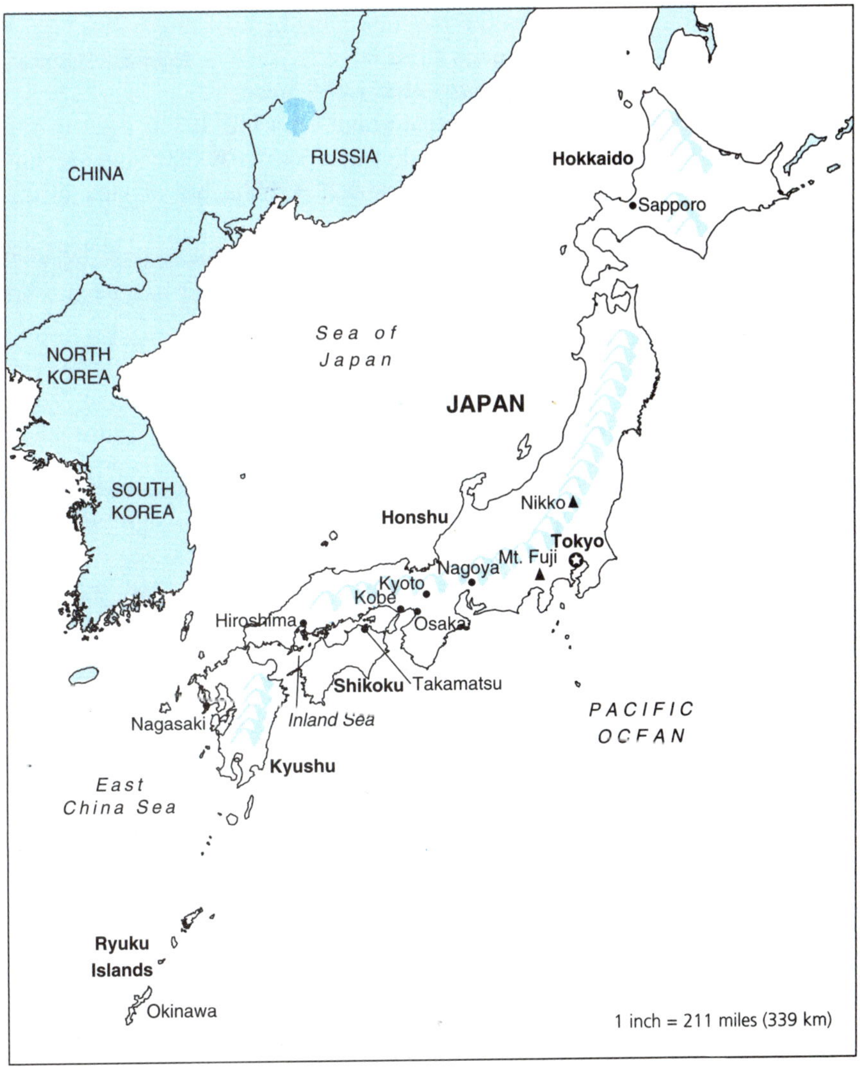

FIGURE 14.7

Japan

- Ueno, in the city's north. It is home to one of Tokyo's biggest parks (a favorite place for cherry-blossom viewing) and the Tokyo National Museum, where art lovers can view everything from woodblock prints, calligraphy, and samurai swords to modern art.
- Nightlife. Visitors can see sumo wrestling, enjoy Kabuki theater (Japanese opera), or find a karaoke place. Singing along with an electronic orchestra is an integral part of the city's social life.

Temple in Kyoto, Japan

Kyoto For more than a thousand years, Kyoto (*kee OH toh*) was Japan's capital and the center of art, culture, religion, and thought. The city is in central Honshu, 318 miles (513 km) southwest of Tokyo, about three hours by fast train. The only major city to escape damage in World War II, Kyoto retains the atmosphere of feudal Japan and abounds with temples, shrines, and museums.

The Kinkakuji Temple (Golden Pavilion) is a standout. The temple's walls are covered in gold leaf. It was burned to the ground by a deranged priest in 1950 and rebuilt exactly as before.

The Zen Buddhist Ryoanji Temple is another of Kyoto's revered sites. On the outskirts of the city, it contains one of the world's oldest stone gardens. Designed in 1499 as an aid to meditation, the garden consists of fifteen large stones set in a sea of gray-white gravel carefully raked into place daily.

Netsuke are the miniature carvings created by Japanese artists to serve as a counterbalance for the *inro*, which are boxes that were used to hold personal belongings in the *obi* (sash) when men wore the kimono. Netsuke are collected as artwork by connoisseurs.

Osaka Three hours by express train or one hour by air from Tokyo, Osaka (*oh SAH kuh*) on Honshu is Japan's third-largest city. It is sometimes called the *Venice of Japan* because of its many canals and rivers.

Osaka Castle overlooks the city from high on a hill. It was built in the 16th century by a powerful shogun and destroyed twice. In 1931 it was rebuilt mostly out of concrete. The castle has historical exhibits, but its view of the city is the main attraction.

Bunraku puppetry was born in Osaka. The National Bunraku Theater's puppets are one-third life-size, manipulated by skilled handlers, and accompanied by chanted narrative and musical instruments.

Other Places to Visit

Although leisure travel to Japan is sparse, corporate travel is extensive. The corporate traveler is often in the country on long-term assignment and wants to know what to do on weekends or short vacations. Most confine their excursions to Honshu, but the other islands offer equally entertaining experiences.

Fujikyu Highlands and Mount Fuji, Japan

Mount Fuji A few hours to the southwest of Tokyo, Mount Fuji is the focus of an area that might be called Tokyo's playground, part of the Fuji-Hakone-Izu National Park. It is a mountainous region with volcanoes and many hot springs.

Mount Fuji is Japan's highest and holiest mountain. A dormant volcano that last erupted in 1707, it is revered by Shintoists and Buddhists. The mountain has many temples and shrines, some even at the bottom of its crater.

For most of the year, the mountain is covered with snow or shrouded in fog. Although expeditions challenge the mountain throughout the year, the official climbing season is July and August, when the snow melts and thousands of pilgrims climb to the top. Mountain huts and services along the trails are open only during these two months.

Nikko Day excursions from Tokyo reach Nikko to the north. The name *Nikko* means "sunlight," a fittingly beautiful name for one of Japan's greatest shrines. In 1617 Shogun Ieyasu was buried at the mountain village of Nikko, and his tomb, the Toshogu Shrine, became a center of pilgrimage. Most of the sites were originally Buddhist, but in later centuries Nikko became predominantly Shinto.

The mausoleum's main building is covered in vermilion lacquer and decorated with more than 2 million sheets of gold leaf. It is the setting for an annual May pageant in which men parade in the costumes of samurai warriors.

Hokkaido The northernmost island, Hokkaido, is the most rural and traditional. **Sapporo** is its cultural, political, and economic center. The island has forested mountains and is popular as a recreation area. Long winters and heavy snowfall make Hokkaido ideal for winter sports and festivals.

Shikoku The smallest of Japan's four main islands, Shikoku is very scenic, part of the Inland Sea National Park. The island has many holy temples and is a favorite destination for Japanese pilgrims. The city of **Takamatsu** is the gateway.

Kyushu Japan's southernmost island, Kyushu is mountainous, with volcanoes, subtropical scenery, hot springs, and numerous historical sites. It is also a center for Japan's electronics industry, earning itself the nickname of *Silicon Island.*

On the west coast, **Nagasaki** (*nah guh SAH kee*) is the city with which Westerners have had the longest contact. In 1857 it was one of the first Japanese ports to open to foreign trade. Nagasaki's Peace Park is a reminder of the atomic bomb that destroyed 40 percent of the city in 1945.

ON THE SPOT

Mr. and Mrs. Weiler are about to take a tour to Japan. They are very experienced travelers who can spend what they need to get what they want. When they travel in Europe, they always rent a car and like the freedom that private transportation allows. They want to rent a car in Japan. Should they?

If they cannot read Japanese, understanding road signs will be a problem. Furthermore, city traffic is congested. It takes hours just to cross from one side of Tokyo to the other. Parking is another headache. In some cities, Japanese citizens cannot buy a car until they can prove they have a place to park it. You might suggest renting a car with a driver. Japan is the ideal country for this option.

✔ CHECK-UP

Honshu, Japan's largest and most populous island, is the site of

- ✔ Tokyo, the capital and site of the Imperial Palace.
- ✔ Kyoto, an ancient capital.
- ✔ Osaka, famous for its castle.
- ✔ Mount Fuji and the Fuji-Hakone-Izu National Park.
- ✔ Nikko and its shrines.

The other major islands of Japan are

- ✔ Hokkaido, the most northerly island, with the city of Sapporo.
- ✔ Shikoku, with its gateway city Takamatsu.
- ✔ Kyushu, the most southerly island, with its port of Nagasaki.

Planning the Trip

The prospect of planning a trip to Asia can be daunting. The choices are many and varied, the languages a barrier, and the trip a long one, making both distance and price potential barriers. Trip planning must include research into documentation requirements as well as careful monitoring of political, safety, and health concerns. In addition, Asia is a crowded region: advance reservations for hotels and especially for planes and trains are a must.

Beyond concerns about distance, price, health, language, and personal security, potential travelers to the region may be concerned about the services

> **➤ PROFILE**
>
> ### Shopping in Asia
>
> Throughout the area, bargaining is common in markets and with street vendors, though not in all shops. Specialties of each country include
>
> - In India: saris, shawls, and silks. Spices and jewelry are widely sought.
> - In Thailand: silk, colored gems such as rubies and sapphires, celadon, and handicrafts.
> - In Singapore: Asian antiques, jewelry, silks, and items such as briefcases, wallets, and purses made of reptile skin and snakeskin.
> - In China: silk, jade, jewelry, cloisonné enamelware, carvings, bamboo items, screens, and lacquer furniture. Favorite souvenirs are items with a communist theme (watches with Mao on the face, workers' posters), found for sale in antique stores, at flea markets, from street vendors, and at the store at Mao's Mausoleum.
> - In Japan: pearls, *ukiyoe* (woodblock prints), netsuke, watches, dolls, silk goods, and two-toed socks.

they will find when they get there. The infrastructure for tourists varies from place to place. In particular, India has fine hotels, good ground services, sightseeing, shopping, and spas. Its hospitality to visitors is legendary. Thailand and Singapore have well-structured tourism industries (although travel off the beaten track in Thailand should raise security concerns). China lacks tourism facilities outside the cities, but in Japan facilities are ample.

Most tourists visit China as part of an organized tour with hotel reservations, transportation, and sightseeing prearranged by tour operators working with Chinese ground service companies. The official state travel agency, China International Travel Service (CITS), continues to be part of Chinese travel. It has offices in most tourist towns, usually in the large hotels. The provinces, however, have set up their own ground operations. Independent travel is possible, but the coordinating services of an experienced tour operator are invaluable. International tour operators offer trips that follow traditional routes as well as trips organized around themes such as calligraphy, acupuncture, or Chinese cuisine.

When to Go

In general, the best time to visit India and Southeast Asia is from November to February. May through October is the time of the most rain, heat, and humidity. In India, summer is hot and dry for most of the country but humid along the coasts. The World Meteorological Organization has declared Bangkok to be the world's hottest city.

The best times to visit China are in spring and fall, but this vast country has a wide range of weather. May, September, and October are peak travel times.

The best time to travel in Japan is also in spring and fall. For business travelers, there is no off-season. Within their islands, the Japanese travel extensively, especially during holiday seasons. The New Year is one such period; mid-August is another. Golden Week, April 29 through the first week of May, is Japan's third holiday period.

Preparing the Traveler

The visitor to Asia encounters all the hassles of the truly foreign. In China, potential difficulties for travelers go beyond the lack of tourist infrastructure and the country's vast size to include some strange travel differences; for example, Beijing time (GMT + 8) is standard throughout China. For experienced travelers, Asia can be just the challenge they are looking for; for others, the benefits of a group tour should be strongly emphasized.

> A supply of business cards printed in English and Japanese is essential for corporate travelers. When meeting someone, a businessperson should present the card with both hands. Appointments should be made. Punctuality is important.

Health Health insurance is strongly recommended because of the high cost of treatment and the lack of reciprocal insurance agreements. Depending on the destination, either carelessness or hypochondria can guarantee a miserable time.

In India, all water should be regarded as being potentially contaminated. If travelers stick to bottled drinks (making sure the bottles are properly sealed) and well-cooked food, serious problems are rare. A touch of Delhi belly is unavoidable when a person is not used to spicy food.

Cholera is a risk in Thailand, and precautions are essential. Up-to-date advice should be sought before travel.

Levels of hygiene are high in Singapore and Japan. It is unlikely that travelers will become ill as a result of what they eat or drink in those countries.

Travel to China requires cautionary health procedures: drink bottled beverages; eat cooked foods; peel all fruits; and avoid salads, ice, and raw or undercooked seafood. Colds and respiratory problems are common. SARS scares require extra precautions. Swimming in lakes, streams, and rivers is not advised. The bilharzia parasite is present, and malaria exists throughout the country.

Money Each country has a national currency, and facilities for money exchange vary. Banks are the best places to convert traveler's checks and cash to the local currency.

ATMs and credit cards are widely used in India, Thailand, Singapore, and Japan. In China, major hotels, restaurants, and state-run Friendship Stores accept credit cards and traveler's checks, but visitors should be prepared to pay cash in small shops and restaurants. Chinese money is not traded outside the country. China's one national bank, the People's Bank, has branches in hotels and Friendship Stores.

Language The region's many languages present a barrier. In India, English is widely spoken in tourist areas but cannot be counted on outside the cities.

In several Asian languages, tonal differences determine meaning, and the countries use a different alphabet. Travelers should carry with them the name and address of their hotel in writing. They might carry a postcard, piece of stationery, or book of matches, or they might ask the tour escort or someone at the hotel to write out the information. When language barriers are hard to overcome, translation services are useful, especially to the business traveler.

Customs Travelers in Asia soon realize that people do things differently, very differently. In China, for example, spitting on a sidewalk or blowing your nose without a handkerchief is not considered rude, but blowing your nose into a handkerchief and returning it to your pocket is considered vulgar. Throughout Asia, tipping is increasingly common and expected. Bargain in markets, but not in stores where prices are marked.

In Muslim areas, travel can be difficult during Ramadan, the Islamic holy month when the faithful may not eat or drink from morning until night. Food service outside the major hotels may be hard to find, and people tend to resent the foreigner who does not take part in observances.

India has little nightlife as the term is understood in the West. In almost all cities, the sale of liquor is not permitted on certain days of the week. Many Hindus are vegetarians, and many, especially women, do not drink alcohol. Visitors must show respect when entering places of worship and private homes. Shoes must be removed. Avoid taking leather goods into temples as this can cause offense in a country that worships the cow.

In Thailand, it is customary to remove one's shoes before entering a home. Hindus believe that the head is the fount of wisdom and the feet are unclean. For this reason, it is insulting to touch another person on the head, point one's feet at someone, or step over someone. Disrespect toward Buddha images, temples, or monks is not taken lightly.

In Singapore, jaywalking, littering, smoking in public places, and forgetting to flush a public toilet are punished with stiff fines. Islanders are admonished not to waste water when cleaning their teeth. Cars carrying fewer than four people cannot enter the center during peak traffic hours without a special pass. Drug trafficking is punishable by death.

Along the rural roads of China, people sell puppies—not intended as pets. Dog meat is supposed to be good for what ails you. In Chinese cities other than Beijing and Shanghai, stores close early, and people eat dinner

➤ PROFILE

Cuisine of Asia

The staple food of Asia is rice, accompanied by garnishes, spices, and sauces. Singapore has more than thirty cooking styles. Chinese meals seek harmony with contrasts. A crisp dish is followed by a softer one. A spicy course is served with a sweet garnish. Preparation is divided into four regional styles, including

- Cantonese (southeast China): use of rice and cooking methods based on parboiling, steaming, and quick stir-frying.
- Beijing (northern China): noodles and bread, with deep-frying and spicy sauces.
- Shanghai (eastern or coastal China): food diced or shredded and stewed in soya or fried in sesame oil with lots of garlic.
- Szechuan (southwestern China): hot and spicy with lots of chilis.

Other specialties of the region include

- In India: cuisine based on rice, spices, and fruits. The British used curries and chutneys, but these foods are not representative of authentic Indian cooking.
- In Thailand: hot and spicy sauces, coconut milk soups, sticky rice and mangoes, and the durian, a fruit so smelly that most hotels will not allow it on the premises.
- In Japan: specialties such as *teriyaki* (marinated beef, chicken, or fish seared on a hot plate), *sukiyaki* (thin slices of beef, bean curd, and vegetables cooked in soy sauce and then dipped in egg), *tempura* (deep-fried seafood and vegetables), *sushi* (slices of raw seafood rolled in rice balls), and *sashimi* (slices of raw seafood dipped in soy sauce). Green tea and saki (hot rice wine) are the most popular beverages.

around 1800 or 1900. During the week, the Chinese eat their main meal at night; on weekends, the main meal is eaten at noon.

In Japan, pushing and shoving in crowds is tolerated, but a strict code of politeness is followed in other situations. A nod or a slight bow is the appropriate greeting. Do not attempt to bargain in a shop. Sunday is a major shopping day because many people work a six-day week; shops are often closed one day in midweek. Dinner is from 1800 to 2000. Service charges are added to bills at hotels and restaurants.

Remember, though: customs change. It is always best to check locally to keep informed.

A traditional Japanese breakfast includes soup with bean curd, dried seaweed, hot boiled fish, radish pickles, and green tea.

Transportation

Travel from North America to Asia is usually by air. Internal travel can be by air, rail, or even elephant, but rarely by rental car.

By Air International gateways are usually each country's capital or major city, although alternate gateways are frequently introduced.

India and Thailand have extensive internal air service. Singapore's modern Changi Airport is an Asian hub.

China's principal international gateways are Beijing, Hong Kong, Shanghai, and Guangzhou. The approximate flight time from Los Angeles to Beijing is twelve hours. Within China, most long-distance travel is by air. The Civil Aviation Administration of China (CAAC) operates more than eighty routes linking Beijing to other cities.

The approximate flight time from Los Angeles to Tokyo is eleven hours. Japan has extensive service from North America to its international gateway at Tokyo's Narita Airport, 40 miles (65 km) northeast of the city. Taking a taxi can cost hundreds of dollars. Shuttle buses link the airport with major hotels. Japan Railways' Narita Express runs from a terminal located beneath the airport to Tokyo (travel time: 53 minutes).

By Water Both world and local cruises visit the area's ports. River cruises bring travelers to areas difficult to reach by land.

India has few internal water routes. Ferry services to nearby islands are seasonal and generally suspended during monsoon season.

Thailand has, depending on the season, more than 1,000 miles (1,610 km) of navigable inland waterways. Luxury cruises are available. Reduced services operate during the monsoon season from May through October.

Ocean cruising is one of the fastest-growing tourist attractions in Singapore, and there are plans to considerably expand the already extensive port facilities. Asian travelers are a booming market for the cruise product.

China's principal seaports are Shanghai, Guangzhou, and Hong Kong. Cruises offer passengers land excursions by rail or air; passengers leave the ship in one city and pick it up a few days later at another, spending the intervening time sightseeing inland—at extra cost, of course. The best time to cruise the Ch'ang is May and June or late August and September. July to early August is extremely hot and humid.

In Japan, Yokohama (the port of Tokyo) and Kobe (near Osaka and Kyoto) are busy ports. International shipping also calls at others, including Nagasaki and Nagoya. Cruises operate among the Japanese islands.

By Rail The colonial powers left a legacy of railroads, especially in India. The state-run Indian railway system is the largest in Asia and the second largest in the world. Express service links the main cities, and local service connects other parts of the country. Indian Railways offers discounts and special passes to foreign nationals. When conditions are suitable, tour companies operate luxury trains on selected itineraries.

The state railways of Thailand link most towns. The journeys are slow but comfortable, and travel by train is one of the best ways to get around the country.

Rail is the major means of public transportation in China. Trains have four types of fares: hard seat, soft seat (only on short-distance trains), hard sleeper, and soft sleeper. Those traveling first-class have access to a separate waiting room in railway stations. The world's first high-speed maglev (magnetic levitation train) runs from Shanghai's Pudong International Airport to an outlying subway station.

Outside Nagoya, Japan, a slower maglev is starting up, designed for short-hop routes. The Japan Railways Group (JR) runs one of the best rail networks in the world and is widely used by both business and pleasure travelers. The transportation system is clean, safe, and efficient—though crowded. Express trains such as the *Shinkansen* (the "Bullet Train"), which travels up to 136 miles (219 km) per hour, offer alternatives to air travel. Rail passes for foreign tourists must be purchased before arrival in Japan through authorized travel agencies.

Tokyo's subway system is most efficient. Signs are in English as well as Japanese. At some stations at rush hour, white-gloved employees called *pushers* shove passengers into cars to make room for more. Avoid rush hours if at all possible.

ON THE SPOT

Margaret Landon wants to tour India by herself. She has planned a three-week itinerary to major cities and sights. She would like to travel within India by train. What advice would you give her?

Indian trains carry more than 12 million passengers a day, with express services linking all the main cities. There are seven classes of travel. A woman traveling alone would do best taking first-class passage and having confirmed reservations for each trip. The Indrail Pass might be appropriate. Information about how to obtain the pass and make reservations is available from the Indian Tourism Office.

By Road Road travel is often the only way to reach places of outstanding interest. Driving is on the left in India, Singapore, and Thailand. Although traffic in China drives on the right, in Hong Kong it continues to drive on the left, British style. In Japan, driving is also on the left.

Unless a private car is absolutely necessary, visitors to this region should forget driving and hire a chauffeur or take public transportation. In the cities, traffic is many times worse than L.A. freeways at their most congested. Road signs are in the local language and alphabet. In China, roads are not always of the best quality, and distances should not be underestimated.

Accommodations

Asia is home to some of the world's finest hotels. Resorts are among the most beautiful in terms of their natural setting and distinctive architecture. Service levels are excellent.

India features palaces that have been converted into hotels. The Taj Lake Palace Hotel in Udaipur in northern India is a white marble structure that was built in 1746 on an island in a lake by Maharajah Jagat Singh II. It has no grounds. The palace walls extend to the edge of the island. Guests, when not concentrating on their palatial lifestyle, are likely to feel they are on a cruise ship. Visits to the hotel (refurbished in 2004) begin with a boat ride from Udaipur across the lake. On arrival, guests are greeted by men holding fly whisks and dressed in the attire of the maharajah's court.

Lake Palace, Udaipur, India

Thailand also has some of Asia's finest hotels. Many belong to the large international chains. The country has no official grading system; price is usually the best indication of standards.

Singapore's deluxe hotels are world renowned. In 1887 Raffles Hotel opened as a haven for adventurous travelers. In the words of Somerset Maugham, "Raffles stands for all the fables of the exotic East."

Major chains operate in China, with rooms and service that meet international standards. Many include convenient facilities such as shopping malls, banks, and post offices. Hong Kong has some of the world's most deluxe properties. Chinese hotels often provide hot water ready for the guest's cup of tea.

Japanese hotels are "Western" or "Japanese" style. Western-style hotels range from deluxe to modest. Japanese-style accommodations provide new experiences for the adventurous. *Minshuku* in resort areas are the Japanese equivalent of B&Bs. Rates are modest, but guests should expect few amenities.

One deluxe Japanese-style hotel that is fast disappearing in its original form is the *ryokan* (*rio khan*)—a small inn—decorated and operated in a manner set hundreds of years ago. Usually ryokans have from six to fifty rooms and are surrounded by a garden or natural scenery. Public floors are made of polished wood. Room floors are covered by *tatami*, thick mats made of reeds bordered with fabric. Guests take off their shoes in the entry foyer and put on soft slippers, but they leave the slippers outside their rooms. In their rooms, guests wear *yukatas* (robes) and sleep on *futons* (sleeping mats) on the floor at night.

Inner doors are made of sliding paper panels that cannot be locked. Each room has a maid to serve the honored guest. Maids come and go without knocking and serve dinner and drinks in the room. Lunch is never served.

Bathing is done in small private baths that accommodate a couple or in larger baths that fit several dozen people, nowadays separated by sex. Guests undress in their rooms, don their yukatas, put on their slippers, and proceed to the bathing areas.

The ryokan is not a budget property, and the modern world is changing traditions. Nowadays, ryokans have mini-refrigerators for snacks and drinks, and the larger ryokans are building conference rooms.

✔ CHECK-UP

Travelers to Asia should
- ✔ Prepare themselves for cultural differences.
- ✔ Pay particular attention to the political situation and other safety concerns.
- ✔ Exercise caution in eating and drinking.
- ✔ Have confirmed reservations.
- ✔ Use an experienced tour operator.

For transportation
- ✔ Indian train service covers the subcontinent.
- ✔ Thailand's rail network links most towns.
- ✔ Chinese rail service is extensive although somewhat primitive.
- ✔ Japan is known for its Shinkansen—high-speed rail service.
- ✔ Tourists should avoid driving unless absolutely necessary.

Unique options in the region include
- ✔ Using accommodations at former royal palaces in India.
- ✔ River cruising in China.
- ✔ Staying in a ryokan in Japan.

OTHER DESTINATIONS IN ASIA

Asia offers unlimited possibilities to the traveler in search of adventure. In addition to the countries discussed so far, several destinations have significant attractions for travelers, although some are currently off the path of U.S. tourists. This section briefly discusses these destinations, dividing them into South, Southeast, and East Asia.

SOUTH ASIA

Bangladesh Known for tropical cyclones and poverty, the small and densely populated country of Bangladesh lies north of the Bay of Bengal. It separated from Pakistan in 1971. **Dhaka** is the capital. Bangladesh is low and flat. During monsoons, water sometimes submerges as much as two-thirds of the country. Tourism to the country is rare.

Maldives The Maldives is Asia's smallest independent country. It consists of coral atolls north of the equator in the Indian Ocean. (Look again at Figure 14.1.) It is in danger of disappearing altogether if the sea rises. Graceful coconut palms lean over crystal-clear lagoons, coral reefs promise great snorkeling and scuba diving, and there is plenty of sunshine. The islands are popular beach resorts.

The people of the Maldives are Muslim. Outside the resorts, rules regarding dress and alcohol consumption are strictly enforced. Visitors are housed in self-contained resorts, distanced from the native population. Most tourists come on charter flights from Europe to the airport near **Malé**, the capital. Hotel boats meet guests and take them to their accommodations.

Sri Lanka An island in the Indian Ocean off the southeast tip of India, Sri Lanka is about the size of West Virginia. The beautiful green land is rolling, with mountains in the south central region. Tea plantations dominate the highlands, and coconut trees grow in plantations along the sandy coastal lowlands. Sri Jayewardenepura Kolte (**Colombo**) is the capital and largest city. Called *Ceylon* until 1972, Sri Lanka is in a state of civil war between two ethnic groups: the Tamil minority, primarily Hindus, who claim the north, and the Sinhalese majority, primarily Buddhist, who control the south.

Nepal Nepal is a landlocked kingdom the size of Illinois and lies between India and Tibet, China. It is one of the world's most remote and beautiful places. The land is impressively diverse—with lush plains in the lowlands, hills clothed in green forests, the Valley of Kathmandu, layer upon layer of foothills, and finally, in the north, the *Roof of the World*, the Himalaya. Nepal's mountains include Mount Everest, the world's highest peak at 29,035 feet (8,850 m) and still growing.

One of the principal reasons for visiting Nepal is either to see or to climb its mountains. **Kathmandu** is the capital and the hub for treks. The trekking season is from September to May, but many think the best periods are from October to December and from March to April. For the athletically challenged, Nepal's domestic airlines offer flights in light aircraft over the peaks.

Two Nepalese groups are known for their special skills: the Sherpas have won fame as guides and porters for mountain-climbing expeditions; the Gurkhas, as brave soldiers.

Bhutan Mountainous Bhutan, the size of Massachusetts, is situated on the southeast slope of the Himalaya, bordered by Tibet and India. **Thimphu** is the capital and largest city.

The kingdom of Bhutan has adopted a very cautious approach to tourism in an effort to avoid negative effects on the country's culture and environment. All travel must be on a preplanned, prepaid, guided tour. Independent travel is not permitted.

SOUTHEAST ASIA

Myanmar Located on the Bay of Bengal between Bangladesh and Thailand, Myanmar is nearly the size of Texas and has a mountain-backed coastline. It is struggling to overcome years of ethnic strife and military rule. Myanmar is a place for the adventurous traveler who has seen just about everything and respects a country's culture.

Yangon (Rangoon) is the capital. Its tallest buildings are pagodas, and the city is surrounded on three sides by water. At the city's heart is the Sule Pagoda, a gold-crowned stupa believed to have been built in the 3rd century. Nearby are stores where visitors are encouraged to buy the precious rubies on which Myanmar's government has a monopoly.

Travelers cruise upstream on the Irrawaddy River to view the ruins of **Pagan**. Between 1057 and its conquest by Kublai Khan, some 13,000 temples, pagodas, and other religious structures were built on a vast plain along the river. Today, 2,217 structures remain.

Mandalay is on the Upper Irrawaddy, 350 miles (563 km) north of Yangon. This old royal city is the center of Buddhist learning, and about 70,000 orange-robed monks fill the city. Small temples dot the famous stairway on Mandalay Hill. On the climb, astrologers and souvenir peddlers ply their trades.

For the wind is in the palm trees,
and the temple bells they say
"Come ye back, you British soldier;
come ye back to Mandalay."

—Rudyard Kipling, "The Road to Mandalay" (1887)

Malaysia Malaysia consists of the eleven states on the southern part of the Malay Peninsula plus the two states (Sarawak and Sabah) known as East Malaysia on the island of Borneo, about 400 miles (640 km) across the South China Sea (see Figure 14.8). In area, the country is slightly larger than New Mexico.

Malaysia's capital and largest city is **Kuala Lumpur** (*KWAHL uh loom POOR*), on the west coast of Peninsular Malaysia. It is a huge city with high-rise buildings, shops, and many mosques. The skyscrapers include the Petronas Towers. On its completion in 1996, the Petronas was the world's tallest skyscraper, but it has since been surpassed by ones in Taipei and Shanghai.

Penang, the *Pearl of the Orient*, is the best known of Malaysia's many islands. It is off the northwest coast near the border with Thailand; the world's third-longest bridge links Penang to the mainland. **Georgetown**, the island's town, is one of the country's most important ports. Its unusual attraction is the Temple of the Azure Cloud, also known as the Snake Temple, where venomous snakes hang from the rafters and slither about the floor.

The durian is one of the unique fruits of Southeast Asia. It has a most delicious taste and a most obnoxious smell. Some believe it is an aphrodisiac.

Indonesia By far the world's biggest island chain, Indonesia is between Asia and Australia in the Indian and Pacific Oceans. Its many islands straddle the equator, curving through miles and miles of ocean—farther than the distance across the continental United States (see Figure 14.8). Most of the islands are mere specks with no official names or inhabitants. The main islands are mountainous.

The turbulence of the country's active volcanoes is matched by the turbulence of its political life. In the 16th century, the Netherlands seized control and named the islands the Dutch East Indies. Indonesia declared its independence in 1945 after being under Japanese rule during much of World War II, but peace has not come easily. Terrorist attacks in Bali in 2002 targeted Western tourists.

FIGURE 14.8

Malaysia and Indonesia

1 inch = 519 miles (835 km)

Indonesia's islands are heavily populated. Nearly 90 percent of the people follow the Islamic faith, making it the world's largest Muslim country.

The island of **Java** is home to about 60 percent of the republic's people. **Jakarta** (*juh KAHR tuh*), Indonesia's capital and one of the world's largest cities, is on the northwest coast of the island. Most of Java's sights, however, are not in Jakarta but in and around **Yogyakarta** (*yog yah KAHR tuh*). Near Yogyakarta are the Buddhist site of Borobudur (*bore uh buh DUR*) and the Hindu temple complex of Prambanan.

Borobudur is the world's largest Buddhist monument. As seen from the air, Borobudur looks like a huge stone birthday cake with six or seven layers, each with icing, topped by a giant stone bell. The layers are terraces and the bell is the central shrine, the *stupa*.

Prambanan is east of Yogyakarta. Its temples look like rockets. Ancient ruins litter the surrounding plain, which the Javanese call the "Valley of the Kings."

To the east of Java, **Bali** is Indonesia's most densely populated and developed island. Unlike the rest of Indonesia, the predominant religious faith is Hinduism, although in a special form known as Agama-Hindu. **Denpasar** (*DEN pah sar*) is the island's capital and airport gateway. Once viewed as the most idyllic of destinations, leisure travel to the island slowed to a trickle after a 2002 terrorist bombing there.

Sulawesi is in the center of the Indonesian archipelago. It is an island of high mountains, lakes, geysers, and hot springs. The island is the home of the highland Toraja. The Toraja bury their dead in vertical cliffside tombs sealed with decorative wooden doors. Wooden statues of the deceased stand in balconies on the cliff. The clothed figures, their white eyes painted perpetually open, gaze across the rice fields. Family members regularly replace the statues' clothing.

Irian Jaya (*IH ree ahn JYE uh*)—which is the western half of the huge island of New Guinea—is also part of Indonesia. It is probably the earth's most isolated and primitive region. In Irian Jaya, strangely adorned tourists on treks can meet strangely adorned aboriginal tribespeople. What thoughts each must have of the other! Entry is by plane or boat; roads are almost nonexistent.

The best batik comes from Java. Wearing batik can indicate status, bring good luck, or placate the spirits. The word *batik* refers to the process as well as the printed cloth.

Laos The only landlocked country in Southeast Asia is Laos. It is also the poorest state in the region. Once the home of the 14th-century Million Elephant Kingdom, it became a French protectorate in 1893 and gained independence in 1953. From 1964 onward, Laos was fought over by royalists, communists, and conservatives. Used as a military supply route by the North Vietnamese, it was heavily bombed with defoliants by the United States during the late 1960s. The country's primitive infrastructure is a major handicap to tourism.

Cambodia The kingdom of Cambodia is tucked in a steamy corner of Southeast Asia. It is bordered by Thailand, Laos, Vietnam, and the South China Sea. **Phnom Penh** (*nawm pen*) is the capital. Before 1953, the country was a French protectorate. In the mid to late 1970s, Pol Pot's Khmer Rouge dictatorship controlled the country. The Vietnamese overthrew Pol Pot in 1978.

Siem Reap is the gateway to Cambodia's principal attraction, the monumental Hindu temple complex known as **Angkor** (*ANG kohr*) **Wat** (see Figure 14.1). Angkor was the administrative center for the Khmer kingdom. Each king built a temple to glorify himself. Constructed in the early 12th century, Angkor Wat was intended as the tomb of its builder. After foreign invasions, Angkor was abandoned to the jungle in the 15th century—except for Angkor Wat. Preserved by Buddhist monks, it became a pilgrimage site. To Europeans, however, it remained a lost world. In the 1860s, the French "discovered" the site and began a reconstruction program. The temple complexes are considered among the supreme architectural achievements of their time.

Vietnam Vietnam opened to tourism in the 1990s. **Hanoi** (*ha NOY*), the capital and largest city, retains an air of faded French colonial elegance. The Ho Chi Minh Mausoleum draws Vietnamese pilgrims to pay their respects to the man who was the leader of their revolution and then president until his death in 1969. Elsewhere, the

Vietnamese food is justly famous, but tourists might find some specialties not exactly what they bargained for. Dog is a popular meat, and restaurants advertising *thit cho* are devoted to this dish—be warned.

wide boulevards of the French Quarter contrast with the narrow streets of the Old Quarter. Colorful pagodas and temples, including the Temple of Literature founded in 1070 and dedicated to Confucius, rise throughout the city.

Brunei Darussalam About the size of Delaware, Brunei is on the northwest coast of Borneo, wedged between the Malayan states of Sabah and Sarawak. Three-quarters of the country is covered with tropical rain forest. The country's oil and gas wealth provides its citizens with cradle-to-grave care. **Bandar Seri Begawan** is the capital. Brunei is one of the last absolute monarchies. Business travel is tolerated, but leisure tourism is not promoted.

Philippines The Philippines consist of more than 7,000 islands off the southeast coast of Asia, north of the equator. In total, the land area is comparable to Arizona. The archipelago has three main island groupings: the Luzon group, the Visayan group, and the Mindanao (*mihn dah NOW*) and Sulu Islands. The two largest islands, Luzon in the north and Mindanao in the south, account for 65 percent of the land. Common to the islands are narrow coastal belts, mountainous interiors, and active volcanoes. Mount Pinatubo on Luzon erupted in 1991 after being dormant for more than 600 years.

Manila is the capital, largest city, and busiest port. Accessible from Manila by hydrofoil, Corregidor Island is a memorial to those killed during the Japanese invasion in World War II. Recent political conflict has discouraged tourism.

EAST ASIA

Mongolia During the 1200s, the Mongols—led by Genghis Khan, "lord of all people living in felt tents," and his grandson Kublai Khan—were the most savage of conquerors. Their empire stretched from the Yellow Sea to Europe, but by the 1300s it was gone. China ruled the Mongols from the 1680s to 1911.

Today, Mongolia borders Siberia to the north and China to the south. It is the world's largest and most thinly populated landlocked country. The Gobi (meaning "desert") covers one-third of the land.

Mongolia's deserts, severe climate, and widely scattered population of nomadic people tend to shut it off from modern life. It is among the last places left for exploration. **Ulan Bator** ("Red Hero") is the capital and largest city. Although independent travel is becoming more common, travel outside the capital is usually only by prior arrangement. The most popular tours include trekking, mountaineering, bird-watching, horseback riding, rafting, camel riding, riding on yak caravans, and going on overland motorcycle tours.

South Korea South Korea occupies the southern half of the Korean Peninsula (look again at Figure 14.1). Mountains cover most of the land, but South Korea is a land of contrasts—from flat plains to high mountains, from hot, hot summers to very cold winters.

The *yogwan*, a Korean inn, is a true budget property. Bedding is a mattress, a quilt, and a hard pillow (filled with wheat husks). Most tourists prefer one of Korea's fine Western-style hotels.

Korea became a country in the 7th century; however, from the 14th century onward, China and Japan dominated its history. After World War II, the peninsula was divided along the 38th parallel. In 1950 North Korea invaded the south. A three-year war (1950–1953) involving the United States followed.

Most visitors start their tours in **Seoul**, the capital and largest city. Four of the city's original gates remain. The Great South Gate of Seoul, called *Namdaemun*, is regarded as Korea's foremost national treasure.

South Korea is cutting edge when it comes to technology, yet it is an ancient land where the monuments of imperial dynasties remain. On the southeast coast about 200 miles (322 km) from Seoul, Kyongju's (*quong ju*) temples, tombs, and fortresses have been lovingly restored. Kyongju can be reached from Seoul by road in four and a half hours and by rail in three and a half hours.

Pusan, South Korea's second-largest city and busiest port, is on the southeast coast across the Korean Strait from Japan. Stretching west from Pusan is the Hallyo Waterway, Korea's inland sea and a national park.

Taiwan Taiwan (*ty wahn*) is an island in the South China Sea about 90 miles (145 km) off the coast of China. The Chinese call the island *Taiwan*, meaning "terraced bay." The forested beauty of the land led Portuguese sailors to name it *Formosa*—"beautiful island."

In 1949 the Chinese communists defeated Chiang Kai-Shek's forces and took control of mainland China. Chiang escaped to Taiwan and took over the island. Taiwan today maintains that it is an independent country, but China disagrees, claiming that Taiwan is part of China. Prospective travelers should, of course, monitor the political situation.

Taipei (*ty PAY*), the capital and largest city, is at the north end of the island. It is one of the world's megacities. One skyscraper, Taiwan 101 (named for the number of stories), is among the world's tallest buildings. Overcrowding has produced double-decker sidewalks with shops on two levels.

The National Palace Museum in Taipei is rated as one of the world's top four museums. The collection was started in AD 960 and added to by a succession of Chinese emperors who hoarded the best of jade, paintings, porcelains, bronzes, and antiques. The treasures piled up in the Forbidden City. In the 1930s and 1940s, the heritage was moved around the country to protect it from the Japanese. In 1949 Chiang Kai-Shek brought the treasures to Taiwan, where they remained hidden until 1965.

Two-thirds of Taiwan is covered by the Chungyand Shanmo mountain range. In the mountains, the Taroko Gorge, with its hot springs and outdoor activities, is a big draw.

CHAPTER WRAP-UP

SUMMARY

Here is a review of the objectives with which we began the chapter.

1. **Describe the environment and people of Asia.** The Indian subcontinent has the Himalaya, the world's highest mountains, which provide a barrier in the north; a plain drained by three great rivers; the Deccan Plateau in the center; and sandy beaches rimming the southern coasts. The Hindu religion plays an important part in the culture, providing a fascinating legacy of art and architecture.

   Southeast Asia is a lush land with rain forests, green plains planted with rice, mountains, and beautiful sand beaches. Traditions of the Hindu, Muslim, and Buddhist religions dominate people's lives.

   East Asia is home to about one-fourth of the world's population, and China makes up most of the region. China's principal landforms include the high plateau of Tibet and the Taklimakan and Gobi Deserts in the northwest, north, and northeast. China's most important rivers are the Huang He (Yellow River) and the Ch'ang (the Yangtze).

   Japan's four principal islands are, from south to north, Kyushu, Shikoku, Honshu, and Hokkaido. The country is on the Ring of Fire, the wide loop of active volcanoes that circles the Pacific Ocean, and is subject to frequent earthquakes.

   Climate throughout South and Southeast Asia depends on the monsoon. In most areas, it provides three seasons: a cool, dry season from November to March; a hot, dry season during April and May; and a rainy, humid season from June to October. Huge China has many climate variations. Tibet and northern China have long, cold winters and hot summers; southeast China is pleasantly warm and dry in winter and hot and humid in summer. Regions of Japan on the same latitude as North America have similar climates to those of the eastern United States.

2. **Identify the most-visited attractions, matching travelers and destinations best suited for each other.** India, Thailand, Singapore, China, and Japan are the

countries in Asia that are most likely to attract travelers. In India, Agra is the site of the Taj Mahal, a must-see on any tourist's list. Nearby Jaipur has the Palace of the Winds (Hawa Mahal), with a beautiful façade of windows built for the harem ladies. Thailand's principal attractions are the city of Bangkok, the mountainous north with the gateway city of Chiang Mai, and the beach resorts of the Kra Isthmus south of the capital. Singapore attracts business and leisure travelers interested in shopping opportunities, restaurants, and fine hotels.

Travelers to China must go to Beijing, where they can see the Forbidden City, visit the Ming Tombs, and view the Great Wall. If time permits, they might take a cruise on the Ch'ang River. History buffs will want to see the Terracotta Warriors near Xi'an. A boat trip on the Li River near Guilin or an excursion to the Stone Forest near Kunming satisfies the scenery lover. The adventurous might relish a tour to the roof of the world in Tibet or along the Silk Road to the grottos of the Mogao Caves.

In Japan, tourists can enjoy the shopping possibilities of Tokyo and visit the Mount Fuji area or the Toshogu Shrine at Nikko. Kyoto is Japan's cultural capital and will please those wanting to learn more about the country's feudal period. Its Kinkakuji Temple dates from those times.

3. **Recall factors limiting tourism to Asia.** Distance, health concerns, language differences, expense, and security concerns are among the factors limiting tourism to the region. Asia's size requires travel by air from destination to destination. Health concerns affect travel to India. Thailand presents problems with distance, expense, and security in out-of-the-way destinations. In China, barriers include the country's huge size, language, and lack of tourism infrastructure outside the main cities. Japan has ample tourism facilities and a compact size; its barriers are primarily those of cost and language.

4. **Provide or find the information needed to plan a trip to Asia.** Planning a trip requires careful confirmation of air and hotel reservations or, better yet, use of a reliable tour operator to do the work. Monitoring of political situations and research into safety concerns, documentation issues, and travel logistics are also needed. Government sources, tourist boards, trade papers, and Web sites provide the necessary information.

   Reservations for peak travel times should be made well in advance. Within the countries, travelers should not plan to drive on their own.

QUESTIONS FOR DISCUSSION AND REVIEW

1. What are some of the problems that must be solved before Asia can begin to attract more travelers?

2. How has China's vastness influenced tourism?

3. Travel to many countries in Asia is not appropriate for everyone. What steps do you think the Asian tourism industry should take to increase demand?

CHAPTER 15

The Pacific

- Australia
- New Zealand
- Oceania: Melanesia, Micronesia, and Polynesia

OBJECTIVES

When you have completed Chapter 15, you should be able to

1. Describe the environment and people of Australia, New Zealand, and Oceania.
2. Identify and locate the region's main attractions.
3. Match travelers and destinations best suited for each other.
4. Provide or find the information needed to plan a trip to the region.

Antipodes is a name sometimes used for lands in the Pacific. More than 200 years ago, the word was coined to refer to places at opposite points on the globe, particularly points opposite Great Britain, then the world's dominant power. Despite jet travel and telecommunications, in many ways the antipodes are still faraway places. The lands of the Pacific—**Australia, New Zealand,** and **Oceania**—offer visitors a unique ends-of-the-earth experience.

The Environment and Its People

Geographers use the term *Oceania* to include Australia and New Zealand, but the name seems more suitable for the scattered and remote islands of the Pacific, fabled places such as Tahiti, Fiji, and Samoa. The Pacific islands range both north and south of the equator and east and west of the international date line (see Figure 15.1). Size and culture distinguish these islands from Australia and New Zealand.

The Land

Australia is the smallest, flattest, and least populated of the major continents, and it is the only one housing a single country. It is surrounded by the South Pacific and Indian Oceans and by the **Timor**, **Arufura**, **Coral**, and **Tasman Seas**. The waters surrounding the continent are some of Australia's principal attractions. Coral reefs separate the mainland from the open sea. The **Great Barrier Reef**, the world's longest coral reef, extends more than 1,250 miles (2,013 km) along the continent's northeast coast.

English explorers imagined that Australia's interior held mighty rivers and green prairies like those of North America, but that hope was soon dashed. Australia's huge interior is mostly desert or dry grassland, a region called the **Outback**. About 90 percent of the continent consists of plains and plateaus, with few lakes and rivers. Dry lakes called **playas** are common in the south and west; they fill with water only after heavy rains. Most of the country's rivers fill with water only during the rainy season.

Australians call their remote countryside the *bush*. The term *Outback* refers specifically to the interior.

The main mountain range—the **Great Dividing Range**—runs down the east coast. Highlands extend along this coast from the **Cape York Peninsula** in the north to the island state of **Tasmania** in the south. In contrast to the dryness elsewhere, the Cape York Peninsula has rain forests, and vegetation on Tasmania is lush. The highlands peak in the southeast in a region called the **Australian Alps**. There, **Mount Kosciuszko** (*kahs ee UHS koh*) in the Snowy Mountains is the range's highest peak (7,310 feet [2,228 m]).

The world's largest single rock lies in just about the middle of Australia: **Ayers Rock**, known by its Aboriginal name, **Uluru** (*oo LOO roo*). A vast treeless plateau called the **Nullarbor Plain** extends along the southern edge of the continent. Western Australia is a land of plateaus and deserts.

About 1,000 miles (1,610 km) southeast of Australia, across the Tasman Sea, are the islands of New Zealand. They are volcanic islands, about the size of Colorado, with some of the world's most beautiful scenery. Unlike Australia, New Zealand is rich in water. On a map the country looks like an upside-down boot that someone kicked in at the ankle. New Zealand's main

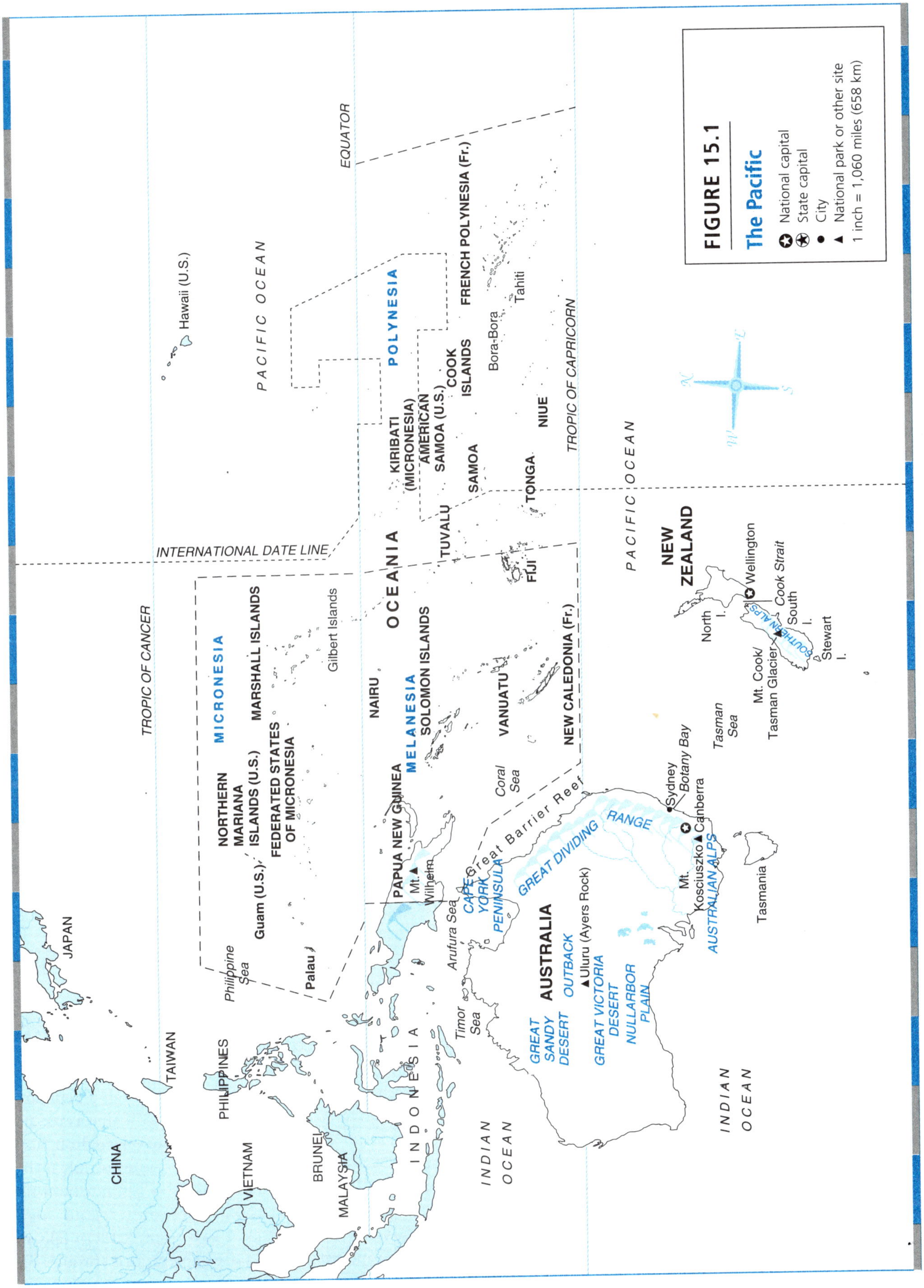

FIGURE 15.1

The Pacific

- National capital
- State capital
- City
- National park or other site

1 inch = 1,060 miles (658 km)

A staff member of the New Zealand tourist board reported receiving a query from a potential tourist: "How much is the toll for the bridge between Australia and New Zealand?"

islands are **North Island** (with the toe of the boot) and **South Island;** they are separated by narrow **Cook Strait**.

North Island—the smaller of the two islands but also the one with more population—has fertile grazing land and a mountainous center with active volcanoes. South Island is dominated by the **Southern Alps**. The highest peaks are near the island's center on **Mount Cook** (12,349 feet [3,764 m]). The **Tasman Glacier**, the largest of New Zealand's many glaciers, flows down Mount Cook's eastern slopes. In the southwest corner of the island, where the mountains meet the sea, the flooded valleys have formed steep fiords. (Note that *fiord* is spelled with an *i* in New Zealand, a *j* in Norway.)

Oceania includes thousands of islands scattered across the Pacific Ocean. Geographers estimate that there are from 20,000 to more than 30,000 islands, but only about 3,000 are large enough to have names. Together they cover less land than the state of Alaska. The islands can be divided into three groups based on location:

- **Melanesia** is west of the international date line and in the Southern Hemisphere.
- **Micronesia** is west of the international date line and mostly in the Northern Hemisphere.
- **Polynesia** is both east and west of the international date line and mostly in the Southern Hemisphere, but some islands (including Hawaii) are in the Northern Hemisphere.

Melanesia means "black islands." The name comes from the word *melanin,* which is the blackish or brownish pigment in the skin. Native Melanesians have very dark skin. Melanesia includes **New Guinea**, the **Solomons, New Caledonia, Vanuatu,** and **Fiji.**

Micronesia means "small islands." Most are low-lying coral islands. **Guam**, the **Federated States of Micronesia**, the **Marianas**, the **Marshall Islands**, and the **Gilbert Islands** are some of the islands in Micronesia.

Polynesia means "many islands." This group spreads across the Pacific. Hawaii and New Zealand are geographically part of Polynesia. Major islands include **Tonga, Samoa, French Polynesia**, the **Cook Islands, Tuvalu,** and **Niue**.

The islands differ greatly. Many, especially those in Polynesia, are famous for their white-sand beaches and swaying palm trees. Others—those in Melanesia, for example—have thick jungles and tall mountain peaks. There are high volcanic islands and low coral reefs. The majority of the low islands are atolls. An **atoll** is a coral reef—or a number of small reefs—surrounding a large lagoon. Coral reefs or atolls lie off the shores of most high islands.

TABLE 15.1

Wet Seasons of the Region

Area	Rainy Season
Australia	June through August
New Zealand	June through August
Guam	June to November
Papua New Guinea	December to March
Islands near the equator	Evenly spread
Pacific north of the equator	June to November
Pacific south of the equator	January to April

The Climate

Australia, New Zealand, and much of Oceania are south of the equator. Thus their seasons are opposite those of North America. Most of the region experiences a wet season and a dry season (see Table 15.1).

A large part of Australia lies in the temperate zone. January and February are generally the hottest months, with the summer season lengthening as you go north. Western and central areas are arid or semiarid, with prolonged droughts.

Except for the far north, New Zealand is in the temperate zone. July is the coldest month, and January and February are the warmest. The northern tip of North Island is warm and humid year-round. On South Island, high rainfall on the west coast contrasts with the drier east. Snow seldom falls in lowland areas, although some mountain peaks are snowcapped throughout the year. The country has about 400 earthquakes every year, but only about one-quarter of them are strong enough to be felt.

Most of the Pacific islands are tropical. The atolls are extremely vulnerable to typhoons—the Pacific version of hurricanes—most of which occur from January to March. Rising tides caused by global warming seem likely to cause the disappearance of several low-lying islands beneath the waves before too long.

The People and Their History

Scholars believe that the first inhabitants of Australia, New Zealand, and the Pacific islands came from Asia over land bridges or by water (see Figure 15.2). Australia's original inhabitants may have reached the continent as early as 50,000 years ago; their descendants today are called Aborigines (*ab uh RIHJ uh neez*). New Zealand was settled between AD 800 and 1000 by people known as the Maori (*MOW ree*). The Polynesian islands were the last to be reached.

Spanish and Portuguese sailors explored the region during the 1500s. They were looking for a land known as *Terra Australis Incognita* ("Unknown Southern Land"), but they reported unfavorably on what they had seen, and the area remained undisturbed for centuries. In 1770 Captain James Cook (1728–1779) of the British navy sighted Australia's east coast. He claimed the land for Great Britain and named it *New South Wales.*

Mark Twain wrote, "Australian history does not read like history but like the most beautiful lies. . . . It is full of surprises, adventures, incongruities, contradictions, and incredibilities; but they are all true; they all happened." Twain's comment pretty much covers the continent's history. After the American Revolution, the British needed a new place to ship convicts, and they decided to establish a penal colony in New South Wales. With eleven ships, 730 male and female convicts, 200 soldiers, 30 soldiers' wives, and a few children, the *First Fleet* sailed from England, reaching Botany Bay nine months later. Botany Bay proved to be swampy and open to winds, but 12 miles (19 km) up the coast, search parties discovered beautiful Sydney Harbor.

The next centuries were for the brave who ventured to the new land. Most settlers considered the Aborigines a primitive people, treated them badly, and occupied their land. When the English came, about 750,000 Aborigines lived in Australia. Today, they represent less than 1 percent of the population.

In 1901 Australia became an independent nation within the British Commonwealth. Through the mid-20th century, most Australians could trace their ancestry back to the British Isles. That changed after World War II. Between 1947 and 1972, more than 2 million emigrants came, and soon communities of Italians, Greeks, Croatians, Macedonians, and Turks were established. Doors were opened to immigrants from Asian countries in the 1970s and 1980s.

Like Australia, New Zealand is a former British colony, but it was never a penal colony, and unlike Australia's gentle Aborigines, its natives, the Maori, were fierce warriors. They would begin a fight by sticking their tongues out and waggling them at their enemies in the belief that this would scare them. (New Zealand sports teams often begin their matches this way.)

On February 6, 1840, Maori chiefs and representatives of the British Crown signed the Treaty of Waitangi. Although fighting between Maori and settlers continued for many years, the day is celebrated each year as New Zealand's national day. New Zealand became a self-governing British colony in 1856, a dominion in 1907, and fully independent in 1947. The Maori today make up 14.5 percent of the population.

FIGURE 15.2

Milestones in the History of the Pacific

43,000 BC Rock art appears in Australia.

c. AD 800s–1000s Maori migrate to New Zealand.

1400 Temple city of Nan Madol is in use in Micronesia.

1568 Spanish sailors visit the Solomon Islands.

1606 Dutch captain Willem Jansz explores the eastern shore of Australia.

1768 British navigator and explorer James Cook maps the Pacific.

1788 Convicts are sent to Sydney, Australia, on the *First Fleet*.

1800s Yankee traders and Christian missionaries challenge cultures in Oceania.

1845–1870 Maori/European wars take place in New Zealand.

1868 Convict transportation to Australia ends.

1893 New Zealand is the world's first country to grant women the right to vote.

1901 The Commonwealth of Australia is created.

1941–1945 Melanesia and Micronesia are battlegrounds in World War II.

1945–1963 Atomic and hydrogen bomb tests are carried out on Micronesian and Polynesian atolls.

1947 New Zealand becomes fully independent.

1960 Australia grants citizenship to Aborigines.

1960s–1980s Independence movements take place in the islands.

2000 Political conflict exists in Fiji between Melanesian and Indian citizens.

Today, the Maori facial tattoo, or *moko*, is applied with paint, but it was originally chiseled into the skin using a knife. Men adorned themselves with *moko* over their entire bodies.

Elsewhere in the Pacific, clashes between European and native cultures took varied forms. Reports of Captain Cook's discoveries brought missionaries who discouraged native customs. Traders, whalers, and slave traders brought diseases and encouraged lawlessness. By 1900, the United States, Germany, Britain, and France controlled most of the islands.

In the 20th century, Japan increased its power across the Pacific. The islands became battlegrounds in World War II. After the war, the United States, Britain, and France used islands in Micronesia and Polynesia for nuclear testing. Since 1962, a number of islands have become independent, and others are working toward this goal.

✔ CHECK-UP

Major physical features of Australia and New Zealand are
- ✔ Outback of Australia.
- ✔ Great Barrier Reef off Australia's east coast.
- ✔ Southern Alps of South Island, New Zealand, dominated by Mount Cook.

Australia's and New Zealand's cultures are notable for
- ✔ Aborigine acceptance of, and Maori resistance to, foreign takeover of their lands.
- ✔ Use of Australia as a dumping ground for British convicts in the 18th century.
- ✔ Dominance of Western customs today.

Among key features of Oceania are
- ✔ Low coral and high volcanic islands.
- ✔ Atolls and lagoons.

Australia

If you put the maps of Australia and the continental United States on top of each other with either one upside down, they almost match in size and physical features. The Cape York Peninsula sticks out like Florida, the highest population density is around Sydney in Australia and around New York in the United States, and Perth and San Francisco are beautiful cities on the west coast of each continent (see Figure 15.3).

Australia has six states and two territories. More than 80 percent of the population lives in the state and territorial capitals. All but one of the cities—the federal capital, **Canberra** (*KAN buhr uh*)—are on the coast, as close as possible to a good harbor. Each is the airport gateway to its region.

This chapter begins where modern Australia itself began, at Sydney in the state of New South Wales, and continues around the continent in a clockwise direction.

New South Wales

Sometimes called the *Gateway to Australia*, New South Wales is in southeastern Australia. The state contains **Sydney**, the country's largest city.

Sydney The capital of New South Wales, Sydney developed from a penal settlement of tents and shacks into one of the world's largest cities, equally famed for its innovative architecture and its vivid lifestyle.

Sydney's harbor dominates the landscape and separates the city from its suburbs across the bay. The Sydney Harbor Bridge and a tunnel connect the areas. Local people call the bridge the "Coat Hanger" because of its shape. Visitors with a head for heights can take the "Bridge Climb," a three-hour tour to the top of the bridge attached by a harness to the safety rail and escorted by experienced guides. The view is spectacular!

An area called the Rocks is on a point near the bridge. The Rocks is the oldest section of the city, a place where convict tents were pitched and the first houses were built.

Circular Quay is the harbor's heart and the center of the transit system of ferries, trains, and buses. The Overseas Passenger Terminal for cruise ships is on the quay. George Street, the city's main street, runs south from the quay through the center of downtown.

On the south side of Circular Quay, located on a promontory, is the Sydney Opera House, Australia's most recognizable structure. It is as much a work of art as a building. Its Danish architect envisioned a construction of concrete sails, and from a distance it appears to be sailing on the harbor water. Farther east is Kings Cross, an area of nightclubs and restaurants—Sydney's answer to London's Soho.

Both north and south of Sydney, there are miles of inviting beaches, including Bondi (*bond EYE*) and Manly. West of the city, the **Blue Mountains**

Sydney Harbor, Australia

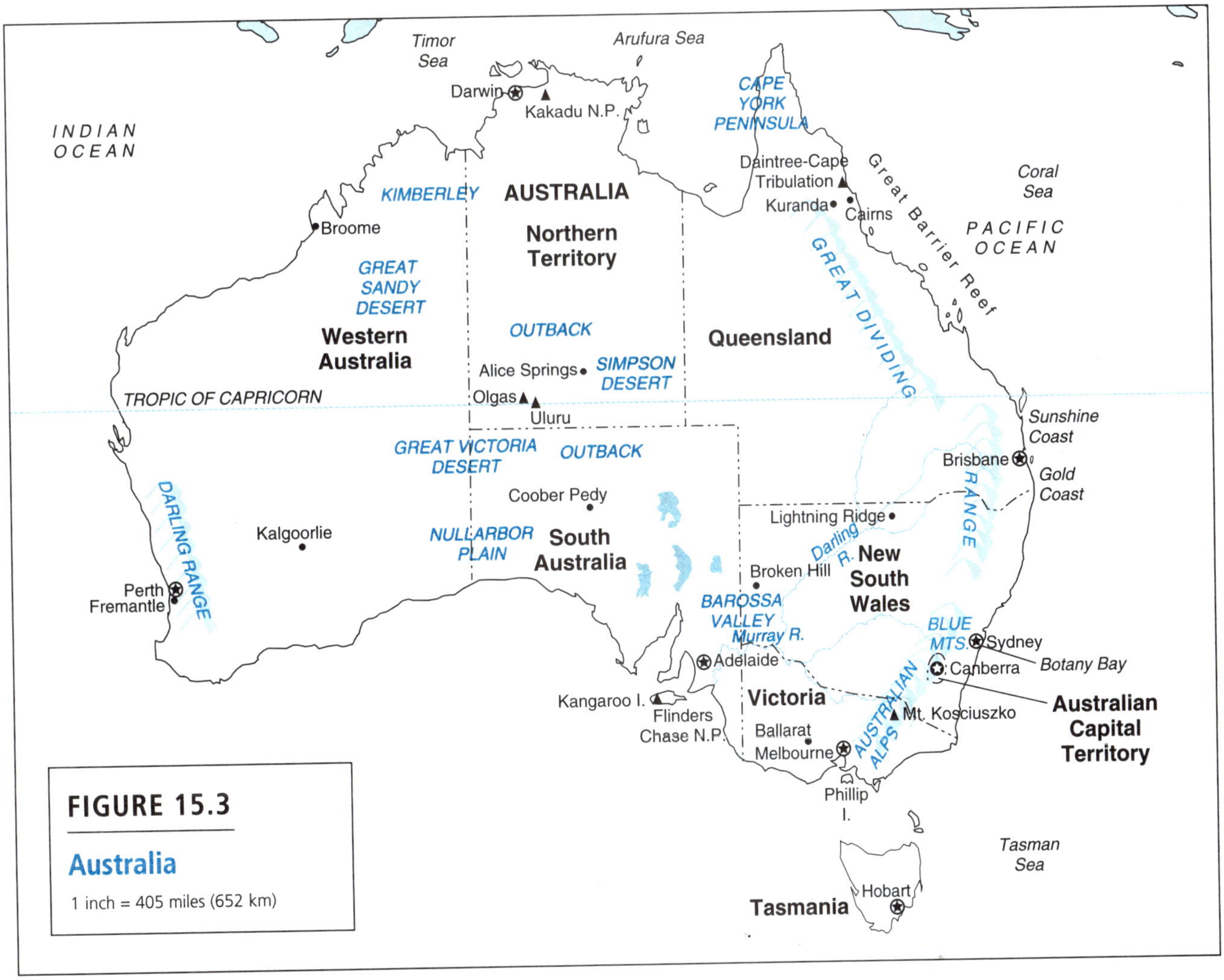

FIGURE 15.3

Australia

1 inch = 405 miles (652 km)

are part of the city's playground. Eucalyptus trees dominate the landscape. At one time these trees grew only in Australia. Their leaves give off droplets of aromatic oil, causing a bluish haze that inspired the mountains' name.

Outback People who want the Outback experience but have limited time might fly (about two and a half hours) to **Lightning Ridge** in the Back of Beyond (another term for the Outback), near the Queensland border. This mining town produces the precious black opal. Another flight west from Sydney can take the traveler to **Broken Hill**, a town built on the riches of silver mining.

In Australia during the 1890s, poems known as "bush ballads" were popular. Banjo Paterson's "Waltzing Matilda" became the country's most popular song. It glorifies a tea-drinking sheep rustler.

Australian Capital Territory (ACT)

In the early 1900s, Australia's leaders recognized the need for a national capital. Compromise between Sydney and Melbourne produced a location midway between the two cities. The government created the Australian Capital Territory (ACT) and named its city Canberra, which is Aboriginal for "meeting place." The capital is built around hills and ridges on a rolling plain.

➤ PROFILE

Australia's Unique Wildlife

Australia's long isolation from any other landmass has produced a number of zoological marvels. Of great interest are 150 species of *marsupials*, animals that give birth to poorly developed offspring that mature in a pouch on the mother's stomach. Some of the best known are

- ➤ Kangaroo. This furry mammal hops on its hind legs at speeds that can reach 30 miles (48 km) per hour.
- ➤ Koala (*koh AH luh*). This arboreal marsupial (which is not a bear) has soft fur, a large hairless nose, round ears, and no tail. It sleeps during the day and spends most of its awake time eating eucalyptus leaves.
- ➤ Platypus. A semiaquatic mammal, the platypus lives in burrows in the banks of streams. Its webbed feet and broad flat tail aid in swimming.
- ➤ Echidna (*ih KIHD nuh*), also called the spiny anteater. This nocturnal mammal has sharp spines on its back and sides. It lays one egg a year, which hatches in a pouch that forms on the female's stomach each mating season.

Victoria

Desert plateau in the northwest, the fertile valleys of the Murray River, and a magnificent coastline attract travelers to Australia's smallest state, Victoria, on the southeast coast. Its capital is **Melbourne** (*MEL bin*).

Australia is a sports-minded country, and Melbourne is perhaps its most sports-minded city. "Footy," Australian-rules football, is a passion; so is cricket. Citizens are so enthusiastic about sports that they stop for a legal holiday on the first Tuesday in November for the Melbourne Cup, a horse race.

The most popular excursion from the city goes southeast to **Phillip Island** to see tiny penguins come out of the sea at dusk and waddle up the beach to their sand dune burrows. The nine-hour excursion to the rookeries is made several nights each week during the nesting season, November through January.

A drive west of Melbourne takes you to gold rush country around **Ballarat**. Visitors can pan for gold and walk through a reconstructed miners' town.

Northeast of Melbourne are the Australian Alps, shared with New South Wales. The mountains attract skiers from July to September; the season is short and not reliable. Ski villages with an Outback theme cater to off-season visitors with horseback riding, bush walking, and wildflower watching.

Tasmania

Southeast of the continent, the island state of Tasmania has spectacular mountain wilderness areas. More than 30 percent of the state is protected World Heritage area, national parks, and reserves. It is as wet and lush as the mainland is dry and arid. Snowcapped Mount Wellington presides over **Hobart**, the state capital. The island is a popular destination for those who want to see the remains of the last convict prison.

The last of the penal colonies, the infamous Port Arthur, is an hour's drive from Hobart, Tasmania's capital. It closed in 1877.

South Australia

West of Victoria, opals, wine, wildlife, and desert are available in South Australia. Its official animal is the hairy-nosed wombat. Like the wombat, South Australia is self-reliant. Everything needed can be found within its borders.

Adelaide, the capital, is a sophisticated city where culture and good living are important. Its museum has the world's largest collection of Aboriginal art.

The **Murray River**, Australia's equivalent of the Mississippi, begins in the Snowy Mountains and finishes its wanderings in South Australia. It is Australia's most important inland waterway. The river waters the **Barossa Valley**, northeast of Adelaide, where German immigrants established Australia's oldest vineyards in the 19th century. One out of every two glasses of Australian wine comes from the Barossa. Visitors enjoy seeing the area from a hot-air balloon or on the Barossa Wine Train.

Kangaroo Island, one of Australia's largest islands, is off Adelaide's south coast. The western end of the island is **Flinders Chase National Park**. Kangaroos, koalas, and emus live there in their natural state but have become extroverts, snuggling up to visitors and stealing food.

Coober Pedy, the opal capital of Australia, is about 525 miles (845 km) north-northwest of Adelaide. The name is Aboriginal for "white fella down a hole." Opals were discovered lying on the surface by a fourteen-year-old boy back in 1915. Now, the opals are all underground as well as stores, the post office, and a hotel. Tourists can stay underground at the Desert Cave Hotel.

The story goes that Captain Cook asked an Aborigine to tell him the name of the strange hopping animal. "Kangaroo" was the answer. Cook told the world. It turned out that "kangaroo" is a native expression for "I don't know."

Western Australia

Bigger than Texas and Alaska combined, Western Australia stretches from the **Nullarbor Plain** to the Indian Ocean. Most of the population enjoys the Mediterranean climate around the capital, **Perth**. It is inland from the country's Indian Ocean port, the city of **Fremantle**. Nearby there are forests, beautiful coastal scenes, and vineyard-covered lands. But most of this vast state is desert, semi-desert, or otherwise difficult, if not impossible, terrain. Inland are gold fields where the precious mineral is still mined.

Unspoiled beaches extend along the coast north of Perth. The city of **Broome** on the north coast at one time supplied 80 percent of the world's mother-of-pearl used to make buttons. Today, the white pearls cultivated in Broome's pure waters are again sought after, this time by jewelers.

Broome is the southern gateway to the **Kimberley**, a rugged Outback region. Attractions include huge cattle stations and Aboriginal culture. One of the world's richest diamond mines gives sparkle to the region. The Argyle diamond field produces the rare pink diamond as well as industrial gems.

ON THE SPOT

Ms. Pakeha is headed off on a trip to Australia and New Zealand and is concerned about tipping. She has heard that you do not tip in these countries, but her well-traveled friends have given her conflicting advice. What's the scoop?

Virtually no one in the service sector in these countries expects to be tipped. Their livelihood does not depend on it. In hotels frequented by foreigners, however, porters are accustomed to receiving tips. In good restaurants, a tip of 5 to 10 percent is a reward for courteous service. Taxi drivers accept but don't expect tips. But it never hurts anyone's feelings if you do give an appreciative tip.

Northern Territory

Tropical **Darwin**, the capital of the Northern Territory, is where Aboriginal, Asian, and European cultures meet. Visitors can tour nature parks by day and play roulette in the city's casino by night or take a cruise across Darwin Harbor for an Aboriginal meal and a *corroboree* ("get-together").

Darwin is the gateway to **Kakadu National Park**, a three-hour drive east of the city. The park is home to Aboriginal tribes as well as crocodiles, water buffalo, birds, waterfalls, and dramatic rock formations. More than 1,000 sites of Aboriginal rock paintings are in the park. Tours and safaris are available from Darwin.

Alice Springs is the only major town between Darwin and Adelaide. It was established late in the 19th century as the first overland telegraph station. The base for exploring the Outback, Alice is an oasis. It has hotels and motels, a casino, restaurants, and facilities for everything from golf and tennis to hot-air ballooning and tandem parachuting. The town is home to the Flying

Australian Outback

Doctor Service and the School of the Air, services for people who live on the remote Outback stations.

Close to the geographic center of Australia, Uluru (Ayers Rock) rises from the middle of the Outback about a five-hour drive southwest of Alice Springs. The world's largest monolith sits alone, the remnant of a sandstone formation that once covered the entire region. When the sun hits its surface at sunset and sunrise, Uluru glows deep red.

Uluru is sacred to the Aborigines. Their Dreamtime creation stories tell of an unformed world that was shaped by giant kangaroos, lizards, snakes, witchetty grubs (worms), and even plants and clouds. Uluru and the nearby **Olgas**, a cluster of smooth-domed boulders, are considered evidence of the creation period. The native people believe that the rock's features represent important people or events in their history. Some of the rock's caves contain paintings of epic journeys made by distant ancestors.

Uluru and the Olgas are known jointly as Uluru-Kata Tjuta National Park. Because of park restrictions, just about the only place to stay while

CLOSE-UP: AUSTRALIA

Who is a good prospect for a trip to Australia? North Americans would feel very comfortable in Australia. The only thing holding them back is the time and money needed for the trip. People with interests in birds and animals—such as those who support zoos or are members of the Audubon Society—are prospects for special interest touring.

Why would they visit Australia? The country provides the comfort of a familiar culture, a common language, and excellent tourism facilities, as well as attractions such as scenic wonders, a taste of adventure, and strange animals.

Where would they go? Half a world away, Australia offers the Aboriginal culture, exotic natural landscapes, wildlife straight out of a nature documentary, and a spirit of today. A first trip might follow this itinerary.

Days 1–2 Fly from North America to Sydney. (As you cross the international date line, you lose a day.)

Day 3 Sydney. You are greeted by a tour representative who will assist you with luggage and transfers to your hotel.

Day 4 Sydney. See the Rocks, Kings Cross, and Bondi Beach on a city tour. Enjoy a luncheon cruise on Sydney's harbor and then a memorable evening with dinner at the Opera House Restaurant.

Day 5 Day at leisure in Sydney. Optional tour to the Blue Mountains.

Day 6 Fly to Melbourne. Dinner this evening on a tramcar.

Day 7 Day at leisure in Melbourne. Optional tour to Phillip Island.

Day 8 Alice Springs. Fly into Australia's Red Center. In the afternoon, take a guided desert discovery tour into the bush.

Day 9 Alice Springs–Uluru. Test your camel-riding skills in the morning before motoring south to Uluru (Ayers Rock). Arrive in time for sunset.

Day 10 Uluru–Cairns. Walk around the base of Uluru before your flight to Cairns. Sightseeing tour of the city.

Days 11–12 Dunk Island. Free time to explore the island, wander the rain forest, or relax on the beach. The next day, board a semi-submersible to view the colorful corals and tropical fish.

Day 13 Cairns. Back to the mainland to enjoy a ride on the Skyrail over the World Heritage rain forest to Kuranda. Travel back on the Kuranda Train.

Day 14 Board your flight for Los Angeles. Regain your lost day.

When is the best time to visit? Natives will say that any time is a good time to visit Australia, and they are quite right. The continent is so big and its terrain so varied that there is something to enjoy in the continent at any time of the year. In general, spring and fall seem to attract most visitors. Aussies vacation in their summer (our winter), and accommodations and sights are apt to be crowded then.

The travelers say, "It's too far." How would you respond? The Australian Travel Commission counters with "From L.A. to G'Day in half a day." Suggest that the travelers plan a trip with stopovers in the islands both going and coming. Excursion airfares to the South Pacific usually allow a certain amount of stopovers at no extra cost. Point out that crossing the international date line makes it appear as though the trip takes forever.

visiting the area is the range of accommodations available at the environmentally sensitive Ayers Rock Resort. It was built in 1985 about 11 miles (18 km) from the rock. No structure is higher than the surrounding sand dunes. Facilities include sites for tents and motor homes as well as a five-star hotel and shops.

Queensland

The state of Queensland has just about everything that makes Australia a special destination: deluxe resorts, beautiful beaches, Outback mining towns, modern cities, rain forests, deserts, and its most outstanding feature, the Great Barrier Reef.

Brisbane (*BRIHZ buhn*) is the sprawling state capital, Australia's third-largest city. Its attractions include the Lone Pine Koala Sanctuary. Koalas breed freely here, and surplus stock goes to zoos throughout the world. The park offers a prime opportunity for visitors to cuddle a koala and have their pictures taken.

An hour's drive south of the city, the Gold Coast resorts have high-rise hotels, a casino open twenty-four hours a day, nightclubs, theme parks, and excellent beaches. To Brisbane's north is the Sunshine Coast, with the same good beaches but not as much development.

The Great Barrier Reef is close to shore in the north of Queensland and slants out to sea as it extends southward. Only four islands—Heron, Green, Lady Elliot, and Lady Musgrave—are on the reef itself, but hundreds of islands are scattered across the water between the coral barrier and the mainland. More than a dozen islands have resorts. Some focus on wildlife; others market to honeymooners, children, game fishermen, rain forest trekkers, and, of course, reef walkers, divers, and snorkelers.

The distance from the mainland to the outer reef is typically 50 miles (80 km). The main gateways are **Cairns** (*canz*) and Port Douglas in the north and Shute Harbor for the Whitsunday Islands in the south. Each day thousands of visitors speed out on catamaran services to the semipermanent pontoons moored at intervals on the reef. The pontoons act as bases for diving, snorkeling, and reef exploring.

From Cairns visitors can also explore the **Daintree–Cape Tribulation** rain forest. Visitors can ride the Skyrail Rainforest Cableway over the forest to the mountain village of **Kuranda**, visit an Aboriginal cultural park, and return by scenic train.

From late October to early May, the box jellyfish abound along Australia's North Queensland coast. Beaches put up warning signs when the stingers are nearby.

✔ CHECK-UP

Australia's divisions and their capitals are

- ✔ New South Wales; its capital is Sydney.
- ✔ Victoria; Melbourne is the state capital.
- ✔ South Australia; its capital is Adelaide.
- ✔ Western Australia; its capital is Perth.
- ✔ Northern Territory; Darwin is the capital.
- ✔ Queensland; Brisbane is the capital.
- ✔ Tasmania; the capital city is Hobart.

Outstanding attractions are

- ✔ Architecture, lively atmosphere, and beaches that can be found in Sydney.
- ✔ Penguins waddling out of the sea at Phillip Island near Melbourne.
- ✔ Hunting for opals in South Australia's Coober Pedy.
- ✔ Tropical Darwin and Kakadu National Park.
- ✔ Alice Springs and Uluru, in the heart of the Outback.
- ✔ Beaches, resorts, and Great Barrier Reef that can be found in Queensland.

New Zealand

New Zealand is midway between the equator and the South Pole (see Figure 15.4). Geographically it is part of Polynesia. Of New Zealand's two major islands, North Island is the more populous; South Island is the more rugged. **Stewart Island** is a small island south of South Island.

New Zealand has an amazing variety of geological and climatic conditions, but its only native mammals are bats, and it has no snakes. In the absence of threatening native predators, some remarkable birds developed—including the *kakapo*, the world's largest parrot, and the *kiwi*, a bird that cannot fly. The kiwi is a shaggy, dull brown bird about the size of a chicken. It is unlikely that the visitor will see a kiwi outside a zoo, although New Zealanders have adopted the nickname "Kiwi" for themselves.

The easiest way to say Maori words is to pronounce each syllable. Every word ends in a vowel, and *wh* is pronounced like an *f*. Practice with *Whakarewarewa* and you'll soon see why the locals call the town "Faka."

Its small size makes New Zealand a satisfying destination. Even with limited time, people can see the country. The standard of living is among the world's highest, and modern infrastructure (transport, hotels, restaurants, attractions, and information centers) makes sightseeing easy.

North Island

Wellington on North Island is New Zealand's capital, although **Auckland** is its largest city. North Island also has long sandy beaches, active volcanoes, geysers, hot springs, boiling mud, Maori culture, caves, fertile grazing land, and grape-growing regions.

FIGURE 15.4 New Zealand

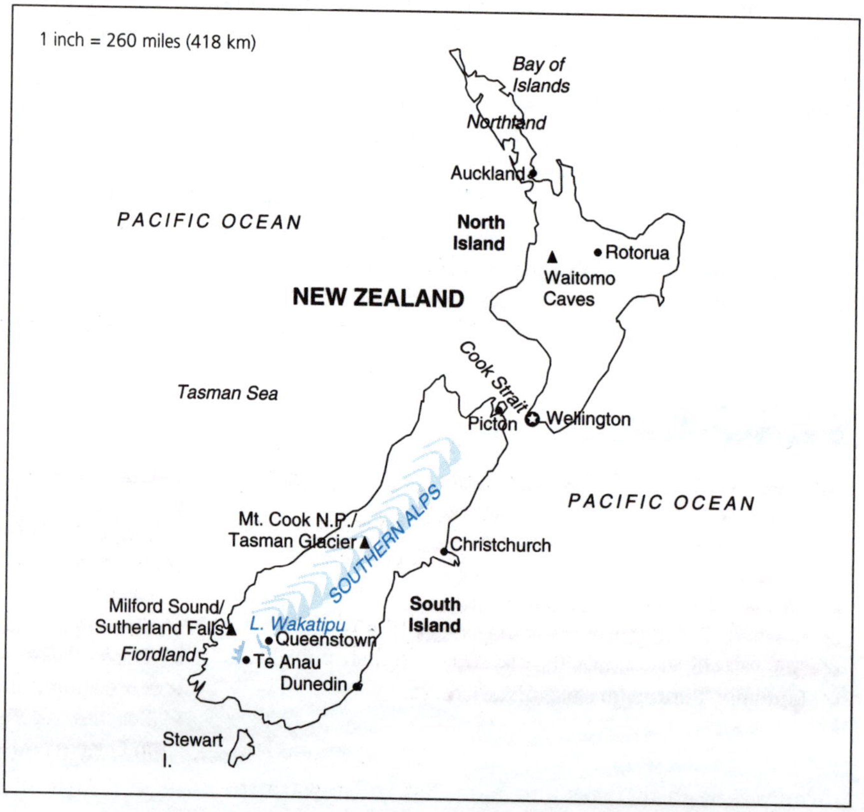

Auckland Most visitors to New Zealand arrive in Auckland (*AWK luhnd*), on the northwest coast of North Island. The waterfront city is on an isthmus that separates two harbors. Mount Eden, an extinct volcano, is Auckland's highest point. Its lookout offers good city views. Lower Queen Street is the city's main artery.

Highlights of the *City of Sails* include harbor excursions and a visit to the War Memorial Museum to see Maori art and handicrafts. Skilled boat builders, the Maoris sailed in huge war canoes. Among the displays are ceremonial meeting houses; these peaked-roof structures with intricate wood carving are the Maoris' most developed art form.

Maori carving

Northland The long finger of land north of Auckland has a warm climate that nurtures the kauri gum trees, considered to be equal in beauty to the California redwoods. Off the northeast coast, the **Bay of Islands** offers fishing, golf, small boat cruises, and yacht charters.

Rotorua Geysers occur principally in three parts of the world: in Iceland, in Yellowstone Park in the United States, and in the center of North Island. It is a thermal wonderland with many plopping, gurgling, hissing geysers, mudpots, and hot springs. Rotorua, an old spa town, is right in the heart of this geothermal activity—so close, in fact, that the place smells of sulfur, an odor reminiscent of rotten eggs.

Rotorua is also the center of Maori culture. At the Maori Arts and Crafts Institute in the Whakarewarewa Reserve, travelers can tour a replica village, take in a show featuring traditional song and dance, and attend a Maori *hangi* ("feast"). If the traveler has time for only one attraction, this is it. It offers a cross section of everything for which the region is famous.

Waitomo Caves West of Rotorua, millions of glowing insect larvae hang from the ceiling at the Waitomo glowworm caves. The lights began to flicker out in the late 1970s, drained by the human bodies who gathered to watch the phenomenon. Now, the number of people allowed to enter the caves at any one time is limited, while humidifiers control the atmosphere. Visitors can tube-raft or slip silently through the caves on a barge. The more adventurous can abseil (rappel) down into huge caverns.

Wellington Centered around a fine harbor at the southern end of North Island is scenic Wellington. Its buildings are a mix of modern and Victorian. Colorful wooden houses spill down the hills. Ferries connect Wellington on North Island to **Picton** on South Island. The trip takes about three hours.

South Island

South Island has some of the world's most unspoiled scenery. Plains fringe the southeast and the central east coast. The snowcapped peaks of the Southern Alps rise from the plains with astonishing suddenness and run the island's length.

Christchurch South Island's largest city and New Zealand's third largest is Christchurch, often called "the most English city outside England." It has a good airport, and tours often start there.

Mount Cook National Park West of Christchurch, the road passes through a land of lakes and hills that roll toward the Southern Alps and

➤ PROFILE

Trekking in New Zealand

New Zealand is laced with miles of paths and trails, or, as the Kiwis call them, walkways and tracks. Some of the best known are

- ➤ Abel Tasman National Park Walk (year-round), a five-day walk along the northwest coastline of Tasman Bay on South Island.
- ➤ Milford Track (November–April), a 34-mile (55 km) walk often described as the "finest walk in the world," in Fiordland National Park on South Island. The guided track takes five days and four nights, and reservations must be booked months in advance.
- ➤ Routeburn Walk (November–April), a three-day trek through primeval forests, over alpine ridges, and across grass valleys in the heart of Fiordland National Park.
- ➤ Tongariro Trek (year-round), a three-day trek into the volcanic plateau of North Island.

Mount Cook (*Aoraki* to the Maori), which towers above other peaks in Mount Cook National Park. The Tasman Glacier, one of the longest outside the Himalaya, is on the south face of the mountain. Spectacular ski plane flights open up this world for all—even the physically challenged—to see. All sorts of ski options, including heliskiing, are available.

Anyone from the age of 13 upward is eligible to bungee-jump (13- to 16-year-olds require parental permission), and anyone over age 60 goes free. The oldest jumper so far was 90 years old.

Queenstown South Island's most popular resort for both summer and winter sports is Queenstown, southwest of Christchurch. It is often called the *Adventure Capital of New Zealand.* In winter, Queenstown is a skiing center; in summer, it is a center of activities ranging from trout fishing to paragliding, from white-water rafting to jet-boat touring on the narrow chasms and shallow rapids of the Shotover River.

Commercial bungee-jumping began in Queenstown in 1988, and more than 100,000 leaps, guided by professionals, have been made. Nearly all the bungee sites have observation platforms for spectators. The original jump is the 141-foot (43 m) drop from the Kawarau Suspension Bridge. The latest is a 335-foot (102 m) drop. All it takes is willpower.

Queenstown is on the shores of S-shaped **Lake Wakatipu**. When wind

CLOSE-UP: NEW ZEALAND

Who is a good prospect for a trip to New Zealand? Lovers of the outdoors and nature, hikers, skiers, those interested in the Maori culture, and people who just want to relax in a beautiful setting are ideal prospects for the country. New Zealand is a popular holiday destination for visitors from Australia, Japan, the United Kingdom, and North America.

Why would they visit New Zealand? The country offers unspoiled countryside and excellent facilities for outdoor recreation.

Where would they go? After the journey from North America, a vacation might include the following itinerary.

Day 1 Arrive in Queenstown on South Island.

Day 2 Queenstown. Day at leisure to experience the endless scenic attractions and outdoor adventures. Perhaps try bungee-jumping or an exciting jet-boat ride on the Shotover River.

Day 3 Milford Sound–Te Anau. Weather permitting, you cruise the fiord to view Mitre Peak and spectacular waterfalls.

Day 4 Te Anau–Dunedin. Travel to Dunedin, the *Edinburgh of the South*, on the southernmost coast. Perhaps take a wildlife cruise to view penguin and albatross colonies.

Day 5 Dunedin–Mount Cook. Journey north to Mount Cook National Park, where you have the opportunity for a scenic flight over the region.

Day 6 Mount Cook–Christchurch. Travel by motorcoach across the plains of Canterbury to the *Garden City* of Christchurch.

Day 7 Christchurch–Wellington. The morning begins with a trip to Kaikoura, a renowned whale-watching area. At Picton, board the interisland ferry to cross Cook Strait bound for New Zealand's capital city, Wellington.

Day 8 Wellington–Taupo. Travel north through orchards and vineyards to Taupo.

Day 9 Taupo–Auckland. Visit the thermal area, and then continue northwest through kiwi fruit country to Auckland, the *City of Sails*.

Day 10 Auckland. City sightseeing includes travel to the volcanic crater of Mount Eden for a panoramic view.

Day 11 Depart for home.

When is the best time to visit? The weather is pleasant year-round. November through April is the most popular time for exploring. The highlands are cool, and it is wise to pack a light weatherproof jacket or coat as rain is possible, especially in the north and west. New Zealand's winter brings extensive snowfalls to the Southern Alps and the North Island mountains, a time skiers would like to visit. New Zealand's unpolluted air makes the sun particularly strong; sunglasses, sunscreen, and hats are recommended.

The traveler says, "I don't have the time." How would you respond? Compare New Zealand to California. What would they expect to do in that time on a California vacation? You can easily see all of New Zealand in that time and experience everything from its sparkling cities to its pristine wilderness.

and atmospheric conditions are right, the lake "breathes." According to Maori legend, the lake is the "Hollow of the Giant," formed when an evil sleeping giant was set on fire by a brave youth, melting the snow and ice of the surrounding mountains to fill the lake. The peculiar rise and fall of the lake's level is the result of the giant's heartbeat.

Lake Wakatipu, New Zealand

Fiordland In the southwest, where the mountains meet the sea, the flooded valleys have formed steep fiords to create Fiordland, the country's largest national park. **Milford Sound** is the most accessible and best known of the fiords. It is lined with mountain peaks that rise sharply, the most famous of which is Mitre Peak, named for its resemblance to the high pointed hat worn by a church bishop. Lush rain forest and majestic waterfalls such as **Sutherland Falls**, the world's twelfth highest, abound.

Te Anau is the park's gateway, about three hours southwest of Queenstown by car. Fiordland has some of New Zealand's rarest birds, as well as some of its best-known hiking tracks.

✔ CHECK-UP

New Zealand's major cities and towns include

- ✔ Auckland, the major air and sea gateway.
- ✔ Rotorua, the center of Maori culture.
- ✔ Wellington, the capital and an important port.
- ✔ Christchurch, South Island's largest city.
- ✔ Queenstown, the center of South Island's resorts.
- ✔ Te Anau, the gateway to Milford Sound.

New Zealand's attractions include

- ✔ Thermal attractions and Maori culture on North Island.
- ✔ Waitomo glowworm caves.
- ✔ Flightseeing over the Tasman Glacier on Mount Cook.
- ✔ Jet-boat rides on white-water rivers.
- ✔ Fiordland National Park and Milford Sound.

Oceania

Thoughts of sunlight on the sand and moonlight on the sea, as well as a relaxed lifestyle, coconut palms, banyan trees, and bananas you can pick right off the tree, have been luring travelers to the Pacific islands for centuries. The number of visitors to Oceania, however, is small. This section looks at the places that attract the most visitors: Fiji in Melanesia, Guam in Micronesia, and French Polynesia in Polynesia (see Figure 15.5). The section at the end of the chapter reviews other islands of interest.

Fiji

Called the *Crossroads of the South Pacific*, the Melanesian country of Fiji (*FEE jee*) is an isolated archipelago in the southwest Pacific, about two-thirds of the way from Hawaii to New Zealand. It is south of the equator and west of the international date line. Located on the air route from Australia to North America's west coast, Fiji is well served by flights, and it attracts an increasing number of tourists. Of all the Melanesian destinations, Fiji has the most extensive tourist infrastructure.

Fiji has hundreds of islands, but two—**Viti Levu** (*vee tee LAY voo*) and **Vanua Levu** (*vahn wah LAY voo*)—account for nearly nine-tenths of the land and 70 percent of the population. The islands are volcanic in origin, with offshore coral reefs and central mountains rising steeply from narrow coastal plains. The western sides of the islands are dry; the eastern sides are subject to cloudy skies and frequent rains. Fiji is subject to cyclones from December through April.

Explorers called the Fijian Islands the *Cannibal Islands*. Violence was an accepted way of life, and cannibalism was a religious practice.

Suva (*SOO vah*) on Viti Levu is Fiji's capital. Fiji's international airport is also on Viti Levu, at **Nandi** (*NAHN dee*). Most resorts are located on Viti Levu along the Coral Coast on the road between Nandi and Suva.

Fiji became an independent country in 1970. About 48 percent of Fiji's people are of Melanesian descent. About 46 percent are descendants of laborers brought in from India. Although Indians control much of the economy, Fijians traditionally had more power. Political conflict between the two groups has flared several times in recent years.

For visitors, Fiji offers diving, surfing, game fishing, and yachting. It also preserves a variety of traditional customs and crafts such as fish driving, tapa cloth making, and kava or *yagona* (*yan gona*) drinking. Yagona is made from powdered pepper plant roots and looks like pale chocolate milk. It is a nonalcoholic drink that numbs the tongue and lips of the drinker after several bowls. Fijians drink yagona when welcoming visitors, making deals, settling arguments, or taking the equivalent of a North American coffee break.

Firewalking is another Fijian tradition. Hotels present performances of the firewalking ceremony and stage a *meke*—a combination of dance, song, and theater.

No Fijian itinerary is complete without a visit to the nearby **Yasawa Islands** in a small ship. On the popular Blue Lagoon Cruises from Lautoka (a town just north of Nandi), passengers visit comparatively uninhabited islands. They might swim, snorkel, visit the Sawa-I-Lau Caves or a coconut plantation, or just relax.

Guam

Guam (*gwahm*) is a U.S. territory in the Mariana Islands of Micronesia. The island is an important U.S. air and naval base. Its residents are U.S. citizens. Guam's international airport serves as a connection point for the smaller islands of Micronesia.

North of the equator and west of the international date line, Guam is a high island with coral reefs off its coast. Rolling hills and cliffs border the sea. The cliffs are tunneled with caves.

Agana (*ah GAN yah*) is the capital and largest town. Its museum has sections dedicated to island culture, natural history, and the Japanese soldier who hid in the caves until 1972, unaware that World War II was over.

French Polynesia

Acclaimed as some of the Pacific's most beautiful islands, the 118 islands of French Polynesia are south of the equator on the eastern side of the international date line, scattered over an area the size of western Europe. Most are high islands protected by encircling coral reefs. The islands are an overseas territory of France. They are divided into five archipelagos: the Australs,

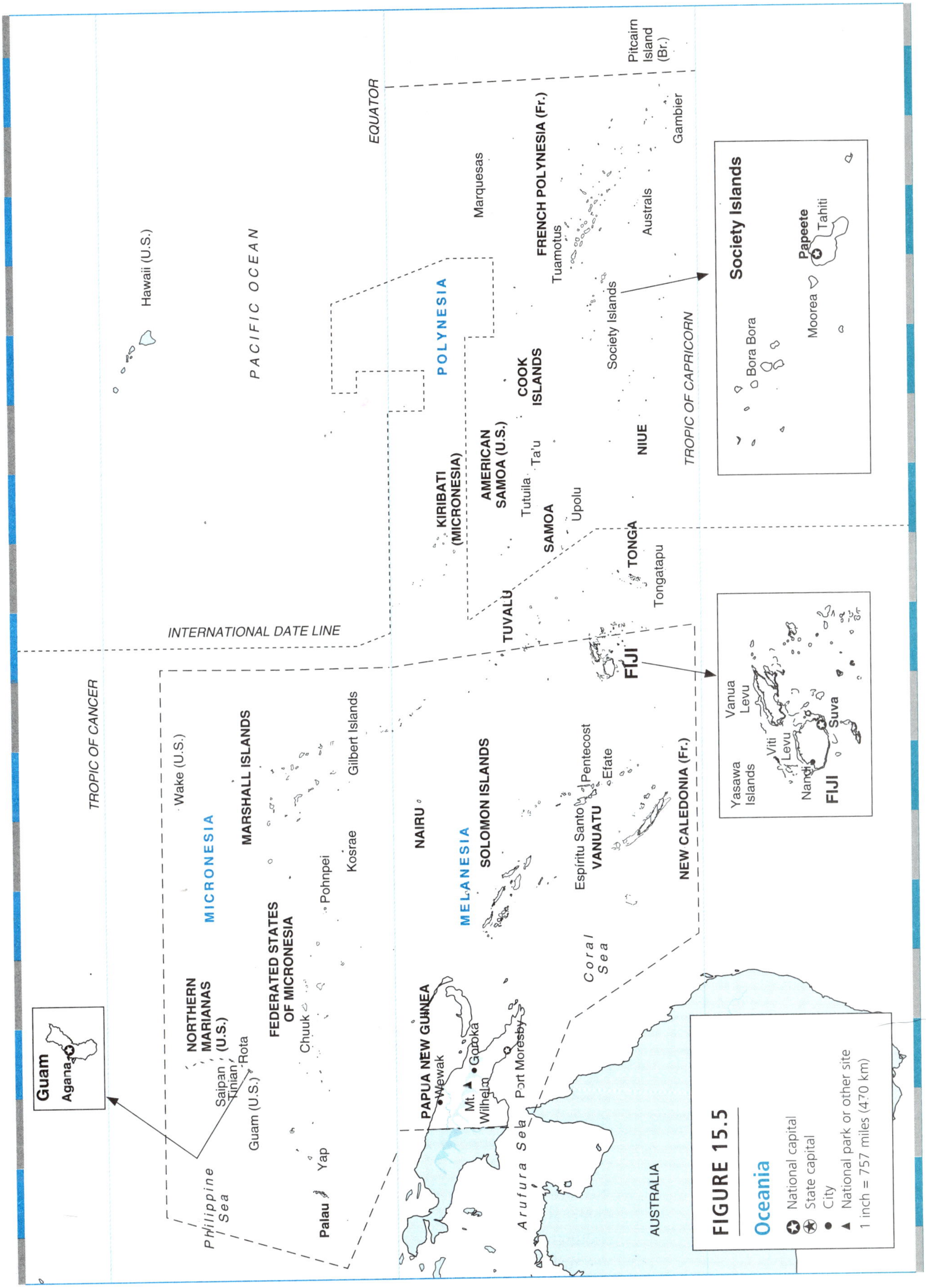
FIGURE 15.5
Oceania
National capital
State capital
City
National park or other site
1 inch = 757 miles (470 km)
PACIFIC OCEAN
TROPIC OF CANCER
EQUATOR
TROPIC OF CAPRICORN
INTERNATIONAL DATE LINE
MICRONESIA
MELANESIA
POLYNESIA
Hawaii (U.S.)
Wake (U.S.)
MARSHALL ISLANDS
NORTHERN MARIANAS (U.S.)
Saipan
Tinian
Rota
Guam (U.S.)
Guam
Agana
FEDERATED STATES OF MICRONESIA
Chuuk
Pohnpei
Kosrae
Yap
Palau
Philippine Sea
Gilbert Islands
NAURU
KIRIBATI (MICRONESIA)
PAPUA NEW GUINEA
Wewak
Mt. Wilhelm
Goroka
Port Moresby
Arafura Sea
Coral Sea
AUSTRALIA
SOLOMON ISLANDS
VANUATU
Espíritu Santo
Pentecost
Efate
NEW CALEDONIA (Fr.)
TUVALU
FIJI
Yasawa Islands
Vanua Levu
Viti Levu
Nandi
Suva
TONGA
Tongatapu
SAMOA
Upolu
AMERICAN SAMOA (U.S.)
Tutuila
Ta'u
NIUE
COOK ISLANDS
FRENCH POLYNESIA (Fr.)
Marquesas
Tuamotus
Society Islands
Australs
Gambier
Pitcairn Island (Br.)
Society Islands
Bora Bora
Moorea
Papeete
Tahiti

Bora Bora, French Polynesia

Gambier (*GAN bee ay*), Marquesas (*mahr KAY suhz*), Society Islands, and Tuamotus. Most tourism is to the Society Islands.

Tahiti (*tuh HEE tee*) in the Society Islands is French Polynesia's largest island, and about 70 percent of the people live there. **Papeete** (*pa pay EH tay*) on Tahiti is the territory's capital, chief port, and gateway to the other islands. It is a modern town with office buildings, big hotels, French restaurants, nightclubs, boutiques, and traffic jams. Nonstop flights connect Los Angeles to Papeete in seven and a half hours.

Moorea, Tahiti's heart-shaped sister island, is visible across the bay from Papeete. It is accessible on a 30-minute ferry trip or by interisland air. Moorea is the laid-back South Sea isle of the brochures. The island offers white-sand beaches, lush volcanic peaks, and a broad blue-green lagoon. Many of the hotels are clusters of thatched-roof bungalows with rooms built over the waters of the lagoon. Room service is delivered by canoe.

A volcano surrounded by a blue lagoon encircled by a reef, **Bora Bora** is everyone's idea of what a South Pacific island should be. This Society Island northwest of Papeete is connected by small plane (a 45-minute flight) and local boat services. From the island's luxury resorts, diving is popular throughout the year; the best diving conditions occur between April and November.

✔ CHECK-UP

Islands of interest to travelers include

- ✔ Fiji in Melanesia; its capital is Suva on the island of Viti Levu.
- ✔ Guam in Micronesia; Agana is the capital and largest town.
- ✔ French Polynesia; Papeete on Tahiti is the capital.

Highlights of a trip to Oceania are

- ✔ Watching firewalkers and sipping yagona in Fiji.
- ✔ Visiting the beautiful islands of French Polynesia.

Planning the Trip

Australia and New Zealand are ideal destinations for North Americans whether they are traveling independently or on an escorted tour. Tour wholesalers provide packages that include air travel, transfers, and accommodations.

When to Go

Considering the reversal of seasons, the best time to visit Australia and New Zealand is the region's spring or fall. Trekkers, divers, and skiers all have their special season. Accommodations may be hard to find, however, when Aussies and Kiwis themselves go traveling during school holidays. These are staggered state by state, but the rush periods are in May, from August to September, and from mid-December to the beginning of February. In New Zealand, reservations are advisable from December to Easter, the local summer holiday period.

In Fiji, the weather is warm and pleasant year-round. The best time to visit is from June to October, when the southeast trade winds prevail. Guam also offers endless summer, but it is located in the breeding grounds of Pacific typhoons. Storm season is June to November. In French Polynesia, the climate is somewhat cooler and drier from May to October. January to April coincides with the hurricane season.

Preparing the Traveler

Travelers should be warned that this region has documentation requirements. They should check current requirements and also should check their insurance. Some policies are invalid if the person engages in any "dangerous activities" such as scuba diving, parasailing, surfing, bungee-jumping, or even riding a motor scooter.

Health Australia and New Zealand have no special health problems unless the visitor goes to isolated areas. Australia's hazards start with the threat of too much sun. Snakes and spiders lurk in many places, and bathers must beware of sharks and, in certain seasons and areas, dangerous jellyfish.

For visitors to the South Seas, food, humidity, and other conditions may tax the system. It is always wise to ask locally if any health precautions need to be observed.

Money Departure taxes collected at the airport in local currencies are fairly common in the region. Travelers should ask about them before they spend all their local currency.

In Australia and New Zealand, credit cards and traveler's checks are commonly accepted, but their use may be restricted in small towns. ATMs are available in the cities. To avoid bank fees, travelers should consider taking checks in pounds sterling.

The resorts of Oceania accept credit cards, but travelers should be prepared to use cash in local restaurants and small shops. Guam uses the U.S. dollar as its currency, and ATMs are widely available.

Language Most everyone speaks English down under, so language is not an issue—unless some Aussie or Kiwi accent causes you to concentrate a bit harder. Accents tend to indicate class rather than region.

The official language of Fiji is English. Although other languages are spoken, travelers should have no trouble. In Guam, English and Chamorro are the official languages, and Japanese is widely spoken. French is the language of French Polynesia as well as native languages; in places where the people are not accustomed to dealing with Americans, tourists might have difficulty communicating.

Transportation

Travelers need to be reminded of Australia's great size. The trip between Sydney and Brisbane takes 1 hour, 15 minutes by air; 16 hours, 30 minutes by car; and 16 hours by train.

By Air Major airlines serve Australia, New Zealand, and the larger islands of the Pacific. Small planes are used to reach the Australian Outback and to travel among Oceania's islands.

➤ PROFILE

Cuisine of the Pacific

In Australia and New Zealand, fish and meat, especially lamb, play a large part in the diet. In the islands, the diet emphasizes fish and native plants. Travelers might like to try

- In Australia: crocodile steaks or an Aboriginal delicacy, *witchetty grubs* cooked over an open fire. A favorite dessert is a meringue pie called *Pavlova*, named after a Russian ballerina who visited. Australian wines are especially fine.
- In New Zealand: lamb and more lamb and real cream. *Vegemite* and *marmite*, salty spreads made from yeast extract, are used like peanut butter and show up in the jam basket at breakfast.
- In Oceania: breadfruit, kumara (a form of sweet potato), dozens of varieties of bananas, exotic fruits, and various starchy root crops such as taro, tarua, and ufi.

➤ PROFILE

Shopping Opportunities of the Pacific

The region is known more for its crafts than for its upscale shopping. Some items people like to bring home include

- From Australia: opals, wool, leather, and sheepskin products. The Northern Territory is a good place to find authentic boomerangs, *didjeridoos* (wind instruments made from tree trunks hollowed out by termites), and Aboriginal art.
- From New Zealand: by-products of the sheep industry converted into everything imaginable; hand-carved Maori tiki pendants and paperweights.
- From Oceania: love sticks, tapa cloth, and shell jewelry; colorful pareus from Polynesia. Primitive art from Papua New Guinea is prized but difficult to obtain.

The Australian Immigration Service allows travel agents to issue electronic visas using the Web. Visit www.immi.gov.au for current information.

Australia has more than 400 airports, but most flights from North America go to Sydney. The average flight time to Sydney is 14 hours from Los Angeles and 25 hours or more from New York, depending on the route. Many tours stop in Fiji one way and Tahiti the other way to break the long flight.

Auckland and Christchurch are the air gateways to New Zealand. The approximate flying time from Los Angeles to Auckland is 12 hours, 45 minutes.

By Water Australian and New Zealand ports are on the itineraries of a number of cruise lines. Within Australia, short cruises on the Murray River are popular. Fiji and Tahiti are port stops on Pacific cruises. Apra Harbor on Guam is the principal port of Micronesia and a destination for cruises from Japan.

By Rail The Australian rail network spans the continent, with many routes of great interest. Each state has its own train company and its own gauge (width of track). Reservations for seats and sleeping berths are essential on all long-distance trains.

The *Great South Pacific Express* operates between Cairns and Brisbane, with the option of continuing south to Sydney. Like a cruise ship, the Express mixes transportation with land excursions, which might include trips to a rain forest and the Great Barrier Reef.

The *Indian Pacific Express* runs from Sydney to Perth, crossing the Nullarbor Plain, where there is scarcely a speck of greenery. The line boasts the world's longest straight stretch of track, almost 310 miles (500 km) without a hint of a curve. The trip takes three days and three nights.

Another historic train is the *Ghan,* named for the camel drivers from Afghanistan who originally explored the Outback. The federally administered railway runs from Port Augusta, north of Adelaide, through the Simpson Desert to Alice Springs and on to Darwin. The transcontinental service began in 2004 when the refurbished Ghan left on its 47-hour, 1,860-mile (2,993 km) journey. The extension of the railway line from Alice Springs north to Darwin has been called one of Australia's greatest engineering and construction feats.

In New Zealand, TranzRail Ltd. operates reliable service and offers many very scenic routes. There is only one class of service.

ON THE SPOT

Mr. and Mrs. Nagelmacker are railroad fans. In *Condé Nast Traveler*, they read about the train called the Great South Pacific Express, which operates from Cairns to Brisbane in Australia. They are interested in traveling on the train but are concerned that if they do they would miss seeing the Great Barrier Reef, a principal reason to travel to northeast Australia. What can you tell them?

Condé Nast Traveler listed the train as one of the "hot new hotels" of the world. Like a hotel, the train mixes accommodations with sightseeing, including a helicopter flight over the Whitsunday Islands to a pontoon platform anchored in a channel of the Great Barrier Reef. The train trip would benefit the Nagelmackers by combining accommodations, transportation, and sightseeing along with their love of railroading.

By Road Driving in Australia, New Zealand, and Fiji is on the left. In Guam and French Polynesia, driving is on the right.

Motoring in Australia's Outback requires special care. Minor roads are unpaved, and a four-wheel-drive vehicle is essential off the beaten track. Water, fuel, a repair kit, and spare parts are necessities. Hazards include stray sheep, cattle, and kangaroos, as well as "road trains" (trucks pulling multitrailers).

Renting a car in New Zealand makes good sense. The islands are compact, and outside the metropolitan areas, traffic congestion is of no special concern. Roads, although mostly two-lane, have good surfaces. Motorist services are available. Oil company credit cards are not accepted, however.

On the islands, travelers can rent cars, scooters, or bicycles. On Tahiti, the basic form of public transportation is *Le Truck*, a brightly painted, open-sided truck with benchlike seats.

Renting a camper is a popular way to view New Zealand, but bringing your own camping equipment is not allowed. A nasty pest could sneak in on the folds of a sleeping bag. In a country highly dependent on agriculture, pests are a disaster.

Accommodations

Accommodations in Australia and New Zealand range from five-star palaces to austere economy-class rooms. New Zealand has a network of deluxe wilderness lodges in beautiful settings. In the 1990s, the Huka Lodge near Taupo on North Island welcomed Queen Elizabeth II and the Duke of Edinburgh.

The islands have some lovely resorts, exclusive private hideaways for upscale clients. In French Polynesia, resorts have followed the island style and built thatched-roof bungalows, called *farés*. Several are built over the water with windows in the floor to provide guests with light from the lagoon and endless fascination. On Fiji, the thatched-roof cabins are called *burés* (*BOO rays*). In Guam, modern hotels line the beaches.

✔ CHECK-UP

Planning a trip to Australia, New Zealand, and Oceania involves

- ✔ Remembering the reversal of seasons in the Southern Hemisphere.
- ✔ Checking documentation needs. The region has great variation.
- ✔ Reading the fine print in a travel insurance policy.

Travelers seeking something different might enjoy

- ✔ Rail trip across Australia.
- ✔ Accommodations in a *faré* over the water in Bora Bora.

OTHER DESTINATIONS IN OCEANIA

Other islands of Oceania offer a variety of soft and hard adventures. But if travelers do not love the ocean and the sun or cannot leave their Western ways behind and slow down, these islands are not for them. Travel to these islands is usually by small plane or ship.

MELANESIA

Melanesia includes high islands in the western Pacific. (Look again at Figure 15.5.) Besides Fiji, Papua New Guinea (PNG) and Vanuatu receive the most visitors, but North American visitors are few.

Papua New Guinea (PNG) An anthropologist's paradise, PNG consists of the eastern half of the island of New Guinea (the other half is Indonesia's Irian Jaya) plus the island of Bougainville and the Bismarck Archipelago. It lies north of northeastern Australia, just south of the equator. **Port Moresby** on the southeast coast is the capital and largest city.

PNG is a high island, very high. Its tallest mountain, **Mount Wilhelm**, is the tallest mountain in the South Pacific. Volcanoes line the north coast, tropical forests cover 80 percent of the land, and mangrove swamps are common in coastal areas.

PNG is a last frontier for travelers. For centuries the Sepik River has been the only road into the interior. Small boat cruises on the Sepik pass by villages with A-frame spirit houses (*haus tambaran*), once used solely by men as a place to speak to their ancestors. Many collectors consider the Sepik basin the world's best source of primitive art. **Wewak** on the north coast is the Sepik's gateway.

The Eastern Highlands have the longest history of contact with the West. The largest town is **Goroka**. Once a year, tribes gather there for a *sing-sing*, an extravaganza of song and dance. Performers wear headdresses of bird-of-paradise plumes, fur neckpieces, shell jewelry, and body paint in bright yellow, blue, and red.

Vanuatu The Republic of Vanuatu (*vah noo AH too*) has thirteen main islands and dozens of smaller ones, forming a Y-shaped archipelago. West of Fiji, they are south of the equator and west of the international date line. Most of the islands are mountainous and volcanic in origin, with coral beaches and offshore reefs. The main islands are Espíritu Santo and Efate, site of the capital, Port-Vila.

In April and May, men on **Pentecost Island** perform the ritual leap (*Naghol*) to ensure a bountiful yam harvest. The ceremony was recently opened to the public for a fee. Performers tie liana vines to their ankles and leap from a rickety tower, falling head first. Each diver carefully selects his vines, calculating the exact length so that his head just brushes the ground at the end of the jump—bungee-jumping in its original form.

According to legend, land diving on Vanuatu began when a woman trying to escape her abusive husband climbed a big tree. He followed her, and when he nearly caught her, she jumped. He jumped after her, not realizing that she had tied vines around her ankles to break her fall. Today, only men have the right to land-dive.

MICRONESIA

Micronesia's tiny bits of land are low coral islands in the Pacific north of the equator. Their beautiful beaches, diving opportunities, good airstrips, and proximity have made them popular among Asian travelers. After Guam, the islands of Micronesia most visited by North Americans are the Northern Marianas and the Federated States of Micronesia.

Northern Marianas The Northern Marianas stretch from Guam almost to Japan. They are the weathered tops of a mountain range rising from the depths of the Marianas Trench, the deepest of the ocean's canyons.

The largest islands—and the ones with airstrips—are **Saipan** (*sigh PAN*), **Rota**, and **Tinian** (*tin ee AN*). Susupe (*sue sue PAY*) on Saipan is the capital and largest settlement. The islands played an important role in World War II. The *Enola Gay* left from Tinian's airfield for Hiroshima carrying the first atomic bomb. Today, luxurious hotels and casinos line beautiful beaches, and more than 85 percent of the visitors are from Japan or Korea.

Federated States of Micronesia (FSM) The Federated States of Micronesia consist of four states—**Pohnpei**, **Chuuk** (or Truk), **Yap**, and **Kosrae**—that are island groups spread out across 2,000 miles (3,220 km) of ocean. They are about halfway between Australia and Japan. Their landscape varies from high mountains to low coral atolls. The United States controlled the islands from 1945 to 1986. The islands now have self-government, but the United States retains responsibility for the country's defense. Palikir on the island of Pohnpei is the capital.

Falus are the islands' native houses. The shelters rest on stone foundations and are open-sided to allow the trade winds to sweep through.

Rich marine life attracts divers to FSM, but poor infrastructure and the country's remoteness hinder the development of tourism. Tourists come to Chuuk to scuba-dive among its lagoon's sixty wartime wrecks, the world's largest collection of sunken ships.

In Yap, visitors can see stone money, large donut-shaped discs of limestone. Even today, the discs are conspicuously displayed against the outside walls of their owners' houses. Women wear grass skirts, and men and women chew betel nuts, which produce a mild high. Most tourists come to Yap to swim with the giant manta rays.

On Pohnpei, Nan Madol is a series of artificial islets built on tidal flats and reefs connected by canals. Nan Madol may have served as a ceremonial center, a royal residence, or both. It was in use during the 12th century. Visitors must approach by motorboat or kayak.

A Micronesian man would carve a stick with symbols that a woman would recognize as his. At night this love stick was pushed through the walls of the woman's thatched house. If she pulled on the stick, it meant yes, come in. If she pushed it out, it meant no. Concrete construction has discouraged the tradition.

POLYNESIA

The islands of Polynesia occupy the South Pacific's largest area. In addition to French Polynesia, Tonga and Samoa are the islands most visited by tourists.

Tonga Located in the southwest Pacific, Tonga (*TAHNG guh*) is a double chain of islands to the east of Fiji. Situated just west of the international date line and south of the equator, Tonga claims to be the first country to greet each new day. Nuku'alofa (*noo koo uh LO fuh*) on Tongatapu Island is the capital.

Tonga was a British protectorate for many years but gained independence in 1970. It is a constitutional monarchy, the only kingdom remaining in the Pacific. The

Royal Palace in Nuku'alofa is a white wooden mansion with Victorian-style spires and turrets completed in 1867.

Cruise ships call on Tonga. White-sand beaches and reef-protected lagoons offer plentiful water sports. Resorts built to resemble island houses provide accommodations.

Tapa cloth made from the bark of the mulberry tree is a favorite Tonga souvenir. The bark is soaked and pounded with a wooden mallet on a log. The tap-tap-tap sound gives the cloth its name.

The Samoas North of Tonga but south of the equator and east of the international date line are the Samoas. Erupting volcanoes formed these high islands, but volcanic activity has not occurred since 1911. The islands' shores are lined with palm trees, and tropical rain forests cover the mountains.

In the 1830s, Britain, Germany, and the United States vied to control the islands. The United States took the seven eastern islands that today make up **American Samoa**. Germany took control of the western islands but lost them after World War II. Western Samoa became independent in 1962 and changed its name to **Samoa** in 1997. Its capital is Apia on the island of Upolu.

Samoa's landmarks include Aggie Grey's Hotel in Apia—frequented over the years by countless writers, movie stars, poets, and adventurers—and Vailima, the house of the author Robert Louis Stevenson (1850–1894). Natives called him *tusitala*—teller of tales.

Among the islands of American Samoa, Tutuila is the largest and most important. Pago Pago (*PAHNG oh PAHNG oh*) on Tutuila is the capital. It has one of the South Pacific's most beautiful harbors. American Samoa's people are U.S. nationals, but not citizens. The islands are under the control of the Department of the Interior.

Blessed with spectacular scenery and a delightful climate, American Samoa is the most southerly of all lands under U.S. sovereignty. Guests often hear the expression *fa'a Samoa*—the relaxed "Samoan way." Visitors who seek complete relaxation can take local flights or interisland boats to untouched islands.

CHAPTER WRAP-UP

SUMMARY

Here is a review of the objectives with which we began the chapter.

1. **Describe the environment and people of Australia, New Zealand, and Oceania.** Australia is the smallest and flattest of the seven continents. Its geographic regions contain interesting animals and terrain. In the center of the country is Uluru, the world's largest single rock.

   New Zealand's mainland is separated into North and South Island by narrow Cook Strait. North Island is the more populous; South Island is home to Mount Cook, the Tasman Glacier, Sutherland Falls, and Fiordland. New Zealand's natives, the Maori, mostly live on North Island around Rotorua.

   Oceania is divided into three sections: Melanesia, Micronesia (north of the equator), and Polynesia. Thousands of islands are spread across the ocean. Some are flat atolls with palm trees and white-sand beaches; others have thick jungles and tall mountain peaks.

   Except for the islands of Micronesia, the region is south of the equator, and the seasons are reversed from those of North America. Climate varies from the arid interior of the Australian Outback to the lush fiord lands of South Island, New Zealand.

2. **Identify and locate the region's main attractions.** Australia's attractions include its beautiful beaches, the Great Barrier Reef off the northeast coast,

Sydney in the southeast, the Outback in the continent's center, an underground opal-mining town called Coober Pedy in the south center, and the landscape and Aboriginal culture at Kakadu National Park in the north.

New Zealand's attractions on North Island are the city of Auckland; the region around Rotorua, with its Maori culture and glowworm caverns; and Wellington, the capital. South Island's top attractions are Mount Cook, Queenstown in the south center, and Fiordland National Park in the southwest coastal area.

The beaches, diving opportunities, and relaxed lifestyle of just about any island in Oceania are attractions. Fiji, Guam, and French Polynesia have the most developed tourism infrastructure.

3. **Match travelers and destinations best suited for each other.** Australia has something for just about everyone but is probably best suited to those with a spirit of adventure and an enjoyment of the open attitudes of the Australian people. Divers and trekkers would be happy with the reef and rain forests, while history fans would enjoy learning about the Aboriginal culture.

   New Zealand appeals to those who enjoy scenic beauty and those who might want to get right in the middle of it all by trekking through Milford Sound, flightseeing over Tasman Glacier, or jet boating on the many rivers.

   Oceania appeals to those who want to enjoy the beauty and water sport opportunities of the region. The resorts of Bora Bora would have great appeal for honeymooners and romantics of any age.

4. **Provide or find the information needed to plan a trip to the region.** The reversal of seasons, the distances, and the documentation requirements involved in trips to the region need to be kept in mind. Good sources of information include the tourist boards of Australia and New Zealand, which maintain Web sites that can answer just about every question.

QUESTIONS FOR DISCUSSION AND REVIEW

1. What geographic factors have strongly influenced life and culture in Australia, New Zealand, and the islands of the Pacific?

2. What problems face promoters of Australia and New Zealand, and how can these problems be overcome?

3. What are the three major island groups that make up Oceania, and how can you distinguish one from the other?

4. How does the international date line affect travel to the region?

APPENDIX
A

Fact File

United States
Area 3,618,765 sq. miles (9,372,610 sq. km)
Capital Washington, D.C. (DCA/Reagan National)
Government Federal republic
Population 294,043,000
Population density 83 per sq. mile
Local divisions 50 states and District of Columbia
Languages English and many others
Currency U.S. dollar
Time zones GMT –5, –6, –7, –8, –9, –10

Alabama
Area 52,419 sq. miles
Capital Montgomery (MGM)
Nicknames Heart of Dixie; Camellia State

Alaska
Area 663,267 sq. miles
Capital Juneau (JNU)
Nickname The Last Frontier

Arizona
Area 113,998 sq. miles
Capital Phoenix (PHX)
Nickname Grand Canyon State

Arkansas
Area 53,179 sq. miles
Capital Little Rock (LIT)
Nickname Razorback State

California
Area 163,696 sq. miles
Capital Sacramento (SMF)
Nickname Golden State

Colorado
Area 104,094 sq. miles
Capital Denver (DEN)
Nickname Centennial State

Connecticut
Area 5,543 sq. miles
Capital Hartford (HFD)
Nicknames Constitution State; Nutmeg State

Delaware
Area 2,489 sq. miles
Capital Dover (use Philadelphia PHL)
Nicknames First State; Diamond State

Florida
Area 65,755 sq. miles
Capital Tallahassee (THL)
Nickname Sunshine State

Georgia
Area 59,424 sq. miles
Capital Atlanta (ATL)
Nicknames Peach State; Empire State of the South

Hawaii
Area 6,459 sq. miles
Capital Honolulu (HNL)
Nickname Aloha State

Idaho
Area 83,570 sq. miles
Capital Boise (BOI)
Nickname Gem State

Illinois
Area 57,914 sq. miles
Capital Springfield
Nickname Prairie State

Indiana
Area 36,418 sq. miles
Capital Indianapolis (IND)
Nickname Hoosier State

Iowa
Area 56,272 sq. miles
Capital Des Moines (DSM)
Nickname Hawkeye State

Kansas
Area 82,277 sq. miles
Capital Topeka (FOE)
Nickname Sunflower State

Kentucky
Area 40,409 sq. miles
Capital Frankfort (FFT)
Nickname Bluegrass State

Louisiana
Area 51,840 sq. miles
Capital Baton Rouge (BTR)
Nickname Pelican State

Maine
Area 35,385 sq. miles
Capital Augusta (AUG)
Nickname Pine Tree State

Maryland
Area 12,407 sq. miles
Capital Annapolis (use Baltimore BWI)
Nicknames Old Line State; Free State

Massachusetts
Area 10,555 sq. miles
Capital Boston (BOS)
Nicknames Bay State; Old Colony

Michigan
Area 96,716 sq. miles
Capital Lansing (LAN)
Nicknames Great Lakes State; Wolverine State

Minnesota
Area 86,939 sq. miles
Capital St. Paul (MSP)
Nickname North Star State; Gopher State

Mississippi
Area 48,430 sq. miles
Capital Jackson (JAN)
Nickname Magnolia State

Missouri
Area 69,704 sq. miles
Capital Jefferson City
Nickname Show Me State

Montana
Area 147,042 sq. miles
Capital Helena (HNL)
Nickname Treasure State

Nebraska
Area 77,354 sq. miles
Capital Lincoln (LNK)
Nickname Cornhusker State

Nevada
Area 110,561 sq. miles
Capital Carson City (use Reno RNO)
Nicknames Sagebrush State; Silver State

New Hampshire
Area 9,350 sq. miles
Capital Concord (CON)
Nickname Granite State

New Jersey
Area 8,721 sq. miles
Capital Trenton (use Newark EWR)
Nickname Garden State

New Mexico
Area 121,589 sq. miles
Capital Santa Fe (use Albuquerque ABQ)
Nickname Land of Enchantment

New York
Area 54,556 sq. miles
Capital Albany (ALB)
Nickname Empire State

North Carolina
Area 58,819 sq. miles
Capital Raleigh (RDU)
Nicknames Tar Heel State; Old North State

North Dakota
Area 70,700 sq. miles
Capital Bismarck (BIS)
Nickname Peace Garden State

Ohio
Area 44,825 sq. miles
Capital Columbus (CMH)
Nickname Buckeye State

Oklahoma
Area 69,898 sq. miles
Capital Oklahoma City (OKC)
Nickname Sooner State

Oregon
Area 98,381 sq. miles
Capital Salem (use Portland PDX)
Nickname Beaver State

Pennsylvania
Area 46,055 sq. miles
Capital Harrisburg (use Philadelphia PHL)
Nickname Keystone State

Rhode Island
Area 1,545 sq. miles
Capital Providence (PRO)
Nicknames Ocean State; Little Rhody

South Carolina
Area 32,020 sq. miles
Capital Columbia (CAE)
Nickname Palmetto State

South Dakota
Area 77,116 sq. miles
Capital Pierre (PIR)
Nicknames Coyote State; Mount Rushmore State

Tennessee
Area 42,143 sq. miles
Capital Nashville (BNA)
Nickname Volunteer State

Texas
Area 268,581 sq. miles
Capital Austin (AUS)
Nickname Lone Star State

Utah
Area 84,899 sq. miles
Capital Salt Lake City (SLC)
Nickname Beehive State

Vermont
Area 9,614 sq. miles
Capital Montpelier (use Burlington BTV)
Nickname Green Mountain State

Virginia
Area 42,774 sq. miles
Capital Richmond (RIC)
Nickname Old Dominion

Washington
Area 71,300 sq. miles
Capital Olympia (OLM)
Nickname Evergreen State

West Virginia
Area 24,230 sq. miles
Capital Charleston (CRW)
Nickname Mountain State

Wisconsin
Area 65,498 sq. miles
Capital Madison (MSN)
Nickname Badger State

Wyoming
Area 97,814 sq. miles
Capital Cheyenne (CYS)
Nicknames Cowboy State; Equality State

Canada
Area 3,851,788 sq. miles (9,976,140 sq. km)
Capital Ottawa (YOW)
Government Confederation with parliamentary democracy
Population 31,510,000 (2001 census)
Population density 9 per sq. mile
Languages Officially bilingual: English and French
Currency Canadian dollar
Time zones GMT –3.5, –4, –5, –6, –7, –8

Alberta
Area 246,422 sq. miles (638,232 sq. km)
Capital Edmonton (YEG)
Language Primarily English
Time zone GMT –7

British Columbia
Area 344,663 sq. miles (892,677 sq. km)
Capital Victoria (YYJ)
Languages Primarily English, many Asian languages
Time zone GMT –8

Manitoba
Area 211,468 sq. miles (547,703 sq. km)
Capital Winnepeg (YWG)
Language Primarily English
Time zone GMT –6

New Brunswick
Area 27,633 sq. miles (71,569 sq. km)
Capital Fredericton (YFC)
Languages English and French
Time zone GMT –4

Newfoundland and Labrador
Area 156,649 sq. miles (393,189 sq. km)
Capital St. John's (YYT)
Languages 95 percent speak English, 5 percent speak French
Time zones Newfoundland, GMT –3.5; Labrador, GMT –4

Northwest Territories
Area 503,951 sq. miles (1,305,233 sq. km)
Capital Yellowknife (YZF)
Language Primarily English
Time zone West of 102°W, GMT –8

Nova Scotia
Area 20,402 sq. miles (52,840 sq. km)
Capital Halifax (YHZ)
Languages Primarily English, some French
Time zone GMT –4

Nunavut
Area 818,959 sq. miles (2,121,104 sq. km)
Capital Iqaluit (YFB)
Languages Inuktitut, also English
Time zones GMT –6, –7, –8

Ontario
Area 353,951 sq. miles (916,733 sq. km)
Capital Toronto (YYZ)
Languages Primarily English, also French
Time zone GMT –5

Québec
Area 524,251 sq. miles (1,357,811 sq. km)
Capital Québec City (YQB)
Language Primarily French
Time zone GMT –5

Prince Edward Island
Area 2,185 sq. miles (5,660 sq. km)
Capital Charlottetown (YYG)
Languages Primarily English, also French
Time zone GMT –4

Saskatchewan
Area 220,121 sq. miles (570,113 sq. km)
Capital Regina (YQR)
Language Primarily English
Time zone GMT –6

Yukon Territories
Area 186,661 sq. miles (483,452 sq. km)
Capital Whitehorse (YXZ)
Language Primarily English
Time zone GMT –8

Bermuda and the West Indies

Anguilla (Leeward Islands)
Area 35 sq. miles (91 sq. km)
Capital The Valley (AXA)
Government Self-governing British dependency
Population 11,407
Population density 326 per sq. mile
Language English
Currency East Caribbean dollar
Time zone GMT –4

Antigua and Barbuda (Leeward Islands)
Area 171 sq. miles (443 sq. km)
Capital Saint Johns (ANU)
Government Constitutional monarchy
Population 67,897
Population density 400 per sq. mile
Language English
Currency East Caribbean dollar
Time zone GMT –4

Aruba (one of the ABCs)
Area 69 sq. miles (179 sq. km)
Capital Oranjestad (AUA)
Government Self-governing part of the Netherlands
Population 68,675
Population density 995 per sq. mile
Languages Dutch, English, Spanish, Papiamento
Currency Euro, U.S. dollar
Time zone GMT –4

Bahamas (southeast of Florida)
Area 5,386 sq. miles (13,950 sq. km)
Capital Nassau (NAS)
Government Independent commonwealth
Population 314,000
Population density 58 per sq. mile
Language English
Currency Bahamian dollar
Time zone GMT –5

Barbados (most easterly of the Windwards)
Area 166 sq. miles (430 sq. km)
Capital Bridgetown (BGI)
Government Parliamentary democracy
Population 270,000
Population density 1,626 per sq. mile
Language English
Currency Barbadian dollar
Time zone GMT –4

Bermuda (in the Atlantic Ocean)
Area 20 sq. mi (52 sq. km)
Capital Hamilton (BDA)
Government Self-governing British dependency
Population 64,482
Population density 3,224 per sq. mile
Language English
Currency Bermudian dollar
Time zone GMT –4

Bonaire (one of the ABCs)
Area 111 sq. miles (287 sq. km)
Capital Kralendijk (BON)
Government Part of the Netherlands Antilles
Population 14,190
Population density 128 per sq. mile
Languages Dutch, Papiamento, English
Currency Euro
Time zone GMT –4

British Virgin Islands (Leeward Islands)
Area 59 sq. miles (153 sq. km)
Capital Road Town (EIS)
Government Self-governing British dependency
Population 21,730
Population density 368 per sq. mile
Language English
Currency U.S. dollar
Time zone GMT –4

Cayman Islands (Greater Antilles)
Area 100 sq. miles (260 sq. km)
Capital Georgetown (GCM)
Government Self-governing British dependency
Population 41,934
Population density 419 per sq. mile
Language English
Currency Caymanian dollar, U.S. dollar
Time zone GMT –5

Cuba (Greater Antilles)
Area 41,620 sq. miles (107,800 sq. km)
Capital Havana (HAV)
Government Communist state
Population 11,300,000
Population density 272 per sq. mile
Language Spanish
Currency Cuban peso
Time zone GMT –5

Curaçao (one of the ABCs)
Area 182 sq. miles (471 sq. km)
Capital Willemstad (CUR)
Government Part of the Netherlands Antilles
Population 152,700
Population density 839 per sq. mile
Languages Dutch, English
Currency Euro
Time zone GMT –4

Dominica (Leeward Islands)
Area 289 sq. miles (749 sq. km)
Capital Roseau (DOM)
Government Parliamentary democracy
Population 70,000
Population density 242 per sq. mile
Language English
Currency East Caribbean dollar
Time zone GMT –4

Dominican Republic (Greater Antilles)
Area 18,657 sq. miles (48,322 sq. km)
Capital Santo Domingo (SDQ)
Government Republic
Population 8,745,000
Population density 469 per sq. mile
Language Spanish
Currency Peso
Time zone GMT –4

Grenada (Windward Islands)
Area 120 sq. miles (311 sq. km)
Capital St. George's (GND)
Government Constitutional monarchy
Population 89,000
Population density 742 per sq. mile
Language English
Currency East Caribbean dollar
Time zone GMT –4

Guadeloupe (Leeward Islands)
Area 582 sq. miles (1,507 sq. km)
Capital Basse-Terre (SKB)
Government French overseas department
Population 420,943
Population density 723 per sq. mile
Language French
Currency Euro
Time zone GMT –4

Haiti (Greater Antilles)
Area 10,714 sq. miles (27,749 sq. km)
Capital Port-au-Prince (PAP)
Government Republic
Population 8,326,000
Population density 782 per sq. mile
Language French
Currency Gourd
Time zone GMT –5

Jamaica (Greater Antilles)
Area 4,471 sq. miles (11,580 sq. km)
Capital Kingston (KIN)
Government Parliamentary democracy
Population 2,651,000
Population density 593 per sq. mile
Languages English, Creole
Currency Jamaican dollar
Time zone GMT –5

Martinique (Windward Islands)
Area 425 sq. miles (1,101 sq. km)
Capital Fort-de-France (FDF)
Government French overseas department
Population 411,439
Population density 968 per sq. mile
Language French
Currency Euro, U.S. dollar
Time zone GMT –4

Montserrat (Leeward Islands)
Area 40 sq. miles (104 sq. km)
Capital Plymouth (use St. Martin)
Government Self-governing British dependency
Population 4,000 (after eruption)
Population density 100 per sq. mile
Language English
Currency Eastern Caribbean dollar
Time zone GMT –4

Puerto Rico (Greater Antilles)
Area 3,435 sq. miles (8,897 sq. km)
Capital San Juan (SJU)
Government U.S. commonwealth
Population 3,890,353
Population density 1,133 per sq. mile
Languages Spanish, English
Currency U.S. dollar
Time zone GMT –4

Saba (Leeward Islands)
Area 5 sq. miles (13 sq. km)
Capital The Bottom (use St. Martin)
Government Part of the Netherlands Antilles
Population 1,466
Population density 293 per sq. mile
Languages Dutch, Papiamento, English
Currency Euro
Time zone GMT –4

St. Barthélemy (Leeward Islands)
Area 37 sq. miles (95 sq. km)
Capital Gustavia (SBH)
Government French overseas separtment
Population Included as part of Guadeloupe
Population density See Guadeloupe
Language French
Currency Euro
Time zone GMT –4

St. Eustatius (Leeward Islands)
Area 8 sq. miles (21 sq. km)
Capital Oranjestad (EUX)
Government Part of the Netherlands Antilles
Population 2,609
Population density 326 per sq. mile
Languages Dutch, Papiamento, English
Currency Euro
Time zone GMT –4

St. Kitts and Nevia (Leeward Islands)
Area 104 sq. miles (269 sq. km)
Capital Basseterre (SKB)
Government Constitutional monarchy
Population 39,000
Population density 386 per sq. mile
Languages English, Creole
Currency East Caribbean dollar
Time zone GMT –4

St. Lucia (Windward Islands)
Area 238 sq. miles (616 sq. km)
Capital Castries (SLU and UVF)
Government Constitutional monarchy
Population 149,000
Population density 626 per sq. mile
Languages English, French-based Creole
Currency East Caribbean dollar
Time zone GMT –4

St. Martin (Leeward Islands)
Area 20 sq. miles (52 sq. km)
Capital Philipsburg/Marigot (SXM)
Government French overseas department
Population 25,518
Population density 1276 per sq. mile
Languages Dutch, Papiamento, English
Currency Euro, U.S. dollar
Time zone GMT –4

St. Maarten (Leeward Islands)
Area 13 sq. miles (34 sq. km)
Capital Philipsburg (SXM)
Government Part of the Netherlands Antilles
Population 36,231
Population density 2,787 per sq. mile
Languages Dutch, Papiamento, English
Currency Euro, U.S. dollar
Time zone GMT –4

St. Vincent and the Grenadines (Windward Islands)
Area 150 sq. miles (389 sq. km)
Capital Kingstown (SVD)
Government Constitutional monarchy
Population 120,000
Population density 800 per sq. mile
Language English
Currency East Caribbean dollar
Time zone GMT –4

Trinidad and Tobago (off the Venezuelan Coast)
Area 1,980 sq. miles (5,128 sq. km)
Capital Port of Spain (POS)
Government Independent republic
Population 1,303,000
Population density 658 per sq. mile
Languages English, French, Spanish, Hindi, Chinese
Currency Trinidad and Tobago dollar
Time zone GMT –4

Turks and Caicos (part of the Bahamas Chain)
Area 166 sq. miles (430 sq. km)
Capital Grand Turk (GDT)
Government Self-governing British dependency
Population 19,359
Population density 117 per sq. mile
Languages English, Creole
Currency U.S. dollar
Time zone GMT –5

U.S. Virgin Islands (Leeward Islands)
Area 133 sq. miles (345 sq. km)
Capital Charlotte Amalie (STT)
Government U.S. territory
Population 119,555
Population density 899 per sq. mile
Language English
Currency U.S. dollar
Time zone GMT –4

Mexico and Central America

Mexico
Area 759,530 sq. miles (1,972,544 sq. km)
Capital Mexico City (MEX)
Government Federal republic
Population 103,457,000
Population density 139 per sq. mile
Language Spanish
Currency Mexican peso
Time zones GMT –6, –7, –8
Central America

Belize
Area 8,867 sq. miles (22,966 sq. km)
Capital Belmopan (BZE)
Government Parliamentary democracy
Population 256,000
Population density 29 per sq. mile
Language English
Currency Belize dollar
Time zone GMT –6

Costa Rica
Area 19,652 sq. miles (50,899 sq. km)
Capital San José (SJO)
Government Republic
Population 4,173,000
Population density 212 per sq. mile
Language Spanish
Currency Colón
Time zone GMT –6

El Salvador
Area 8,260 sq. miles (21,393 sq. km)
Capital San Salvador (SAL)
Government Republic
Population 6,515,000
Population density 789 per sq. mile
Language Spanish
Currency Colón
Time zone GMT –6

Guatemala
Area 42,042 sq. miles (108,889 sq. km)
Capital Guatemala City (GUA)
Government Republic
Population 12,347,000
Population density 294 per sq. mile
Language Spanish
Currency Quetzal
Time zone GMT –6

Honduras
Area 43,277 sq. miles (112,087 sq. km)
Capital Tegucigalpa (TGU)
Government Republic
Population 6,941,000
Population density 160 per sq. mile
Language Spanish
Currency Lempira
Time zone GMT –6

Nicaragua
Area 49,579 sq. miles (128,410 sq. km)
Capital Managua (MGA)
Government Republic
Population 5,466,000
Population density 110 per sq. mile
Language Spanish
Currency Córdoba
Time zone GMT –6

Panama
Area 33,659 sq. miles (87,177 sq. km)
Capital Panama City (PTY)
Government Republic
Population 3,120,000
Population density 93 per sq. mile
Language Spanish
Currency Balboa
Time zone GMT –5

South America

Argentina
Area 1,072,156 sq. miles (2,776,884 sq. km)
Capital Buenos Aires (BUE)
Government Federal republic
Population 38,428,000
Population density 36 per sq. mile
Language Spanish
Currency Argentine peso
Time zone GMT –3

Bolivia
Area 424,162 sq. miles (1,098,579 sq. km)
Capitals La Paz (LPB) and Sucre (SRE)
Government Republic
Population 8,808,000
Population density 21 per sq. mile
Languages Spanish, Quechua, Aymara
Currency Boliviano
Time zone GMT –4

Brazil
Area 3,284,426 sq. miles (8,506,663 sq. km)
Capital Brasília (BSB)
Government Federal republic
Population 178,470,000
Population density 5 per sq. mile
Language Portuguese
Currency Real
Time zones GMT –3, –4, –5

Chile
Area 292,257 sq. miles (11,275,440 sq. km)
Capital Santiago (SCL)
Government Republic
Population 15,805,000
Population density 54 per sq. mile
Language Spanish
Currency Chilean peso
Time zone GMT –4

Colombia
Area 439,735 sq. miles (1,138,914 sq. km)
Capital Bogotá (BOG)
Government Republic
Population 44,222,000
Population density 101 per sq. mile
Language Spanish
Currency Colombian peso
Time zone GMT –5

Ecuador
Area 109,483 sq. miles (283,561 sq. km)
Capital Quito (UIO)
Government Republic
Population 13,003,000
Population density 119 per sq. mile
Language Spanish
Currency Sucre
Time zone GMT –5

Falkland Islands (Islas Malvinas)
Area 4,700 sq. miles (12,173 sq. km)
Capital Stanley (MPN)
Government United Kingdom dependency
Population 2,967
Population density 1 per sq. mile
Language English
Currency Falkland Islands pound
Time zone GMT –3

French Guiana
Area 35,126 sq. miles (90,976 sq. km)
Capital Cayenne (CAY)
Government French republic
Population 186,917
Population density 5 per sq. mile
Language Spanish
Currency Euro
Time zone GMT –3

Guyana
Area 83,000 sq. miles (214,970 sq. km)
Capital Georgetown (GED)
Government Republic
Population 765,000
Population density 9 per sq. mile
Languages English, Creole, Hindi, Urdu, Amerindian dialects
Currency Guyana dollar
Time zone GMT –3

Paraguay
Area 157,043 sq. miles (406,741 sq. km)
Capital Asunción (ASU)
Government Republic
Population 5,878,000
Population density 37 per sq. mile
Languages Spanish, Guarani
Currency Guarani
Time zone GMT –4

Peru
Area 496,222 sq. miles (1,285,215 sq. km)
Capital Lima (LIM)
Government Republic
Population 27,167,000
Population density 55 per sq. mile
Languages Spanish, Quechua, Aymara
Currency Nuevo sol
Time zone GMT –5

Suriname
Area 63,251 sq. miles (163,820 sq. km)
Capital Paramaribo (PBM)
Government Republic
Population 436,000
Population density 7 per sq. mile
Languages Dutch, English, Sranang Tongo, Hindustani, Javanese
Currency Suriname guilder, euro
Time zone GMT –3

Uruguay
Area 68,039 sq. miles (176,221 sq. km)
Capital Montevideo (MVD)
Government Republic
Population 3,415,000
Population density 50 per sq. mile
Languages Spanish, Portuguese
Currency Uruguayan peso
Time zone GMT –3

Venezuela
Area 352,143 sq. miles (912,050 sq. km)
Capital Caracas (CCS)
Government Republic
Population 25,699,000
Population density 73 per sq. mile
Languages Spanish, many dialects
Currency Bolivar
Time zone GMT –4

The British Isles

The United Kingdom
Area 94,251 sq. miles (244,110 sq. km)
Capital London (LHR)
Government Constitutional monarchy
Population 59,251,000
Population density 629 per sq. mile
Language English, many local dialects
Currency Pound
Time zone GMT
EU member Yes

England
Area 50,333 sq. miles (130,362 sq. km)
Capital London (Heathrow LHR/Gatwick LGW)
Government Constitutional monarchy
Population 49,752,900
Population density 988 per sq. mile
Language English, with many local dialects

Scotland
Area 30,418 sq. miles (78,133 sq. km)
Capital Edinburgh (EDI)
Government Constitutional monarchy, Scottish Parliament
Population 5,064,000 (2002)
Population density 166 per sq. mile
Languages English, Gaelic

Wales
Area 8,019 sq. miles (20,779 sq. km)
Capital Cardiff (CWL)
Government Constitutional monarchy, Welsh Assembly
Population 2,903,000 (2001)
Population density 362 per sq. mile
Languages Welsh, English

Northern Ireland
Area 5,452 sq. miles (13,576 sq. km)
Capital Belfast (BFS)
Government Constitutional monarchy, home rule
Population 1,663,300 (1996 estimate)
Population density 305 per sq. mile
Languages English, Gaelic

Republic of Ireland
Area 27,135 sq. miles (70,273 sq. km)
Capital Dublin (DUB)
Government Parliamentary republic
Population 3,956,000 (2003)
Population density 146 per sq. mile
Languages English, Irish Gaelic
Currency Euro
Time zone GMT
EU member Yes

Europe

Albania
Area 11,100 sq. miles (28,749 sq. km)
Capital Tiranë (TIA)
Government Republic
Population 3,166,000
Population density 285 per sq. mile
Languages Albanian, Greek
Currency Lek
Time zone GMT +1
EU member No

Principality of Andorra
Area 180 sq. miles (482 sq. km)
Capital Andorra la Vella; use Barcelona (BCN)
Government Co-principality
Population 69,150
Population density 384 per sq. mile
Languages Catalan, Spanish, French
Currency Euro
Time zone GMT +1
EU member With Spain and France

Austria
Area 32,375 sq. miles (83,851 sq. km)
Capital Vienna (VIE)
Government Federal republic
Population 8,116,000
Population density 254 per sq. mile
Language German
Currency Euro
Time zone GMT +1
EU member Yes

Belarus
Area 80,154 sq. miles (207,599 sq. km)
Capital Minsk (MSQ)
Government Republic
Population 9,895,000
Population density 123 per sq. mile
Languages Belarusian, Russian
Currency Ruble
Time zone GMT +3
EU member No

Kingdom of Belgium
Area 11,781 sq. miles (30,513 sq. km)
Capital Brussels (BRU)
Government Constitutional monarchy
Population 10,318,000
Population density 876 per sq. mile
Languages Dutch, French, German
Currency Euro
Time zone GMT +1
EU member Yes

Bosnia-Herzegovina
Area 19,904 sq. miles (51,750 sq. km)
Capital Sarajevo (SJJ)
Government Republic
Population 4,161,000
Population density 209 per sq. mile
Languages Bosnian, Croatian, Serbian
Currency Marka
Time zone GMT +1
EU member No

Bulgaria
Area 42,823 sq. miles (110,912 sq. km)
Capital Sofia (SOF)
Government Republic
Population 7,897,000
Population density 184 per sq. mile
Languages Bulgarian, Turkish
Currency Lev
Time zone GMT +1
EU member No

Croatia
Area 21,829 sq. miles (56,537 sq. km)
Capital Zagreb (ZAG)
Government Democracy
Population 4,428,000
Population density 203 per sq. mile
Languages Croatian, Serbian
Currency Kuna
Time zone GMT +1
EU member No

Cyprus
Area 3,572 sq. miles (9,251 sq. km)
Capital Nicosia (LCA)
Government Republic
Population 802,000
Population density 225 per sq. mile
Languages Greek, Turkish, English
Currency Cyprus pound
Time zone GMT +2
EU member Yes

Czech Republic
Area 30,450 sq. miles (78,866 sq. km)
Capital Prague (PRG)
Government Republic
Population 10,236,000
Population density 336 per sq. mile
Languages Czech, German, Polish, Romani
Currency Koruna
Time zone GMT +1
EU member Yes

Kingdom of Denmark
Area 16,629 sq. miles (43,069 sq. km)
Capital Copenhagen (CPH)
Government Constitutional monarchy
Population 5,364,000
Population density 323 per sq. mile
Language Danish
Currency Krone
Time zone GMT +1
EU member Yes

Estonia
Area 17,413 sq. miles (45,100 sq. km)
Capital Tallinn (TLL)
Government Republic
Population 1,323,000
Population density 76 per sq. mile
Languages Estonian, Russian, Ukrainian, Finnish
Currency Kroon
Time zone GMT +3
EU member Yes

Finland
Area 130,128 sq. miles (337,032 sq. km)
Capital Helsinki (HEL)
Government Constitutional republic
Population 5,207,000
Population density 40 per sq. mile
Languages Finnish, Swedish
Currency Euro
Time zone GMT +2
EU member Yes

France
Area 212,918 sq. miles (551,458 sq. km)
Capital Paris (CDG)
Government Republic
Population 60,144,000
Population density 285 per sq. mile
Language French
Currency Euro
Time zone GMT +1
EU member Yes

Germany
Area 137,735 sq. mi (356,734 sq. km)
Capital Berlin (Tempelhof THF/Tegel TXL)
Government Federal republic
Population 82,476,000
Population density 599 per sq. mile
Language German
Currency Euro
Time zone GMT +1
EU member Yes

Greece
Area 50,944 sq. miles (131,945 sq. km)
Capital Athens (ATH)
Government Republic
Population 10,976,000
Population density 217 per sq. mile
Languages Greek, English, French
Currency Euro
Time zone GMT +2
EU member Yes

Hungary
Area 35,919 sq. miles (93,030 sq. km)
Capital Budapest (BUD)
Government Republic
Population 9,877,000
Population density 275 per sq. mile
Languages Hungarian, Romani, German, others
Currency Forint
Time zone GMT +1
EU member Yes

Iceland
Area 39,702 sq. miles (102,828 sq. km)
Capital Reykjavik (REK)
Government Constitutional republic
Population 290,000
Population density 7 per sq. mile
Language Icelandic
Currency Krona
Time zone GMT
EU member No

Italy
Area 116,313 sq. miles (301,251 sq. km)
Capital Rome (FCO)
Government Republic
Population 57,423,000
Population density 494 per sq. mile
Language Italian
Currency Euro
Time zone GMT +1
EU member Yes

Latvia
Area 24,595 sq. miles (63,701 sq. km)
Capital Riga (RIX)
Government Republic
Population 2,307,000
Population density 94 per sq. mile
Languages Latvian, Russian, Belarusian, Polish
Currency Lat
Time zone GMT +3
EU member Yes

Principality of Liechtenstein
Area 62 sq. miles (161 sq. km)
Capital Vaduz (no airport)
Government Hereditary constitutional monarchy
Population 33,000
Population density 532 per sq. mile
Language German
Currency Swiss franc
Time zone GMT +1
EU member No

Lithuania
Area 25,174 sq. miles (65,201 sq. km)
Capital Vilnius (VNO)
Government Republic
Population 3,444,000
Population density 139 per sq. mile
Languages Lithuanian, Belarusian, Russian, Polish
Currency Lita
Time zone GMT +3
EU member Yes

Grand Duchy of Luxembourg
Area 999 sq. miles (2,589 sq. km)
Capital Luxembourg (LUX)
Government Constitutional monarchy
Population 453,000
Population density 453 per sq. mile
Languages Luxembourgish, French, German
Currency Euro
Time zone GMT +1
EU member Yes

Macedonia
Area 9,928 sq. miles (25,714 sq. km)
Capital Skopje (SKP)
Government Republic
Population 2,056,000
Population density 207 per sq. mile
Languages Macedonian, Albanian, Turkish, Romani
Currency Denar
Time zone GMT +1
EU member No

Malta
Area 122 sq. miles (316 sq. km)
Capital Valletta (MLA)
Government Republic
Population 394,000
Population density 3,230 per sq. mile
Languages Maltese, English
Currency Maltese lira
Time zone GMT +1
EU member Yes

Moldova
Area 13,012 sq. miles (33,701 sq. km)
Capital Chisinau (KIV)
Government Republic
Population 4,267,000
Population density 328 per sq. mile
Languages Moldovan, Russian, Gagauz
Currency Leu
Time zone GMT +3
EU member No

Principality of Monaco
Area 370 acres (150 hectares)
Capital Use Nice (NCE)
Government Constitutional monarchy
Population 32,000
Population density c. 40,000 per sq. mile
Languages French, Monegasque, Italian
Currency Euro
Time zone GMT +1
EU member With France

Kingdom of the Netherlands
Area 16,033 sq. miles (41,525 sq. km)
Capital Amsterdam/The Hague (AMS)
Government Constitutional monarchy
Population 16,148,000
Population density 1,007 per sq. mile
Language Dutch
Currency Euro
Time zone GMT +1
EU member Yes

Kingdom of Norway
Area 154,790 sq. miles (400,906 sq. km)
Capital Oslo (OSL)
Government Constitutional monarchy
Population 4,533,000
Population density 29 per sq. mile
Language Norwegian
Currency Kroner
Time zone GMT +1
EU member Yes

Poland
Area 120,756 sq. miles (312,758 sq. km)
Capital Warsaw (WAW)
Government Republic
Population 38,587,000
Population density 320 per sq. mile
Language Polish
Currency Zloty
Time zone GMT +1
EU member Yes

Portugal
Area 35,383 sq. miles (91,642 sq. km)
Capital Lisbon (LIS)
Government Republic
Population 10,062,000
Population density 284 per sq. mile
Language Portuguese
Currency Euro
Time zone GMT
EU member Yes

Romania
Area 91,699 sq. miles (237,500 sq. km)
Capital Bucharest (OTP)
Government Republic
Population 22,334,000
Population density 244 per sq. mile
Languages Romanian, Hungarian, Roma
Currency Lei
Time zone GMT +2
EU member No

Russian Federation
Area 6,592,812 sq. miles (17,075,383 sq. km)
Capital Moscow (SVO)
Government Republic
Population 143,246,000
Population density 22 per sq. mile
Languages Russian, many others
Currency Ruble
Time zones GMT +3 to +12
EU member No

Serbia and Montenegro
Area 39,449 sq. miles (102,173 sq. km)
Capital Belgrade (BEG)
Government Republic
Population 10,527,000
Population density 274 per sq. mile
Languages Serbian, Albanian
Currency Dinar
Time zone GMT +1
EU member No

Slovak Republic
Area 18,923 sq. miles (49,011 sq. km)
Capital Bratislava (BTS)
Government Republic
Population 5,402,000
Population density 285 per sq. mile
Languages Slovak, Hungarian
Currency Koruna
Time zone GMT +1
EU member Yes

Slovenia
Area 7,819 sq. miles (20,251sq km)
Capital Ljubljana (LJU)
Government Republic
Population 1,984,000
Population density 254 per sq. mile
Languages Slovenian, Serbo-Croatian
Currency Tolar
Time zone GMT +1
EU member Yes

Kingdom of Spain
Area 194,881 sq. miles (504,742 sq. km)
Capital Madrid (MAD)
Government Constitutional monarchy
Population 41,060,000
Population density 211 per sq. mile
Languages Castilian Spanish, Catalan
Currency Euro
Time zone GMT +1
EU member Yes

Kingdom of Sweden
Area 173,665 sq. miles (449,792 sq. km)
Capital Stockholm (STO)
Government Constitutional monarchy
Population 8,876,000
Population density 51 per sq. mile
Languages Swedish, Finnish, Sami
Currency Krona
Time zone GMT +1
EU member Yes

Switzerland
Area 15,941 sq. miles (41,287 sq. km)
Capital Berne (BRN)
Government Federal republic
Population 7,169,000
Population density 450 per sq. mile
Languages German, French, Italian, Romansch
Currency Swiss franc
Time zone GMT +1
EU member No

Ukraine
Area 233,089 sq. miles (603,701 sq. km)
Capital Kiev (KBP)
Government Republic
Population 48,523,000
Population density 208 per sq. mile
Languages Ukrainian, Russian, others
Currency Hryvnia
Time zone GMT +3
EU member No

Africa and the Middle East

Botswana
Area 219,916 sq. miles (569,582 sq. km)
Capital Gaborone (GBE)
Government Republic
Population 1,785,000
Population density 8 per sq. mile
Languages English, Setswana
Currency Pula
Time zone GMT +2

Egypt
Area 386,900 sq. miles (1,002,071 sq. km)
Capital Cairo (CAI)
Government Republic
Population 71,931,000
Population density 186 per sq. mile
Languages Arabic, English, French
Currency Egyptian pound
Time zone GMT +2

State of Israel
Area 7,992 sq. miles (20,699 sq. km)
Capital Jerusalem (use Tel Aviv TLV)
Government Republic
Population 6,433,000
Population density 805 per sq. mile
Languages Hebrew, Arabic, English
Currency Shekel
Time zone GMT +2

Hashemite Kingdom of Jordan
Area 34,575 sq. miles (89,549 sq. km)
Capital Amman (AMM)
Government Constitutional monarchy
Population 5,473,000
Population density 158 per sq. mile
Languages Arabic, English
Currency Dinar
Time zone GMT +2

Kenya
Area 224,960 sq. miles (582,646 sq. km)
Capital Nairobi (NBO)
Government Republic
Population 31,987,000
Population density 142 per sq. mile
Languages English, Swahil, others
Currency Shilling
Time zone GMT +3

Kingdom of Morocco
Area 172,413 sq. miles (446,550 sq. km)
Capital Rabat (RBA)
Government Constitutional monarchy
Population 30,566,000
Population density 177 per sq. mile
Languages Arabic, Berber, French
Currency Dirham
Time zone GMT +1

Namibia
Area 318,321 sq. miles (824,451 sq. km)
Capital Windhoek (WDH)
Government Republic
Population 1,987,000
Population density 6 per sq. mile
Languages English, Afrikaans, German
Currency Namibia dollar
Time zone GMT +2

Kingdom of Saudi Arabia
Area 865,000 sq. miles (2,240,000 sq. km)
Capital Riyadh (RUH)
Government Monarchy
Population 24,217,000
Population density 28 per sq. mile
Language Arabic
Currency Riyal
Time zone GMT +3

South Africa
Area 471,445 sq. miles (1,221,043 sq. km)
Capitals Cape Town/legislative (CPT), Pretoria/administrative, Bloemfontein/judicial (BFN)
Government Republic
Population 45,026,000
Population density 96 per sq. mile
Languages Afrikaans, English, Ndebele, others
Currency Rand
Time zone GMT +2

Tanzania
Area 364,900 sq. miles (945,091 sq. km)
Capital Dodoma
Government Republic
Population 36,977,000
Population density 101 per sq. mile
Languages Swahili, English
Currency Shilling
Time zone GMT +3

Turkey
Area 301,380 sq. miles (780,574 sq. km)
Capital Ankara (ESB)
Government Republic
Population 71,325,000
Population density 240 per sq. mile
Languages Turkish, Arabic, Armenian, Greek
Currency Lira
Time zone GMT +2

Zambia
Area 290,585 sq. miles (752,615 sq. km)
Capital Lusaka (LUN)
Government Republic
Population 10,812,000
Population density 37 per sq. mile
Languages English, Bemba, others
Currency Kwacha
Time zone GMT +2

Asia

Islamic State of Afganistan
Area 250,001 sq. miles (647,500 sq. km)
Capital Kabul (KBL)
Government Transitional administration
Population 23,897,000
Population density 96 per sq. mile
Languages Dari, Pashtu, Turkic, many others
Currency Afghani
Time zone GMT +4.5

Bangladesh
Area 56,977 sq. miles (147,570 sq. km)
Capital Dhaka (DAC)
Government Republic
Population 131,269,860
Population density 8,895 per sq. mile
Language Bengali
Currency Taka
Time zone GMT +6

Kingdom of Bhutan
Area 16,000 sq. miles (41,440 sq. km)
Capital Thimphu (PBH)
Government Monarchy
Population 2,257,000
Population density 141 per sq. mile
Language Dzongkha
Currency Ngultrum
Time zone GMT +6

State of Brunei Darussalam
Area 2,226 sq. miles (5,765 sq. km)
Capital Bandar Seri Begawan (BWN)
Government Sultanate
Population 358,000
Population density 161 per sq. mile
Languages Malay and Chinese dialects
Currency Brunei dollar
Time zone GMT +8

Kingdom of Cambodia (or Kampuchea)
Area 69,898 sq. miles (181,036 sq. km)
Capital Phnom Penh (PNH)
Government Constitutional monarchy
Population 14,144,000
Population density 202 per sq. mile
Languages Khmer, French, English
Currency Riel
Time zone GMT +7

People's Republic of China
Area 3,700,000 sq. miles (9,583,000 sq. km)
Capital Beijing (BJS)
Government Communist
Population 1,304,196,000
Population density 362 per sq. mile
Languages Mandarin, many others
Currency Yuan
Time zone GMT +8 (Beijing time throughout China)

India
Area 1,704,300 sq. miles (4,414,137 sq. km)
Capital Delhi (DEL)
Government Federal republic
Population 1,065,462,000
Population density 928 per sq. mile
Languages Hindi, English, others
Currency Rupee
Time zone GMT +5.5

Indonesia
Area 779,675 sq. miles (2,019,358 sq. km)
Capital Jakarta (CGK)
Government Republic
Population 219,883,000
Population density 314 per sq. mile
Languages Bahasa Indonesia, many others
Currency Rupiah
Time zones GMT +7, +8, +9

Japan
Area 143,619 sq. miles (371,973 sq. km)
Capital Tokyo (TYO)
Government Democracy with emperor
Population 127,654,000
Population density 838 per sq. mile
Languages Japanese, Ainu, Korean
Currency Yen
Time zone GMT +9

Lao People's Democratic Republic (Laos)
Area 91,428 sq. miles (236,799 sq. km)
Capital Vientiane (VTE)
Government Communist
Population 5,657,000
Population density 63 per sq. mile
Languages Lao plus many tribal languages
Currency Kip
Time zone GMT +7

Malaysia
Area 128,727 sq. miles (333,403 sq. km)
Capital Kuala Lumpur (KUL)
Government Democracy with monarch
Population 24,425,000
Population density 193 per sq. mile
Languages Bahasa Malaysia, English, Chinese dialects
Currency Ringgit
Time zone GMT +8

Maldives
Area 116 sq. miles (298 sq. km)
Capital Male (MLE)
Government Republic
Population 318,000
Population density 2,745 per sq. mile
Languages Dhivehi, Arabic, English
Currency Rufiya
Time zone GMT +5

Mongolia
Area 604,247 sq. miles (1,565,000 sq. km)
Capital Ulan Bator (ULN)
Government Republic
Population 2,594,000
Population density 4 per sq. mile
Languages Khalkha Mongol, Kazakh, others
Currency Tugrug
Time zones GMT +7, +8

Union of Myanmar (Burma)
Area 261,789 sq. miles (678,034 sq. km)
Capital Yangon (RGN)
Government Military
Population 49,485,000
Population density 189 per sq. mile
Languages Burmese, others
Currency Kyat
Time zone GMT +6.5

Kingdom of Nepal
Area 54,362 sq. miles (140,798 sq. km)
Capital Kathmandu (KTM)
Government Constitutional monarchy
Population 25,164,000
Population density 463 per sq. mile
Languages Nepali, others
Currency Rupee
Time zone GMT +5.5

Democratic People's Republic of Korea (North Korea)
Area 46,609 sq. miles (120,717 sq. km)
Capital Pyongyang (FNJ)
Government Communist republic
Population 22,664,000
Population density 486 per sq. mile
Language Korean
Currency Won
Time zone GMT +9

Philippines
Area 115,651 sq. miles (299,536 sq. km)
Capital Manila (MNL)
Government Republic
Population 79,999,000
Population density 695 per sq. mile
Languages Filipino, English, many dialects
Currency Peso
Time zone GMT +8

Singapore
Area 225 sq. miles (583 sq. km)
Capital Singapore (SIN)
Government Republic
Population 4,253,000
Population density 17,653 per sq. mile
Languages Malay, English, Mandarin Chinese, Tamil
Currency Singapore dollar
Time zone GMT +8

South Korea
Area 38,022 sq. miles (98,477 sq. km)
Capital Seoul (SEL)
Government Republic
Population 47,700,000
Population density 1,255 per sq. mile
Language Korean
Currency Won
Time zone GMT +9

Sri Lanka
Area 25,332 sq. miles (65,610 sq. km)
Capital Colombo (CMB)
Government Republic
Population 19,065,000
Population density 763 per sq. mile
Languages Sinhala, Tamil, English
Currency Rupee
Time zone GMT +6

Taiwan (Republic of China)
Area 13,807 sq. miles (35,760 sq. km)
Capital Taipei (TPE)
Government Democracy
Population 22,603,000
Population density 1,637 per sq. mile
Language Mandarin Chinese
Currency Taiwan dollar
Time zone GMT +8

Kingdom of Thailand
Area 198,455 sq. miles (513,998 sq. km)
Capital Bangkok (BKK)
Government Constitutional monarchy
Population 62,833,000
Population density 317 per sq. mile
Languages Thai, Chinese, Malay, Khmer
Currency Baht
Time zone GMT +7

Socialist Republic of Vietnam
Area 127,844 sq. miles (331,114 sq. km)
Capital Hanoi (HAN)
Government Socialist republic
Population 81,377,000
Population density 648 per sq. mile
Languages Vietnamese, French, Chinese, English
Currency Dong
Time zone GMT +7

The Pacific

American Samoa
Area 77 sq. miles (199 sq. km)
Capital Pago Pago (PPG)
Government U.S. territory
Population 70,260
Population density 912 per sq. mile
Language English
Currency U.S. dollar
Time zone GMT –11

Australia
Area 2,967,909 sq. miles (7,686,884 sq. km)
Capital Canberra (CBR)
Government Democracy
Population 19,731,000
Population density 7 per sq. mile
Language English
Currency Australian dollar
Time zones GMT +8, +9, +10

Federated States of Micronesia
Area 1,055 sq. miles (2,733 sq. km)
Capital Palikir on Pohnpei (PNI)
Government Republic
Population 109,000
Population density 103 per sq. mile
Languages English, Trukese, others
Currency U.S. dollar
Time zones GMT +10, +11

Fiji
Area 7,055 sq. miles (18,272 sq. km)
Capital Suva (SUV)
Government Republic
Population 839,000
Population density 119 per sq. mile
Languages English, Fijian, Hindustani
Currency Fiji dollar
Time zone GMT +12

French Polynesia
Area 1,609 sq. miles (4,167 sq. km)
Capital Papeete (PPT)
Government Overseas territory of France
Population 262,125
Population density 163 per sq. mile
Language French
Currency Euro
Time zone GMT –10

Guam
Area 209 sq. miles (541 sq. km)
Capital Agana (GUM)
Government U.S. territory
Population 163,941
Population density 784 per sq. mile
Languages English, Chamorro, Japanese
Currency U.S. dollar
Time zone GMT +10

New Zealand
Area 103,736 sq. miles (268,676 sq. km)
Capital Wellington (WLG)
Government Parliamentary democracy
Population 3,875,000
Population density 37 per sq. mile
Languages English, Maori
Currency New Zealand dollar
Time zone GMT +12

Papua New Guinea
Area 178,260 sq. miles (461,693 sq. km)
Capital Port Moresby (POM)
Government Democracy
Population 5,711,000
Population density 32 per sq. mile
Languages English, pidgin, others
Currency Kina
Time zone GMT +10

Samoa
Area 1,133 sq. miles (2,935 sq. km)
Capital Apia
Government Republic
Population 178,000
Population density 157 per sq. mile
Languages Samoan, English
Currency Tala
Time zone GMT –11

Kingdom of Tonga
Area 270 sq. miles (699 sq. km)
Capital Nuku'alofa (TBU)
Government Constitutional monarchy
Population 104,000
Population density 385 per sq. mile
Languages Tongan, English
Currency Pa'anga
Time zone GMT +12

Vanuatu
Area 5,700 sq. miles (14,763 sq. km)
Capital Port Vila (VLI)
Government Republic
Population 212,000
Population density 37 per sq. mile
Languages Bislama, English, French, others
Currency Vatu
Time zone GMT +11

APPENDIX B

Major City Codes

United States

Albany, NY	ALB
Albuquerque, NM	ABQ
Anchorage, AK	ANC
Atlanta, GA	ATL
Augusta, ME	AUG
Austin, TX	AUS
Baltimore, MD	BWI
Baton Rouge, LA	BTR
Billings, MT	BIL
Birmingham, AL	BHM
Bismarck, ND	BIS
Boise, ID	BOI
Boston, MA	BOS
Buffalo, NY	BUF
Burlington, VT	BTV
Charleston, SC	CHS
Charleston, WV	CRW
Charlotte, NC	CLT
Cheyenne, WY	CYS
Chicago, IL	
Midway	MDW
O'Hare	ORD
Cincinnati, OH	CVG
Cleveland, OH	CLE
Columbia, SC	CAE
Columbus, OH	CMH
Concord, NH	MHT
Dallas/Fort Worth, TX	DFW
Dayton, OH	DAY
Denver, CO	DEN
Des Moines, IA	DSM
Detroit, MI	DTW
Fairbanks, AK	FAI
Fort Lauderdale, FL	FLL
Fort Myers, FL	RSW
Frankfort, KY	LEX
Gulfport, MS	GPT
Harrisburg, PA	MDT
Hartford, CT	HFD
Helena, MT	HLN
Hilo, HI	ITO
Honolulu, HI	HNL
Hoolehua, Molokai, HI	MKK
Houston, TX	IAH
Indianapolis, IN	IND
Jackson, MS	JAN
Jackson Hole, WY	JAC
Jacksonville, FL	JAX
Jefferson City, MO	COU
Juneau, AK	JNU
Kahalui, Maui, HI	OGG
Kansas City, MO/KS	MCI
Kapaa, Lihue, Kauai, HI	LIH
Key West, FL	EYW
Knoxville, TN	TYS
Lanai City, Lanai, HI	LNY
Lansing, MI	LAN
Las Vegas, NV	LAS
Lincoln, NE	LNK
Little Rock, AR	LIT
Los Angeles, CA	LAX
Louisville, KY	SDF
Madison, WI	MSN
Memphis, TN	MEM
Miami, FL	MIA
Milwaukee, WI	MKE
Minneapolis, MN	MSP
Mobile, AL	MOB
Montgomery, AL	MGM
Nashville, TN	BNA
New Orleans, LA	MSY
New York, NY	
Kennedy	JFK
LaGuardia	LGA
Newark, NJ	EWR
Newport News, VA	PHF
Nome, AK	OME
Norfolk, VA	ORF
Oklahoma City, OK	OKC
Olympia, WA	OLM
Omaha, NE	OMA
Orange County, CA	SNA
Orlando, FL	MCO
Philadelphia, PA	PHL
Phoenix, AZ	PHX
Pierre, SD	PIR
Pittsburgh, PA	PIT
Portland, ME	PWM
Portland, OR	PDX
Providence, RI	PVD
Raleigh/Durham, NC	RDU
Reno, NV	RNO
Richmond, VA	RIC
Sacramento, CA	SMF
St. Louis, MO	STL
St. Paul, MN	MSP
Salem, OR	CVO
Salt Lake City, UT	SLC
San Antonio, TX	SAT
San Diego, CA	SAN
San Francisco, CA	SFO
San Jose, CA	SJC
Seattle/Tacoma, WA	SEA
Spokane, WA	GEG
Tallahassee, FL	TLH
Tampa/St. Pete, FL	TPA
Topeka, KS	FOE
Tucson, AZ	TUS
Tulsa, OK	TUL
Washington, DC	
Dulles	IAD
Reagan	DCA
West Palm Beach, FL	PBI

Canada

Calgary	YYC
Chalottetown	YYG
Edmonton	YEG
Fredericton	YFC
Gander	YQX
Halifax	YHZ
Hamilton	YHM
Iqaluit	YFB
Moncton	YQM
Montreal	
Dorval	YUL
Mirabel	YMX
Ottawa	YOW
Québec City	YQB
Regina	YQR
Saskatoon	YXE
St. John's	YYT
Toronto	YYZ
Vancouver	YVR
Whitehorse	YXY
Winnepeg	YWG
Yellowknife	YZF

Bermuda, Caribbean Islands, Mexico, and Central America

Acapulco, Mexico	ACA
Anguilla	AXA
Aruba	AUA
Basseterre, St. Kitts	SKB
Belmopan, Belize	BZE
Bermuda	BDA
Bonaire	BON
Bridgetown, Barbados	BGI
Cabo San Lucas, Mexico	SJD
Castries, St. Lucia	SLU
Cancún, Mexico	CUN
Caymans	GCM
Curaçao	CUR
Fort-de-France, Martinique	FDF
Gustavia, St. Barts	SBH
Guatemala City, Guatemala	GUA
Havana, Cuba	HAV
Kingston, Jamaica	KIN
Kingstown, St. Vincent	SVD
Managua, Nicaragua	MGA
Marigot, St. Martin	SXM
Mérida, Mexico	MID
Mexico City, Mexico	MEX
Montego Bay, Jamaica	MBJ
Nassau, Bahamas	NAS
Oranjestad, St. Eustatius	EUX
Panama City, Panama	PTY
Philipsburg, St. Maarten	SXM
Plymouth, Montserrat	Closed
Providenciales	PLS
Pointe-à-Pitre, Guadeloupe	PTP
Port-au-Prince, Haiti	PAP
Port of Spain, Trinidad	POS
Road Town, Tortola, BVI	EIS
Roseau, Dominica	DOM
San José, Costa Rica	SJO
San Juan, Puerto Rico	SJU
San Salvador, El Salvador	SAP
Santo Domingo, Dominican Republic	SDQ
St. Croix	STX
St. George's, Grenada	GND
St. John's, Antigua	ANU
St. Thomas	STT
Scarborough, Tobago	TAB
Tegucigalpa, Honduras	TGU
The Bottom, Saba	SAB

South America

Asunción, Paraguay	ASU
Bogotá, Colombia	BOG
Brasília, Brazil	BSB
Buenos Aires, Argentina	BUE
Caracas, Venezuela	CCS
Georgetown, Guyana	GEO
La Paz, Bolivia	LPB
Lima, Peru	LIM
Montevideo, Uruguay	MVD
Paramaribo, Suriname	PBM
Quito, Ecuador	UIO
Rio de Janeiro, Brazil	GIG
Santiago, Chile	SCL

São Paulo, Brazil	GRU
Sucre, Bolivia	ABC

Europe

Ajaccio, Corsica	AJA
Alicante, Spain	ALC
Amsterdam, the Netherlands	AMS
Athens, Greece	ATH
Barcelona, Spain	BCN
Basel, Switzerland	BSL
Belfast, Northern Ireland	BFS
Belgrade, Serbia and Montenegro	BEG
Bergen, Norway	BGO
Berlin, Germany	
Tempelhof	THF
Tegel	TXL
Berne, Switzerland	BRN
Bilbao, Spain	BIO
Bordeaux, France	BOD
Bratislava, Slovakia	BTS
Brussels, Belgium	BRU
Bucharest, Romania	OTP
Budapest, Hungary	BUD
Cardiff, Wales	CWL
Chisinau, Moldova	KIV
Cologne, Germany	CGN
Copenhagen, Denmark	CPH
Corfu, Greece	CFU
Cork, Ireland	ORK
Crete, Greece	HER
Dublin, Ireland	DUB
Düsseldorf, Germany	DUS
Edinburgh, Scotland	EDI
Faro, Portugal	FAO
Frankfurt, Germany	FRA
Funchal, Madeira, Portugal	FNC
Geneva, Switzerland	GVA
Glasgow, Scotland	GLA
Hamburg, Germany	HAM
Helsinki, Finland	HEL
Innsbruck, Austria	INN
Inverness, Scotland	INV
Kiev, Ukraine	KBP
Las Palmas, Canary Islands	LPA
Lisbon, Portugal	LIS
Ljubljana, Slovenia	LJU
London, England	
Gatwick	LGW
Heathrow	LHR
Stansted	STN
Luxembourg, Luxembourg	LUX
Madrid, Spain	MAD
Málaga, Spain	AGP
Manchester, England	MAN
Milan, Italy	
Linate	LIN
Malpensa	MXP
Minsk, Belarus	MSQ
Moscow, Russia	SVO
Munich, Germany	MUC
Mykonos, Greece	JMK
Naples, Italy	NAP
Nice, France	NCE
Nicosia, Cyprus	LCA
Oslo, Norway	OSL
Palermo, Sicily, Italy	PMO
Palma, Majorca, Spain	PMI
Paris, France	
Charles de Gaulle	CDG
Orly	ORY
Ponta Delgada, Azores	PDL
Prague, Czech Republic	PRG
Reykjavik, Iceland	REK
Riga, Latvia	RIX
Rhodes, Greece	RHO
Rome, Italy	FCO
Salzburg, Austria	SZG
St. Petersburg, Russia	LED
Santiago de Compostela, Spain	SCQ
Santorini, Greece	JTR
Sarajevo, Bosnia-Herzegovina	SJJ
Seville, Spain	SVQ
Shannon, Ireland	SNN
Skopje, Macedonia	SKP
Sofia, Bulgaria	SOF
Stockholm, Sweden	STO
Stuttgart, Germany	STR
Tallinn, Estonia	TLL
Tenerife, Canary Islands	TCI
Thessalonica, Greece	SKI
Tirané, Albania	TIA
Valencia, Spain	VLC
Valletta, Malta	MLA
Vienna, Austria	VIE
Vilnius, Lithuania	VNO
Warsaw, Poland	WAW
Zagreb, Croatia	ZAG
Zürich, Switzerland	ZHR

Africa and the Middle East

Abidjan, Ivory Coast	ABJ
Abu Dhabi, United Arab Emirates	AUH
Abuja, Nigeria	ABV
Accra, Ghana	ACC
Addis Ababa, Ethiopia	ADD
Algiers, Algeria	ALG
Amman, Jordan	AMM
Antananarivo, Madagascar	TRN
Asmara, Eritrea	ASM
Baghdad, Iraq	BGW
Bamako, Mali	BKO
Bangui, Central African Republic	BGF
Banjul, The Gambia	BJL
Beirut, Lebanon	BEY
Bloemfontein, South Africa	BFN
Brazzaville, Congo Republic	BZV
Bujumbura, Burundi	BJM
Cairo, Egypt	CAI
Cape Town, South Africa	CPT
Conakry, Guinea	CKY
Dakar, Senegal	DKR
Damascus, Syria	DAM
Dar es Salaam, Tanzania	DAR
Djibouti, Djibouti	JIB
Doha, Qatar	DOH
Durban, South Africa	DUR
Freetown, Sierra Leone	FNA
Gaborone, Botswana	GBE
Harare, Zimbabwe	HRE
Johannesburg, South Africa	JNB
Kampala, Uganda	EBB
Khartoum, Sudan	KRT
Kigali, Rwanda	KGL
Kinshasa, Republic of the Congo	FIH
Kuwait City, Kuwait	KWI
Libreville, Gabon	LBV
Lilongwe, Malawi	LLW
Lomé, Togo	LFW
Luanda, Angola	LAD
Lusaka, Zambia	LUN
Malabo, Equatorial Guinea	SSG
Manama, Bahrain	BAH
Maputo, Mozambique	MPM
Maseru, Lesotho	MSU
Mbabane, Swaziland	MTS
Mogadishu, Somalia	MGQ
Monrovia, Liberia	ROB
Moroni, Comoros	HAH
Muscat, Oman	MCT
Nairobi, Kenya	NBO
N'Djamena, Chad	NDJ
Niamey, Niger	NIM
Nouakchott, Mauritania	NKC
Ouagadougou, Burkina Faso	OUA
Porto-Novo, Benin	COO
Praia, Cape Verde	SAI
Rabat, Morocco	RBA
Riyadh, Saudi Arabia	RUH
Sana, Yemen	SAH
São Tomé, São Tomé	TMS
Tehran, Iran	THR
Tel Aviv, Israel	TLV
Tripoli, Libya	TIP
Tunis, Tunisia	TUN
Windhoek, Namibia	WDH
Yaoundé, Cameroon	DLA

Asia

Bandar Seri Begawan, Brunei	BWN
Bangkok, Thailand	BKK
Beijing, China	BJS
Colombo, Sri Lanka	CMB
Dehli, India	DEL
Hanoi, Vietnam	HAN
Hong Kong, China	HKG
Jakarta, Indonesia	CGK
Kathmandu, Nepal	KTM
Kuala Lumpur, Malaysia	KUL
Male, Maldives	MLE
Manila, Philippines	MNL
Phnom Penh, Cambodia	PNH
Pyongyang, North Korea	FNJ
Seoul, South Korea	SEL
Shanghai, China	SHA
Singapore, Singapore	SIN
Taipei, Taiwan	TPE
Tokyo, Japan	TYO
Ulan Bator, Mongolia	ULN
Vientiane, Laos	VTE
Yangon, Myanmar	RGN

Australia, New Zealand, and Oceania

Adelaide, Australia	ADL
Agana, Guam	GUM
Alofi, Niue	IUE
Auckland, New Zealand	AKL
Avarua, Cook Islands	RAR
Brisbane, Australia	BNE
Cairns, Australia	CNS
Canberra, Australia	CBR
Chalan Konoa, Marianas	SPN
Darwin, Australia	DRW
Faunafuti, Tuvalu	FUN
Hobart, Australia	HBA
Honiara, Solomons	HIR
Melbourne, Australia	MEL
Majuro, Marshalls	MAJ
Nadi, Fiji	NAN
Nauru, Nauru	INU
Nouméa, New Caledonia	NOU
Nuku'alofa, Tonga	TBU
Pago Pago, American Samoa	PPG
Palikir, FSM	PNI
Papeete, Tahiti	PPT
Perth, Australia	PER
Port Moresby, Papua New Guinea	POM
Port Vila, Vanuatu	VLI
Suva, Fiji	SUV
Sydney, Australia	SYD
Tarawa, Kiribati	TRW
Townsville, Australia	TSV
Wellington, New Zealand	WLG

APPENDIX C

Guide to Films and Television

Viewing classic films made on location helps you to learn physical and cultural geography and history. Most of the films mentioned here are available at your local library or in the "classics" or "foreign" section of your video rental store. They are also shown on TV. Not all are great movies, but the location shots make them worth viewing, and the story lines keep you watching.

On TV, one source of travel information is the Travel Channel, with dozen of shows airing twenty-four hours a day. All are packed with advice on vacations. The Discovery Channel and PBS stations are also resources. Videos and DVDs are also popular, but their logistical information is quickly dated.

All Creatures Great and Small (1978)	BBC series/Yorkshire
Amadeus (1984)	Vienna, Salzburg, Prague
An American in Paris (1951)	Paris
Anna and the King (1999)	Thailand
The Beach (2000)	Thailand
Big Easy (1986)	New Orleans
Blue Lagoon (1980)	Fiji
Braveheart (1995)	Scotland
Bread and Chocolate (1973)	Switzerland
Brideshead Revisited (1979)	BBC series/Castle Howard
Chariots of Fire (1981)	England and Scotland
Chocolat (1988)	French West Africa
Cinema Paradiso (1989)	Sicily
Coca Cola Kid (1985)	Australia
The Corn Is Green (1979)	Wales
Crocodile Dundee (1986)	Australia
A Cry in the Dark (1988)	Australia
Dangerous Liaisons (1988)	Château country, France
Death on the Nile (1978)	Egypt
The Deep (1977)	Bermuda
Divorce Italian Style (1961)	Italy
Doctor Zhivago (1965)	Russia
Eiger Sanction (1975)	Switzerland
Elizabeth (1999)	England
Empire of the Sun (1987)	Singapore
The English Patient (1996)	Egypt and Italy
Far from the Madding Crowd (1967)	Wiltshire and Dorset
Farewell My Concubine (1993)	China
French Kiss (1995)	Paris, south of France
The French Lieutenant's Woman (1981)	Dorset and Devon, England
Gandhi (1982)	India
The Gods Must Be Crazy (1980)	South Africa
Golden Bowl (2000)	Lincolnshire, England
Greek Tycoon (1978)	Greece
Guns of Navarone (1961)	Greece
Haman (1997)	Turkey
Hawaii (1966)	Hawaii
The Hawaiians (1970)	Hawaii
Heavenly Creatures (1994)	New Zealand
Heimat (1984)	Germany
How Green Was My Valley (1975)	BBC series/Wales
How Stella Got Her Groove Back (1998)	Jamaica
I Dreamed of Africa (2000)	Kenya
If It's Tuesday It Must Be Belgium (1969)	Group tour of Europe
Il Postino (1994)	Italy
Indochine (1992)	Indochina
Jean de Florette (1986)	Provence, France
Jewel in the Crown (1978)	BBC series/India
Khartoum (1966)	Sudan
Kundun (1997)	Tibet
La Dolce Vita (1960)	Italy
Last Emperor (1987)	China

Last Samurai (2003)	Japan
Lawrence of Arabia (1962)	Jordan
The Leopard (1963)	Sicily
Like Water for Chocolate (1991)	Mexico
Local Hero (1983)	Scotland
Lord of the Rings Trilogy (1999–2003)	New Zealand
Lost in Translation (2003)	Japan
Man from Snowy River (1982)	Australia
Manon of the Spring (1986)	Provence, France
Michael Collins (1996)	Ireland
Midnight in the Garden of Good and Evil (1998)	*Savannah, Georgia*
Monsoon Wedding (2001)	India
A Month by the Lake (1994)	Lake Como, Italy
Mrs. Brown (1997)	England and Scotland
Murder on the Orient Express (1974)	Orient Express train
My Brilliant Career (1979)	Australia
My Father's Glory (1980)	Provence, France
My Mother's Castle (1990)	Provence, France
Nicholas and Alexandra (1971)	Russia
Night of the Shooting Stars (1981)	Italy
On Golden Pond (1981)	Squam Lake, New Hampshire
On Her Majesty's Secret Service (1969)	Switzerland
Once Were Warriors (1994)	New Zealand
Out of Africa (1985)	Kenya
Padre Padrone (1977)	Sardinia
Pascali's Island (1988)	Greece
A Passage to India (1984)	India
The Piano (1993)	New Zealand
Poldark (1975)	BBC series/Cornwall
Priscilla, Queen of the Desert (1993)	Australia
The Quiet Man (1952)	Ireland
A River Runs through It (1992)	Montana
Rob Roy (1995)	Scotland
Roman Holiday (1953)	Rome, Italy
A Room with a View (1985)	England and Italy
Ryan's Daughter (1970)	Ireland
Sense and Sensibility (1995)	England
Seven Years in Tibet (1997)	Tibet
The Shining (1980)	Estes Park, Colorado
Shirley Valentine (1989)	England and Greece
Shogun (1980s)	TV series/Japan
The Sicilian (1987)	Sicily
Smiles of a Summer Night (1955)	Sweden
Snows of Kilimanjaro (1952)	Africa
Song of Norway (1970)	Norway
The Sound of Music (1965)	Salzburg, Austria
South Pacific (1958)	Kauai, Hawaii
Stage Coach (1939)	Monument Valley, Utah
Summertime (1955)	Venice, Italy
Surviving Picasso (1996)	Paris, France
The Talented Mr. Ripley (1999)	Italy
10 (1979)	Manzanillo, Mexico
Three Coins in the Fountain (1954)	Italy
To Catch a Thief (1955)	French Riviera
Topkapi (1964)	Istanbul, Turkey
A Town Like Alice (1993)	BBC series/Australia
Under the Tuscan Sun (2003)	Italy
Upstairs Downstairs (1971–1974)	BBC series/London
Utu (1963)	New Zealand
Waking Ned Devine (1998)	Ireland
We of the Never Never (1982)	Australia
Wings of the Dove (1997)	Venice, Italy
Zorba the Greek (1964)	Crete
Zulu (1964)	South Africa

Glossary

A

acclimatization The way in which an organism adjusts to a new environment.

acropolis A Greek word meaning "high point of the city"; a raised area, natural or artificial, topped with buildings, that was the religious and military center of an ancient Greek city-state. The acropolis in Athens, Greece, is the best known.

adventure travel Travel with an element of risk.

alluvial Refers to the mud, silt, and sand deposited by rivers and streams.

alpine A treeless area on mountains that is above the tree line but below the limit of permanent snow.

alpine skiing Downhill skiing.

altiplano The high plains area of Ecuador, Bolivia, and Peru.

altitude The height in the atmosphere reflecting the distance above sea level.

aqueduct A gravity-fed water channel originally developed by the Romans, frequently elevated and supported by arches.

archipelago A group of islands clustered together; from the Greek word meaning "chief sea."

arctic The part of the earth where in summer the sun never sets and in winter it never rises. In biological terms, it refers to the cold polar regions where trees will not grow.

atlas A book of maps.

atmospheric pressure The weight of the overhead atmosphere as measured by a barometer.

atoll A coral reef enclosing a lagoon; found primarily in the Pacific Ocean.

aurora The colorful light display that shimmers in the dark polar sky. In the Northern Hemisphere, it is called the northern lights, or *aurora borealis;* in the Southern Hemisphere, the *aurora australis.*

avalanche A mass of snow, rock, ice, or other material sliding swiftly down a mountainside.

B

barrier islands Landforms parallel to shorelines.

basin A low spot in the land.

bay A body of water partly surrounded by land, with a wide opening to the ocean.

bayou A sluggish, swampy backwater of a river or a lake.

beach A narrow, gently sloping strip of land that lies along the edge of an ocean or a lake.

Benguela Current The cold current flowing north along the west coast of South Africa.

bilharzia A dangerous water-borne parasitic disease acquired by skin contact with fresh water containing worm larvae; also called **schistosomiasis.** The worms exist in rivers, lakes, streams, and water holes throughout Africa, Asia, the Caribbean, and South America.

blue hole A deep-blue ring of water in the sea coming from what was a cave on an island of limestone that has sunk into the sea.

bluff A cliff or steep wall of rock or soil that borders a river or its floodplain.

bog Wetland in which soil conditions hinder the decay of plant and animal matter until the decayed matter accumulates as peat. A bog is often called a moor in Europe and a muskeg in Canada.

bore A wall-like wave of swift-running water formed in a bay or river mouth by a rapidly rising tide.

boreal Refers to the evergreen forests of the Northern Hemisphere.

breakwater A pile of rock or concrete built parallel to the shore to prevent erosion or damage to watercraft.

butte A lonely tower of rock that rises sharply from the surrounding area and has sloping sides and a flat top.

C

caldera A large crater formed after a volcano explodes and collapses in on itself.

calving The breaking off of blocks of glacial ice into the ocean to form icebergs.

canal An artificial waterway.

canyon A deep, narrow valley with steep sides formed by mountains or hills.

cape A piece of land projecting into the sea; smaller than a peninsula.

cartography The science of mapmaking.

cataract A waterfall that forms a single long drop.

cay A low-lying island formed of coral or sand.

Celsius scale The scale for measuring temperature on the metric system in which 0° is the freezing point of water and 100° is the boiling point; also called the **Centrigrade scale.**

cenote A deep pool on the surface of limestone formed by underground water.

channel A wide waterway between two large landmasses that lie close to each other.

chaparral The shrubs and small trees that grow in regions with mild, moist winters and hot, dry summers.

Chinook A warm, dry wind that blows down the eastern slopes of the Rockies, rapidly melting snow.

cliff A high, steep face of rock.

climate The average of weather conditions over a period of time.

clouds Visible masses of tiny water droplets or ice crystals.

coast The edge of land that borders the ocean along a continent or an island; also called **seacoast** or **shore.**

coastal plain A large area of low, flat land lying next to the ocean.

compass rose A symbol on a map that indicates the map's orientation.

continent A large landmass. The seven continents are Asia, Africa, North America, South America, Antarctica, Europe, and Australia.

continental divide A stretch of high ground that separates a continent's water flow.

continental island A piece of land surrounded by water that was once connected to a continent.

continental shelf The area where the sea meets land at the edge of a continent.

coral island A low island formed in warm waters by tiny sea animals called coral polyps.

coral reef A ridge created by corals, tiny, soft-bodied marine animals that have hard outer skeletons.

cordillera Parallel mountain ranges.

Coriolis effect The result of the earth's rotation that causes a moving object or fluid to turn toward the right in the Northern Hemisphere and to the left in the Southern Hemisphere.

coulee A trenchlike dry canyon with steep walls.

cove A small bay; an inlet of water protected by surrounding land.

crater The depression around the opening of a volcano.

crevasse A deep, wedge-shaped opening in a moving mass of ice called a glacier.

crust The rocky outermost layer of the earth.

culture Every feature of an area's way of life, including language, religion, dress, diet, arts, manners, recreation, and government.

current A cold or warm moving stream of water or air.

cyclone A storm or system of winds in the Indian Ocean that rotates around a center of low atmospheric pressure; called a **hurricane** in North America, a **typhoon** in the Pacific.

D

daylight saving time The time during which clocks are set one hour or more ahead of standard time; also called **summer time**.

delta A low-lying plain at a river's mouth where it enters the sea; often fan-shaped.

desert An area with less than 10 inches (250 mm) of rainfall a year. Deserts may be hot or cold.

destination geography The application of the knowledge of geography to the travel, tourism, and hospitality industry.

dike A barrier built to hold back water from drained lands.

doldrums The often windless area of the ocean near the equator.

dune A mound of loose sand found along seacoasts, near rivers and lakes, and in deserts.

E

earthquake Movement in the earth's crust.

ecology The interrelationship between life forms and the natural environment.

ecosystem A group of organisms and the environment with which they interact.

ecotourism A form of tourism that emphasizes limited impact on the natural environment.

elapsed travel time How long it takes to get to a destination.

elevation The height of a physical feature above sea level on the surface of the earth.

El Niño The warming of the normally cold seawater off the coast of Peru that occurs naturally every three to seven years. It often affects the western coast of America as far north as California.

enclave A territory, such as the Vatican City, that is surrounded by another political unit.

environment The sum of conditions that surround and influence an organism.

equator The line of latitude that circles the earth at an equal distance from the North and South poles; the 0° latitude line.

equinox The time when the sun appears directly overhead to observers at the equator.

erosion Changes in the earth's surface made by water, air, or ice.

escarpment A cliff or steep slope that separates two levels of land.

esplanade A level area of paved or grassy land.

estuary An arm of the sea at the mouth of a river.

etesian wind A wind blowing from the north and northwest in the eastern Mediterranean and the Aegean, often creating rough seas.

Eurasia The combination of Europe and Asia as one continent.

F

fall line The place at the edge of a continent where the land begins to flatten out; where rivers drop from a hilly region to flatland and form waterfalls.

Fahrenheit scale The temperature scale used in the United States; 32° is the freezing point of water, and 212° is the boiling point of water.

fault A break in the earth's crust along which there is movement.

fen A marshlike area partially covered with water.

firth The Scottish equivalent of a fjord.

fjord A narrow arm of the sea bordered by steep hills formed after a glacier has gouged out the bottom of a river valley.

floodplain A flat area along a river or stream that is subject to flooding.

foehn A warm, dry wind blowing down the leeward slope of a mountain, melting snow and causing avalanches.

fog Cloud at ground level that reduces visibility.

fold Rock layers lifted up or pushed down relative to the surrounding area.

forest A large area covered with trees.

fringing reef A reef along the shore of an island.

fumarole A vent in the earth's surface.

G

gap A narrow valley or gorge cut by water across land.

garúa The heavy mist on the Pacific slope of the Andes in a normally very dry part of the coast.

geoglyphs Marks in rocks that give evidence of past geological events.

geographic grid A network of evenly spaced lines on maps that indicate longitude and latitude.

geographic information system (GIS) The computers and software programs that record, retrieve, analyze, and manipulate information gathered by satellites and use such to make maps.

geography The study of the relationships between people and their environments.

geyser A hot spring that, when heated to the boiling point by geothermal energy, is forced upward under pressure into a water jet.

glacier A mass of ice formed by compressed snow that gradually moves down a valley under the force of gravity.

glen A secluded, narrow valley in Scotland.

globe A scale model of the earth.

gorge A steep-sided valley.

grasslands Flat or rolling open areas where grasses are the natural vegetation.

great circle Any circle that divides the earth into two equal parts.

great circle route A phrase used by airline navigators to refer to the shortest distance between two points.

Greenwich Mean Time (GMT) The time at the prime meridian located in Greenwich, England; also called **Universal Time**.

gulf A large area of ocean partly surrounded by land.

Gulf Stream The warm ocean current that flows northeast along the coast of North America from the Gulf of Mexico. After passing Newfoundland, it divides and follows three separate routes.

gyre A circular pattern of wind-driven ocean currents that move clockwise in the Northern Hemisphere and counterclockwise in the Southern Hemisphere.

H

harbor A body of water sheltered by natural or artificial barriers.

hemisphere A half of the earth.

high season The time when a destination is in most demand.

hills Elevated landforms more rounded and with less elevation than mountains.

horizon The line where the earth and sky seem to meet.

hosted tour A prepaid package, including air, ground transportation at the destination, and lodging, plus a host available at the destination to assist travelers.

hot springs Thermal springs with heated waters of more than 98.6° F.

human geography The study of people and their patterns of settlement and activity on the earth.

Humboldt Current The cold current flowing north along the west coast of South America that cools the coast as far north as the equator; also called the **Peru Current**.

humidity The measurement of water vapor in the air.

hurricane A storm with winds of at least 74 miles (119 km) per hour and heavy rains. Called a **typhoon** in the western Pacific; called a **cyclone** when it forms in the Bay of Bengal and the northern Indian Ocean.

I

iceberg A large chunk of ice that breaks off, or calves, from a glacier and falls into the sea.

ice cap A thick layer of ice and snow that has formed a permanent crust over areas of land, found primarily in the polar regions.

independent tour A prepaid package of three elements, usually air, ground transportation at the destination, and lodging; at the destination travelers are free to do as they wish.

inlet A narrow strip of water cutting into the land.

interactive mapping The process whereby a GIS user asks for information and the computer guides the user toward answers.

international date line The point

180° from Greenwich, England, in the middle of the Pacific Ocean where the next day begins.

intertropical convergence zone (ITCZ) The place where the trade winds of the Northern and Southern hemispheres meet.

island A naturally formed body of land, completely surrounded by water and above water at high tide.

isthmus A narrow bridge of land that connects two large landmasses.

J

jet stream A band of swiftly moving air located high in the atmosphere.

jungle A thick, tangled mass of tropical vegetation.

K

karst A limestone landscape where water is carried by underground channels rather than on the surface by streams and rivers. The water activity creates caves and sinkholes.

key An explanation of the symbols used on a map; also called a **legend**.

khamsin A hot, dry wind blowing from the south and southeast in the eastern Mediterranean, warming the coastal region and helping to create dust storms and a hazy atmosphere.

L

Labrador Current The cold current flowing south along the east coast of Canada, which carries icebergs and keeps the coastal region relatively cool during the summer.

lagoon A shallow body of water isolated from the sea by a strip of land such as a reef.

lake A body of water surrounded by land.

landform A natural feature of the earth's surface.

landmass A huge division of land on the earth.

La Niña The opposite to El Niño. Warm surface water flows toward Asia and colder water from the ocean depths moves to the surface in the eastern equatorial Pacific.

latitude A horizontal line on a map that shows the distance north or south of the equator.

lava Molten rock, or its later solidified form, produced when a volcano erupts.

leeward The side sheltered from the wind.

levee A ridge of gravel, silt, or other material built up by a stream or constructed by engineers along the edges of a channel in a floodplain.

limestone A type of rock formed chiefly of organic remains such as shells or coral.

littoral Land along the coast.

llanos The treeless grasslands of Venezuela and northern Colombia.

local time The time at any particular place.

loch A Scottish lake or a long narrow arm of the sea.

loess Fertile silt or dust blown by the wind.

longitude A vertical line on a map that measures the distance east or west from the prime meridian.

low season The time when a destination is in least demand.

M

magma Molten, mobile rock that lies beneath the earth's surface.

mangrove A tropical shrub capable of living in salt water, with roots that form dense tickets along tidal shores.

map A symbolic representation on a flat surface of a whole or part of an area.

marsh A wetland; an area of land where surface water covers the ground.

meridians Vertical lines that measure longitude on a map of the earth.

mesa A broad, flat-topped landform with steep sides formed by streams cutting through a raised area of flat land. *Mesa* means "table" in Spanish.

mist Cloud at ground level.

mistral A strong, cold, dry wind blowing from the Alps into southern France, most often in winter and spring.

monadnock A hill or low mountain of rock that did not wear down when all surrounding land was leveled by erosion.

monolith A single, very large rock.

monsoon A regional wind that reverses direction between summer and winter and dominates coastal Asia from Pakistan to Japan. In the dry season, the northeast monsoon blows dry air from the land; in the wet season, the southwest monsoon blows wet air from the ocean.

moor A wasteland of soft, spongy ground consisting chiefly of partially decayed plant matter called peat; also called a **bog**.

moraine A deposit of rocks and debris left behind by a glacier's movement.

mountain A landform higher than its surroundings with some kind of peak or summit.

mouth The end of a river.

Mozambique Current A warm current flowing south and west along the coast of Mozambique and eastern South Africa.

muskeg bog A mossy bog found in northern North America.

N

norther A cold, strong wind bringing falling temperatures across Texas and the Gulf of Mexico. In Mexico and Central America, it is called **El Norte**.

North Atlantic Current The extension of the Gulf Stream that helps maintain relatively mild winters in the British Isles and along the Norwegian coast.

notch A pass through granite mountains.

O

oasis A small fertile area in the desert.

ocean The interconnected body of salt water that covers about 70 percent of the earth's surface.

Outback The dry, isolated interior of Australia.

oxbow lake A crescent-shaped lake or swamp (such as a bayou) that occupies an abandoned channel left by a river or stream.

P

Pampas Level, treeless, grassy plains of southern South America.

panhandle A long, narrow projection of land within a state's boundary, as in western Florida and Oklahoma.

parallels Horizontal lines that measure latitude on a map of the earth.

peat The partly decayed plant matter that has collected in swamps and marshes over long periods of time. Dried peat is used as a fuel in places such as Ireland where coal and oil are scarce.

peninsula A piece of land that extends from a continent and is almost surrounded by water.

permafrost Permanently frozen ground that prevents surface water from draining, resulting in a summer landscape of lakes and marshes.

Peru Current See **Humboldt Current**.

physical geography The study of the earth's natural features and the climatic, geologic, and other processes that shape it.

piedmont The land at the base of a mountain.

plains Flat or gently rolling lands that are less than 1,000 feet (305 m) above sea level.

plateau An area of flatland raised above its surroundings; also called **tableland**.

playa A dry lake that fills with water only after rain. The term is used mostly in Australia.

polder Land reclaimed from the sea.

poles The North and South poles are at the ends of the earth's axis of rotation (an invisible line through the earth's center).

population density The average number of people per square mile or square kilometer.

prairie An open area of fertile land covered by tall grass.

precipitation Any form of moisture that falls from the atmosphere to the ground.

prevailing winds Winds that blow in a fairly constant pattern.

prime meridian The line of 0° degree longitude; the starting point for measuring distance both east and west around the globe.

projection The transfer of information about the spherical earth onto flat paper.

R

rain forest A lush, wet, generally warm area with a high canopy of trees and low underbrush.

rain shadow Dry area on the leeward side of a mountain.

rapids Areas of broken, fast-flowing water in a stream that is making a slight descent.

ravine A small, narrow canyon.

reef A ridge of rocks or sand at or near the surface of the water along the coast.

relief map A map that shows differences in elevation.

rift valley A valley formed when land sinks between two parallel faults.

Ring of Fire An arc of volcanoes that circles much of the Pacific Ocean.

river A ribbon of water flowing over the land.

S

Sahel A semiarid area in Africa south of the Sahara.

savanna Tropical grassland with clumps of grasses and widely scattered trees.

scale The indication of the relationship between the distances on a map and the actual distances on the earth.

scarplands Lines of cliffs produced by faulting or erosion.

sea A division of the ocean.

seamount A submerged volcano.

sediment Solid material such as stones and sand deposited by water, wind, or a glacier.

selva A tropical rain forest.

skerry A rocky reef off the west coast of Norway.

shield A geologically stable region of the earth's crust that formed during its early history.

shoal A shallow sandbar or mudbank.

shore The contact area where waves wash over the land surface.

shoulder season The time when a destination is in neither the most nor the least demand.

sierra A high mountain range with jagged peaks that resemble the teeth of a saw. The Spanish word *sierra* means "saw."

sinkhole A surface depression resulting from ground collapsing into a cave.

sirocco A hot, dusty wind blowing toward Europe from North Africa.

solstice A celestial event occurring twice a year, when the sun appears directly overhead to observers at the Tropic of Cancer or at the Tropic of Capricorn.

soroche High-altitude sickness.

sound A long, wide inlet of the ocean that connects two bodies of water.

source The beginning of a river; also called a **headwater**.

steppes Grassy plains of eastern Europe and central Asia; semiarid, treeless regions that receive between 10 and 20 inches (25–51 cm) of precipitation per year.

strait A narrow body of water connecting two larger bodies of water.

straths The broad, rolling valleys of Scotland.

subcontinent A landmass that has its own continental shelf and its own continental plate. Currently, India is the only subcontinent.

swamp An area of land permanently saturated with water.

T

tableland See **plateau**.

taiga The coniferous forests of the subarctic climate zones.

temperature The degree of hotness or coldness as measured by a thermometer with a numerical scale.

tepuís The flat-topped mountains of Venezuela, much like the mesas of Arizona.

tidal bore An abrupt front of high water from the sea rushing up the mouth of a river.

tides The rhythmic rise and fall of the ocean waters that occur twice daily; caused by the gravitational pull of the moon and sun.

tidewater Water that overflows the land during high tide; also, the area of land near water that is subject to tidal flooding.

timberline The boundary above which forest vegetation ends.

topographical map A map that represents an area's surface features.

tor A tower of rocks.

tornado A violent and destructive whirlwind.

trade winds Constant winds that blow from northeast to southwest toward the equator in the Northern Hemisphere, and from southeast to northwest toward the equator in the Southern Hemisphere.

tree line The elevation above which it is too cold for trees to grow.

trench Ocean depth marking the point where one tectonic plate wedges under another.

tsunami A large wave, caused by an underwater earthquake or volcano that moves rapidly through water and can be more than 100 feet (30 m) high.

tributary A stream that feeds, or flows into, a larger stream.

tropics The area between the Tropic of Cancer and the Tropic of Capricorn.

tundra A treeless area with grass, moss, and small flowering plants in its warm season. The ground beneath the soil is always frozen. There are Arctic and alpine tundra areas.

24-hour clock A clock that eliminates the AM/PM distinction and provides a different numeral for each hour of the day.

typhoon A violent storm, similar to a hurricane, that forms over the northern Pacific Ocean.

V

valley A depression between hills or mountains.

veld The open grassland area of South Africa.

volcanic island A mountainous island formed by the eruption of a volcano on the sea floor.

volcano An opening in the earth's surface through which lava, hot gases, and rock fragments erupt.

W

wadi A streambed in southwestern Asia and northern Africa that is dry except during a period of heavy rain.

waterfall The steep descent of a river over a rocky ledge.

water gap A valley between two mountains that has a river running through it.

waterspout A column of rotating wind that descends to an ocean or a lake.

wave A ridge or swell on the surface of water, caused by wind.

weather The state of the atmosphere over short periods of time.

westerlies Currents of air high above the earth that blow from the southwest in the Northern Hemisphere and from the northwest in the Southern Hemisphere.

wetlands An area of land that is covered by water or that is saturated with water long enough to support vegetation adapted to wet conditions.

wind The movement of air over the earth caused by the uneven heating of the sun.

wind gap A dry valley that funnels winds between mountains.

windward The side on which the wind blows.

world ocean The connected waters of the Atlantic, Pacific, and Indian oceans.

Index

Numbers in **bold** indicate photographs.

C

G

H

■ M ■

P

Q

R

■ S ■

T

■ U ■

■ V ■

Photo Credits

Argentine Tourist Office, 202
Australian Tourism Commission, 399, 402
Austrian National Tourist Office: Wiesenhofer 257; Ascher, 258
Bahamas Tourist Office, 140
Banff & Lake Louise Tourism Bureau, 122
Belgian National Tourist Office, 246
Bermuda Department of Tourism, 138
Canadian Tourism Commission Image, 107, 115, 116
China National Tourist Office, 374, 376 (both)
City of Chicago: © Peter J. Schulz, 63
Credit: © Kindra Clineff, 303
The Colonial Williamsburg Foundation, 41
Czech Tourist Authority, 279, 280
Delta Queen News Bureau, 52
Destination Mexico, 163, 167, 168, 171, 174
Egyptian Tourist Authority, 336
Everett Clay Associates, 155
French Government Tourist Office, Daniel Thierry, 309
German National Tourist Office, 250, 252
Greek National Tourist Organization, 293, 318, 319
Hawai'i Visitors and Convention Bureau/Joe Solem, 102
Holland America Line, 95, 179
India Tourist Office, New York, 365, 385
Japan National Tourist Organization, 380 (both)
Moroccan National Tourist Office, 327, 334 (both)
Northwest Territories Tourism, Canada, 121
Norwegian Tourist Board, 261
NYC & Company—the Convention & Visitors Bureau, 31
Philadelphia Convention & Visitors Bureau: © Nick Kelsh, 21
Photo Courtesy of the Washington, DC, Convention & Visitors Association, 39
Polish National Tourist Office, 276
Portuguese National Tourist Office: João Paulo, 299; José Manuel, 300
PromPerú, 1, 8, 196
Renaissance Cruises, 187, 205, 225, 346, 357, 410
Romanian Tourismas, 290
Royal Caribbean International, 133
Russian Embassy Information Office, 285
San Antonio Convention & Visitors Bureau: Al Rendon, 57, 72
Seattle-King County Convention & Visitors Bureau, 94
Norberto Seebach/Embassy of Chile, 200
Courtesy of Somak Safaris, 338 (both), 342
South Pacific Tourism Organisation, 393
Nona Starr, 239, 313, 314, 315
St. Louis Convention & Visitors Commission, 66
St. Lucia Tourist Board, 151
Switzerland Tourism, 256
Tourism Authority of Thailand, 368
Tourism Ireland 233
Tourism New Zealand, 405, 407
Tourism Nova Scotia, 113
Turkish Tourist Office, 350, 351
VisitBritain, 213, 219, 221, 223, 226, 227
The Walt Disney Company, 47
Luanna Wheatley, Martin Public Relations, 147
World Landmarks and Travel 13, 14, 69, 75, 85, 91, 146, 206, 271, 307, 310, 372